"EVEN NONROYAL-WATCHERS WILL FIND THIS BOOK ENLIGHTENING AND, MORE IMPORTANTLY, FULL OF ENTERTAINING REPORTAGE AND GOOD OLD JUICY GOSSIP."

—Joseph Wambaugh

* * *

"THERE IS A GREAT DEAL OF VERY SEXY STUFF IN THE NEW BOOK ON THE ROYALS."

—The Philadelphia Daily News

* * *

"A PERCEPTIVE VIEW OF THE ROYAL COUPLE."

—Entertainment Today

CHARLES HIGHAM is the author of the bestsellers *The Duchess of Windsor*; *Kate: The Life of Katharine Hepburn*; and *Bette: The Life of Bette Davis*. A former *New York Times* feature writer, Mr. Higham lives in Los Angeles.

ROY MOSELEY is the author of *A Life with the Stars*; *Bette Davis: An Intimate Memoir*; and biographies of Sir Rex Harrison and Roger Moore. With co-author Charles Higham, he has also written biographies of Cary Grant and M Oberon. Mr. Moseley lives in Los Angeles and Lo

ELIZABETH AND PHILIP

The Untold Story of the Queen of England and Her Prince

CHARLES HIGHAM AND ROY MOSELEY

BERKLEY BOOKS, NEW YORK

ELIZABETH AND PHILIP

A Berkley Book / published by arrangement with
Doubleday, a division of Bantam Doubleday Dell Publishing Group, Inc.

PRINTING HISTORY
Doubleday edition / February 1991
Berkley edition / March 1993

ISBN: 0-425-13757-0

A BERKLEY BOOK ® TM 757,375
Berkley Books are published by The Berkley Publishing Group,
200 Madison Avenue, New York, New York 10016.
The name "BERKLEY" and the "B" logo
are trademarks belonging to Berkley Publishing Corporation.

PRINTED IN THE UNITED STATES OF AMERICA

10 9 8 7 6 5 4 3 2 1

DEDICATIONS

* * *

*Charles Higham dedicates this book to
Richard V. Palafox.*

*Roy Moseley dedicates this book to
his mother and father, now and forever.*

1

***

IN 1926, WHEN PRINCESS Elizabeth was born, London, with a population of 7,655,000 people, was the largest city in the world. Over half a century of soot, spewed out of factory and domestic chimneys, covered the city's ancient stones with a black and noxious pall. The streets were jammed with a bewildering array of open-topped double-decker omnibuses, steam-driven trucks, donkey carts, brewers' vans, and newspaper delivery boys on bicycles, screaming out the latest news. Against the imposing grandeur of the palaces and cathedrals, and the lushness of the parks and gardens, could be set the sprawling, noisome slums of the East End, the sinister alleys of Limehouse, the swirling muddy blackness of the River Thames.

London was the nerve center of the British Empire. The vast territories of those people who swore allegiance to the King (Elizabeth's grandfather) encompassed the mountains, lakes, and forests of Canada, the jungles, swamps, and plains of Africa, the swarming cities of India, the frowning, red Stone Age deserts of Australia, and the volcanic dark green hills and shining fjords of New Zealand. The Nile, the Niger, the St. Lawrence, the Irrawaddy, the Ganges, the Murray, and the Thames were among the arteries; a man could climb a Himalayan peak, the Canadian Rockies, the Mountains of the Moon, the slopes of the Snowy Mountains, Australia, or the glaciers of New Zealand and still be within royal territory.

The rich of England enjoyed privileges that today assume a nostalgic and mythical appeal. Members of the upper class could afford a country household, consisting typically of a housekeeper, a butler, a valet, a chauffeur, a lady's maid, an upstairs maid, a downstairs maid, a parlor maid, a kitchen maid, a skivvy, a groom, a head gardener, and an assistant gardener. Luxury flats in London often came complete with staff, all of whom were housed conveniently in the basement or attic of the actual premises, in, of course, considerably less commodious accommodations. Radio was still a novelty; movies were silent; the theater was the thing: a Shaw, Coward, Galsworthy, or Somerset Maugham opening called for every man to arrive in black tie, his lady in an evening gown.

Records show that the British royal family, for all of its possessions, including jewelry, priceless furniture, paintings and stamps, and unlimited land, did not enjoy an especially happy existence. Elizabeth's father, the later George VI, known as Bertie, was a miserable child, whose wretched digestion, knock-knees, and recurrent stammer ill-fitted him for royal office. Shy, nervous, and retiring, though at times of an explosive temperament, he was in every way overshadowed by his athletic and glamorous older brother, the Prince of Wales, known to everyone in the royal family as David, and by his youngest brother, Prince George. He came sixty-first out of sixty-seven at the Royal Naval College at Dartmouth. He suffered from recurring stomach ulcers, almost certainly of psychosomatic origin brought on by the inferiority complex he experienced in the face of his autocratic father and his flighty but glamorous elder sibling. During World War I, he was operated on for appendicitis, spent long drawn-out weeks in sick bays, and, on the eve of the Battle of Jutland, lay ill after eating some herring. At the tender age of twenty-two, he had a duodenal ulcer, which called for a serious operation.

Along with his physical frailty he displayed a courage that also transfigured his father: for all of his illnesses, he managed to serve decently in both the Navy and the Air Force. But at Cambridge, he was an isolated, lonely figure, and it was surprising that he was able to pull himself together sufficiently to win, as an excellent player, the RAF Tennis Doubles at Wimbledon in 1920.

The most sensible thing he did in his life was to marry the strong, sweet, ambitious, and forceful Lady Elizabeth Bowes-Lyon, attractive youngest daughter of the fourteenth Earl of Strathmore and the remarkable Nina Cavendish-Bentinck. Lady Elizabeth was raised with great love and attention, in part at Glamis Castle in Scotland, and in part at St. Paul's Walden Bury, in Hertfordshire. The enormous, gloomy Glamis seemed to present no terrors to this strong, sensible, and amazingly self-assured child. She does not appear to have shared the fears of many guests in the matter of the alleged monster of Glamis, a supposed ancestor who resembled a somewhat hairy Easter egg and occupied a sinister stone chamber in a remote wing, from whence it was taken moaning disagreeably on chains, drawn along the corridors at night while the guests were forbidden to open their doors on pain of instant death or worse. Nor did this pragmatic youngster recognize the existence of a number of ghosts, whose busy activities were reported by impressionable servants. Elizabeth Bowes-Lyon was a law unto herself. If she decided to be late for an appointment, she was late. If she decided to be helpful, she was helpful, if not, not. If she felt like flaring up in a temper, she would do so, and few had the temerity to try to control her. On the other hand, and more often, she could switch on a degree of radiant charm that would conquer even the most formidable. Along with her Scottish common sense, she had the capacity to confront without seeming to do so; she had the strength of sweetness, along with an inexorable will. Of all the British royal family, she was from the beginning unquestionably the strongest. At time of writing, it seems that even death itself is unwilling to take her on.

There are different accounts of the first meetings of the Duke of York and Lady Elizabeth. The most likely story is that they met at a party at Lord Farquhar's on May 20, 1920, and then when she stood in for her mother during the latter's illness when the King and Queen came to stay at Glamis; they were impressed by her, and so, particularly, was the Duke of York. She set out, with matchless skill, to conquer the King and Queen. Although she was a commoner, they adored her from the outset.

On January 13, 1923, when the Duke of York was staying with the Strathmores at St. Paul's Walden Bury, he took a walk with Elizabeth in the nearby Fairy Wood and proposed, stammeringly and touchingly. She accepted at last; if, as has been alleged, she had thought of marrying the Prince of Wales instead, she had sensibly put that thought out of her mind. Two days later, the elated Duke appeared at the royal residence of Sandringham House in Norfolk and advised his father of the situation. The King was pleased to learn the news. He wrote in his diary following the Strathmores' inevitable appearance at Sandringham just under a week later, ''[Elizabeth] is a pretty and charming girl. Bertie is a lucky fellow." The Court Circular announced the official engagement.

The King, who ran his life with Germanic meticulousness, was known never to tolerate the slightest lateness in anyone, especially his own family. However, he could forgive Elizabeth even the ultimate sin of unpunctuality.

Shortly after the announcement of the engagement, the Duke of York made a serious mistake. He let it be known that, according to the terms of the dispersement of royal monies, he would be entitled to receive an additional £15,000 on his present annuity on the occasion of his marriage. The timing of this was unfortunate. Over a million were unemployed in England, and a million more were living in work houses, the conditions of which were abject. Many starved. A coal strike crippled the country. And now (although legally they were quite entitled to it) this newly engaged couple was making an excessive demand.

On February 15, 1923, a storm broke in the House of Commons. David Kirkwood, a radical Labor member from Scotland, insisted on knowing whether Parliament had been consulted on the increase and whether it would be taxable. Stanley Baldwin, Chancellor of the Exchequer, replied that the grant was authorized and that in fact taxes would be paid. Kirkwood demanded that "Economics should begin at the top." Several Labor backbenchers besieged the ministers, using such colorful language that the Conservatives called for order. The debate turned out to be futile, since the Civil List was set anyway.

The wedding was fixed for April. Not displaying a customary Scottish thrift, Elizabeth began spending a great deal of the Strathmore money on clothes. The *New York Times* announced, "When Lady Elizabeth Bowes-Lyon is married on April 26, she will have one of the most sumptuous wardrobes in the world, as well as a wealth of priceless jewels and enough furniture and gifts to fill a dozen homes." The article went on to disclose that fashion designers in New York, Paris, London, Rome, and Australia were contributing their skills to the creation of the bride's trousseau. With twelve days to go before the wedding, the prospective bride had acquired no less than sixty-five formal gowns and over a hundred morning, tea, and evening dresses, and six dozen fur coats and hats.

Gifts to the equivalent of over $1 million arrived from every part of the world. Of these, the most remarkable was a marvelous clock, given by the city of Gloucester, which showed the day of the week and month and the phases of the moon. As each hour struck, the clock played a royal march. The dial showed King George V, Queen Mary, and every other member of the family walking in a circle. The makers of the clock showed an appropriate respect for the Sabbath. It declined to play marches on Sundays.

A total of fourteen wedding cakes was supplied, the most elaborate of which weighed three hundred pounds and was constructed of nine tiers with a replica of the royal couple in formal garments on the top. On the first tier were reproductions of Windsor Castle and St. George's Chapel. Glamis Castle appeared on the second tier, and on the third there was a masonic emblem symbolizing that both the Duke of York and the Earl of Strathmore were Masons. There were Cupid figures on ladders, leading all the way to the top of the cake; operated by clockwork, they moved up and down and rang tiny silver wedding bells.

The Prince of Wales presented the couple with a touring automobile, and gave Lady Elizabeth a sable stole. Leslie Field, the royal jewelry historian, has confirmed some of the magnificent gifts of diamonds the Duchess received. The Earl of Strathmore presented her with a platinum-and-diamond tiara fashioned of five large roses of gems separated by sprays of diamonds. King George V gave her a diamond ribbon-bow brooch, her godmother gave her a diamond-and-emerald arrow, and the Duke of York excelled in giving her a replica in diamonds of the badge of his Naval cap and a diamond cluster corsage brooch designed as a spray of flowers with three diamond pendants suspended from a chain of platinum.

On the night of April 25, the King and Queen gave a pre-wedding party so that everyone in society could meet the bride and groom. London was lashed with wind-driven rain, which reduced the elaborate decorations in the streets to a soggy, pathetic mess.

On the morning of the twenty-sixth, Elizabeth, magnificently dressed in ivory chiffon, with a Flanders lace veil supplied by Queen Mary, left her parents' house at Bruton Street to be greeted by the State coach, which had made its way along an immense human barrier of police. As she saw the coach in gilded splendor, she stopped for a moment, turned pale, and seemed to be reluctant to step into it. It was as though, at that moment, she realized the enormity of the future. But she composed herself with characteristic speed, entered the coach and sat absolutely still, her face as pale as frost, as the vehicle rolled creakily toward its destination. She was greeted with cheers by the thousands in the bitter rain and cold. Her father sat next to her, gripping her hand to increase her courage.

Sunshine broke through murky clouds as the guests entered Westminster Abbey; the edifice was almost devoid of displays of flowers or special decorations by request of the King, perhaps because of criticism of extravagance in Britain's time of need. The pews provided a spectacle, with the scarlet and gold or navy blue uniforms of the men and the white satin gowns, silver and green sashes, and elaborate hats of the ladies. In a solemn procession, the Archbishop of Canterbury, followed by the Archbishop of York, the Bishop of London, and the Primate of Scotland, proceeded to the altar. As the band and choir struck up the national anthem, followed by Elgar's "Imperial March," the royal party appeared, walking slowly down the nave, and the entire congregation rose in one body. The Princess Mary and her husband, Viscount Lascelles, preceded Prince George, dressed as a midshipman, and flanked by Alexandra, the Queen Mother, and her sister Marie, the dowager Empress of Russia. The King and Queen were next, he wearing the full-dress uniform of an admiral, and she ablaze in diamonds, with a silver and aquamarine gown, decorated with the sash of the Order of the Garter.

The Duke of York stepped from the royal coach in his RAF Group Captain's uniform, and, with the Prince of Wales at his side in Welsh Guard's uniform, and Prince Henry in a Hussar's outfit, he was greeted by the Queen Mother. Lady Elizabeth Bowes-Lyon was last to appear. She still looked nervous, literally trembling as she made her way up the nave. She had been so afraid of being late for the first, and perhaps last time in her life, she was actually early. Two minutes ahead of time, she pushed ahead out of order and unwittingly upstaged her prospective husband by preceding him to the sacrarium. She placed with dramatic emphasis her white rose and heather wedding bouquet upon the Tomb of the Unknown Warrior. To the strains of the sacred hymn "Lead Us, Heavenly Father, Lead Us," she was presented by her father to the Duke of York, and then the couple stood, looking touchingly slight against the vastness of the Abbey, as the Dean of Westminster carefully commenced the Office of Holy Matrimony.

Returning to the Palace at the ceremony's end, the newly wed couple appeared on the balcony. Elizabeth was presented formally, curtsying to the King with visible unease; smiling, he raised her to her feet with the words, "Come, Your Royal Highness." He kissed her affectionately on the cheek and gripped her hands in his in a gesture of reassurance. She seemed more composed at the wedding breakfast.

Three hours later, the couple emerged from the Palace. The family pelted them with rose-petal confetti; Prince George took a large ball of it and struck the Duke of York on the face, doubling up with laughter as he did so. Then the State coach, pulled by its eight handsomely caparisoned horses, took the couple through an excited crowd to Waterloo Station.

The couple traveled to Dorking in Surrey, where they stayed at Polesden Lacey, the home of Mrs. Ronald Greville, illegitimate daughter of a Scottish brewer and wife of the grandson of the Duke of Montrose. They proceeded from her opulent residence to Glamis Castle, where they waited for their future home, White Lodge, in Richmond Park, Surrey, to be prepared. It was at Glamis that the Duchess had an unromantic attack of whooping cough, of which the *New York Times,* in an unnecessary but amusing aside, observed, "It has attacked persons of all ranks." The royal couple then went to Frogmore, another favored residence, before they proceeded to White Lodge.

Situated in the well-groomed greenery of Richmond Park, White Lodge was a pleasant but undistinguished Georgian residence, once a hunting lodge of the Hanoverian King George II and the domicile of Queen Mary when she was a child. Mary was an amateur interior decorator and had been there for weeks, redoing the house, making sure that the Duke of York's favorite cigarettes were placed in silver boxes, organizing the Duchess's most beloved roses in elaborate arrangements, redesigning the kennels for the Duchess's Labrador and the Duke's red setter, and having the lawns perfectly mowed.

She briskly instructed the substantial staff in the matter of her son and daughter-in-law's personal requirements. The result was a pleasant honeymoon, marred only by the fact that the public would sometimes peer through the windows of the drawing room, so accessible was the house from the public road, and that some occasional rain spoiled the couple's golf and their walks through the lushly green, handsomely planted grounds. Photographs show the pair as relaxed and happy, ideally suited to each other. Elizabeth's nervousness now vanished for good. Despite the fact that the house had no electricity, bad plumbing, and insufficient bathrooms, and that its heating system left much to be desired, the couple, out of politeness to Queen Mary, saved their grumblings for an appropriate future date.

The King declared Elizabeth, despite her commoner status, Royal Highness, and she was elevated to Princess. After Queen Mary, Queen Alexandra, and the Princess Royal, she was the fourth lady in England; she would soon be the first commoner since Catherine Parr, last wife of Henry VIII, to become Queen.

Back from a State visit to Italy, the King continued to admire his daughter-in-law. He, who ran his life with a metronome, again proved to be tolerant of her unpunctuality. One night, the King invited the Yorks to dinner at Holyroodhouse, the fabled residence of Mary Queen of Scots in Edinburgh. Even though the couple had started early, they were an unthinkable several minutes late for dinner. The monarch, following a life-long custom, ordered the dining room doors firmly shut at the stroke of eight. The Yorks arrived. The Duke said to his wife, "It is too late. The dining room doors are closed." The Duchess did the impossible. She flung open the double doors of the dining room, marched in, and placed herself firmly in her chair to the right of the King. Everyone looked aghast. The Duke of York hung back awkwardly. The King and Queen flushed crimson. Then, with her sweetest smile, the Duchess exclaimed, "I'm so sorry, Papa, I'm afraid we are two minutes late!" The King melted at her glance. To everyone's amazement, he replied, "No, you are not, my dear. We must accidentally have sat down two minutes early."

The Yorks traveled: they attended the christening of Crown Prince Peter, eldest son of King Alexander I of Yugoslavia, and the marriage of Prince Paul of Greece and the Princess Olga. They visited Northern Ireland. At the end of 1924, they sailed to Africa, at which time, once again, parliamentary criticism was heard. The cost of the trip was again castigated in the House of Commons.

In November, no longer able to endure the plumbing at

White Lodge, the Yorks moved into Curzon House, Curzon Street, which was to be their winter home. Five vans brought their possessions, excluding their furnishings, to the new address, and a crowd filled the Mayfair streets to see hundreds of suitcases and trunks borne by servants into the new residence. One newspaper described the house as ''small as royal dwellings go, having only twenty-odd bedrooms.'' Some commentators noted that they would have been more comfortable at York House, St. James's Palace, but the Prince of Wales had refused to make room for them there, or at Marlborough House; the illness of Queen Alexandra, who liked Marlborough House as her London residence, precluded others living there. Actually, the reason the Yorks wanted to live in Curzon House was that it was close to the home of the Princess Royal and her husband at Chesterfield House. The Duchess was now four months' pregnant and needed to discuss the baby with the Princess Royal, who already had two children. Curzon House had been virtually unoccupied for twenty years.

Now, as later, the Duchess of York showed no inclination to have her child in any of the larger royal residences. In fact, she was restless at Curzon House, and considered moving almost the moment she had established her household. With Scottish independence, she decided that she would become a mother in one of her parents' residences, either Glamis or their London home at 17 Bruton Street, which she at last settled on.

2
* * *

IN MARCH 1926, THE Duke of York fell ill with influenza. There was concern that the Duchess might also become sick, and that the baby might be affected. But, sturdy as she was to remain throughout her long life, she did not even catch cold. The Duchess experienced labor pains. April 12 was dark and dismal, lashed by driving rain. The doctors in attendance were Sir Henry Simson and Walter Jagger. Some complications developed, and, in the early hours of the morning of April 21, Sir Henry decided to use cesarean section. At that moment, the Home Secretary, Sir William Joynson-Hicks, appeared on the scene, according to a time-honored custom, which had begun as a result of an incident in 1688, when there was a "warming pan plot" discovered to place a substitute baby in the bed of the Queen of England. The presence of the Home Secretary was greatly annoying to the Duke of York, who, for all of his gentle nature, was capable of being irritated. Sir William sent a messenger to the Lord Mayor shortly after 2 A.M. to advise of "the intimation of the birth" and, presumably, to report that no changeling had been introduced to the Royal Household. The child, a healthy, noisy daughter, was born at 2:40 A.M. At Windsor Castle the King and Queen were telephoned with the good news. The King ordered the royal automobile to convey him and his wife to London at dawn. The Duke cabled his brother at Biarritz, France. Even at that chilly, early morning hour, a crowd stood outside, cheering excitedly when the news was conveyed to them.

Princess Mary was among the first to call in the morning; she was followed by Mabell, Countess of Airlie, who was carrying with her a bottle of Jordan water brought by the British Ambassador from Palestine for the christening. The King and

Queen arrived in the afternoon. Reporters were not admitted to the house, but were sent tea and sandwiches as they stood huddled under umbrellas in the rain. The decision was made to name the child Elizabeth Alexandra Mary, after her mother, great-grandmother, and grandmother. Gifts poured into the house, making it almost impossible to walk through the entrance hall; hundreds of presents from strangers were returned, no matter how valuable, according to royal custom that had not varied in decades. The robust Duchess wasted little time in issuing instructions to the nannies. The christening took place on May 29, with the baby dressed in a robe brought by Queen Mary; it had been worn by both the Prince of Wales and his father the King, among other royal children. It was made of finest lace, tied with pink ribbons, packed in bags of lavender. The Duchess saw the long skirt and instantly called in a dressmaker to cut it down, announcing, "I don't want Elizabeth to have too many frills!"

The christening took place in the Private Chapel of Buckingham Palace at noon that clouded day. The King and Queen attended with the parents, the Strathmores, the Prince of Wales, the Princess Royal, the Duke of Connaught, and Prince and Princess Arthur of Connaught. After the precentor, the choirboys, and the royal organist took their places, the Queen presented the baby to the Archbishop of York, who made the sign of the cross with the Jordan water on her puckered forehead. As he lowered her into a gold font borrowed from Windsor Castle, his words, "In token and hereafter she shall not be ashamed to confess her faith in Christ crucified," were drowned out by the baby's screams, the echoes reverberating up through the apse. Nor did the child's exclamation of distress cease when the choir sang the Duchess's favorite hymn, "Praise the Lord, Ye Heavens, Adore Him!" The nanny dosed the baby with some unpleasant-tasting dill water used in bottling pickles, which made her scream all the louder. The Prince of Wales bent double in a gust of laughter.

The Princess Elizabeth was at once made aware of Buckingham Palace. The formidable structure, not noted for its beauty or elegant classical proportions, fronted by heavy black iron gates and railings, proved daunting even to its royal inhabitants. Yet it would one day be the Princess's home.

With its long, echoing corridors, vast collection of statues and paintings and period furnishings, all of which tended to assume a musty, gloomy character with the passage of time, the Palace was maintained by an army of servants who lived like the inhabitants of Middle Eastern caves. The servant quarters, accommodating as many as 240, scarcely offered the comforts available from the ground floor up. The floors were bare, few of the ceiling light bulbs had glass covers, and the windows were barred. Had the baby been admitted to the nether regions, an unlikely contingency at any age, she would have seen scores of staff busying themselves with washing up enormous quantities of cutlery, glassware, and dishes, polishing silver trays, piling up freshly laundered towels in the giant linen closets, folding and ironing sheets, or scrubbing out stoves. In these subterranean realms, a visitor would see vast storage rooms, filled from Victorian times with a range of bric-a-brac, Minton, Crown Derby, or Spode china, and golden goblets, candelabra, and even spare door handles.

The child was often present at Queen Mary's afternoon tea, as ritualistic an occasion as anything else at the Palace. It took place at the stroke of 4 P.M. Three trolleys arrived, wheeled by liveried staff, the first carrying a Queen Anne silver teapot, jugs of cream and milk, and a sugar bowl, the second bearing a spirit stove and a singing kettle, and the third supporting a pyramid of every description of cake, including lemon sponge, marzipan, icing and raisin, Dundee cakes bristling with almonds, and cucumber sandwiches; alongside these tasty if fattening delights could be found white stone pots of Dundee marmalade and a vivid array of loganberry, raspberry, gooseberry, strawberry, and greengage jam.

On June 7, a letter arrived at Bruton Street. Its author announced that the baby Princess would be kidnapped and the Duchess of York would be murdered. The guard was doubled about the house; Scotland Yard investigated to no effect; and on June 21, a madman was seized, wandering through the grounds of Buckingham Palace, announcing dementedly that he would take action against the royal child. He was confined to an asylum.

There was always a large crowd outside, waiting to see the baby in her black carriage as her nurse wheeled her through Berkeley Square. She would sit up animatedly, missing nothing. At first, she was smuggled through the back door, to take her airing. But later, such evasive attempts were altered to allow people to look at her. She was from the outset pretty, with her big blue eyes and rapidly growing golden hair. At three months, she went by train to Glamis Castle, and a ritual was observed. Immediately after breakfast, she was taken into the Morning Room, where each item of furniture was discussed with her. After tea, she was led to the Oak Room and the silver service was explained to her. She was given a conducted tour of Queen Mary's writing desk, where she was shown the official seals. The Countess of Strathmore accompanied her as she was wheeled through the Dutch garden, past the Cupid fountain and the terraces. She could have understood almost nothing.

Untoward events in that year darkened the child's first months of life. In May, the country was temporarily crippled by a general strike. The King arranged for a cut in his royal income. The middle class took to driving buses and serving in restaurants. The strike resulted in losses for the workers; the bitterness remained, but the loyalty to the royal family was unswerving. Conditions in England didn't improve; by December 1926, the country was suffering from a severe coal shortage, and, on Christmas Eve, families were pushing what little coal they could obtain to their homes in wheelbarrows or prams or pushcarts.

For the young Princess, insofar as she had awareness, Christmas was a magical time. According to tradition, the royal family took off to Sandringham House, in Norfolk, for the holidays. The night before the royal departure, the King and Queen presided over a turkey and Christmas pudding dinner, accompanied by ample amounts of port, whiskey, and beer for the Palace staff.

A great entourage followed the royals on their journey to Norfolk. The drafty mansion stood on grounds of sand and silt, a bleak and barren territory, relieved by fir forests planted in the late nineteenth century. It was beloved by King Edward VII; the rooms were filled with bric-a-brac; visitors had to thread their way gingerly through tables covered in ornaments, tapestry chairs, display cabinets, rocking chairs, screens, poufs, footstools, and occasional tables. The drawing room was a riot of overstuffed settees, richly woven Indian rugs, potted palms, and great brass bowls. The library had books going almost to the ceiling, in mahogany open shelves, topped with military paintings and portraits and classical busts and vases; the ballroom was strewn with tiger and bear skins and decorated with classical columns. The magnificently decorated eighteen-foot Christmas tree freshly cut from the Sandringham Forest stood in a corner of the ballroom. Next to it stood a mahogany table piled high with exquisitely wrapped gifts labeled individually by the royal couple for their countless guests. The King and Queen joined their children in hanging the gifts from the branches.

The fires were lit for the royal arrival, consisting, in view of the coal prices, of logs cut by royal instruction to exactly the same size and stacked immaculately in piles in wicker baskets placed beside the fire irons. Everyone talked excitedly as the flames leaped up from the wood into the ancient chimneys where owls and other birds were known to nest, causing problems. Christmas Eve was a big occasion. At exactly 4 P.M., not a second earlier or later, and regardless of whether there was snow or rain, the King marched off to inspect the stables. When he returned, there was high tea for the staff. The King was first to carve the juicy sides of prime beef and not a single employee was denied the delicious repast. This was known as the Ceremony of the King's Beef. At 6:30 P.M., to the second, the carol singers appeared to entertain the staff.

Everyone went to bed before 11 P.M. Elizabeth, of course, had been tucked in long since. On Christmas morning, the royal family walked off across the snow-smothered lawn to the local Church of St. Mary Magdalene. They returned to Sandringham for lunch at one-fifteen, where they were greeted by the baleful stare of a boar's head on the dining room sideboard. The head, complete with tusks, was filled with forcemeat and truffles. It was flanked by an extraordinary variety of meats, and with displays of candied fruit, raisins, and nuts. Lunch was a five-course meal. Afternoon tea was served at four. After tea, the overstuffed family somehow summoned the energy to present Christmas gifts to a long line of staff, who entered the ballroom one by one, bowing as they did so. A mere three hours later, a six-course dinner was served.

Between Christmas and New Year's Eve, much of the time was occupied with shooting birds. On New Year's Eve, there were games, and just before midnight, liveried flunkies served drinks. At the exact stroke of midnight, a page in medieval uniform arrived, announcing the wishes of the season, for which he was rewarded with a glass of Johnnie Walker whiskey. The entire staff was given a drink.

Such was the baby Elizabeth's introduction to a world of unmatched privilege and wealth. She learned to walk with remarkable determination, starting her basic training on the arm of a chair. She rode briskly a rocking horse that was the favorite of the Countess of Strathmore as a child. Her first words were "Gan-Gan," a corruption of "grandmother" addressed to Queen Mary. Guests were often flabbergasted by the sight of the King allowing the baby to play with his precious World War I souvenirs or acting as a horse while she rode on his back, or crawling after her along the nursery floor, despite the difficulty he had in getting up afterward. Her parents were strict; she was not permitted to be untidy or throw things on the floor, and she was particularly discouraged from upsetting the Duke's pin-neat bedroom, which was sacrosanct against all invaders.

As early as July 1926, the King was insisting the Duke and Duchess of York should make an official visit to Australia and New Zealand, in part to open the Australian Parliament Building in Canberra. The Duchess of York was very unhappy about the separation from her child, but the King's decision could not be countermanded.

On January 5, 1927, the Duke and Duchess appeared at a farewell dinner in their honor at Buckingham Palace. Elizabeth would not remain in Bruton Street but at Buckingham Palace in the charge of her grandparents; this was changed, so that she went to St. Paul's Walden Bury, then the Palace.

The Princess accompanied her parents to the railway station before their journey to Portsmouth for their sailing aboard the battle cruiser *Renown*. The child was already capable of royal control: she did not cry as her mother said good-bye to her, and the Duchess, whatever her feelings, also showed little emotion. As the couple went up the platform to the train, the baby was held up at the window of the royal car to catch one final glimpse of the Duke and Duchess. Arrived at Portsmouth, in blazing sunshine, the Yorks were piped aboard the vessel, greeted by rows of sailors linked arm in arm. Twenty-one guns rang out across the harbor as the *Renown*, with its full escort of flying boats, other airplanes, and ships, moved slowly down the channel, and a military band struck up a tune in honor of the Princess, "The Girl I Left Behind Me."

In February, Princess Elizabeth found herself ensconced happily at Buckingham Palace, plans to take her to Sandringham temporarily delayed. On the eleventh, the Princess noisily cut her first tooth. The Queen was advised by her ladies-in-waiting of this momentous event; the King was not informed until two days later. He rushed in to tell his wife of his great excitement, and she, with charming discretion, feigned surprise. He immediately sat down at his desk and wrote out a wireless message to his son and daughter-in-law on board the *Renown* announcing the thrilling development.

Even her parents were not as devoted to the Princess as her grandparents. The King insisted upon her visiting him after breakfast each morning, when, sometimes a little too vigorously, she would pull at his beard. The Queen would entertain her at least three times a day. She was given her own area of the Palace garden, into which no member of the staff other than her devoted nurse Alla was permitted to intrude. She was brought word of her parents' progress almost every day. For her first birthday, she was given a handsome new cot, all in pink satin and cream, in which she could bawl away to her heart's content.

The Princess's schedule was crowded. She would toddle about, even at nine months, giggling excitedly over the coral necklace her mother had given her just before departure. Behind the tall windows of the Palace streaming with rain or beaten by snow and sleet, she was always on show. She was irresistible in starched skirts that were decorated with multicolored sashes; her insecure curtsies made everyone burst out with laughter. Her solemnity of demeanor proved vastly amusing for everyone at the Palace. She sat for new portrait photographs every four weeks, which were to be telegraphed to the Yorks at ports of call. She posed expertly, seeming to have an almost preternatural understanding of what was required.

Her chief expeditions were to Chesterfield House; there, she'd dominated her favorite cousins George and Gerald Lascelles. Early made aware of her superior importance, these two boys would place their toy soldiers or golliwogs before her, and if she felt like abducting the playthings, the brothers were unable to oppose her.

Elizabeth's first birthday celebration was held at the Palace, and celebrated with an extra-special Queen Mary tea party. On this occasion, a fourth trolley was wheeled in decorated by one single angel-food cake with a large red wax candle lit at its center. So many were the gifts presented to the child that a special room had to be set aside from which the furniture was removed in order to provide enough space.

Soon afterward, she was taken to her maternal grandparents at their home at St. Paul's Walden Bury. This delightful red brick Queen Anne home with its kitchen garden and white wicker gate, rambler roses and foxgloves, was an English dream of domestic comfort. The Princess was especially interested in a statue of Father Time which did service as a sundial. Adults were often uneasy in the presence of this all-too-visible reminder of fate. But the one-year-old child embraced Father Time; she knew what she was doing.

Elizabeth was always playing games, exhausting the Strathmores. As soon as she could walk properly, she would put her favorite teddy bear in its tiny pram and propel it in circles around the drawing room, at considerable speeds, everyone pretending they couldn't catch up with her. Then the entire family would fall on the floor helpless with laughter. At one stage, the Princess was taken to see the ocean for the first time. After she witnessed the sea at Bognor, she announced herself unimpressed.

The Princess was not noted for her fondness of dolls. She showed a surprisingly boyish love of soldiers, and while the dolls would be thrown recklessly around the room, the toy cavalry would be lined up in rows for her inspection.

The Princess had an irritating habit of testing her new teeth on the Queen's valuable necklaces. The Queen was never known to be without the diamonds or pearls which were part of her royal privilege, and she soon realized that none would escape her granddaughter's savage mouth. So she made a visit to the Home Arts and Industries Exhibition to buy cheap beads for the baby. But not before Elizabeth had bitten through the silk thread of a valuable pearl necklace, which broke, compelling a great many servants to scramble about seeking to retrieve the pieces.

It was at St. Paul's Walden Bury that the child developed her lifelong passion for dogs. The Strathmores had two Chows, Brownie and Blackie. They never failed to follow her, and at night would bark and scratch irritably if they were not permitted past the green baize door of her bedroom, which had once accommodated the Duchess of York as a child. She had a mania for disappearing, driving everyone mad while they searched for her. Her favorite custom was to sit in the exact center of the Persian rug in the library, throwing several packs of cards around the floor, spinning out wool balls or spilling boxes of matchsticks. Her obsession with the piano invoked many headaches.

The Duke and Duchess at last returned to London from their twenty-five-thousand-mile journey. The hold of the *Renown* was stuffed with an array of gifts for Princess Elizabeth. These amounted to a total of three tons of cargo, including several hundred dolls as well as teddy bears, knickknacks, and souvenirs of every description; many of them, especially some antique toys discovered in Melbourne, were of great value. There were dresses, shoes, coats by the score. In drenching rain, thousands stood to see the royals as they journeyed from Victoria Station to Buckingham Palace. Queen Mary was present at the station; when the couple arrived at the Palace, the Princess toddled in to greet them. Her mother could scarcely restrain the tears as she hugged the Princess and carried her to the balcony, gripping her tightly as the crowd cheered.

In their absence, the King and Queen had supervised the preparation of the Yorks' new residence at 145 Piccadilly. Even before they had left on their tour, the Yorks had settled upon it; the house, obtained on a special rental after protracted discussions with the Crown Estates Office, was a nineteenth-century Portland stone, four-story townhouse situated near Hyde Park Corner and opposite the grim pile of St. George's Hospital. Queen Mary had moved in as decorator, continuing the work the Duchess had begun in furnishing the place. No expense was spared to make this a lavishly comfortable royal establishment.

The house had twenty-five bedrooms, an electric passenger elevator, a conservatory, and a handsome drawing room, dining room, ballroom, study, and library. The nursery and children's bedrooms were on the top floor under a Victorian glass dome. The Queen and her daughter-in-law decorated these rooms in delicate pastels and wallpaper with scenes from children's fairy tales. Large glass-doored cupboards were supplied to accommodate the enormous number of objets d'art which the young girl acquired, including ivory, jade, and porcelain figures and glass birds and animals.

The family settled in comfortably. A popular sight was Alla

wheeling the Princess in her pram through Hamilton Gardens behind the house. The Yorks, their affection for Elizabeth deepened, if that were possible, by their long absence, had again to fight hard not to spoil her outrageously.

In September, the Princess traveled from her August stay at Glamis Castle to Balmoral, the Scottish castle with its tartan furniture and curtains, and its amusing full-size statue of Queen Victoria's beloved Prince Albert in a kilt. During one garden party in the grounds, Elizabeth was received with rapture by several hundred inhabitants of Deeside. She was almost constantly in motion. When she traveled to Sandringham for her second Christmas, the King and Queen converted her personal railway coach into what one eyewitness described as "a fairy land." He added: "Around the side of her coach, bunches of holly were intertwined with glittering silver foil. From the roof hung a huge Christmas cracker, the cushions covered with printed chintz, representing fairy stories, and on the floor was a picture rug."

The King and Queen and the Duke and Duchess of York followed a British custom. During the night, they stole on tiptoe into the nursery and placed exquisitely wrapped gifts in gold or silver on the child's bed. They stuffed the stockings hung from the mantelpiece. Then as later, Elizabeth would awaken to feel the unfamiliar pressure on her feet, but she was forbidden to make a move until everyone could assemble and see her face as she gazed at the generous pile of presents.

For all except the royal family and some of the very privileged, 1927 had not been a good year. There were over 1 million unemployed, hunger and poverty were everywhere, and many people lived in verminous, filthy, and squalid conditions. The aftermath of the strike showed that nothing had been accomplished by it. The coal strike in fact did not end until November. Paralysis affected everything. Coal had to be imported in vast quantities. All the elements of class war existed in full measure.

Nineteen twenty-eight was to show little improvement. And even the Princess's second birthday was darkened by a sad event: Queen Mary's nephew Lord Trematon died suddenly and unexpectedly. The traditional birthday party was canceled as a result. However, the occasion was celebrated quietly at Windsor Castle, in the Princess's special nursery in the Queen's Tower. The Princess received a large number of adult guests with a delightfully exaggerated curtsy, which, as usual, amused everyone. The Prince of Wales gave her a Sealyham puppy, the Duchess of York gave her a china tea set decorated with magpie motifs, and the King and Queen a large box of chocolates designed in velvet. There was a slight distraction when the president of the Royal Academy of Art and the painter A. G. Walker unwrapped a portrait of the Princess to be shown at Burlington House and the King expressed his displeasure with it. The day was saved by the Duchess of York, who swept into the room, clapped her hands with delight over the picture, and conquered the King, who crumbled before her will.

In 1928, a visitor to Sandringham, quoted by the historian Kenneth Rose, observed the twenty-one-month-old child exchanging little jokes with the King, feeding his dog with cookies, and grandly addressing the imposing Countess of Airlie as "Airlie." Winston Churchill met her at Balmoral. He described her: "She has an air of authority and reflectiveness astonishing in an infant." Sir Owen Morshead described a morning at Windsor Castle, when the officer in charge of the Royal Guard approached her pram and asked for permission to march off. She nodded her head, waved her hand, and thus graciously bestowed her permission. She was still less than two years old.

There were few incidents during most of 1928. Then, on November 21, the sixty-three-year-old King became exhausted by his round of public appearances and contracted a severe cold and fever. Bronchitis, the traditional complaint of the family line, turned into pleurisy and toxemia. The news came as a shock to the monarch's millions of royal subjects. Elizabeth, who had been staying at Naseby Hall in Northamptonshire, where she was taken to her first hunting meet, came to Buckingham Palace as often as the doctors would permit, to cheer her stricken grandfather. By the beginning of December, the monarch's condition caused grave concern. He seemed to be hanging between life and death.

In December, a so-called Council of State was formed that included the Queen, the Prince of Wales, who was absent in Africa, the Duke of York, the Archbishop of Canterbury, Prime Minister Baldwin, and the Lord Chancellor. The King was not helped by occasional bulletins that filtered through on what seemed to be the collapse of Britain's economic system and the now overwhelming increase in unemployment. He could not help but hear of his severely divided government. He lay in misery, tortured both mentally and physically, for weeks on end, the occasional visit from his granddaughter among a few consolations.

Crowds gathered outside Buckingham Palace, anxiously waiting for bulletins from the royal bedchamber. The Prince of Wales came to London, leaving the cruiser *Enterprise* at the Suez Canal and traveling sleeplessly by train to Alexandria and thence to Brindisi in Italy aboard the *Frobisher*, when Mussolini, no doubt recalling King George V's visit with him in 1923, sent out a special train. The King was operated on soon after the Prince of Wales returned. He was given ultraviolet rays, thought to be effective against emphysema, but he remained weak, feverish, and sleepless. Elizabeth was forbidden to see her grandfather as his condition was so grave. She insisted on messages and tiny gifts being taken to him constantly, seemed to be broodingly aware of the nature of the crisis, even at her age, and played only desultorily with her Sealyham and golden retriever.

All plans to go to Sandringham for the season were abandoned. The Princess joined her family at the table for dinner at Buckingham Palace. It was the first time since 1918, when President Wilson was in London, the family had been in London for Christmas.

The King was a little better and had a reasonably restful Christmas Day. The Queen was able to lead the family in to see him for about ten minutes in the late morning. Princess Elizabeth had wrapped a present for the Queen the night before, issuing solemn instructions as she handed it over that it must on no account be opened until lunchtime the following day. It was, in the presence of the Duke and Duchess of York, during a very small, unfussy luncheon in the private dining room. That evening, the Prince of Wales, who had made a dramatic speech on the BBC calling for help for the unemployed coal miners, joined the King's sister, Princess Victoria, the Yorks, Queen Maud of Norway, and Viscount Lascelles for dinner. On Boxing Day, December 26, Queen Mary gave a small tea party for the Princess and for a four-year-old cousin, Lady Mary Cambridge. As she presented Charlotte, the King's beloved parrot, with a sugar lump, the Princess exclaimed, "Poor Charlotte! You look so sad! Poor Grandfather!"

Even in this grave period, she showed a good deal of childish mischief. One afternoon, when it was still light, she suddenly turned on all the chandeliers she could in the Palace, saying, "It's much too dark!" When her mother told her to stop, she flew round and round the rooms turning the lights on and off at an alarming speed. When some of her Christmas gifts arrived, she pulled out boxes full of shavings and threw them all over the room, flinging many at her mother's head.

At last the King seemed to rally somewhat, and repaired to Bognor to convalesce by the sea. Princess Elizabeth was permitted to visit him. He was absolutely thrilled as she sat on a chair next to him, feeding his dogs with biscuits. Then she sat on his lap, tugged at his beard, and made him laugh, only to see him dissolve in fits of post-pneumonia coughing.

3

***

THE YEAR OF THE Wall Street crash was marked by changes in Great Britain. The country's discontent in the so-called Jazz Age was expressed in the return of the Labor government in the general election of May 30. Prime Minister Ramsay MacDonald was triumphantly back in office.

The vestiges of imperialism were slowly but surely vanishing as the British Commonwealth countries became increasingly independent, and the grumblings in London clubs grew louder. As he recovered at Bognor, the King was disturbed by talk of radical movements and possible revolution in his beloved India. These were hard times for the monarch; so much was crumbling, so much that his parents and grandparents had lived for was disappearing before the onward march of modernism.

But whatever happened, nothing must be made to disturb the fairy-tale existence of Princess Elizabeth. In keeping with the more democratic times, she shared her third birthday cake at Naseby with the local village children, and rode her pony among them. Her favorite gifts were a cairn terrier puppy given her by the Prince of Wales, and an amusing clockwork monkey presented by Queen Mary. She continued to display royal airs. When her mother announced that she was going to give a visitor a gift of a powder box, she preempted her parent, handed over the box herself as though it were her own gift, and declared haughtily, "This is for you to powder your nose!" When the recipient curtsied, the Princess, to general delight, bowed from the waist.

Another lady guest arriving at the house in Piccadilly did not please Elizabeth, who objected to her looks. The child was also restless and bored as the lady talked about society matters with the Duchess of York. In mid-conversation, the Princess pressed an electric bell button. A footman appeared. The three-year-old child piped up with "Kindly ring for a taxi! Our guest is leaving!" As it turned out, the only one who left was Princess Elizabeth, who was dispatched to her room without supper.

The Princess disliked having her portrait painted. Unable to sit still for an instant, she would shift around, unsettling the painter badly. Every so often she would rise from her chair, examine the painting critically, with her hands placed on her hips and her head to one side, and she would demand that certain colors be altered to conform more accurately to the exact tint of her garment. Unhappily for him, the painter would have to accept her criticism, since it was invariably correct.

By summer, the King was partly recovered, only to collapse twice, the second time following a fit of laughter on July 7; a rib had to be removed in an emergency operation. It was some weeks before he was sufficiently well to resume a certain number of official duties. It came as a considerable shock to the people of Europe when, on November 3, 1929, the French radio station Radio-Paris announced during a musical program at 6:30 P.M. that he had died of a sudden heart attack. Although the station corrected the statement after an angry phone call from Buckingham Palace, the distress caused by the announcement was considerable. Ironically, the King did have another temporary relapse and was unable to attend the Armistice Day service on November 11.

He was stronger at Christmas, urging the Duke and Duchess of York to attend the marriage of Crown Prince Umberto, Prince of Piedmont and son of Victor Emmanuel III, to Princess Marie-José of Belgium in Rome. The Duchess made her excuses when the time came in January, announcing an attack of bronchitis; it would be nice to think that she was expressing her disapproval for a fascist regime. The Duke was compelled to make the trip alone, fretting constantly over the separation from his wife and daughter.

Three months after he returned, Elizabeth gave him cheering news. She was going to have another child. When Princess Elizabeth was informed of this, she expressed her requirement haughtily that it be a son. She was told that even she could not exercise control over the course of destiny.

Much of the spring of 1930 was spent by the royal couple at

their beloved Naseby. But they were constantly in movement. By April, the Duchess had canceled all her official engagements.

The Princess's fourth birthday was celebrated at Windsor Castle. She undertook a shopping trip into the local town with her mother to buy Easter eggs, candies, and gold-wrapped chocolates to celebrate Easter weekend. Her birthday coincided with the Bank Holiday: at 10:30 A.M., she came out into the Grand Quadrangle of the Castle to acknowledge the crowd at the Norman Gate and St. George's Gate. A moment later, the Scots Guards, magnificently tartaned and kilted, performed the changing of the guard as she clapped her hands in delight. The Princess walked up and down the row of bagpipers expressing her approval, quietly took the officer's salute, her back ramrod-straight, then smiled and waved, blowing kisses to the crowd.

Once again, after a brief respite, England was in critical condition during these fairy-tale scenes. The Depression returned in full force, and the Labor government was unable to fulfill its promises of a year before. The Imperial Conference of 1930 seemed to spell the final death of Empire, the radical reshaping of British international power causing so much pain in high places that the historian Sir Philip Gibbs was moved to write, ''Britain is being changed into a middle-class, bourgeois nation like Belgium or Holland.'' As if the ruling classes did not have enough to put up with, a government resolution brought about a surtax on large estates and called for State operation of the Bank of England. It is no wonder in the circumstances that the royal family provided the only escape into romantic fantasy supplied to the public other than the daydreams concocted by Hollywood.

And the expected advent of another royal child was the most popular of escapist diversions. More and more articles appeared on Princess Elizabeth, illustrating the sort of life that her brother or sister might expect. In a piece in the *New York Times Magazine*, American readers were regaled with details of her fabled existence: ''In her nursery suites at Naseby Hall, Northamptonshire, and at 145 Piccadilly, Princess Elizabeth is surrounded only by carefully selected objects—the furniture is rare and old and beautiful, and the pictures are chosen for their aesthetic value, which the Duchess believes will aid in cultivating the child's tastes.''

The article continued: "For a brief second (on her birthday), England's small idol held the scepter in her hand . . . one gift was a Shetland pony given to her by her grandfather . . . Elizabeth is allowed only to use two toys a day. They are chosen early in the morning, then the cupboard door is closed on the rest. Whenever she travels, a clockwork monkey and a phonograph, presents of Queen Mary and Prince George, [her son] have a place in her luggage . . . Occasionally Princess Elizabeth is permitted to have a 'tea party' and 'Grandma' honors her with her presence . . . These fetes sometimes occur in the Queen Victoria Tower at Windsor, in which the nursery is located, or in a wind-tight hut in the castle park, built by Canadian troops during the war."

Princess Elizabeth received the Queen with a full court curtsy; in the evening, she would visit the King at 6 P.M., and be given a good night kiss, saying, very gravely, "I trust Your Majesty will sleep well." Then she would make a deep bow and back out of the room.

One day, Princess Elizabeth and her mother went shopping at Forfar. They ventured into a bookstore. The child picked up several books, a few of which she couldn't even begin to understand, and when the saleslady offered her some children's picture books, she handed them back with the cool remark, "I've seen that already." So many books had been sent to her suitable for her age group (and some not) that she was hard put to find a single one published in the last four years that she had not already been given. At last, a particular book met with her satisfaction. She asked the price. She then took out a small jeweled purse, removed some coins from it, and presented them to the saleslady, asking firmly for a written receipt. She would almost never use money again.

The Duchess of York characteristically decided to have her second child not in a royal residence or even at 145 Piccadilly, but in her parents' home. Since she had had her first child at Bruton Street, the second, she categorically decided, would be at Glamis Castle.

On August 4, the Duchess, expecting the arrival of her child within hours, quietly enjoyed her thirtieth birthday and the pleasure of having her daughter share the cutting of the cake. There was no celebration. The King and Queen were visiting the Isle of Wight, and called to give their best wishes. Sir Henry Simson, who had, of course, brought Elizabeth into the world, moved into rooms at the Castle. Meanwhile, the Home Secretary, now J. R. Clynes, left by train from London so that he could confirm the authenticity of the child. This was again a matter of annoyance to the Duke of York. For some reason, perhaps because he was not entirely welcome, Clynes did not actually move into Glamis. Instead, he was housed at Airlie Castle, eight miles away, with a chauffeur-driven automobile to bring him to the spot when the appointed hour arrived.

The Duchess awaited the arrival of her baby in the Tapestry Room, in a large four-poster bed covered in cloth of gold. There was a considerable delay before labor. In fact, two weeks went by as everyone in England, and to some extent in the rest of the world, was in a state of extreme suspense. The *New York Times* commented, ''The good folk of the British Isles have concluded that royal babies, like those of lesser rank, are born when they are born, and not before.'' A giant pile of branches was built on nearby Hunters' Hill, to be lit the moment labor began. At the foot of the hill, the Earl of Strathmore had supplied wooden casks bubbling with ale, guarded by soldiers who were instructed to turn the taps only when the birth occurred. Then, on August 20, a storm swept across Forfarshire, accompanied by streaks of lightning appropriate to Glamis, the real-life setting of *Macbeth*. In the Tapestry Room, preparations began as the Duchess went into labor. Inevitably, her second child would have to be delivered by cesarean section. The pains were anesthetized. Thunderclaps burst over the Cairngorms, the nearby mountain range, as rumors fluttered through the Castle. There was talk among the staff that the famous Gray Lady, the residence's best-known ghost, was praying in the chapel; there were whispers that the Monster of Glamis was abroad in clanking chains, that the figure of a dead knight in armor was supposed to be making his perambulations through the corridors.

The Home Secretary had already turned up on a false alarm earlier that night. Now, in answer to an urgent phone call, he took off again, through the rain and lightning, down a poorly paved road to Glamis. He dashed up to the front door, asking if he was in time. The answer was ''Barely.'' The angry Duke of York was compelled to admit this *bête noir* to the Tapestry Room. The Home Secretary entered, observing that the newly born child was a girl and running headlong to a telephone, he called London to announce that no warming pan baby had been introduced into the royal bed.

The new Princess emerged into the world twenty-two minutes after the tower clock struck nine. The Duchess was weakened by the second cesarean surgery, but she rejoiced in having another daughter. The Duke of York was enraptured, and Princess Elizabeth clapped her hands with pleasure. Everyone was relieved when the Home Secretary left. The King and Queen were informed of the good news at the Isle of Wight. The storm continued, making it impossible to light the Hunters' Hill bonfire and preventing the opening of the casks of beer. This melodramatic beginning to the life of the child who would be known as Princess Margaret Rose was entirely appropriate.

The baby weighed six pounds, eleven ounces. There was a forty-one gun salute from the Tower of London, and the Royal Horse Artillery paraded in Hyde Park in celebration. All of England rang with thousands of bells. At last, as sunset came, the storm cleared, and next day a crowd surrounded Glamis, pounding through seas of liquid mud, struggling and slipping as they made their way to imbibe the free beer, climbing to the top of Hunters' Hill to join in the lighting of the bonfire. Elizabeth wrapped her beloved toys in a pink petticoat and placed them next to the baby's freshly prepared cot with its sprigs of heather, before walking to a window to see the bonfire. As she gazed out, the flares leaping into the sky, she thrilled to the sound of the Glamis Pipe Band, fully dressed in tartans, as the kilted players strode up the hill. Turning to her parents, the Princess allegedly said, "We've always played Three Bears. Now we can play Four Bears!"

The cheering, scrambling crowds covered the hill, undisturbed when an occasional gust of rain returned. It was a week of weeks in England, and few who experienced it would ever forget it. Movie houses across the nation flashed messages on the screen. It was only the second time a royal child had been born in Scotland in over three hundred years. Charles I had been born at Dunfermline in November 1600. The Earl of Strathmore remembered that night that there was a Gaelic prophecy inscribed in the stones of the ancient Castle walls. It promised that an August baby born in the Castle would be happy in life and lucky in love. It was unfortunate that, like so many prophecies, this one turned out to be inaccurate.

There was talk of the child's name. As squads of motorcyclist dispatch riders roared through the Castle gates, their satchels filled with cables of congratulations from all over the world, they brought innumerable suggestions of appropriate nomenclatures. In the Tapestry Room, in the four-poster bed, the Duchess was still too exhausted as the night wore on to discuss the name. The first choice had been Anne Margaret. There was much opposition to this. The Duke of York disliked Anne, because it made him think of Anne Boleyn, the notorious wife of King Henry VIII, who had been executed for adultery and treason on royal instructions. Margaret was acceptable to him: it had been the name of three Scottish Queens. Soon after, Rose would be added, completely satisfactory because it was the name of a favorite sister of the Duchess of York.

With her robust health, the Duchess recovered quickly. Meanwhile, in London, the nursery at 145 Piccadilly was being elaborately reconstructed to accommodate the new arrival. There was now some talk of the child being named Cecilia Victoria Margaret. The King and Queen arrived at Glamis via Aberdeen, beaming (the Queen somewhat uncharacteristically) at the welcoming crowds. There was a family conference on the final decision on the child's name. After lunch on August 30, the Duke led his parents into the Tapestry Room for their first inspection of their grandchild, now nine days old. The King was dressed in Highland costume, with a Balmoral hat and an Inverness cape.

Princess Elizabeth could scarcely contain her excitement in those days. She could not be restrained from running in and out of the Tapestry Room at all kinds of hours, just for another peek into the cradle. At last, after much discussion, the name Margaret Rose was finally decided upon. The christening ceremony would take place in October at Buckingham Palace according to inescapable tradition. Several commentators noted that naming the child Margaret was a complete break with tradition, that a British Princess should be given a name used by royal family members.

On October 2, the Princess's birth was registered by her father in person at the Glamis Village Post Office. Some fiddling occurred to prevent the baby being listed thirteenth on the registration list. Fortunately, another child was entered just ahead of her and she could be numbered fourteen.

The Yorks and their two children returned to London on the

Aberdeen Express, which made an unscheduled stop at Glamis to pick them up. A welcoming crowd was discouraged by royal request, so that the family could make its way with the least possible fuss from the station to 145 Piccadilly. Alla Knight was, of course, in charge of the two children. She was aided by Margaret and Ruby MacDonald; Margaret's nickname was Bobo.

The christening took place on October 30. Once again, the gold font was borrowed from Windsor Castle. The child, unlike her sister, was subdued and well behaved. There was no need to feed her with pickle water, and even the splashing of the Jordan water from Palestine didn't bother her. Elizabeth and the Lascelles boys were present, all three on their best behavior. Now ten weeks old, Margaret was an even prettier baby than her sister.

One forty-five Piccadilly had undergone some changes in the past few weeks. Much of the clutter of bric-a-brac Queen Mary had filled it with had been eased out, and visitors in 1930 reported that the house had a rather cold, Art Deco atmosphere, almost like the operating theater of a hospital. Apart from the deerhound chintz that covered armchairs and sofas, most of the rooms were quite plain.

According to Margaret's biographer James Brough, the Yorks' second daughter was "taught to share everything with her doll-like sister, including the stuffed animals on four wheels, which had to be unsaddled, fed, and watered every night." Brough reported that as soon as Margaret could propel herself, she would join Elizabeth at the window and gaze down at Piccadilly, watching a brewer cart stopped at a traffic light, a scrubby pony dragging another cart, or, from another window, Rotten Row in Hyde Park, where society rode on horseback past autumn trees.

They could also see mounted policemen, choking traffic, including red double-decker buses, bronze horses cast in commemoration of the Crimean War, a statue of Achilles and of Byron with his dog. And of course Margaret could, as soon as she was able to crawl, explore the Chinese-wallpapered schoolroom, exclaim as her sister made train noises, gaze at the Chinese dishes, marvel at the fantastic number of toys as well as cottages and palaces, filigree furniture, tiny dolls, and a glass menagerie of animals and birds. Bath time was a riot of splashing, giant sponges, flourished soaps, and screams of laughter. Loofahs were vigorously applied, shampoos poured on in good measure. The house was filled with joy from morning to night.

Christmas was dark and grim in London. The year before had been comparatively mild, but now one of the notorious sulfur fogs, yellow and crawling and all-invading, blanketed London in toxic fumes. On December 22, 1930, half a million Londoners were stranded on their way home, seven were killed in street accidents, and several hundred cars were abandoned when their drivers were unable to see more than a few inches beyond the ends of their noses. Buses crashed into front gardens, automobiles careered off highways into meadows, and there were multiple pile-ups. Shipping along the Thames was completely deactivated, and a chorus of foghorns pierced the night. London shops lost at least 5 million dollars' worth of business. But the royal family took off to Sandringham through the swirling yellow clouds in a brisk mood. Surprisingly, the King did not suffer from bronchitis or emphysema despite the poor quality of the air. Ahead of the royal car, so-called link men stood with white handkerchiefs on their backs, guiding the automobile foot by foot along the way. As the family entered the train, the news was brought to them that two steamers had collided in the River Humber and another ship had run aground off the Suffolk coast.

The train chugged with agonizing slowness through the fog until at last it made its way to its Norfolk destination. With the additional child present and the King and Queen in rare good spirits, it was the most joyous season Princess Elizabeth had experienced to date. Never had there been such vivid celebrations at Sandringham, and, despite the fog that crept through the crevices and cloaked the tall windows, everyone laughed and ate and drank and rejoiced without constraint. Even Queen Mary, normally a pillar of icy rectitude, melted for the occasion.

Reality was not entirely absent from this charmed world. The pinched conditions of England even reached as far as Buckingham Palace. The royal family actually had to cut corners in 1931. Before long, the King would agree to have his Civil List income reduced by £50,000 a year. The Prince of Wales would soon contribute an equivalent amount to the National Exchequer. The Duke of York would be informed that he must sell six of his favorite horses and not hunt during the forthcoming season.

Some consolation was provided by the fact that, in order to give the Yorks a country residence, the King made the Royal Lodge in Windsor Great Park available. It had been given by his son, the Duke of Cumberland, to his secretary and official draftsman, Thomas Sandby, in 1746. George, Prince of Wales, occupied the house, formerly called Lower Lodge, after he assumed the role of Prince Regent. He continued to live there part of the time as George IV. He made additions to the house, which became popular among members of the royal family during the reign of Queen Victoria. When the Yorks went to look at Royal Lodge in September, it was run-down, and part of the roof had fallen in. However, they were delighted with the possibilities of this well-constructed residence. The Duke, who liked to garden, saw opportunities in the grounds, and decided to use his restricted income to landscape.

Burglar alarms were installed, iron grilles placed over the windows. There was fear of kidnapping; threatening notes had been received. Weekends were spent with the whole family, except Princess Margaret, trudging around in Wellington boots, pulling up weeds, burning them in bonfires, and remodeling the house with the aid of the architect and landscape designer Geoffrey Jellicoe.

Elizabeth was starting to read now, at the age of five, using rag books, which she could not pull to pieces as she sometimes was apt to do with picture books, stand-up books, and albums; she was aided by Alla in using letter blocks for spelling. Princess Margaret was extremely precocious. She amazed the Countess of Strathmore by humming the "Merry Widow Waltz" at the age of eleven months, had a tendency to spill her dolls out of her preambulator, in order to gain attention, and talked incessantly at the slightest opportunity. However, she did not join her sister in throwing dolls down from the topmost staircase of 145 Piccadilly, hitting unsuspecting guests as they arrived for lunch.

4

***

IN THE SPRING OF 1931, the Duke and Duchess of York employed a remarkable young woman: the twenty-two-year-old Marion Crawford, destined to be known to the world as "Crawfie." She was born in 1909, in a Scottish country village, and studied at Moray House Training College in Edinburgh. She was engaged by Lady Elgin. While teaching Lady Elgin's son, Lord Bruce, she met the Duchess of York's sister, Lady Rose Leveson-Gower, who was impressed with her. She agreed to teach the Leveson-Gowers' daughter. Lady Rose felt that Crawfie would be appropriate for her royal nieces.

The Yorks turned up at the Elgin house at Broomhall, Dunfermline, in Scotland in late February. The Duke and Duchess approved of Crawfie, and, after two weeks, Lady Rose Leveson-Gower informed the excited nursery governess that the Yorks were considering her. Crawfie wrote to the Duchess of York expressing her pleasure at the honor bestowed upon her and suggesting she should go to Royal Lodge just before Easter to see whether there would be a mutual degree of rapport. Crawfie went to Windsor, where she was met at the station by a chauffeur-driven car. She was met at the Castle by Ainsley, the butler. The royal couple were not there to receive her. They were visiting Princess Victoria, the King's sister, who was unwell. Crawfie was taken to the night nursery, where she met Alla Knight, and the sisters Margaret and Ruby MacDonald. Princess Elizabeth was seated in bed, wearing a lace nightgown decorated with pink roses. She was pretending she was in a carriage, crying out to an imaginary team of horses. The Princess addressed her Scottish visitor with the words, "Why have you no hair?" Crawfie replied sharply, "I have enough to go on with. It's an Eton crop.'' She went on, even more boldly, to ask the Princess, ''Do you usually drive [your horses] in bed?'' Elizabeth was not to be outdone. She snapped back with, ''I mostly go once or twice around the park before I go to sleep . . . It *exercises* my horses!''

It seemed by this stage that the Princess had been delegated to conduct the job interview by her absent parents, an assignment which, at the age of five, she did not hesitate to undertake. She tacitly approved Miss Crawford, and, not quite sure how she felt, the new employee made her way to the sitting room. Late that evening, the Duchess arrived; her husband had remained in London for some official engagements, including an address to the House of Lords on town planning, a major concern of his. The Duchess approved her elder daughter's choice, and, next morning, Crawfie learned a benefit of working for royalty when a maid brought her breakfast in bed.

She was granted a signal honor, a personal tour of the Little House, given by Elizabeth. The Little House was a miniature cottage whose one bedroom was a perfect replica of a Tudor sleeping chamber. A gift of the Welsh people, the cottage was named *Y Bwthyn Bach*; Morgan Willmott designed it.

Crawfie was pleased to enter *Y Bwthyn Bach* on all fours. The Princess delightedly showed her the oak dresser, the embroidered linen, an insurance policy signed by the Princess in a primitive hand, a set of Beatrix Potter's children's books, and amply furnished linen closets. The Princess explained to Crawfie how she always wrapped the sterling silver monogrammed table service in newspapers, and how each blanket and sheet had to be folded to her requirements.

Crawfie was surprised to find that the Duke and Duchess had separate bedrooms at Royal Lodge, and that both were on the main floor. The Duke's bedroom, similar to that at 145 Piccadilly, was very much like a ship's cabin. Princess Elizabeth seemed to be in constant motion, visiting her sister, setting up a bird table at which the winged denizens of the garden could find provender, going out with the large number of dogs including the lion dog Choo Choo, and King George's cairn, Bob, which sometimes visited. Crawfie was under instruction to see that Elizabeth and Margaret had matching clothes. Favored colors were cherry red, pink, and blue, and pale pink and white, and there were literally dozens of dresses to choose from every morning, all made virtually in duplicate.

Both the Yorks were busy that summer and fall. Princess Elizabeth was always under guard. When Crawfie took her for a ride on the London Underground or on top of a double-decker bus, security men filled most of the available space. There were reports that the Irish Republican Army might blow up the children. None of these threats came to anything, but constant care had to be exercised.

Typical family scenes would show the Duchess of York listening to Chopin, Brahms, or Schubert on the walnut radio gramophone with the children attending quietly, or pounding out black spirituals, Scottish and English folk songs on the living room grand piano. The dog population greatly increased; Elizabeth began riding lessons that year with Owen, the groom.

Both she and her sister were still being photographed constantly, and by now the Princess had learned to sit still during posing sessions. Marcus Adams, official photographer, took captivating shots of the two Princesses, both of whom were charmingly photogenic; the photos filled the press week after week, so insatiable the demand of editors that literally scores of pictures were taken each year. Reporters hung around 145 Piccadilly and Royal Lodge trying in vain to get inside information from the servants. Enterprising journalists infiltrated St. George's Chapel, Windsor, watching while the sisters put their money into the collection plate or knelt in silent prayer. All over England, women did their best to match the royal children's clothing, emphasizing pink, blue, and tartan. Countless schoolgirls filled their bulging scrapbooks with articles and photographs about the Princesses. When they ventured into Hyde Park, gazing at the ducks that quacked on the silver surface of the Serpentine, other children would freeze into semicircles around the lake, gazing at them transfixed.

Life at 145 Piccadilly had all of the tranquility of the family's country existence. Almost every evening, the two little girls would kneel on a window seat and point out the automobiles and buses that passed below their nursery. Elizabeth soon introduced Margaret, now two and a half, to her beloved thirty toy horses, each of which was one foot tall and was set upon a platform with well-oiled wood and metal wheels. She would instruct Margaret in saddling them and bridling them afresh; as evening fell, she would advise Margaret how to take off the saddles, feed and water her team. She would also walk up and down in front of lines of tin soldiers, making sure they were correctly deployed. If one should fall over, it was reprimanded severely.

In addition to rejoicing in every new development of the Princesses, the nation was encouraged by an improvement of the country's affairs under a coalition government formed in a national emergency of August 1931. Yet by the end of the year, the economic situation was worse than ever: unemployment was well over 2.5 million. But in the tight cocoon of the Royal Households, there was still no sharp awareness of reality.

The only troublesome matter was still comparatively minor: soon it would loom large: the Prince of Wales had met, momentously, an obscure but ambitious American woman named Mrs. Ernest Simpson. The Prince's interest in Wallis was disturbing to his parents, although the full weight of the potential problem had not yet been felt. The King's health was much improved, and he seemed extraordinarily mellow.

His broadcast from York Cottage on Christmas Day, 1932, was a triumph not only of broadcasting and public relations, but of a sincere and decent man's success over numerous physical problems. Although Princess Margaret was too young to appreciate it, Elizabeth was enthralled. To make the broadcast through a mahogany and gilt microphone, the monarch sat, rather oddly, in a tiny chamber tucked under the narrow cottage stairs. It was a deeply moving speech, in which the King delightedly stated that he could talk to his millions of subjects through "one of the marvels of modern science."

The difference between the Princesses' characters became clear as time went on. By 1933, Margaret already had a fully formed personality of her own. She was boisterous, brisk, and not particularly disciplined. After her first more random years, Elizabeth was now a model of exactitude and precision, pin-neat in everything. In their special, individual gardens at Royal Lodge, Elizabeth exquisitely planted flower beds; Margaret, more rugged and down-to-earth, would soon develop a potato patch, getting happily grubby in the process of planting and digging up her king-sized spuds. Their doll collections, not as appreciated as the soldiers, were kept religiously separate; Elizabeth's were always the most well groomed and best dressed. Elizabeth would accept mild punishment for an occasional harmless malfeasance; Margaret contrived to discover the existence of an imaginary Cousin Halifax. Accused of naughtiness, she would place the blame firmly on this invisible character.

Whereas Elizabeth had no business with fantasy, Margaret had two other imaginary companions, a person of indeterminate gender called Inderbombanks and a human being with bird wings named Pinkle Ponkle. Their favorite relative was the Prince of Wales, who invariably brought a succession of glorious gifts including A. A. Milne's classic *Winnie-the-Pooh* and *When We Were Very Young*. Elizabeth responded with gracious curtsies and thank-yous, while Margaret sent printed "grateful" cards. At Glamis, Margaret searched the corridors for evidence of ghosts or monsters, while Elizabeth would remain in her room, diligently studying. Margaret was thrilled with a comic book that Elizabeth despised: discovered in a chest at the old Scottish castle, it contained gruesome accounts of bloody murders, and it took a good deal of effort to extract it from her.

Nineteen thirty-three and nineteen thirty-four were peaceful, uneventful years, the Depression deepening still further, the golden life of the royal Princesses more peaceful and delectable than ever. Elizabeth was more and more meticulous. She would remain a perfectionist for the rest of her life. Her handwriting was of almost copper-plate quality. Margaret would enjoy "ragging" with the Lascelles boys; Princess Elizabeth would not. She was beginning to assume the character of her great-grandmother, Queen Victoria, exact, solemn, and composed.

During a military tattoo at Aldershot, an official suggested that, because hundreds of children were staring at the Princesses, they might eschew the royal automobile and travel past their admirers in a convertible. Informed of this, the seven-year-old Elizabeth said, disdainfully, "I'm not going to ride in that awful-looking thing. Take it away. I want my own car." Soon afterward, she was taken to visit a battleship, and when the captain assisted her into the launch, using the words, "There, little lady!" she drew herself up to her full height of two and a half feet and said furiously, "I am not a little lady! I am a Princess!"

The royal family was upset in 1934 by the increasing involvement of the Prince of Wales with Mrs. Simpson. And at the same time, events in continental Europe were proving to be disturbing. Hitler's accession to power at the beginning of 1933 gave great cause for alarm. There was fear that he might upset the balance of British power in Europe, and perhaps join with his fellow fascist Mussolini in threatening the Mediterranean basin and cutting off the British trade routes to India. There was concern over Japan's threatened withdrawal from the League of Nations, her building of a giant Navy, and the extreme arrogance of her military leaders suggested serious crisis directly ahead. In his speech and Christmas greeting to the British Empire, delivered at Sandringham House on Christmas Day, the King referred to "anxieties," expressing confidence that they would be overcome if met "in the spirit of one family."

He was not only referring indirectly to the continuing economic problems of his country, but to the unrest in Imperial India. His final words, "God bless you all!" brought cheers from people listening in the streets. Once again, it was a beautiful speech.

But the King's health again faltered. By now, he was acutely distressed over his son's misbehavior with the infamous Wallis. She was everywhere in London, triumphant, ablaze with emeralds. She dared to turn up with the Prince in Lady Cunard's box at the Royal Opera House, Covent Garden. And her sensational public appearances occurred, most unfortunately, during extensive preparations for the King's Silver Jubilee.

The King decided that neither of the two Princesses would go to school. They were to be taught at home, according to a precise series of regulations under designated teachers. Christopher Warwick, authorized biographer of Princess Margaret, has given us the curriculum. At nine-thirty on Monday morning, there was always a half hour of religious instruction. The following mornings began with arithmetic, history, English, grammar, geography, and literature "or writing." French teacher Madame Montaudon-Smith, supplemented by Mademoiselle Georgina Guerin, specialized in French conversation. Between eleven and noon, Crawfie took the Princesses for glasses of orange juice and games in the enclosed greenery of Hamilton Gardens. Before lunch, which was served at exactly one o'clock, there was a reading session; then, the afternoons were laid out with absolute precision. On Mondays at two, they were taught dancing; on Tuesdays at the same hour, they were taught singing at the home of the Countess of Cavan; on Wednesdays there were drawing lessons, on Thursdays music, and on Friday the entire family drove to Royal Lodge. Saturdays were devoted to going over the week's work, riding, and visiting the Duke and Duchess. There was a constant stream of visitors. One of the least favorite of these was the much-disliked Dr. Cosmo Gordon Lang, Archbishop of Canterbury, who would, to Margaret's great irritation, put his hand on her head and declare, "Bless you, my child."

The only visits to the theater permitted by the royal parents were those to the pantomime every Christmas. It is almost impossible today to imagine the degree of innocence of Elizabeth and Margaret in the mid-1930s. Even their history lessons were scrupulously doctored; they were to know nothing of the world. They did not even go to the seaside anymore. The biggest events in their lives were the horse show of Olympia and the Aldershot Tattoo. The Yorks seldom entertained now, so there was scarcely an invasion of adults into this enclosed world. Newspapers and magazines were locked away from the children's gaze. Even Crawfie, whose own life was somewhat sheltered, marveled at the extreme simplicity of the Princesses' outlook on life.

They were models of deportment: when Crawfie went for a vacation to Scotland, and sent a copy of *Pinocchio* to Elizabeth, she replied from Windsor Castle with exquisite consideration, reporting on her reading of *Ivanhoe* by Sir Walter Scott and thanking her governess for "the lovely book." Nor, like so many children, did Elizabeth have to be ordered to send a thank-you note. She decided upon it and composed it herself.

Even though she was only eight in 1934, Elizabeth was aware of what being a royal personage would entail. There would be a constant round of duties to be performed, few of them stimulating, many of them actually of a numbing dullness. There would have to be the laying of cornerstones, the opening of hospital wings, new government buildings, presidings over garden parties or levees, literally hundreds of public events per annum, which would have to be divided according to their importance between members of the family. It was reported in the press that Princess Mary, now given the title of Princess Royal, collapsed from the strain of public appearances, often undertaken because of her father's poor health.

She was compelled to have a six-month complete rest at home. It was almost unheard of for a royal personage not to appear at an occasion to which he had been invited and which he had accepted.

From new roads to new bridges, from blocks of worker apartments to new Army barracks, from mayoral lunches to committee meetings and visits to the poor and humble, there seemed to be no end to the smiling, hand-shaking, walking, or train-taking. The Princess must have known even at that stage that she would not be permitted to exhibit the frailties of normal mortals; she would have to bear up even if she had a headache, or was tired, or felt ill. Fortunately, the protectiveness and cossetting of her royal upbringing gave her the sense of security, the cozy absence of anxiety and stress, which would provide her with a healthy mental and physical constitution for the indefinite future. She learned early the appearance of effortlessness. The sound of cheers was as familiar to her as the voices of her own family. She had ample opportunity to follow the authority and style of her grandparents and the more informal charm of her parents. And she could see how the apparent lack of character, the perfunctoriness and excessive formality that critics of royalty attributed to her clan were entirely incorrect: they were human, after all.

Nor were they invulnerable. The Princesses Elizabeth and Margaret, along with their parents, were under armed guard at Glamis for their summer holidays, the gates bolted and double-locked. Police and game-keepers roamed the grounds, or patrolled the driveway and the wooded avenues leading to the keep.

A big event of August 1934 was the engagement of Prince George, the Princesses' uncle, to Princess Marina of Greece, cousin of Prince Philip. The announcement of the betrothal took place when Prince George was visiting Yugoslavia as a guest of the Crown Prince and Princess Paul of that country. Princess Marina was also a guest. Princess Elizabeth was excited by the news, looking forward to being a bridesmaid. In October, Prince George became Duke of Kent. There had been talk of his being made the Duke of Edinburgh, but the title Kent was chosen instead. In late November, Princess Elizabeth was dressed in exquisite clothes as an attendant to the bride, along with more senior bridesmaids, Princess Irene of Greece, Princess Juliana of Holland, and Grand Duchess Kyra of

Russia. Princess Margaret was a guest. Once again, severe questions were asked in the House of Commons about the addition £15,000 a year the Duke of Kent would receive after the marriage.

London was ablaze with pageantry for the wedding on November 29, 1934. Such dazzling displays had not been seen since the last coronation in 1910. Thousands lined up to see the wedding decorations in fog and rain. The closeness to the Christmas season enhanced the excitement. Wedding souvenirs were sold; Bond Street was given an archway of flowers and hung with twelve-foot silver wedding bells, and similarly sized gold crowns and wreaths. Marina was the trademark of the hour: every girl worth her salt had to have a Marina dress, coat, and hat, and in the theaters people offered each other chocolates with the Marina stamp on them.

Elizabeth and Margaret were delighted to attend an elaborate house party at 145 Piccadilly on the wedding eve. That night, the Queen, the Duke of York, Princess Marina, and Princess Nicholas of Greece, Marina's mother, went to a theater, to be received by loud applause. The audience attended little to the play, but instead stared at them through most of the performance. Elizabeth and two other bridesmaids, Lady Mary Cambridge, age ten, and Lady Iris Mountbatten, age fourteen, were sent to their rooms for an early night, to be fully rested up for the ceremony next day. Even London public house licensing hours were suspended for the occasion. And the wedding cake at eight hundred pounds was five hundred pounds heavier than that supplied for the Duke and Duchess of York.

Next morning, "the wedding breakfast" was actually a lavish and very substantial lunch. It consisted of soup, fish, lamb cutlets, followed by chicken, ham, fruit, wafers, and wedding cake. Pheasants and strawberries were also served. Elizabeth was composed, pink-cheeked, and solemn as she made her way with her family into Westminster Abbey. She helped carry the bride's four-yard-long train, all in what was described by the press as "Moonlight Silver." King George was dressed as an Admiral of the Fleet, and Queen Mary was in silvery blue and a magnificent diamond necklace, one of her treasures. The marriage was doubly celebrated, the second ceremony occurring in the presence of immediate family in the Buckingham Palace Chapel. This was a Greek Orthodox rite, presided over by the Metropolitan Dr. Germanos. The Archbishop of Canterbury stood beside him as the couple drank from the ritual cup before a gold-bound edition of the Greek gospels. Again, the little Princesses behaved impeccably. They then accompanied their parents, the King and Queen, and their uncle the Prince of Wales to the balcony as the bridal couple waved farewell. It was a triumph for the Greek royal family over the terrible memory of King Constantine's collaboration with the Germans in World War I.

Next year, there was to be another wedding, of Lady Alice Montagu-Douglas-Scott to the Duke of Gloucester; Elizabeth and Margaret would be bridesmaids. The elaborate jubilee celebration in May, for which the King fortunately recovered his health, was another grand display of the wealth and power of England and the British Commonwealth. Again, thousands thronged the London streets; on this occasion, the setting for the divine service, followed by the thanksgiving service, was at St. Paul's Cathedral. Princess Elizabeth and her sister were conveyed through the cheering crowds in the golden coach. Waving and smiling with practiced expertise, they and countless other people of England rejoiced on Silver Jubilee night as the King lit the first of a long string of bonfires, two thousand in number, in Hyde Park. The twenty-foot-high main bonfire, constructed so that it consumed its own smoke, and would not topple over, was made of stout timber, crammed with electric cables, tar barrels, old packing cases, and shavings. St. Paul's was illuminated by floodlighting and so were the royal castles and countless other buildings including the Admiralty, St. James's Palace, and the Bank of England. London was ablaze with light, drenching the Thames with the illuminations and burning like a beacon to vessels sailing out to sea.

Two State dinners took place in the Grand Ballroom at Buckingham Palace; the guests were served off the £3,375,000 plate collection. Each guest had a separate liveried footman and waiter in attendance. But in all of the pageantry and State occasions, Elizabeth and Margaret were the main attractions. Their bubbling excitement and enthusiasm were received with rapture by the crowds. Jubilee week ended at midnight on May 12, with scenes of almost violent enthusiasm. A quarter of a million people milled around the gates of Buckingham Palace to express their adoration as the King, in a Derby hat and a heavy overcoat slung over his dinner jacket, and the Queen, wrapped in ermine against the cold, stood quietly in a blaze of floodlights. As the crowd rushed forward, five hundred people were injured. Many were rushed to hospitals. One woman was trampled, her ribs crushed. Piccadilly Circus and Trafalgar Square were jammed with dancing and cheering people, while seventy thousand children added their cries to the excited multitude.

In November came the wedding of the Duke and Duchess of Gloucester. The ceremonies were subdued and confined to the royal family and one hundred very privileged guests, since the bride's father, the Duke of Buccleuch, had died the previous month. Despite proclamations that the wedding was to be a quiet one, ten thousand people ignored the advice and turned out to celebrate.

Once more, King George V succumbed to the miseries of the English winter. It was almost as though the jubilee had marked, with great and imposing dignity, the end of a reign and the end of a life. On January 16, 1936, the King was confined to his bed; he had not relinquished his unfortunate habit of smoking after his last bout of emphysema and a devastating bronchial catarrh savaged his body and caused him to have violent fits of coughing.

5

***

THE DUCHESS OF YORK was also ill, suffering from an almost equally severe case of bronchial pneumonia; in those days, there were no antibiotics, and all that was recommended was patent medicine, constant rest, a restricted diet, liquids, and prayer.

Her grandfather's illness was deeply distressing to Princess Elizabeth, who continued to adore him. The Princess seemed instinctively to understand that death was close. Already, and, if truth be told, from the beginning of her life, this remarkable child had been treated as though she would one day be Queen; the advent of Mrs. Simpson had done nothing to alleviate the family view that the Prince of Wales would leave no heirs, and by now that prospect pleased. The thought of Mrs. Simpson giving birth would add the unbearable to the unthinkable. In no event would the child of a notorious divorcée and woman of ill repute be considered for the throne of England. And it was also known that the Duke of York did not enjoy robust health, inherited the family problem of bronchial weakness, and emulated his father in the unfortunate practice of chain-smoking.

On January 16, Queen Mary, with customary understatement, sent a note to the Prince of Wales at his residence, Fort Belvedere, reading, "I think you ought to know that Papa is not very well." The Queen suggested that the Prince should go to Sandringham, where the King was failing fast.

The Princesses were kept informed as much as possible of the old monarch's decline. His sons and daughter were in attendance day and night; they noted with sadness that his resonant voice had sunk to a mere whisper and that his body, never strong despite the uniforms that gave it an appearance of size and power, was shrunken, frail, the muscles weakened by age and sickness. Even his perfect Germanic posture had gone, so that he slumped in his chair in his favorite Tibetan robe. It was apparently considered too shocking for the Princesses to see him *in extremis*. On January 17, the Prince of Wales and the Duke of York drove to London from Sandringham to confer with the Prime Minister, Stanley Baldwin; on the nineteenth, the King began to slip away. He murmured to his Principal Private Secretary Lord Wigram, "How is the Empire?" "All is well, Sir, with the Empire," Wigram replied, generously overlooking the fact that the Empire had virtually ceased to exist following the Imperial Conference in 1930.

At noon, the King scrawled a barely legible signature appointing all Counsellors of State. By 10 P.M., he had sunk into a comatose condition; it was shortly thereafter that the physician Lord Dawson of Penn made a questionable decision. The law clearly forbade euthanasia. But if the King lived past midnight, his death announcement would miss the morning edition of the *London Times*. In view of this unfortunate potentiality, and the monarch's grievous suffering, Lord Dawson quite literally killed the King. He injected three quarters of a grain of morphia and one grain of cocaine into the jugular vein, and fifteen minutes later the royal life was extinct.

According to James Brough, author of *Margaret: The Tragic Princess,* at the moment the King died, the Queen stooped to kiss the hand of the Prince of Wales, symbolically announcing that he would now be King. It was decided immediately that Elizabeth would attend the funeral, but that Margaret was too young to do so. The Duke of York advised Crawfie, "Don't let all this depress the children more than is absolutely necessary . . . they are so young." Elizabeth cried helplessly when she heard the news, no doubt wishing she had been permitted to see the dying monarch; Margaret appeared to be cheerful, saying, "Grandpapa is in Heaven now, and I'm sure God finds him very useful."

The Duchess of York grieved most acutely in her still drastically weakened physical condition. Queen Mary proved to be a marvel of discipline and self-control, despite her grave concern about the situation between her eldest son and the inescapable Wallis. England mourned with all of the agonizing grief that had accompanied the passing of Queen Victoria. Numerous houses in England had some black decoration or other, from wreaths down to mantelpiece drapery of black velvet; few monarchs had been as beloved.

On the morning of January 23, the King's body was taken from Sandringham Church to the nearby Wolferton Railway Station, whence it was borne by train to London and in simple procession through the streets to Westminster Hall. The King's sons stood through the early hours of one morning between the officers of the household brigade, stationed at the four corners of the funerary platform. The Yorks had much to endure following the royal burial, not least the much-quoted remark of Mrs. Simpson that she hadn't worn black stockings since she gave up the can-can, and wouldn't wear them now. The Duke of York took his family, including the ailing Duchess, to Compton Place, a residence of the Duke of Devonshire at Eastbourne.

The Princesses, as children will, recovered rapidly from their distress; they took a special interest in the move of Queen Mary from Buckingham Palace to Marlborough House, which, with great resolution, the dowager Queen furnished according to her Victorian tastes.

In April, the Prince of Wales boldly brought Mrs. Simpson to Royal Lodge to meet his nieces. They stared fascinated at this raw-boned, harsh American woman with her powerful stride and sharply etched features as she walked into the drawing room as though she owned it. She had never lacked nerve, and her behavior revealed her character: she took the King to the windows and said to him with an air of royal authority, which cannot have sat well with the Duke and Duchess, "David, don't you think those trees could be cut down and replanted, and part of that hill removed? There'd be a much better view then." Neither of the Yorks showed a trace of their feelings; but the Duchess wasted little time in saying, "Crawfie, would you like to take Lilibet and Margaret into the woods for a while?" As the relieved nursery governess conducted her charges out of the house, she had the awkward task of trying to explain who this strange woman was. It is probable that the most she could say was that the personage was an American acquaintance of Uncle David's.

These were troublesome times for the Yorks. The King flouted convention at every turn, upsetting the Royal Household by consulting with Wallis on the royal budget, insisting

that his unnamed future Queen be granted £50,000 a year by
Parliament, staring at her directly during a Westminster Abbey
pre-Easter ceremony, firing ancient and valued retainers from
the royal residences, and welcoming Hitler's reoccupation of
the Rhineland. Now that Princess Elizabeth was closer to the
throne, Queen Mary moved into Royal Lodge for a month,
revising the methods applied by Miss Crawford to the children's education, and insisting upon an increased emphasis on
the historical and dynastic genealogy of the royal family. She
wanted the children to learn poetry by heart, and to give a much
closer study to geography, particularly that of the British
Empire, with a necessary emphasis on India. Even more than
when her husband was alive, the Queen Mother devoted herself
with energy and concentration to grooming Elizabeth for the
throne. The child was taught to dance in preparation for her
appearance at royal balls, her instructress, Betty Vacani of the
Vacani School of Dancing reporting enthusiastically, ''Margaret Rose may be quicksilver, but Elizabeth is pure gold.''
Inspired by the Queen Mother, Crawfie added strong dramatic
touches to history lessons, bringing the affairs of ancient Kings
and Queens miraculously to life.

By now, Elizabeth was beginning to display occasional and
alarming notes of precocity. She greeted former Prime Minister
Ramsay MacDonald with the unfortunate observation that she
had seen him grotesquely caricatured in *Punch*. However, it
was the Queen Mother's special ability to suppress such
occasional shows of high spirits, making the Princess aware of
the importance of a modest demeanor. Simultaneously, the
Duke of York, aware that he might eventually be sovereign,
returned to earlier treatments with an Australian speech thera-
pist, Lionel Logue. Logue worked on the Duke's stammer,
determining that it was not the result of any physical problem
but was a symptom of insecurity, shyness, and a sense of
inferiority, very probably brought on by his father during
childhood. While the British public appeared to be looking
forward to a long and golden reign of their new, much beloved
monarch, the royal family was preparing secretly for a different
eventuality.

The Duke and Duchess made sure that the children were
unaware of the crisis that lay just ahead. On no account must
reality even now intrude deeply into their lives. They moved in
a cycle from 145 Piccadilly to Royal Lodge, to Birkhall, a

Scottish house built in 1715 near Balmoral, lit by oil lamps and filled with gloomy Lanseer oil paintings and Spy caricatures, to Sandringham, and then back to Piccadilly again. Their only intrusion into the real world, apart from Elizabeth's appearance at her grandfather's funeral, was when they were taught swimming and the location chosen was the Swimming Bath Club in Mayfair. They proved to be relaxed and natural among the ordinary children, responding expertly to the instruction of a Miss Daly; the Yorks turned up to clap loudly as the children overcame any problems of breaststroke or sidestroke with athletic ease. Once again, Elizabeth was far more disciplined during practice than Margaret, and, while behaving with a normal degree of childish enthusiasm, exuded an atmosphere of royal authority no one could ignore.

The sisters sometimes indulged in sibling squabbles, but generally achieved a closeness which would mark their relationship for the rest of their lives. For all their differences of character, they might have been twins, so intimate was their interlocking, profound affection for each other. In photographs, Elizabeth would sit symbolically with her arm around her sister, at once protective and slightly dominating.

The Duke of York's responsibilities increased as heir presumptive to the throne. When the King, besotted with Mrs. Simpson, took off with her on a prolonged yacht cruise of the Mediterranean late that summer, his unfortunate brother was left to carry a burden of official engagements. On July 15, the Yorks and their daughters attended divine service at St. Paul's Cathedral. The two Princesses' birthdays were celebrated with Elizabeth firmly at the head of the table, distributing *bon mots* to her amused family in her now quite official position.

The last months of 1936 were overwhelmed by the abdication crisis. Just how much the Princesses understood of it is uncertain. However, they cannot have been unaware of their parents' moods of depression, concern, and, finally, acute anxiety over the future. In October, Mrs. Simpson obtained her divorce; the night afterward, she was awarded by the King with an engagement ring which contained the fabulous Mogul Emerald, obtained at vast expense and after a worldwide search from a syndicate in Baghdad. Winston Churchill and Lord Beaverbrook together engineered a real or imaginary bomb plot against Wallis, and a window of her house in Cumberland Terrace was broken by a vigorously tossed brick. By December

3, it was clear that the British Empire would never accept Wallis as Queen or morganatic wife. Mrs. Simpson fled to friends in the South of France; after a dramatic journey through severe weather, she wrote to the monarch begging him not to abdicate. But he would not rule in England without her as Queen; after much anguished self-questioning, and meetings with his brothers, the King decided he must abdicate. At 1:52 P.M., on December 10, Elizabeth asked a footman the reason for the crowd gathering at her front door. The footman informed her that Uncle David had left the throne. She ran to the nursery and told Margaret what had happened. Margaret asked her if that meant that Elizabeth would be the next Queen of England. The response was in the affirmative. "Poor you!" Margaret exclaimed. The former King made his moving speech of farewell to the nation at 10 P.M. on December 10, 1936. Then he left for a long exile in Europe.

As each day ended with a deeper and more painful awareness of the future, the Yorks knew that there would be no escaping their fate or that of their children. It was only a question of time before the frail Duke and his commoner Duchess would have to ascend to the throne, with all of the severe responsibilities that the new position would entail. For weeks past, the Yorks had been forced to be absent from their happy homes, as the Duke was required to travel to his brother's side, trying to give him last-minute advice, and no doubt begging him to abandon his thought of giving up his inheritance for the sake of a notorious woman. The children must never be made to feel that their parents feared the future. They must be given an impression of optimism, cheerful acceptance of destiny, and of joy in patriotic responsibility. Yet the Duke of York's haggard appearance, strained eyes, and sagging physique could not be hidden from his now piercingly observant elder daughter. Only his wife's strength and cheerfulness sustained him as, on December 12, at 11 A.M., he attended the Accession Council.

According to his wishes, the King watched the ceremony of proclamation of his new reign from a window overlooking Friary Court, St. James's Palace. At the stroke of ten, the heralds and pursuivants appeared in vivid scarlet and gold tabards, while trumpeters played a royal fanfare. A cannon boomed across the park, heard at the York residence, where the children clapped. They remained in the house; when the King returned from the ceremony, they curtsied to him for the first time in their lives; he looked astonished before bursting into laughter and kissing them with deep affection. All through lunch, the Yorks laughed uproariously at the fact that they were now King, Queen, and heiresses presumptive.

Yet it was with a sense of sadness that the loving family realized they would be moving into Buckingham Palace with its armies of footmen, maids, and cooks. King Edward had only been resident in the Palace for two months. He had hardly made a mark on the building, merely modernizing his bathroom and exchanging an ordinary double bed for the fourposter with its royal Arms that had been used by the previous royal occupants. Fortunately or unfortunately, plans for the decorator Lady Mendl to refurbish the Palace according to Mrs. Simpson's instructions had been stalled by the abdication.

Buckingham Palace proved to be a challenge to the homemaking capacities of the royal couple. When Crawfie sat herself down on a brocaded chair in the Belgian Suite, it collapsed beneath her and she fell to the floor amid gusts of merriment from her employers and youthful charges. The mishap was symbolic: the Palace, Miss Crawford wrote in her memoirs, presented little in terms of luxury or even comfort, was in a notable state of dilapidation, and somewhat resembled a disused museum. Electric light had only recently been installed; King George and Queen Mary had developed eye strain through years of reading by gaslight. When a maid attempted to pull bedroom curtains, they crashed to the floor, narrowly missing the Princesses' heads. It took all of the skills of both Queen Elizabeth and Queen Mary to brighten the rooms in the front of the Palace to which the children were assigned. The Princesses' toy horses were reinstated in a place of honor in the corridor outside the playroom, the vast amounts of figurines were stored in their glass-fronted cupboards, and a dank and depressing schoolroom on the top floor, fronted by a grim balustrade of stone, in which the King had once been educated, was abandoned for a more attractive room overlooking the royal gardens. But, despite every effort, the family was not happy in the Palace. It was sunless, cheerless, the cold London winds whining in the chimneys, as Crawfie described them, "like a thousand ghosts." She wrote: "At 145 Piccadilly . . . we had been a small, utterly happy family. I did not think I was going to like the change at all. Now we were separated from one another by interminable corridors.''

In a rare radio interview, Princess Margaret has said that, to her, the apartments assigned to the children overlooking the Palace gardens had great appeal and charm; she appears to have been alone in that judgment. Already, she was considerably overshadowed by her sister and, unhappily, her grandmother, Queen Mary, did not appreciate her. Before too long, the matriarch would observe, quite cruelly, "How small you are! Why don't you grow up?" Princess Margaret never forgave her.

While this younger child, made to feel inferior because of the four-year difference in their ages, seemed less than overwhelmed by the prospect of the Coronation that lay just ahead, Princess Elizabeth was ecstatic. She was beside herself when she was told that she would wear a coronet and be attended for the first time by a lady-in-waiting. She was told she would have the honor of placing the diamond circlet on her head immediately after her mother was crowned. Princess Margaret would have an identical honor; the circlet would be made of silver gilt adorned with crosses and fleur-de-lis over purple velvet, ermine-edged caps. Elizabeth flushed with pleasure as she was fitted for her purple velvet robe trimmed with ermine, lace floor-length gown, and elbow-length white kid gloves. It was understood that she would wear a pearl necklace of three matched rows given her by King George V on the occasion of the Silver Jubilee. Queen Mary supervised every detail of Princess Elizabeth's clothing and jewelry. She was so overexcited that the Queen had her sent to bed one half hour before normal in order to try to relax her, but sleep was probably impossible.

Indications of the regime to come were given when the new King made drastic revisions expressed in the Civil List. He bought back the racing stables sold by Edward VIII, rehired the numerous aged family retainers whom Wallis Simpson had insisted Edward dismiss, and renounced voluntarily £60,000 per annum of the £470,000 permitted for royal use. Actually, the results were slightly deceptive: King Edward had saved £104,000 by the mere fact that the absence of a Prince of Wales invested the revenues of the Duchy of Cornwall in the crown. George VI announced that, with the larger income from the Duchy, he would rebate £106,000 of the totals carried in the

Civil List and the consolidated fund. Also, Edward had not drawn £40,000 of the privy purse income since he did not have a Queen.

On May 6, a few days before the Coronation, the King and Queen received the elite of British and foreign society at a reception in Buckingham Palace, a more elaborate occasion than any held in that building for many years. The U.S. Ambassador Robert W. Bingham was present, followed by his family and the entire Embassy staff, along with Mrs. Homer Cummings, wife of the U.S. Attorney General. It was a red, white, and blue ball, the older women dressed in blue and red, and a majority of the debutantes in white or off-white. Queen Elizabeth displayed her passion for jewelry and luxury by wearing a magnificent gown fashioned of gold brocade, and a long gold lamé train embroidered by Indian seamstresses in gold thread. She wore a blazing tiara and a necklace of diamonds and rubies. The men were in gold-braided uniforms, equipped with court swords, or full-dress Naval, Army, and Air Force uniforms. By royal suggestion, everyone was encouraged to restore to the royal occasion the glamour to be found in the time of Queen Victoria and Edward VII. The glitter of gems under the Palace chandeliers created an atmosphere of festivity for which few parallels could be found in memory. History has tended to color King George VI and his wife with drab de-emphasis: nothing could be further from the truth.

Queen Mary, who had quite shaken off her despair following her husband's death, was everywhere to be seen, issuing commands and rejoicing in the splendor of preparations for the big event. London was in a state of a carnival, and every seat along the procession route was sold. Few seemed to regret the absence of King Edward, now Duke of Windsor and living in pathetic exile. Two absentees would be regretted by the royal family: their friend and financial adviser J. P. Morgan, who was ill, and the aged Duke of Connaught, who hoped to watch the parade from the window of his house in the Mall.

For that whole week, sixty cooks supervised by Prupart, the royal chef, prepared for the Coronation banquet. The Queen herself named a number of dishes after her mother-in-law and personally prepared the complex menus. Throughout the tenth, with the banquet set for that evening, the King and Queen and their daughters were at Westminster Abbey for a dress rehearsal of the ceremonies. The throng outside broke through the police cordons and swamped the royal cars as they swept into the courtyard.

The banquet that night once again recalled Victorian times. Among the four hundred guests were Crown Princess Juliana and her husband Prince Bernhard of the Netherlands, and the Crown Princes and Crown Princesses of Denmark, Norway, and Sweden. They ate off gold plate and drank from Venetian crystal. The knives, forks, and spoons were also of gold. As the banquet broke up close to midnight, fifty thousand people chanted through the Palace railings, "We want the King and Queen!" But the exhausted couple had left the banquet before its conclusion and retired for the night.

Two hundred thousand visitors were in London for the occasion, including at least twenty thousand from the United States. One hundred million dollars in passage money was paid. A hundred and fifty thousand more people would appear for the post-Coronation celebrations by train. There were eighty-five thousand in the official stands and a hundred and fifty thousand more in windows; for the best seats, the price was $40, or at least $800 in present-day money. Over £1 million was expended on seating and refreshments. Virtually everyone camped out in the streets the night before the Coronation, and even the eight thousand privileged obtaining access to the Abbey would have to rise at dawn. Thieves had a field day as they ripped Coronation decorations and street flags and wreaths from their positions, and few were ever caught.

The Queen, with the strong support and advice of her mother-in-law, had a crown specially made for her, of great value and brilliant configuration. Once again, Leslie Field, on royal authorization, has supplied the particulars. The circlet, made for Queen Victoria, displayed the fabled Koh-I-Noor diamond, one of the largest gems of its kind in the world. It had been given to Victoria by Lord Dalhousie on behalf of the East India Company in 1850, and after recuttings was by 1937 108.9 carats and measured 1¼ by 1⁷⁄₁₆ inches. Known as the Mountain of Light, this legendary stone was said to bring bad luck to any male person who wore it; fortunately, no such prediction applied to the female members of the Royal Household. Among the diamonds in the Queen's new crown was a gift of the Sultan of Turkey to Victoria and a drop diamond from that same monarch's gift of a necklace. The King's and Queen's crowns weighed about five and a half pounds each.

The robes were also heavy, but the Queen was in the highest spirits trying them on, hugely enjoying the magnificence of her status. Her husband was considerably less sanguine, and on the morning of the Coronation found himself unable to eat his breakfast. It is clear that he was already missing the intimate, happy, sheltered existence he had enjoyed with his family before the awesome terror of his new prospect.

The morning of Wednesday, May 12, 1937, was somber with rain clouds, the soot-blackened buildings looming glumly in the near-darkness. The royal family, following a 7:15 A.M. breakfast, was dressed by a team of maids and valets, the King notably pale and silent. Queen Mary was uncharacteristically mellow, obviously relieved that her erring eldest son was out of the picture. She had decided to wear most of her diamond collection, valued at about $2 million.

By common decision, the Princesses left for Westminster Abbey first, accompanied by Queen Mary, the Princess Royal, and their cousin Viscount Lascelles. As the glass coach rolled by, the Princesses barely able to sit still, cheers filled the air with a roar like that of thunder, and a chaplain fainted beside the King's coach. About 3 million people, at a conservative estimate, were present. It is hard to believe that Princess Elizabeth's heart did not flutter at the sight.

She saw a grand spectacle in the Abbey. Chandeliers cast a stream of light from the ceiling, augmented by the grayness refracted through the stained-glass windows. The length of the nave was lined in a rich blue Indian carpet, while a carpet of cloth of gold covered the sacristy and the triforium. Two thrones of crimson and gold stood on the triforium at the joining of the nave, chancel, and transept. The crimson, ermine, gold, navy blue, and pale blue colors created an extraordinary spectacle, along with the thousands of gems that sparkled in the light.

The Princess Royal walked ahead of the rest of the family with the Princesses, then sat down with them in the royal gallery. An oversight was that footstools had not been supplied for the Princesses. Queen Mary followed in a train of purple velvet, over a dress of cloth of gold, and took the Princesses from her daughter, walking with them to the royal box. The music had a somewhat mixed reception; the Countess of Oxford and Asquith, reporting on the occasion, wrote: "Our long wait was not enlivened by the meandering on the organ. I wish they had played something fine from Bach or Handel; but no, they went on playing their own special voluntaries.''

Buoyant up to the moment she entered the Abbey, the Queen soon showed the nervousness and tension she had displayed at her wedding. She may have been encumbered by the train carried by six ladies-in-waiting, or, possibly, the enormity of office once more struck home to her. Unhappily, although Princess Elizabeth's behavior was impeccable, Princess Margaret's was not. She showed an excessive amount of enthusiasm by tapping her feet loudly as she stared at the crowd. She was barely restrained from jumping to her feet when her parents entered the nave. She began squirming about, twisting the service book around her fingers, jabbing a finger in one eye, and even wiggling her ears; then suddenly she ran a finger up and down her sister's arm, wiggled about again, and, when required to stand, twisted her head in every direction on the wooden ledge of the box. She even yawned; she placed her head sideways on her hand with visible and rebellious indications of boredom. Princess Elizabeth was maddened by this behavior and sternly reprimanded her. Princess Margaret ignored even the icy stares of the dowager Queen.

There were other problems. According to the historian Kenneth Rose, the Archbishop of Canterbury jiggled the St. Edward's Crown before depositing it on his sovereign's head;[1] while holding the Form of Service for the King to read, because two bishops failed to find it, he also managed to obscure the Coronation oath with his thumb. While fixing the Sword of State to the King's belt, the Lord Chamberlain almost knocked him out with the hilt. The King nearly put on the garment known as the Colobium Sindonis the wrong way round. As the monarch left the Coronation Chair, a bishop trod on the King's robe and almost sent him tumbling. The King was forced to make a sharp remark to save a public humiliation.

As the Archbishop of Canterbury placed the crown on the King's head, the trumpets sounded, the crowd cried, ''God save the King,'' cannons boomed across London, and the choir sang. At the last, the King received and returned the Holy Bible. He mounted the throne, lifted by the archbishops, bishops, and peers of the kingdom. Still another ceremony

1. In some versions, he almost put it on back to front.

followed, of homage. The Archbishop and bishops pledged to be faithful and true, and the Archbishop kissed the King on the left cheek; the entourage knelt and repeated the pledge. The Queen was crowned. The order of the Communion service was resumed, and bread and wine were taken; post-Communion was followed by prayers of thanksgiving and the singing of an anthem, with the couple standing side by side before the altar.

6

***

THE PEOPLE CELEBRATED WITH King George VI and Queen Elizabeth, responding vibrantly to his celebratory radio address on the night of the Coronation, and sending countless tokens of enthusiasm to the Palace.

On May 14, the King and Queen, seated on thrones, presided over a festive court ball, the first of their reign. Much to Elizabeth's and Margaret's disappointment, they were confined to bed. The King opened the ball with a fox-trot, Crown Princess Martha of Norway chosen as his partner; the Queen danced with Crown Prince Olav of the same country. The monarchs only once danced together, to the popular tune "Harbor Lights." Toward midnight, the King picked up his ceremonial sword from the Lord Chamberlain and carried it up to the supper room, leading the throng. On two occasions, between twelve midnight and two in the morning, the couple left their two thousand guests to receive the cheers of a hundred thousand gathered below the balcony.

Patient, measured, always guiding, yet commanding when need be, the Queen continued to be the power behind her husband. She had his speeches written to avoid words over which he might be expected to stammer; when he threatened to become incomprehensible during an address she gave him an unfailing signal, a tight squeeze of the hand; when he grew dull and awkward she would whisper "Shall we twinkle?" into his ear; and when he broke into a temper fit as children broke through a police cordon and tore off his buttons (at Cardiff, in Wales) she calmed him with a grip on the arm. There were times when even she could not appease his temper; at a Lord Mayor's Luncheon, people were asked to change places because a large microphone was stuck up before the Queen's place, and he screamed, ''For God's sake, sit in the bloody seats you were told to sit in!''

Years later, he was capable of noticing that the performers in a Shakespeare play had ''his'' garter on back to front; even when he was dying, he would notice an error in a cipher. Along with his love of jazz, collecting eggs from birds' nests, poring over the crossword puzzle in the *Times,* and shooting, he remained as long as he lived a grumpy perfectionist, putty in nobody's hands except his wife's.

In the wake of the crowning, Prime Minister Stanley Baldwin, worn out after a storm-tossed career that had reached its apogee with his historic speech to the House of Commons at the time of the abdication crisis, announced his resignation. It was declared that the arch-conservative Neville Chamberlain, fragile Chancellor of the Exchequer, would take over his duties.

On May 28, 1937, Chamberlain entered 10 Downing Street; Anthony Eden was Secretary of State for Foreign Affairs. The defense program increased drastically: that year, twenty-five hundred military planes were completed for immediate service, numerous battleships and battle cruisers were launched, and a total of £1.5 billion was called for in a five-year plan not dissimilar to Goering's in Germany.

The defenses of Singapore, Hong Kong, Malta, and Gibraltar were strengthened and, in view of Mussolini's threat to the Suez Canal, the Naval base at Simonstown at the Cape of Good Hope, South Africa, was reconstructed in order to continue the all-important trade, Naval, and military routes to India. Even at this early stage, evacuation camps were built in parts of the countryside, so that populations could be shifted from cities overnight, and millions of gas masks were issued.

The Imperial Conference held from May 14 to June 15, 1937, brought about major decisions concerning the uniform and independent defense programs of the Commonwealth. These were dangerous times: the German, Italian, and Japanese tripartite pact called for mutual action if any one of the three were to be assailed. Efforts were made to keep Mussolini and Hitler apart, largely without success.

As always, the two Princesses were hidden away from events; newspapers were secreted; only children's books admitted. Their memories in later life were innocent of experience of the world: Margaret's most vivid recollection of the time was marching up and down the driveway of Birkhall with her sister, to the tune of the Royal Marine Band playing Sousa's "King Cotton," singing lustily in chorus with the Lascelles brothers, and Elizabeth remembered mostly games of Rummy, Happy Families, Snap, or Bagatelle, a pin table game enormously popular in upper-class homes at the time.

At night at the Palace, in those first glorious weeks of the new reign, the royal children sat enchanted, giggling happily, as newsreels of the Coronation, the Naval review at Spithead, and various processions were shown. They were especially amused when, in one shot, the Queen was seen entering a coach, rashly hiking up her skirt above the knee; she led the laughter. Part of the greatness the world would soon recognize in this remarkable woman was her sportiveness and capacity for unaffected merriment.

She and the King were at their best during their visit to 10 Downing Street—the first of any monarch in a quarter of a century; they arrived for a farewell dinner to Stanley Baldwin, whom both admired deeply, and whom the King toasted joyously.

George and Elizabeth interrupted the new reign's festivities to consider the matter of whether the notorious Mrs. Simpson would be granted the title of Her Royal Highness upon the occasion of her wedding to the Duke of Windsor in France on June 3. Although there was a precedent in law to permit such a decision, they agreed unequivocally that no such title could be used by her for the rest of her life. This proved to be a matter of great distress to Windsor, who never forgave his brother and sister-in-law and spent the next several decades grumbling loudly about the matter to anyone who would listen.

The extravagance of royal expenditure in 1937 beggars description, but few voices were heard in protest; it may be said that the lavishness reintroduced by the King and Queen had a morale-building effect on the public when world war did not seem too remote a possibility. The King continued to work on his stammer in order to increase the image of an important leader that his wife most strongly encouraged.

It was hard to find suitable child companions for the growing Princesses, aside from the sons of the Princess Royal, George, Viscount Lascelles, and his brother Gerald. One of their few friends was Georgina, daughter of Sir Harold Wernher of

Electrolux Industries; but she was eighteen, and did not have a great deal in common with the two girls. The result of this isolation from the rough-and-tumble of other children was a certain distantness, a coldness that, in particular, would at times mark Princess Elizabeth's character. The Princesses did make good friends of the grooms and stable hands involved in their favorite sport of riding. Horses became Princess Elizabeth's beloved companions. She established an extraordinary rapport with these animals.

The round of royal engagements became crushing by the beginning of 1938. In January, the King and Queen had some dozen commitments; in February as many again. The Princesses were busy, too: Elizabeth visited the London Museum, rejoiced with her sister in the excitements of Walt Disney's masterpiece *Snow White and the Seven Dwarfs,* shown privately at Buckingham Palace, attended the National Pony Show, and officially accepted a bluebell-decorated calendar from Banstead Hospital. The King and Queen were up to their eyes in preparations for a State visit to France, inspired by the strong royal desire to cement relations with that nation, to assist in setting up a common front against Germany. It would be one of the most costly visits by a sovereign in the twentieth century.

In 1937 it was an accepted fallacy in some circles that Britain was not only following a policy of appeasement in Europe, but was unprepared for war. Nobody attending the royal celebrations in London could doubt the military character of the King as Colonel-in-Chief of the Household Brigades, nor could anyone ignore the joy the public took in every display of the Colors. The warlike preparations were not unnoticed by Dr. Goebbels and his propaganda ministry in Berlin. Both Germany and Britain were arming, vigorously blaming each other for threatening peace.

The year 1938 was an appalling one in Europe. Hilter consumed Austria without firing a shot. Playing for time, the British Government, as Dr. Hjalmar Schacht would contemptuously announce at the Nuremberg Trial, was soon to hand Hitler the Czech nation on "a silver platter." One commentator wrote, "Two decades after the humiliation of the Reich at Versailles, it was generally admitted that Hitler had won the World War." By summer, Germany was second only to the United States as an industrial nation. Hitler's anti-Jewish excesses, struggle with the Protestant and Catholic churches, and suppression of all free thought filled the King and Queen of England with grave concern. That was the year of the Munich Conference, at which Hitler duped Chamberlain into believing that he intended never to go to war. It seems probable that King George and Queen Elizabeth were similarly duped, since they publicly welcomed Chamberlain and appeared to endorse his policy of appeasement.

The King devoted himself rigorously to his duties. In view of his wife's Scottish background and his own need to cement the disparate elements in the British nation, he held certain of his royal courts in Scotland, and he made a special point of appearing among the depressed people of the Welsh coal-mining districts and in the horse-breeding parts of Northern Ireland. He proved to be surprisingly tough, expertly dealing with hecklers who tried to disrupt his public meetings.

That summer brought a severe blow: the beloved Countess of Strathmore died, that woman whose influence over the Queen, her daughter, had always been strong, forceful but benign. Her passing caused a postponement of the trip to Paris, and a further postponement was caused when the King fell ill of bronchitis and gastric influenza; but at last the elaborate plans for the journey came to fruition.

The visit to Paris confirmed that the image of drabness so often associated with King George VI and his consort had been quite misplaced.

On July 18, 1938, the King and Queen arrived at the Gâre du Nord by boat-train, specially painted with the royal coat-of-arms and drawn by a golden locomotive engine.

Once again, Queen Elizabeth's extravagance was displayed. It is possible that no female monarch in British history had ever been so bedecked in jewels as she, who had insisted that 7 million dollars' worth of gems accompany her. These included the Koh-I-Noor diamond, now extracted from the crown into which it had been set for the Coronation, and affixed to a diadem she wore at the Paris Opera. She took with her fifty trunks of clothes, all of royal blue and stamped "THE KING" in elaborate gold letters; her evening gowns were copies of the Empress Eugénie's, several of her day dresses copied from paintings by Winterhalter.

One ominous moment of the royal journey remained stamped in the King and Queen's memory, and recalled the fact that the last tour of Paris and its surroundings by a reigning

British monarch had been in 1914, on the brink of World War I. During a concert of Monteverdi choral works at Versailles, a military flypast shook the chandeliers and made everyone glance anxiously upward. Two months later, the Munich agreement was signed, and the doom of a Europe that would never return was firmly and finally sealed.

The Princesses, who had missed their parents desperately, were given a reward following the French sojourn; at the beginning of August, the family set sail on the *Victoria and Albert,* north from the Thames along the Suffolk and Norfolk coasts. On August 2, they visited the Suffolk Summer Camp for boys the King had started up some eighteen years earlier; by barge and rowboat through rough, tossing waves the King was hauled ashore by the boys themselves, who swam out to greet him. At sundown, the family departed to the strains of "Auld Lang Syne." It was a memorable day. The Queen celebrated her thirty-eighth birthday aboard the yacht, the children rushing in at top speed before breakfast, carrying piles of beautifully wrapped gifts.

At Balmoral in mid-August, the royal parents were deep in discussion of a possible visit to the United States and Canada; no British King or Queen had visited Canada before. It was agreed that it would be desirable for them to make the trip, to help ensure support in the event of war. But in view of the King's uncertain health, it would be unwise to attempt a winter journey; they would have to go in the summer of 1939.

Princess Margaret's birthday was celebrated at Balmoral; the King added four pearls to the necklace which was to be completed on her twenty-first.[1] The joyful occasion was followed by great stress as Chamberlain went to Berchtesgaden to confer with Adolf Hitler; and by considerable grief as, in mid-September, the beloved Prince Arthur of Connaught, cousin to the King, died.

In pouring rain on August 30, Chamberlain returned from another mission to Germany with a declaration of the "desire of our two peoples never to go to war with one another again."

At the end of September, Chamberlain came to Buckingham Palace to report on his meeting with Hitler. At 10 P.M. that night, the King summoned the Privy Council, Chamberlain

---

1. He did the same, of course, for Elizabeth.

held a series of urgent conferences with Premier Daladier of France, and the French Foreign Minister and Chief of Staff. In answer to King George's royal proclamation, every port of England was fully manned, policemen's holidays were canceled, and blind and handicapped children were taken out of London. Air raid shelters were dug everywhere, even in the hallowed Eton playing fields and in the cloisters of Oxford and Cambridge. Guns and searchlights were set up in the heart of London. Theaters and cinemas were half empty, theater first nights were postponed, roads out of London were crammed.

The King extended his prerogatives by extravagantly supporting Chamberlain on the radio on the night of October 2, 1938. He offered his "thanks to the Almighty, for saving us the horrors of war." He spoke of the "magnificent efforts of the Prime Minister in the cause of peace" and of "friendship and prosperity in the relations of England with the world." Next day, Hitler began to move into the Sudetenland; soon he would be in Czechoslovakia. A delay of world conflict had been bought at the expense of that nation.

On January 28, 1939, Chamberlain, who had despaired of all the hopes he had excited the King with the previous autumn, warned in a dramatic broadcast, timed to precede Hitler's forthcoming speech to the Reichstag, that any attempt to dominate the world by force would be met by a uniting of the democracies, a direct reference to America. On that same day, Elizabeth and Margaret gazed excitedly from the lawn of Sandringham as three Royal Air Force planes staged a phony bomb attack on the house, while the staff put on gas masks and ran to newly constructed bomb shelters. The children were overjoyed by the drill, and probably were sorry they did not themselves take part in it.

Another, more immediate danger than Hitler now presented itself, and the family moved hastily to the greater security of Royal Lodge. The IRA was bombing various locations in England, its quartermaster Sean Russell ordering a reign of terror; all visitors to St. George's Chapel or the Windsor State apartments were searched for bombs or weapons. When the family went to church in Aldershot on February 5, an unprecedented police escort was supplied; explosions and arsonist fires were discovered in several cities and ten thousand police volunteers were added.

There were happy trivial occasions in those painful months: one was the marriage of Cecilia Bowes-Lyon, the Queen's niece, to Kenneth Harington. Another was the Princesses' joining the Girl Guides, equivalent to Girl Scouts of America. But then, on April 12, reality again intruded into the Princesses' cellophane world: with the King and Queen and the Duchess of Kent, they this time did take part in an air raid drill, at Windsor. A test air raid siren was sounded—that high, unpleasant wail which would soon be heard repeatedly throughout England—as they all ran down the stairs to an air raid shelter in the ancient Castle dungeons. The same week, it was announced that the American trip would not be made, as long since planned, on the *Repulse,* but on a passenger vessel, the *Empress of Australia,* with the *Repulse* as escort ship.

On April 20, the King and Queen, without their daughters, watched from behind barbed wire as a fake battle was staged in Hampshire. A heath was set on fire, and anti-aircraft artillery was demonstrated. Next day, Elizabeth celebrated her thirteenth birthday by putting on, rather gingerly, her first silk stockings, a gift from her mother; she was a young lady at last, and her favorite half-length socks were banished—but only for a day. She took pictures of her birthday tea with a brand-new movie camera her uncle David had sent her from Paris. Among her guests were Prince Edward and Princess Alexandra.

In those weeks, her mother and grandmother were teaching her the backhanded wave customarily given by royalty to public acclaim. She worked constantly on knot-tying, bed-making (much to the delight of her maids), campfire building and signaling, first aid work and tracking, to obtain her Guides test badge. Her life in those days was French, German, and Spanish, the dreaded math, swimming, knitting, piano playing, and poring over the royal stamp collection, to which she was adding rare and precious items. And then, of course, there was learning about money: she opened an account at the Post Office Savings Bank.

After many last-minute qualms and agonized discussions, with some talk of canceling, the royal couple sailed on May 6, 1939, from Portsmouth on the *Empress of Australia* on their transatlantic voyage; with their entourage, twenty-eight carefully chosen guests and security guards, they occupied the entire large passenger vessel. About ten thousand people were lined up to see them off as, to the tune of the national anthem

and "The Maple Leaf Forever," the royal pair stood on the
bridge, he in admiral's uniform. Cries of "God bless you!" and
"Give our love to America" rang out across the sea. The
Princesses, dreading the separation, had to fight back the tears,
clinging to the Queen Mother's hand as the white-painted ship,
accompanied by the cruisers *Southampton* and *Glasgow,* and
by the *Repulse,* drew out. Guns boomed in farewell, and the
Princesses safely returned to London. They hated the experience as much as the King and Queen did; for their mother, it
was her worst suffering since the journey to Australia when
Elizabeth was a baby.

The Princesses followed eagerly every nautical mile of the
voyage; they received daily radio telephone calls from their
mother aboard ship; they shouted as loud as they could at the
sound of Queen Elizabeth's voice crackling through the static.
A storm hit the *Empress,* hurling sixty-foot waves over the
decks; then another danger threatened, recalling the *Titanic*
disaster of April 1912. East of Cape Race, a white fog closed
in, clammy and clinging; icebergs were sighted, the ship's fog
warning sounding eerily as from the bridge the King and Queen
watched the ice banks scrape the vessel's side.

The danger increased, so that the engines had to be cut off,
and all other vessels in the vicinity, including the escort ships,
sounded their own warnings. Through the swirling near-
darkness there were false rumors that a Canadian vessel sent to
accompany the *Empress* had struck an iceberg and that German
U-boats had been sighted. The ship was delayed, costly
Canadian preparations drastically postponed and rearranged.

The Princesses were told of the danger; the Queen gave them
a carefully moderated account by radio telephone. At last, two
days late, Their Majesties arrived to a tremendous reception in
Quebec. At the same time, the Princesses were involved in a
spin of distracting activities in London, largely engineered by
their grandmother: a boat trip down the Thames to a running
commentary on the ships moored in the Pool of London; a visit
to the Royal Mint, soon to be followed by the royal tournament
at Olympia; even a trip on the Underground railway; only an
excess of newspaper attention prevented them from attending
the Epsom Derby. And twice a week Elizabeth was with
Crawfie at Eton, to take lessons in constitutional history from
the authority C. H. K. Marten, Vice Provost.

The royal tour was a great success. The visit to Washington,

D.C., where six hundred thousand citizens hailed the couple as they were driven to the White House, was the high spot of their trip. New York also put on a grand welcome, with British displays in the stores and the avenues hung with Union Jacks. Walter Winchell's nationally broadcast "Well, Britain chose the right pair!" expressed the feelings of a nation and provided a slap in the face for the Duke and Duchess of Windsor.

The visit to Hyde Park, the Roosevelts' country estate, was marred by the sudden collapse of an elaborately laden table, carrying dishes, glasses, and candlesticks to the floor. Everyone laughed; the Roosevelts were enchanted with the informality of their royal guests.

The American trip won all hearts, save the militant Irish and the left-wing radicals, and performed the political purpose for which it was intended. The King and Queen sailed home on the *Empress of Britain,* arriving at Southampton just seven weeks and two days after their departure. The Princesses sailed out aboard the destroyer *Kempenfelt* to greet them. They never stopped talking, describing all of their adventures in the past few weeks; at lunch, they played with the balloons that decorated the saloon, batting them across the table or out of the portholes with loud screams; they besieged the ship's shop to buy Canadian Royal Mounted Police dolls, then, with their white half-socks clinging to their ankles, made their way to the bridge to wave to the crowd. In London, as the royal carriage rolled into Buckingham Palace, Margaret's tam-o'-shanter fell off; but by now the King and Queen were far too elated to care. The King was so exhilarated by the trip that he lost his stammer when he addressed the Guildhall audience on June 24.

On June 29, cheered on by the Queen, the Princesses won races at the Mayfair Swimming Bath Club; they had practiced countless hours in the Buckingham Palace pool. Then, on July 21, there was an occasion that would alter the royal family's life forever.

The King had decided to retire the *Victoria and Albert,* which was no longer fully seaworthy; she was now just under forty years old. He always remembered being on her decks as a boy, and insisted that he and his family make a nostalgic last voyage aboard her to Dartmouth Naval College. It was at Dartmouth that Elizabeth met again a young man she had noticed at the wedding of the Duke and Duchess of Kent, and at the jubilee: a tow-haired bumptious youth, Prince Philip of

Greece. According to a Foreign Office document of April 18, 1939:

> Consequent on a request from Buckingham Palace, arrangements have been made for H.R.H. Prince Philip of Greece and Denmark to enter the Royal Navy as a cadet this month. He will do the ordinary special entry cadets' training which will consist of one term at the R.N. College, Dartmouth, followed by two terms in the training cruiser. It is not intended that he shall remain in the Royal Navy after he has reached the rank of Acting Sub Lieutenant . . . the detailed arrangements have been made by Captain the Lord Louis Mountbatten, G.C.V.O., R.N., who is Prince Philip's uncle.

The "request from Buckingham Palace" can only mean from the King and Queen.

7

***

THE CONVENTIONAL VIEW IS that there was no question, in 1939, of anyone so considering this insignificant young man as Elizabeth's possible consort, and that Philip, certainly, was not on any list of possible swains. Yet the following paragraph had appeared in the respected American magazine *Literary Digest* on January 2, 1937:

> Tho' Elizabeth has not been told she will reign as Queen, court gossips have already speculated on her future husbands: Prince Charles of Luxembourg, aged nine; Prince Gorn, 17, and Prince Olaf, 13, of Denmark; Prince Philippe [sic] of Greece, fifteen; and Prince William Victor, seventeen year old grandson of the Kaiser, have been mentioned as possible consorts of this child . . .

Philip was born, in 1921, into a family whose tormented history involved assassination, death by blood poisoning, judicial murder, slaughter of the innocent, exile and disgrace, all figuring in the perpetual melodrama of a nation that was by the 1920s a grotesque shadow of the ancient classical state. The royal clan existed not as a self-contained dynasty, exercising its limited powers through parliamentary government, but as a muddled series of mediocre rulers, ill-equipped to govern, summoned or dismissed according to the whimsical or ruthless ambitions of successive Prime Ministers, enthroned or debased or exiled according to heavily rigged plebiscites.

Insecurity was the very air this family breathed; they would return from Switzerland or Italy after long, ignominious banishments, refurbish battered Palaces or country residences, dredge money from the privy purse to recarpet and paint and add antiques by the cartload, only to find that, within a year or two, they were again threatened with a journey to a meaningless destination where the only power they had was in attracting guests to their parties.

The family name had an imposing Germanic sound: the German-Danish house of Schleswig-Holstein-Sonderburg-Glucksburg. Released from the long bondage of the Ottoman Empire in 1829–1830, the Greeks had, as their first foreign monarch, Otto I, son of Ludwig of Bavaria, who came to power on January 25, 1833. The government expelled him because he was without heirs in 1862. He was followed by Prince William, brother of Princess Alexandra of Denmark (who would later be Queen Consort of Edward VII of England), and of Maria Fedorovna, future Czarina of all the Russias.

At eighteen, William left for Athens, jocularly told by his father, who foresaw bounty and honors accruing to the Danish-German dynasty, that he would be shot dead if he did not assume the throne. He proved popular, and his reign as George I continued for half a century; he married a niece of the Czar, Grand Duchess Olga, who was only fifteen, and they raised a family, of whom Andrew, Philip's father, was the seventh-born.

In March 1913, George I was shot in the back by a fanatical anarchist while out walking at Salonika, and immediately some fifty years of peace came to an end. His successor was his eldest son, King Constantine I, who married Princess Sophie of Prussia, a sister of the Kaiser. It was a disastrous choice since Britain had for long been the supporter, bulwark, and financial savior of Greece.[1] During World War I, Greece maintained an uneasy neutrality; influenced by his wife, by his own dynastic connections and ties, and by the fact that Germany was the chief importer of Greek tobacco, Constantine proved helpful to Germany in refusing to allow aid to the British and Australian forces in the Near East. Yet he vacillated constantly, secretly giving permission for Allied landings in Greek territory against the German-allied Turks.

On December 1, 1916, a sanguinary incident occurred, which was to influence the future of the still unborn Philip. In an attempt to force Constantine's hand, a British and French

---

1. It should be noted that she was the daughter of the then Princess Royal of England, sister of King George V. The Kaiser was the King's cousin.

landing party disembarked at Phaleron for Athens; breaking his promise not to attack Allied forces, the King and his brothers, including Prince Andrew, Philip's future father, ordered the attacking troops to be fired on; several were killed and the others conducted ignominiously back to their ships. The pro-Allied mayor of Athens was beaten, his beard torn out by the roots, and scores of his supporters were shot or blinded. The *London Spectator* echoed furious public opinion when it said, "The Royalist government at Athens has become an open enemy and must be treated as such. The King must know he is recognized as our enemy." The *New York Times* wrote of "the hideous treachery of King Constantine." It was reported that Queen Sophie was leaking crucial information to Germany via Sweden; she telegramed the Kaiser on December 2, "It [the attack on the British and French] was a great victory."

The victory was short-lived: Constantine's downfall in 1917 came about because of the joint schemings of Lloyd George, the fiery Welsh Prime Minister of England, and of the devious, ascetic Greek political leader Eleuthérios Venizélos, who seemed to exercise as much power when he was out of his prime ministerial office as when he was in it. Lloyd George and Venizélos were jointly determined to prevent the Turkish Empire from its resurgence. When Constantine proved vacillating, he was conveniently exiled. The Greek Government now awarded the throne to Constantine's second son, Prince Alexander, since the actual heir, the Diadoch (Crown Prince) George, was considered too pro-German.

King Alexander, a weakling of twenty-three when he assumed the throne, at once became Venizélos's puppet. Lloyd George and Venizélos wasted little time in having the car-loving Alexander, whose interest in affairs of state was less than in the internal combustion engine, authorize an attack on Turkey and the seizure of Smyrna; in June 1920, the British-backed campaign extended to a full-scale and bloody invasion of Anatolia, the Greeks defeating the Turks at Alashehr, taking Bursa, and overwhelming Adrianople.

On September 17, Alexander went for a walk in the wooded grounds of his palace at Tatoi; his Alsatian made its way into a gamekeeper's cottage, where it attacked the gamekeeper's rabid pet monkey. In trying to separate them, Alexander was bitten severely by the monkey; his leg was swollen with poison, but doctors refused to amputate. As a result, he died.

In 1920, Constantine reassumed the throne; encouraged by the arms agent Sir Basil Zaharoff, who had made vast profits from Alexander's campaign, and by Lloyd George, Constantine prepared for a further onslaught on Turkey, and another grab at Black Sea oil. The new offensive cost Zaharoff an estimated £4 million. But it was a serious mistake; the Turkish leader Kemal Atatürk ended his own civil war by the usual adjustments. He was fully prepared to meet, with any amount of bloodshed, fire, and pillage, the badly generaled force of three hundred thousand hastily mustered by Constantine and his Prime Minister, Pangalos.

Prince Andrew and his wife, the Princess Alice of Battenberg, set up residence in Corfu after Constantine returned to Athens. Alice was the daughter of Prince Louis of Battenberg, first Marquess of Milford Haven, who had been First Sea Lord of England; he had been forced to resign from the Admiralty only weeks after the outbreak of World War I, officially because a campaign in the press (actually only in the worthless *Globe* and *John Bull*, which no one took seriously) had damaged him, charging that, born a German with extensive properties in Germany, he was unfit for high office in wartime. It has been claimed that in truth his (and First Lord of the Admiralty Winston Churchill's) career after the war broke out was marked by wanton inefficiency that resulted in the loss of a very large number of lives, especially at the Battle of Coronel. He also seems (after rallying the Navy to service very promptly before war was declared) to have been notably lacking in belligerent initiative thereafter, perhaps because he could not bear to kill his German blood kindred.

Whatever the truth, Alice suffered greatly from his resignation, as did her younger brother Louis, later Lord Mountbatten, and her sister Louise, later Crown Princess and finally Queen of Sweden. She was already laboring under the painful handicap of being born deaf, a matter of concern to her loving grandmother, Queen Victoria.

Using sign language, she had married Prince Andrew on October 7, 1903, at Darmstadt, the ancient Hesse family seat in Germany. The drunken, chaotic nuptials were followed by years of great financial difficulty raising four daughters in Athens, exile in Switzerland, and Corfu.

The burdens of her husband's skittishness and unreliability, as well as his poor service in the campaign against the Turks, her father's destruction at the Admiralty, and her mother's, the eccentric and Germanic Victoria, Marchioness of Milford Haven, constant railing against the government that had allegedly ill-treated Prince Louis, all helped to make Alice a tortured woman by the time she conceived Philip in 1920. Mon Repos, the home she shared occasionally with Andrew, had been built in Corfu by the British governor Sir Frederick Ashton in 1832, for his mustachioed Greek wife; the house's setting was attractive, with lavish plantings of cypress, lemon, fig, and banana; the view across the sea to Albania was famous, and it was here that, in legend, Odysseus had drifted naked ashore.

But the house itself, once a handsome residence in the Henry Holland style, was in a wretched state of disrepair. There was no electricity, no hot water, and no heating system; the "footmen" were dirty and unkempt, and had no uniforms; the maids were slovenly peasant girls; baths were taken in water heated on a stove.

All through her pregnancy, Alice was in a state of hysteria: her brother-in-law the King was extremely ill. The fact that he was *persona non grata* with the Allies drove him into screaming fits followed by breakdowns. There was almost no money in the royal coffers; Andrew was constantly on call for action against the Turks.

In March 1921, Alice's anxieties increased as, after a lull, Kemal Atatürk joined forces with the Soviet Union and began a full-scale onslaught on the Greeks. Andrew was given the command of the 2nd Division of the Army at the battle of Eskishehr; routed in a viciously intense attack, he lost many of his men. On April 4, Alice, now over seven months' pregnant, was told the horrifying news that Andrew had been killed at the front, bayoneted to death with his regiment; she collapsed, but next day received a telegram that he was alive. He had abandoned the front line, fled the Baghdad railway; demoralized, his men were in rags, burning villages as they ran.

On May 28[2] Alice went into labor. Because of her neurosis, it was a nightmarish ordeal. The unpracticed Corfu doctor delivered the big, robust baby boy Philip on the dining room table.

2. The Julian Calendar later changed the date to June 10.

The boy's nanny, Nurse Roose, was British; baptized in the Greek Orthodox Church, he was raised to learn sign language, so that he could communicate with his mother. English was his first language, German and French his second and third, and Greek not at all. In view of his unstable family, he was astonishing: an unadulterated, loudly bawling extrovert, a tease, nuisance, and prankster, dominantly masculine and greedy in gobbling his heavy English foods. While his father and uncles were plagued by bedbugs in Smyrna, traveling by a fetid train to the front line, clashing with Turks in mortal combat, or crossing the Great Salt Desert scraping away wind-driven silt that made their eyelids stick together, Alice was restless, in agony, at the ironically named Mon Repos.

On June 10, 1921, the day of Philip's birth, Andrew, with his brothers Constantine and Nicholas, had returned to Smyrna from Athens. There followed an incident which would almost cost the Prince his life, and displayed very clearly his rebellious and controversial character. His 2nd Corps was at the front line in the basin of the Sakharia River in Turkey, readying for its part in a battle. Suddenly and impetuously wearying of the conflict, he proposed to General Papoulas, the Greek Commander-in-Chief, that he should retreat at 7 P.M. on September 9; he would make arrangements for a reinforced regiment to protect the right flank of the 1st Corps. At three thirty-five that afternoon, Papoulas categorically refused permission. His instructions were that Prince Andrew's corps would remain in position; it was to attack the Turks immediately they advanced. Papoulas reminded Prince Andrew that he was the only person authorized to issue such instructions. The following day, the tenth, Prince Andrew announced that he wished to be replaced, since his request for retreat had not been treated with sufficient importance. Papoulas responded with the words, "There is no reason for you to be replaced." Whereupon, Prince Andrew disobeyed Papoulas's command and retreated. This was, according to the laws, outright desertion, mutiny, and treason, and was punishable by death following a court-martial. Thus (and the appropriate exchange has only just been obtained after years of being classified in the Turkish archives of seized Greek documents), the subsequent trial of Prince Andrew, in which he has always been described as a scapegoat, was entirely proper and legal.

In 1922, the Greek Government collapsed; King Constantine abdicated in favor of his son, the Diadoch George; the armed forces mutinied. Refused asylum in British Malta because of the disgrace of 1916, the King was covertly assisted into exile in Mussolini's Sicily by the British Government; transported aboard the filthy *Patris*, Constantine, Nicholas, and their wives moved into a depressing hotel in Palermo.

Stubbornly, Andrew refused to leave Corfu, and the revolutionary government, controlled in absentia by the exiled former Prime Minister Venizélos, ordered his arrest. In a much misreported incident, a military party headed by Colonel Lufas landed in Corfu and seized him for treason and desertion. Andrew's defense was weak and confused and he was shipped off, his wife and children crying, to house arrest in Athens.

While Andrew was a prisoner in that city, several members of King Constantine's Cabinet were put on trial for treason, for seeking to undermine the Army's morale, handing supplies, ammunitions, and guns to the Turks, fleeing from the front, making illegal arrangements with the British Government, and arranging a secret government under Andrew's brother Prince Nicholas. On November 28, 1922, they were lined up against a hospital wall in their top hats and morning coats and shot; the former Prime Minister, Dimitrios Gounaris, was suffering from typhoid and was dragged from a hospital bed to be slaughtered along with the others.[3]

Constantine collapsed when he heard the news. Alice was terrified for her husband's safety. King George V in London was deeply anxious. With Nicholas, Alice begged the British monarch, the Pope, and the King of Spain for help; the Pontiff contacted British Foreign Secretary Lord Curzon, who was at the Lausanne Conference, and Curzon in turn spoke to his fellow conference delegate Venizélos, who agreed on papal advice to urge the Greeks to clemency and to send Gerald Talbot, a special Vickers munitions company agent, to Athens to make "arrangements." Through bribery and promises Talbot managed to have the Revolutionary Committee agree that Andrew would go through a form of trial but would be

3. On November 28, Jefferson Caffery, chargé d'affaires in Athens, had telegraphed the U.S. Secretary of State that several hundred Venizélist officers had demanded of the Revolutionary Committee that these Cabinet members should be executed and if they were not the committee would be. This was the real reason for the trial being rushed through and the six principals condemned and executed.

banished and disgraced rather than killed. At the trial, the unfortunate Prince was forced into a humiliating admission of "inexperience and incompetence"—but the truth was he had had long service and was a trained military officer.

Preferring dishonor to death was a stain on this feckless princeling's character. Picking up Alice, the children, Nurse Roose, governess, and ladies' maid on the way, Andrew sailed under British protection aboard the Royal Navy's *Calypso* to Brindisi on December 5, 1922, and thence to Rome, where he and Alice thanked the Pope in person.

They were out of funds; British Ambassador to Italy Sir Ronald Graham had to advance them the cash for the train fare to Paris. Sharp questions were asked in the House of Commons as to the desirability of using British Royal Navy vessels for removing deposed Princes; and the true initiator of the rescue was revealed in a note by Alexander Cadogan of the Foreign Office on December 8:

> The original source of the instructions (the King) cannot be quoted, but perhaps the Prime Minister will be prepared to say that he instructed the Admiralty to issue the necessary orders.

He was not prepared. As it turned out, nobody dared admit the responsibility; the Greek royal family was too much of a political problem. Andrew, Alice, and the children were met in Paris by Andrew's brother Prince Christopher and his wife, the ailing American Anastasia, popularly known as "The Dollar Princess"; Princess Marie Bonaparte, and her husband, Philip's uncle Prince George of Greece, his father's elder brother, accommodated them at the Princess's house in St. Cloud.

The Princess Bonaparte, a dark, pale, dreamy-eyed and tortured *belle laide*, was the great-granddaughter of Lucien Bonaparte, brother of Napoleon; on her mother's side she was descended from the immensely rich François Blanc, her maternal grandfather, virtual owner of the Monte Carlo casino. Her mother died shortly after giving birth to her, and Marie grew up lonely and loveless, neglected by her father, the cold and ineffectual Prince Roland. Romantic, a daydreamer, and easy victim of men, the unhappy, neurotic girl was subjected to blackmail and extortion, and was at her wits' end to find a husband until she met Prince George of Greece. They were married in November 1907, but the marriage, begun with high hopes, was a disaster: Marie was restless, oversexed, and promiscuous, George cold, distant, and unfaithful. They had two children but spent much of their lives apart; she obtained as a lover no less a personage than Aristide Briand, many times Prime Minister of France. Increasingly unstable, but generous and fiercely intelligent, Marie was an astonishing figure in Philip's life; soon she would embrace Freud as both friend and inspiration, and would become his patroness, savior, and disciple.

It was imposed on the Foreign Office by King George V that the Greek royals must not come to England until Parliament was in recess and the press was mostly on vacation; their presence as guests of Buckingham Palace would cause a furor. "The Prime Minister agrees with the King in thinking it most undesirable that Prince Andrew should come to England at the present time," a Foreign Office report dated December 7, 1922, reads. They were sneaked into Marlborough House and thence into Kensington Palace, where Philip's grandmother, the dowager marchioness of Milford Haven, received them with gruff Germanic welcomes and chain-smoked cigarettes, incessantly grumbling about the murder of her two sisters, Grand Duchess Elizabeth and the Czarina Alix, at the hands of the Communists in 1918.

It was thus in terror, exile, and disgrace that Philip had his first taste of life. The wrangling between the Treasury and the Admiralty over who should pay for the Greek royal family's rescue and travel expenses dragged on for years. The King made sure that the dowager Marchioness of Milford Haven paid the out-of-pocket costs; the Admiralty secretly paid the rest. This unhappy family of exiles, impoverished, dependent on others, owed everything to their chief benefactresses.

In January 1923, after depositing Philip and his sisters in Paris, Prince Andrew and Princess Alice went to the United States as guests of Christopher and his wife Anastasia in Palm Beach; they were aboard ship when news of King Constantine's death reached them. On their return, they devoted little time to raising their children; irresponsible and vague, they drifted rapidly apart. It took constant British intervention for Mon Repos to be rescued from confiscation by the Greeks; this intervention was at the behest of the King and Lady Milford of Haven, and was drastically opposed within the Foreign Office.

Through royal influence, the family silver was stored at the British consulate in Corfu.

In an atmosphere of secret deals, conspiracy, disgrace and family squabbles, Philip grew up an arrogant but vividly handsome, casually cheerful, and athletic young Viking forced to hold his own in an army of formidable women and determined to wipe out his family disgrace. And soon, in his childhood, he became aware of his strange family: the need to communicate in sign language with his mother, the rages at her husband's treatment by the dowager Marchioness of Milford Haven, Princess Marie Bonaparte's nymphomaniac behavior, his father's and uncle's inflammatory attacks on Greece, and the fact that the French hated all of them for their role in attacking French troops in 1916.

The situation scarcely made conditions in Paris comfortable, despite the impeccable support of that eminent political figure, the ugly but impressive Aristide Briand, whose prolonged romantic devotion to Princess Bonaparte, given scant response from her in a physical sense, was an obscure wonder of the age. A main presence in Philip's life was his exiled cousin King George II of Greece, the power of whose Glucksburg dynasty, as it was familiarly known, was ended on March 25, 1924, when Greece became a republic. The small, oily-haired, and dapper George II, who wore built-up shoes to conceal his lack of height and who enjoyed prizefights, tennis, shooting game and circuses, fast cars and pretty men and women, and hated intellectuals ("I distrust the professor and the pedant," he once said. "The world is too full of bookworms . . . ") drifted from Bucharest to Copenhagen to Paris, where he dabbled in screen writing and talked vaguely of being an actor. Later, he moved to Brown's Hotel in London, a silly lost figure for all his extrovert charm, destined to be a pawn of Churchillian wartime politics.

At the age of three, Philip was frequently at the home of the wealthy Greek Anna Foufounis, at Berck-Plage in France. He was fond of the Foufounis children, Jean, their son, and the two daughters Helene and Ria. Anna Foufounis recalled, "My Philip used to race excitedly in heavy wooden *sabots* through the gardens of my home outside Marseilles."

She described him vividly:

His hair was white-blond and fine, like that of his father . . . his features were chiseled like his mother's, and his eyes were the penetrating blue of his Danish forebears. He stood there solemnly, a well-mannered child in rather long shorts of gray corduroy and a pullover . . .

Philip enjoyed taking photographs with a box Brownie; from the beginning, photography was his hobby. He was passionately interested in cars, and asked for a real one, complaining when Anna Foufounis sent him a "gorgeous little red push-pedal automobile." He hated to be introduced as Prince Philip, grandson of the King of Greece, and would shout at Mrs. Foufounis, "I'm just Philip. Just Philip, that's all!" With Jean, who was two years older than he, he would wade in pools at Berck-Plage, echo the cries of fisherwomen as they caught shrimps in nets; on one occasion, they were almost drowned in a shrimp pool. Mrs. Foufounis remembered that Philip was from the beginning taught by his Nurse Roose to be an English gentleman. All his clothes came from the best London children's shops. He'd recite English nursery rhymes set to music, including "Ride a Cock Horse to Banbury Cross" and "Hi Diddle Diddle." He had odd habits: at a tea party at Berck-Plage, he was missing after the group dispersed, and was found drinking every drop of tea from the leftovers in the cups. Nurse Roose was appalled.

When, during a game of tennis in the entrance hall, Philip and Jean Foufounis broke an expensive vase, Jean's nurse, Mrs. MacDonald, approached Philip to spank him. He said sharply, Mrs. Foufounis remembered, "Nobody's allowed to spank me but my own nanny!"

On one occasion, at the Foufounis house at Marseilles, the family was disturbed to find the two boys missing. They noticed that two expensive rugs had also vanished. It turned out that the boys were imitating the local Moroccan rug sellers and had gone down the road and sold the carpets to buy toys with.

Philip's favorite animals were pigs. Much as he liked the family's pet goat, cows, horses, and dogs, pigs were paramount in his life. He turned prophet when he said to Jean, "I shall play a pig. You'll let me. Someday, I'll be an important man—a King even! If you'll let me be pig now, when I'm grown up I'll take you out in my car!" He enjoyed farming, taking apart and reassembling clocks, constructing a primitive version of an airplane out of two-by-fours, and chasing the neighborhood children ecstatically.

In 1927, Philip, age six, was a pupil at The Elms, Donald McJannet's famous school for wealthy Americans at St. Cloud. The very high fees were met by Princess Marie Bonaparte, and by Prince Christopher, who had by now inherited his dead wife's American tin-plate millions.[4] Alice opened a boutique to make some money; Andrew disappeared often; Philip's sisters were farmed out to the Hesses and others in Germany.

Between the ages of four and six, Philip was often at Cotrocene, the royal Palace of Bucharest, or at Sinaia, the royal residence in the Transylvanian Alps, visiting his cousins Prince Michael of Rumania and Princess Alexandra. The Glamorous Queen Marie of Rumania was their hostess; Philip called her affectionately Aunt Missie. She told the children marvelous fairy stories in her bedroom. An early memory of Philip's was this amazing woman blazing with diamonds; on one occasion, she dropped a priceless diadem; Alexandra picked it up, and Marie gave it to her.

He would also visit his aunt, the Kaiser's sister, Queen Sophie of Greece, at Pankau on the Baltic coast; the Baltic fishermen would carry him shoulder high to their boats, and he early learned a love of the sea. He was a prankster: he let all the pigs at Pankau out of the sties, and the animals charged an elaborate tea party and upset the guests and the tables. He was also often at Wolfsgarten, the Hesse estate.

In England, Philip stayed at his mother's brother Lord Mountbatten's country home, Adsdean, a rambling Victorian folly, or at Lynden Manor, his uncle George's house. His family was still working for months on end protecting Mon Repos. Louis Mountbatten even leased the property to save it. It was also protected by Sir Harold Wernher, wealthy brother-in-law of Nadejda (always called Nada), the wife of George, Marquess of Milford Haven.

The ménage of the Milford Havens, who were very prominent in European society, was, to say the least, sexually peculiar, and would become more so over the years. Nada was an overpowering presence in the young Philip's life. She was thirty-four years old, a dark, slender, exquisitely dressed and

---

4. Her first husband had been the multimillionaire William B. Leeds, who gave her a son.

jeweled beauty, when Philip moved in to the house. She was widely understood to be a lesbian, the lover of Lady Louis Mountbatten, her sister-in-law, and the year before at Cannes she had fallen in love with Gloria Vanderbilt, Sr. They had become fiercely attracted during a big do at the Cannes Sporting Casino when Nada and Prince George triumphed in a Charleston competition; Nada was seen bathing her sore feet in a golden bath of champagne. She sent her hostess the bill for the wine.

Nada's background was almost excessively exotic. She was a great-granddaughter of the celebrated Russian poet Alexander Pushkin; her mother, the ravishing Countess Torby, was as widely gossiped about as her husband, the Grand Duke Michael of Russia. When they married morganatically, Czar Nicholas II refused to acknowledge the match, and the pair fled to England with bags of gold ingots stuffed into their personally owned railroad train. The hoard of gold was described by the Bank of England's governor as the biggest deposit in the bank's history. Grand Duke Michael's possessions included three oceangoing yachts, private cars on every major railway in Europe, a villa in the South of France, and an Adam-designed house, Kenwood, on Hampstead Heath in London. It was whispered that Nada had black blood; one of her ancestors was said to have been an Abyssinian Prince, seized from the Sultan's seraglio in Constantinople. People talked incessantly behind her back about her almost jet eyes and the crispy curls of her black hair. Her marriage to George Milford Haven (then Battenberg) in November 1916 was a huge social event and was attended by the King and Queen of England and Queen Alexandra.

Philip spent many Lynden Manor days with Nada and Gloria Vanderbilt, both exotically gorgeous, or with his uncle, who was equally bizarre, or at the barn where Uncle George had his fabled miniature railroad. The trains covered two miles of winding track, brilliantly constructed within the barn's confines, with tunnels carved through the thick old Tudor walls. Finished in 1929, the railroad cost the Milford Havens the present-day equivalent of $120,000. There were hills and dales made of papier-mâché, goods sheds and sidings, imitation forests made of metal, and mountain ranges with imitation ice.

It is uncertain whether Philip was allowed to investigate the secret, locked bookcases in the library. There, the odd owner of the house maintained one of the most extraordinary porno-graphic book collections in the world. It was supplemented by several albums of photographs of people in various positions of sexual intercourse. There were books on bondage and whip-ping, thumbscrews and racks, photographs in which there were incestuous orgies between every member of a family. George collected garish advertisements for dildos and the 1930s version of vibrators, as well as condoms with stimulating chemicals introduced into them. Had the unsuspecting Philip explored the collection, and it is not impossible he may have done so, he would have found such books as *The Awful Confessions of Maria Monk,* the story of a nun's nightly ravishment in a convent, *Raped on the Railway,* about the violent ill-treatment of a woman on the Flying Scotsman, *A Tale of the Birch,* or *Lady Gay: Sparkling Tales of Fun and Flagellation.* At night, after tucking the children into bed, Lord Milford Haven would settle down to a pleasant evening's reading, perhaps finding consolation for his wife's frequent absences with Gloria Vanderbilt.

Philip's fondness for the saxophone, performing practical jokes, and playing noisy games with George and Nada's children Elizabeth and David got on everyone's nerves. He and David took off to Dover, returning by Thames barge, to everyone's combined despair and relief. Soon, Gloria Vander-bilt, to make things more confusing, would break off her engagement to the Czech-Austrian Prince Gottfried von Hohenlohe-Langenburg, great-grandson of Queen Victoria. He would, instead, marry Princess Margarita, Philip's sister.

That marriage took place in 1931; and in a twelve-month period, so did the marriages of Philip's other three sisters: Theodora to Gottfried, Margrave of Baden; Cecilia to Georg Donatus, author and Hereditary Grand Duke of Hesse and by Rhine, another great-grandson of Queen Victoria; and Sophie to Prince Christoph of Hesse, who would soon be enlisting in Himmler's Order of the Death's Head.

On May 26, 1932, Andrew wrote from Basel, Switzerland, to the royalist papers in Greece attacking Venizélos's critiques of the royal family and describing himself and his brothers, "wandering in foreign parts in poverty, deprived by Monsieur Venizélos of fatherland and nationality at a moment when he, now an extremely wealthy man, abandons an unhappy and exhausted Greece whose people are poverty-stricken and miserable." He referred to the five ministers and a general executed in 1922 as "national martyrs, assassinated by Monsieur Venizélos" and to the late King Constantine as "dying in foreign parts and still unburied in Florence." His refusal to admit Venizélos's attempt to save his life infuriated the British.

It was decided that Philip should have a German education, and after four years at Old Tabor School, Cheam, Surrey, he was sent briefly to Salem, the German school near Lake Constance that had been founded by his brother-in-law's father, the famous Prince Max. The ghostly, overwhelming presence at Salem was the pedagogue Kurt Hahn, who left just before Philip arrived, and would soon be his headmaster in Scotland. He was among the most important influences in Philip's early life.

Educated at Oxford, the gaunt, stooped, and despotic Hahn had returned to his native Germany just before the outbreak of World War I. Appointed head of the Berlin Foreign Ministry's British information-gathering desk, he determined that the *Lusitania* was carrying 4,200 chests of Springfield cartridges and 11 tons of black gunpowder, intelligence which led to the *Lusitania*'s sinking in 1915; he also was able to predict British troop movements, which led to the slaughter in the trenches. Ironically, the sinking of the *Lusitania* helped cause the German defeat, since it was instrumental in provoking America's entry into the war. As special adviser to Chancellor Prince Max von Baden, Hahn became the chief negotiator for peace in 1918, working closely with William Bullitt of the U.S. State Department; but he was unable to achieve his purpose: to allow Germany to retain her colonies and to be permitted defeat with honor—a result of this failure was the devastating agreement of Versailles.

Von Baden and Hahn set up school in a wing of Schloss Salem—a vast thirteenth-century converted Cistercian monastery at Lake Constance—with a class of forty-five girls and boys, who were raised on principles of mental and physical health; meantime, Hahn was, as a part-Jew, in difficulties with the Nazi regime that came to power in January 1933. At first a supporter of the Nazis, he now favored the centrist or moderate elements in the party, believing, along with Prince Max, that the Old Germany, of the Junker class, and of the aristocratic elite, was preferable to an extremist gangsterdom; he tried to influence Hitler against too drastic measures.

Before Philip arrived at Salem in 1934, Hahn had been arrested and put in prison; according to T. C. Worsley in the book *Flanneled Fool,* Hahn begged Hitler to be allowed to stay in Germany, but had to go because he was part-Jewish; according to other sources, former British Prime Minister Ramsay MacDonald interceded for him and got him out.

Next to Hahn, Prince Max's son, the amiable Gottfried (married to Philip's sister) was the chief influence on Philip at the school. Legend has it that the Nazi youth movement was present at Schloss Salem and that Philip laughed at the swastikas and the goose-stepping and refused to heil Hitler; but again there is no evidence, simply oft-repeated tales. But it is certain he learned the Hahnian principles: suppression of sexual desire, "self-contemplation" (today we would call it meditation), severe physical training, including gardening and construction, forced marches, Marine-style pack drill, and swimming, along with the less emphasized academic curriculum.

Transferred to Scotland in 1933, Hahn began the Salemish Platonic school of Gordonstoun, while at the same time acting as a self-appointed adviser to the Foreign Office in London, urging policies of restraint and appeasement and appeals to the "middle" Nazis. Oddly, one of the governor-founders was Lord Tweedsmuir (John Buchan), whose novels were grossly anti-Semitic. It would not be long before Hahn, who probably was frustrated by his own Jewishness since it forced him out of Germany, would embrace Christianity in front of the whole school: a process of self-Aryanization of which Dr. Goebbels himself would have approved.

The talk, not to say the hubbub, of Lynden Manor while Philip was waiting to be admitted to Gordonstoun for the fall term, was the involvement of his brother-in-law, Prince Gottfried von Hohenlohe-Langenburg and his sister Margarita, and more importantly, his protectress and aunt Nadejda, Marchioness of Milford Haven, in the most sensational American court case of the year. Gloria Vanderbilt was in the middle of a ferocious custody battle against Mrs. Harry Payne Whitney for possession of one of the world's wealthiest brats—Gloria's own daughter and namesake.

On October 4, Nada, her eyes flashing fire, her cheeks flushed, stormed into Lynden Manor and screamed at her husband that she had been falsely accused of lesbianism by

Mrs. Vanderbilt's former maid, who had testified under oath she had seen Nada embrace Mrs. Vanderbilt in her bedroom at Cannes and kiss her "like a lover." As the wife of a descendant of Queen Victoria, she was answerable to the Palace, and within hours—no doubt to Philip's fascination—she was summoned to answer the charges against her. She denied them, but they stuck especially because she did not at once sail to the United States to give evidence.

Instead, she made sure that Gloria's former lover, Hohenlohe-Langenburg, testified, along with Philip's sister, that the charges were false: the Hohenlohes at once took ship to New York, fielded a storm of questions from the press, and on the witness stand, denied charges of lesbianism against Gloria, and asserted that she was a fit mother; Prince Gottfried's statements were ruinously undermined by the testimony of another maid, Emma Sullivan Keislich, who stated point-blank that she had seen Gloria, still a married woman, in bed with the Prince, and that he had cohabited with her for one entire summer at Biarritz.

The Hohenlohe-Langenburgs arrived at Lynden Manor wishing they had never crossed the Atlantic. In the midst of the scandal, David and Nada Milford Haven had the scalding effrontery to drive Philip to Gordonstoun, where Kurt Hahn, no doubt smacking his lips over gossip, but hoping (presumably in vain) no word would leak to his pupils, received his future protégé with open arms.

At Gordonstoun, Philip, with his perfect Nordic looks, became a prize pupil of Hahn and his German imported master, Dr. Erich Meissner. The result of the training was that he became a juvenile superman, domineering, contemptuous of theoretical learning, cold before displays of emotion, devoted to athletic accomplishment, the picture of fitness, hard, insolent, and Germanic to his fingertips.

Life at Gordonstoun (where Prince Charles, Prince Andrew, and Prince Edward would one day be pupils) was unpleasant, rugged, and demanding; the boys were wakened in the early morning hours, plunged into a hot and then a cold shower, followed by runs and lessons; periods of the day were spent in silence, recalling Salem's monastic origins; punishments were strict. Hahn's looming dark presence was everywhere, snooping into corners, running everyone into the ground with Germanic insistence, invoking the authoritarian principles of

Plato; he strode around with shoulders hunched like an ape's, his coattails flapping behind him, his head always covered with a gigantic wide-brimmed German hat, designed to keep the feeble Scottish sunlight off his skull, which had a large metal plate set into it as a result of some mysterious operation or mishap during his years at Oxford. Hated, worshiped, feared, loved, he was a force like thunder.

Philip was noted for his practical jokes, including sewing up a master's pajama bottoms, and filling shoes with water; nevertheless, he was a favorite of Hahn's; he and his fellow pupils literally helped build the school—a neat way of Hahn's obtaining free labor. He proved to be an expert seaman aboard the *Prince Louis*,[5] named for his grandfather and used as a Gordonstoun training vessel; he also captained a school cutter without sails in the North Sea—or so he told his cousin, Princess Alexandra.

At thirteen, Philip was a magnificent-looking boy, the Aryan product of a Jewish schoolmaster's version of strength-through-joy principles. In school holidays, escaping the hothouse world of George and Nada Milford Haven, he spent much time in Europe with his cousin Princess Alexandra of Rumania and with his sisters.

Philip's brother-in-law and Sophie's husband, Prince Christoph of Hesse, was by 1935 chief of the Forschungsamt, a Special Intelligence operation run by Goering.[6] He was also Standartenführer (colonel) of the SS on Himmler's personal staff—one of the first aristocrats, with his brother Wilhelm, to join. The organization, which we shall call the F.G., infiltrated the officer corps in the armed forces, seeking out members who were subversive of Hitler. The leaders of the Nazi party were investigated and so was the Catholic Church, and the findings of the F.G. resulted in the devastation of the Catholics in Germany. In collaboration with the Gestapo, the F.G. investigated all Jews, the trade unions, all the labor organizations, and the German people as a whole. Himmler had a major role in the F.G. When Captain Ernst Roehm of the Stormtroopers (SA) was suspected of homosexuality and subversive activity, the

5. It is probable that Edwina Mountbatten and Louis's fund-raising campaigns materially assisted the school.
6. His brother, Prince Philipp, was Nazi governor of Hesse, under the aegis of Goering, and was to become Hitler's chief emissary to Mussolini.

F.G. took the lead in investigating him and his followers, through microphones concealed in lamps, clocks, or telephones. As a result, Hitler brought about the Night of the Long Knives. The dreaded F.G. played a special role in undermining the inner structure of the Austrian and Czechoslovakian governments. It created and broke codes. The headquarters was the Hotel Knie in Charlottenberg, Berlin.

Christoph and Sophie had five children. The eldest of two sons was named Karl Adolf, after Hitler; his education would one day be aided by Philip as royal husband and Duke of Edinburgh.

In 1935, Philip's cousin George II was returned to the Greek throne after a long exile in London; the plebiscite was notoriously rigged through British influence.

The following year Philip attended a ceremony of reburial of King Constantine, Queen Sophie, and Queen Olga at Tatoi, the royal seat near Athens; the fickle Greek public cheered the family they had ignominiously exiled. Always greedy, Philip overate the lobster served at the funerary banquet and became so violently ill he could not walk behind the coffin during the solemn procession.

On November 16, 1937, Philip heard desolating news on the radio: Georg Donatus, Hereditary Grand Duke of Hesse and by Rhine, and Cecilia left Ostend for London in one of Goering's crack junkers for Georg's brother's[7] wedding to Margaret Campbell Geddes, daughter of the former British Ambassador to Washington. On the plane, Cecilia was apparently seized by labor pains, and the pilot, acting on instructions, attempted a landing in fog to obtain help. Banking for the turn, he crashed into a factory chimney at Steene and the entire family, except for a baby daughter who had been left behind—she died two years later—and including two young sons, was burned to death. The wedding was held in black. Philip took the news with the manfully controlled emotion and rigid calm that had been taught him at Gordonstoun.

Another severe bereavement occurred when the intriguingly decadent George Milford Haven died of cancer after a long struggle at the age of forty-eight; again calm and stoical, Philip

---

7. Prince Ludwig of Hesse and by Rhine, sometime associate and chargé d'affaires for Joachim von Ribbentrop, German Ambassador to the Court of St. James's.

was a great consolation to his flamboyant aunt Nada, who moved to her home in the South of France.

In Paris, Philip saw his wayward benefactress Princess Marie Bonaparte; in Athens, he attended the expensive wedding of Princess Friederike, granddaughter of the Kaiser and former Hitler Youth member, to his cousin by marriage Prince Paul of Greece in January 1938; he continued to Venice, as the guest of his aunt by marriage, King Alexander III's commoner widow, Aspasia, a former nurse. At the famous Harry's Bar and on two other occasions he met the beautiful Cobina Wright, Jr., famous debutante and soon to be mascot of the New York World's Fair. Her mother, Cobina Senior, a leading American socialite, pushed her daughter in the matter; Philip spent many evenings dancing Cobina Junior off her feet; but the likelihood is that his chief romantic interest in Venice was his pretty cousin, Princess Alexandra. And then, half the girls of Venice were in pursuit of the dashing, flirtatious, hot-tempered blond Prince, who was enjoying the bounty of his aunt, even though he had not a penny of his own. On a subsequent trip to Europe, he visited his father, who had taken as mistress a well-known actress.

When he left Gordonstoun after being guardian, or head boy, at seventeen, it was felt that Philip should do service in the Royal Navy, but only for purposes of manhood training, not reasons of a career. It was at Dartmouth that, as we know, he met Elizabeth, and the course of history was set.

The circumstances of the 1939 meeting were unexciting: Philip was still fretting from being made to dig a trench and undertake solo drill on his birthday weeks earlier. He half-heartedly showed the Princesses how to operate a model train at the home of Captain (later Admiral) Frederick Dalrymple-Hamilton, C.O. of Dartmouth. Later, the youngsters played croquet, and Philip demonstrated his athletic skill by leaping over a tennis net. A restless Elizabeth kept asking when she could go back to the yacht. He was twice aboard the *Victoria and Albert,* the first at dinner that night, the second to see the Princesses. His frisky temper allied him more closely to Margaret than to her more severe elder sister, who was dismayed by his boisterous extroversion but attracted to his good looks. When the yacht left next day, the cadets from Dartmouth, in a state of high excitement, provided a noisy unofficial escort; the King declared their maneuvers unsafe and ordered them back to port, but Philip typically disobeyed. According to Crawfie, the King exclaimed, "The young fool! He must go back!" Yelled at through the yacht's public address system, the irrepressible Philip at last yielded. One of the vivid memories of Princess Elizabeth's lifetime was seeing the dashing young cadet as he turned his boat, waving until he vanished from sight.

8
***

THE MEETING OF ELIZABETH and Philip was engineered by Lord Louis Mountbatten, and by King George II of Greece; the intention was to bring off a royal betrothal, even though Elizabeth was only thirteen. Such an alliance arranged in youth was not uncommon in royal families at the time; and it had every advantage for the Greeks.

The ghastly memories of 1916 could be expunged; the hole-in-the-corner existence of the Greeks in Paris might well change for the better; and perhaps the behavior of Philip's two sisters in marrying Nazis, one of whom was a Secret Intelligence chief, might be papered over with British royal influence. Of course, when the wedding took place a few years hence, there could be no question of those sisters attending it, and, if war broke out, no communication with them would be possible; nevertheless, with Britain on the verge of war, to even consider a man as a prospective Prince Consort whose family was steeped in Nazism (his cousin Friederike was under grave suspicion, with four brothers in the Nazi armies) was bold and mysterious. And wasn't there fear of a security leak, that Philip might inadvertently send information in letters to his German clan? Presumably he was warned to restrict his mail to meaningless generalities, and not to discuss Dartmouth or anything else of significance in England.

From the Mountbatten point of view, there was the advantage that Philip would help to rub out the unfortunate memory of his grandfather's forced resignation as First Sea Lord and the widespread rumors of illegitimacy in the family line. And one cannot put it past Lord Louis that he would be furthering his own soaring ambition in fostering the alliance. Money played a part: Philip was notably short of even the most meager funds.

As for Philip's parents, they seem to have played no role in the conspiracy and in fact Princess Alice, his mother, was backing him to assume the throne of Greece after the death or abdication of King George II.

Boisterous and aggravating, Philip nevertheless charmed Elizabeth, though not Princess Margaret or Crawfie, who wrote of the encounter with less than enthusiasm in her memoirs. For Elizabeth, he was Prince Charming, with his athletic bearing, his chiseled face (very similar to that of his uncle Prince George of Greece in Paris), his apparent freshness, wholesomeness, and normalcy despite his bizarre upbringing. From then on, he was the only man she loved or would ever love. His interest in her was casual, indifferent; he was in no mood to be committed to anyone, with the world of young and pretty girls waiting for a handsome cadet in Navy uniform.

A few weeks after the meeting, war broke out. The royal family was in residence at Balmoral, according to tradition; the King and Queen left for London at once. "Who is this Hitler spoiling everything?" Margaret is supposed to have remarked. They moved to Birkhall, which was felt to be less obvious a target for German bombers. Elizabeth wrote to Philip constantly; now that the war had started, his plans to train for the Royal Navy and then leave the service were abandoned, and he became a fully enlisted seaman, passing out of Dartmouth as special entry cadet and winner of the King's Dirk.

Louis Mountbatten arranged a posting; the chosen vessel was the *Ramillies;* Prince Philip went aboard on February 24, 1940, in Colombo, Ceylon, with letters to the ship's captain, Harold Baillie-Grohman. He confided in his commander, "My uncle has ideas for me; he thinks I should marry Princess Elizabeth." "Are you fond of her?" he was asked. "Oh yes," he replied. "I write to her every week."

The *Ramillies* sailed via Australia to Middle Eastern waters, and in April was at Aden, a hot, burned-out township traditionally used as a port for vessels en route to Australia. After a brief posting to an Australian cruiser he returned to the *Ramillies.*

Even in 1940, Britain's royals were able to keep in touch with his sisters in Germany, through his uncle Lord Louis Mountbatten and the dowager Marchioness of Milford Haven. They forwarded letters, via the Swedish Embassy in London, and Louis's sister, Louise, Crown Princess of Sweden, a nation at that time in league with the Nazis.

Many of the documents concerning the royal correspondence through Sweden have disappeared, thanks to the weeders who periodically remove sensitive information from the Public Record Office at Kew, London; but a few documents have survived from September through November 1940. They show how Victor Mallet, the British Minister in Stockholm, pleaded continually with the Foreign Office to allow the letters to go through the diplomatic bag.

By November, Mallet's pleas had worked and Lord Halifax, Foreign Secretary, had yielded; this surrender to an inadvisable arrangement occurred when R. A. Butler at the Foreign Office was making some disgraceful government-authorized peace feelers behind Churchill's back, communicating with the Germans via Sweden, and organizing Swiss meetings to replace Hitler with Goering.

Life at Birkhall was overshadowed by word of sinkings of British ships, with great loss of life; the royal family would grimace or make sharp comments during the broadcasts from Berlin of the British traitor William Joyce (Lord Haw-Haw); they followed the rationing and blackout regulations like any citizens, equipped with the customary garb of British people at the time; sensible tweeds, scarves, rubber boots, and gas masks during drills; they learned how to man hoses in rescue exercises and served tea and cakes to the locals. Then, rather oddly, the Princesses were moved to the far more vulnerable and identifiable Royal Lodge. The King and Queen could not bear their absence so far from London.

War or no war, Christmas was spent at Sandringham, with the entire family present; the King even held his Privy Council there. Talk of the family—or at least the Princesses—going to Canada was instantly quashed: they would soldier on to the end. It was a great aid to British morale when the King played in an ice hockey match at Sandringham in January. And the Queen abandoned the extravagance and indulgence in displays of pomp and wealth that had marked her prewar career; she became every British housewife rolled into one, marching with felt hat, mackintosh and umbrella, in smart street clothes with three strands of pearls, through evacuee camps and old folks' homes, in that period of the phony war before the bombs started to fall. It was a time when, instead of attacking and

crushing Germany from the air, the British seemed to be
incapable and passive, the enfeebled and cancer-stricken
Chamberlain giving an ear to appeasers and the Duchess of
Gloucester's brother, the Duke of Buccleuch, actually insisting
peace be made, an attitude which soon would cost him his job
as Lord Steward of the royal household.

Chamberlain's attitude was more and more obstructionist
and stubborn in the early part of 1940; he refused the Labor
demands to mobilize Britain's plagued economy under one
single director.

Britain spent those strange months of nonbelligerence in
economic war and blockade, forcing neutral countries to favor
Whitehall and prevent supplies from reaching Germany, but
still not seizing the initiative and attacking Hitler. Then came
the surprise German invasion of Denmark and Norway on
April 9; the disastrous failure of the British Expeditionary
Force in Norway infuriated the British public and brought the
government to its knees. A resounding victory would have
frightened Hitler and stemmed his march of conquest. When
Chamberlain tried to form the coalition, Labor members
refused to serve under him. When Hitler invaded the Netherlands on May 10, Chamberlain was finished, and the King
wanted the questionable Lord Halifax to replace him; but God
smiled on England, and Churchill was appointed, and also
became Minister of Defense, with Halifax as Foreign Secretary; by degrees, the King overcame his unease over Churchill
and succumbed to his energy and charm. By the end of May,
Hitler had destroyed Belgium and, by June, France lay defeated
and betrayed. On May 13, Churchill delivered his famous
"blood, sweat and tears speech." On June 30 and July 1,
Germany occupied the Channel Islands.

Much attention was given that summer of 1940 to the matter
of the royal protection; surprisingly, no bomb shelter was at
that time built under the Palace, but rather a housemaids' joint
sitting room was appropriated, situated as it was in a basement.
Queen Mary was evacuated from Marlborough House to
Badminton, the family home of the tenth Duke of Beaufort,
Master of the Horse, where she proved to be a tetchy,
demanding guest; the Duchess of Gloucester and the Duchess
of Kent did not abandon their houses.

The two Princesses were removed to Windsor Castle, where
they would remain for the duration. Princess Margaret recalled,

"We packed for the weekend and . . . stayed for five years." Why they were not at this stage sent back to Scotland with the Germans in the Channel Islands can again only be explained by both the need for family unity and the necessity to keep up British morale. If the nation would fight on the beaches, then they would stand firm in the country citadel of the kingdom, with the King and Queen (who learned to fire a revolver) unshaken at Buckingham Palace.

The air raids on Britain in July and August found the royal family more determined and unbudgeable then ever. On the night of July 11, the King was inspecting a military camp in the south of England when German bombers leveled a village he had left just minutes before; Churchill had to take shelter in a trench during a similar attack. On August 1, the King and Queen toured the East Midlands. Families whose homes had been totally destroyed lined up to shake hands with them.

Sugar rationing precluded Margaret (as it had Elizabeth) from having icing on her birthday cake that season; she had allegedly saved food coupons for a month to provide enough sugar for the cake itself. In the third week of August, the King was busy inspecting Free French troops in the South of England; the Queen joined him in leaving London in the middle of an air raid through the blackout for a train journey to the north to look at gun emplacements.

In September, the Germans' most severe attacks took place. Princess Margaret discussed in a broadcast many years later the feeble attempts at a defense of Windsor, bombs falling nearby; actually, it was surrounded by anti-aircraft guns, among the most powerfully guarded sites in England. Its art treasures were moved to tin mines in Cornwall.

On September 9, a bomb crashed outside the Regency Room near the Buckingham Palace swimming pool. It did not explode at once, and neither the King nor the Queen was present in the Palace. Most of the staff moved out; it proved impossible to dig the bomb out of the concrete. Then, in the early morning hours of September 10, the bomb did explode, shattering the pool and throwing a two-ton piece of Portland stone about twenty feet. It blew smaller pieces over the roof and shattered the glass in the North Front of the royal residential quarters. It buried a staircase and seven stone pillars; at that moment the King and Queen were in the East End, and had to join their bedraggled subjects in a cellar as the air raid signal sounded.

On the thirteenth, while the King and Queen were in the maids' sitting room under the North Wing, two sticks of three bombs each landed at Buckingham Palace; one destroyed the Private Chapel where the Princesses were christened, another shattered a water main and fire hydrant, sending water spurting, two fell in the forecourt, and others fell in the quadrangle and the garden. The King and Queen lunched in their shelter.

The Princesses had been trained by their grandmother to show no displays of fear or emotion during those perilous weeks of 1940; in fact, Elizabeth continued to take her lessons in constitutional history from Vice Provost of Eton C. H. K. (later Sir Henry) Marten with absolutely no certainty that she would live long enough to need what he taught her. For other children, the war was in many ways a big adventure, Hitler and Mussolini seen as comically insignificant as the figures in coconut shies, the propaganda machinery engineered in Whitehall carefully put together to defuse any sense of awe the humorous and skeptical British public might be tempted to feel for the common enemy. But the Princesses had been taught to know better.

By now, Elizabeth was dutiful and severe; she was a tender guide to her sister in everything. Margaret never lost her wit, sparkle, and sense of mischief, which, if the two sisters had not been so utterly close, might have caused irritation.

The royal historian Sir John Wheeler-Bennett wrote, "[Margaret] it was who would always make her father laugh, even when he was angry with her."

On September 23, the Princesses listened enthralled as their father broadcast from the Palace, talking of "the armies of invasion massed across the Channel, only twenty miles from our shores . . ." and of the fact that London was, for the time being, "bearing the brunt of the enemy's spite." He spoke of recently introduced new honors, the George Cross, and Medal, for civilian service in war, and, with Churchillian overtones, he said, "The walls of London may be battered, but the spirit of the Londoner stands resolute and undismayed . . . Winter lies before us, cold and dark. Let us be of good cheer. After winter comes spring, and after our recent trials will surely come victory . . ." He closed with a reference to "the unconquerable spirit of the British people."

On October 13, while Philip was serving on the *Shropshire,* Elizabeth broke custom by turning up on the BBC "Children's

Hour" to express in a high, sweet voice, her conviction that all would be well. At the end, she said (and who that heard the broadcast would ever forget it?), "My sister is by my side . . . and we are both going to say good night to you. Come on, Margaret." And Margaret, aged ten, said, with great strength, "Good night, and good luck to you all!"

It would be fair to say that almost everyone in England heard the broadcast, offices and factories stopping work at 5 P.M. so that the words of encouragement could be enjoyed. When Elizabeth said that she and her family were "trying . . . to bear our own share of the danger and sadness of war," not a decent soul could argue with her.

That same spirit infused the brave young men of the Royal Air Force who, with cheerful gallantry, decimated the Luftwaffe's choicest pilots and planes in the Battle of Britain; as the sirens, the sandbags, the lines for food in the rain, and the steady crump of bombs went on and on, the nation was bound to a common purpose it had not shared since 1918. There were many new crosses to bear that dreary autumn of 1940: Coventry was leveled on November 15, U-boat sinkings of British ships were a heavy and grievous burden; but still, when Parliament opened on November 21, the pomp and ceremony were deliberately retained, and Churchill's speech was rousing.

For the King, the death of Chamberlain and the posting of Lord Halifax to Washington (where he could do little harm) were disturbing; but after much early reluctance he at last accepted Churchill completely. He and his wife and children were also heartened by the news that the United States supplied, before Lend Lease, six hundred thousand rifles, eighty thousand machine guns, and eight hundred 75-mm field guns, along with mothball destroyers and some merchantmen.

Christmas 1940 was spent at Windsor, where the Princesses took part in a nativity play, with Elizabeth as one of the three kings and Margaret as the child Jesus. To the Princesses' delight, their parents began to stay at the Castle each weekend as well as at night. The shoal of Christmas gifts from New York, even though so many had to be given away or returned, was welcome.

In January 1941, after service on the *Shropshire,* Philip was at Athens off the decks of the battleship *Valiant,* visiting his mother; Greece was fighting desperately against Mussolini for its survival. The inexhaustible British diarist Henry ("Chips")

Channon met Philip at a party that month and wrote, "He is to be our Prince Consort and that is why he is serving in our Navy." One can hardly doubt that the Prince was the source of this interesting information; he has been notably testy on the matter of the diary entry ever since. Philip served aboard the battleship *Valiant* that March, against the Italian fleet at the Battle of Cape Matapan. The captain of the *Greyhound,* a British vessel which joined the *Valiant,* ordered the ship's searchlights trained on the enemy and the other British ships followed suit. Philip was in charge of the *Valiant*'s searchlight unit; he was mentioned in dispatches and received from his uncle King George II the Greek War Cross of Valor.

The German invasion of Greece drove Philip's family headlong from Athens, first by seaplane to Crete, where George II tried to continue with a provisional government supported by the British, but unrecognized by his people, and thence aboard the British warship *Decoy,* to Alexandria, Egypt; only Princess Helen of Greece, Philip's aunt by marriage, wife of Prince Nicholas, and mother of the Duchess of Kent, and his mother Princess Alice elected to stay on under German occupation, their correspondence conveyed to them, rather surprisingly in view of the conditions of war, by no less than Thomas Cook and Son. Why were they allowed this peculiar privilege? Some correspondence of Prince Philip indicates that it was because Alice's daughters, his sisters, were all married to figures involved with the Nazis. Presumably, the fact that both were involved in charitable work entitled them to this arrangement with the pro-Nazi puppet government of Greece. As for Prince Andrew, he was in Monaco, which was some-what immorally preserving a convenient "neutrality" by accommodating British, Americans, Italians, and Germans at the same casino tables, with his mistress, a former actress.

Later that year, at the specific request of King George VI, who did not want any "dynastic heirs" of the Greeks to enter England (he had not forgotten 1916, but he had forgotten—or had he?—Prince Philip), the Greek royals were dispatched as far away as possible—to South Africa, where they became the house guests of General Jan Smuts. Philip saw a good deal of them before their departure from Egypt that spring, especially his appealing Greek cousin Alexandra (daughter of King Alexander I) of Venice days; with his cousin David Mountbatten he went swimming with them, drove them helter-skelter through the crowded, noisome streets of Cairo, drank lustily at the Ghezire Club, visited the pyramids and the Sphinx, and dined with them among the potted palms at the grand old Mena House Hotel. When they took off to Cape Town he turned up to surprise them, having come off a Canadian troopship, looking impressive in tropical whites. Then he sailed by a roundabout route to England for an officer training course.

In April the Princesses were overjoyed to receive a model of a Spitfire, fashioned by a Czech pilot from the scrap of a downed German Dornier bomber, sent to Windsor by the Czechs in exile. The children were busy "digging for victory" in the Windsor gardens, dressing their favorite dolls for the auction for injured war heroes, putting up with the depressing slaughter of half the royal deer in Windsor Great Park for venison to feed evacuees, joining their parents at St. George's Chapel (the King dressed as a field marshal), in a service of prayer for deliverance. Elizabeth's fifteenth birthday was celebrated at Windsor (still described as "somewhere in England" in the security-conscious press); she received from her parents her first major gift of jewelry, a turquoise necklace, brooch, and bracelet set that had belonged to Queen Victoria. She showed home movies taken by herself. The Princesses were fascinated to hear from their mother that she had found a picture of them in the bomb ruins of a London girls school. There must have been thousands of such pictures in homes and offices in London. On April 30, 1941, nine days after her birthday, Elizabeth, with Margaret beside her at a desk, would jointly write a "Thank you, Americans," letter, which Mrs. Kermit Roosevelt circulated in Washington, D.C., through the Young America Wants to Help Organization. It was the beginning of a lifelong love affair between the Princesses (marred only by the unfortunate habit the Americans had of calling Elizabeth Princess Betty) and the United States that continues to this day.

Nineteen forty-one was the year of the most ferocious of German onslaughts on the capital, and the year of greatest courage of the British people. St. Paul's Cathedral, Westminster Abbey, the British Museum, were all damaged and the House of Commons was gutted. Civil defense became compulsory for civilians who were fit enough and over forty-two. Two million tons of shipping were lost, almost fifty thousand killed in bombing raids; and these figures related to only the first six months of the year. Restaurants could merely serve soup or dessert and one main dish; cheese and clothing were rationed. But Lend Lease and victories in the Atlantic heartened the royal family and their peoples.

On July 20, the Princesses gave a concert of songs, dances, and pianism at Windsor for the King and Queen, the Duchess of Kent, and a large audience, to raise money for wool for knitting comforters for the armed services. They sang excellently in duets in French; they also helped design and paint the scenery. At the end of the concert they gave the V for Victory sign, whose use by the public had just been initiated by Churchill and by the BBC on American Independence Day when all Allied or defeated countries were called upon to use that letter in morse code.

The Queen was as unpunctual as ever in 1941, irritating the King constantly with her lateness; he did not have the forgiving attitude of his father, and sometimes her behavior led to sharp domestic quarrels. She rose at nine (the King was up and about by eight), took care of her many letters, answering each one personally, conferred with Sir Hill Child, master of the Royal Household, and with the chefs, then met the King for the first time in the day just before lunch. Half the prewar Palace staff were serving in the Forces, and this made managing the vast old Palace a major problem. The Queen knew every detail of the food stocks, the linen (over which she would brood with the housekeeper Mrs. Ferguson), kept a careful eye on press coverage of her children, spoke to them every day at Windsor when she was in London, supervised their six teachers (they were now learning American history, with Lord Bryce's *The American Commonwealth* as authorized text), saw to it that they learned German (!) and Spanish, and insisted Scottish history be part of the curriculum.

On December 19, the Princesses were watched by their parents acting in the pantomime *Cinderella* in the Waterloo Room at Windsor; Margaret was Cinders and Elizabeth a dashing Prince Charming; the chorus and orchestra were made up of Grenadier guardsmen, there was a supporting cast of thirty, and the audience of six hundred included refugee children. The pumpkin coach was Queen Anne's sedan chair. Afterward, the whole company was entertained to tea by the King and Queen.

The King's routine was precise; when he woke at exactly

eight, he was served a cup of his favorite black Indian tea, so strong that in British parlance you "could stand a spoon up in it"; by nine-thirty, when the Queen was applying her makeup after her bath, he had already had (with less than six inches of water and lukewarm besides) a bath, taken a simple breakfast of rationed food, and read all of the London papers, starting with *The Times.*

He went to his office and met one of his two Private Secretaries, who brought dispatches, marked "SECRET," from the War Office, the Air Ministry, and the War Cabinet Office. He was required to sign a number of documents, and he read every word of every one. Eleven to one was spent with official visitors, including Army, Navy, and Air Force chiefs or Americans like Eisenhower or Spaatz, or Australian, New Zealand, Canadian, and other Commonwealth figures. He chain-smoked throughout despite warnings from his doctors. Lunch was at one o'clock on the dot; a brisk thirty-minute walk, his only serious exercise, followed the meal. Churchill dined with him one day a week, always on Tuesdays. Their favorite repasts were Dover sole and cold roast beef, obtained from the royal fisheries and farms, and accompanied by scotch and soda rather than wine. They often laughed, sharing the same sense of humor, along with much serious discussion of the war.

After dinner, the family joined in listening to jazz records or "ITMA" ("It's That Man Again") with Tommy Handley, the greatest British radio comedy program of the war years. *Time* magazine reported that the family would celebrate with drinks and dinner on Saturdays, when the King, who shared his mother's love of risqué stories, would stand and drink and smoke and roar with laughter as leaders of the services told the latest tales dredged up from the rank and file. These (along with the times shared with Elizabeth and Margaret) were the best nights of all.

In September 1941, Philip was reunited in London with his Greek royal relatives. King George II was firmly installed at Claridge's Hotel and Philip at 16 Chester Street, owned by his uncle Louis: the monarch set up the Greek Government-in-exile in London and in Cairo. Precisely why King George VI had changed his mind about the dynastic heirs of the family being allowed to live in England is unclear, but the dowager Marchioness of Milford Haven and Lord Louis may well have

played a crucial role in the decision. Alice remained with
Helen, Nicholas's wife and mother of the Duchess of Kent, in
Athens in her strange "neutral" role, working for the Swiss
and Swedish Red Cross on child relief, while still correspond-
ing with her daughters in Germany through Crown Princess
Louise of Sweden, a continuing anomaly.

Princess Helen's situation was equally anomalous: she was
in touch with her daughters, also through Louise; of these,
Elizabeth was married to Count Toerring-Jettenbach, who was
serving as an officer in the German Army, and Olga was
married to Prince Paul of Yugoslavia, who signed a pact with
the Axis that helped in the downfall of Greece, while Princess
Marina was commandant of the WRNS (Women's Navy) in
England.

It is unsettling to report that when a German commandant
appeared at Helen's house he politely asked her if he could
requisition it as a hospital; she successfully talked him out of it;
also, she obtained permission to perform charitable duties and
visit the family graveyard at Tatoi. Would he have conceded to
her wishes if she was not at least considered friendly to the
German cause? She was a White Russian Grand Duchess by
birth, and a Hesse, which may have helped. What the King of
England and Winston Churchill thought of these arrangements
has not been recorded.

Philip cut a dashing figure in London society in the last part
of 1941 and into 1942. Nada, Marchioness of Milford Haven,
arranged for him to meet Queen Mary at Marlborough House;
he enchanted her with risqué Naval stories, to which she was
addicted; she dubbed him "a very bright young man." In the
West End, he was seen constantly with his favorite Greek
cousin Alexandra and with beautiful and fashionable debutantes at the 400 Club, the Savoy Grill, and other popular
nightspots. He was a guest of the Duke and Duchess of Kent at
their home at Coppins, Iver; he still adored his cousin Marina,
and was very fond of her children, particularly her middle
child, Princess of Kent, Alexandra, who was to become one of
his most intimate lifelong friends. He was also received at
Buckingham Palace, where he saw the Princesses. Then he was
posted as sublieutenant to Rosyth in Scotland, joining the HMS
Wallace, a destroyers' flotilla leader, in risky convoy duties,
dodging mines and torpedoes in the choppy North Sea.

Princess Elizabeth's confirmation took place in St. George's

Chapel on March 28. The *Times* published the fact two days later, unwisely revealing the Princesses' carefully hidden, "somewhere in England" whereabouts to the enemy; but the Castle was still not demolished. On April 10, Margaret became a Girl Guide. On her sixteenth birthday, Elizabeth took part in her first public ceremony since childhood, reviewing selected detachments of the Grenadier Guards as Colonel-in-Chief. She gave her first royal audience to Col. John Prescott of the Guards to discuss details of the ceremony. After the parade, she and her sister entertained the regiment with songs and dances at the Castle.

She also offered her first Princess Elizabeth essay prize, open to all children of Wales on the enterprising subject of metal salvage, and made her first registration at a Labor Exchange; in May, she became a patron of the new Queen Elizabeth Hospital. She was growing up.

August 1942 brought the joyous events of Prince Michael of Kent's baptism and Princess Margaret's birthday. But tragically, in a still unexplained flying boat crash in Scotland, the Princesses' beloved uncle George, the Duke of Kent, was killed on a mission to Iceland. This shocking bereavement deeply depressed the whole family; the funeral at St. George's Chapel was the first Royal Air Force ceremony to take place there. Noël Coward, one of the Duke's closest friends, collapsed, sobbing uncontrollably. Many others wept as the Duke's favorite musical work, Sinding's "Intermezzo Number One," was played. The Princesses were not permitted to attend.

The increase of Japanese power in Asia caused grave concern in England; French Indochina collapsed, and the attack on Pearl Harbor followed on December 7. The entry of America into the war, following Hitler's intense commitment to the Russian campaign, the error which would destroy him, greatly relieved England and was received with rejoicing at Buckingham Palace and at Windsor. Three million more men were drafted for military service, the age limit was increased to fifty-one, and at least sixty thousand women were in uniform.

Life in the royal residences continued with British calm. The poet and essayist Sir Osbert Sitwell was often at the Palace to advise the Queen on reading good books, to keep her mind off the air raids. She enjoyed Harding, Kipling, and Conrad while the King read the war dispatches. At weekends at Windsor, she played Ravel, Debussy, Beethoven, and Bach for her family on the piano. The circle was composed of David Bowes-Lyon, the Queen's brother, Lady Helen Graham, daughter of the Duke of Montrose, and (mysteriously, in view of her pro-Nazi politics before the war) an ailing Hon. Mrs. Ronnie Greville.

Nineteen forty-two was a year of other tribulations. Churchill was embattled following the fall of Singapore, severe setbacks in North Africa, and the sinking of British ships; in February, he was forced to reshuffle the Cabinet. In June, there was the devastating news of the British Eighth Army's defeat at Tobruk, and many called for Churchill's resignation. In August, half the British landing party at Dieppe was killed. But there was a change which heartened the royal family and brought rejoicing throughout England: the Eighth Army turned the tables on Rommel, Anglo-American landings in North Africa proved successful, and Russia fought back against the German invader. Despite coal rationing, a grievous burden to the British public, coal strikes, and drastically increased conscription, public morale remained as high as ever. And there was something unassailable about England, from the royals down, that attracted millions of Americans and made having their sons and husbands in the war more acceptable to troubled parents in Omaha or Dubuque or Pomona: croquet was still played on well-mown English lawns, rose shows still took place in villages, the vicar still had people to tea and biscuits, and schoolboys still tied strings to chestnut "conkers" and fought with them or got drenched in mud on rainswept football fields.

By June it was costing the nation £10 million a day to run the war. Famine swept Philip's Greece; cholera, typhoid, and pneumonia killed off thousands. A weird situation developed in which the Germans actually allowed the Allies to ship food-stuffs to Athens and to permit thousands of children to be evacuated. Princess Alice was working day and night in conditions of disease and starvation.

In October and November, Eleanor Roosevelt was in Lon-don; visiting the Palace, she found the King and Queen living in a building that was icy, drafty, and miserable; both monarchs were suffering from colds, and the Queen's bedroom windows were unrepaired from the recent bomb blasts, fitted up with slats. The food was terrible, though the best gold and silver service was used. When Mrs. Roosevelt was asked what was in her postbirthday cake, the Queen laughed and exclaimed, "Probably sawdust!''

There were other burdens that fall: rats invaded the Palace, and the entire staff, headed by the royal family, became involved in a bizarre, blackly comic adventure in catching and shooting the creatures. While visiting Windsor Castle one weekend, the Queen repaired to her bedroom, separate from the King's, and heard a strange sound from behind the curtains. She scarcely had time to cross the room to see what was there when a man jumped out at her. She froze; then, instead of attacking her, the intruder embraced her feet and begged to be excused for deserting the Army. She heard him out, edging every minute toward an emergency bell which at last she managed to push, and help came. A similar incident was to occur almost forty years later to the Queen, who no doubt learned from her mother's example: keep them talking and try to get to a bell button.

On November 26, the Princesses joined their parents in receiving two hundred officers of the U. S. Army and Navy and twenty nurses at the first Thanksgiving party held at Buckingham Palace. By a miracle, the chilly Palace, its heating virtually nonexistent because of shortages, managed to come up with pumpkin pie and sweet potatoes for the occasion. On December 12, the Princesses entertained the family in *Sleeping Beauty,* with Elizabeth as Prince. Although Princess Margaret was listed as Beauty in the press, she has categorically denied she took the role; she played a supporting part.

On January 7, 1943, Margaret received £20,000 in the will of the recently deceased the Hon. Mrs. Ronnie Greville, whose jewels were divided between Queen Elizabeth and Victoria Eugénie of Spain. Princess Elizabeth was not named in the will; the great estate of Polesden Lacey, where her parents had spent their honeymoon, was left to the National Trust. Margaret's first investment was to buy, with her sister, the first two of the newly issued government savings certificates; the rest of the cash was put in Coutts Bank to gather interest for years. Just as exciting a gift as the legacy was Lord Louis Mountbatten arriving with a bunch of African bananas; the Princesses instantly asked their mother to take the fruit to injured children at Lewisham Hospital. Presented with an unfamiliar yellow object, one little girl asked, "Do I have to eat it?'' The nurses joined the Queen in laughter.

At the time, rationing allowed the family only one serving of meat per week, while the King worked two nights a week at a factory, turning out precision parts for RAF guns. Irritated when he returned from his humble labors to see Buckingham Palace staff in tailcoats and white ties, he ordered them to wear plain livery. Soon they would be given royal orders to wear "battledress" livery, designed by himself.

An assistant to Lord Woolton, Minister of Food, appeared at the Palace and advised how the Queen could give Buckingham Palace tea parties for the first time in years without breaching the rationing regulations. She served bridge rolls with watercress, fish paste, Hovis bread smeared with Marmite, and cake with marzipan made from soya bean flour. The parties were held in the Grand Hall and the Princesses joined their parents in welcoming their guests.

Princess Elizabeth became a Sea Ranger, sending a carrier-pigeon message of good cheer to a rally of Brownies and Girl Guides in London. She helped distribute a vat of Argentinean honey to two thousand Edinburgh children, inspected (as honorary colonel) her favorite Grenadier Guards, attended a poetry reading in aid of the French in Britain Fund (she understood the French verses perfectly and indeed spoke fluent French), and, on May 3, became, to her delight, and by the King's special nomination, president of the Royal College of Music.

Seventeen days later, she and her sister attended a thanksgiving service in St. Paul's for the British victory over Rommel in North Africa. In the bomb-scarred building, lilies were among the few decorations as the choir sang the "Te Deum Laudamus"; the King was in admiral's uniform and the Lord Mayor in State robes. The *London Times* noted significant details: "Near the monument to Lord Nelson sat a group of war workers which included a Land Army girl in breeches and green jersey and a bus driver in his white overalls . . ." The Archbishop of Canterbury and Bishop of London were officiating. The high, thin voices of the Princesses joined their parents in the hymns "Praise My Soul, the King of Heaven" and "Now Thank We All Our God." In June, the Princesses were at the Strand Theater to see the antic comedy *Arsenic and Old Lace* with Dame Lilian Braithwaite and Mary Jerrold, the first time they ever attended a play at an evening performance. As they entered the box, they were cheered, and afterward they went backstage to congratulate the company. It was their celebration of the King's birthday; the play ran for over one thousand performances.

In February of that year, Eyre Crowe of the Foreign Office, whose father had played a special role in the matter of Philip's and Prince Andrew's removal from Athens in 1922, now assisted Princess Alice and Princess Helen by sending them thirty gallons of precious gasoline petrol in Nazi-occupied Athens; it may seem odd that, whether or not the gasoline was used for the purpose of aiding war victims, its supply to persons under German control was arranged (via Sweden) by the Minister of Economic Warfare and (presumably) approved by the German equivalent. "There would be no question of consignments [being] specifically earmarked for these ladies and labeled accordingly," states a memorandum from the Ministry, signed by Anthony Camps, and dated February 15, 1943.

That spring, Philip was serving aboard the destroyer *Wallace* in the Mediterranean, escorting the Canadian landings in Sicily. When the vessel was harbored at Velletta, Malta, for extensive refittings, he again returned to England, staying as usual in his uncle and aunt Mountbatten's house. The mood of London was elated: by late July, Mussolini was finished following the Allied invasion in which Philip had played a tiny role, and by September the Badoglio government had given up. Lord Louis Mountbatten was made head of Southeast Asia Command, to reopen the trade route to India, release the British fleet for service in the eastern waters, and help the United States destroy Japanese control of the Orient. Threatened by the collapse of Italy, Germany intensified its military hold on Greece. Heroic guerrilla armies seemed about to seize power when the Communist and anti-Communist factions clashed in bitter conflict and the Germans instituted a new reign of terror; thousands died of famine in Athens and the Germans looted and burned the city. Philip had difficulty contacting his mother through many painful months.

Meanwhile, following the King's triumphant tour of the North African war front that summer of 1943, he sought a revision of his own instituted Regency Act of 1937, so that after Princess Elizabeth reached her eighteenth birthday the following April, she could be included among the Counsellors of State in certain eventualities and thus learn some of the duties of a Queen at first hand. It was anticipated that in certain circumstances she might become regent.

The bill was debated in the House of Commons and passed; Campbell Stephen, Independent Labor member, observed, "This is the beginning of her apprenticeship. I do not think eighteen is the wrong age in regard to her apprenticeship to a trade which is going to occupy her in the future, and consequently I feel there is no objection I should take to the measure."

On October 7, 1943, Prince Christoph of Hesse, Philip's brother-in-law, husband of Princess Sophie, the infamous SS leader and Luftwaffe pilot, who had been involved in the bombing of London, was shot down by the RAF over the Apennines. One would have thought the news of the death of this deadly enemy of the Allies would have caused rejoicing among the Mountbattens, but Lady Edwina cabled Lord Louis in New Delhi, India, her sorrow for Princess Sophie's bereavement. Lady Edwina's father, Lord Mount Temple, was a leading Nazi sympathizer of the 1930s; Lady Edwina was Jewish and Commandant of the St. John's Ambulance.

Unhappily for his admirers, Lord Louis then wrote to his mother, the Marchioness of Milford Haven, at Kensington Palace, also expressing his sorrow over Princess Sophie's bereavement. Those who suffered from the bombing raids on London and countless Jews whose lives were ruined or destroyed would not share such loyal family sentiments.

In his speech opening Parliament at the House of Lords on November 24, the King, radiant with joy, announced, "The enemy has been cast out of Africa, freedom has been brought to Sicily, Sardinia, and Corsica, and in Italy my forces and those of my American Ally are now engaging the enemy on the mainland of Europe." He pledged dedication to the defeat of Japan, once the war in Europe was at an end. "Many believe the next opening of Parliament will be held after the defeat of Germany," said the *New York Times*'s David Anderson. That night, the Princesses joined their parents at a Thanksgiving Eve party in the Bow Room at Buckingham Palace for Captain Quentin Roosevelt and three hundred U.S. officers and WACs.

Philip attended the royal family's Christmas pantomime, *Aladdin,* at Windsor Castle; Princess Elizabeth was in the starring role and Margaret played Roxana. Among the royal cast of forty were the Duke of Kent and Princess Alexandra.

Elizabeth made an exciting first stage entrance by bursting unexpectedly out of a laundry basket dressed in a Chinese kimono and white silk pantaloons. Margaret was dazzling in silver and blue robes. Everyone laughed uproariously as the Princesses tap-danced and sang solos and duets and expertly rattled off the funny and sometimes risqué lines. There was laughter and applause when they played in a famous slapstick Chinese laundry scene as washer women in sackcloth dresses and aprons singing along with office boy Cyril Woods, ''We're Three Daily 'Elps.'' Elizabeth delighted the crowd by expertly tap-dancing and singing ''In My Arms.'' Philip was in the front row, applauding loudly with the King and Queen, the Duchess of Kent, and Princess Helena Victoria. He had unsportingly refused to take part in the play.

In the early months of 1944, King George II of Greece was pressing hard for his cousin Philip's position as husband of the heiress presumptive to the British throne. He urged George VI to take the matter seriously: George II was still under suspicion of the Greek people for collaborating with the Germans at the outset of the war, and he stood unfairly accused of failing to give more than hypocritical vocal support to the admitted leftwing guerrilla armies of his nation. Should Churchill and George VI attempt to return him to the throne, once the war was over, he could not feel confident that an alternative monarch might not be selected by plebiscite; it could not be his brother Paul, whose supposed collaboration had been alleged to be as serious, and who was married to the Kaiser's grand-daughter, a former member of the Hitler Jugend; nor could it be Prince Andrew, who was questionably in residence in ''neu-tralist'' Monaco, and whose craven self-abasement in 1922 was not easily to be forgotten. The surviving brothers were similarly tainted for the 1916 incident; only Philip was impeccable, a hero, and beyond reproach; and Alice wanted him for monarch. By supporting Philip in his need to acquire British nationality, seeking his rejection of both Greek nationality and membership in the Greek Orthodox Church, and above all by marrying him off to Princess Elizabeth, the King could remove the one serious challenge to his cardboard throne that re-mained. However, King George VI resisted his efforts to achieve a betrothal with the quiet, steely stubbornness that marked his character.

The monarch wrote to his mother, who was living at Badminton, that Elizabeth was far too young to be betrothed, and (an odd statement) had never met any young men of her age. The King concluded, "We are going to tell George that P. had better not think any more about it for the present." In contrast, the King did approve the marriage of Philip's favorite cousin Alexandra to King Peter of Yugoslavia in March, and acted as best man.

Nineteen forty-four was a tremendous year for England and the United States, and for Elizabeth. It was the year of her eighteenth birthday, the time at which, as a royal person, she came of age; and it was also the year of the Allies' great triumphs over Germany. At the outset of the year, the invasion of Europe was fully planned; 250,000 acres of airfields were made available for the RAF; on April 17, all foreign diplomats were forbidden communication with their countries; travel abroad for anyone not on official duties was suspended ten days later. Every available man was trained and ready for action by early May.

In a mood of exhilaration, Churchill, the King and Queen, the Princesses, and the rest of the royal family waited for the glorious moment that lay ahead. And who, now, was this girl of eighteen, whose future would include the throne?

She was well balanced, an all-rounder: not brilliant, but sensible and composed; not intellectual, but intelligent and grave. She was a fine swimmer and horsewoman, she spoke French and German with fluent expertise; she had, through C. H. K. Marten, a command of history, was an accomplished pianist and choir singer, and a devoted president of the Royal College of Music.

The King had made it his purpose to instruct her in reigning over her Commonwealth, equipped to advise and warn, never actually to govern. Above all, she exuded wholesomeness, cleanliness, a spirit decent, untainted, sheltered, and eminently sane. Was she then a saint, and must at this stage any biographer be forced into the role of hagiographer? No, because she had faults: she could be stubborn, resistant, imperious, often cold, and she inherited a temper and a strength that were very human. She was somewhat inflexible even now; her understanding of life was limited by her enclosed circumstances, her virginity, and by a not surprising lack of sophistication. Her sister was always more open, more vulnerable, more surprising, more intriguingly unpredictable, more "human." They were closer than ever.

In certain respects, the Princess's education had been conspicuously neglected and, so, more markedly, had her sister's. Despite the fact that Elizabeth was honorary head of the College of Music, she had, so far as is known, seldom attended the Albert Hall or (until it was bombed) the Queens Hall or indeed very few places in which music was professionally performed; nor had she and her sister been to the Old Vic to see performances of Shakespeare, whose untoward chronicles of ancient royalty might not have been comforting to a prospective monarch, though she could have learned profitably from their example; nor had they been to ballet or the opera or serious plays—Ibsen, Strindberg, the reader can add his favorite names to the list.

Margaret's education in history had been so poorly attended that she was even denied, rather unkindly, the ministrations of the Vice Provost of Eton, who still had the peculiar habit of addressing her sister as "Gentlemen," having come directly from a class at his school and forgetting temporarily that he was in a more august presence. Typically, Elizabeth's birthday treat was not a performance of a great British classic at the Old Vic but the lighthearted musical *Something in the Air* at the Palace Theater. The day was quiet; she received no honors; the King had decided not to make her Princess of Wales despite the urgings of Lloyd George, a decision with which she concurred. She appeared on the parade ground at Windsor (this time the erring *Times* did not mention the address) and received from Colonel Prescott of the Grenadiers a replica of the King's Color—made of crimson silk decorated with the Princess's monogram in all four corners, surmounted by gold coronets.

She still enjoyed £6,000 ($30,000) a year, of which £1 a week was permitted her and the rest invested by the royal treasurer. She was a regular visitor to the fashion salon of Norman Hartnell, and he fitted her personally. She gave herself a mink coat on the royal account just before her birthday. She still had not been on a bus or inside a movie theater. She had forty-four clothing coupons a year, and already had run out.

Elizabeth's birthday gifts were her thirty-fifth and thirty-sixth necklace pearls from her father, a horse from both her parents, and a diamond brooch from Queen Mary. Prince Philip's card was especially welcome; it is not known whether he sent a gift; he was posted in Newcastle upon Tyne in the North of England, in a modest hotel, while the destroyer

Whelp, to which he had been seconded, was prepared for sailing.

She rejoiced with the Allied peoples when D-Day, the sixth of June, dawned; all that morning, the skies of London were filled with the roar of aircraft—few who heard that sound or saw the great flight of planes would ever forget it. At twelve o'clock as Big Ben struck, Winston Churchill walked into the House of Commons to announce, to a tremendous outburst of cheers, "During the night and the. early hours of this morning a series of landings in force upon the European continent has taken place." There were more cheers, and then he proudly added: "An immense armada of four thousand ships, together with several thousand smaller craft, crossed the Channel."[1]

Magnificent though the moment was, it reaped a whirlwind. The Germans had threatened that if the invasion took place there would be brutal and violent retaliations in the form of new secret weapons—and there now came the dreaded "doodle bugs," pilotless robot bombs, rockets aimed at the heart of England.

By summer, Princess Elizabeth was already serving as a Counsellor of State, and in July, while her father was absent in Italy,[2] she signed Acts of Parliament. She visited South Wales mining districts, factories, and civilian defense posts, and, that fall, an American Eighth Air Force bomber base, and christened a Flying Fortress.

According to Chips Channon, Elizabeth met Philip on very intimate (but innocent) terms at Coppins, Iver, Bucks, the home of the Duchess of Kent, in the months before he sailed on the *Whelp.*

There was an unfortunate and revealing incident in London at the time, reported by E. H. Cookridge in *From Battenberg to Mountbatten:* at a meeting with King George VI, King George II of Greece said, in the hearing of others, "What a pity Philip and [Princess] Alexandra [of Greece] did not get hitched up,

1. Ten days later, the King crossed the Channel to visit General Montgomery's headquarters.
2. This was a very awkward visit in view of King Victor Emmanuel's reception of King George V in 1926 and also that monarch's fascist connections; the Pope also had obtained a questionable neutrality during the war. The King met neither—Italian ruler nor Pope—on Churchill's and Eden's advice.

but it might be for the best. How nice it would be if we could reunite our families and countries through Prince Philip.''

The King, very embarrassed and annoyed, remained silent. Then George continued, ''It seems Lilibet is in love with Philip and I know that he adores her.'' King George VI scowled with anger. He said to George II, ''Philip had better . . . not think . . . any more about it at present . . . They are both too young.''

So now King George II, with Lord Louis Mountbatten, decided to alter the campaign for their own benefit and change is so that Philip would merely become a British citizen, and then they could proceed to their next move.

Their plans for the future marriage had been advanced. Mountbatten had been in London, arguing with the Chiefs of Staff about his conduct of the Southeast Asian campaign. He stopped at Cairo on the way back to India, for a meeting with Lord Killearn, then British Ambassador to Egypt, Prince Paul of Greece (George II's brother, who was married to the Kaiser's granddaughter), and Philip, whose *Whelp* was docked in Alexandria.

The luncheon meeting took place at the British Embassy at a time of drastic unrest and bloody warfare in Greece. The British were determined that a reluctant and ailing George II should return to the throne, whether by plebiscite or (more probably) not, to ensure a foothold in the Mediterranean. The EAM, the Greek resistance organization bent upon eliminating Nazi power, lost British support when it was feared that it might introduce communism into the country; almost the whole population was committed to EAM, and by early 1944 the Greek armed forces in Egypt mutinied against George II, convinced (along with most Greeks) that he was against Greek unity and that he did not support resistance to Germany.

Paul agreed with Mountbatten's approach as there was clearly no future for Philip in the Greek Navy; George pointed out to Mountbatten that since there were several in the family line before Philip there was no point in his settling in Greece in the future; George told Mountbatten that Andrew would not care as he had lost all interest in his native country; Alice, however, might not welcome the move as she had backed Philip for the throne. George added, ''I could never agree to this as the legal succession must be adhered to and Pavlo [Crown Prince Paul] and his son are both in line.'' He neglected to mention that he might, in fact, abdicate or renounce the throne, as the public did not seem to want him and he wasn't eager to return; that if he were not returned by plebiscite Paul might be equally unpopular because of his wife's former Nazi connections; and their son was too young. Had he forgotten the fact that he himself had been overruled in favor of his brother Alexander, or that Philip was one of the very few members of the Greek royal family who had no stain on his political character?

King George did not like the idea of backing Philip as a rival candidate; his statement showed that he took Philip's potential threat seriously—and at lunch that day, he signed the document authorizing Philip's change of citizenship. Philip signed an agreement to change nationalities, which Mountbatten sent at once to King George VI.

Mountbatten agreed that he willingly shared the responsibility for pushing the change of nationality through, and stated that this must take place before the "armistice" with Germany. What does "armistice" mean in this context? Was it a slip of the pen or was Mountbatten indulging in the foolish dream, never backed by action or by more than opportunism, of his German family members that there might be a separate peace with the more moderate levels of the Nazis—a dream also of Philip's egregious former schoolmaster, Kurt Hahn?

9

***

IN OCTOBER 1944, HAROLD Macmillan, the resident minister in the Near East, and acting president of the Allied Commission, visited (at the request of Lord Mountbatten, and by extension Philip) Prince Philip's mother in Athens. He found her living in "humble, not to say squalid" conditions; he saw her as "a rather blowsy, lumpish and very *hausfrau* type." He thought her "not intelligent—and seemed very nervous and clumsy." She had been working with the Swedish Relief Scheme and with the Swiss Red Cross. She had no sugar, tea, rice, coffee, or canned foods. She spoke of Philip; she hoped he would be in the Mediterranean, and regretted he was in the Orient.

By contrast, Princess Helen of Greece, after years under Nazi rule still living in luxury, was under suspicion in Whitehall of German sympathies; but like seemingly everyone else in high society, Macmillan thought it a "courtesy" to visit her. She spoke predictably against communism over the teacups; German sympathies or not, the future Prime Minister of England found her appealing, and sympathized with her loss of a cultivated, civilized, prewar world. It seems that this White Russian neutralist was to be forgiven everything—because she was the mother of the Duchess of Kent.

Both the royal family and Philip were bereaved in those last months of 1944. The Earl of Strathmore passed away in November, his body cremated and interred at his beloved Glamis Castle, the simple ceremony accompanied by the Black Watch Regiment playing a bagpipe lament. In December, the ineffectual and impoverished Prince Andrew, after wasted years in Monaco, died of a heart attack. Notes in the Mountbatten files show that he had grown so distant from his son that his demise brought Philip no great grief; he was moved to Tatoi, to the family burial ground, in a Greece that was now torn apart more violently than ever by conflict, between the Communist-backed EAM and the more democratic revolutionary party, both of which had effectively dislodged the Germans.

Philip received word of his father's death from the dowager Marchioness of Milford Haven, while he was aboard the *Whelp* in Trincomalee, Ceylon; soon thereafter, the Mountbatten letters reveal, Princess Alice wrote to Philip stating that she had changed her earlier position, had apparently given up all thought of his being a Greek King, and wanted him to take British citizenship. Philip had been very worried about her reluctance in the matter. Princess Alice was now in England, and she saw the King, no doubt to make sure everything would go through; the Queen invited her to tea with Lady Milford Haven. In a note to the latter (February 9, 1945) Mountbatten expressed concern because, despite the fact that all parties were agreed, George VI had not officially advised Philip that he approved. Mountbatten also fretted that Alice might indiscreetly press the issue of Philip and Elizabeth with the British King. He worried that she would reveal his and King George II's ambitions too much, instead of concentrating on the citizenship.

As he continued to serve in the Pacific, heading back slowly to England, Philip had much to lament of in the state of his native Greece. In October, the Germans left, but in their wake the warring revolutionary factions bathed the streets in blood. The British troops were far outnumbered by the EAMs; a bizarre situation followed in which, of all people, General Nikolaos Plastiras, who had threatened the life of Prince Andrew in 1922, became Prime Minister by choice of George II; Archbishop Damaskinos, Greek primate, became regent. It seemed that Churchill was prepared to play any card, wild or ecclesiastical, to ensure that the exiled monarch should return, despite the fact that almost none of his people, influenced as they were by EAM propaganda, wanted him to.

Through Mountbatten, and Crown Princess Louise of Sweden, Philip yet again obtained news of his sisters in Germany; their husbands had been dismissed from the Army because Hitler incorrectly suspected all aristocrats of being sympathetic to the bomb plot against his life.

In a letter to his mother,[1] Mountbatten expressed a belief that his German relatives were all anti-Nazi in their heart of hearts—an assumption that suggests he was either hopelessly naive (how could they have served Hitler, why did they not revolt or mutiny?) or put family considerations before patriotism in lying to the dowager Marchioness. He can scarcely not have known the truth through the Intelligence grapevine.

He also showed a questionable interest in the fate of Prince Philip's dead sister's brother-in-law, Prince Ludwig of Hesse and by Rhine. Prince Ludwig had been Ribbentrop's right-hand man and some-time chargé d'affaires in London in the 1930s, and was later in Field Marshal Keitel's army and the Volkssturm, or home guard. Mountbatten had been in constant touch via his sister Louise of Sweden; Ludwig was in a camp because of Hitler's suspicions but was released by the U.S. forces. Mountbatten passed on word of Ludwig and his wife, the former Hon. Margaret Campbell Geddes, to Philip, who was in the Pacific region fighting the Japanese.

Princess Elizabeth's engagements became crushingly heavy in early 1945. She saw off her uncle, the Duke of Gloucester, and the Duchess, when they left for Australia, where he would be Governor-General; she visited gas and electricity exhibitions, attended chapel at Eton, and toured the Lancashire factories. She was at commemoration services, memorial services, march pasts, official gallery visits, hospital board meetings, tours of bomb sites, horse shows—already the burdens of office were upon her, and she seemed to enjoy everything, her famous fixed smile already in place.

She learned at nineteen that the order of the household was as rigid as ever: the Royal Household came first, with their own sitting room and dining room, then the clerks and stenographers, then the so-called upper servants and lower servants. The royal caterer Frederick Corbitt wrote in his memoirs:

It is absolutely forbidden for a servant, for instance, from the Stewards' room to go into Official's Mess except on some very special occasion, and no official would dream of intruding into the Household Dining Room any more than any member of the Royal Household would dream of barging into the Sovereign's Dining Room.

1. February 9, 1945.

The inescapable Ainsley was the Palace steward, an imposing, dignified presence who had been butler at 145 Piccadilly. He was the butt of the King's not infrequent irritable complaints: the nervous monarch had never lost his foul temper, but Ainsley, during the royal tantrums, resembled a lighthouse against which a stormy sea was beating. It was only afterward that his friend Corbitt noticed he was pale and shaking. The King's valet was the cautious, secretive Tom Jerram, who often went sleepless to ensure the immaculate condition of the royal uniforms and the glittering mirror-polish of the royal shoes. Bobo MacDonald continued at the Palace and with her Alla Knight, who did not long survive the war. Bobo took care of the Queen like a baby, and to this day tends her like a daughter.

Food was ordered by Corbitt, only from those who held the Royals Warrant of Appointment; the royal chef phoned in the orders to the Comptroller of Supply each day; deliveries were made only to the Trade Door; each item was checked in, as in a large hotel. The kitchens and larders were vast: the cold storage room alone was fifteen feet square, and eight feet six inches high, and could contain hundreds of sides of beef, venison, veal, and birds of every description.

The royal chef prepared the menus after lunch each afternoon and presented them to the Queen, who would nod or shake her head at each item. Breakfast was usually porridge or cereal and bacon and eggs and toast and marmalade with cups of tea; lunch was roast lamb or fish, dessert crêpes suzette or a luscious *mille-feuille*—thin layers of pastry and cream and jam filling, all managed despite rationing.

Dinner parties were meticulously prepared. Corbitt described the details: the guests' names were on cards, and the Queen arranged them on a large board with pins, so there could be no question of the seating. Just before the meal, an equerry took the board to the drawing room so that the guests could see where they were to sit without peering round the table. Place cards and menus were not put before the guests.

That winter, Elizabeth won a prolonged battle against her father's stubborn dislike of her being in uniform and enlisted as a second subaltern in the auxiliary Territorial Service; part of her driver's training was putting on khaki coveralls and working on truck and automobile engines. By spring, she had her own rooms at Buckingham Palace; they were softly feminine in decor, with chintz-covered armchairs and white occasional chairs. She at last had two ladies-in-waiting for herself alone, Lady Mary Strachey, who had been appointed the previous year, and a young war widow, the Hon. Mrs. Vicary Gibbs, a member of the Hambro banking family, which had strong connections in Greece.

There were occasional dances at which the Princess and her more buoyant sister acted as hostesses, and sometimes the King would lead a conga line down the Palace corridors. Everyone noted that Elizabeth was charming and appealing to her guests; she was not only attractive, but was one of the prettiest girls in London. She missed Philip, and we may suppose she was concerned that the matter of his British citizenship was still not settled. She was also made nervous by the restrictions of her education in arms and commerce and her lack of worldly knowledge; Lady Longford, one of her biographers, has noted that she told a friend, "I [would] think, 'Oh, who am I going to sit by [at meals] and what are they going to talk about?' I'm absolutely terrified of sitting next to people in case they talk about things I have never heard of."

In addition to thinking about the future, and of the prospect of attending countless public occasions, she and her family were very much looking forward to the official visit of President Roosevelt, following the San Francisco Conference. And she was, with them all, sorrowful on hearing that he died at his home in Georgia on April 12. But he left a magnificent legacy, a victory that, it is sad to recall, he never lived to see. On April 28, Mussolini was executed at Mezzagra, and, just two days later, Hitler killed himself in the Chancellery Bunker in Berlin. At 2:41 A.M. on May 7, 1945, Colonel-General Alfred Jödl cosigned the instrument of unconditional surrender in a schoolroom in Reims.

The war was not yet over: Japan remained to be defeated, and there was fear of a protracted war in the Pacific. Elizabeth must have cast her thoughts to Philip, aboard his destroyer *Whelp* in that distant battle zone. But even her concern could not quell her rapturous joy in the events of May 8, 1945, VE Day.

The Prime Minister lunched with the King at Buckingham Palace, while outside the crowds had already started to gather; preparations had gone on apace for some time. Nature provided its own dramatic accompaniment: the night before there had been a violent electrical storm and, on the morning of the great day, there was another heavy burst of rain; before it cleared, the crowds began pouring into the streets, and for those left at home, the BBC kept up first the victorious themes of a cinema organist and then the joyous clamor of a radio church service, culminating in "Now Thank We All Our God." At 3 P.M., Churchill went to the microphone and the Princesses and their parents sat enraptured as they heard him say, in his beloved resonant gruff tones, "The German war is . . . at an end. God save the King!"

Again and again, as many as eight times, the royal family came out on the crimson and gold draped balcony (which was shaky due to war damage) to join in the ecstasy of their subjects; the entire Mall was thronged from one end to another, a sea of black umbrellas under heavy rain. At five twenty-five, Churchill appeared with the royal family for the first time that day; he did not give his famous V for Victory sign as he was in the royal presence, nor, for the same reason, did he smoke his omnipresent cigar. As he stepped forward, a strange silence settled over the throng, and then he bowed to the people of England a deep bow of gratitude and acknowledgment, and a cheer rose up and startled flocks of pigeons from the rooftops. The royal family, in a unique gesture of warmth and friendship, turned toward him.

As night fell, searchlights, recently used for spotting enemy aircraft, now swept an unthreatened sky. People dragged out petrol cans, banged tin cups, let off fireworks, clanged dustbin lids together like cymbals, dressed up in bizarre costumes and fancy hats from long-forgotten parties, circled the big bonfires in the parks, jitterbugged in the shadow of Big Ben, crammed the river bridges to see the fireworks; for once the over-reserved British talked to strangers or laughed or celebrated with them—even on trains.

The King and Queen made the radical and unprecedented decision to let their children join in. It was enterprising Margaret's idea to be let out of the Palace by a side exit to join in the crowd; her parents said yes, so long as the Princesses went with friends and had a Guard's escort.

The small party, which included Princess Elizabeth in uniform, two guardsmen, the Princesses' lively uncle David Bowes-Lyon, a Major Phillips, and Crawfie, made their way out and joined the hundred thousand in the streets, most of whom were singing such popular refrains as "Roll Out the

Barrel," "Knees Up, Mother Brown," and "Run, Rabbit, Run." They managed to get as far as Piccadilly, and not more than a handful recognized them. David Bowes-Lyon knocked a policeman's helmet off. They returned to the Palace, but not before yelling out with the rest, "We want the King!" or "We want the Queen!"

The second day of celebrations was quieter, as many returned to work; but at night the city went completely mad. In the afternoon, the Princesses joined their parents for an exciting drive through the devastated East End. At 8:30 P.M., Churchill, this time flourishing his cigar and giving the V-sign, climbed onto a car roof at 10 Downing Street and was driven down Whitehall to loud cheers. Between 7 P.M. and midnight the royal family appeared seven times on the balcony to the tune of the Coldstream Guards Band.

A few days later, the Princesses were overjoyed to be taken to Edinburgh for the Scottish celebrations: they had never been to the ancient city before. On May 13, there was a service of thanksgiving at St. Paul's. The golden State coach, with its full escort of Household Cavalry, moved toward Temple Bar, where the Lord Mayor handed the pearl-handled City Sword to the King. The tumultuous welcome continued all the way up to Ludgate Hill and the cathedral, which was surrounded by heaped-up bricks and ruined walls.

On May 24, the Princesses joined their parents at a celebratory concert at the Royal Albert Hall.

In many respects, that concert was ironical, because, the day before, Winston Churchill had resigned the office he had adorned for five glorious years. He had urged the political parties to continue the coalition government until Japan should be defeated; Clement Attlee, the dry and ascetic leader of the Labor party, declined the arrangement. Churchill's resignation was to force a general election; he was reappointed head of a caretaker government until the polling on June 16.

Unfortunately, the great man overplayed his hand in attacking Labor during his electioneering campaign, talking rashly on the BBC of "Gestapo rule" that would prevail under a prospective Labor government; nevertheless, the landslide victory of Attlee can only be thought of as an insult to a hero; it was an ignoble day for England when the Prime Minister tendered his resignation to the King.

August brought the grand visit of President Truman to

London, the dropping of the atom bombs on Hiroshima and Nagasaki, and victory. After a visit to Australia, where he cut a swathe through the local girls, Prince Philip was on board the *Whelp* in Tokyo Bay when the Japanese surrender was signed; by now he was exchanging letters with Elizabeth almost weekly.

In London, on August 15, the events of May were repeated: one hundred thousand in the Mall to see the royal family wave back at them; the Princesses passing into the crowds again to share in the jubilations; the failure of all but a handful to recognize them. On the family's third appearance, the crowd sang, "For He's a Jolly Good Fellow!" Because of the immense crowd outside, distinguished visitors had to be let in through the Electricians' Gate in Buckingham Palace Road. Something awkward happened when Foreign Secretary Ernest Bevin arrived. The Electricians' Gate was swamped and he was told he would have to go through the Trade Entrance; when his car drew up he furiously announced that he would not enter that humble door—he who was supposedly a working man's working man. The royal family teased him as he made his way, flustered and panting and red-faced, through the Electricians' Gate into their presence.

The pouring rain again did nothing to dampen the public spirit, and then, at last, in the late afternoon the sun broke through. Churchill, responding to cries of "We Want Winnie!" as he was driven across London, buried whatever bitterness he may have felt and magnificently addressed the Commons; Attlee was less inspiring, rather resembling a shoe salesman announcing to a customer an interesting new example of footwear. The King's speeches on radio and on the Palace balcony were confident and stirring, and, in a nice touch, his BBC broadcast was introduced by an obscure soldier, twenty-one-year-old Sergeant Philip Gray. A service of thanksgiving at which the royal family was gratefully present again took place at St. Paul's. As the old cathedral's bells rang out from the northwest tower across all London, a *Times* correspondent was moved to note some previous occasions for this clamor: the victory of Trafalgar, Queen Victoria's Diamond Jubilee, King George V's jubilee, and successive Coronations; he could have added Waterloo and the end of the Boer War and World War I, and the relief of Mafeking. It was a sound that would ring in the ears of the two Princesses forever, as they rode in the royal open landau to and from the service.

Soon afterward, the King joined King George II of Greece for a train journey from Edinburgh to London; no doubt the matter of Philip was earnestly discussed, as well as the circumstances in which George would return to the Greek throne and perhaps the major problem of Philip's German relatives. The time was not propitious either for Philip to become British or to be betrothed to Elizabeth, because the issue was in the air of Britain's backing George's return; it must not be known what Britain's policy was in the matter, and Philip's change of citizenship could give the game away. So secret were Britain's plans that when, in the Commons, Richard Crossman, Labor MP for Coventry, asked the Foreign Secretary about the matter, Philip Noel-Baker, Minister of State, was forced to deny that any such scheme was afoot. The lie was greeted with unknowing cheers. The Communist member, Willie Gallacher, whose sympathies of course lay with the Greek EAM movement, asked Noel-Baker whether General Scobie of the British Army and the Ambassador would be withdrawn from Athens as they were overt royalists. His question was shrewdly brushed aside.

Thus yet again, Philip's future was part of a game of politics, his desires blocked frustratingly because of the deceptions of diplomacy. Princess Elizabeth was understandably aggravated by the situation, but neither George II nor George VI could move in the matter. There is no indication that Philip cared very much; if he had to wait for his goals of citizenship and his cousin and uncle's goal of marriage, well, there was much to enjoy in the Orient and he was twenty-four and handsome and the world was at his feet.

On September 15, 1945, Elizabeth was thrown from a horse at Balmoral and was badly bruised; while she was recovering, an article appeared in the *New York Times* entitled "Marriage à la Mode," saying that of the most likely candidates for her hand, Prince Philip of Greece was the first. ("This tale, which circulated in Greek diplomatic circles, has been officially denied.") Others mentioned were "an unspecified American," a "Guards Officer" and those familiars, the Duke of Rutland and Lord Euston.

In October, King George VI, anxious about possible damage from the press to his brother the Duke of Windsor, and perhaps to his daughter's chief romantic interest, sent Anthony Blunt, Surveyor of the Queen's Pictures and a British secret agent, to Schloss Krönberg, family home of the Princes of Hesse, near Frankfurt. The King authorized the collection of a secret set of documents that could well have revealed not only such inconvenient matters as the Duke of Windsor's conversations with Hitler but also Prince Christoph of Hesse's activities with Goering's secret service, and the similar activities of his brothers Wilhelm and Philipp, the latter a special contact between Hitler and Mussolini.

When Blunt and his associate Owen Morshead arrived, Princess Margaret had left and an American WAC officer was in charge. Blunt engaged the officer in conversation as Morshead and his team stole military documents and carried them down the stairs to a truck. The Hesse documents wound up in Windsor Castle. Prince Philip probably did not know of this maneuver at the time.

In his Christmas speech on the radio, his family gathered round, the King spoke of much that remained to be done and how "a little would have to go a long way." It was a dismal and depressing forecast of a coming Age of Austerity.

While Elizabeth thought of Philip, his photograph in a bristling beard always present on her bedside table at Sandringham, Balmoral, Windsor, or Buckingham Palace, another romantic presence was at court: the attractive Wing Commander Peter Townsend, to whose handsome face and figure Princess Margaret, though only fifteen, was already not indifferent; he was acting as an equerry to the King.

Philip returned to England in the early weeks of 1946 and spent his weekend leaves at the Mountbatten townhouse, 16 Chester Street, Belgravia. Although Brook House, the Mountbatten residence in London, was in process of being returned to its owners after being commandeered by the government, the Mountbattens seemed to like this smaller and more intimate house, despite the fact that the dining room could only accommodate twelve people. It was elegant and exquisitely furnished, reflecting Edwina Mountbatten's perfect taste. Philip was fond of the cook, Mrs. Cable, a cozy body with an immense bosom, and the housekeeper, dear old Jessie. He would drive up very fast in his black MG from the coast when the Mountbattens were away at weekends and settle into his favorite room, from which he could venture night after night into the world of the West End with his cousin David.

On a visit to Paris to see his old benefactress, the ailing Marie Bonaparte, Philip also saw a good deal of Helene Foufounis, his sprightly childhood companion, who had had an affair with an airman, Max Boisot. Philip was godfather to her two children, Max and Louise. He had seen Helene from time to time when on leave, so much unfounded gossip swirled that he was the children's father. The impoverished Helene met him at the Ritz; he rode up on a small woman's bicycle and the sight of him made her double up in laughter. They raced each other to a location on the Rue Pierre Charron, she by subway, he by bicycle; she won. She saw him frantically pedaling down the Champs-Élysées while she stood laughingly awaiting him. They rode in a fiacre to the Air Force Club; she dared to invade the sacred male precincts of the Travelers' Club, where he was staying. It was an exciting time; Philip lingered on into the spring, and it is possible that he and his old friend had romantic feelings for each other. He took an interest in the children as if they were, in fact, his own.[2]

Philip was still in Paris when Elizabeth celebrated her twentieth birthday at Windsor; it was a quiet celebration, no more lavish than any during the war, and indeed the mood of the nation was now more grimly austere than ever; Attlee's England was still a gray and dismal place, not reflecting the camaraderie and humor of the war years. Rationing continued; the country looked and felt impoverished. London had the air not of a victorious city, but of one that had been defeated. Only royalty seemed to escape the constant complaints of most people, still lining up in the rain for chocolate bars or whale meat or Spam. The King wrote to his brother the Duke of Gloucester on January 21, 1946, in Australia, "I have been suffering from an awful reaction to the strain of war . . . I really want a rest away from people and papers but that, of course, is impossible." He felt no rapport with Attlee, and spent grim, desultory hours talking about the food, fuel, and housing shortage with him.

Like everyone else in England, the king was irritated and depressed at the news that bread would now be rationed. Of the

2. Later, he sent Max to Gordonstoun.

Labor Cabinet he only liked the fussy Ernest Bevin, whose appointment as Foreign Minister he had recommended. Churchill's famous Fulton-Missouri speech on March 5 spoke of the Kremlin's dreams of "indefinite expansion of their power and doctrine"; back in London, a grateful monarch expressed his support of Churchill's feelings: the wartime alliance with Russia had never been popular at the Palace. The King was cheered also by discussions about a tour of South Africa with his wife and daughters, to take place the following year.

So heavy were the taxes of the beleaguered nation that in 1945 only sixty individuals kept as much as £16,850 after tax. Yet nobody resented the royal income, unchanged since before the war. Most people felt the family was worth it, especially when Princess Elizabeth gave a stirring Empire Day speech on the BBC and then at the Royal Albert Hall. She attacked those who charged the Empire with growing up through "cunning and force." The government also tried to whip up enthusiasm by staging a belated Victory Parade to celebrate the first anniversary of D-Day.

Reality was still something the charmed Princesses knew little about. There were glamorous weddings which they attended as bridesmaids, most notably the exquisitely staged nuptials of the Duke of Northumberland to Lady Elizabeth Montagu-Douglas-Scott, daughter of the Duke and Duchess of Buccleuch and niece of the Duchess of Gloucester. The dashing groom had followed the tradition of the House of Percy in riding from his ancestral home one hundred miles on a black horse to Drumlanrig Castle in Dumfrieshire to offer his proposal to his lady fair.

Philip often met Princess Elizabeth at Coppins, Iver, Bucks, that summer, under the benevolent and encouraging eye of the house's owner, the Duchess of Kent. After a brief sojourn in Wales, he was training petty officers aboard the HMS *Royal Arthur* at Corsham. As second in command, he worked very hard on the eighty trainees in his "house." He was a good batsman at cricket, and quite enjoyed the evenings at the "local," the Methuen Arms, playing darts or skittles and drinking mild and bitters. But it was a dreary, unrewarding existence. Soon, the ambitious Lord Louis would be chosen to be Viceroy of India: the present summit of his hopes.

* * *

The Greek September 1 plebiscite, rigged or not, returned King George II to the Greek throne. Soon, tragic Greece would again be the scene of bitter conflict—the first arena of post-war Soviet-British confrontation. When the monarch packed up his bags at Claridge's and returned to Athens, the fickle public clapping him not long after they had burned him in effigy in the squares, he decided to force George VI's hand by leaking the news that Philip and Elizabeth were engaged—an act of *folie de grandeur* typical of him and also an act of desperation for reasons this narrative has already made clear.

On September 7, the *New York Times* said, "Londoners were briefly thrilled today by a report that Princess Elizabeth, who will one day rule over them, was to become engaged to her second cousin, Prince Philip of Greece, but their expectations of marriage were ended by a denial from the Royal House-hold." Of course, the memories of 1916 still rankled with the British monarch. It cannot have appeased the King's temper that the Greek royal family was always being backed not for its own sake (though the King does seem to have found some liking for George II) but because they could protect British interests in the Mediterranean and Suez and oppose commu-nism on their native soil.

Philip fulfilled his uncle Louis's and cousin King George II's ambitions by asking Elizabeth's hand in marriage. She accepted without parental approval, but her father still was irritably obdurate; in addition to the royal unease about Philip becoming British just when his uncle had been returned by plebiscite to the throne, which might indicate lack of support for him, there was the South African tour to consider: an official engagement might detract from cementing a nation within the Commonwealth that already was showing cracks in its commitment to Britain.

In tense discussions with the King in his study, Philip, probably wishing himself somewhere else, had to talk over at length the question of whether he would renounce his Greek titles. That was certainly no problem for Philip: he despised the Greeks, and refused to speak their language. Philip pleased the monarch when he said (as a person who—particularly in dealing with the rank and file of the Navy—was greatly embarrassed by titles of any sort) he would like to be known as "Lieutenant Philip, RN." But he still had to have a surname, and certainly the Glucksburg string of names would not do: if anything the German connection was even more embarrassing than the Greek. And there were those awkward sisters and brothers-in-law with whom he was in touch in Germany. Philip recommended Oldcastle, a version of Oldenburgh, but when this was submitted to the College of Heralds, they declared it inappropriate: there were other Oldcastles about. It would later be agreed that he would assume the name Mountbatten. As for renouncing the Greek Orthodox religion, that was a joy, in view of the heavy ritualistic elements of the church. He hadn't attended other than simple shipboard services or weddings in the Protestant faith in years.

It must have been painful for the sheltered, subdued, but willful and single-minded Princess Elizabeth to put up with wranglings over her future, which had so little to do with her own emotional state, and merely obstructed her romantic daydreams of days and nights with Prince Charming. Her father's obduracy must have been far more painful to her because she knew almost nothing of Greek politics or of the carefully hidden history of the Greek royal family. It was a wearisome summer at Balmoral, despite the bagpipes and highland reels. And perhaps the worst aspect was that Philip found out that Group Captain Peter Townsend, whom he detested, was behind the idea that he be subjected to Balmoral to see if he would fit the royal idea of a husband. ("What infernal cheek!" he exploded later.) Townsend, who would one day suffer from his own royal mishandling, did not warm to Philip; and there were others in the King's circle who had grave doubts about the young man. But rumors of the engagement persisted after the Balmoral summer season. Philip did not like Balmoral—as he later admitted to his cousin, Queen Alexandra: she gave a grisly account of his experiences there in a book about him. There was no running bathtub or basin water; hot brown bog water was brought into the rooms in tin jugs for the guests.

Philip did not appreciate his noisy ground-floor bedroom, furnished in tartan, from carpet to furniture, and decorated with pale, washed-out wallpaper chosen by Queen Victoria and never replaced. Ralphe M. White, royal footman, wrote in his memoirs: "In the narrow corridors of the castle, the glassy eyes of long dead stags surveyed him from the walls as he passed by." He did not look impressive to a King who was a stickler for perfect clothing: his shoes were scuffed and worn and had to be repaired at a local cobbler's, his tuxedo didn't fit (it belonged to his uncle Louis, who was broader), and, no doubt to the King's horror, he went hunting not in knickerbockers but in gray flannels. All this was a deliberate act of defiance: he had been sent, according to custom, a complete list of clothing that he must wear for the grouse season, as well as the instruction that no shirt should be worn twice. Horror of horrors, he didn't even have his own gun. Was this to be the future husband of Elizabeth? The consort of the future Queen?

He did not enjoy wearing a kilt, which seemed to him "sissified"; such garb was a mandatory requirement, along with killing deer, at Balmoral. On the first occasion he wore the sacred Scottish garment (jokes about sporrans were endemic in World War II), he entered the royal presence and dropped a curtsy to the King. The joke was not appreciated.

In every way, his cheerful, relaxed, indifferent, and boisterous personality grated on the King, who was, of course, Victorian: correct, rigid, his father's son. Propriety and deportment were still paramount in his lexicon of life, his attitudes stern and his temper as explosive as ever when he was crossed. It is easy to envisage the thunderous atmosphere that prevailed at Balmoral in the midst of all the premature press and radio announcements of the engagement and the stubborn Princess's insistent announcements to her parents that she was betrothed.

For Philip, not everything was deadly at Balmoral. He discovered the pleasures of the gillies' ball—restored after many years. The gillies, farm hands and estate workers, were all brought in to dance with the royal family; over three hundred and fifty were present that season in the ballroom, with dancing from nine-thirty to eleven-thirty, followed by a buffet. Grouse shooting and deerstalking were required rituals: later, Prince Philip would be an advocate of preserving wildlife. A breakfast buffet in large chafing dishes on the sideboard was followed by a ride in a station wagon or shooting brake to the moors. The royals and their guests followed by gun loaders; venison pies and stuffed rolls, finger rolls, and pudding were served in a rigged-up tent for lunch. There was another break for tea: Chelsea buns and sandwiches. Books were meticulously kept, recording the hunters' beat and the number of grouse that had been shot. The King was furious, Frederick Corbitt recalled, if the slightest mistake was made in the entries. Deerstalking was next in the royal curriculum: gillies selected stags for the kill, then, with King, Queen, Princesses, and guests, followed the animal's tracks. Amply stoked with obligatory scotch, the gillie would make sure he found the beast. It had to be standing still, stationary in its magnificence, before the King or a member of his family entourage would fire the fatal shot.

Stalking took up tedious hours. It is reported that Princess Elizabeth bagged a handsome beast during Philip's stay. When Philip killed his first stag, he would normally have had to sling it over his neck on a pole—a hefty load even in his prime athletic condition. He was permitted to carry it in his arms and toss it over the back of a pony, a pampering of a guest of which King George V would have noisily disapproved. He had to beat off swarms of mosquitoes and flies that plagued the great estate.

When not on Naval duty at Corsham, which in his case seems to have provided a remarkably flexible curriculum, or stopping at weekends at his uncle Louis's townhouse, Philip spent his days at Kensington Palace, which his mother was visiting, and the now ancient dowager Marchioness of Milford Haven still roamed about issuing High German expletives in a cloud of bitterness, cigarettes, and reminiscence. He had a bedroom adjoining his cousin David, the Marchioness's gadabout ill-tempered grandson, and a valet; his first, the loquacious John Dean. Philip and David were astonishingly juvenile in their behavior, racing down the corridors or disappearing into nightclubs at all hours of the night, returning silently so the touchy old Marchioness would not catch them at their pranks. Philip smoked constantly, so much that the hard-pressed Dean had an endless fight to keep the silver cigarette boxes full and the ashtrays empty, threw his clothes about the room to be picked up, only had one baggy gray suit and a blazer and slacks, and never bought new socks; they had to be darned over and over again. One night he went out with a tuxedo and suede shoes; he could not tie his tie; he kept his hands pushed in his pockets until the jacket sagged and became shapeless. The habit is still his trademark. His only jewelry was his father's signet ring.

He even got his father's clothes from storage in Monaco and had the moth holes repaired and the coats let out and then proceeded to wear those hopelessly out-of-fashion garments.

That year, Philip's favorite sister, "Tiny," Princess Sophie of Greece and Denmark, married for the second time. Her new husband was Prince Georg Wilhelm of Hanover, the grandson of the Kaiser and brother of Queen Friederike of Greece. He had been taught at Salem, with Philip and, during the mid-1930s, had joined the Reichswehr, the military arm of the Nazi party. By World War II, he was in active service; he first served in the Army in Poland, and then became General Staff Officer with the 2nd Panzer Group under the command of General Guderian, and fought in battles at Smolensk, Kiev, and Orel. He was removed from the Army in January 1944, at the same time as Prince von Hohenlohe-Langenburg because of Hitler's paranoia over members of the German royal family supposedly militating against him. There was no real basis for such a belief.

After the war, Prince Georg Wilhelm and his mother, Princess Viktoria Luise, were living at Blankenburg Castle when British military officers took over. They charged mother and son with hiding weapons, and at the same time abstracted from the cellar numerous of the crucial German Foreign Office documents concerning the Duke and Duchess of Windsor's Nazi connections. Later, strings were pulled and they were reasonably well treated. Princess Viktoria angrily informed the British authorities that her son should not be manhandled because he was a Prince of Great Britain and Ireland, in the Guelph Line; the astonished officials checked with London and released them both.

Kurt Hahn, busying himself as usual, appointed Sophie's husband Georg Wilhelm headmaster of Salem in succession to Prince Gottfried von Baden, Philip's other brother-in-law.

There were many exciting events that winter to divert the Princess from her problems: a dazzling, vividly staged, and exciting first Royal Film Performance, at the grand old Empire in Leicester Square, with its big red carpeted staircase and deep crimson velvet curtain; the movie was Michael Powell and Emeric Pressburger's expensive romantic fantasy of the supernatural, *A Matter of Life and Death (Stairway to Heaven* in America). A legion of stars led by Vivien Leigh, Ray Milland, and Joan Bennett, the latter two heading a contingency from Hollywood, was greeted rapturously by the crowd thronging the square under a blaze of searchlights and moving spotlights;

many fainted in the crush; the royal car was delayed twelve minutes by the throng, and the King, who was furious when the crowds rocked his Daimler, was heard to remark, "We barely got here—I didn't think we would; we had to make our way through on two wheels!" The royals were met by the manager, and led into the lobby. Children of industry executives presented bouquets to the Queen, the Princesses, and other female members of the royal family. The royals were introduced to industry leaders, taking from fifteen to no more than thirty seconds with each person. Ladies were required to wear elbow-length gloves and evening gowns.

The lineup of stars awaited the royal family upstairs in the dress-circle foyer; not to ruffle sensitive egos, the lumniaries were placed in alphabetical order from right to left. The lineup included the film's star, David Niven, and its director-writer; again, thirty seconds was the maximum for each chat. The family was escorted into the circle and as they entered, a trumpet fanfare by royal bandsmen was sounded from the stage. They took their seats; the audience stood and many faced the King and Queen. The national anthem followed; the royals sat, and the house was darkened. The film began.

Just four days later, there was the almost equally glittering Royal Command Variety Performance at the London Palladium. The royal box was magnificently bedecked in flowers; two boxes were combined on the right-hand side of the theater on the first level. The excited audience was seated by request half an hour before the royals arrived. Fifteen minutes later, the Crazy Gang, among the most popular comedy groups in England, and the King's personal favorites, noted for their bawdy humor and irreverence to everyone, invaded the audience, and, while the famous Bud Flanagan gave a satirical running commentary on the royal progress to the theater, his partner Teddy Knox appeared as a salesgirl tossing ice creams at the fashionably dressed women, splattering their expensive gowns. Jimmy Nervo appeared in the royal box with a coffee urn shouting, "Well, the royals might get thirsty!" then waved a dead fish over the side with, "They might get hungry!" Pandemonium broke loose; the audience was hysterical with laughter.

As the Crazy Gang learned that the royals had arrived they evaporated with amazing speed and the royal drumroll began. The audience stood; most looked up at the royal box; a spotlight pierced the darkness and disclosed the King and Queen. The national anthem followed; the audience greeted the family with rapturous applause.

A comic episode occurred during the intermission: the King was talking to the theater manager, asking him how it was possible that immediately when the family was seated in the box, the show would proceed. The manager pointed to a telephone in the box itself. This was a special private line from the box to the stage manager, so that the manager could inform his colleague that the royals were about to take their seats. The King asked if he could do the job himself. The manager agreed, and the monarch delightedly picked up the receiver.

In his halting voice, he informed the stage manager, "The royals are entering the box!" The stage manager screamed out a stream of four-letter words, saying, "Who the bloody hell are you? Get off the bloody line!" The King roared with laughter and handed the manager the receiver. The show resumed; the manager told his colleague that the King had been on the telephone. The stage manager was close to collapse.

Prince Philip was at neither of these occasions but the stories of the engagement kept leaking, and Sir Alan Lascelles, the King's Principal Private Secretary, was much put about denying the truth. Fuel was again added to the fire of gossip when it got out that Prince Philip's application for citizenship had been put at the front of a very long line—Labor MP George Jager wrested an admission from Home Secretary Chuter Ede in the Commons. Then, at last, on December 16, the *New York Times* went front page: Raymond Daniell reported from London that "only politics, which has blighted so many royal romances, is delaying the announcement of the engagement of Princess Elizabeth, heiress to the British throne, and Prince Philip of Greece."

In January 1947, on the verge of the tour of South Africa, King George was obliged to inform his possible future son-in-law that he would not be allowed aboard the battleship *Vanguard* to say farewell to—much less kiss good-bye—the Princess, who was no doubt in a combined state of ecstasy at thought of the trip and misery because of the separation.

Philip consoled himself with a lavish dinner party, supervised by his valet John Dean, at the Mountbatten townhouse in January. The King, Queen, and Princesses, and Noël Coward, who sang some of his marvelous songs, were among the guests.

He also had the consolation that the King finally gave his approval for British citizenship, ensuring him a lifelong career in the Navy. Princess Elizabeth could not have been happy about the latter prospect: it would mean constant and lengthy separations.

10

***

THE QUEEN AND THE Princesses spent many hours of January 1947 reading (probably doctored) histories of South Africa; and had numerous fittings for their magnificent, ration-defying wardrobe that would be worn on the trip, the first the Princesses would make outside the British Isles. According to the *New York Times:*

> Pearls and diamonds, cloth of gold, endless yards of material, interminable work by dozens and dozens of seamstresses, have gone into the most sumptuous wardrobe that British royalty has worn for generations.

Meanwhile, in January, the *Sunday Pictorial* took a poll of its two and a half million readers to see how they felt about a marriage of Elizabeth and Philip. Forty percent opposed it outright; some declared that if she insisted on going ahead, she should at once renounce the throne. A great many of the letters in response to the poll pointed out that the Greek royal family was politically disgraceful; other newspapers reached a similar conclusion from their readers. The Palace continued to remain silent in the matter; the fact was that the betrothal had still not been approved by the King.

The trip to South Africa was not subjected to wide criticism, but in many ways was a mistake. Britain was suffering from a severe winter, pipes frozen and bursting, snowdrifts piled high, traffic immobile, icy winds lashing the coast; the economic conditions were worse than ever; there were threats of major uprisings in India to denounce the appointment as Viceroy of Lord Louis Mountbatten, and the King was weighed down with worry that he might be leaving at the wrong time. Moreover, though this was not much discussed, the entire tour was in essence a publicity stunt of Field Marshal Jan Smuts. His dictatorship of South Africa, where blacks were grimly suppressed, was severely troubled, most of all by the Afrikaans political faction, which was in revolt; he needed to cement the black races and the militant Afrikaans, if only temporarily, by an appeal to patriotism and a display of the royal trump cards in his questionable pack. The King's motives in acceding to Smuts's blandishments were probably as much a desire to separate Elizabeth from Philip and allow her to come to her senses as they were to get some sunshine and overcome the republican elements in this controversial far-flung corner of the Commonwealth.

A meat strike left Londoners without beef, lamb, mutton, or chicken for days in mid-January; the royal family, of course, had ample stocks from their country residences and farms. Meanwhile, the 42,500-ton *Vanguard,* which the royals had recently launched, was being preened and cleaned and fussed over from morning to midnight.

The King saw to it that the restless Philip was kept away from Elizabeth in public. The Prince's powerful ego took a beating as he was marooned in his seedy rooms at Kensington Palace or in his Nissen hut at Corsham, in order to dampen down the tittle-tattle of Fleet Street and the foreign press. He was notable by his absence from the farewell luncheon at the Palace that preceded the royal departure. The most extraordinary situation imaginable prevailed in England: because of the expected long royal absence, it was crucial that a Council of State remain to sign Parliamentary bills and reprieves; in the first instance, such a bill might be of critical moment, in the second, justice and human life were at stake. Yet of the council, the Duke of Gloucester was in Australia, and Viscount Lascelles, son of the Princess Royal, was in Canada, as A.D.C. to the Governor-General. Thus, only the Princess Royal, whose husband the Earl of Harewood was distractingly unwell, was left; as a result, the Duke of Gloucester had to be rushed back to London—and he was quite put out by the sudden move.

Next day, as snow floated down from an iron-gray sky, the royal family braved the elements in their open landau. The cavalry, still not in the Colors because of austerity rules, trotted beside, umbrellaed crowds standing six deep on the sidewalks to cheer them on their journey; they traveled from Waterloo

Station to Portsmouth, many of their subjects gathered in backyards waving Union Jacks as the train chugged by. They were sent off from Portsmouth with cheers of half a million people in wind-driven sleet; a forty-one-gun salute boomed across the sound as the *Vanguard* sailed, accompanied by virtually the entire Home Fleet and every private craft in harbor.

Thus they sailed to their African adventure—and perilously close to a disaster. After *Vanguard* steamed along a great lane of ships, past the Isle of Wight, the family gazing excitedly out of the portholes, a German mine was reported to the bridge, drifting toward the vessel, less than two miles away in a very strong current. The captain had to make an immediate adjustment, setting course south-southwest; the danger was narrowly averted as thin sunshine broke through and the last cheers and sirens and whistles of the fleet faded away and *Vanguard* moved out into the Channel.

There were exciting moments in the next days: a helicopter landing on the ship's tossing deck, a grand salute from the French vessel *Richelieu*. Otherwise, the voyage was something of an ordeal: the great wallowing battleship rolled and pitched alarmingly in the notoriously choppy waters of the Bay of Biscay, and Princess Elizabeth was hopelessly seasick; Margaret did a little better, easily winning over her sister in shipboard shooting matches, and was consoled by the presence on board of her adored Peter Townsend.

When the ship crossed the equator, everyone joined in the traditional Crossing the Line ceremony, King Neptune and Queen Neptune "baptizing" members of the royals' entourage in the pool. The Princesses longed to be christened, but much to their annoyance were not. Instead, they were covered with flour from giant mops made into imitation powder puffs. The King and Queen dissolved in laughter at the sight; already he, who had grown haggard with cares, looked somewhat better, and handsomely tanned by the tropical sun.

But his appearance was deceptive: he was, as always, irritable and fretful, constantly grumbling that he should not have made the trip at that particular time, with radio reports coming in of England's wintry plight. He hated the fact that the old and children were dying of influenza and pneumonia, and London was muffled and dead, while he was disporting himself at costume parties and skeet-shooting in the sun.

Meanwhile, in South Africa, there were ill omens: a bakers' strike took place in Capetown, following a three-week goldminers' strike in the Witwatersrand, and bitter protests against racism and oppression from the Nationalist Opposition party. Bitter denunciations that Field Marshal Smuts was using the trip to bolster his regime were not without foundation. The monarch listened to the ship's shortwave radio. He heard that more blizzards swept England; London was crippled by a dock strike; the Austin automobile factory was closed. For five hours each day, not a soul in London enjoyed electricity; a state of emergency was declared in Britain's most severe industrial crisis since 1926. Just before the ship docked in Capetown, the King's guilt, tension, and anxiety burst out in a telegram to Attlee in London, expressing his anguish at British conditions. In a city ablaze with sunshine, security precautions were tripled as threats came from Indian nationalists and militant Afrikaans against the royals. As the ship docked, word came of Ernest Bevin's utter failure to deal with a major crisis in Palestine—and he had been the King's choice. Burma was talking of secession from the Commonwealth. Attlee was about to hand India—George V's beloved India—back to the Indians. It was all a nightmare for a King marooned at the end of the world.

The Princesses were seriously disturbed by his temper and his very bad nerves; the Queen, strong as ever, managed to cushion most of his outbursts by rigorous nannying. The magic name of royalty had already sent the bakers and gold miners back to work—and Capetown was *en fête* for the royal arrival, a blaze of flags and bunting under a brilliant blue sky as *Vanguard* sailed in with her accompanying vessels on February 16.

The Princesses, in particular, were excited by the sight of Table Mountain and the Cape of Good Hope, and the ceremonies and street parades. But within two days the severe heat had left the royal party drained and weary. Even the Queen, who was never heard to voice a complaint, was moved to ask Field Marshal Smuts, ''Is it always as hot as this?''

The tortures of the next weeks of travel were considerable, despite the luxury of the famous air-conditioned White Train, which was placed at the King's disposal for a journey that went from Cape Province to the Orange Free State to Basutoland to Natal to the Transvaal, to Northern Rhodesia and Bechuanaland. There was a triumphal entry into Grahamstown, as a storm came after four months of drought and nine thousand blacks hailed the family as bringers of rain. Elizabeth delivered a strong speech to the youth of South Africa as she opened a dry dock at East London.

The Queen made an unprecedented gesture at Ladybrand in thanking a black children's choir along with the white, and in Basutoland the King refused to obey government rules against pinning medals on blacks' uniforms or suits. His address of praise there to the crowd of eighty thousand, mentioning the gallant service by black regiments in the world wars, was also impressive.

On April 1, news reached the royal party of the death in Athens of the troublesome George II of Greece; Philip had by now obtained his British citizenship, and George's death cleared the way once and for all to a future betrothal; the King's brother Paul would now assume the throne. Princess Elizabeth was radiant for the rest of the tour; Princess Margaret was equally happy, because Peter Townsend was constantly attending to her, taking horse rides with her on remote beaches.

The King remained tense despite the diplomatic and political triumph achieved during the immense journey. He was annoyed when Margaret started to giggle at an arthritic old lady's awkward curtsy and her helpless laughter when an African tribal chieftain stumbled repeatedly over lines in a prepared speech at Paarl; at one town, a burst of wind aggravated him, and still more so when it tossed a shoal of acorns onto their hats—but he laughed loudly, always a good sport, when everyone else did. On a tour of the Rand mining towns, he was especially difficult, flustering a hard-pressed chauffeur with a maddening display of backseat driving; suddenly a Zulu appeared, rushing headlong at the Daimler, and thrust something at the royal family's faces. The King shrank back, but the doughty Queen slammed her parasol hard over the intruder's head several times, as the King screamed at the driver to accelerate. The black turned out to be wanting to give Princess Elizabeth a ten-shilling note.

The royal family had to stand repeatedly in severe heat while blacks sang every single verse of the national anthem; they saw zebras and birds, visited lepers, attended balls, descended a gold mine, trudged past the Victoria Falls, climbed up to Cecil Rhodes's grave where the Queen's shoes pinched and Princess Elizabeth handed over hers. Margaret fell ill on the White

Train, tossing in fever; and then at last there was Capetown again, and Elizabeth's twenty-first birthday on April 21.

She was in a buoyant mood, sustained by telegrams from Philip, and even a phone call or two; enchanted by the seven-thousand-mile tour, she was shadowed only by her father's increasing depression. Gala balls and fireworks and rejoicing turned Capetown into a dazzling, festive place. She was showered with gifts: a diamond necklace from Smuts, more diamonds from Kimberley and the De Beers and from the Royal Household, the Grenadier Guards, the Diplomatic Corps in London, the King's pilots. And now she gave her first birthday radio address: in her high-pitched, cool voice, broken by an occasional quaver of nervousness more marked toward the end, she spoke of a "solemn act of dedication with a whole Empire [sic] listening. . . . I declare before you that my whole life, whether it be long or short, shall be devoted to your service and the service of the great imperial family to which we all belong."

It was bravery in the face of a troubled and divided Commonwealth; it was defiance in the mere mention of Empire; it was a summation of the tour's purpose; it was an indication that the Princess was still a Victorian and that her sheltered statements were not without a sincere utilitarianism. That night, Field Marshal Smuts, at a luxurious and splendid reception under the chandeliers of City Hall, gave her twenty-one more diamonds to form a new necklace; she was also awarded a gold key to Capetown and—joy of all joys—her loving father at last gave her the forty-second pearl that formed the most treasured of all her possessions: her simplest necklace.

At the farewell luncheon on the twenty-fourth, Smuts gave the King 399 diamonds for mounting in his Star of the Order of the Garter, the Queen a gold tea service and a 9-carat diamond, and Margaret 35 bracelet stones. The family collapsed into the *Vanguard* cabin suite that evening and spent much of the home voyage asleep.

The King was seventeen pounds lighter than when he had left. As the bells of Westminster Abbey rang out and the royal carriage rolled from Waterloo Station across Westminster Bridge to the Palace, many in the tumultuous throng noted that he looked drawn and ill. He had much to face: the conflicts in Palestine, the withdrawal of British troops from Egypt, the Indian situation, the crisis at home. It was too great a burden for a frail and unhealthy man. In his speech of good cheer at the Guildhall on May 15, he was at times almost inaudible: his voice was hoarse and guttural, and he broke into coughing, causing an embarrassed, painful silence in the banqueting hall.

He was even now, with Elizabeth's feelings for Philip further enhanced by distance, not prepared to allow any formal announcement of an engagement; but it is probable that he did inform her that he would put the matter into process, by seeking Attlee's advice and that of the Dominion Prime Ministers; Attlee in turn would speak to Churchill as leader of the Opposition.

On June 8, Elizabeth, who returned full-tilt to the theaters and parties of London, was given her first Private Secretary, thirty-three-year-old John Rupert Colville, grandson of the first Viscount Colville of Culross. Three days later, she received the freedom of the City of London, the first woman since Florence Nightingale to be so honored. She impressed everyone when she described the Commonwealth at a Guildhall speech as "not so much a single act of stagecraft as a miracle of faith." At the time of the King's birthday honors, she and Princess Margaret were appointed to the Imperial Order of the Crown of India—supremely ironical since India would in days be gone from the Commonwealth. They rejoiced at the knighthood of Laurence Olivier. And on June 26, Elizabeth received her first personal automobile—a Daimler.

But the crowning glory of her summer came on July 9, when, after weighing every possible objection and brooding over every possible disadvantage, the King at long last gave his official and public consent to the betrothal of his beloved daughter to Lieutenant Philip Mountbatten. Philip had lately renounced all his Greek titles[1] and was now a commoner, soon to embrace (on the pertinent advice of the Archbishop of Canterbury) the Church of England, and renouncing the Greek Orthodox Church, in which he had been baptized. As it turned out, his rejection of Greek nationality was unnecessary: all descendants of the mother of King George I were automatically granted British citizenship; at that point in time, George VI and his genealogical advisers didn't know it, or the monarch might have used the necessity of his acquiring British nationality as a

1. But not his right of succession to the throne.

delaying tactic. The King was still uneasy about the marriage. Apart from anything else, he may not have overlooked the consanguinity of distant cousins; but there was no gainsaying one of the most determined young women alive. Aside from Group Captain Townsend, there were few at the Palace who complained. The Court Circular brought front-page stories and rejoicings all over the world: at last, in a tortured world, a real-life fairy tale was about to have a happy ending.

Since Philip could not afford to buy an engagement ring, his mother sent him from Athens her favorite tiara to be broken up, eleven of its diamonds to be used in the setting. When he put the ring on Elizabeth's finger, it fell off; much to everyone's annoyance the band had to be narrowed. It was barely ready in time for the official portrait.

There was a service of celebration at Westminster Abbey; in the afternoon, the happy couple appeared together for the first time at the Palace garden party; at night, the huge welcoming crowd summoned them to the balcony; the people, one hundred thousand in all, were kept waiting until they finished dinner. At last, Elizabeth emerged in a white ball gown, Philip in Naval uniform, the King smiling bravely, the Queen fighting her doubts over the match, looking as serene and relaxed as always.

Two days later, the family was at Lords for the Eton-Harrow cricket match, animatedly talking among themselves. Joy was interrupted when, right after that, the King was constrained to sign the Indian Independence Bill, which he had recently but painfully supported; at the House of Lords Robing Room ceremony, the finale of another chapter in the history of Empire was glumly celebrated. It was the end of a world, devastating to the King and Queen, and a nail in the coffin of an England which was, to all intents and purposes, utterly bankrupt.

A momentous meeting took place at the Palace that week. The prominent fashion designer Norman Hartnell came to see the Queen. She gave him her thoughts on the wedding dress; he worked round the clock searching for the perfect design. He combed the galleries, at last finding in a book a most striking Botticelli painting, *Primavera,* that proved to be the basis for his inspiration. The figure of Flora in the painting was wearing what appeared to be a white silk garment; the Princess's wedding dress would be fashioned of white satin, and would be sewn with an embroidery of ten thousand seed pearls, and an equal number of crystals, creating a magical illusion of flower decorations of white York roses, syringa, jasmine, wheat ears, and smilax. The veil would be of white tulle; the eighteen-foot train would be alive with the same flower motifs as the dress, a fairy-tale creation of exquisite artistry. Elizabeth would wear a diamond tiara which the Queen had worn originally in 1937.

On July 14, Princess Elizabeth met her eccentric future mother-in-law, Princess Alice, who was visiting London from Athens for the ceremonies and staying with the dowager Marchioness of Milford Haven at Kensington Palace. It is possible that Philip had kept them apart because of the peculiar character of his mother's background and history, and the fact that, like the tempestuous dowager, she was prone to drag out, in the very loud voice of the deaf, old family skeletons and prejudices; furthermore, it might disturb the Princess if she were to learn that the Princess Alice had been treated in sanitariums for emotional disturbances. However, a meeting had to take place sooner or later; it cannot have been comfortable, and must have been unsettling for Elizabeth. The aging figure before her in her strange convent garments was not the sort of person the Princess would have been accustomed to having to tea.

The King obtained Sunninghill Park, near Ascot, a twenty-five-room house with six hundred and sixty-eight acres of grounds, for his daughter and future son-in-law. It had been used as a headquarters for the U.S. Army Air Force and the RAF. It was an odd choice, since it was virtually uninhabitable and would have to be converted at great expense back to domestic use; it had already been severely damaged by fire. Sixteen days after it was requisitioned, another fire destroyed the south wing; this was caused by a workman's carelessly tossed cigarette. The royal family arranged for a lease on another, smaller house, Windlesham Moor.

On September 11, the excited Princess, barely able to sleep for all her rigid training, chose her eight bridesmaids, including, of course, Princess Margaret, and Princess Alexandra of Kent and Lady Pamela Mountbatten. Then, while she and Margaret were at Balmoral, she heard the news that Norman Hartnell had finished the wedding dress. She decreed that nobody outside of the salon other than her parents and sister should see it until the wedding day.

She spent the beginning of October going over various designs for her wedding cake. She selected one that was fashioned at considerable expense. The first tier displayed the bride and groom's insignia and carvings of Windsor, Balmoral, and Buckingham Palace; the second showed her taking the salute as Honorary Colonel of the Grenadier Guards, as well as a searchlighted night scene of the Battle of Matapan, and musical sporting motifs illustrating the couple's several interests; the third had a cupid with initialed shields, ATS and Girl Guide badges, and a representation of the *Valiant,* two lifetimes in icing and paint; the fourth tier flourished the symbols of the Commonwealth.

The already uncomfortable Palace was a cacophony of stone masons, pneumatic drill teams, and carpenters sawing as all the war damage was repaired; the balcony on which the family had so often courageously stood was at last rendered safe, pictures still in storage brought back, new curtains made, carpets tacked down, walls and ceilings painted, kitchens freshly scrubbed, flues cleaned. The royal family had to thread their way through dust-sheeted armchairs, canvas floor coverings, newly arrived crates, ladders, disrupted floorboards, sawdust.

By mid-October, the invitation lists were proving as much of a headache as the day-and-night redecoratings and plans for the Abbey; there was no mention of the name of the hated Duchess of Windsor, whose Nazi connections alone would preclude her from the ceremony, nor would the King and Queen consider the presence in London of Philip's three sisters from Germany, whose appearance would not only cause untoward gossip that might wreck the marriage (suppose it were discovered that his brother-in-law had been Goering's Intelligence boss?) but would be quite against their principles. Kurt Hahn, perhaps because he was too controversial and too questionable in terms of World War I, was not included.

By October 19, some spectator seats were selling for as much as £3,000—$30,000 today. One room in Whitehall went for £3,600. By now, Philip was staying at the Palace and at Windsor while Elizabeth was in a whirl of shopping, presenting prizes, antiquing, laying cornerstones, opening building wings. During the engagement, the rule was that Princess Elizabeth had to be home by 10 P.M., and it was well known among Philip's Naval comrades that, after dropping her off in the MG at the Palace, he would go off and meet his friends for late-night drinks and laughter, with his handsome future Secretary, the fun-loving Australian Michael Parker.

On October 21, quiet in a pink dress, Elizabeth attended her first State opening of Parliament, seated on a chair attended by heralds in medieval scarlet and gold livery, listening to her father's stiff and unhappy speech emphasizing further difficulties, as the curbing of certain powers of the House of Lords as well as the nationalization of all industry was debated. She looked blank and expressionless, staring ahead at the crowd before her.

Next day, Philip, driving his MG very fast through the Gloucestershire countryside, skidded into a hedge and was bruised, his knee badly twisted. The King was probably not amused.

A heap of 2,667 gifts was displayed at St. James's Palace. Winston Churchill sent an autographed set of his book *The World Crisis*—a singular error since it contained unflattering references to Greek activities in the 1920s. On October 23, Lord Louis Mountbatten was to be created Earl of Mountbatten of Burma and Baron Romsey.

Between mid-October and the wedding, the Princess was showered with an astounding and dazzling array of gifts of jewels from all over the world. Her grandmother, Queen Mary, excelled everyone by giving presents that she herself had received: a priceless tiara, spiked and studded with diamonds, given to her for her own wedding in 1893 by thousands of young British girls; an antique diamond stomacher of exquisite design; diamond-studded Indian bangle brooches fit for an Empress; the legendary Devon earrings; the ruby earrings King George V had given her for her fifty-ninth birthday.

The King and Queen gave Elizabeth chandelier earrings featuring every cut of diamond then available; a sapphire-and-diamond necklace mirroring the colors of the Order of the Garter and almost a hundred years old; and two valuable strands of antique pearls worn in a double string, combining favorite possessions of Queen Anne of England and Queen Caroline, consort of King George II.

The Overseas League's more than fifty thousand members gave her a galleon clip with deck and sails of rubies, diamonds, and emeralds; the Burmese people, soon to be severed from the Commonwealth, a dazzling shoal of rubies; the Nizam of Hyderabad a diamond bandeau and tiara; the diamond king John T. Williamson a 54.5-caret uncut pink diamond; the Victoria, British Columbia, citizens an emerald and diamond necklace. But the gift which probably meant the most was among the simplest: Philip's. It was a miniature brooch of diamonds fashioned, like the engagement ring, from his mother's tiara, and formed in the shape of a Royal Navy badge.

In addition to this blizzard of gems, consider the other gifts which God or nature bestowed upon the Princess at the age of twenty-one. As Queen, she would not be subject to arrest, even if she killed her husband in public; she had almost never since childhood carried money; she would never pay income tax; she would need no passport or driver's license; even now she had no need of alarm clocks or wake-up calls because Bobo or her favorite bagpiper would summon her from sleep; she had seldom drawn a bath or prepared a meal; she had not had to worry over investments, because Coutts Bank and her investment counsellors Rowe and Pitman took care of everything; she had seldom paid a bill in person, or insurance, or taken, since childhood, a bus or subway or even a taxi. So sheltered had she been, she had not even contracted chicken pox or measles or mumps. She suffered from no taint of neurosis or emotional disturbance, only a natural concern over her father's health and, at present, the problem of learning by heart the order of her wedding service and making sure her exquisite Botticellian dress fit. She could indulge to the limit her love of dogs and horses. She was to the people a goddess—above the stars of stage and screen, because most of those were plagued with insecurities, and egomania, and terror of failure, age, and the public. Is it any wonder that countless millions of women focused their fantasies on her?

Although no expense was spared in the shower of gifts, corners would have to be cut in the wedding arrangements, and it was announced that few extra seats would be built in the Abbey, because of labor costs; there would be no more than $60,000 spent on decorations. There would be no general floodlighting of all of central London, because electricity was at a premium; the trousseau would be less lavish than at the 1937 Coronation or the King and Queen's wedding. A honeymoon abroad was out of the question. However, the Treasury would have to stretch itself to the limit to import the official guests. Among those on the list of some twenty-five hundred invited were the Kings of Denmark, Norway, Rumania, and

Iraq. Queen Friederike of Greece, Prince Bernhard of the Netherlands, the Crown Prince and Princess of Sweden, Queen Helen of Rumania; Philip must have taken special pleasure in including his old benefactresses the dowager Marchioness of Milford Haven and Marie Bonaparte, now famous as the rescuer of Freud from Hitler in 1938 (and a noted author and psychoanalyst), and her husband, Prince George, Philip's uncle. Field Marshal Smuts was especially welcome among the Dominion Prime Ministers, and of course Lord Louis Mountbatten would fly in from India to observe the results of his machinations in person.

The normal order of a Church of England service would be followed, and the Princess would promise to "obey" her husband, although, in practice, that would not always be possible. The musical side of the ceremony was a considerable burden for the organizers: the Westminster Abbey organist Dr. William McKie was at work composing a motet; Sir Arnold Bax, Master of the King's Musick, was busy preparing fanfares. Princess Elizabeth had a good deal to do with the musical selections. She wanted to include the Psalm, "The Lord is My Shepherd," set to a traditional Scottish tune, which one of her ladies-in-waiting, Lady Margaret Egerton, sang sweetly to her and her family and friends at Balmoral. But it proved impossible to discover any written score, and it appeared that Lady Egerton had learned the setting by heart. There was no gainsaying the Princess as a search went on in every music library in England and many abroad; her staff at the Royal College of Music, of which she remained president, was especially hard-pressed. At last, all were forced to confess failure. Since the Princess would never admit defeat, she arranged for Lady Margaret to sing the Psalm in its appropriate setting *a cappella* to both organist and precentor of Westminster Abbey, who made shorthand notes on music sheets and handed them to the choirmaster for transcription.

Before the eagerly awaited ceremony, the King bestowed the Order of the Garter on Elizabeth; he wanted to be sure that she was senior in the order to Philip, who received his Garter on the nineteenth; they would be officially and publicly invested the following spring. The King made Philip His Royal Highness, Baron Greenwich, Earl of Merioneth and Duke of Edinburgh—the last a time-honored royal title, useful in enlisting nationalist Scots' support, that had died out.[2] The King wrote to his mother, "It is a great deal to give a man all at once, but I know Philip understands his new responsibilities on his marriage to Lilibet."

The honors were kept a secret until the wedding day; thus, the invitation cards carried only the name, "Lieutenant Philip Mountbatten, R.N." There was one curious aspect of the matter: Philip was not made Prince, or Prince Consort, a title used by Queen Victoria's husband, and customary in all royal families. This bizarre anomaly is hard to explain: was it because all memory of his Greek princedom was to be expunged, or was it because the King could not bring himself to accord this final and most absolute of honors? Philip was not to receive the title of Prince for almost a decade; oddly, the King used Prince Philip as a courtesy title for years; Philip never became Prince Consort.

There was much discussion of Elizabeth's and Philip's increased income: a Select Committee on the Civil List recommended £10,000 a year for Philip. He would be included in all National High Church service orders of prayer for the royal family.

The couple was very busy right up to the day of the ceremony. There was a splendid party at the Palace just before the wedding; John (later Sir John) Colville recalled in his memoirs two untoward events at that occasion: an Indian Maharajah became belligerently drunk and physically attacked the Duke of Devonshire, and Field Marshal Smuts said to an unsettled and displeased Queen Mary, "You are the big potato; all the other Queens are small potatoes." *Time* magazine noted that Princess Juliana of the Netherlands was dancing with the Duke of Gloucester when she slipped to the floor and lay there, large and plump and gasping, while everyone froze including the royal family; in the awkward silence, Gloucester helped her awkwardly to her feet, and the band continued.

At a second party the following night, the comedienne Beatrice Lillie was unable to resist smoking, a forbidden practice in the royal presence. When Princess Margaret came up to talk to her she was at a loss: where could she put the

2. Alfred, Duke of Edinburgh, fourth child of Queen Victoria, was grandfather of Elizabeth, first consort of King George II of Greece—a Philippean connection.

cigarette? There were no ashtrays And she could scarcely stamp it out on the marble floor. She stuffed it down her dress front, and smoke began to float up from between her breasts. Somebody doused the fire with a well-aimed glass of water.

Following a full-scale dress rehearsal on November 19, the Abbey was at last made ready for the great ceremony. The morning of the twentieth was gray, murky, and threatened rain, but both Princess Elizabeth and Philip were up at about 7 A.M. Wakened by the customary bagpipes and given a cup of tea by Bobo MacDonald, the Princess took a bath and breakfast and at about 9 A.M. the Hartnell team arrived with their boss to start the long drawn-out process of dressing her. She stood, smiling and patient, as they busied themselves about her person, checking every stitch and seam and (though this had been rehearsed before) the exact fall and pull of the long train; one hour and ten minutes later, the work was completed and Charles Joerin (Monsieur Henri), arrived to fuss over her hair.

Philip had spent the night at Kensington Palace, as it was not thought appropriate that he and the Princess should emerge from the same residence. He had had farewell stag parties, the most riotous at the Dorchester Hotel, arranged by his uncle Louis; he was tired from these, and needed strong cups of tea supplied by John Dean. He went on to coffee and toast for breakfast, then dressed, not in the full-dress uniform which his uncle might have preferred, but because the King was in admiral's full dress, in regulation blues. But he did wear his controversial grandfather Prince Louis of Battenberg's ceremonial sword.

He itched for a cigarette, but had foresworn the habit for life, obeying a rule. He couldn't resist a quick gin and tonic as a stimulant, rather surprising for ten o'clock in the morning. His mother and the dowager Marchioness of Milford Haven left before Philip could see them; now, he became nervous and impatient and after much pacing up and down talking at a rapid pace to his cousin David Milford Haven, who would be best man, Philip strode out of the door only to be sent back by a policeman who was looking at a watch. He had to sit or stand restlessly for an agonizing hour more before he was finally informed that it was time to leave. As he walked out with Milford Haven, he noted that there was just a small knot of people to observe him—everyone else was lining the route of the procession or thronging the outside of the Abbey.

Shortly before she was to leave Buckingham Palace, the overexcited Princess Elizabeth made a sudden decision. She felt she must wear the magnificent double pearl necklace her parents had given her: it would add the final perfect touch to her wedding ensemble. Where was it? She suddenly remembered that it had not been retrieved from the 2,667 gifts displayed at St. James's Palace. How, with a hundred thousand people cramming the streets between the two royal residences, could she possibly retrieve it?

She summoned her hard-pressed Secretary John Colville. He must at once fetch the necklace. He was appalled at the prospect, but the Princess's will was inflexible. He raced down corridor and staircase to the quadrangle. The first car he saw was King Haakon of Norway's Daimler. He jumped into it and screamed at the chauffeur to put on full speed—but the car at once ran into the crowd in the Mall and could not move. He had to get out and fight his way through unaided. At last he reached St. James's, which was deserted as everyone was on their way to the Abbey. An aged janitor heard his tale of woe and proved to be unbelieving and obstructionist; at last the almost hysterical Secretary managed to reach the police guards on duty at the collection; they called the Palace to check on him, but the switchboard operators had the day off. He had no driver's license, no other form of identification. Then he had a brainwave: show the police the program for the wedding and point to his name in it. At last they gave in and he snatched up the priceless pearls, put them in his pocket, and fought his way back to the Palace just as the irritable Princess was about to leave.

In the meantime, two other disasters occurred. The Princess's tiara, her gift from Queen Mary, broke in half when she put it on. She turned in desperation to the Queen Mother, who said, "There's time and more than one tiara in this house!" and called for another. Now, extremely nervous, she asked a lady-in-waiting to bring her bouquet. It was missing! It took all of her royal control not to burst out in a storm of rage. Two of Hartnell's dressers and whatever staff could be summoned were dispatched to search the vast Palace from top to bottom. They raced down corridors, flung open rooms—and there was less than half an hour to spare. Finally, they negotiated flights of stairs, invaded staff quarters and cellars in a headlong rush until at long last someone said the bouquet was in the porter's lodge icebox, being kept cool and to be given to the Princess at the last minute.

Meanwhile, at the Abbey, commoners and minor royalty turned up first. Delayed by some unforeseen circumstance, or perhaps because he had confused the time, Winston Churchill was late, appearing after everyone had been seated, and bringing a cold stare from Clement and Mrs. Attlee. As Big Ben struck 11 A.M., Queen Mary, magnificently dressed, sat bolt upright in an ancient Daimler, leading the procession to the Abbey. She was followed by the Life Guardsmen, restored after many years to their prewar glory of plumed helmets, scarlet or blue tunics, white buckskins, and polished leather boots; Queen Elizabeth and Princess Margaret followed, Elizabeth the Queen waving cheerfully, Margaret strangely still and glum; then Philip's car, then the Horse Guards, then, finally, King George in Naval uniform and Princess Elizabeth. Women screamed, ''God bless you! God bless you!'' over and over again, and the Princess, exhausted from tension and anxiety over pearls and tiara and bouquet, smiled pallidly back.

As she arrived at the Abbey, she looked as acutely nervous as her mother had been at the Coronation, startled by the sheer size of the congregation. The ancient edifice was ablaze with gems and dashing uniforms of white or blue, rows of medals glinting under the gleam of ceiling lights, the sounds of the brass band outside subdued, muffled through the thick ancient walls. There were twenty-five hundred people there, from sheiks in white robes to Maharajahs in turbans, from choirboys in surplices and scarlet chasubles to dowagers dressed like Christmas trees in family diamonds, emeralds, and rubies. Down the entire length of the aisle, a red carpet awaited the royal progress; Philip and the Marquess of Milford Haven had already entered quietly through the Poet's Corner door.

Ahead of Elizabeth and the King, the royal standard was ceremonially dipped to the floor, and then there was absolute silence as father and daughter stood dramatically framed in the doorway. An instant later, as she stepped forward, there was a tremendous roll of drums and the full trumpet voluntary was sounded from a squadron of instrumentalists, soaring up into the high gray arches above the nave. Two pages appeared, the boy Prince William of Gloucester and Prince Michael of Kent, the latter only five, to carry her train; both were in kilts. As the Princess walked forward, she felt a tugging sensation: Prince

William was so nervous he had trodden on the train, but luckily it did not tear. Swarms of eyes glared at him: a unique ordeal for a child. Prince Michael, determined not to make a similar mistake, clutched the train so tightly he caused a mishap: he committed the pardonable sin of walking clean over the Tomb of the Unknown Soldier, on which, following her mother's gesture in 1937, the Princess was supposed to place her elusive orchid bouquet. She forgot.

According to the musical program she had prescribed, Parry's bridal hymn echoed upward from organ and choristers as she walked, a little ruffled by these mishaps but smiling sweetly, up the aisle. Philip made a ceremonial bow to the King, whose arm supported the Princess's hand, and grinned directly at Elizabeth, who responded in kind. The Dean of Westminster began the rite of solemnization and the Archbishop of Canterbury, the Most Reverend Geoffrey Fisher, performed the ceremony itself. The responding voices of bride and groom were almost inaudible to the congregation, but the BBC microphones caught the words perfectly and relayed them all over the world.

Philip placed the gold ring, fashioned from the same Welsh nugget from which Elizabeth Bowes-Lyon's had been made, upon his bride's finger. As they moved to the high altar, the King had to bend down and help Prince Michael lift the train, which was now too heavy for him. The litany and the Lord's Prayer were followed by a favorite motet of the Princess; the venerable Archbishop of York spoke briefly and paternally, then came the long sought metrical version of "The Lord Is My Shepherd," sung to the notes taken in shorthand, and the Princess, Philip, the King, the Queen, and a very few others walked off to sign the register in the Chapel of the Kings; as they returned, a Wesley anthem soared from the choir, trumpets announced Mendelssohn's wedding march, and then, once again, the royal progress was impeded by Prince Michael, who so delayed the train that Prince Philip looked backward several times to make sure he kept step. The bells of St. Margaret's pealed in triumph, and at last the couple emerged, and seemingly every soul in London cried out in glory that there was at least one fairy tale come true in a sad world.

The procession returned to a luncheon for a hundred and fifty at the Palace. The great crowd outside broke the barriers and rushed headlong to fling themselves against the black railings; over one hundred and fifty thousand people screamed in unison, "We want the bride!" At one-thirty, Elizabeth and Philip stepped out, as perfect and formalized as ever; the rest of the family joined them, and then again, they were alone, and at three-thirty they appeared once more. As they ran to the coach to take off for their honeymoon at the appropriately chosen Mountbatten estate at Broadlands—he who had fixed the match had provided comfort for its consummation—the King, Queen, Queen Mary, and Princess Margaret, and the Duke and Duchess of Gloucester pelted the couple with rose petal confetti. The coach disappeared, as fairy-tale coaches will do, into a romantic mist, for its journey to Waterloo Station.

11

* * *

THE ROYAL TRAIN WAS ready at the red-carpeted and
flower-banked platform at Waterloo. John Dean accompanied
Bobo MacDonald in the royal entourage; with the Princess's
favorite corgi dog, Sue, the royal couple arrived at the station
shortly after four in the afternoon accompanied by staff
carrying seventeen pieces of luggage—fifteen were the Princess's, two Philip's. The dining car was elaborately set out for
tea, with the finest of china and an ample supply of hot scones,
jam, and Dundee cake.

At dusk, the honeymooners drove up to Broadlands in a
black Rolls-Royce; Edwina Mountbatten, before leaving for
India with her husband—they had flown four days and nights
into London from New Delhi and were already on their way
back—had made arrangements with Frank Randall, the butler,
and Charles Smith, the valet, to take care of the royal couple.
Smith recorded that the bedroom chosen for them was the
Portico Room, the heart of Countess Mountbatten's suite,
which included separate dressing rooms and a lavish bathroom;
the Mountbattens had spent their wedding night in the same
four-poster Tudor bed, with its ivory satin padded bedhead,
heavy damask covers, and ghastly pink sheets, surrounded by
Salvador Dali *gouaches*. The view over the Test River valley
and the forest beyond was already darkened as the heavy
curtains were drawn and dinner prepared in the kitchen.

The couple went to bed just before midnight. Next day
(Charles Smith recalled) he supervised the breakfast—they had
called from the room for grapefruit and boiled eggs. They spent
the days walking and riding—they enjoyed a feast of local
beef, lamb, veal, pheasant, fish, with champagne cocktails; in
the evenings, Smith wrote in his memoirs, they are in the sitting

room by a roaring wood fire, bathed in the candlelight the Princess favored, and would favor always. The flowers, bone china, heirloom silver, and cut Venetian and Waterford crystal were brought out, as Countess Mountbatten had instructed, along with the best vintage wines in the cellars.

The idyll was soon spoiled: the public would not let the couple alone, nor would the press, cramming the church where they went on Sunday for divine service, following them on horseback, peering at them from treetops, training binoculars on the royal bedroom. Princess Elizabeth was consoled by a touching letter from her father, who was sad and fretful in London, but wished her well; Philip was not consoled; he screamed at the invading pressmen. He was already getting a foretaste of what it meant to be a royal husband in the full glare of publicity.

Much of the post-Christmas season was spent in anxious inspections of the couple's London residence, Clarence House, which was a disaster from any point of view: the rooms were still lit by gaslight, the walls of many corridors were mildewed, carpets were frayed, ceilings fallen down; bomb damage left unrepaired; there was no central heating or hot water. The Queen, Queen Mary, and Princess Margaret arrived to give much-needed advice, and the Department of Works' staff was busy for countless hours. Isley Donald, a friend of Lady Louis Mountbatten, was hired as decorator. Elizabeth and Philip were housed in the Bühl Suite at Buckingham Palace throughout January; Philip was working at the Admiralty, a paper-shuffling job he hated, and would stride home in all weathers, very few passers-by taking much notice of him; he had yet to acquire a substantial public following on his own, separate from his wife—and that was a pleasure to him. He and the Princess would most enjoy their weekends redecorating Windlesham Moor: their tastes were in conflict, she very much a latter-day Victorian, loving bric-a-brac and antiques, he a modern man, who wanted a simple, uncluttered decor. She won: she was loving and honoring, but already she was firmly, if charmingly, disobeying. They moved into Kensington Palace on January 27, making the best of mediocre but immaculately neat quarters vacated by the ill-tempered Earl of Athlone, Queen Mary's brother, who was off to South Africa.

The Princess became pregnant in February; but there would be no announcement until June. Next month, Philip left the

Operations Room at the Admiralty, and took an Officer Training course at the Royal Naval College at Greenwich. Meanwhile, Elizabeth, though not feeling well, agreed to open an exposition of eight hundred years of British life in Paris on the occasion of a State visit to that city in the spring. The Cold War had begun, and, with much fear that Russia might prove dangerous in the Mediterranean—only Greece was not under direct control of the Soviet Union in the Balkans region—the visit was felt to be as necessary as her parents' had been in 1938. As usual, Labor members of Parliament attacked the cost of the trip, the royal wardrobe, the fortune being spent on Clarence House, the increase in the Princess's income—and also as usual, few were listening.

Paris was floodlit for the royal visitors on May 14, 1948. The arrival at the Gare du Nord was a riot of excitement; after a rainy morning the sun broke through, and the city was *en fête,* from President Vincent Auriol, who awarded the Princess the Légion d'Honneur and Philip (tactfully) the Croix de Guerre at the Élysée Palace to the humblest *poilu* who gave up his Whitsunday vacation for the event. In immaculate French, the Princess gave a graceful speech, delivered and broadcast from the entry of the Galliéra Museum, where the British exhibition was opening; the Opera gala was a great occasion, and the Princess's Hartnell and Molyneux wardrobe, though more modest than that which her mother had worn in the 1930s, was much admired. But there were jarring elements in the trip.

For all her charming manners, Elizabeth was still feeling ill in her third month of pregnancy; and Philip not only was suffering from a case of food poisoning from the boat-train, he was irritable and showed sudden outbursts of temper. He was already feeling the unpleasantness of being a mere appendage to his wife; he was maddened by the ritualistic elements of a royal visit. On a trip to Longchamp Racecourse, where he won a hundred francs, he was increasingly sickly and moody, and the Princess asked him to cancel his engagements but he would not.

At dinner at the Tour d'Argent, Philip screamed at a photographer who was hiding under a table; the Princess did not appreciate this outburst. Back in London, the couple ran into a storm, albeit one in an ecclesiastical teacup: the Scottish Association of the Lord's Day Observance Society of Scotland, supported by the General Assembly of the Free Church of

Scotland, roundly condemned the couple's attendance at Paris theaters and racetracks, omitting any mention of the fact that they had, despite illness, twice attended church.

The Archdeacon of Lewes assailed the Church of Scotland in the matter, and a furor broke loose, with the Dean of Westminster joining in the fray against the Scots clerics, the Cardiff churches supporting the Princess when she received the freedom of the city, Philip sounding off against Scotland, and British and Scottish ministers arguing themselves blue in the face.

There was much animated clerical discussion when the Princess and Duke arrived at a U.S. Embassy costume ball disguised as a waiter and waitress, and turned up in the Distinguished Strangers' Gallery at the House of Commons to hear a debate. Philip's cutting through red tape and protocol, rewriting speeches written for him, and generally trying to assert his masculine pride in impossible circumstances, added fuel to the sacred fires, until the fury died down with the first authorized announcement that the Princess would make no more official engagements as a baby was on the way. Sir William Gilliatt, who had delivered the Duchess of Kent's children, was appointed gynecologist.

That summer of 1948, Philip's mother, Princess Alice, for so many years a lay sister of the Greek Orthodox Church, established her own order of nuns, the Sisterhood of Martha and Mary, on the Greek island of Tinos; she became Mother Alice Elizabeth. The order was described in E. E. Tisdall's *Royal Destiny* as "a working order group, offering active charity to the needy and different from other Greek orders, which lead contemplative lives in convents." The following year, Alice would move the order to North Heraklion, a suburb of Athens.

She had been inspired by the example of her aunt, the dowager Marchioness of Milford Haven's sister, the Grand Duchess Elizabeth, who had founded an identically named order of nuns before her husband, Grand Duke Serge, brother of Czar Alexander III, was assassinated in 1905. Princess Alice copied the order's plain gray habit. In 1918, the Grand Duchess and the other members of her sisterhood had been thrown down a mineshaft to their deaths. White Russians rescued her body and carried it via Peking to Jerusalem, where it was interred in the Greek Orthodox Church of St. Magdalene, near the Mount of Olives; the Grand Duchess's sister Alix was, of course, murdered by the Communists along with her husband, Czar Nicholas, at Ekaterinburg.

Despite the announcement she would cease all activities in June, Elizabeth's calendar was more crowded than ever in July. During her pregnancy, she was busy day and night, scarcely missing a single London stage show, presenting medals, attending the marriage of Lord Derby, going to Greenwich to see Philip work. On July 21, Elizabeth sat with the Countess Mountbatten, in the Civil Servants' Gallery of the House of Lords to see Philip take his seat as Duke of Edinburgh; in scarlet and ermine robes, he declared firmly his allegiance to the "King, his heirs and successors."

In 1948, Prince Philip engaged Lieutenant Commander Michael Parker as his equerry. Parker was his closest friend; although he was a rank outsider in Palace circles as a Roman Catholic and an Australian, his charm and magnetism overcame all obstacles. Handsome and rugged, he was twenty-eight years old; his early life was spent in the Navy, as captain of escort vessels doing convoy duty in the choppy North Sea; while on East Coast Patrol off Scapa Flow, he met Prince Philip; released from the Navy because of war wounds toward the end of the war (he had met Prince Philip again in the Pacific theater), he married an attractive Scotswoman, Eileen Allen, who was in the WRNS. Parker was working in the lowly job of selling ropes by sample for his father-in-law when Philip asked him to be equerry.

They joined in all-male parties, one of which, in October 1953, would actually take place at the Palace, in a room that the Prince, imitating his uncle Louis Mountbatten, had turned into a replica of a captain's cabin; according to the *Sunday Graphic,* "No woman is allowed in . . . even the Queen."

Princess Margaret, possessed of a sense of inferiority because she realized every day her sister's importance as heiress presumptive, and because her own education had been, by comparison, inadequate, now emerged in her full colors as a vivid, strong-willed, moody, and independent modern young woman. She was impatient with trains and ships, and liked to fly; she enjoyed cocktails and cigarettes in long holders and Les Ambassadeurs, the very exclusive Milroy Club above that restaurant, and young men in fast cars; not even her staid father, who said of her, "She could charm the pearl out of an oyster,'' could quell her insistence on late-night hours and trips abroad. She liked practical jokes and painting, good food and liquor; in short, she was fun. She was also very beautiful, more beautiful than all but the best photographs revealed—the Artists' Association of America listed her as having the most beautiful eyes in the world.

A chief influence upon her was Sharman Douglas, daughter of the U.S. Ambassador to the Court of St. James's, a honey-blond, fun-loving, charming, and attractive girl who entertained at the Connaught Hotel and at the ambassadorial residence in Regents Park.

Margaret was up almost every night until well after midnight. The Palace staff would already be in bed and a policeman on duty had to let her through the entrance of the private apartments, and thence by elevator to her third-floor suite, where she was attended by Bobo MacDonald's sister.

Now that Margaret was of marriageable age, the decision was made by the King and Queen that she must ''marry British.'' After all the problems of Philip's background, they could not cast the net too wide, and there were few of her European cousins who were without some taint from World War II. She must be discouraged from Group Captain Peter Townsend, since the idea of her bringing about a divorce would be unacceptable, and no member of the royal family could marry a divorced man; and she should marry into the aristocracy. She was taken out at night, sometimes in a group, sometimes individually, by a number of eligible bachelors, including the Marquess of Blandford (''Sunny''), the son of the wealthy Duke of Marlborough, who was not handsome enough to physically attract her, and the Earl of Dalkeith, son of the Duke of Buccleuch, who had, as we know, been fired from the Royal Household for his appeasement-defeatist attitudes at the outbreak of war.

Another of her magic circle was the wealthy William (''Billy'') Wallace, who was introduced to her by her closest friend, the equally rich Judy Montagu; Wallace was grandson of Sir Edwin Lutyens, the leading British architect, whose Cenotaph, BBC building in Portland Place, and Queen Mary's dollhouse had admirers. Wallace suffered from recurring ailments and later would be stricken tragically with cancer. But he shared Margaret's love of the arts; most of her circle lacked that serious interest.

In February 1948, a new and extraordinary presence entered her life. The brilliant thirty-five-year-old Brooklyn-born comedian Danny Kaye opened at the London Palladium in an evening of entertainment that has perhaps never been equaled in the history of variety in England. He was virtually unknown in the United Kingdom at the time, as his Hollywood films had made little impression and his great career on Broadway had not had echoes in London. He was the rage of the nobility, and was befriended by David, Marquess of Milford Haven, during the early days of the season, finally becoming irritated by Milford Haven's constant invasions of his dressing room, accompanied by his friends.

One evening, Milford Haven said that two cousins wanted very much to come backstage and meet him. Kaye said he was too tired to see anybody else, until the theater manager explained to him that the cousins were Princess Elizabeth and Margaret. Delightedly yielding, he entertained them hugely with his manic humor.

Princess Elizabeth reported to the King that Kaye was as excellent as the reviews said, and that her parents must see him. The King said he would order the royal box for the family. Elizabeth said it was impossible to appreciate him from the box and he had to be seen from the front of the house. Shortly thereafter, the King and Queen and the two Princesses saw a performance from the center of the front row of the stalls. They were dazzled by Kaye's brilliance and Kaye was introduced to the monarch, who invited him to have dinner at Buckingham Palace—a very rare privilege for an entertainer. The King had always like American comedy.

Princess Margaret became romantically attached to Kaye, fascinated by his copper hair, handsome face, and lithe figure. At first, the King and Queen were amused by the friendship, and charmed by it. But gradually, the extent of Margaret's interest disturbed her parents. There was something grostesquely improbable in the thought that she might even want to marry him. And he was married; his wife, the gifted lyricist Sylvia Fine, was in and out of London. The entire matter threatened to erupt into a scandal. It was not until three years later that Princess Margaret finally yielded to pressure and broke off the intimate friendship, and Danny Kaye was discouraged from making public visits to London.

At the end of summer, 1948, Margaret and Philip undertook

Elizabeth's—and the ailing King's—official duties, including attendance at the installation of Princess Juliana of the Netherlands as Queen in September. The constant whirl of activity took its toll: Margaret suffered from "migraine headaches" (or hangovers) and frequently would take to her bed.

The King's condition troubled Elizabeth. He had never recovered from the South African trip; he was still drawn and painfully thin, with great bags under his eyes—the "Windsor bags"—unnaturally pronounced; he was insomniac, with puzzling, gnawing pains in his legs. Exhausted from a State visit of the King and Queen of Denmark, the full-dress opening of Parliament in October, and angrily disobeying doctors' orders not to attend official occasions, he at last took medical advice and agreed to postpone a planned 1949 Australian tour—a severe disappointment to him.

He learned that he had arteriosclerosis and might have to have his right leg amputated. Although that crisis was averted, he was in wretched health.

Princess Elizabeth moved into the Bühl Suite at Buckingham Palace in November to await the birth of her child.

It would be the first time since Queen Anne that an heiress presumptive had had a child. About one matter the King was adamant. He would not countenance the appearance of the Home Secretary to confirm that no warming pan baby had been introduced into the royal bed. Sir Alan Lascelles announced, using the King's own deeply felt words, that such attendance at a birth was "not a statutory requirement or a constitutional necessity. It is merely a survival of an archaic custom, and the King feels it is unnecessary. . . ."

A temporary nursery was furnished at the Palace, adjoining the Bühl Suite; Philip was housed in a separate suite. Princess Elizabeth's own cradle was brought out of storage for the occasion, complete with chiffon head curtain and blue bows, and accompanied by a wicker hamper full of baby clothes and rattles. Sir William Gilliatt announced that the local anesthetic trilene would be used.

Sir John Weir, the King's homeopathic physician, was in attendance on the Princess; Sir William Gilliatt moved into the Palace on November 12. That night, Philip's valet, John Dean, was sent to a pharmacy in Wigmore Street to obtain sleeping tablets for the Princess; since this might attract publicity, he picked up the prescription in his own name. On the fourteenth, surprisingly, Elizabeth and Philip actually left the Palace and were driving to dine at the Mountbatten house at 16 Chester Street with Earl Mountbatten's daughter Patricia and her husband, Lord Brabourne. If she had given birth at the time, then the child would have been born, by no means inappropriately, in Earl Mountbatten's house.

By now, the Bühl Suite at the Palace had been stripped of its furniture and become an operating theater, very well equipped, with three nurses on Gilliatt's special team in attendance along with the midwife Sister Helen Rowe. Philip became so tense over the waiting that he decided, just after 4 P.M. on the afternoon of the fourteenth, that he would play a brisk game of squash with Michael Parker, followed by a swim in the garden pool. The Princess went into labor shortly after 7 P.M. The crowd outside the Palace was silent and nervous; there was no sense of fierce excitement or festivity as there had been when Elizabeth and Margaret were born, though the bonfires were waiting to be lit across England and countless drinkers in pubs and families at home were at the radios listening.

There were no complications; there was no call for cesarean section. The Princess had learned relaxation techniques; the painkiller worked effectively without causing any side effects. The baby was born at 9:14 P.M., rosy and plump and healthy, loudly bawling: a boy, weighing seven pounds and six ounces.

A boy! A future King on the throne of England! Even Henry VIII at the birth of his first and only son, King Edward VI, could scarcely have been more excited than Philip, who ran carrying an immense bouquet of camellias, lilies, carnations, and roses into his wife's bedroom in response to Sir Allan Lascelles's announcement of the news. The King and Queen were there, the King temporarily cheered; Queen Mary was summoned from Marlborough House, where she had been anxiously awaiting Lascelles's phone call; of the immediate royal family, Margaret was the only one out of town, staying with the Earl and Countess of Scarborough at their country estate.

The forty-one-gun salute rang out, the bells of St. Paul's and Westminster Abbey pealed as many as five thousand changes each for three hours, four thousand telegrams of congratulation swamped the Palace, and the fountains in Trafalgar Square were colored little boy blue.

It had already been decided by both parents that if the child

were of the male sex he would be called Charles Philip Arthur
George. The choice of Charles was odd: it had been centuries
since the name had been used in the royal family, one
exception being that egregious Nazi, the Duke of Saxe-Coburg-
Gotha. Neither King Charles I nor King Charles II had lent any
particular distinction to the throne, and, of course, the first of
the monarchs ended up on the execution block. When asked for
an explanation, the Princess always said that Charles was
simply her favorite name; there may also have been a need to
maintain, just as the title of Duke of Edinburgh did, the
all-important links with Scotland, by referring back directly to
the Stuart line and by de-emphasizing yet again the German
line, since the Georges were Hanoverians. The name George
thus became last in order; Arthur was the name of the
much-beloved Prince Arthur, Duke of Connaught (1850–
1942), son of Queen Victoria. When apprised of the confirmed
selection of names, Princess Margaret is said to have observed,
"Oh, dear! Now they will now be calling me Charlie's aunt."

The King rallied, stimulated by Prince Charles's advent and
by Elizabeth's radiant health; sadly, he had an almost immediate relapse. The Princess was told for the first time, three
days after her son's birth, of the gravity of the situation. On
November 16, he was ordered a complete rest by his doctors as
there was an acute obstruction to the arteries of his legs. Thus,
the Princess's greatest joy was tempered by the greatest of all
fears concerning her beloved father. The news came as a
tremendous shock to the Commonwealth.

The King underwent massages and homeopathic remedies;
he was no easier a patient now than before. He hated to be idle,
insisting upon holding Privy Council meetings in his rooms.

On November 27, 1948, Prince Charles received his first
play house, a ten-foot-high Tudor cottage with doors that only
a child could get through. Three firemen had spent a year
building and furnishing it at their own expense; the rule against
accepting unsolicited gifts from commoners was waived for
once by the delighted parents. The cottage drew crowds when
it was exhibited at Olympia. As one of the worst pea-soup fogs
in memory blanketed London, the Princess was at last up and
about; she immediately began checking through the no less
than fifty-five expensive garments in the layette. Charles was

sporting a beautiful head of golden hair, inherited from his father and grandfather, and he was a robust picture of health.

The christening took place on December 15 in the gold and white Music Room under the glitter of chandeliers, before an immense bow window because the Private Chapel had not been restored after the bombings of World War II. The Archbishop of Canterbury presided; Princess Margaret as godmother held the baby; the dowager Marchioness of Milford Haven was among those present along with the King and Queen. Despite the Palestinian troubles, Jordan water had been safely brought from Jerusalem, and the gilded font had been driven, according to tradition, from Windsor Castle.

Charles did not issue plaintive cries like his mother, but behaved chucklingly well, like his aunt; no dill water was necessary in order to quell him.

The Princess breast-fed the baby, who was in the charge of his nanny, Helen Lightbody, and was visited, as he grew older, only twice a day by his mother, for an hour in the morning and for an hour in the late afternoon. In view of the King's state of health, the family made the disappointing decision not to go to Sandringham until January, and the Christmas festivities, which were very subdued on this occasion, were held at Buckingham Palace.

On the eighth, the King and Queen at last did leave for Sandringham by the recently nationalized British Railways; they had been preceded by the Princess, who had brought with her Philip and Charles. Within a few days, Elizabeth was suddenly stricken with measles, which, due to her sheltered condition, she had never suffered from as a child. The highly contagious disease was considered dangerous for a small baby, and she was not permitted to see Charles until she was out of quarantine.

Prince Philip was restless at Sandringham, and was glad to return to London; he took off with Elizabeth for a national tour, to meet the people. In more than one official speech, he mentioned his urgent need for "a home of our own." Prince Charles was left behind on the prolonged journey. They returned when the King underwent a successful sympathectomy operation.

In an extraordinary break of protocol totally hidden from the press, Princess Elizabeth and Prince Philip celebrated her twenty-third birthday on April 21, 1949, at the Café de Paris, one of the most fashionable nightclubs in London. She loved the club, and personally named its famous central room with the big staircase down which the great stars of the world descended, the Pink Room. Her sister Margaret was also in love with the club, and often went there at the time with a devoted but much older beau, Major John Profumo, an immensely rich descendant of an Italian noble family who would one day become the most notorious figure in the nation. His love for her was never mentioned in the press.

On her birthday night, Elizabeth was the guest of a close friend, Sir Eric Miéville, who was to become her husband's stand-in at the rehearsals of the Coronation. The whole party went to see the vivid and unforgettable performance of *The School for Scandal* with Sir Laurence Olivier and his wife Vivien Leigh as Sir Peter and Lady Teazle. Close to midnight, the Oliviers joined the royal party; at a table decorated with the Princess's favorite maidenhair fern and white Scottish heather, they dined on smoked salmon, breast of chicken, peas, and new potatoes, followed by strawberries and ice cream, cookies and coffee. Few in England could have dreamed of such a feast.

At 11:10 P.M. exactly, the chef produced a ten-pound birthday cake; the "Z" in the Elizabeth inscribed on the cake was back to front and everyone laughed. The whole party danced and drank happily until, to cries from the crowd of "Happy Birthday," they went to the 400 Club for nightcaps and rhumbas.

In May, Elizabeth and Philip were in Northern Ireland. The almost sixty public appearances before the end of June wore down Philip's patience and provoked a decision to apply for reenlistment in the Royal Navy. He rejected all of the speeches prepared for him, quite annoying Lieutenant General Sir Frederick Browning, who composed several of them, rewriting the speeches Michael Parker put together for him. Even the sumptuous royal train, in which the Princess and the Duke had handsomely appointed adjoining bedrooms (they never slept in the same room, even at Buckingham Palace), and on which the food served was as good as any in a three-star restaurant, with the finest of silver, cutlery, and napery, left him dissatisfied. When asked to sign autographs, he gruffly announced that royalty was not allowed to sign, adding rudely that he was not a film star; but gradually the enthusiasm of the people in the impoverished Midlands, which he hated, reached through to him and made him feel better.

At last, the redecoration and rebuilding of Clarence House were completed, and the royal couple could move in. Much of the mansion was restored to its original, 1825 John Nash glory; Princess Elizabeth's bedroom was a symphony of peach and rose-colored satins and silks, Philip's a severely handsome Regency room, his dressing room fixed up like an officer's cabin in the Royal Navy. Charles's primrose-colored nursery was part of a four-room private suite, and he had a separate night nursery in motifs of blue and white. The enormous dining room and drawing room were rendered livable by carefully thought-out designs, contributed to in part by Queen Mary and Princess Margaret.

The overall effect was elegantly "period" and cool; Canada and Australia, Lancashire, and the city of Glasgow, among other nations and municipalities, had raised funds to supply elements in the decor, according to the royal requirements, but the cost was still a staggering £20,000 more than that originally voted for in the House of Commons; in modern terms over $1,800,000.

Looking out of her window onto the richly planted garden, gazing at her rosewood-paneled walls, the fine paintings and the glories of the Lancaster Room, the library, and the splendid reception rooms, the Princess, for all of her Midlands and Scottish tours, still knew little of reality. The King's health was improved; Margaret was in high spirits after a grand tour of Europe, when the family gathered at Balmoral. At that gathering Philip, amid all the deerstalking and grouse shooting, pressed the King for the umpteenth time on the matter of being allowed to go to sea. The King at last agreed, though Princess Elizabeth can only have had twinges of distress, since Philip did not want a job in home waters. He was appointed first lieutenant on the destroyer *Chequers,* in the Mediterranean fleet, where he would be close to Earl Mountbatten, who commanded the 1st Cruiser Squadron.

Philip left for his Naval duties in Valletta, Malta, on November 17. Elizabeth followed, without Charles, and also by plane, four days later. Although the trip was described as a semi-vacation for her, it was in fact filled with activities. Major Alfred Briffa, OBE, a friend of the royal couple, remembers those days well: Princess Elizabeth was happier than at any other time of her life before or since; she was a Naval wife and had no responsibilities; she was allowed to roam around Malta unescorted; she drove her sports car with a scarf on her head, and went to the movies with her husband, paying the one shilling and sixpence entrance to go in and sitting with him in the back row, holding hands.

The couple often went to friends', sitting on the floor and enjoying picnic-style dishes of timpana, a local favorite; after dinner, they would play card games; when Prince Philip got the king of hearts in his hand, he would exclaim, "It's that man again!" Initially, the royal couple lived with Sir Gerald Creasy, the English governor; later, they moved to the Mountbatten house, the Villa Guardamangia, which means, in Italian, "Look and eat."

On December 12, Charles fell ill with tonsillitis, a very serious matter at his age, yet neither Elizabeth nor Philip returned to London to be at his side, leaving the matter in their parents' hands, knowing he would enjoy the best of care, a very royal response to a child's emergency. Philip was by now in a black temper again: he had longed for, and was badgering Earl Mountbatten for, command of a vessel; it was not easy to take orders in his position as first lieutenant. But he failed the Command Examination, no doubt because of his numerous absences from the course at Greenwich.

Michael Parker gave him the bad news. Explosive with frustration, Philip feared that someone might try to fix the results and threatened to resign if anyone did.

Elizabeth was able to soothe him some of the time. She was pregnant with her second child and enjoying Malta's sunshine, sea breezes, and weekend swims and picnics. She did not return to Charles for Christmas at Sandringham.

Elizabeth extended her stay in Malta. Earl Mountbatten found her to be so sensitive and loving that when, during a local amateur play performance, rain came down on the roof, she gripped his arm and asked him in agony whether he thought the storm might affect the paint Philip had ordered for *Chequers*. Mountbatten—and everyone else in Malta—adored her.

The New Year found Philip in the Middle East. Returning at last to London, Princess Elizabeth could now devote more attention to Prince Charles; he was an enchanting baby, not at all petulant as she had been, almost too angelic, and the absence of his father at that early age didn't seem too important. His grandparents remained captivated by him ("He is too sweet stumping around a room," the King noted), and he greatly relieved the monarch's nervous disposition.

A pleasure for Elizabeth was winning both the Queen Elizabeth and Hurst Park races in January and February; she was enthusiastic about her victorious horse Monaveen, and racing was unquestionably, and always would be, the passion of her life. She loved the sweet smell of straw, the scent of leather, the rippling, polished, black or chestnut hides of horses in prime condition; she was endlessly at the royal stables at Wolferton near Sandringham, checking on foals, attending their births, going over saddles and bits, smiling as she fed the horses sugar lumps or grass with her flat palm, jumping up and down as she watched them romp home at the finish. Horses! Only her husband and son and beloved parents could outmatch them . . . they were, with her dogs, her best, her most adored friends; and Monaveen was the most beloved.

Princess Elizabeth returned happily to Malta at the end of March, staying at the house of the governor of San Antonio because Earl Mountbatten was suddenly bereft of staff; she and Philip would move back into the lavish Villa Guardamangia in mid-April. Earl Mountbatten arranged a spectacle for her: on April 1, she stood at Fort St. Elmo, watching the ten ships of his cruiser squadron, in five columns of two ships each, deploy and dock at Grand Harbor and Sliema.

In March 1950, Philip took up his uncle Louis's favorite sport of polo, at first suffering a glorious defeat but later improving greatly; watching the matches was a great excitement for the Princess. Earl Mountbatten took Philip on a quick and most memorably exciting flight to the headquarters of the Foreign Legion in French Morocco; Mountbatten had been their commander in Indochina. The French, German, Austrian, Czech, and Hungarian Legionnaires were fascinating company; these were glorious days for Philip, filled with adventure and pleasure, travel in exotic regions, a young and beautiful girl waiting for him in Malta—and he was not yet twenty-nine.

Princess Elizabeth celebrated her twenty-fourth birthday at the Villa Guardamangia; later that month, Philip made another visit to the Arab countries. He was the guest of King Abdullah of Jordan. The Anglo-Arab connection was very important in the wake of the war with Israel; with Russian influences operating in the Middle East, a husband of the heir to the British throne could do much good in that region. It was important that the sea-lanes be kept open and supported through Suez, the Red Sea, and the Gulf of Arabia; Britain (and the royal family in particular) had substantial oil interests in the region.

The Princess left for London on May 9 via the South of France, but no sooner had the Viking aircraft of the King's Flight left Nice at 2:30 P.M. than it ran into a violent storm. Word came from a preceding Viking, carrying the Princess's mountainous luggage, that the conditions ahead were dangerous, and the King's pilot, Air Commodore Fielden, was forced to radio Buckingham Palace (a direct line had been organized by Prince Philip) that he was turning back. The Hotel Negresco managed to provide a suite at a moment's notice and the Mayor arranged for all the lights along the Promenade des Anglais to be dimmed at midnight because they might bother the Princess as they shone through her semi-transparent bedroom curtains.

In late May, while the Princess enjoyed the pleasures of London and the reunion with her son, Philip learned the results of the Naval examination he had taken in February; he was overjoyed that he would now be qualified to command a vessel. He was told he would be able to take up a position in late August as captain of the frigate *Magpie.*

Elizabeth hung on in England all summer, a long separation from Philip; because she was awaiting her second child (the official announcement was made as late as April 17), she curtailed her engagements again—but only somewhat; she was, of course, at Ascot and the Derby and all of the other racing events.

On June 25, the Soviet- and Chinese-influenced North Korean Government launched its infamous attack on South Korea; the King at once consulted with Prime Minister Attlee, and the decision was made to commit an impoverished nation to the unqualified support of the Seoul Government and the United States. Britain had to find money to rearm and raise millions for defense in case the Korean War should escalate into a global conflict. By August, as much as £3,400,000 was voted for this purpose: one tenth of the entire national revenue.

This dark news shadowed the summer of 1950; there was fear in England of a third world war, in which atom bombs might destroy all life on the planet.

Everyone was overjoyed when Elizabeth delivered a girl at 11:50 A.M. on August 15; the baby weighed six pounds. She was named Anne Elizabeth Alice Louise, the last two names, of course, for Philip's mother and for Lord Mountbatten's sister, Crown Princess of Sweden.[1] Philip called the King at once and the Queen drove over excitedly. A stream of people filed past the announcement boards outside Clarence House, but it was not until 3 P.M. that the crowd became really large. Half an hour later the King's Troop of the Royal Horse Artillery fired off a forty-one-gun salute, and all England rejoiced.

Mysteriously, Princess Margaret did not travel to London to see the baby, but instead went on to Balmoral, where the Queen, who had spent less than forty-eight hours with her daughter, joined her on the seventeenth, to celebrate her birthday four days later. Child or no child, the Balmoral August vacation was sacrosanct.

Then, in late October, just two days after Princess Anne's christening, news reached Princess Elizabeth that the dowager Marchioness of Milford Haven had at last died after a long struggle; the entire royal family—Philip flew in from Malta— was gathered for the solemn obsequies in the flower-banked Chapel Royal at St. James's Palace. As in many large families, the juxtaposition of a christening and a funeral was quite typical, the cycles of birth and death, or loss and renewal, constant and providing many conflicting emotions for the rejoicers and mourners.

Half-hidden among the long list of attendees published in the London *Times* was Philip's sister Margarita, wife of Prince Gottfried von Hohenlohe-Langenburg, whose service as commander of a Panzer division on the Russian front seemed not to disqualify his own or his wife's acceptance in international society; his brother Max had been a double agent for the British and the Germans during the war. This was the first time that one of Philip's sisters had dared to make a semi-public appearance in London, and fortunately, it went almost unnoticed. The Princess von Hohenlohe-Langenburg was Princess Anne's godmother; another godmother was Mother Alice Elizabeth; the godfathers were Earl Mountbatten and the Hon. Andrew Elphinstone, cousin to the Queen.

1. Louise would become Queen on October 29, following the death of King Gustav V.

John Dean coolly recorded in his memoirs that another sister, Sophie, was in London at the time without her husband, Prince Georg of Hanover, grandson of the Kaiser. She was received at Clarence House and met the Princess.

For all the nation's pleasure in Anne's birth, the critical state of the economy and the Korean War meant that there were few spectacular scenes such as had marked the birth of her mother and Aunt Margaret; those days in England were long gone. Philip continued to cement relations in the Near East by sailing the frigate *Magpie* to Izmir, scene of his father's and grandfather's disasters in the 1920s, and to Yalova, Turkey, proceeding to Istanbul aboard Turkish President Celâl Bayar's handsomely appointed launch. It was the first visit of a member of British royal family to that country since 1936, when the Duke of Windsor was there; and the first visit of a member of the Greek royal family to his nation's traditional enemy in anyone's memory. It was a valuable visit because the dangerous liaison between Turkey and the Soviet Union might surface again, to England's detriment, and the trip confirmed that ancient Greco-Turkish wars should be forgotten. Philip proceeded to Athens for a five-day visit with his mother.

Princess Elizabeth's days were very carefully ordered while she was in London: she awoke at seven-thirty in the morning, Bobo MacDonald bringing her tea; she took a bath and ate (she was dieting now—coffee, fruit, and toast) at exactly eight-thirty, and went through every one of the then very skimpy London newspapers, no matter of what quality—the *Times* printed a rag paper royal edition; then she saw her children. She was at her desk at the stroke of nine-thirty, personally reading her mail and dictating to her assistant secretaries the answers she required; at ten-thirty she conferred with her Private Secretary, Major Martin Charteris, until he left for Canada to prepare a prospective royal tour; at eleven-thirty she met the comptroller of her household, Sir Frederick Browning, to discuss the royal expenditures, and she would meet her councellors on her holdings in Manhattan, and continental Europe, especially West Germany. At twelve-thirty she had her fittings, since she seldom wore the same dress publicly twice; at one o'clock she would have a light lunch and at two-thirty most days of the month attend a public occasion. At five she had another hour with her children; dinner was followed by a family evening at Clarence House (her mother would come over for canasta), or, very often, a visit to a theater.

Philip was back in the Mediterranean by early November, and in December, Princess Elizabeth joined him for a prolonged visit to Greece. They were guests at the summer palace at Tatoi of King Paul and Queen Friederike and, such are the ironies of history, saw much of Sophocles Venizélos, son of the man whom Philip's family hated more than any other (but who had saved Prince Andrew's life) in his newly assumed role as Prime Minister. Greece was at peace (of a sort) following the crushing of the Communists in August 1949, but there were still serious guerrilla forays on the borders. It was important that the Princess and Philip be there, to cement the royal family in the eyes of the people.

Meanwhile, something odd had occurred in London. On December 28, 1950, Hugh Gaitskell, Chancellor of the Exchequer, sent a memorandum to the Prime Minister. This contained proposals for alterations to the Civil List Act of 1937, revised in 1943. Gaitskell pointed out that the Consolidated Fund was drawn from officially for payment for each member of the royal family, but Princess Margaret had been accidentally omitted. There was thus no statutory authority to make the payments, to take place when she was twenty-one (next year).

There is therefore the possibility of some embarrassment when Princess Margaret reaches the age of 21. There is the question of amending the Civil List itself, since if the Treasury authorized the issue of £6,000 from the Consolidated Fund, their action may be challenged by the Comptroller and Auditor General, and that would mean a certain amount of tiresome publicity, etc. Probably the wisest solution is the most honest one: to introduce a one-clause Bill late in the summer on the assumption that Parliament will pass it without question just before the recess. In order to do it with the least fuss, it might be wiser, since Princess Margaret does not become 21 until August 1951, but nothing should be said to anybody at the moment.

She did on her maturity receive a Civil List.

Nineteen fifty-one began excitingly for both Elizabeth and Philip. They learned that they would be making a tour of Canada that fall. In April, they were in Rome, where Elizabeth celebrated her birthday and was received in an audience, following her sister's recent example, by the Pope.

In late May, during the Festival of Britain, the King was again unwell; and on the twenty-fourth, at a ceremony in Westminster Abbey, at which the Duke of Gloucester was installed as Great Master of the Order of the Bath, he felt appalling; he came down with severe influenza, his left lung was infected, and doctors saw a suspicious shadow. He was severely wearied, looking shockingly drawn under his tan makeup. Princess Elizabeth had to deputize for him at the Trooping the Color.

By the middle of June, it was clear that Princess Elizabeth might soon have to become regent, and Prince Philip, in a black mood, was forced to surrender his often-interrupted command of the *Magpie* and return to his wife's side. He was depressed as he addressed the crew for the last time.

There was now agonized discussion as to whether the trip to Canada, officially announced on July 4, should be canceled. Then came a severe blow: Monaveen, Princess Elizabeth's beloved racehorse, was injured during a race and had to be destroyed. The tragedy came close to breaking her heart, but she was careful to show no emotion in public.

Within a few months of Princess Anne's birth, it was clear that Charles was loving and protective of his sister; he was always attentive, helping Nurse Lightbody to bathe and dress her and comb her hair. At just under two, Charles's only serious aversion was to photographers; he tended to run away when they appeared; at his sister's christening he had hidden behind a vase. He was fond of the traditional British game of hide and seek, firmly insisting that all visitors to his household should join him, no matter how heavy or old or infirm.

Aside from his worry over Korea and the still chronic economic misery of his nation, the ailing King was concerned over Princess Margaret: she was still talking of such improbable matters as her fondness for Danny Kaye, who remained married; she was not by any means ready to relinquish Peter Townsend, still married also, and living in the grace-and-favor Adelaide Cottage with his wife and children in Windsor Great Park. Princess Margaret was still seeing her circle, including Billy Wallace and the Marquess of Blandford. The King wished with all his heart that she would marry and settle down.

Princess Margaret's twenty-first birthday was celebrated at Balmoral. The King's condition worsened; the harsh weather at his beloved retreat of Balmoral for once disagreed with him, and in September he returned to London for X-rays. He was advised by the doctors to undergo a bronchos-copy, the removal of a fragment of lung tissue for careful examination. It was determined then that he had cancer.

The blow to the Queen, Princess Elizabeth, her sister, and the whole family was unbearably severe. Everyone decided that no mention of this horrifying truth would appear in the press, and that the King must never know; for all his courage, his nervous and fragile disposition probably could not have withstood the shock. His left lung must be removed at once; he was told the reason was a blockage of a bronchial tube. He was terrified of the operation, writing to a friend that the very idea of a surgeon's knife was "hell," but he steeled himself to the ordeal.

Outside the Palace, the crowd greeted Elizabeth with shouts of sympathy when she drove in from Clarence House at 5 P.M. on September 22. Queen Mary followed, her face set and grim. The Queen, Princesses Elizabeth and Margaret, and Philip all prayed earnestly. The following morning, with virtually the whole family at the Palace, the King underwent the resection in the Bühl Suite, which was still set up as an operating theater. All over England, people stood in groups, praying and weeping. At last, the operation was over, and the monarch was wheeled past darkly shuttered windows to his rooms. Only the Queen, who had not slept for several nights and was fighting exhaustion, was allowed to see him before evening. Prince Philip left early, not visiting the King at all; the Princesses tiptoed in for a few minutes in the evening and were severely shocked by their father's appearance.

The government collapsed that week. After fighting a losing battle for survival, it was clear that Clement Attlee would have to accede to a general election. Princess Elizabeth joined the Queen at a Privy Council meeting held at Buckingham Palace, to sign an Order for Prorogation of Parliament; the King, very feebly, spoke the word "Approved" from his pillow, his voice the hoarsest of whispers, while the counsellors waited outside: that one word meant that Parliament could be dissolved.

Meanwhile, despite her father's condition, Princess Elizabeth, after consulting with her mother and the royal doctors, decided to proceed on the delayed Canadian tour. In time of the Korean War, it was vitally important to cement the Commonwealth, and there was fear that Canada, in an escalated conflict in the Pacific basin, might be invaded by Russia across the Bering Strait.

Accompanied by the royal party's 189 suitcases, the Princess and Philip left for Montreal by plane on October 8, 1951. Though she was in anguish over her father's condition, and spoke to the Palace daily to have word of him (and of her children), she was delighted by the Canadians' robust expressions of welcome, and showed no public sign of stress. The spectacular journey in a richly accoutred private car of the Canadian Pacific Railway took the royal couple from Ottawa to Toronto to Niagara Falls, to Calgary for the stampede, to Winnipeg, a grand journey through the snowy peaks of the Rockies, to Vancouver. At Eaglecrest, a huge log house in Victoria decorated with the severed heads of moose, and strewn with polar bear rugs, they heard through a crackling telephone their children's voices, and learned that the King had at last taken a few faltering steps from his bedroom. On October 25, the public decided for a Conservative government, and the following day Winston Churchill came to see his ailing monarch and received with joy his mandate.

To relieve the tension of the journey, Philip would indulge in practical jokes; he placed a tin of mixed nuts on the Princess's dressing table and she opened it—only to find an imitation snake popping out. He would pursue her down the train corridor wearing a huge pair of false teeth obtained from a magic shop. "We heard screams of laughter coming from the royal car," John Dean wrote.

But at times Philip's darker self showed—screaming at irritating reporters, occasionally turning brusque with officialdom. On balance, however, he and Princess Elizabeth loved Canada in the fall—an unforgettable impression of clean, clear skies, swirling blizzards, Indians dancing in war feathers in snow, mountains capped with ice, forests alive with the golden colors of fall, logging camps, modern cities rising on great plains—a vision of the Commonwealth nation that would remain close to the couple's hearts.

The Princess narrowly escaped death in Montreal when a concrete slab, loosened by wind, crashed onto the spot she had vacated seconds before. The royal couple continued to a tremendous reception of half a million people in the streets of Washington, D.C., where the highlight of their visit was almost certainly the very simple and comfortable family luncheon that President and Mrs. Truman gave for them at Blair House,[2] served off the favorite Woodrow Wilson china. They very much liked the Trumans, and the Trumans shared their feelings.

The official program called for the royal couple to go to Mount Vernon to pay their respects to its illustrious former occupant, George Washington; everywhere they went they were sportingly at pains, like Elizabeth's parents before her, to show admiration for the founders of democracy and the opponents of her Hanoverian royal ancestor.

The departure was dramatic: a storm hurled sixteen-foot waves onto the wharf as, in driving rain, they managed to struggle aboard the waiting tender that would take them out to the *Empress of Scotland.* The 189 pieces of luggage, including 25 crates crammed with gifts for the children, were squeezed into accompanying tenders. The official farewell party slipped and slid on the violently pitching vessel, and Elizabeth's condition was not improved when three oilskinned fishermen dashed up and handed her a basket filled with dead codfish. She could barely stand up as the pitching grew more violent; Philip, despite his years as a Naval officer, became seasick.

As the couple boarded the *Empress,* Philip ran vomiting to his cabin, raging that people had seen him. The Princess, much the worst sailor, smiled as radiantly as if she were at a picnic. She had learned already, and long before the end of a glorious eighteen-thousand-mile journey, how to be Queen.

2. The White House was being redecorated.

12

***

THE KING SEEMED MUCH improved by Christmas, although the speech the nation heard on radio, cobbled together from several prerecordings, was spoken in a harrowingly hoarse, weak, and exhausted voice; by now, plans were advanced for Princess Elizabeth and Philip to proceed to Australasia without him. The Princess made a request—unusual for royalty—to vary the itinerary; she wanted to see Kenya, and the wild animal reserves. It was agreed that the royal party should include Lady Pamela Mountbatten as lady-in-waiting and Martin Charteris as Secretary, with Michael Parker as Philip's A.D.C., and Bobo MacDonald and John Dean in the party.

On January 30, 1952, the King and Queen, the Princesses, and Philip were at a performance of *South Pacific* starring Mary Martin at the Theater Royal, Drury Lane.

Next day, the King, hatless, his hair blowing in the wind, accompanied by the Queen, Princess Margaret, and other family members, said farewell to Princess Elizabeth and Philip. They took off in fine weather on the BOAC Argonaut charter *Atalanta*. According to John Dean, eight seats were removed to make room for a special compartment, with two berths and a lounge.

The aircraft touched down at Nairobi next day at 10:12 A.M. in very severe heat; the governor, Sir Philip Mitchell, greeted the royal party at the gangway, a twenty-one-gun salute rang out, and the Royal Air Force Brass Band played the national anthem. Four hundred African tribal chiefs in leopard skins did a war dance. With no time to rest, and barely time to wash and brush up, the Princess and Philip were rushed at once into a grueling series of official engagements, starting with a visit to a maternity hospital, and concluding with a reception at Government House, attended by close to three thousand guests.

The second day was partly spent in a visit to Nairobi National Park, where the Princess took pictures of wild animals with her moving picture camera; Philip took stills. She came within ten feet of a lion, which was eating a wildebeest; it looked at the heiress to the British throne, ambled forward, yawned, then ambled back to finish its meal under the shade of a giant tree.

At a celebration that evening, thousands of children gathered on the Government House lawns to sing to the Princess. By now, she was fascinated by Kenya, glad that she had added it to the Australasian schedule. As always, she talked to the Palace every day, and the King seemed well and the children very happy.

Very early on Sunday, February 3, the royal party was driven in a fleet of cars almost one hundred miles along bumpy, pitted, unpaved roads, past clumps of banana leaves and mud hut villages, until at last they began to climb up, up, beyond the shimmering heat of the plains to Nyeri, at the foot of snow-capped Mount Kenya; the Princess, Philip, Lady Pamela Mountbatten, and the staff were covered in red dust, and the Princess was overjoyed. The cedarwood log cottage amusingly known as Royal Lodge had been given her by the government of Kenya years before, and she liked it at once; it only could accommodate six—which meant that John Dean, Bobo Mac-Donald, and others in the party slept in tents and Martin Charteris was accommodated at a hotel. Next day, John Dean wrote:

The Royals were out riding at dawn, when the rising sun colored snowy peaks with pink and gold and there was still sufficient nip in the air to make exercise pleasant.

On the fourth, after a much-needed morning of rest, the Princess and Philip were told that elephants had been seen not more than six miles distant; they drove at once to the spot and photographed thirty magnificent beasts ambling along, swatting flies with their long gray trunks. They lunched off a tasty trout that Michael Parker had caught; Philip played a game of polo in the afternoon.

On the fifth, the royal couple went from the Royal Lodge to

the famous Treetops Hotel, which was constructed inside an enormous fig tree, with a fine view of a water hole used by many animals; the jovial host, Sherbrooke Walter, told the couple cheerfully that if a rhinoceros should charge them they should at once climb a ladder to a height of no less than eight feet; if an elephant did, the height was to be eighteen feet. Walter also showed them the remnants of lampshades that had been happily devoured by baboons, and his descriptive speech was counterpointed by a loud buzzing of locusts, which had also plagued the couple in Nairobi.

The night of the fifth was unforgettable: the half moon in the black satin sky was augmented by an exquisite effect of artificial lunar light, and the Princess, Philip, Parker, and many guests sat in the soft glow cast about Treetops watching the wild animals—elephants, rhinoceroses, baboons—come down to drink. It was the most exciting experience the royal couple had known, as the Princess said to her Kenyan friends next morning.

At exactly 7:30 A.M. on the sixth, 11:30 A.M. in Kenya, when the Princess and Philip were returning to the lodge from a photographic and fishing expedition, James MacDonald, second valet to the King, walked into the royal bedroom at Sandringham carrying a breakfast tray with a pot of tea and two slices of thinly cut, buttered brown bread. The King was very still and silent, so MacDonald decided not to disturb him at once. He set the tray down on the bedside table and went into the bathroom to run the bath.

He returned; the King had not stirred, as he customarily did, at the sound of the water running. MacDonald tried to waken him; there was no response. The valet summoned help. There was no pulse; Dr. James Ansell, surgeon apothecary, arrived at once and pronounced life extinct. Only now did Sir Harold Campbell, equerry-in-charge, advise the Queen in her nearby room.

She hurried to her husband's chamber without the slightest show of emotion, even though her heart was breaking. She walked up to the King's bed, saw his face as still and cold as marble, and kissed his forehead for the last time. Then she said, "Lilibet must be informed." She at once corrected herself. "The *Queen* must be informed," she said.

She walked over to Princess Margaret's chamber and told her the news. Margaret, inconsolable, locked herself in. The new Queen Mother returned, desolate, to her bedrooms. Sir Harold Campbell tried to get through to Nyeri, but a tropical storm, which had driven the new Queen and her husband indoors, had cut off the lines. He then telephoned Reuters, the most trusted of the news services.

He asked them to make sure the new Queen received the news. Then Campbell went to call Queen Mary at Marlborough House, the Duke of Windsor in New York, the Duke of Gloucester at his home in Barnwell Manor, Northamptonshire, and the Duchess of Kent in Germany. His staff contacted Mother Superior Alice-Elizabeth in Chicago, where she was collecting funds for her Sisterhood of Martha and Mary, and other family members.

In the meantime, the Reuters correspondent in Kenya advised Granville Roberts of the *East African Standard,* who was covering the royal visit to Nyeri, and was staying at the Outspan Hotel in that town, to get the news to Philip before it came through on the radio. Martin Charteris, the Queen's Private Secretary, was also staying at the hotel. Roberts found him in the bar and conveyed the news to him. Charteris somehow got through to Michael Parker at the lodge and Parker checked the authenticity of the news at the Palace. Wakened from sleep, Philip now had the terrible task of informing his wife, who was resting in her room, that her beloved father, who meant more to her than any human being, was dead. She broke into tears, but only for a moment. Now she was Queen; she had been trained from childhood to behave with perfect majestic control when this shocking and unbearable moment should occur. She at once ordered Charteris to send cables of condolence to her mother, grandmother, and sister; she sat at her desk and neatly wrote out apologies to the people who were expecting to be with her that afternoon and next day, she had Charteris advise the captain of the *Gothic,* waiting at Mombasa, and the government of Ceylon, Australia, and New Zealand, that she must postpone her antipodean trip, and she ordered a plane from East African Airways to take her to Entebbe, Uganda, where a BOAC four-engine Argonaut was to be placed in readiness.

All this she did without showing any distress before her husband and staff. Finally, she autographed pictures, sent notes of thanks, and, as the storm temporarily broke, walked with Philip through the dripping tropical gardens of the lodge, past the swollen river and wind-tossed palms, the soaking banks of bougainvillea and the bedraggled flame trees, and said a silent farewell to the place she loved so much.

The royal couple sent out a request that the people of Kenya not mob them as they left the country. The roads were almost deserted as they made their journey, the suitcases packed at record speed under Bobo MacDonald's and John Dean's expert supervision. They had scarcely landed when the storm came back in full fury, tremendous claps of thunder and streaks of lightning filling the sky. They had to sit in the airport for three hours, waiting, the Queen expressionless, staring straight ahead, Philip pacing restlessly about, until at last it was safe to fly.

When the plane landed in London, the Duke of Gloucester and Lord Mountbatten climbed the gangway with Sir Alan Lascelles. The Queen, according to John Dean, asked, "Do I go down alone?" The reply was in the affirmative. Philip was not Prince Consort; he would follow just behind.

At the foot of the gangway stood a long line of members of the three political parties, in somber black overcoats, hatless out of respect; Winston Churchill was in tears, bent, a white scarf wound around his neck to keep out the cold. He greeted the Queen as she set foot on English soil for the first time as monarch, and she took his hand. Attlee and other parliamentarians followed in greeting her. She thanked every member of the aircraft crew individually. Then the royal party left by Daimler.

As the car drove up to Clarence House, the lights began to come on in London to relieve the gathering dusk. At the moment the Queen entered, the royal standard was raised. Queen Mary was awaiting for her as she walked in. With difficulty, the aged Queen managed a curtsy.

After thirty minutes of conversation with her grandmother, the Queen telephoned Sandringham to speak to the Queen Mother (as she would henceforth be known) and Princess Margaret. She met the Lord Chamberlain, the Earl of Clarendon, and the Duke of Norfolk, Earl Marshal, to discuss arrangements for the funeral. Then at last, exhausted after two nights without sleep, she was able to go to bed.

She walked next morning to St. James's Palace next door, followed by Philip some steps behind, to meet her Privy Council in the matter of the accession. As snow fell outside the tall windows, she entered the chamber; Philip left her side to join the 192 other council members arrayed in dark suits before her, headed by Churchill, and the Lord High Chancellor, Lord Simonds. Very pale, but steady and composed, the Queen read the declaration from a paper, speaking of the heavy task laid upon her so early in her life, then with a firm hand signed the two copies of the oath and proceeded to the Throne Room with her husband and the Duke of Gloucester. Arrangements had been completed for her to travel to Sandringham, where the King's body was to be embalmed that night.

Next day, the public proclamation was read at various locations to a vast and respectful public. Artillery salutes rang out across the dark city. The Queen watched the ceremony on television at Clarence House as Sir George Bellew, Garter King of Arms, walked out onto the balcony at Friary Court and spoke through a microphone—a last-minute, modern addition—to the throng; as the St. James's clock rang out 11 A.M., four trumpeters sounded their instruments, the Kings of Arms carried their maces, the heralds and pursuivants in their scarlet and gold and their white plumed hats appeared in medieval finery. The Guards dipped their rich standards at the sound of "God Save the Queen!" The Guards band played the anthem and the crowd repeated the words, the sound swelling until a surging roar of loyalty and affection engulfed the capital.

Before she left London, the Queen austerely decreed that there should be no public holiday at the time of the royal funeral, but that a two-minute silence should be observed. It is possible that she feared a mobbing of the funerary procession such as had taken place during her grandfather George V's funeral in 1936. In future, after the accession, the female family members were bound to curtsy to her and Philip to bow. When the occasion was required for mother and daughter to be together, the Queen Mother had to wait for her daughter to proceed before she could do so. It was often observed how distasteful this practice of protocol was to the Queen. She would always stretch her arm out to her mother to walk forward, breaking protocol. At meals, nobody could sit before the Queen was seated; nor could anyone sit in her presence until she bade them. Visitors to her office had to back out from her presence. When finished, she would press a hidden button under her desk and a page would come in to show them out.

In Sandringham Church on February 9, 1952, over nine

hundred estate tenants and servants—many in tears—filed past the coffin, draped in the royal standard on which lay three wreaths—the Queen Mother's, the Queen's, and Princess Margaret's. One hundred officers of the U.S. Air Force bomber base at Sculthorpe joined the mourners. The coffin was guarded not by military men, but, at the Queen's request, by gamekeepers and foresters. The press, except for Reuters and A.P., and two photographers, were kept out.

Meanwhile, jewelers were busy at the Tower of London, cleaning the State crown which was to be set upon the coffin for the monarch's final journey.

The Princess was driven by Philip in the Rolls-Royce part of the way very fast from London to Sandringham, then a chauffeur took over. They arrived at 4:30 P.M., entering through the Jubilee Gate, instead of the main Norwich Gate, to avoid the photographers and press, who anyway had been asked to move back by the police. The Queen Mother was bravely composed when she greeted her daughter with a curtsy, but Margaret, more temperamental and nervous, was utterly distraught with grief and beyond consolation.

At a private service on Sunday, the tenth, the royals attended the coffin, the Queen Mother kneeling beside it, her face pale, her eyes swollen from weeping. In London, St. Paul's, Westminster Abbey, and St.-Martin's-in-the-Fields all had services. Agencies sold seats at record prices in windows along the funeral route, and hotels at King's Cross and Paddington Stations were packed out.

The coffin was brought to London on the afternoon of the eleventh, watched sadly by thousands who stood in their backyards weeping as the train chugged by. The three pale and haggard Queens, in deepest mourning, their faces scarcely perceptible behind the black veils, met at King's Cross Station to take a maroon Daimler to Westminster Hall while the green-painted bier was drawn by gun carriage. The Dukes of Edinburgh and Gloucester walked behind the coffin as bitter rain and sleet lashed the procession; there was absolute silence in the gray city. The Queens met the coffin at Westminster Hall; there was a brief service; the coffin was placed on a catafalque flanked by funerary candles.

On February 15, after hundreds of thousands had been to visit the coffin, the King was taken to St. George's Chapel, Windsor. Now joined by the Duke of Windsor, newly arrived from America, the Dukes of Edinburgh, Gloucester, and Kent walked behind the gun carriage in the snow flurries to Waterloo Station. Drums were like muffled thunder; solemn bells tolled across the city; a funerary march filled the dark air. Thousands stood silent and shivering in the cold. The Queen and Queen Mother rode behind in the Irish State Coach; Queen Mary was too infirm to attend the funeral.

Pipe music and bosun's whistles accompanied the boarding of the train, providing a plaintive, shrill lament. There followed the service and interment, attended by the Kings and Queens of Europe, including the monarchs of Norway, Sweden, the Netherlands, Denmark, and Greece.

After the funeral, the Queen Mother, who was inconsolable in her grief, retired to Birkhall and let it be known she was in retreat. But grief-stricken though she was, the new Queen—the photographs and records show it—exulted in her newly ac-quired power, while carefully encouraging the fantasy through her Press Secretary, Commander Richard Colville, that she had little or none.

She knew from the moment she became Queen she must show no emotion in public; if a guardsman fainted on a parade she must seem not to notice it; if a bee settled on a churchman's nose in the course of Divine Service, she must not even smile; she must never be heard using her favorite swear words, "Damn!" and "Bloody!" Perennially seasick, she must "brace up" (her words) so that nobody of the public must see it; she would soon be reproving Princess Margaret for her public boisterousness, and would receive the reply, "You look after your empire and I'll look after my life." Like her father, she would know at once if a belt buckle was unpolished or a shoelace undone; she would never go out in public without a pin to secure her hat; she would never not know the full history and botanical particulars of the maple (Canada) or the wattle (Australia), never not have a clip on her handbag to prevent it tumbling, never be without extra stockings in her lady-in-waiting's hands or a slit petticoat allowing for freedom in walking; she would never not know the name of every horse, its breed and pedigree, even at a horse display in a circus.

She was always at least as strong as her domineering husband. If he dismissed a zealous photographer, she would summon him back; when he proved restive at a portrait sitting, she snapped, "You just stand there!" When an old courtier slumped in her presence, she demanded to know if he were tired or ill. He said he was not. "Then don't you think you should stand erect when you talk to the sovereign?" she asked coldly.

Contrary to carefully fostered public relations, to the support of mythology that goes with all prominence, the Queen had considerable power. The public was made to feel that she was simply a figurehead, as colorful but useless as the manatee that was flourished on the prows of ancient ships, while at the same time a lovable, universal aunt, concerned only with grouse shooting, horses, dogs, and opening buildings.

The truth is that the Queen was considerably more than a mere consultant, appendage, or front for Parliament; she could, as just one example, declare war; in her constant meetings with her ministers and in particular Winston Churchill, who in 1953 was her humble and attentive servant, she was a commanding and most influential presence. By encouraging and warning according to the paradoxically expansive restrictions of her office, she in a sense became her own *éminence grise*. Even the choice of those whom she would honor could be taken as indicating a policy. And when we shall come to such personal crises as the matter of Princess Margaret and Peter Townsend, it would be unwise to think, no matter how loyal or cosmetic her sister's account of the matter might be, that the ultimate decision to separate the couple could not have been the Queen's, or that she was not fully aware of the constitutional issues involved.

Her conduit to all her Ministers, and the person who conveyed their thoughts to her, and hers to them, was that pillar of propriety, her austere, bloodless, and bespectacled Principal Private Secretary, Sir Alan Lascelles. Each morning as the ormolu clock struck ten, he would enter the Queen's study with a stiff, military but stoop-shouldered gait, and she, seated bolt-upright at her desk, which was filled from end to end with family photographs, decorated with a leather and mahogany rack of her scarlet-crested stationery, and with the funeral-black blotting paper that was devised to prevent some snoop from reading the impress of her royal hand, would greet this latter-day Victorian pedant and proceed at once to the day's business.

They, with the other staff members, would go over every hour with minute precision; Lascelles would attend to the royal dispatch boxes (the only person in her entourage so privileged); he would discuss her tours and visits and the texts of some of her speeches, which, unhappily due to his influence, or drafting, were remarkably lifeless until his resignation in late 1953.

She was, of course, the richest woman in the world, by the mere fact of succeeding to the throne; she was said to own parts of the West Forties in New York, and at least one building on Broadway; she owned Balmoral and Sandringham and the capital of the Crown Estates, she owned much of London, and was rivaled in that respect only by the Duke of Westminster; she had U.S. railroad shares and British Government stocks; she enjoyed the fifty-two thousand acres of the Duchy of Lancaster as well as her Civil List; she owned thirty-five horses and her income from them and from her wins was the equivalent of a quarter million dollars a year; her jewels were incalculable in value, as we have seen, the largest collection in the world; she had the greatest array of paintings in private hands, including Holbeins, Canalettos, Vandykes, Michelangelos, Leonardo da Vincis, Raphaels; a tremendous collection, begun by King George IV, of French antique furniture; a 5-million-dollar stamp collection, including the Mauritius Penny Orange Red, worth $15,000. She of course paid no income tax, nor did she require a passport or driver's license.

Made painfully aware of the uncertainty of human life by her father's death, the Queen, in 1952, was conscious of a major problem. She realized that Prince Charles or Princess Anne might accede to the throne while under the age of eighteen, and that it would be necessary to appoint a regent. Were she to be incapacitated by illness or accident, a regent would be equally necessary. Since a minor could not effectively be regent, it would be necessary to make a special appointment.

Princess Margaret seemed increasingly wrong for the task. It was generally considered that the heiress presumptive to the throne should be regent. In every way, it seemed more desirable that Philip, Duke of Edinburgh, should be regent and thus charged with the guardianship of the person of the new sovereign. She decided that she would seek advice on this, but, with her formidable grasp of constitutional law, she already understood that such an arrangement would be possible.

She also felt it desirable that her mother should be added to the Council of State, in order to run royal functions. She would in due course plan to present the proposed amendment directly to Parliament.

She entered into discussions with Prime Minister Churchill, who supported her in the proposed plan. She was not unaware of the fact that Prince Albert, consort of Queen Victoria, had been placed in this position after application by his wife. However, this was not a matter to be entered into immediately, and there would be a series of meetings on it over the next many months.

Also in the wake of the King's funeral, a controversy blew up. The shrewd, wise, and now grief-stricken Queen Mary had long since, together with her late son, sniffed the plot by which Earl Mountbatten, in collusion with the King of Greece, had engineered Philip's involvement with the present Queen, her granddaughter. She had little time for Mountbatten's peerless ambition. She was appalled to learn that Mountbatten, at a party at Broadlands, had made the startling announcement, "The House of Mountbatten now reigns!" He had at last overplayed his Machiavellian hand; the truth was out.

At the same time, Philip compounded the error by sending a long, carefully worded plea for Mountbatten-Windsor to be used in place of Windsor in the royal family in a memorandum to Churchill, whom Queen Mary had advised of the incident at Broadlands, and who was already ablaze with anger. This latest missive was the last straw. He and his friend Lord Beaverbrook exploded—and at once Churchill called the Cabinet. However, in order to avoid a direct conflict with Philip, he did not attend himself. Instead, he asked John Colville, his principal Private Secretary since 1951, to appear at the meeting with the members in his name, and a very stern joint letter was forwarded, co-signed by the Lord Chancellor, the Lord Privy Seal, and the Home Secretary, among others, to the Queen and Prince Philip. The unanimous decision was that the name Mountbatten would not be used by the family. On her birthday, the Queen, much to the fury of her husband, who yelled, "I'm just a bloody amoeba! That's all!" signed the authorizing order in council.

Prince Philip consumed his frustration in radical inspections of Buckingham Palace. He strode through the vast maze of servants' quarters, the kitchens, the staff canteen, the offices of the Royal Household; he explored the private post office, the telephone switchboard, and even counted the rooms—there were 611. He asked questions constantly, irritating many of the old retainers.

He was maddened by the complex rituals and protocol of life at the Palace. If he wanted sandwiches and coffee prepared for his late-night return, he had to filter his request down a long pipeline of command, from a page to the Comptroller of Supply to the chef to the footmen; he at once eliminated this tiresome procedure and ordered his nocturnal repasts directly from the kitchen.

He detested having flunkies carry his bags or chauffeurs driving his car; the sight of a grown male opening a door for him drove him into transports of rage and contempt. He disliked having drinks served and insisted on serving them from his own cocktail cabinet. He installed a direct telephone system within the Palace, enabling him to contact everybody from the monarch down direct without going through the switchboard. He refused to deal with the ancient, far distant kitchen and instead put his own kitchenette into his suite; the Queen already had her own. He pounded corridors, causing havoc among the staff as they sought to follow his loudly radical, and quite revolutionary, ideas. He dismissed footmen who sought to run the bird cage-like elevator at the Palace, and operated it himself; he often drove his family; he would not allow a projectionist to thread up and show movies, but did the job himself; he speeded constantly; police looked the other way; he would not have speeches written for him but instead checked them out by listening to them on tapes; his speeches combined the provocative, the humorous, the muscularly Christian, and the incentive-increasing in more or less equal parts. He was seen dragging chairs and couches about to provide less stiffly formal rooms.

Given a mountain of African mahogany, he fashioned it into doors; his rooms at the Palace would be like ships' cabins, and he built in and designed every shelf and closet and lighting device to make him feel he was back in the Navy he loved. He sent messages to everyone, starting with his wife, on tape, because he was maddened by people's short attention span on the telephone, and was too impatient to write a letter (though he was forced to write hundreds or more in his lifetime). Pushed to the limit of perfection by his uncle Lord Louis and by Kurt Hahn, he expected that same perfection in everyone, from his children down. Many learned to dread his stalking about, hands clasped behind his back to prevent round shoulders, long neck thrust forward, face inquisitive, frowning, aquiline, like a fierce if humorous, quizzical eagle's—he was challenging, sharp, dangerous, sporty, funny: a handful. For a lifetime, his stoical wife would have to put up with behavior such as shouting at the press, snapping "This is a bloody waste of time!" or "Let's get the hell out of here!" when the endless factory tours and hand-shakings and receptions and banquets went beyond the limits of the tolerable. The press wrecked his happiness; there cannot have been a week in his life that he would not miss the bumptious pleasures of the quarterdeck. His role in life called for a heroism which no amount of sea battles could demand, and if he cracked sometimes, could one blame him?

He was all too painfully aware of his exclusion from the absolute top of power. He was not permitted to examine the contents of the dispatch boxes that were sent by Victorian horse-drawn brougham for royal inspection from the government each day, and which the Queen meticulously read; as a member of the Privy Council, he was obliged to bow when the Queen entered the appropriate chamber. He was to address her as ma'am in public. In March, he was fairly active, but was restricted by the period of full mourning which, the Queen decreed, was to last until May 31. Deprived unhappily of the Navy, he turned his attention to the Royal Air Force, and to giving a special attention to Britain's only trump cards in the international game: atomic energy and advanced science.

Unable to exercise authority in the wider arena, or do more than bestow his handsome, joking, irascible presence on coastal command headquarters, chemical research laboratories, wild fowl reserves, flower shows, and flypasts, he felt totally frustrated.

One of the major problems the Queen faced when she assumed the throne was Windsor Castle. It had no central heating to relieve the grim winters, and only about half a dozen electric fires. The public rooms were lit by coal or wood fires, which caused chimney problems and much scattering of ash. The corridors were very cold at all times. The staff joined their employers in wearing overcoats indoors from December to March (or Easter).

The Queen and Prince Philip were determined to improve the Castle. The Duke worked overtime installing wall lights and electric fires; but more problems existed. The Queen's personal bathroom was so small that she could not get into the bathtub unless she entered it from the back. The ceiling was absurdly high, over twenty feet, thus rendering the room even more disproportionate. The Queen enlarged the room by putting in a six-and-a-half-foot false ceiling.

The Queen detested the royal bed occupied by her parents, and replaced it with a Victorian acquisition exactly seven feet six inches wide, with a hard, uncomfortable horsehair mattress that nevertheless was good for the back. She replaced the old, burningly hot metal water bottles in their woolen covers with rubber bottles. But unfortunately, the water wore out the rubber and William Ellis, chief steward of Windsor Castle, had to have them replaced continuously.

One Monday, Ellis recalled, he came in and found all the furniture in the Green Drawing Room completely rearranged. The couple had been pushing and dragging settees and chairs all weekend, many of the items of furniture extremely heavy. Much to the Queen and Prince Philip's annoyance, a porter and housekeeper, thinking that some intruder had disarranged the drawing room, put everything back in place. Prince Philip flew into a tantrum; the room was rearranged as the couple wanted it.

The Queen was tight with money. She fretted and fussed over every expense, despite the fact that her unparalleled personal fortune was augmented by colossal sums allocated to her by the government. If curtains could be darned instead of replaced, she would prefer that. When William Ellis brought her a pattern book of chintzes, she shook her head and said they were too costly for her. When sheets wore down and shredded, she would have them turned sides to middle and continue using them. Every light switch in the castle was marked with a notice reading, ''Please turn off the light when you leave the room.'' Carpets were never replaced, but simply patched; they were underlaid with canvas. Moreover, the pay for staff was poor. Ellis said that in nine years he had advanced from only £500 to £1,000 a year, or about four times that amount in dollars. He had to pay for all his own clothes, including ceremonial suits, and his own car. The only advantage he had was that he had a grace-and-favor home, the Garter House.

Apart from the delicate matter of appeasing her husband, and not adding salt to his wounds, the twenty-five-year-old Queen had to face a daunting challenge: the state of the nation, and the world as a whole, was still not inspiring. The British census showed appalling figures: 4,500,000 people had no bathtub, over 900,000 had no toilet, 690,000 had no water. Rationing was even now, seven years after the war, a harsh reality of everyone's lives—excepting royalty and the very rich, who had their own lands and their own produce.

The Queen was constantly and exhaustingly busy, fulfilling no less than 140 public engagements until the end of the mourning period, naming the date of the Coronation, June 2, 1953, conferring with her beloved Winston Churchill, meeting with General Eisenhower, with Field Marshal Earl Alexander of Tunis, who had received her in Canada as Governor-General, Anthony Eden, Foreign Secretary, Lord Ismay, Secretary of State for Commonwealth Relations—the list of visitors went on and on as she learned, and guided, and learned still more.

Sometimes she would see as many as a dozen dignitaries a day. Between 5 and 6 P.M. was, as always, the best hour, sacrosanct to her children, except on Tuesday, when she saw the Prime Minister. Anne was crawling or trying to toddle, and Charles was ready for hide-and seek or a primitive form of football or "tag"; Philip and Helen Lightbody were run off their feet keeping up with the antic, suddenly informal though still saddened Queen. But at the stroke of six, Charles and Anne were off to bed and the evening's events loomed. That May, mourning or not, the Queen must entertain the King and Queen of Denmark and the Regent of Iraq. She was still busy day and night until mourning ended on May 31 with the promise of Ascot and the other summer racing events. There were pictures to be taken by Dorothy Wilding for the new issue of stamps, and sittings for no fewer than eight portrait painters, chosen from lists of hundreds of applicants. The Queen launched her first big party for the Diplomatic Corps at the Court of St. James's on July 16; she wore a magnificent satin gown and diamond tiara; a thousand guests were entertained in a style more lavish than at any time since before the war.

That August, the Queen had to confront the all-important matter of the Coronation dress. She decreed that the ceremony would only take two and a half hours, and that the garment must be the most magnificent Norman Hartnell had ever designed, and that he must prepare a number of sketches from which she would choose. It must be in white satin and it must surpass her wedding dress.

Hartnell worked desperately hard. He settled on eight possible designs; the Queen discarded them one by one, settling finally on the eighth and last—with silver and crystal motifs and emblems of all the flowers of England; modified into a ninth design, the costume included at her command all emblems of the Commonwealth. Keeping that mystical or phantasmal corpus of nations remained her greatest concern.

Hartnell faced a problem at once. He had thought that the traditional symbol of Wales was the daffodil, but was horrified to find it was a leek. He managed to incorporate that humble vegetable nonetheless, in a representation in emerald green that glamorized it effectively. He used mauve Scottish thistles, green Ireland grass, pink English roses, Canadian maple leaves, Australian golden wattles, New Zealand ferns, South African proteas, Pakistani wheat, Ceylon lotus petals—a marvelous creation. He also designed the shift the Queen would wear for her anointing: a plain white linen garment with huge cloth buttons, easy to handle by her ladies-in-waiting.

Hartnell, working eighteen hours a day, also designed the clothes for the other family members: the Queen Mother would wear gold and diamonds, Princess Margaret white satin, with pearls sewn into the bodice, the Queen's aunt, the Princess Royal silver—this fairy-tale display of clothing cost thousands. The discussions and fittings began in August and continued into the autumn, past the Queen's first opening of Parliament in November.

At the beginning of 1953, the Queen, her desk crowded with documents and notes, her inkwell often threatening to run dry, her husband a frequent absentee, had another burden to carry, more personal and pressing than any of her royal offices, or even a crisis in Egypt. The problem was Princess Margaret. She had by now lost certain of her prospects for marriage; Danny Kaye was back in the United States; and she had become more deeply interested in Peter Townsend, CVO, who was promoted, paradoxically, by the Queen Mother, from Deputy Master of the Royal Household to Comptroller of the Queen Mother's Household at Clarence House, into which the Queen Mother and Princess Margaret moved in early spring. In effect, Townsend was not only living in a grace-and-favor house next door to the woman who loved him (cause for radical gossip in itself), but he was also in charge of all of the domestic and financial affairs which she and her mother must need attended to—a constant, burning presence in the Princess's life. Could she, she asked the Queen, marry him?

Townsend's own marriage had disintegrated: he was divorced in December 1952. But marriage to a divorced man, or physical involvement with a married one, was against the Queen's religious precepts.

It is unfortunate that the teachings of C. H. K. (now Sir Henry) Marten, Vice Provost of Eton, in constitutional history, had apparently not been extended to Princess Margaret, and that she was presumably not taught, as her sister undoubtedly was, the provisions of the Royal Marriage (not Royal Marriages) Act of 1772, of which more later. It is impossible to believe that she was so ignorant of ecclesiastical law that she did not know that marriage to a divorced person was unacceptable to the Church of England, at least officially, and thus not to the Queen as supreme governor. She was encouraged toward optimism over any future desire to marry.

As she told her authorized biographer Christopher Warwick, she was at the time advised by Sir Alan Lascelles (she was loyal enough not to mention her sister) that such a provision would be possible in her case, and that if she would wait a year or two (as Elizabeth had waited for Philip), all would be well. We seem to be in Looking Glass Land here, in which a Princess of much sophistication can be so deceived by royal sleight of hand; it is hard to know whether to be more impressed by the deceptive and histrionic skills of Sir Alan Lascelles as royal representative or the incomprehensible naïveté of the victim.

Consider the origins and terms of the Royal Marriage Act itself, whose poisonous shadow was cast over, and in many ways ruined, Princess Margaret's life. It began in the contentious brain of King George III, whose problems were by no means restricted to the colossal mishap of losing the American colonies. His younger brother, Henry, the Duke of Cumberland, in 1770 had become embroiled in a divorce case, the first member of a British royal family ever to be cited as corespondent; he was named in lurid terms by Lord Grosvenor, whose wife he had vigorously seduced, and his illiterate and foolish love letters caused a riot of laughter, and the monarch unique chagrin, when they were read in court. Cumberland caused the King further distress when he married a wanton widow, Mrs.

Anne Horton, with the result that he was banished from Britain.

The terms of the Act were punitive: no individual might marry without permission of the reigning monarch, if he were in the line of descent of George II, unless that person were the child of a marriage between a Princess of the blood and a foreign royal; if that successor should refuse to obey the instruction not to wed, he or she could, if over the age of twenty-five, give a year's notice to the Privy Council, which would then be required to grant permission, provided that both Houses of Parliament did not object. If the heir should disobey the rules, then those who solemnized, associated with, or were present at the celebration of such marriage would be stripped of their moneys and sent to prison under the ancient law of Premunire, which went back to the time of Richard II.

The bill ran into a storm in the House of Lords, provoking streams of vituperation from the great Charles James Fox, who resigned from the Admiralty and became a Whig out of disgust at the Act "big with mischief"; there was objection that the descendants of the Georges might run into thousands; that if an individual could be King or Queen at twenty-one, that person should be allowed to marry at that age; that potentially royal children would be reduced to servitude; that the bill was oppressive, absurd, whimsical, and despotic. Nevertheless, and its reception in the Commons was equally tempestuous, the bill was passed into law on March 3, 1772.

Once Princess Margaret announced to her sister that she intended eventually to marry Group Captain Peter Townsend, consent could have been given on the ground that it had been accorded by King George VI to David Milford Haven, also a descendent of King George II. He was not required to make application to the Privy Council, or even to obey the rules of the Church that marriage to the divorced woman, Mrs. Simpson, was unacceptable, that rule being overcome by a civil wedding in a foreign country, the United States.[1] The British public would at once have rejoiced, as later newspaper opinion polls showed, in this romantic eventuality. However, Sir Alan

1. The Duke of Windsor was never refused permission to marry that other Mrs. Simpson, his Duchess, nor was he excommunicated from the Church, nor did the Reverend Jardine, a British cleric, performing his office in France, suffer loss of property or imprisonment under the terms of the Royal Marriage Act.

Lascelles convinced the Queen (supported by the Press Secretary, Commander Richard Colville, and others) that she must not grant permission, but instead must ask Princess Margaret to wait for a year. It seems appalling that neither the Princess nor Townsend looked up the Act itself or cited the Milford Haven matter, to unlock the royal determination, if they should one day wish to marry. Instead, Lascelles deceived the couple, as indicated earlier in this narrative, that all would be well if they waited, while at the same time making sure that it would not.

Why was Lascelles put in such a punitive position? And why did the Queen, Prince Philip, and Churchill stand with him? Perhaps because they were determined (Churchill's initial response was to let love take its course—he was a die-hard romantic—but Lady Churchill overrode him) not to have a repetition of the Windsor affair, a sensational marriage to a divorced woman, in Coronation year. If that is the case, then Princess Margaret and Peter Townsend were, like many before and after them, offered up not on a sacred altar, but on the Aztec pyramid of public relations, where the priests awaited them with knives.

There is another matter to be noted: the couple was incorrectly informed, two years later, when their attitude proved obdurate, that if they proceeded with their determination, then Princess Margaret would be stripped of her property and all income under the Civil List and would have to surrender her position as third in line to the throne. Publicly, she blamed Lascelles for this; privately, the Queen Mother. Those who have followed the narrative thus far will have realized that no such provision exists in the Royal Marriage Act, which as of 1991, had yet to be repealed. So drastic a revision of the Act could scarcely have passed both Houses of Parliament, since the Queen happily did not follow the policy of her Hanoverian ancestor in paying off or locking out her members or packing the two Houses. It may be useful to note also that, if Philip had remained a member of the Greek royal family when she married him, she, as Princess, could not, under the provisions of the Act, have denied her two elder children the right to marry whom they chose. Was the then King and Queen's opposition to him as royal husband based in part upon the provisions of the Act?

The tension was added to by the fact that Philip, Duke of Edinburgh, had little in common with Townsend, who found

Philip brusque, brash, and excessively hearty; Townsend, the commoner, was by contrast elegant, introspective, careful, overcivilized; and Philip could not forget how Townsend had opposed his own marriage. Obviously, a scandal would erupt if Townsend continued to live under the same roof with Margaret, so the Queen made him an equerry at Buckingham Palace, thus demoting him and saving his neck at the same time.

The challenge of the Coronation lay ahead.

Then, on March 24, the Queen suffered another heavy blow. Her grandmother, Queen Mary, had long been failing, and had been generally depressed, even permanently shattered, by her beloved second son's death. She went into a coma and died on March 24.

13

* * *

A MAJOR QUESTION SURROUNDED the two crowns that the Queen would wear at the Coronation on June 2, 1953. The St. Edward's Crown would be worn at the moment of the actual crowning, while the Imperial State Crown would be worn in the walk down the aisle that followed, and on the journey by coach back to the Palace.

The St. Edward's Crown weighed over five pounds. This cumbersome object had been fashioned for the coronation of King Charles II; it was made of gold, studded with no less than 275 precious stones. Some effort was made by members of the Queen's family to dissuade her from wearing this particular crown, since it was known to be uncomfortable; they wanted her to replace it with the lighter crown, containing the Koh-I-Noor diamond, that had been fashioned for her mother in 1937. But she characteristically would not agree to wearing any crown that had not been worn previously by her father and grandfather.

Rebuilt for the Queen, the Imperial State Crown, because of a blending of platinum and silver with gold, was, at just under three pounds, less heavy than the St. Edward's Crown despite the fact that fixed into it were 2,783 diamonds, 273 large pearls, 16 sapphires, 11 emeralds, and 5 rubies. The front of the crown was embellished with the 317.4-carat Cullinan II, the second Star of Africa. Above it, set into a Maltese cross of rare value, was the legendary ruby spinel of the Black Prince, worn, according to legend, by King Henry V in his helmet at the Battle of Agincourt. This second crown was scarcely more wearable than the first. At a State opening of Parliament, King George V had complained that it gave him a headache and that he could scarcely have endured it for very much longer than twenty minutes. He was a man of some strength; the Queen was slight of figure. But there was no gainsaying her determination.

She would have to carry, both at the height of the ceremony and while leaving the Abbey down the aisle, the heavy royal scepter and orb. She would have to proceed on a long walk, watched by a very large number of her subjects, with close to three pounds on her head and a total of more than five and a half pounds in her hands, plus the suffocating weight of the heavy purple velvet and ermine robe over the Coronation gown with its long train, not to mention a heavy Queen Victoria diamond necklace and earrings.

Not only did she have to rehearse the difficult movement continuously in the ivory and gold Imperial State Ballroom of Buckingham Palace, but she also had to deal with numerous problems involving the Coronation dress itself. Madame Isabelle, imported from Paris by Norman Hartnell to be in charge of the gown, explained to the Queen that the dress was so completely smothered in jewels that it would swing to the left in a most awkward and cumbersome movement. Finally, in consultation with Her Majesty, the couturière lined the dress with layers of taffeta and crinoline, stiffening the whole with horsehair, which added considerably to its bulk and weight. So concerned was Hartnell over the dress in some way stumbling the Queen, who would not relent on the richness of its embellishments, that, without her knowledge, he sewed a tiny four-leaf clover of emerald spangles into it for luck.

She had placed Philip as head of the Coronation Council; the Roman Catholic Duke of Norfolk as Earl Marshal of England was immediately under him, and the members were, in fact, her Cabinet. However, she personally was involved in every detail of the forthcoming event, meticulously checking the guest list of over four thousand, which, rather boldly, included Philip's three sisters (but not, be it noted, their husbands), and the Abbey color scheme, which she ordained a rich blue, not quite a royal blue, which perhaps would have been considered too obvious. She chose the Coronation stamp after rejecting seventy-three designs. She selected the flowers, and the hangings, which were to have an almost medieval sense of luxury and beauty. She approved the addition of a very large number of seats, about 690, to avoid the situation which had taken place

at her parents' Coronation, when many had been excluded.[1]
She was annoyed to learn that the Archbishop of Canterbury
and Sir Winston Churchill were opposed to the idea of
televising the sacred occasion. Given the fact that the Commonwealth and her mystical and symbolic rule over its many
nations were of paramount importance to her, she was determined that each and every citizen of that far-flung communion
of human beings should not only picture her in their imagina-
tions through the medium of radio, but should actually see her
on film crowned in vivid and striking images.[2] With her
customary instinct and acumen, she knew that her singular
decision would cement the basis of her new reign and assist in
preventing any disagreeable moves toward republicanism that
might occur in the indefinite future.

Both Archbishop and Prime Minister argued vigorously
against the matter, using secular and religious arguments, but
they were soon to discover that the Queen was immutable.
They were compelled to submit to her inexorable royal will.

The preparations for the Coronation were not without
problems. One of these was the matter of the all-important holy
oil that would be used in the Ceremony of Anointment.
According to the Coronation Council's investigators, the place
in which it had been preserved in the appropriate jars at the
Abbey had been destroyed by enemy action in World War II,
and when a search was made for the original manufacturer, it
was discovered that he had gone out of business and had
apparently left the country. The Queen instructed her husband
to make sure the formula was located. This proved impossible.
Finally, a member of the staff discovered an ancient record
book in an obscure library which provided the formula dating
from the time of Charles I's accession. On royal request, a
Bond Street chemist re-created the oil to the Queen's expressed
satisfaction.

The Imperial State Coach, a rococo fantasy of tritons and
shells, encrusted with gold, that seemed to have been devised
for King Neptune himself, had to be completely refitted at vast
expense. The wheels were lined with rubber to provide a less

---

1. For members of both Houses of Parliament and their wives, 1,710 seats
would be required.
2. Australia, New Zealand, and South Africa did not have television in
1953.

bumpy ride. However, the Queen pointed out that no matter how smooth the journey back to Buckingham Palace, there would be the serious question of having to hold the heavy scepter and orb in her hands, as her weary and fragile father had, for that progress. She ordained that special metal rests should be inserted into the coach, upon which her insignia of State could rest, giving the optical illusion that they were supported by her hands.

For the first time, the pink interior lighting of the coach was revamped, so that it could be controlled by a rheostat through a system of batteries. The wood panels of the coach had suffered from time and weather, so that the rich and glowing Cipriani paintings were removed by scalpels one by one and, with infinite delicacy, affixed to restored surfaces.

The Queen also thought of another discomfort her father had suffered, the matter of the then Archbishop of Canterbury almost putting St. Edward's Crown on back to front. After some research, she discovered that the reason for the error was that red cotton thread had been sewn into the inside of the crown to indicate which side was the front. An inept person had thought that the cotton was misplaced, and had removed it. In this case, she instructed two small, unremovable silver gilt stars to be affixed to the appropriate place. Elizabeth also selected Queen Mary's tiara, given that monarch by the girls of Great Britain and Ireland for her own crowning, to wear on the way to the Abbey.

Buckingham Palace was in an uproar over the preparations. It was decided that Philip would kneel before the Queen to give homage at a certain point in the ceremony. Unfortunately, his natural jocularity emerged and he made light of this self-humiliating gesture. The Queen was heard to say, "Don't be silly. Come back and do it properly!" It goes without saying that he did. The Duchess of Norfolk and that favorite of the royal family's, Sir Eric Miéville, took part in four rehearsals, acting as the Queen and Philip. The Queen observed carefully the last run-through from various positions. On May 22, the Queen herself rehearsed part of the ceremony, in which she delivered the crown, scepter, and orb to the Lord Great Chamberlain; and she also rehearsed the Recess, in which her crimson velvet robe was placed upon her instead of her red Robe Royal and she proceeded, crowned, down the aisle with the orb and scepter to the Imperial State Coach. She wore both crowns during this rehearsal, but did not attend the final full-dress rehearsal, in which her place was again taken by the Duchess of Norfolk.

So determined was she to get used to the crowns, particularly the St. Edward's Crown, she was actually seen wearing it while seated at her desk answering her correspondence.

She troubled herself deeply over makeup. Knowing that millions of people all over the world would be watching her, she realized that the regular makeup she used would be inappropriate, and she had specialists come in to match her cosmetics to the difficult golden shine of the Abbey floodlights and the specially controlled batter-operated pink lights in the Imperial State Coach. She even had herself photographed in both color and black and white, and examined the photographs minutely and made changes in her macquillage accordingly. She had a lipstick prepared for her exclusive use, an unusual blend of red and pale blue that looked odd to the naked eye, but was ideal for television.

In the meantime, the staff of hundreds at the Palace was involved in last-minute removal from storage of the magnificent livery which would be worn by the royal attendants, laying out the newly fashioned cotton stockings that would be used to replace those which had been eaten away by age. From many long-since closed cupboards in the Gold Pantry, sumptuous plates, cutlery, ornate vases, candlesticks, and sets of gold cups were carried onto massive tables for polishing and rouging. Furniture was reupholstered and regilded, mirrors were polished, chandeliers were taken apart crystal by crystal and refitted and cleaned. The cost of all this was remarkable, but the Queen was determined that, at over £4 million,[3] this would be the most magnificent Coronation in British history. If the official coffers had to be stripped for the occasion, so be it. She added a new feature: following the ceremony, she would go down Northumberland Avenue and Victoria Embankment on the route from Palace to Abbey, so that thousands of children could see her. She would undertake four drives through London between June 6 and June 9, so that more people would see her than had seen any sovereign before.

Over a million people poured into London in Coronation

---

3. About $50 million in 1991 money.

week. Once again, landlords made fortunes in renting rooms
and apartments, hotels were crammed, and countless Americans and those from other countries were unable to obtain
accommodation. One Texas woman, desperate to see the
procession, took the bold step of writing to the Queen directly,
begging her to help. The Queen was so amused by the
effrontery of the note that she organized a room for the woman
at a hotel at Kensington. Few others were as lucky.

For the citizens who would brave the dismal weather of an
English summer to actually see the procession, it was a major
feat of preparation. Yet the British public, seasoned by years of
the blitz, thought little of spending a soaking night on chilly
sidewalks. Thermos flasks, sandwiches, cakes, and plastic
raincoats were packed into tens of thousands of paper carrier
bags as the throngs left their homes, jamming subways and
buses or proceeding on foot to their destination. As they
struggled into position, shoulder to shoulder with their neigh-
bors, starting the day before the crowning, they laid down
bedding, set up camp chairs, put down battery-operated radios,
set out playing cards, checked their cameras, wrapped themselves in blankets or rugs, and bought innumerable numbers of
colored balloons or ribbons from an army of street salesmen.

It was a long night, damp and chilly as an English summer
night could be, yet the brave camaraderie of the people and
their numerous Commonwealth cousins could only inspire
admiration. Over ten thousand spirit lamps glowed like fireflies
in the drizzly darkness. The Queen peeped out of the tall
windows of her suite at the great crowd that awaited her. Then,
a true champion, she went to bed and slept soundly till
morning.

It was a bleak, funerally black dawn, with no hint of sunlight
over the great city. The people, shivering in the damp, listened
to jazz music blared through a public address system, and sang
among themselves, favorite tunes of World War II and of that
present day. Reporters arrived, followed by television teams.
The Queen was up and about at seven, along with Philip,
checking over every last-minute detail as Norman Hartnell
arrived with his assistants to make sure there were no mishaps
as had occurred before the royal wedding.

Every last stitch in place when the Queen, pale but extremely
calm, and Philip, dressed in the uniform of the Admiral of the
Fleet (he had been elevated in January), went down to enter the

coach just one minute early, at 10:29 A.M. They had been
preceded to the Abbey by the vast congregation of peers, other
highly placed social figures and distinguished foreign visitors,
including several monarchs, Philip's mother and sisters and the
Greek royals. The Queen Mother and Princess Margaret had
been driven to the Palace and then left in the Irish State Coach,
which was scarcely less splendid than the Queen's own. As the
Imperial State Coach, drawn by eight royal grays, the best
horses selected according to long tradition, left the Palace with
his Guards escort, the Queen seemed genuinely startled by the
immense thunderburst of welcome that sprang from the thousands lining the route. Some observers fancied they even saw
tears in her eyes.

The coach trundled up to the Abbey at the exact moment of
11 A.M. The Queen with Prince Philip walked in to behold a
scene even more dazzling than that which had greeted her
upon the occasion of her parents' Coronation and of her
wedding. With the exception of one incorrigible rebel, Aneurin
Bevan, Labor member of Ebbw Vale, who wore a blue business
suit, the peers present were in robes or dress uniforms. Sir
Winston Churchill was outstandingly resplendent in a garter
robe and the uniform of the Warden of the Cinque Ports, almost
matched by the glowing-garbed Knights of the Garter, to
whose number he had recently been added.[4]

Ahead of the Queen, flanked by the immense throng of
standing figures, the women so blindingly aglitter with diamonds that they threatened to ruin the television shots, the
Queen could see the Archbishop of Canterbury in his miter and
cope, standing near St. Edward's Crown, fixed upon its velvet
cushion and guarded by Viscount Cunningham of Hyndhope;
she could also see certain lords carrying the regalia and
ceremonial swords. She was attended by the Bishop of Bath
and Wells, and by the Bishop of Durham, the train of her robe
followed by the dowager Duchess of Devonshire, Mistress of
the Robes, and carried by six ladies-in-waiting. The Queen
Mary tiara sparkled vividly in her carefully combed and

---

4. Even these individuals came close to being upstaged by the towering,
irrepressibly cheerful Queen Salote of Tonga, who was accompanied by an
official. Noël Coward was asked the identity of her companion. "Her
lunch," Coward replied.

brushed chestnut-colored hair; she was unwavering, calm, upright, and lightly flushed with pleasure and pride of office.

As she knelt briefly, she made a fairy-tale picture, her ladies-in-waiting in their virginal white like attendants in *Swan Lake,* their heads garlanded, their satin dresses stylish and stylized against the gray Abbey pillars.

The music of Purcell swelled up from the organ to greet the Queen at the Choir, followed by Parry's rousing version of the Coronation anthem. The pupils of Westminster School, exercising a time-honored privilege, cried out in unison, "Vivat Regina Elizabetha!"

She looked straight ahead from the Chair of Estate; she stood at the four points of the compass at the King Edward's Chair and showed herself ritually to her people as the congregation cried, "God Save Queen Elizabeth!" and a fanfare of trumpets sounded. She returned to the Chair of Estate and was seated; the loudly coughing Archbishop of Canterbury ministered the Queen the questions contained in the Order of Service. These the Queen answered; then she rose and, preceded by the carrying of the Sword of State, went to the altar, knelt, and took the Coronation oath, kissed the Bible, and was about to set her Royal Sign Manual to the oath text when she found the inkwell empty. "Pretend you are signing!" the Lord Chamberlain hissed in her ear. She did.

At that moment, as she rose, she could not resist an anxious glance at the Royal Gallery, where Prince Charles, in a white silk suit, brought in late to the service, was alternately jumping up and down with excitement and sinking chin on hand in an expression of boredom, barely controlled by his aunt Margaret and maternal grandmother. His rain of questions could scarcely be suppressed, breaking the temporary silence after the oath.

Now the Queen was back at the Chair of Estate; she was presented with the Bible by a Scottish dignitary and returned it; she could proceed to Communion. She knelt at a faldstool; the Archbishop began the hymn, "Come Holy Ghost, Our Souls Inspire," and then spoke the prayer of Consecration. The Queen and her people stood, and the choir sang the Handel anthem, "Zadok the Priest."

The Lord Chamberlain divested the Queen of her crimson and ermine robe; she removed her tiara and Garter collar, and then, with the Sword of State borne before her, proceeded to King Edward's Chair and was again seated. Four Knights of the Garter held the cloth of gold canopy over her head for the hallowing, and the Dean of Westminster in the Ceremony of the Ampulla poured holy oil into the spoon and anointed the Queen on the forehead. The Queen knelt, and the archbishop blessed her; she was invested with the ceremonial robes known as the Colobium Sindonis and the Supertunica, followed by the Girdle; and she touched the spurs. The Queen was given a ceremonial jeweled sword to carry—the Sword of State was too heavy—and she walked with it to the altar.

She offered the sword, giving it to the Dean, who delivered it to the Marquess of Salisbury, for the traditional fee of one hundred silver shillings in a velvet bag; the Archbishop placed the Armills, or ceremonial bracelets, on the Queen's wrists. The Queen was invested with the Stole Royal, and with the Pallium or Robe Royal of cloth of gold; she was given the orb; then the ring was placed on the fourth finger of her right hand and upon that hand she was helped to place the glove. She received the scepter and orb; there followed the prayer of Benediction. She was crowned, took Communion, and received the homages.

A near mishap occurred; although the blue carpet of the nave had been meticulously laid down, according to the Queen's prescription, the gold carpet at the altar had been laid in the wrong direction, so that the metal-fringed mantel of the newly donned Robe Royal caught in it. She signaled to the Archbishop of Canterbury, whispering, "Get me started!" Somebody released her, and a near disaster was averted.

Back at the Palace, the Queen was remarkably fresh, as always rejoicing in her power, and not at all drained and exhausted as her parents had been. The atmosphere in the royal rooms was one of jubilation, and Cecil Beaton, arriving to take the authorized pictures of the family group, noted that everyone was extraordinarily informal, the Queen parading about in purple robes and crown, quite unwilling to remove them, Prince Charles and Princess Anne jumping up and down and racing to and fro, chasing each other in a circle around the laughing Queen Mother, the Duke of Gloucester popping his eyes and grimacing, the Duchess of Kent snapping at her children, Philip impatiently cheerful, and Princess Margaret looking pink and white and remarkably sexy. Although the Queen did admit to Beaton that the crown got rather heavy, and her eyes showed some inkling of tiredness, she was in the very best of form, and rejoiced in several trips to the Palace balcony to acknowledge the cheers. In London, the celebrations continued well into the night, though oddly, they did not quite have the ecstatic release of those in 1937. Probably, the heavy rain which had marred the procession back to the Palace and threatened not to leave for the indefinite future had finally dampened even the most rugged of British spirits. Molly Panter-Downes, the *New Yorker* correspondent, observed:

> The . . . rain . . . turned khaki uniforms to greenish black as they clung to the soldiers' backs, took the crispness out of the marvelous Pakistan turbans, and so bedewed the footguard's bearskins that they looked as gray as the grizzled mops of the elder Fiji chieftains. The stout white-stockinged calves of the footmen . . . were pale-strawberry pink with the dye from their crimson velvet pantaloons.

There were fireworks over the Thames, every major restaurant offered champagne dinners, the public houses were crammed with singing customers, and the entire city was drenched in dance music. Everyone trailed home not long after midnight, leaving behind soggy gold and red heraldic draperies, soaked flags of many nations, and the glitter of gold crowns shining above the Mall. Shortly before dawn, men in white coats appeared and started pulling down the stands. The moment of a generation was over.

14
***

THUS, THE NEW ELIZABETHAN age began; the world rejoiced; it seemed that at last England would emerge from the new Dark Age. But, in a single gesture, Princess Margaret precipitated a wave of publicity that within weeks threatened to engulf the throne.

In view of the awkward situation with Townsend, it was of crucial importance that she retain a tactful distance from him, both at the two State balls that marked the Coronation, and at the gatherings of the royal family at the Abbey. However, this vital and rebellious Princess openly displayed her sentiments immediately following the ceremony of Coronation, at a meeting of royalty and aristocracy in the Great Hall of the Abbey. She brushed some fluff off a lapel of Townsend's Royal Air Force uniform. The couple laughed, and the New York reporters, led by those from the *Journal-American* and the *Daily News,* rushed to the telephones.

At once, the matter was in American headlines. However, the Queen, via her Press Secretary, Commander Colville, had an extraordinary control over the press, unthinkable today, and the matter was not allowed to be mentioned in the British newspapers or on British radio and television. Inconceivable as it may seem, Britain was so insulated that even the most scandalous of American tales would be restricted from the British public. Even when the episode was headlined in continental Europe, the public remained in ignorance. Colville declined to issue an official denial that the gesture at the Abbey was an expression of romantic interest on the Princess's part.

It was not until June 14 that *The People,* a Sunday newspaper, published in London, repeated the rumors. There can be no measuring the Queen's dismay. She could not now prevent other London papers from taking up the issue. Her incapacity to suppress inconvenient news would become an increasing problem for her in the new age of communications. She at once, and with great determination, set in motion a campaign.

She held a series of meetings with Lascelles and Colville, both of whom foolishly advised her that the only way to escape the situation was for Townsend to be exiled, like some dangerous courtier in the Middle Ages. Stuffy and blind to reality, they failed to realize that, by making this arrangement, they would instantly confirm the newspapers' allegations and would expose the crown to excessive amounts of criticism. She decided not to act upon their advice immediately.

Her first step was to withdraw Townsend from the imminent tour of the Queen Mother and Princess Margaret of Southern Rhodesia, planned for the end of June, and instead she would have him accompany herself and her husband on a journey to Northern Ireland, departing at almost exactly the same time. She consulted with Sir Winston Churchill in the matter. Influenced by his wife, he confirmed the views of her two immediate advisers, and in a meeting with the Secretary of State for Air, the Lord De L'Isle and Dudley, requested that gentleman to obtain a position for Townsend abroad. De L'Isle suggested three possible appointments, as air attaché to Singapore, Johannesburg, or Brussels. Lascelles, receiving Townsend icily in his office, informed him of the choice. Townsend smiled bitterly. After all, his two sons, aged eleven and eight, the younger of whom was the godson of King George VI, were in the custody of Mrs. Townsend. It was absurd to expect him to see them regularly if he were posted to Malaya or South Africa. He elected to go to Brussels.

This taken care of, Colville advised the Queen that not a word would be said to the press other than that the appointment had been made. Townsend was not to be advised of the appointment until he actually would be in Ireland.

On June 29, at Clarence House, Townsend said good-bye to Margaret; they had both been advised by the Queen Mother that he would not actually leave for Brussels until the Princess returned from Rhodesia on July 17. Next day, he left for Belfast, and the news of his appointment broke in the press. The Queen acted out her role carefully, never showing anything but public admiration and warmth toward Townsend, both then and later, in London. However, when Townsend

returned to his royal residence, Lascelles informed him of the
appalling news that he would now have to go to Brussels on
July 15, giving him no opportunity to see Princess Margaret
again for at least a year. The Palace was implacable. A reporter
brought up the mater of Townsend having been Comptroller of
the Queen Mother's Household, only to receive the lying reply
from Colville that, ''The Queen Mother never had a comptroller.'' When an official of Lord De L'Isle was asked about the
Brussels posting, he pretended that it was a good career move.
It was nothing of the sort: it was a demotion; an appropriate
promotion would have been to a major Air Force base, of
which he would have been appointed commanding officer.

Townsend was obliged to inform by telephone Princess
Margaret, who had been suffering from a severe cold at the
Leopard Rock Hotel at Umtari during her tour. With royal
control, she showed no inkling of her annoyance during her
frequent public appearances thereafter, but, from that moment
on, she never forgave Lascelles, whom she regarded, not quite
accurately, as Churchill's ally in a devilish plot against her.

In the midst of the crisis, the question was revived of her
position as regent should the Queen become incapacitated or
die while Prince Charles was still below the age of eighteen. It
was now obvious to the Queen that this matter must be brought
to a swift conclusion. Winston Churchill, who had been most
useful during the early discussions, was out of action after a
stroke which had occurred at a dinner at 10 Downing Street in
honor of the Italian Prime Minister, followed by another which
partly paralyzed him. It thus fell upon Chancellor of the
Exchequer R. A. Butler, as unofficial surrogate Prime Minister,
to continue the matter of the regency. It is unfortunate that the
government felt compelled to announce, in the midst of the
Margaret-Townsend controversy, that the decision had been
again made to present the matter to the Lords and Commons in
the new Parliamentary session in November. It would then be
debated; but there was something peremptory about the announcement that seemed to indicate rather more than the usual
amount of royal privilege and raised a number of questions, of
which more later.

In the meantime, Townsend was pursued brutally by reporters day and night in Brussels; he was made to feel extraordinarily awkward, his comings and goings at his modest hotel
monitored. On the day, July 22, that Butler in his official role

as Chancellor of the Exchequer announced the proposed introduction of the Regency Bill, Townsend was seen moping at an otherwise buoyant cocktail party; he had been pursued in his green Ford Zephyr through the streets by an army of paparazzi, and even when he took a sandwich at his office, drably furnished with slanting studio windows, decorated only by a map of Europe and pictures of the Queen, her mother and father (and not of Margaret), the phone never stopped ringing, nor did intruders stop banging on the door. Fond of horses, he was unable to obtain a moment of privacy at the races. He suffered from depression, and made no secret of it in public.

By contrast, Margaret remembered her royal position, and matched her sister's and brother-in-law's capacity for histrionics (in disguising from her the fact that she could never be married) with her own simulation of lack of distress at the brutal separation from her lover. In August, at Balmoral, she went out of her way to make sure that her seeming *joie de vivre* was noticed by everyone. On August 21, she was unusually buoyant at two birthday parties in her honor, the first in picnic-style on the edge of Lake Muick, and the second, a "do" at the Castle, at which she was seen openly flirting with the Hon. Richard Beaumont, second son of Viscount Allendale, who whirled her onto the floor for an unusual number of dances, and whom she joined in the Eightsome Reel. She shared dances with the charming young Lord Carnegie and with Robin McEwen.

The only inkling that she was upset lay in the fact that she, always religious, increased her church attendance considerably in those weeks. Secretly, she and Townsend corresponded, pouring out their feelings in a succession of love letters. In September, she was a guest of the Duke of Buccleuch at Drumlanrig Castle, visiting her old and now married flame, the duke's energetic son; otherwise, she avoided social engagements.

The Queen was preoccupied much of that middle and late summer, not only with the matter of her sister, but also with the performance of her racehorses. Her favorite colt was Aureole, a chestnut-and-white racer of unusually spirited temperament; she was obsessed with Aureole; even as she had left for her Coronation, she had wanted to have up-to-date news of the horse. It was a great disappointment to her that Aureole was beaten at the Epsom Derby. His problem was rebelliousness;

she certainly had enough of rebelliousness that season. She was so anxious about the problem that she actually called in a neurologist, Dr. Charles Brook, who massaged the beast, caressed it, and at last made it relax. But still, Aureole's performance was unsatisfactory, and the Queen became increasingly concerned. It would be several months before Brook's expertise finally paid off.

There was trouble in the Commonwealth. Foreign Secretary Anthony Eden had been ill for months following surgery in the United States for a gall bladder problem, and although Churchill returned to 10 Downing Street in amazing fettle, he was, quite unmistakably, seventy-eight years old. The Mau Mau terrorists devastated Kenya; there was a constitutional crisis in Nigeria, resulting in the injury of three British officials; the Gold Coast demanded independence and the sacking of all British civil servants. There was concern over the Federation of Rhodesia and Nyasaland.

The Queen was faced with a new burden in her own home. In the midst of the Margaret affair, tittle-tattle had begun to circulate concerning the untoward behavior of Philip himself. Since 1946, he had been a secret member of the obnoxious Thursday Club, which met once a week, quite unnoticed in the press, upstairs at the popular fish restaurant Wheeler's in Old Compton Street, London. It seems that his favorite cousin, David, Marquess of Milford Haven, had introduced him. Other members included the editor of the *Tatler,* the London correspondent of the *New York Post,* the politician Iain Macleod, and (according to the author Anthony Summers and his associate Stephen Dorril) Peter Ustinov, the well-known radio and television personality Gilbert Harding, and the harmonica virtuoso Larry Adler.

The member who was to become most notorious was Stephen Ward, a well-known osteopath and portrait sketch artist of weak good looks and dubious habits who would one day cause a colossal political crisis in England. The members would drink heavily, tell dirty stories, and award a prize to the teller of the most tasteless joke. The visitors' books were filled with vulgar and repellent examples of humor. According to Summers and Dorril, Philip went beyond the confines of the Thursday Club into an even more dubious nocturnal world. It is claimed that he appeared at certain of Stephen Ward's dubious parties in Cavendish Square, bringing with him a pretty Canadian model named Mitzi Taylor. Philip also turned up at parties given by his friend the photographer Baron, who was a well-known bisexual with a preference for men. Summers and Dorril do not state whether Philip attended his cousin Milford Haven's sex parties that apparently took place between 1953 and 1956. The authors wrote:

> Selected men would be invited to the Marquess's flat at 35-37 Grosvenor Square. The evening would begin with card-playing, and then, when the drink had flowed for a good while, girls would be brought in. Then the betting would be on the women, in games with names like "Chase the Bitch" and "Find the Lady." Winners won the obvious prize—intercourse in one of the luxurious bedrooms.

How deeply involved Philip was in these indulgences, or whether he enjoyed the inherited collection of pornographic literature and photographs that the Marquess of Milford Haven had inherited from his ill-fated father, is unclear. If the rumors did reach the Palace, the Queen's distress can only be imagined. On top of everything else that year, she seemed to have more than a sufficient number of burdens.

It is surprising that Philip had time for such misbehavior, since in July alone he had over thirty official engagements, not to mention playing in polo matches, attending cricket matches, and going to the theater.

It was probably just as well that the twice-postponed tour of Australia and New Zealand was back on the drawing board. The decision was made to travel, not via the threatened and potentially dangerous Suez Canal, but via the Panama Canal, the first such journey undertaken by members of the royal family. *Gothic* was yet again withdrawn from the Shaw-Savill Australia passenger run to be reconverted for the voyage. The Queen would once more be accompanied by Lady Pamela Mountbatten, and Philip by Michael Parker. The Queen spent countless hours with Norman Hartnell working on the over two hundred dresses she would wear.

Before the couple left, the Queen opened Parliament in an atmosphere of customary splendor, and on this occasion, since she had now been crowned, the Imperial State Crown did not lie beside her upon a cushion but, most uncomfortably, on her head. She was still concerned with the matter of the revised

Regency Bill, the introduction of which precipitated a lively debate. The Home Secretary, Sir David Maxwell-Fyfe, skillfully presented a number of arguments for the Duke of Edinburgh being regent in the event of the Queen's death or incapacity. He referred to a line of precedent of previous Regency Acts in which the sovereign's parent became regent during his or her minority. Princess Augusta, widow of Frederick, Prince of Wales, had been made regent in 1751 in the event of the death of George II, before his grandson attained the age of eighteen. In 1830, the Duchess of Kent was designated regent if William IV died before Princess Victoria attained her equivalent majority. In 1840, Prince Albert was designated to be regent should Queen Victoria die while her eldest child was a minor. And in 1910, Queen Mary was given an identical designation should King George V die before the majority of the Prince of Wales.

It emerged in the debate that, contrary to popular belief, Princess Margaret would in fact become regent if Philip should be appointed regent and then die or be unable to pursue his duties; thus, press statements that her removal from the regency was inappropriate had no substance. Certain members criticized the revised bill; the Rt. Hon. Gordon Walker was not happy with the idea of having Counsellors of State appointed during the Queen's absence; he wanted the appointment of a Governor-General instead. It was pointed out during the debate that it might be difficult for Counsellors of State to get together on major decisions in the event of a national crisis, while others stated that a Governor-General might collide with the governor of Northern Ireland, who has a separate and special office. One member made mention of the fact that Philip was not Prince Consort and was not privy to the royal dispatch boxes, and thus was insufficiently familiar with the affairs of State to take the position of regent in any eventuality. Another, Mr. Jay McGovern, member for Shettleston, Glasgow, said:

> I wonder what the reasons are when the Home Secretary says that Princess Margaret has been consulted and has agreed. I wonder whether that is the sort of answer they get behind the Iron Curtain when a prisoner comes before the court and agrees to all that is taking place and admits all he is charged with. A sensible reason should be given for the change. Has Princess Margaret really been consulted in a proper manner?

Has she given her agreement, or is this being forced upon her?

The question seemed to fly in the face of R. A. Butler's promise to the House that Princess Margaret had concurred with the arrangement. However, there were those who still wondered whether Princess Margaret had in fact authorized the matter, and Sir David Maxwell-Fyfe was compelled to confirm that she had done so. Some members of the press were unconvinced.

Nobody during the debate raised the issue that the greatest likelihood of a crisis would be that, since the Queen and Philip were traveling together, they might be involved in a plane crash, and therefore Princess Margaret would anyway be regent. The appointment of the Queen Mother to the group of counsellors was not argued with, probably because her fellow members could scarcely have functioned without her guidance. The bill allowing for her presence was passed after a third reading on November 12, 1953.

Twelve days later, the Queen and Philip traveled from London, by air, for their first landfall in Bermuda. It was painful for them to leave Charles and Anne. Charles was at last beginning to assume a clear personality; except for one misadventure when he dropped an ice cube down the collar of an unfortunate footman, he was still well behaved, "serious," gentle, and considerate. Like his mother, he loved soldiers, and spent countless hours playing with his toy cavalry, as well as with his own toy infantry, at the Palace. His favorite rabbit, named Harvey after the imaginary creature featured in the celebrated stage play, was the center of his existence. At five, he was fond of birds, spending as much time as possible with budgerigars in the Royal Lodge aviary. He would bow in the presence of his mother, shake hands solemnly with visitors, and rejoice in the company of the corgis, Sue and Sugar, and Honeybun, the Queen Mother's dog. He was, in every way, a normal, robust, not outstanding child. His sister, apart from a crying fit when forbidden to go to the Coronation, also showed a balanced and subdued temperament.[1] It was arranged that, during the royal tour, he would enter into full-scale tuition, and would be trained, in reading, writing, and other simple studies, by Catherine Peebles, his nursery governess.

1. She would change.

* * *

Bermuda was alive with excitement at the royal arrival. Perhaps because she had Philip to herself for the next six months, perhaps because she had left the "Margaret crisis" behind, and, certainly, because she knew of the importance of visiting the furthest outposts of the Commonwealth, the Queen looked·unusually glamorous and vividly happy on this first leg of the tour. However, her joy was not unmixed; she was quite annoyed that racist Bermuda excluded all blacks from the dinner in her honor at Government House.

The passage through the Panama Canal was marvelous; soon, the *Gothic* was in the Southern Hemisphere. Fiji was exotically appealing, stiflingly hot, the small, wooden town of Suva flanked by luscious green trees and flowering bushes. The Queen had to partake of arguably the world's most unpleasant drink from a scooped-out shell; the potion was known, familiarly, as *Kava*. Even with her extraordinary composure, she could scarcely stifle a look of disgust. However, she behaved with aplomb when she received a disagreeable-looking whale's tooth or *tabua*, the most valued object in Fiji.

The royal vessel continued to the island of Tonga, where the massive Queen Salote, that scene-stealer of the Coronation, greeted the couple with an elaborate dinner of pork and yams at which her imperial band played flutes through their nostrils. At another banquet given by the British Consul, there was a power failure and the black Queen and her royal guests joined everyone else in running around looking for candles.

Auckland, New Zealand, was mild and rainy, the surrounding countryside volcanic and brilliantly green. A highlight of this part of the journey was a subterranean voyage through the legendary Glowworm Grotto at Waitomo. The royal couple was warned that a single word would ruin the experience, as the glowworms were extremely sensitive to sound. The small boat carrying them floated, as if in a dream, through the immense dark cavern, whose roof was spangled with what seemed to be a million stars. The tiny glowworms lowered long, glistening silk threads into the water to catch even smaller insects, which were attracted by the light. The Queen and Philip agreed that this was the most magical experience they had ever known.

Hailed everywhere by their loyal subjects, the royal couple

proceeded in high spirits to Sydney, Australia. The robust, bronzed Australians greeted them with boisterous and energetic humor, more than a million people cheering them from the shores. In Canberra, the Queen opened a new session of Federal Parliament. From Tasmania they flew to Brisbane.

It was in every way a glorious trip, the Queen's charm almost never faltering, Philip's good looks and athletic physique appealing to the fitness-mad Australians. But, above all, it achieved a cementing of sentiment in the Antipodes that might never have been possible otherwise. In Sydney, the Queen had not too subtly reminded Australians that she was *their* monarch; and only the most die-hard Republicans were heard complaining that final decisions in major matters were still referred to her Privy Council in London. Whatever cracks might exist in other parts of the Commonwealth, the Queen could leave confident that that vast southern Dominion was hers for the indefinite future.

The royal couple stopped off in Malta and posed for a photograph with officers of the Royal Malta Artillery, the Queen being Colonel-in-Chief. The Queen walked in, followed by Prince Philip. She took her place in the center front row, with her husband walking a few paces behind. Suddenly, he stopped, looking at a large portrait of King Edward VII hanging on the wall.

The King was holding his field marshal's baton across his chest. "Do I have to pose like that, too?" Philip asked. The Queen was annoyed. "Come along, come along!" she whispered loudly as she waved him to his place.

The Queen's children, in a touching gesture, were brought from Britain aboard the royal yacht *Britannia*, via Gibraltar to Tobruk, to meet the returning couple. The Queen was overjoyed to be reunited with them; she had been in touch with them almost every day of the trip, eagerly learning of the progress of Charles's lessons. Despite the colossal challenge of the journey, which covered countless thousands of miles in 173 days, the Queen and Philip looked as fresh as though they had arisen on a normal day in London.

London was *en fête* for them, and the Queen Mother's and Princess Margaret's joy in seeing them again was profound. The end of rationing, soon after they arrived, was cause for rejoicing after so many weary years.

* * *

The Queen's main concern was the performance of her beloved Aureole. She was beside herself with excitement when he won the crucial Coronation Cup race at Epsom, quite losing her royal composure and jumping up and down ecstatically, waving her binoculars. Next came Ascot and the Hardwicke Stakes. Could he possibly succeed again? She was horrified to learn that, due to an accident in his stall, Aureole's left eye was injured. But he was not blinded, and he romped home in a photo-finish.

She was tormented, pacing up and down waiting for the verdict. When she heard that Aureole was the winner, she jumped in the air. Finally, there was the biggest race of the year, the King George VI and Queen Elizabeth Stakes, which offered a prize equivalent to $65,000. Her state of mind was indescribable as she made her way to the royal box. Just before the start of the race, Aureole, showing his old temperament, startled by a suddenly opening umbrella, rose up on his forelegs, tossing the jockey, Eph Smith, to the ground. As the signal was given to begin, Aureole made a swerving turn and fell behind. The Queen grimaced with agonized displeasure. But Aureole recovered and finished three quarters of a length ahead of the field. For the first time in her life, the Queen broke into something close to a run to embrace Aureole. She was now without question the leading racehorse owner in England.

Elizabeth was tolerant of Princess Margaret's latest misadventure, directing, of all things, a play in the West End of London: *The Frog,* by Edgar Wallace. The production was a disaster, and proved embarrassing to most members of the royal family. The audience, which had waited in line at the box office to obtain tickets, groaned through most of it and laughed in the wrong places.

Margaret was going out of her way to give the impression that she was not pining for Peter Townsend. She was constantly in the company of Judy Montagu and others of the old gang, including Colin Tennant. Townsend came to see her under cover, rather like the hero of an old operetta, sneaking into the country (but with the Queen's permission) disguised as a Mr. Carter, meeting the Princess through an intermediary encountered at Harrods' book department, taken thence to Clarence House for a chaste reunion. Townsend recalled in his memoirs that their feelings for each other were as tender as ever and, incredibly, they seemed still convinced that once Margaret was twenty-five nothing would stand in the way of their religious union.

Philip, restless after his return from the Australian trip, his calendar crammed from morning to night, took off on his own on a royal visit to Canada.

As the Queen left with him for Balmoral for the Christmas holidays, the Queen had reason to be pleased with Charles and Anne's progress. From the age of three, the Prince had enjoyed the privilege of his own automobile and chauffeur. He had a personal footman, Richard Brown, who, according to one source, he grandiosely knighted with a table knife when the diligent slave bent down and retrieved some food Charles had accidentally let fall to the floor. He had his own detective, and he acted with that quaint imitation of adulthood that had marked his mother during her own earliest years.

He was a stickler for protocol, under his mother's and grandmother's careful guidance. He bowed, and Princess Anne curtsied, at least when he nudged her, when they were in the presence of older royalty. His mother specifically had taught him to thank train crews, stationmasters, captains and crews on boats, and anyone else conveying the royal persons from place to place. He delighted in making a special gesture of striding firmly within the eye line of Palace guardsmen, so that he could see them snap to attention like clockwork soldiers and officially present arms.

A much-criticized event occurred in January 1955. Prince Charles was taken to a meet of the West Norfolk Fox Hounds at Harpley Dams. He was lifted into the saddle by Hunt Major Robert Hoare, everyone laughing loudly as Charles struggled to blow notes on the Master's horn. Either at that occasion or later (accounts vary), he had his first ''blooding''; this involved a ritual of initiation to those attending their first hunt in which the fox's brush or tail was cut off and their faces were smeared with the dead animal's blood.

In March, the first of a series of new press statements on the Townsend matter appeared in the *Sunday Pictorial;* one writer said that the Princess had ''a choice between marrying Townsend or not succeeding to the throne.'' There was nothing whatever in the Royal Marriage Act allowing for any such provision, but it cannot be ruled out that such an assertion, designed to deceive Margaret, emanated from an official source. The popular newspapers began announcing that Margaret would in fact marry Townsend, no matter what. The *Sunday Pictorial* led the other papers with enormous Sunday headlines: PRINCESS MARGARET SENSATION.

The *New York Daily News* firmly announced the couple would be married in St. James's Palace, basing this unfounded statement upon the fact that the St. James's Chapel was being especially restored. Commander Colville and the new Principal Private Secretary to the Queen, Michael Adeane, who had replaced Sir Alan Lascelles in October 1953, did not issue a denial of these statements about the marriage. Townsend, in his memoirs, says they should have spoken, but what could they have said? If they had issued a denial that the couple intended to marry once Princess Margaret was twenty-five, it would have been a lie; and if they had confirmed it, it would have been against the Queen's desire to keep the matter quiet. They would also have added fuel to the fire of those who wanted the marriage.

There can be little doubt that the matter was as embarrassing to the Queen as it was to Margaret and Townsend, and that every day these reckless stories appeared, the couple's chances of happiness were dimmed still further. The traditional British hatred of being exposed to personal discussion in public places was considerably enhanced at the royal level. Philip was fortunate in escaping the situation in March by leaving for Nice and Malta to see the fleet exercises and to represent the Queen at the opening of Malta Parliament. At home, the Queen had to carry the brunt of the matter without him. She made the rounds of receptions and school and hospital visits, instructing Colville and everyone else to say nothing.

An extraordinary and feudal matter greatly concerned the Queen, whose interest in the Crown Lands never ceased. Seven hundred and twenty-six acres of prime farming land at Crichel Downs, Dorset, had, before World War II, been owned by a number of individuals, of whom one, Lord Alington, owned three hundred and twenty-eight; it had been requisitioned in 1939, with some modest compensation, by the Royal Air Force as a bombing range, the property to be restored after the war. Instead, in 1953, it was obtained by the Ministry of Agriculture, then in turn by the Commissioners of Crown Lands for the Queen, the capital technically if not disposably hers. The owners were understandably incensed.

Lord Alington's nephew, Lieutenant Commander G. G. Marten of Dorset, headed up a protest committee; he tried hard to outbid the crown for the land to refarm it under its previous tenants, but his letters of request were bounced about departments, passed from the Air Ministry to the Ministry of Agriculture. The Minister of Agriculture, Sir Thomas Dugdale, declined to respond or allow an inquiry into the matter. Marten charged that the land was being sold at below market price because government (i.e. the Queen) was involved.

At a stormy meeting of the National Farmer's Union in London, the matter, in October 1953, was angrily discussed. The Country Landowners' Association demanded that the property go into private, not royal, hands. The Minister of Agriculture stood firm against a rising tide; Conservative members of Parliament from Dorset stood wisely with the farmers against the crown. Finally, Dugdale was forced to agree to a public inquiry. Even the London *Times* was compelled to describe the affair as "a sorry and tangled tale," and stated that the crown commissioners had not only obtained the land behind the backs of former owners and sitting tenants, but had, underhandedly, arranged for a Queen's tenant to occupy and refarm the entire territory concerned.

The public inquiry opened at Blandford, Dorset, on April 21—the Queen's birthday. It showed an amazing number of deceptions used to pull the wool over the eyes of the original owners; the court heard instance after instance of callous disregard of individuals in the interests of the crown; of a wholesale annexation of the land by the Queen's commission rather than the "negotiations" which Dugdale pretended had taken place. Nothing as feudal had been heard of in England since the Middle Ages.

The official report on the story of intrigue and deception appeared on June 15. It outright attacked C. H. M. Wilcox, Under Secretary of the Ministry of Agriculture, G. C. Eastwood, Permanent Commissioner of Crown Lands, and H. A. R. Thomson, Crown Receiver, for a "most regrettable attitude of hostility" to Lieutenant Commander Marten, and stated that this attitude was the result of irritation that anyone should have the temerity to confront the government. During a tempestuous debate in the Commons, Dugdale answered cries of "Robbery!" and, when he announced that no further action would be taken on the report, there were gasps and shouts of absolute astonishment and horror.

He was compelled to resign and handed in his papers to the Queen, whose name had carefully been kept out of the entire matter, despite the fact that she was now the full owner of Crichel Downs. Lord Carrington, Parliamentary Secretary to the Ministry of Agriculture, and Mr. G. R. H. Nugent, as Parliamentary Secretary, resigned but Winston Churchill refused to accept their resignations. Both had been named unflatteringly in connection with the case. Churchill decided that Dugdale, and Dugdale alone, should be held responsible. But the land was never surrendered by the Queen; it remained in her possession, maintained by the State, and apart from costs, Marten was never compensated.

Apparently out of concern that she was not fully apprised of her ownerships by the government, and thus did not realize she was depriving individuals of their birthright, the Queen ordered a special document to be prepared by the Commission for the Crown Lands, which was actually published (and seemingly undiscovered since by historians) by Her Majesty's Stationery Office, in June 1955. It was put together under the direct orders of the Prime Minister.

This extraordinary report contradicted all public statements before or since, that the Queen did not "own" the Crown Properties; Part I, Section Five categorically stated, "Crown Lands are a trust estate, of which the capital belongs to the Sovereign." The upkeep was maintained by the State; the income was surrendered by the Queen in return for the Civil List. No list of the Queen's English properties was supposed to exist, yet the report contained one: over two thousand buildings in London, with rents at the time in Regent Street of over half a million pounds, or ten times that much in present-day money; most of Regent's Park, Millbank, the sites of several embassies, Victoria Park; most of Kingsway; several stores, including Liberty's; Regent's Park Terrace and Carlton House Terrace (the latter supplying the German Embassy before the war—the Ambassador's house was Neville Chamberlain's); Swan and Edgar's store, the Regent Palace Hotel, Canada House, and South Africa House. Almost four hundred thousand acres outside London, the bed of the sea three miles off shore, almost all foreshores; holdings included Ascot Race Course, Swinley golf courses, Delamere in Cheshire, Bryanston in Dorset,

Clearwell in Gloucestershire, Gorhambury in Hertfordshire, Croxton in Norfolk, Pynings in Sussex . . . the list was overwhelming.

A sad event occurred at the beginning of April. In his old age, with the uncertainties of health and the future, Sir Winston Churchill had decided, with the Queen's reluctant consent, to step down as Prime Minister. It was a poignant moment when members of the Cabinet held a farewell meeting at 10 Downing Street at noon on April 6, shaking the grand old man's hand one by one. The Queen attended a moving and beautifully organized dinner party at the Prime Ministerial residence, at which Churchill toasted the monarch he loved so well. Romantic and nostalgic as always, he recalled toasting Queen Victoria as a young cavalry subaltern. He spoke of the "deep and lively sense of gratitude" which he and all her peoples felt for the Queen, and the inspiration she provided in an "anxious and darkling age." The Queen rose and, in a rare royal act, proposed her retiring Prime Minister's health. Everyone applauded.

Next day, the Queen called the volatile and neurotic Sir Anthony Eden to the Palace to ask him to form a new government. The House of Commons cheered him as he promised to do "all I can to serve our country." He would combine the role of First Lord of the Treasury with the premiership. But for him to continue as Foreign Secretary would clearly be too burdensome. Harold Macmillan, with his specialized knowledge of the Near and Middle East acquired when he was resident minister in Athens and afterward, was the perfect choice for that office.

The change of Prime Minister[2] provided only a temporary distraction from the ongoing (and increasingly irritating) newspaper campaign in the matter of Princess Margaret. Referring not too indirectly to this, Philip addressed the Newspaper Press Fund at a dinner at Grosvenor House, London, on the subject of "the royal family and the press." He said, "With ordinary people, which we are—unlike presidents and prime ministers, who are usually rather special people—the more one is quoted and reported, the less one is inclined to leave to chance both

---

2. Eden would call a general election on May 26, ending in a Conservative victory.

what one says and what one does in public, and the more
jealous one becomes of one's private life.

"The result, of course, is very dull for newspaper men and
make us appear to be rather unenterprising, but remember that
our mistakes, instead of ending up in obscurity, are never
forgotten, although of course they may be forgiven." He went
rather close to the edge with his next remarks. He referred to
the recent newspaper strike: "I found it a most interesting
experience—breakfast seemed to take no time at all. I must
confess that I only really missed the strip cartoons, but what a
relief it was without the usual flood of gossip."

Gavin Astor, chairman (standing in for Col. J. J. Astor) of
the London *Times,* gracefully fielded these observations, saying that, "if ever there came a day when a responsible editor
forgot that the royal family was news, it would be time for that
editor to put on his hat and look for another job."

Philip's statements were jovial and superficial, bringing the
required laughter from those very journalists who had fought a
losing battle with Commander Colville to obtain one single
word on Princess Margaret's proposed activities following her
twenty-fifth birthday in August. Privately, Philip is certain to
have been furious with the press hubbub, and there is reason to
believe that he was finding the whole affair so tasteless and
annoying that he was turning against the notion of the marriage
as being highly damaging to the Palace's image.

The Princess distracted herself with a visit to Germany in
that last week of May. Townsend was not happy in Brussels. In
August, at Balmoral, her every move continued to be observed,
but on her twenty-fifth birthday, she, perhaps significantly, did
not file (nor, apparently, had she prepared) the necessary
application to the Privy Council which she was now entitled to
make. And even when Townsend turned up at the European Air
Attaché's conference at the Air Ministry in London and at the
Farnborough Air Show, there is no indication that she made
any effort to meet him. He did manage to get messages to her
through her former lady-in-waiting, Lady Elizabeth Cavendish.

Then, on October 1, for reasons that are obscure, Sir
Anthony Eden proposed a Bill of Renunciation which would be
introduced into Parliament, depriving Princess Margaret of her
Civil List income, and the money which she would receive
upon marriage, if she went ahead with her plans. She would
also be deprived of her right to function as Counsellor of State.

He and his wife went to Balmoral to advise the Queen of his decision. He was sure that the bill would be carried through both Houses of Parliament. He was mistaken: at a meeting of the Civil List Select Committee in June 1952, Clement Attlee had made it clear that the Labor party wanted the Princess to marry whom she chose; he was still leader, and would be until his retirement in December. But apparently the Queen accepted Eden's statement, and Princess Margaret was supposed to be, and presumably was, impressed by it. There was no mention of the Queen consulting either with Attlee—she knew what he would say—or with her Commonwealth Prime Ministers in the matter.

On October 12, Townsend was permitted a meeting with the Princess, approved, it seems, by Her Majesty. It was a strained encounter at Clarence House: Townsend had a sore throat and Margaret a headache. She still had not filed her application to the Privy Council. The couple were in each other's company a good deal in those days. They spent a weekend staying with the Queen's cousin, John Lycett Wills, and his wife; the following weekend, Margaret went to Windsor alone to discuss the matter with her sister and with Philip. She is said to have been distressed by the tenor of the conversation: it was clear by now that she would have little chance of happiness. The Queen Mother had sensibly withdrawn to the Castle of Mey in Scotland. The Palace still refused to comment on the couple's various meetings. The press dogged them everywhere, Margaret dealing with them more satisfactorily than the sensitive Townsend, who was, he wrote in his memoirs, "demolished by the physical and mental strain."

Even when he went shopping to buy a suit in the West End, Townsend could not escape. Meanwhile, the Marquess of Salisbury was in full support of Eden in their threat to prepare a Bill of Renunciation. He said he would resign from the government if the marriage went through. The Queen Mother was now said to be firmly opposed. It was an unpleasant time for everyone in the royal family, with constant and maddening speculation on the engagement in virtually every public house and restaurant, every household in England. Police cordons had to be drawn about the country houses where the couple stayed. On October 19, the royal family dined with the Archbishop of Canterbury and the bishops of the Anglican Church at Lambeth Palace to celebrate the reopening of the chapel there. There was no indication of distress on the Princess's face. And in fact it is likely that she had already decided she was worn out by the whole affair and, fond as she was of Townsend, she could no longer endure the spotlight on the matter.

Although the press and public saw her as an intensely romantic figure, bewitched by a handsome man, the truth was that she was still in her heart deeply religious and intensely royal, and above all placed her devotion to her sister above her physical and emotional attraction to her possible future husband. Eden's threat to introduce a Bill of Renunciation was unnecessary in the circumstances, since in the last analysis, if her sister, who had perhaps unwisely encouraged her hopes in the first years of the affair, ultimately was opposed to the match, she could never have flown in the face of such an attitude. Anyone who thought she was impervious to church, duty, and sovereignty would have been grossly mistaken. She was still the same Princess who, even in her dizziest days in Mayfair, sternly corrected anyone who improperly referred to her father King George VI in her presence. And when, on October 21, she was presented at the unveiling by the Queen of the national memorial statue of the King in Carlton Gardens, she cannot have been unmindful of the Queen's words:

> Much was asked of my father in personal sacrifice and endeavor, often in the face of illness; his courage in overcoming it endeared him to everybody. He shirked no task, however difficult, and to the end he never faltered in his duty to his peoples.

Thus, the issue of the terms of the Royal Marriage Act or the still imaginary Bill of Renunciation were in the long run insignificant; what mattered was that the continuing publicity was embarrassing to the Palace, the public relations of the new reign were much embattled, and the Prime Minister of England was single-mindedly, if hypocritically, in concord with the Palace's views. Townsend was the victim of the entire affair. Not only did he have to give up the woman he loved, but he would lose the extraordinary advantages of entering into the royal family, which would undoubtedly have resulted in a peerage. The *London Times* added its thunder to those who criticized the possible union. Princess Margaret went to see the Archbishop of Canterbury, who gave her no further hope. That was the end. Townsend wrote out the notes for the Princess's renunciation speech, handed her the draft at Clarence House, and she read it and accepted it. Meanwhile, at a Cabinet meeting at Downing Street, the Attorney General, Sir Reginald Manningham-Buller, called in from the Queen's Bench Division, advised on the terms of the Bill of Renunciation.

Rather appropriately on Halloween, October 31, 1955, Princess Margaret issued the personal message that Townsend had drafted. She said:

> I've been aware that, subject to my renouncing my rights of succession, it might have been possible for me to contract a civil marriage. But, mindful of the church's teaching that Christian marriage is indissoluble, and conscious of my duty to the Commonwealth, I have resolved to put these considerations before any others. I have reached this decision entirely alone, and in doing so I have been strengthened by the unfailing support and devotion of Group Captain Townsend. I am deeply grateful for the concern of all those who have constantly prayed for my happiness.

As the Labor politician Richard Crossman pointed out in his diary at the time, the renunciatory statement made by the Princess was "bad law" indeed. He based his statement upon a telephone call he received from the former Solicitor General, Lynn Ungoed-Thomas. Ungoed-Thomas, later to become High Court Judge in the Chancery Division, said:

> Princess Margaret's (is) a view of the church's attitude toward divorce which may be the Archbishop of Canterbury's but certainly doesn't cover the whole church, and she has somehow identified the interests of the Commonwealth with the maintenance of the Archbishop's view of divorce. All this has been done without the Queen's consulting the British[3] or Commonwealth Prime Ministers.

Crossman added, "The explanation is that Eden and three other members of the Cabinet, who are divorced, are desperately anxious not to proffer any advice during this crisis, and, if they had been obliged to proffer it, they could not possibly have supported the Archbishop." Crossman clearly did not understand the devious ways of the Prime Minister.

---

3. He was wrong there.

15
* * *

CHRISTMAS AT SANDRINGHAM HAD all the appearances of family unity and good cheer; it would seem that no crisis had taken place. But it would not be long before a far greater crisis would absorb the Queen's attention.

The monarch began preparations for a rare early spring holiday, a Mediterranean cruise in which she and her husband would be accompanied by Princess Alexandra of Kent, aboard the royal yacht *Britannia*. Just as she was in the midst of packing, and the yacht, already lavish, was yet again refurbished, she received disturbing news.

For decades, the anti-Semitic Sir John Glubb, familiarly known as Glubb Pasha, had been, despite his portly figure and red face, regarded by British imperialists as being something of a natural successor to Lawrence of Arabia. As commander of the Arab Legion, a miscellaneous body of anti-Israel soldiery headquartered in Jordan, he had had a remarkable degree of autonomy; he was both patriot and symbol of British influence in the Arab countries.

He had been a proponent of Jordan and of its monarch, the young King Hussein, joining in the 1955 Baghdad Pact, designed to restrict Soviet influence in the Middle East. The youthful King Faisal of Iraq, much admired by the Queen, also joined the pact, with Turkey, Pakistan, and Iran.

When Jordan failed to join the pact, Glubb Pasha's influence was seen to be dwindling. During riots by Palestinians in Jordan in January of 1956, Glubb all too brutally maintained order and his days were clearly numbered. King Hussein removed him on March 1, thereby making a clear statement that the British had little or no business in continuing to try to run (or interfere with) Arab affairs.

The dismissal of an official whose name appealed to the old guard of the Conservatives proved to be a shock to the Prime Minister. The extremely right-wing Conservative element in Parliament known as the Suez Group influenced Eden; he falsely charged Egypt's President Nasser with provoking the dismissal. They could not endure the fact that England was essentially finished in the Middle East and that its Kiplingesque visions of power and glory were in tatters. Foreign Secretary Selwyn Lloyd returned from a visit to Cairo, falsely confirming Nasser's involvement.

Eden was convinced that Nasser must go. Later, he would shout at Anthony Nutting of the Foreign Office, "I want [Nasser] destroyed. Can't you understand? I want him removed, and if you and the Foreign Office don't agree, then you'd better come to the Cabinet and explain why!" Eden found accord in French Premier Guy Mollet, whose onslaughts on Algeria, provoked by riots in Paris inspired by the French population of that nation, involved suppression and slaughter. Both Premiers would use as excuses for anti-Egyptian policy its belligerent attitude to Israel and its Russian deals. The Queen took off on her cruise in mid-March—to Sardinia and Corsica—thus missing two all-important Tuesday meetings with her Prime Minister in this critical period.

On April 23, after a visit to Sweden at the invitation of King Gustav and that useful World War II mail drop Queen Louise, the Queen received the Russian leaders Bulganin and Khrushchev—understandably without much enthusiasm—to tea at Windsor.

On May 16, Nasser, annoyed by charges of engineering the Glubb dismissal, and threatened by a reduction of the arms supplies from Britain that had helped him bring about his coup against his predecessor, General Naguib, deliberately recognized Communist China. It had become clear to Eden and to his Cabinet that Nasser was interlocked with the Communist bloc, despite the fact that Moslems were suppressed in Russia and Communists were suppressed in Egypt. The cynical marriage of political convenience was, Eden saw correctly, intended only to upset the balance of British power in the Mediterranean.

Two months after the Queen returned from her cruise, she was given disturbing information. The one serious chance that Britain and the United States had to retain a foothold in Egypt and to counteract Russian influence was to cofinance, with the World Bank, the new multimillion-dollar Aswan High Dam, to which they had made a substantial commitment some months before the spring of 1956. It would not only irrigate much of upper Egypt but would bring new resources of hydroelectric power to the country, greatly improving its position as an industrial nation.

The High Dam would have been an unanswerable argument in favor of Arabic acceptance of Anglo-American beneficence, at least in the all-important Mediterranean basin. It would have served a purpose in view of the desperate situation in Cyprus, where militant insurgents were threatening British power. Yet, in actions of great unwisdom, inspired by fear of misuse of the dam funds by the Soviets and paranoid unease over Nasser's supposed unreliability, first the United States, then the World Bank and Great Britain canceled the proposed loans.

Nasser was furious at the abrupt, offensive, and misguided cancellation of a full-fledged agreement. He turned crisis to advantage. On July 21, his police seized the Anglo-French Suez Canal Company. Though efficient in terms of piloting and operating the canal, the company had been a moribund, old-fashioned, and badly operated corporation. Although his method of annexation was illegal, the annexation itself was not.[1] Nasser timed the annexation to coincide with his rival King Faisal's visit to the Queen, and to Sir Anthony Eden, who was dining with Faisal when the news broke. Faisal is supposed to have said, "Get Nasser and get him now!"

Nasser addressed a crowd of two hundred thousand people at Alexandria, attacking with inflammatory force the "gross exploitation" of the Suez Canal Company, reminding his audience of the scores of thousands who died building the canal under Ferdinand de Lesseps—always a useful target for Egyptian dictators.

As he had calculated, Nasser was acclaimed as the hero of Suez; his action was warmly received by two thirds of the world, represented by thirty-two individual governments. Spain followed suit by talking of annexing Gibraltar; Iran cried out for Bahrein; the Panamanian government muttered about seizing the Panama Canal.

---

1. As a former Queen's Counsel and student of international law, Foreign Secretary Selwyn Lloyd knew this from the beginning.

Nasser's action was modified by a promise to compensate the French and British shareholders with the equal value of their holdings according to the present prices on the Cairo Stock Exchange. Eden saw as large an opportunity to acquire national support as Nasser did. He and Gaitskell in the Commons began bandying about words like "Hitler" and "Mussolini." Egyptian sterling holdings were blocked in London. There was talk in the House of Commons of "answering force with force." Lord Mountbatten was consulted by the Prime Minister (he would be Admiral of the Fleet by October 22), and he advised that, through a joint Naval and commando attack from Malta and Cyprus, Port Said could be occupied within three or four days. So could the first twenty-five miles of Canal Causeway. Eden was delighted. At first, Mountbatten, who kept the Queen informed throughout the period, was inspired by visions of Empire and gunboat diplomacy, but that cool and calculating man soon saw the danger of the attack backfiring. He wrote a note urging Eden to use sanctions rather than force. But he had not the courage to send the letter to 10 Downing Street.

From the beginning, the Queen was opposed to radical action. Since Mountbatten had her ear, and since, with her sober, conservative, and balanced nature she could scarcely be impressed by Eden's charges and threats, she saw clearly the wisdom of caution and negotiation.

In August 1956, First Lord of the Admiralty Lord Hailsham (whose knowledge, as a distinguished legalist and expert in international law should have caused him to discourage the adventure), with Mountbatten, began assembling every available vessel, including pleasure cruisers and mothball ships, for the so-called Operation Musketeer, to be embarked upon in conjunction with an all-out Israeli attack on Egypt. Since President Eisenhower and U.S. Secretary of State John Foster Dulles were anxious to avoid a Middle Eastern conflict in an election year (despite the fact that both were intricately involved in the secret war against Russia in the Arab countries), they could not be relied upon to help. This knowledge was most frustrating to Eden; knowing that it would be futile to bring the matter of collusion with Israel to Washington's attention, he unwisely embarked with the approval of Lord Chancellor Harold Macmillan (and, surely, with the Queen's knowledge but not approval) upon a full-scale clandestine

arrangement. Israel would be encouraged to invade Egypt's
Sinai territory (as if it needed encouraging); Eden would make
the false announcement that he was interceding with a request
for a cease-fire to prevent full-scale war between Israel's
Premier David Ben-Gurion and President Nasser. Ben-Gurion,
by prearrangement, would agree to a cease-fire; it was calculated that Nasser would also agree; then, with Guy Mollet,
Ben-Gurion would organize an Anglo-British force to "separate the combatants"—i.e., illegally invade Egypt—and seize
the Suez Canal.

Sir Winston Churchill was in agreement with the scheme.
The cost to an almost bankrupt nation would be at least £12
million, or over $25 million, for the attack alone; it would take
another £100 million to secure a garrison and set up an invasion
force with military headquarters in Cairo for just one year; a
further £1.6 billion would be required for the next several years
of occupancy—an insane and meaningless extravagance.

Hugh Gaitskell, as leader of the Opposition, pointed out in
an August Commons debate that any such proposed action by
Britain (he did not know of the Israeli coconspiracy) would
result in humiliation, condemnation by the United Nations
Security Council, and a serious loss of international prestige.
Eden was unimpressed by such warnings. As an old Empire
man, he saw the secretly planned invasion as a way of restoring
the glories of the British Empire.

These critical developments occurred while the Queen was
at Balmoral, and there is no record that the Prime Minister
visited her there. He must have been glad of her absence; the
summer recess of Parliament also proved advantageous to him
and his fellow conspirators. Eden and Macmillan, with the rest
of the Cabinet, went on struggling with an increasingly irritable
Mountbatten and with other Naval and military leaders, to
engineer the attack.

On August 16, at the London Conference, with twenty-two
nations represented, it was decided that the best way out of the
crisis was to arrange for international management of the Canal
Company. Australian Prime Minister Robert Menzies was
chosen to discuss the matter with the Egyptian dictator. A
Churchillian Empire man, representing a politically insignificant country, Menzies failed to impress Nasser, and nothing
came of the meetings.

Shortly thereafter, Mountbatten, appalled by Eden's refusal

to relent, scribbled a note of resignation as First Sea Lord—and failed to send it. He had learned that Eden (rashly supported by Antony Head, Secretary of State for War, and not opposed by anybody) wanted to bomb Cairo, Port Said, and Alexandria from the air. It was unfortunate that Mountbatten did not go through with his resignation: it might have alerted Eisenhower and Dulles to the secret plan, which the CIA was proving lamentably deficient in exploring. However, the Russians got wind of it and published it through Tass, the Moscow news agency, on September 15. The announcement was treated everywhere as Communist propaganda.

By mid-September, Eden and Selwyn Lloyd were on British television, trying to inflame the British public with rallying cries to war. The young were opposed to belligerent measures against a poorly equipped, poverty-stricken, and largely helpless minor nation; the majority of their parents and grandparents, captivated by Eden's record of years with Churchill and his romantic good looks, as well as nostalgia for the days of Empire, gave general support.

Eden had to continue to keep his scheme from his people, as well as from the rest of the world, but it is doubtful whether he was able to keep everything from the Queen, even given her ill-timed, if traditional, sojourn in Scotland. She was at Balmoral into October, while the meetings and plots went on and on. British and French pilots of the Canal Company were withdrawn in mid-September; much to the annoyance of Eden, Mollet, and Ben-Gurion; Nasser continued to run the canal efficiently without them. He shrewdly allowed transit to British and French (though not Israeli) ships, thus avoiding international calumny or a valid excuse for an attack.

On September 25, Harold Macmillan, representing Eden, was at the White House; Eisenhower dodged the subject of Egypt completely, leaving it to Dulles to tell Macmillan that the President was quite opposed to any conflict and, whatever happened, not to do anything until after the election. Macmillan returned to London empty-handed. On October 3, the British Cabinet secretly sanctioned, once and for all, the attack with Israel upon Egypt. On October 24, British, French, and Israeli representatives signed the clandestine, ultrasecret Sèvres Protocol, naming a date for the undeclared war's commencement of October 29. Mountbatten had organized the fleet in the

Mediterranean, and the 16th Paratroop Brigade and the commandos were ready to be dropped from Cyprus.

Again without the knowledge of Eisenhower, who was in the last throes of his election campaign, Israel illegally invaded Sinai, without United Nations approval, on October 29. Exaggerated accounts of the Israeli advance, deliberately designed to sanctify the so-called Anglo-French intervention force, stated that Israel was already at the Suez Canal approaches when in fact the Army was 130 miles distant, and the paratroops were at least 40 miles away. The same day, Mountbatten was entertaining the Queen for the weekend at Broadlands, and told her of the execution of the scheme. She was very upset; from the beginning, and through the receipt of handwritten minutes of certain Cabinet meetings vis-à-vis Israel, she had had to learn piece by piece the truth of a warlike operation she hated and that could risk the world's safety by escalating into a nuclear conflict. Mountbatten urged her to use her influence on Eden to stop the next stages of Operation Musketeer. But it was too late; and now she had another agonizing worry. Philip was due to arrive in Singapore that day: bloody anti-British riots were threatening his life, and the fanatic rebel leader Lim Chion Song was screaming for a royal death. The Chinese rioters, who had swept through the streets, killing, burning buildings, and who had besieged the British Embassy and military headquarters, were violently repressed by police, who clashed with crowds carrying iron bars, stones, crowbars, and acid. A total of one thousand people were arrested; Philip's visit was canceled.

That night, the Queen had to appear at the royal film performance of *The Battle of the River Plate* smiling and talking to movie stars as though her husband was not in danger and the war had not begun against Egypt.

On October 30, Britain and France issued their prearranged ultimatum to Cairo and Tel Aviv to end the fighting they had overtly encouraged and it was rejected, as Eden and Mollet had estimated it would be. They met for lunch at 10 Downing Street to go over the last details.

At dusk on Halloween, October 31, the French and British Air Forces bombed eight Canal Zone airfields and four near Cairo, damaging Russian-supplied aircraft. Because the bombers were operating at forty thousand feet instead of in dive-bombing attacks, comparatively little damage was caused. Nasser evacu-

ated Sinai; Israel's Army marched into an almost defenseless and
deserted region, announcing a great victory. Next morning,
Nasser blocked the canal; Eden had not advised Parliament or the
country.

On November 1, the Prime Minister opened a Commons
debate on the crisis. The Labor members laughed in his face
when he said that the government "could not associate itself"
with the United Nations resolution condemning Israel as the
aggressor; the Conservatives cheered him; they also cheered
him when he referred to the Egyptian radio and press campaign
against Israel; he was cheered when he charged that the crisis
sprang from Egyptian policies; he was hailed with cries of
"You sent arms!" "Hypocrite!" and "What about the Cen-
turion tanks?" from the Labor members. When he spoke of the
advance of Britain's troops toward the canal, there were cries
of "Now tell us, what is your role?" Challenged directly by
Philip Noel Baker, Labor member for Derby South, as to
whether the present government had revealed its triple-pronged
attack to U.S. Government representatives, the Prime Minister
failed to respond adequately, and was besieged by screams of
"Answer!" from the Opposition.

He repeatedly dodged the question of whether troops had
landed in Egypt at all. Infuriated by James Callaghan, Labor
member for Cardiff, he shouted, "He is a master at sitting and
shouting. He seldom stands!" Callaghan replied angrily, "I
would like you to answer a question that 50 million people in
this country will want to know. Are British troops engaged in
Egypt at this moment? Have they landed, and where are they?"

The Speaker called for order; and when Eden said, incredibly, "I am not prepared to give the House any details," there
were cries of "Resign!" "Sit down!" and "Shame!" Try as
he might, Eden could not avoid the fact that he had undertaken
the attack without advising Parliament or the United Nations
Security Council or Washington.

Within hours, the truth of Anglo-French attack was confirmed. Virtually the entire world condemned Eden's, Mollet's,
and Ben-Gurion's actions. The Queen was upset; the Russians
threatened nuclear intervention. As for Eisenhower, with the
election just days away, he exploded at the White House in
language that, according to one witness, "had not been heard
[in that residence] since the days of General Grant." Dulles
was equally enraged, and to save himself Eisenhower had it

announced that America neither backed nor approved this miscalculated adventure in neocolonialism. Rendered nervous by the sheer weight of international contempt, Air Minister Nigel Birch did not go ahead with precision bombing of Nasser's vessels, which instead were sunk by Nasser himself; these "block" ships effectively prevented any craft from making transit through the canal.

Nasser saw his moment. He summoned the male civilian population, including boys over eleven, to arms. Knowing that he could not succeed in local war, he recruited even the old and the sick for guerrilla attacks.[2] On November 5, the British and French invaded Port Said from the air. The Egyptians fought against them with single-minded courage, and though thousands died, they inflicted numerous casualties on the invaders. Nasser became both martyr and hero.

By November 6, the Egyptians had delayed the invasion from advancing beyond the site of El Cap. The British and French, with all of their modern weaponry, had only managed to seize twenty-three miles of territory in two days. The plan for capture of the Canal Zone in six days was doomed. The pressure from Washington was extreme, and from an outraged President, who thus helped to achieve his imminent election. Eisenhower authorized a run on sterling by the Federal Reserve Bank, virtually froze British deposits in the International Monetary Fund, and cut off all credit. Britain was threatened with ruin. Two more weeks would have destroyed the nation. The Archbishop of Canterbury threatened to exclude the Tory party from the Church of England's prayers; the service chiefs, the Treasury (Macmillan turning coat), the BBC, and the Law Offices of the Crown unanimously fled Eden's sinking ship. Eden was forced to the humiliation of a cease-fire.

A UN security force replaced the invading armies, which were to be withdrawn by December 22. The Queen canceled the royal variety performance. She was compelled to open Parliament on November 6, delivering her Prime Minister's bland and meaningless statements in what must have been a

2. In the midst of the most severe crisis in recent history, the Queen continued with her public appearances; on November 2, with the drama at its height, she appeared at a bun-throwing ceremony at Abingdon, Berkshire. Alderman in cocked hats and black robes hurled two thousand buns into the crowd of twenty-five hundred.

very painful state of mind. She was obliged to say, following an innocuous announcement of a proposed visit to Portugal, France, and Denmark:

> My government will continue their efforts to achieve, by all possible means, a prompt and just settlement of the many problems arising from the grave situation in the Middle East. To this end they will welcome the broadest measure of cooperation of the Commonwealth, with our Allies in the Atlantic Alliance and in Europe, and with those international agencies of which the United Kingdom is a member.

Nothing could have been more saccharine. Yet controversial statements, exposés of international intrigue, or even the most tacit critiques of policy could have no place in the Queen's Gracious Speech. If she had warned, she had not been heeded; if she had advised, her advice had not been taken. It was not a happy moment in her life.

The results of the failure of Suez was incalculable. The British nation had seldom been so divided. The working classes and the lower middle classes found themselves especially split; on November 5, Suez Sunday, forty thousand people had rallied in Trafalgar Square, London, and the public uncharacteristically had clashed with the police in the first riots since the General Strike of 1926. Over 2,100 university lecturers and 377 Oxford dons protested vigorously; two Cabinet members, Anthony Nutting and Sir Edward Boyle, had resigned during the crisis, and the veteran Sir Walter Monckton, who had a particular knowledge of international law, had been given the vacant and meaningless sinecure post of Paymaster General. Nutting would go on to become an excessive fan of General Nasser, author of an overgenerous biography of that egregious personage.

England lost power and prestige in the Arab countries forever. The financial cost of the defeat of 80,000 men, 500 aircraft, and 140 warships by a disorganized but fanatical rabble was incalculable. The crisis proved a windfall for the American cotton lobby and for Texas and Oklahoma oil, since Egyptian cotton, already exported to the Communist countries, was no longer available to the British and French, and the Arabs applied an oil embargo that brought petroleum rationing to England. Eden was finished. Ill both mentally and physically, he managed to rally sufficiently to provide an eloquent if lying defense of his position in the Commons immediately after the invasion, his position reiterated in a fraudulent memoir, published some years later.

The end of 1956 found the Queen at Sandringham in what can only have been a depressed mood. What she had witnessed, and had been powerless to prevent, was public exposure of the end of Empire, which had, in fact, taken place as early as 1947.

It is doubtful if, among all of the Christmas-tree decorating, giving of presents and country walks she showed less than absolute composure. Whatever else should happen to England, she must hold her firm and loyal place as the Commonwealth's unassailable center. But she must have missed her husband, who was in Australia for the Olympic Games. Some indication of royal inflexibility and Philip's position even as a subpolitical figure is indicated by the fact that, even when the crisis was at its deepest, the Queen told him not to fly home, even though he very much wanted to do so. Similarly, in view of his Greek origins and special knowledge of the Mediterranean region and the Middle East based upon his years in Malta and the Arab countries, he would, surely, in normal circumstances have remained to play a role, if only a public relations one, in the present bitter struggles between the British and the rebels in Cyprus, and the ancillary problems between Cyprus and Greece, of which his cousin, King Paul, was still monarch.[3]

Sir Anthony Eden did not assist his already damaged image by disappearing from London at a time when he was most needed, and flying to Jamaica for a vacation, with his wife, at the borrowed home of Ian Fleming, creator of the James Bond novels. He returned suntanned, but still a broken man. While the royal family was at Sandringham for Christmas, there was much discussion in political circles of whether Eden, haunted and sickened by his failure, should resign. He was greeted with silence and dismay in the House of Commons. He suffered from severe insomnia and mental disturbances, and Sir Horace Evans, his personal physician, was called to Chequers. The Queen was kept informed as the diagnosis proved unfavorable. He was stricken with fever and pain from adhesions resulting from gallbladder operations in 1953; the mental burden of the

3. King Paul was so impoverished at the time that he had to vacate the royal palace in Athens.

Suez catastrophe was undoubtedly a major contributing factor to his appalling condition.

By the new year, it was abundantly clear that a new Prime Minister would have to be found. Even if Eden's health had proved adequate to the challenge of his high office, it is doubtful whether he could possibly have sustained it. R. A. Butler was mentioned as a replacement, but he had vacillated during the Suez crisis, never fighting against the attack, and Macmillan, for one, began telling people he would never serve under him. Conservative opinion shifted toward Macmillan himself, who had at least changed his position on Suez toward the eleventh hour, his role of chief architect of the fiasco in the crucial early stages conveniently forgotten. He was known to have a special relationship with the Americans, and he was also known to be Churchill's choice. Despite the fact that Churchill was, according to Richard Crossman, virtually senile by this stage, every word he uttered carried considerable weight, as always, from the Palace level down.

The unhappy Eden contacted the Queen at Sandringham and asked to be received; she invited him and Lady Eden to stay. In his biography of Eden, Robert Rhodes James states that the Prime Minister prepared three memoranda on the meeting, two of which "cannot be published at this stage." The reason must be the controversial nature of the discussions and the royal rule against revealing the contents of private meetings between the monarch and any of her ministers. However, it cannot have been a comfortable encounter: the still elegant, handsome, exquisitely tailored but sick, neurotic, and broken Prime Minister, with his strong and forceful wife, every inch a Churchill, forced to admit to the Queen, who from the beginning had disliked his policies on Suez, that the result of his ignoring her recommendations was the termination of his career.

Some light upon the meeting at Sandringham was cast by the published diaries of Richard Crossman. He cites the evidence of David Ormsby-Gore, Parliamentary Under Secretary of State for Foreign Affairs, who was present when the Edens arrived at Sandringham. The Queen had not told Ormsby-Gore that Eden would be there.

According to Ormsby-Gore, Eden told the Queen, during a forty-minute discussion before dinner, that he wanted to resign, although he was careful not to mention this at the semi-formal repast. During the meal, Eden began discussing the Suez affair.

He told the Queen he had always believed that America would not have opposed something Britain and France would do, especially when it was in conjunction with Israel. He had thought Eisenhower would provide sufficient time to perform the strike against Egypt successfully and prevent the United Nations from being organized "a hundred percent against us." What the Queen thought of these comments, which showed a complete blindness to Eisenhower's election promises and foreign policy, was not recorded by Ormsby-Gore. The Queen had now the substantial task, for the first time in her reign, of "selecting" a successor.

She must have leaned toward Macmillan. She was aware that he had in the end shared her own and Lord Mountbatten's views of Suez. However, she certainly thought well of Butler, who had been acting Prime Minister on and off when Eden was ill. She began conferring with the appropriate statesmen. Eden was definitely in favor of Butler, which may have led him to urge the Queen to consult with Lord Salisbury, since Salisbury was known to disapprove of Macmillan's policies vis-à-vis Greece and Cyprus.

On January 9, Eden returned from Sandringham and assembled his Cabinet members at 5 P.M. at 10 Downing Street; he read them a memorandum in which he revealed the "health" reasons for his departure. Then, utterly depressed, he was received by the Queen, who had only just arrived, at midnight at Buckingham Palace. She accepted his formal resignation during a fifty-minute conversation. It was not only a dismal, miserably chilly winter's night, but it was deep winter in the Queen's heart. Eden had been Prime Minister for only twenty-one months.

The Queen summoned Salisbury and Churchill to hear their opposing views on a successor. Salisbury and the Lord Chancellor, Lord Kilmuir (formerly Sir David Maxwell-Fyfe), met the Cabinet ministers in Salisbury's offices in the Privy Council chambers; meanwhile, a generalized and rather scattered survey of the Conservatives had been made to obtain a range of opinions. The decision, no doubt much to Salisbury's dismay, was for Macmillan. It would only be a few months before Salisbury would resign.

All of these discussions were held in secret. The public was not advised. At 2 P.M. on January 10, Macmillan drove to the Palace. The Queen informed him that he should proceed to

form a new government. One day later, Eden resigned his
Parliamentary seat and, in his deep unhappiness, declined an
Earldom. The question of whether there would be a general
election was held in suspense for the time being. Many figures
of the Opposition were absent inopportunely from the country
when the momentous decision was made; the leader, Hugh
Gaitskell, was visiting Harvard University, Aneurin Bevan was
on his pig farm in Wales, Richard Crossman was in Paris, and
Morgan Phillips was in Vienna. Labor party representatives
telephoned Gaitskell at Harvard, urging him to call for a
general election. No such move was made.

There was talk of a debate, urged by Aneurin Bevan, but the
Royal Prerogative, seldom mentioned or exercised, precluded
any such discussion, since, for once, the monarchical decision
was final and unarguable, even in the Commons.

On January 13, Macmillan announced the details of his
government. It is impossible to believe that this was not agreed
to by all parties in advance. Essentially, the decisions indicated
a characteristic closing of the ranks. Selwyn Lloyd, one of the
most unfortunate figures of the Suez affair, was not removed as
Foreign Secretary, perhaps because to have done so would
have been a public admission of guilt. Lord Salisbury, who was
numbering his own days, remained leader of the House of
Lords. Lord President of the Council Butler was, with shrewdness, retained as leader of the House, and was granted, as an
additional sop, the role of Home Secretary. Peter Thorneycroft
became Chancellor of the Exchequer, and, in a solitary concession to public criticism, the Minister of Defense, Antony
Head, quietly resigned, his departure somewhat obscured. The
recently resigned Sir Edward Boyle returned to assume the
inoffensive and ordinary position of Parliamentary Secretary of
the Ministry of Education.

In the meantime, the Queen, after weighing the new Cabinet
with sympathetic interest, began to face yet another major
concern. She returned to Windsor Castle to prepare for her visit
to Portugal, where she would meet her long-absent husband,
when that husband's name was bandied about in the most
alarming manner. Reports of a rift between the couple had been
appearing sporadically in American newspapers for some time;
it had been said that he and Lieutenant Commander Michael
Parker, on their prolonged journey through Southeast Asia and

Australia preceding a trip to Antarctica, had been involved in questionable activities with women. They are supposed to have gone to "wild" parties, where their behavior was scarcely calculated to appeal to the Queen; she must have wished she had responded to Philip's request to return to England during the Suez crisis.

Then a series of events at the beginning of February brought a storm of rumor: Parker's wife announced that she was separating from him, allegedly talking to friends about events at the Mayfair home of Baron, Philip's friend and court photographer, who had died on October 15, 1956, a few days before Philip and Parker left on their Antipodean trip. Immediately following the announcement of the separation, Parker handed in his resignation aboard ship en route from Gambia to Gibraltar, where the news first broke through Reuters. There was talk of "three or four mystery women" in Philip's life. One of these was a popular singer and dancer, another an actress who lived over a tobacco shop, another still a Greek cabaret singer, and the fourth a "Mrs. S," whom he had allegedly visited at a flat in Chelsea.

It was suggested that Mrs. Parker would summon Philip as a witness at the divorce hearing to testify to her husband's alleged adulteries. This was unthinkable, and it appears that the Queen acted promptly in consulting with her new Prime Minister before leaving for Lisbon on February 18. She had for some time been considering making Philip a Prince of the United Kingdom; Queen Victoria had bestowed the same dignity upon Prince Albert some ten years after their marriage, and it was now close to ten years from the Queen's and Philip's wedding.

The announcement of the decision to call Philip His Royal Highness the Prince Philip, Duke of Edinburgh, by Letters Patent under the Great Seal, was to take place, very shrewdly, the day after the royal couple would return to London. The honor would serve the further purpose of scotching the gossips. Of course, it did nothing of the kind, and the Palace could only go on issuing denials of a rift. Sir Michael Adeane and Sir Martin Charteris had the unenviable task of dealing with the matter. Meanwhile, RAF Squadron Leader Henry Moresby Chinnery replaced Parker, whose estranged wife spoke, surprisingly, to the *New York Post*. She said:

My advice to Mrs. Chinnery is that it would be better if she lived in London rather than Buckinghamshire. Then she would be sure of seeing her husband fairly often.

The press seemed to take the view that Lord Salisbury had been responsible for Parker's dismissal, and, as during the Margaret crisis, charged the government with gross hypocrisy. It was observed that at least two members of the Cabinet were separated from their wives and had not been required to resign. The Queen looked grim and somber wherever she went. Meanwhile, the press campaign against Prince Philip grew stronger and stronger.

The timing of this gossip was unfortunate, since not only did it take place in the wake of Suez, but it occurred when Prince Charles was for the first time a pupil at school. He had started at half-term on November 7, 1956, just when Britain stood defeated and in abject withdrawal from Suez.

The Queen and Philip had decided to send their son to Hill House, in Hans Place, behind Harrods in Knightsbridge, about a mile away from Buckingham Palace. This was a break with tradition, an indication that the royal couple wanted their children to have as normal an upbringing as possible. It was understood that Hill House would be ideal, since sons of members of Parliament and the grandson of Harold Macmillan were there.

The pre-prep school had been established in London by Col. Henry Townend, OBE. Its basic principle was that the school pupils would be half English and half foreign. At that time, almost all preparatory schools in England prepared their students only for English public schools; Hill House prepared them for higher education in many countries. When he was criticized for allowing foreigners to enroll, Townend replied that he had suffered from wounds in the war, did not want to see any future wars, and felt that it was necessary for pupils of different nations to get to know each other.

It was understood that Charles would not be called "Prince Charles" by either teachers or fellow pupils, and that he would not be granted unusual privileges. The only exception was that, when he walked the streets or went to play games, Mrs. Townend always walked with him to protect him. He was just one of a hundred pupils briskly enjoying the gym, where the boys could work out. Although gentle by nature, Charles would

Elizabeth Bowes-Lyon leaves her London home for her marriage to the Duke of York on April 26, 1923. (POPPERFOTO)

Princess Margaret with her mother in 1930. (POPPERFOTO)

A 1927 picture of Princess Elizabeth out for a ride with her nurse.

Nadesda Milford Haven, who married the second Marquess of Milford Haven in 1916. (THE HULTON-DEUTSCH COLLECTION)

Left: Prince Philip, second from right, acting in a Shakespearean play at Gordonstoun School (TOPHAM) and *(right)* going out to bat in a school cricket match in 1939. (POPPERFOTO)

The cast of a Christmas pantomime given at
Windsor Castle in December 1941. (POPPERFOTO)

Princess Elizabeth, watched by Princess Margaret, makes her
first radio broadcast, a message to children of
the Empire, on October 13, 1940. (TOPHAM)

The Prince of Wales, Wallis Simpson, and
Lord Mountbatten in Monte Carlo in 1935. (POPPERFOTO)

The Duke and Duchess of
Windsor meet Hitler during a
trip to Germany in 1937.
(THE HULTON-DEUTSCH COLLECTION)

The King and Queen in a
London air raid shelter
in 1940. (POPPERFOTO)

The King broadcasting to the British nation on the first evening of the war, September 3, 1939. (ASSOCIATED PRESS/TOPHAM)

Lieutenant Philip Mountbatten with his three sisters, Princess Margarita von Hohenlohe-Langenburg, Princess Sophie of Hanover, and Princess Theodora of Baden, shortly before his wedding in 1947. (POPPERFOTO)

During World War II, Princess Elizabeth served in the Women's Corps of the British Armed Forces. At the time of this photograph, she was nineteen years old. (POPPERFOTO)

A twenty-first birthday party photograph of Princess Elizabeth *(right),* seen here with Princess Margaret on the grounds of the King's house, Durban, South Africa. (ASSOCIATED PRESS/TOPHAM)

Earl Mountbatten and the Duke of Edinburgh in 1948. (POPPERFOTO)

Leaving Westminster Abbey after the royal wedding on November 20, 1947. (POPPERFOTO)

Princess Elizabeth with her
son Prince Charles shortly
after the christening
ceremony on December 15, 1948.
(PRESS ASSOCIATION/TOPHAM)

Dancing at the Government
House "Cowboy-Dress Party"
in Ottawa during their tour of
Canada in the autumn of 1951.
(POPPERFOTO)

Princess Margaret and Group Captain Peter Townsend,
sight-seeing with the royal party during the
South Africa tour of 1947. (POPPERFOTO)

Queen Elizabeth and Queen Mary *(right)* try to get Prince Charles interested in the camera. His mother is holding Princess Anne.
(POPPERFOTO)

Queen Elizabeth, dressed in black, leaves the aircraft that rushed her back from Kenya after her father's death in February 1952.
(POPPERFOTO)

The Queen, with her husband and children and her mother *(right),* watches the RAF Flypast Salute from the balcony of Buckingham Palace on her return from her Coronation at Westminster Abbey. (THE HULTON-DEUTSCH COLLECTION)

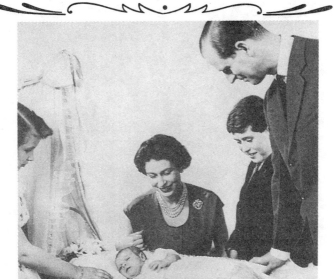

Prince Andrew with the family, 1960. (ASSOCIATED PRESS/TOPHAM)

Official engagement picture of Princess Margaret and
Antony Armstrong-Jones, February 27, 1960. (TOPHAM)

Prince Philip and Princess Alice of Greece at the memorial service for Lady Mountbatten, March 9, 1960.
(THE HULTON-DEUTSCH COLLECTION)

Cecil King, chairman of the Daily Mirror Newspapers, Limited, pictured in 1961.
(PRESS ASSOCIATION/TOPHAM)

Prince Bernard of the Netherlands. (POPPERFOTO)

Prince Charles drowns flies in a fly-catching bottle at Timbertop, the bushland annex of Geelong Grammar School, where he spent three and a half months. (TOPHAM)

A young man is led away by police after an incident in the crowd during the investiture of Prince Charles as Prince of Wales at Caernarvon in 1969. (POPPERFOTO)

Princess Anne and Captain Mark Phillips leave Westminster
Abbey after their wedding in 1973. (PRESS ASSOCIATION/TOPHAM)

Princess Anne talking to one of the men who was
injured during the attempted kidnap. (POPPERFOTO)

The Queen in Bahrain in 1979, with Emir and Prime Minister. (THE HULTON-DEUTSCH COLLECTION)

Prince Charles and Prince Philip at the funeral of Lord Louis Mountbatten. (POPPERFOTO)

Prime Minister Margaret Thatcher with the Queen at the
Commonwealth Conference in Zambia in 1979. (POPPERFOTO)

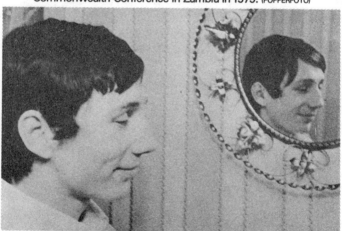

Michael Fagan, the man who broke into the Queen's bedroom
at Buckingham Palace, shown here in an earlier
family photograph. (POPPERFOTO)

Sub Lieutenant H.R.H. Prince Andrew ashore in Port Stanley with a fellow crew member from his Sea King helicopter during the Falklands conflict in 1982. (PRESS ASSOCIATION/TOPHAM)

Prince Edward with some Fijian women during a 1983 visit. (POPPERFOTO)

Prince Charles and Princess Diana of Wales on the
balcony of Buckingham Palace after their
wedding on July 29, 1981. (POPPERFOTO)

join in a fight and in games with as much energy and natural
vitality as any other child. Mrs. Townend, who had designed
the school uniform, proved to be a motherly presence, warm
and thoughtful, and she alternated with her husband in meeting
Prince Charles when he arrived by chauffeur-driven car at nine
each weekday morning.

Corporal punishment was forbidden at Hill House. All
punishments were light; according to the authorized royal
biographer Dermot Morrah, the worst were confiscating the
school tie or having the boys stay in after hours for detention.

Apart from the usual subjects at Hill House, Charles learned
drawing and elementary anatomy (Mrs. Townend had been an
assistant nurse to the royal homeopath Sir John Weir and
supervised the anatomy lessons). At four o'clock each afternoon, a car would arrive and take Prince Charles back to
Buckingham Palace, except for Fridays, when he would stay
after school, and he would sit with Mrs. Townend on a small
stool in the sitting room and have tea waiting for his car to take
him to Windsor. Sometimes, the Queen would accompany the
Prince to the Castle.

Once a week, the Townends would take Charles's class to
Buckingham Palace to take swimming lessons in the royal
pool. The Queen was not amused when this fact was leaked to
the press.

A school report on Charles (Lent, 1957) signed by Townend
indicated reading, very good indeed; writing, good, firm, clear,
well formed; arithmetic, below form,[4] average, careful, but
slow—not very keen;[5] scripture, shows keen interest; geography, good; history, loves this subject; French, shows promise;
Latin, made a fair start; art, good, and simply loves drawing
and painting; singing, a sweet voice, especially in lower
register; football, enjoying the game; and gymnastics, good.

There was no avoiding the presence of reporters outside the
school. But they were forbidden entrance to it. Some inexhaustible pressmen determined that Charles enjoyed the cook's
meals of beef, vegetables, and apple pie, painting a picture of
the royal yacht *Britannia*, sailing under Tower Bridge, doing
well at football, gaining much confidence, and losing the
shyness he had inherited from his mother and grandfather.

4. This is contradicted by the actual pages from the exercise books.
5. Like his mother.

The most important aspect of the exercise book pages, seen today, is the perfect neatness of the handwriting and his arithmetical figures, with none of the scratches and crossings-out normally found in schoolchildren's work.

With Charles at school, scandal breaking over Philip, a new government to deal with, Suez still on everyone's mind, the Queen departed for Lisbon under a heavy burden. She returned with Philip to London, Charles enjoying the Easter holidays at Windsor, when news came of the death of Princess Helen of Greece, mother of the Duchess of Kent.

It had been hoped that Princess Margaret would, after the conclusion of the Townsend affair, have found an aristocratic or foreign titled cousin whom she might marry. However, there appeared to be no one suitable. When it was mentioned that Margaret had an interest in her cousin, Prince Christopher of Hanover, it cannot have escaped the Queen's attention that he was a brother of the much-criticized former Hitler Youth member Queen Friederike of Greece and the grandson of the Kaiser—quite apart from the fact that he was considerably older than Margaret. The Princess turned her attentions to a commoner.

His name was Antony Armstrong-Jones. Slight, good-looking, boyish, just turned twenty-seven, Jewish on his mother's side, Armstrong-Jones had a delicate, equine face, light brown hair and eyes; he limped slightly from an attack of polio. He chain-smoked for hours on end. He had a refined, heartwarming charm, enormous energy and drive, a very English quality of sensitivity and civility, not unlike Townsend's; but, unlike Townsend, he was outgoing, amusing, and not particularly religious. He was considerate, kind, and generous by nature, and, like Margaret, dearly loved the theater, ballet, and all forms of popular entertainment in which he was occupied as a photographer. His father was a well-known Welsh barrister; his beautiful mother Anne was the sister of the brilliant theatrical designer Oliver Messel; the couple was divorced when Armstrong-Jones was four.

His mother remarried; her second husband was the sixth Earl of Rosse. His father married the Australian actress Carol Coombe, who raised Armstrong-Jones partly in London and at their country home, Tickeridge Mill,[6] near Uckfield, Sussex; he also lived with his stepfather and mother in Ireland and Yorkshire. Leaving his studies in architecture at Cambridge without graduating because he wanted to be a full-time photographer, Armstrong-Jones had been apprenticed to the photographer Baron at his studio in Mayfair; after Baron's death, Armstrong-Jones secured modest premises at 20 Pimlico Road, a depressed, lower-middle-class building.

His basement studio apartment was reached by a precipitous winding staircase. His theater-lobby photographs for such shows as *Cranks* and *Irma La Douce* were among the most striking and widely discussed of their era. Sir Laurence Olivier would request Armstrong-Jones to do the photographs for *The Entertainer*, John Osborne's famous play, in which Olivier starred. He had a knack of getting to the heart of the subject without being cruel or deliberately unflattering. His mastery of lighting produced the effect of sculpturing features that went beyond even such talented rivals as the distinguished Angus MacBean. The Duchess of Kent, an inveterate theater-goer, so admired Armstrong-Jones's work that she invited him to take the twenty-first birthday photographs of her eldest son. In 1957, the Queen summoned him via Commander Colville to Buckingham Palace to discuss photographing her children.

With quiet but definite boldness (for he was not lacking in courage and ambition), Armstrong-Jones, who was very per-suasive, asked the Queen if he could depart from the normal custom of very posed photographs as exemplified by Cecil Beaton and Dorothy Wilding and could instead take informal shots of Prince Charles and Princess Anne at play, some of them in the Palace gardens. The Queen agreed. For one shot, he chose a stream, a tributary of the Palace lake, and posed the children playing. Looking through his lens, he was surprised to see the Queen sitting on the footbridge wall. He coolly asked her if she would agree to be included. She approved laughingly and the result was one of the most appealingly informal of all royal family photographs.

Armstrong-Jones was said to be involved at the time he met Princess Margaret with the Chinese-Russian actress Jacqueline Chan, who was appearing in *The Teahouse of the August Moon*.

6. Later the country home of Vivien Leigh.

The Princess first met him in April 1956, when she attended her old beau Colin Tennant's wedding to Carey, daughter of the Earl of Leicester. Later, he took several striking photographs of her; she liked his original and daringly informal approach, less static and rigid than Cecil Beaton's; she lingered after the sessions to talk of photography as an art form, and of the theater. Later, she met him at a formal party given by one of her extra ladies-in-waiting, Lady Elizabeth Cavendish. She took the royal initiative by inviting him to small and intimate dinner parties at the home of friends she could trust. They could not go to shows together, nor even movies; too much would be written in the press. And it was too early to invite him to Clarence House. But he did soon spend evenings with her at Clarence House, right under the Queen Mother's nose. He had to hide his car blocks away, tiptoe up the stairs, and look to right and left as he departed in the small hours.

She began to descend the perilous spiral staircase at Pimlico Road, entering the purple and violet bedroom that was like some early set for Mae West. Gradually they began to take risks, slipping, in simple clothes, into small, cheap restaurants and pubs, or taking coffee at street stalls very late at night. Princess Margaret first told the Queen Mother of her interest in Tony; she found her a strong support; and then she told the Queen, who was not displeased. The Queen loved her sister deeply; she still felt with her the pain of the Townsend debacle; she wanted her to be happy.

Armstrong-Jones acquired a house at Rotherhithe, working hard on remodeling it, smoking furiously and swigging wine, showered with sawdust and shreds of white plaster, toiling very long hours in a decorator's frenzy, recruiting local boys from the wharves, laying down tatami matting. He crammed The Room, as he called it, with a mass of objects described in *Tony's Room*, a memoir by his landlord, William Glenton: a cage with stuffed birds, a blackamoor, china cows, a French locket with strands of human hair, wax flowers in a bowl, a musical box, two figures in porcelain getting into bed, with the legend, "The last in will put out the light"—and, oddly, a Navy hammock, swung from the ceiling. The whole was dominated by a hideous, enormous Victorian portrait of an admiral. Agile, he enjoyed descending from The Room to the dockside down a long chain; sometimes, the photographic models who came to pose for him would, with loud screams, struggle down the chain themselves and fall to the ground, much to the delight of the dock workers gathered to see them.

Princess Margaret visited him there, with the aid of Lady Elizabeth Cavendish, so secretly that even William Glenton did not at first suspect her presence. Since Glenton was a journalist, it was extremely difficult for him to keep the affair a secret. But he loyally did. By the spring of 1958 the romance would be in full bloom.

Many matters, both personal and political, caused the Queen distractions that year. In February, a favorite horse, Winston, fell and had to be destroyed; she was heartbroken. Shortly after her return from Portugal with Prince Philip she was plagued by the illness of her beloved Bobo MacDonald, the indispensable ladies' maid and dresser who had been with her all of her life. In a very rare gesture from a monarch, the Queen was driven to the London Hospital to see Bobo, for whom she had arranged a special private room. She brought Bobo's favorite flowers and sat by her bedside doing her best to cheer her up. The Queen was patron of the London Hospital. That institution was always favored when treatment was called for during the illnesses of friends of the Queen and royal servants.

Consolations for her private concerns and stresses came to the Queen that spring. She very much enjoyed (whatever her problems may have been with Prince Philip) an elaborate State visit with him to Paris, particularly valuable at that time because of the widespread criticism in anti-government circles that it was quite inappropriate for the British to have made secret arrangements with the French and Israelis in the matter of Suez. The Queen spoke at a banquet at the Élysée Palace of the value of a cordial relationship between the two countries, even though it is doubtful whether she would have had the unqualified approval of many in commercial and political circles in London. The evening at the Opera surpassed the glamour and splendor of the earlier visit, and an expensive river pageant was staged in the royal couple's honor. Prince Philip received the Légion d'Honneur, and even the French Communists joined in the festive greetings.

Back in England, the Queen's horse Doutelle romped away to the winning post in the royal colors in the Two Thousand Guineas race at Kempton Park. She showered praise on the Boyd-Rochfort Stables, which repeatedly earned her prizes.

But the greatest of her victories was to come when her Carrozza won the Oaks. It seemed that Carrozza might have lost, as the horse was nostril-to-nostril with its chief rival, but when the anxious monarch discovered that the photo finish film showed Carrozza to be the champ, she lost all composure and jumped up and down in a state of ecstasy. Not since King George VI's Sun Chariot achieved his wins of the One Thousand Guineas, the Oaks, and the St. Leger, in the same year, had the royal family enjoyed anything approaching such a triumph.

Unhappily, these racehorse victories were mere flashes of glory in a continuing national darkness. The country was having to pay the costs of the waste and folly of Suez. The malcontents in the unions, the malaise of the people as a whole, the debt-ridden Exchequer: the Queen was reminded every day of her nation's troubles as the horse-drawn brougham rattled over the asphalt to the Palace with the latest dispatches in the red official boxes. By the later weeks of that bleak winter and spring, there was talk of devaluing sterling.

There was disturbing news from overseas as well. The government of Syria, joining with the rest of the Arab countries in a now quite undisguised contempt for traditional British influence, cut off the pipelines carrying British petroleum. In India, there was much serious discussion of secession from the Commonwealth. Starting with an attempt to inject some echo of a Churchillian spirit into a defeatist nation with a broadcast speech filled with buoyancy and encouragement in January, Macmillan was being received by the people with a characteristic blend of skepticism, humor, and despair. Each Tuesday evening at five-twenty—the Queen had altered her father's policy of lunching with her Prime Minister on that day— Macmillan would meet the Queen at the Palace, finding her, as he wrote in his diary in February, "incredibly well informed." From this we may deduce that every aspect of England's plight, and of the Queen's and her Prime Minister's fragile hopes for the future, were discussed at the Palace at those invaluable meetings. It can be said that she concurred with Macmillan that Britain must reassert itself as a world power, overcome those dissentient elements in the Commonwealth that had had qualms or worse over Suez, and patch up the badly deteriorated state of political relations with the United States in order to form a secure political alliance with that dominant nation.

The Queen took a keen interest in the March Bermuda
conference to discuss Anglo-American relations, which had
been initiated by Eisenhower and at his particular request was
taking place on ''British'' soil. It was fortunate that Macmillan
was an old friend of Eisenhower's, and was well placed to
recement broken bonds. Macmillan's main purpose was to bind
the two great English-speaking countries in a unified stand
against the Soviet Union. That was the year in which all
attempts at conciliation by the Russian Government, which
offered promises of withdrawing troops from Hungary and
lessening its depotism over the Eastern bloc, would be deci-
sively rejected in Whitehall and Washington. When Macmillan
returned to London, he was able to report to the Queen that the
United States was keeping its promise to supply Britain with
the all-important Thor missiles and that a certain accord had
been reached in the matter of the anti-Soviet *cordon sanitaire*.
A matter that seemed to have little attention was the Russian
coup of building the Aswan High Dam, which the American
and British governments had so unwisely failed to construct.

In April, Britain's first hydrogen bomb was exploded,
securing the country's role as a nuclear power, but provoking
widespread public fear and concern and some vociferous
opposition from the Labor party. For months, stretching into
the following year, the substantial membership of the Campaign for Nuclear Disarmament was loudly evident. Young
protesters swarmed through public squares or lay down, in an
imitation of Gandhi's passive resistance, in front of the Prime
Ministerial car. The Queen almost certainly did not oppose the
H-bomb, one of England's few claims to potency in the
post-Suez twilight and fragile Macmillan-era dawn.

There were those at the time who felt that the Queen herself
was increasingly a victim of mediocre advisers and had become
not much more than a ventriloquist's doll, uttering blameless
but meaningless public statements. She was continuously
peppered by minor but irritating journalistic gunshot. Her
family's attendance at fox hunts was disapproved noisily. The
League Against Cruel Sports took exception to her children's
being exposed to bloodings and ''unnecessary slaughter,''
including deerstalking at Balmoral. Even if the Queen made the

most modest concession to popular demands on a Sunday, the Lord's Day Observance Society attacked her unmercifully.

Particularly vocal were those professional gadflies, the journalist Malcolm Muggeridge, the angry young playwright John Osborne, the novelist John Braine, and Lord Altrincham, all of whom seized the choppy wake of Suez to expatiate on their prejudices. Although in retrospect these critics of the Queen seem more self-advertising than genuinely liberal, there was some justice in their opinion that the Queen too readily submitted to lifeless, flat, and meaningless speeches put together by her Principal Private Secretary. The problem was still (and they chose to overlook it) that the Queen was not permitted by the Constitution an opinion per se, nor indeed any expression of policy, whether it was her own or her Prime Minister's. She was charged with dowdiness; but to have displayed the ostentatious glamour of her mother in the last years before World War II would have been at once tasteless and provocative to a public that was still suffering from financial constraints. Lord Altrincham, in the *National and English Review,* of which he was editor, wrote that the Queen's speeches were "a pain in the neck," and that the "personality conveyed by the utterances put into her mouth" was that of "a priggish schoolgirl." This was largely misunderstood to mean that the Queen herself was priggish, schoolgirlish, and painful. On August 6, 1957, as Altrincham left Television House in London after an ITV interview, a sixty-four-year-old man stepped forward from the crowd of newspapermen and photographers and struck him across the face, shouting, "Take that from the League of Empire Loyalists!" Altrincham, a sturdy thirty-three, scarcely felt the older man's feeble and halfhearted slap, and laughed it off in a subsequent interview. He then, in the pages of the *National and English Review,* declined to withdraw his previous statements, merely clarifying them instead.

The Commonwealth Prime Ministers, led by Robert Menzies, rushed to the Queen's defense. The Archbishop of Canterbury dismissed the matter in an interview. It is doubtful if the Queen was concerned.

She was preoccupied with Princess Anne, and with Prince Charles's education at Hill House. Apart from her visits to Portugal, France, and Denmark, she spent as much time with Charles and Anne as possible, watching every detail of

Charles's education with the keenest interest. Hill House was run expertly, one of the reasons she had chosen it. Every morning, the boys' uniforms, caps, shoes, and fingernails were inspected, and any sign of uncleanliness, untidiness, or poor posture was corrected with a polite but firm Victorian rigidity. The curriculum was devised according to Victorian principles to be so utterly time-consuming that there was little or no room for the various pranks or bullying that disfigured most schools.

As the year progressed, Prince Charles was increasingly popular; he was pleased that his fellow pupils called him by his Christian name alone; he was lucky in that he was reasonably good at everything without being in any way exceptional or outstanding: averageness was, of course, the most desirable attribute of a schoolboy in England or elsewhere. He was an all-rounder, plumpish but handsome and cheerful, neither too virtuous to be unbearable, nor so rebellious that he would annoy. The Queen and Prince Philip were pleased with his evident normalcy and happy, uncomplicated progress.

That summer, Charles's tonsils were removed at Buckingham Palace, in that timeworn operating theater, the Bühl Suite. He convalesced at the home of the Earl of Leicester in Norfolk. In August, he disappointed his father by not proving to be a good sailor during a voyage aboard *Bluebottle,* the royal yacht at Cowes. Quite firmly, though not yet despotically, Prince Philip was pushing Charles day and night to improve his athletics and seamanship. He drove him into clipping seconds off his speed in swimming the Palace pool, and he dwelt constantly on his effectiveness in other competitive sports.

It became a strong conviction of Charles's parents that he should proceed to a prep school, and the question that arose which school that might be. No predecessor in the direct royal line had been at such a school, but of course his father had attended the highly disciplined educational establishment of Cheam. Several considerations had to be borne in mind. Seclusion of location was of vital importance, since the press was even more aggressive in pursuing him, and in fact an excessive amount of reportorial spying and sleuthing could wreck his whole life as a pupil. He himself had become understandably nervous about reporters.

The Queen and Prince Philip had to face the thought that every year Charles grew older he would be increasingly caught up in a maelstrom of publicity.

They at last settled upon Cheam, which had moved, in the years since Prince Philip was educated there, from Surrey to Hampshire. The Queen and Prince Philip, by arrangement with the two headmasters, Peter Beck and Mark Wheeler, did an exhaustive tour, along with both the royal children. The Queen pushed her fingers into several hard horsehair mattresses in the dormitory, noted the absence of springs, and said, with a laugh, "Well, Charles won't be able to bounce on these!" The school floors were bare, and there was no central heating to alleviate the English winters. The classrooms had old, wooden desks deeply marked with initials, rude remarks, and slogans cut into their surface by generations of penknives. No doubt the conditions pleased Prince Philip, with his emphasis upon lack of privilege for his son, and his feeling that rigid and spartan circumstances were necessary for boys, to improve their character and physical constitution.

Prince Charles joined the school on September 23, 1957.

It was a very strained trip from Balmoral, Prince Philip bent upon overcoming his son's distress, not allowing any displays of tears, the Queen expressing a natural maternal concern tempered by the royal refusal to allow any public displays of emotion. As the royal automobile rolled up to the school building, joint headmaster Peter Beck was present to receive the family. Charles was a picture of misery as his parents drove off. His hair was too long to fit the school requirements, and he had gained weight and looked too chubby for his clothes. He stood back nervously when David Munir, the mathematics teacher delegated to look after his special care, did his best to introduce him informally to the other pupils. That night, after an uncomfortable evening meal, no doubt of lamentable quality compared with the Buckingham Palace cuisine, he learned his first lesson in the radical democracy of school by having to clean and polish his shoes.

He wore a blue cap when out walking, a gray school uniform, and at times a blue blazer. He was almost too immaculate for a schoolboy, his fingernails trimmed whereas others' were either clumsily cut or actually dirty, and he earned some ragging because of his too-meticulous folding of his clothes in the basket placed under his bed.

Each morning, the boys were wakened with cries of "Rise and shine!" at seven-fifteen, had to run into an echoing, spartan shower room, dress hastily but neatly, and then be inspected from head to foot by that imperious figure of all British prep schools, the white-starched uniformed personage known as Matron.

The heir to the throne had to make his own bed, clean the classrooms, sweep the floors, attend drill on an icy playground, get covered in mud on rainy days on the football field, trudge out on endless Sunday afternoon walks, fight to hold his own in slipper fights or fistfights, and endure the combination of awestruck respect and threatening rebelliousness inevitable in schoolchildren of that age. Again, his averageness helped, and his lack of brilliance or neurosis ensured that at least he could survive in that particular little jungle. Looming ahead of him was the supreme challenge of the Common Entrance Examination, which would allow him, if that were thought desirable, to progress to public school. But his lack of mathematics was again a stumbling block.

Meanwhile, Princess Margaret was still further cementing her bonds with Antony Armstrong-Jones. He had quite ceased to see his former flame Jacqueline Chan, and devoted much of his spare time to the Princess. She was able to disguise herself successfully, dodging reporters in scarf and simple overcoat as she made her way by Austin Mini to Armstrong-Jones's lair on the Thames. He visited Buckingham Palace and Windsor Castle, where the Queen received him warmly; Philip, with whom he had little in common, was at least polite. And the Queen Mother still romantically fostered the affair.

16
***

WHEN THE ROYAL COUPLE was at Windsor Castle, they followed the practice of attending polo matches at Smiths Lawn, also used for many years as an airstrip. Philip still was captain of the home team, which combated vigorously with visitors.

If the weather was good, the matches were played on the number-one pitch, and if it was raining, on the number-two pitch, which did not tend to flood or grow muddy, threatening the horses and riders.

The number-one pitch was flanked by the Royal Enclosure, and the number-two pitch had a large marquee, with a private royal section situated behind the spectator seats. It would take very violent weather conditions for these popular events to be canceled.

The Queen and Prince Philip drove themselves to the polo ground. Philip drove a station wagon, the Queen her favorite Rover. Oddly, instead of changing into polo gear at the Castle, Prince Philip was seen changing, quite uncomfortably, in his automobile, sitting sideways, the door thrown open, pulling his breeches on. Then he stood up to fasten the belt.

The Queen drove her car quite fast to the back of the tent on wet days. The Queen Mother was seen seated beside her, with a tartan rug rolled up in her arms, along with various magazines. The Queen pulled up sharply, jumped out of the Rover, walked briskly up to a white-coated attendant, and asked about the pitch and whether the rain had damaged the grass or would threaten the horses. The Queen Mother was left behind to get out of the car and make her way to her daughter, and thence to the spectator seats.

On one occasion, the passenger door refused to open; the

Queen Mother called out for assistance. The Queen heard her, but since she could scarcely be seen wrenching a door open herself, she ordered a young attendant to help. He climbed into the car over the back seat and tried to push the door open. It wouldn't budge. The Queen rushed to the car, flung open the driver's door, and stretched across the Queen Mother's lap, furiously trying to open the door herself. The Queen finally gave up and told her mother that she would have to force herself over the gears and get out by the driver's door. With her rug and papers, the Queen Mother, disheveled and drastically unqueenly, most awkwardly squeezed her way out. But as she stood up, she smoothed down her dress, waved and smiled, and walked, seemingly unruffled, to the royal section. And all of this in rain.

Though not mentioned by the press, and observed only by a handful of staff and a small knot of determined royal watchers (fans who followed the monarchs everywhere), episodes like this were talked about and deeply endeared mother and daughter to the public. They were so "human," so unlike the allegedly frosty and supercilious aristocratic class of England: they were more like middle-class people, simple, accident-prone, capable of clumsiness and absentmindedness like anybody else. Without calculation, the two Queens were so much part of their people that they were indivisible. It was in those years, and in the 1960s, before the IRA and other terrorists cut them off to a great extent from the public, and surrounded them with security, that they achieved their greatest and most deserved popularity.

The public, led by the press, eagerly followed every royal action. The behavior of the Queen's corgi dogs was endlessly fascinating to the royal watchers. One temperamental animal would be greeted with laughs by the Queen, even when he was most poorly behaved, and had to be tied on a tight leash to the leg of her canvas chair at polo matches. The Queen would simply address the dog quietly, as though addressing a human being, but firmly, with the words "Shut up!"

After each chukka, the Queen would rise and ask the royal watchers if they would join her in leveling out the turf of the polo pitch by tramping on it in unison. She was very considerate to her fans. When one of them asked if he could take a picture of her, instead of reacting adversely, as Prince Philip would have done, she said, sweetly, "If my detective sees your camera, he will confiscate it. So be quick!'' She posed for the shot, adjusting the corgi's collar deliberately to assist the photographer.

There was an episode when a woman walked her poodle at the other end of the pitch. The Queen's obstreperous corgi noticed the dog and suddenly sprang out toward it, dragging the Queen on the leash. She was forced to run with the animal, so powerful was its headlong movement. The terrified poodle began whimpering, and its mistress frantically picked him up to get him out of the way. The woman was astonished when she saw the Queen, who by now was in danger of falling forward. The Queen, to the woman's amazement, told her the incident was not her fault, and in fact it was the corgi's. Narrowly avoiding a dog fight, the Queen pulled the corgi away and slapped it.

On one occasion, Prince Philip's team won the match. When Philip walked up to her to receive the silver cup, she was about to hand it to him when it refused to come loose from the base. She wrestled with it vigorously, and at last the base fell off the table. The Queen and her husband bent down to pick it up and banged their heads together. Everyone burst out laughing. The Queen insisted the team celebrate with champagne in the area behind the tent; then she came out to chat with the royal watchers.

Once, when tea was being served, a footman pushed a button too hard, lifting up a wooden flap on the side of a trolley carrying cakes and sandwiches, and a cream *gâteau* went spinning onto the monarch's bosom. While Prince Philip was driving the Queen near Windsor, he accidentally hit a small automobile. This took place outside a modest pub. The publican's wife ran out to yank the passengers free, and to her astonishment found herself dragging the Queen. The other car's owner was fined.

On one occasion, the Queen Mother arrived at an officers' dance, and was introduced to a young man by the commanding officer. She asked the youth to dance with her; no one could make such a request of a royal. Halfway around the floor, the Queen Mother noticed a friend and asked her partner to wait for her while she went to make her greetings. At that moment, the Queen arrived, and the commanding officer signaled to the youth and introduced him to the Queen. She requested that he dance with her. He could not explain he was still theoretically the Queen Mother's partner, and embarked on a waltz. As the Queen and the young man spun around the floor, the Queen Mother shouted out, "Snob!" to the Queen's partner. Such informal behavior was pleasantly typical of these private occasions.

It was in July 1958, shortly before she was due to go to Balmoral for the summer holidays, that the Queen fell ill of a sinus problem. She was compelled to cancel the balance of a Scottish tour, following a brave descent down a colliery at Rothes, in order to make her way back to Buckingham Palace to see her physicians. Refusing typically to change previous arrangements, according to royal protocol, Philip left her for an official visit to Belgium. He toured Wales, opened the British Empire Games, went to the Scilly Isles, and his well-remembered Royal Naval College at Dartmouth, and to the other colleges at Plymouth and Portsmouth, all during the Queen's illness, which was not relieved until the very end of July. She underwent surgery in the Bühl Suite, and was in pain with a high fever. Philip at last returned to London to take investitures of certain honors in her place. Princess Margaret was in Canada.

Meanwhile, the rumors of Philip refused to die down. That summer, the tabloid papers were describing the continuing meetings of the Thursday Club, now taking place on Mondays, and moved to Kensington. It was noted that Lieutenant Commander Michael Parker, in the wake of his dismissal or resignation the year before, was present at the Monday Club gatherings, and there were murmurings about revealing photographs which might prove distressing to the royal family if they were to be made public.

And all through that summer of the Queen's physical distress, there were continuing crises on the international scene.

Yet, under Macmillan, there were indications of a slow but sure improvement in the British economy and the British morale. The Queen shared increasingly the Prime Minister's warm relationship with Eisenhower, his feeling that only a trans-Atlantic brotherhood would ensure future security for Great Britain. The Queen corresponded happily with the American President, sometimes in her own bold and striking handwriting, sending him recipes and notes of affection and admiration. The arguments over the hydrogen bomb went on repeatedly; the Liberal party demanded that the bomb be abandoned unilaterally, and threatened, along with the Labor party, serious action in the rank and file if there were no improvement in legislation against the racist stance of the government. Further, there was disagreement over the refusal to improve conditions following the notorious Notting Hill riots in London at the beginning of September, as three thousand infuriated whites attacked black residents with sticks and gasoline bombs.

Against such troubles could be set successes: the building of Britain's second atomic power station, supplying plutonium for military purposes, and the triumph of launching commercial jet airplane service for the first time across the Atlantic. Never before had Americans read British newspapers the morning after they were published, nor had British readers been able to pick up the *New York Times* or the *Washington Post* within an identical time frame. The Queen and Prince Philip could note with pleasure that the Black Knight, Britain's pioneer ballistic rocket, was spectacularly fired from Woomera, Australia, on September 7, and that there was a very successful H-bomb test in the central Pacific four days later. Macmillan remained generally popular, his ''never-had-it-so-good'' optimism more or less improving the bruised morale of the post-war nation. As the 1950s neared their end, the Queen's health was improved, but it was decided that she would not accompany Prince Philip on his extensive world tour in January 1959, and a careful examination of her engagements at the time shows a quite drastic reduction. She was still not in the condition of health she had been in at her best.

Macmillan sought to cap his successful unification of British-American alliances with a serious effort to improve relations with the Soviet Union. He was in Moscow in the last week of February and the first few days of March, but despite the slow thawing of his hosts' attitudes toward him, he was unable to bring about a rapprochement on the issue of Berlin and West Germany. A considerable feat was brought off in easing the Cold War: it was agreed, following a British trade mission in May, that Britain would import Soviet automobiles, musical instruments, and toys, and that the Soviets would import British trucks, buses, textiles, and knitwear. Macmillan worked very hard on improving relations with President Charles de Gaulle in France. By May 30, Britain had taken off 80 percent of total restrictions on American goods, and soon virtually all dollar restrictions would be removed. Macmillan was able to announce that the country could afford to repay the Export-Import Bank's 250-million-dollar loan of 1957.

Philip was in India, helping to improve relations with that perpetually troubled nation, in Pakistan, Burma, Singapore, and Borneo, aboard the royal yacht *Britannia* or on jets which he often piloted himself. The tour took two and a half months and covered thirty-six thousand miles, continuing via Guadalcanal, the Solomon Islands, Panama, and the Caribbean, ending on May 1. His behavior had become increasingly rude as he finally lost all patience with the press. He forbade any newspaperman aboard the yacht or on his private jet. If they came too close on an outboard motorboat or launch, he shouted at them. When photographers turned up *en masse* at his meeting with Prime Minister Nehru in New Delhi, he snapped, "Who are all these damned people? I thought there was supposed to be a film shortage in India!"

When he toured the Taj Mahal, he snarled at a reporter, "Get on with your bloody business and stop talking!" At a horse show in Lahore, a Pakistani photographer slipped off a flag-pole, from which he was trying to get a close shot, and tumbled to the ground. Philip screamed, "I hope to God he breaks his bloody neck!"

Several Indian newspapers remembered an earlier occasion in Gibraltar when, in a direct reference to the monkeys that inhabited that port, he had screamed, "Which are the press and which are the bloody apes?" He repeatedly demanded that various journalists and cameramen "bugger off." The Queen no doubt found this behavior unfortunate (though in private the Queen would laugh easily at his bad language), nor could she have been happy with the continuing rumors of romantic encounters with women.

The columnist Rex North set the cat among the pigeons when he wrote, addressing the Queen directly, and referring to Prince Philip's tour, "You and the Duke are symbols of happy family life. It is wrong that duty should keep you apart for weeks and months on end."

He advised the Queen to "cut out pomp, garden parties, meetings with local bigwigs, banquets, dull speeches." He added, "Let me be frank. Occasionally I have seen you abroad looking taut, tense and tight-lipped . . . Get more fun out of life. Be yourself."

Such views, with their scarcely veiled implications of a royal separation, were shared by many in the somewhat hostile and irritated offices of Fleet Street. The continuing appeal by Commander Colville for the press to "go easy" on the royal family, and the annoyance many felt at Prince Philip's aggressive behavior, set the tone for an awkward relationship that would deteriorate quite rapidly and bring about a crisis in the not-too-distant future.

Antony Armstrong-Jones had been in New York for a fourteen-page layout for *Vogue* magazine; he took striking photographs of Manhattan. He spent the early new year in Ireland, where Margaret visited him at Birr Castle. At Harewood House, he jived energetically with Margaret at a party given by the Earl and Countess of Harewood. In April, Margaret accompanied the Queen Mother to Italy for a brief vacation, and then plucked up her courage to tell her sister and brother-in-law that she had grown deeply fond of Armstrong-Jones; it was obvious the matter could no longer be written off as a lighthearted romance. The photographs he took of Margaret at Royal Lodge, Windsor, late that spring, were alive with the sensitivity and warmth of a man who was already very much in love. They would be released officially when the Princess reached her twenty-ninth birthday.

Like Townsend before him, Armstrong-Jones spent a great deal of time at Clarence House, where he and the Queen Mother still maintained an intense rapport, sharing the same sense of humor, enjoying many of the same things. Armstrong-Jones was careful not to overload the conversation with too many intellectual references. He still got along quite well with Philip, despite the drastic differences between them in temperament, and the fact that they had very little in common. He was sufficiently sensitive and adroit to deal with Philip's blunt and sometimes tasteless humors.

Amazingly, the press remained muffled or oblivious, scarcely ever indicating the fact that the Princess and Armstrong-Jones were virtually inseparable, apart from her public engagements, when his presence would have attracted far too many unfavorable comments. According to all reliable sources, Peter Townsend had last seen Princess Margaret in March 1959. But in fact, as exhaustively described by her footman, David-John Payne, he did return again to Clarence

House that summer.[1] It was a painful meeting; the Princess was still in love with Townsend. She was notably tense and highstrung as she asked Payne to make sure that tea was served at exactly 4:30 P.M., and would include the China tea that Townsend especially liked, thinly sliced sandwiches, and small cream cakes. When Townsend's car rolled through the gate, and he rang the doorbell, the Princess broke protocol by not allowing her mother to be the first to greet the guest; though the Queen Mother gripped her arm very tight, she broke free, forcibly and sharply, and ran up to Townsend, putting her hands on his shoulders and drawing him to her. This was unheard of in front of servants. She crushed herself against him; he ran his hands down her; even when at last she stood back, and the Queen Mother took his hand, she devoured Townsend with her eyes.

The tea lasted barely thirty minutes. The bell for the footman rang; Margaret walked out with Townsend, again breaking protocol by preceding the Queen Mother. She was flushed, visibly depressed, her eyes were damp with tears. In the entrance hall, Townsend gave a profound and painful sigh as he kissed the Queen Mother in farewell on both cheeks; then he raised Princess Margaret up to him and embraced her with great tenderness, his eyes boring deeply into hers. Now, the Princess could not restrain her weeping; she did not utter a word, and nor did he. He walked down to his car; he turned to look at the woman he loved and at her mother as they stood in the doorway. Then he was gone.

That night, the Princess could eat no dinner. At 9:30 P.M. she was driven to Buckingham Palace for a long and heartfelt talk with her sister. She never saw Peter Townsend again.

In anguish, Princess Margaret embarked on a heavy social life, attending a banquet for the Shah of Persia, presenting regimental colors to the Royal Highland Fusiliers, attending balls and film premieres, touring Portugal and the Channel Islands. As the Queen and Prince Philip took off for an extensive Canadian visit that summer, thoughts of her sister's future were undoubtedly uppermost in the Queen's mind.

Three days before their departure for Canada, the Queen

---

1. Payne said of his cell-like room at Clarence House that the bed was so small his legs hung over it; he had to share it with three dogs, which grunted and snored all night, keeping him miserably awake.

discovered that she was pregnant. There seems some evidence that the first two of her pregnancies were planned; this one emphatically was not. Prince Philip urged his wife to discontinue the visit, because of its exceptional arduousness, but she categorically refused to listen. As always, she took with her a seamstress who could assist her dresser should she begin to gain weight.

Though the heat was severe during the tour, the Queen at first showed no signs of faltering, as she unhesitatingly trudged through factories and even descended an iron mine; she was constantly in consultation with her physician, Surgeon-Captain Steele-Perkins. But she was visibly worn out, her makeup threatened by perspiration, as she continued through fourteen-hour days in Toronto, battled a storm at Port Arthur, and survived an exhausting thirteen hours in Chicago, to which she sailed across Lake Michigan aboard the royal yacht *Britannia*. The couple negotiated 2,300 feet of carpet at the International Trade Fair, explored the Art Institute and Museum of Science and Industry, and attended a luncheon given by Mayor Richard Daley for forty mayors and seven state governors. She opened the St. Lawrence Seaway, entertaining President and Mrs. Eisenhower aboard her yacht. Even now, very few knew she was pregnant; but the Queen could no longer keep it an absolute secret, and she was unable to resist confiding in Mamie Eisenhower, of whom she was deeply fond. Mamie was overjoyed, and for a long time the two women discussed baby clothes.

At Nanaimo, where an Indian tribe appointed her their Princess, the Queen at last began to crumble. She was forced to curtail a trip to the Yukon. She flatly refused to discontinue the visit, and doggedly went on, with only one day in bed. At the end of the tour, she was in a severe state of exhaustion. Her physician insisted she fly to London at once for a checkup.

In July, unnoted by Court Circular or press, the Queen Mother gave a dinner for the High Commissioner for Rhodesia; it was the first ceremonial occasion in which Antony Armstrong-Jones was invited to Clarence House, and he arrived with Princess Alexandra of Kent; David-John Payne noted how he drank in with pleasure the sumptuous gold and cream decor, the sights of a row of liveried flunkies, the exquisite period china, the gold curtains; but above all, how, as he talked softly and affectionately to Alexandra, his eyes never left Margaret's.

The Queen was at Balmoral when the announcement of her expected baby occurred. Armstrong-Jones was staying with the Queen Mother in her beloved Castle of Mey, also in Scotland. Immediately the press was alerted, huge crowds of newspapermen and royal watchers descended on Balmoral, so completely surrounding the local church that the Sunday services took place in the Castle instead. Yet, despite the most careful surveillance, no one was able to take a picture of Margaret with Armstrong-Jones, and it is possible, though not on record, that the Queen personally asked newspaper owners not to publish anything at the time, until the couple was ready; the ghastly events surrounding Townsend must not be repeated in any circumstances. Margaret's twenty-ninth birthday, in August, was held under locked doors at the Castle. That evening, the Queen, as was her custom, for she very seldom went to public film performances, was putting on a film for a strictly controlled circle of royal guests: *The Bridal Path,* starring the popular British comedian George Cole. Just before the screening, the Princess advised her mother, sister, and the rest of the family that she had accepted Armstrong-Jones's proposal. They were delighted, and within minutes agreed that there would be no announcement of an engagement until the following spring. Even now, the press, either by accident or common consent, was kept firmly in the dark.

It was a happy August at Balmoral, a new baby on the way and the Princess at last able to find personal happiness. Even the heavy, unseasonal rain could not dampen the family's buoyant spirits. The Queen announced that she would not be opening Parliament that fall.

In October, Princess Margaret and Armstrong-Jones were constantly at Clarence House together; they would sit night after night in the private cinema theater, puffing out clouds of smoke. Even when a photographic assignment drew him away, he would send a letter by messenger or telephone two or three times. He would arrive there in the early evening with large brown carrier bags, stuffed with smoked salmon, steaks, wine; she would peek inside as he told her, to her delight, what they would be picnicking on; then he would drive her to his studio in Pimlico Road for the evening; she would return in the small hours. A police guard accompanied them always; they were used to that.

There were two jolts that season: first, the Princess learned that Lady Pamela Mountbatten was going to marry the interior decorator David Hicks. Margaret was furious, complaining loudly at the lunch and dinner table, though nobody knew what she had against him. Second, and more important, in September, she read in the evening newspapers that Peter Townsend was engaged to be married. She stared unbelieving at the paper; she flung it to the floor, and cup and saucer followed it; she stared angrily and silently into the fire. Then she picked up her phone and called her close friend and former flame Billy Wallace and insisted they go out on the town. They did not return until 8 A.M., laughing loudly.

In a state of shock, the Princess—despite her feelings for Armstrong-Jones—was still not over Townsend, and never would be. She became testy, screaming at a footman when he dropped a glass decanter, lingering endlessly in her bath, scrubbing dogs which weren't supposed to be scrubbed; trying to relax from stress, sometimes as much as an hour and a half at a time, after her normal waking up time of 11:30 A.M. She would issue streams of instructions to her maid, Ruby, sister of Bobo MacDonald, whom she had retained since babyhood, then take lunch with the Queen Mother, pouring out wickedly accurate and scandalous stories about society figures while the various guests stared at each other significantly. After lunch, she spent two hours and more with her secret diary, locking it afterward with a tiny key; she also pasted up her photographic album; like the Queen, she shared an enthusiasm for taking snapshots, another link to Armstrong-Jones.

Suffering from Townsend's impending plans, she threw caution to the winds and spent long weekends with Armstrong-Jones at Royal Lodge, Windsor; only when the Queen was coming to dinner would he disappear. At night, they would swim in the pool—it was a mysteriously hot, humid fall—and then, she in a bikini, he in tiny shorts, summon the footman for 5 A.M. drinks. They indulged in strange fetishistic games: he would wear her dresses, and elaborate party hats, squeezing his feet into sandals when her high-heeled shoes would not fit; she would wear his suits and ties and hat; then they would photograph each other. She shot him wearing a period gown, and also took a photograph of him dressed as a child; he had her posing in his tuxedo, brandishing a cigar.

Prince Charles was improving steadily at school. He was learning the piano, singing in the school choir, with a fine, steady soprano voice, appearing in plays, in which, like his mother and aunt, he showed considerable flair; in February 1960 he would appear in the play *The Last Baron,* as the hunchbacked Duke of Gloucester, who was to become the sinister, implacable King Richard III; he copied Sir Laurence Olivier's unforgettable playing of the role, though, according to Dermot Morrah, he was compelled to call for the removal of unsuitable lines, including "and soon may I ascend the throne."

To his father's pleasure, he did reasonably well at soccer and rugby football, but he was something of a flop at cricket. There was always a commotion at the school, no matter how the Queen tried to avoid it, when she arrived, alone, driving her Rover, swapping her comfortable driving shoes for more elegant pumps as she climbed out, scarfed and smiling, like any other mother. Again, the press was considerate in failing to take pictures of the young Prince. But Detective Donald Green was always present in case of danger from cranks or from the Irish Republican Army.

Princess Anne remained as boisterous, energetic, and pugnacious as ever. She was especially fond of Margaret, who, in so many ways, she resembled. She took to sailing as vigorously as her father, whom she also resembled, far more than Charles. And, according to a newspaper report, while sailing with Prince Michael of Kent, she ordered him away from the wheel and turned herself into a temporary captain of his oceangoing yacht. She went rock-climbing, much to the dismay of the Queen, who forbade any further adventures of this kind, and, also to the Queen's astonishment, insisted on learning to drive a car; her father actually taught her to drive at Windsor before she was ten.

She shared her mother's passion for horse racing. In the saddle from (it is claimed) the age of three, she was a proficient rider by 1959. When she heard that her mother was to have another child, she insisted it be a Prince and would not consider any other possibility. Anne became so violently restless and nervous during the pregnancy it was virtually impossible to control her. Her manic energy, questionable manners, and drastic dartings about recalled her mother's behavior at the same age. She would be extremely "royal," and had to be reminded continuously to behave properly, according to the deliberately fostered middle-class image of the family as a whole.

At her age, she was probably bored by her aunt's and Armstrong-Jones's romance, but the thought of a royal wedding had her in a tizzy. It seemed that her whole life was a series of excitements, alarums and excursions, upheavals and thrills.

At the next election, Harold Macmillan achieved victory with polish and ease; it was the third consecutive triumph for the Conservative party. The Queen seemed comfortable with Macmillan's return to office. She still enjoyed the Tuesday late-afternoon audiences, Macmillan following the custom of submitting to the monarch in advance the various matters he felt should be discussed; in addition to placing before her the important political issues of the moment, he had discovered in her a mutual interest in the relationship between church and state, never neglecting her position as supreme governor of the Church of England, never pressing her to the edge of her prerogatives, and always remembering that she had a great sense of humor, a healthy enjoyment of discussing persons and positions, and a relish in her royal stature that only the ignorant would disbelieve in view of her apparent shyness and modesty. A profound royalist, the Prime Minister was also a wit, and the Queen appreciated that as much as anything else. But it would be unwise to say that she was a friend of Macmillan's. She would have stepped beyond the bounds of her particular role if she had embraced him as more than a satisfactory acquaintance. Friendliness rather than friendship was what she correctly extended to her Prime Ministers and Cabinets.

In February 1960, shortly after her return from Sandringham, and with her child only a few days from being born, the Queen was troubled that her husband did not accompany her but stayed behind for shooting and fishing. The press nagged away at the Prince's apparent indifference toward his wife. And yet, on February 8, she fulfilled one of his major ambitions, shared by his uncle Louis Mountbatten, that the name Mountbatten-Windsor would be used by her descendants other than those entitled to the style and title of Royal Highness and Prince or Princess in the future; it was added, however, that she would herself, and her son, daughter, and next child, retain the name of Windsor alone.

The declaration of her will and pleasure was made at a meeting of the Privy Council; she had first discussed the matter with Macmillan before he was swallowed up in preparations for his trip to Africa. She also made sure that the Commonwealth Prime Ministers and Governors-General were advised. What her edict meant was that the grandchildren of the new child, if a boy, would be called Mountbatten-Windsor; it was a way of perpetuating her husband's family name into the very distant future. This was the second substantial revision of the existing arrangements for the titling and naming of heirs: the last major move had been that of King George VI in Letters Patent under the Great Seal of October 22, 1948, whereby his grandchildren would become Princes or Princesses, normally denied to all except first-generation royal children. There was the additional oddity that Mountbatten was an invented name, used, as we know, to replace Battenberg, with its unfortunate reminder of the family's German connections. Parliamentary approval was not required for the alteration.

There was considerable rejoicing among Philip's questionable German family members that they were now even more concretely connected to the British royal line. The town of Battenberg celebrated, the burgomaster calling for a local holiday and forwarding gifts to the Queen in gratitude. On February 19, 1960, the Queen gave birth to a second son, Prince Andrew. There were no medical complications; the nation celebrated, though not with the unbridled ecstasy that had greeted the birth of the two Princesses. The child was robust and healthy. The Queen recovered with considerable swiftness, astonishing her doctors with her vibrant energy and enthusiasm; she was not yet thirty-four. Antony Armstrong-Jones took impressive photographs. The atmosphere at Buckingham Palace was bustling, excitable, and full of rejoicing. The occasion was shadowed only by the sudden death of Countess Mountbatten in Borneo. The Queen was unable to attend the memorial service, coming as it did so soon after Andrew's birth.

It was announced that the marriage of Margaret and Antony Armstrong-Jones would also take place at Westminster Abbey, on May 6. The Duke of Edinburgh would give the bride away, and the ceremony would be presided over by the Archbishop of Canterbury, Dr. Geoffrey Fisher.

The Queen made the announcement to Macmillan, at his first audience with her since February 19. She chose the date to coincide with the Commonwealth Prime Ministers' Conference, a clever example of public relations, designed to help sustain that body of nations which was dearest to her heart. Another reason for the choice was that May was the social season, when most of the debutantes would emerge at balls and festive dinners, and many of the "County" or landed gentry would be in London. There was a good deal of mulling over the possibility of the wedding being televised by BBC and ITV, but, at that time, no decision was reached; permission was slow in coming.

Norman Hartnell was again hard at work. He surpassed his wedding dress for the Queen by following its elaborate, fairy-tale luxuriousness with a dress of ethereal, virginal purity and simplicity. He wanted to provide the Princess, who was at the height of her beauty, with an exquisitely simple and cloud-like garment, suggestive of the portraits of angels in medieval paintings.

She proved to be a good judge of what was best for her, and worked closely with Hartnell, settling finally on the most magical of the designs. Because she was barely five feet tall, the white clothing and veil and vertical panelings were to give an illusion of taller stature. Hartnell turned over most of his salon to designing the clothes for the bridesmaids—theoretical at the present, since they were not immediately selected. However, to her bouncing delight, Princess Anne was informed that she would now make her second appearance as bridesmaid; the first had been at the January wedding of Mountbatten's daughter, Lady Pamela, to David Hicks. Victor Stiebel, noted for his elegant work and made famous by, among others, Vivien Leigh, would design the trousseau. The *Britannia* was refitted at a cost of $70,000 for the honeymoon.

It was decided that the royal couple would live eventually in the grace-and-favor apartments known as Number Ten, on the north side of Kensington Palace, near the State rooms; the former occupant had been Lord Carisbrooke, who had died in 1959. There were ten rooms in the apartment, with well-equipped quarters for the servants. But the residence was not particularly large, no bigger than that occupied by the Duchess of Kent. It was to be redone at vast expense and to the usual chorus of disapproval from the Labor party members.

By 8 P.M. on the wedding eve, Buckingham Palace was surrounded by a vast crowd of people. Up to the last minute, Princess Margaret was in a dither of fittings and refittings of her dress, made of thirty yards of white silk organza, devoid of sewn jewels, with a plain, tight bodice, and a twelve-panel crinoline skirt drifting into an exquisite, very long white train. The veil was also of white silk organza. Her sister was on hand every minute to give advice. Prince Charles and Princess Anne darted about. The Queen and Queen Mother were in a state of near rapture, seeing the solution at last to Margaret's prolonged emotional problems. Meanwhile, Armstrong-Jones had moved into Buckingham Palace on the day the engagement was announced; he told almost nobody in his circle of friends. He made sure there were to be no close-ups of the Queen during the telecast. Despite severe back pain, an inheritance from an early bout with infantile paralysis, Armstrong-Jones showed no sign of strain.

At dawn on May 6, the sky was a delicate, pale blue, and the sun shone brightly on the great crowds along the Mall, Whitehall, and the Horse Guards' Parade. Public address systems blared the popular songs "June Is Busting Out All Over," "So in Love," and "Once in a While." The younger crowd, irritated by these conventional standards, began yelling out Elvis Presley's "Jailhouse Rock." One enterprising girl had brought an enormous balloon with the words "Dear Mum, this is us," inscribed on it, along with her name, so that her family could see her on television.

The procession took place in the late morning, beginning with a stream of coaches. Princess Anne and her seven accompanying bridesmaids were especially well received. Armstrong-Jones and his best man Roger Gilliatt followed, then the Queen and Queen Mother, with Prince Charles seated opposite them. Prince Philip assisted Margaret into the fairy-tale glass coach as thousands of children waved Union Jacks. In her romantic gown and diamond tiara, her veil tossed lightly by the breeze, Princess Margaret had never looked more beautiful. The arches of red and pink roses and banners, with the initials of the couple inscribed in crimson, above the Mall, shone in the light over the dash and glitter of the Household

Cavalry. At every clip-clop of the Windsor gray horses, the crowd cheered and the Princess waved.

The Abbey was filled with over two thousand spectators, few of whom would see the ceremony itself. The building was lit by immense arc lights to make televising possible. This dazzling blaze of illumination overcame the gentle shimmer of candlelight from the massive candelabras; everywhere there were flowers: myrtle, daffodils, and lilies. A special murmur greeted the arrival of the hunched but determined Sir Winston Churchill, dressed on this occasion in sober gray. The gentlemen of arms took their places in scarlet and plumed helmets. Armstrong-Jones stood below the sacrarium. Handel's "Overture to Arminius" rang out from the organ, followed by a trumpet voluntary. At that moment, Margaret appeared at the west door, leaning on Prince Philip's arm. The hymn, "Christ Is Made the Sure Foundation," burst from the choir as the bride joined her husband in place. The Queen looked surprisingly somber, almost displeased; she was unwell. The Queen Mother gave a tender hint of a smile. Princess Anne and the other child attendants behaved impeccably, Anne especially acting with surprising gravity as she received the bouquet and took her place with it. She stood daintily and primly behind the bride as the couple walked slowly to the altar.

The Dean of Westminster read the introduction from the 1928 prayer book. The Archbishop of Canterbury, in his cope and miter, asked the questions calling for the exchange of vows, using the 1662 prayer book form, requiring, as arranged by the couple, the bride's obedience. The couple both responded, "I will," unhesitatingly and strongly. The only flaw in the ceremony was that, in a moment of nervousness, Princess Margaret spoke the words "for better or for worse," before she was supposed to, temporarily unsettling the archbishop. She had memorized the response so well she had preceded the question.

Armstrong-Jones placed the band of Welsh gold on his bride's fourth left-hand finger, and the couple was blessed. They then proceeded to the high altar steps, and Psalm 121 ("I will lift up mine eyes unto the hills") and the hymn "Immortal, Invisible, God Only Wise" were sung. The beatitudes were included. The national anthem followed, and the registers signed. This time there was ink in the inkwells.

Again, the trumpets sounded and the wedding procession

moved down the sanctuary along the nave, where the more than twenty-five hundred people rose from their golden chairs.

The couple rode back along the processional route together in the glass coach. When they appeared with the royal family on the Buckingham Palace balcony, "We want Margaret!" echoed from thousands through the brilliant sunlit air. Even the police began to laugh happily as they at last allowed the people to swarm up to the railings fronting the Palace yard. The wedding breakfast in the white-and-gold supper room was a tremendous occasion, lit by five crystal chandeliers; 120 guests attended, to the accompaniment of the Grenadier Guards' string band. Each of the bridesmaids was given a gold traveling clock in a red leather case.

Among the wedding gifts were a Rolls-Royce Silver Cloud automobile, fifteen hundred daisies creating a floral tribute in the form of the letter M; superb coromandel screens; a 175-piece crystal service, and mountains of silver, glassware, and gems.

So dense were the crowds as the couple made their way to the *Britannia,* moored on the River Thames, as the people cried, "Good luck!" and "God bless you!" they were actually delayed in their progress, forced to stop several times when dozens fainted; 1,215 people in all collapsed that day. Margaret was dressed in pale yellow silk shantung; as she and her husband stepped out onto Battle Bridge Tier Wharf and went aboard the royal barge, there was a chorus of ship sirens, church bells, whistles, and hooters. As the yacht slowly moved down the river, people ran along the embankments, waving ecstatically, and hundreds of bells rang out across London.

17

***

WITH HER NEW COAT of blue paint and red water line, the *Britannia* made a brave sight, steaming at an average of twenty knots per hour, her pennants fluttering in the breeze, more than 260 crew engaged to tend to the honeymooners' every possible wish. Except for their immediate attendants, there were no other passengers. The press had been asked to respect their privacy as they landed on various islands, including Mustique, as guests of its owners the Colin Tennants, who had given them a plot of land on which to build a house, Trinidad, and Tobago. They enjoyed perfect weather, and they swam in such paradisal spots as the Buccoo Reef off Tobago, with its underwater gardens of marine flowers and its exquisitely multicolored fish. Everywhere they went, continuing to Grenada and Jamaica, they were greeted by large and excited crowds. In St. John's, Antigua, some excitement was added to the trip: three earthquakes rippled through the blue sea surrounding the island, causing the *Britannia* to rock and tremble violently. Unfazed, and mindful of royal protocol, the couple did not cancel their trip ashore by motor launch, but instead braved a violent sea to arrive in the midst of an ovation from the somewhat shaken Antiguans.

The couple returned on June 18. Meanwhile, there were tensions between the Queen and Prince Philip. At the Derby, the Queen, according to custom, left the royal box to go to the paddock. She indicated she would like her husband to accompany her, but, to her visible annoyance, he did not. He defiantly sipped champagne as she, unable to repress a royal frown, mingled with horses and jockeys. She was having a bad year at the track, without one winner in many weeks, and this race was no exception. When she sportingly applauded the winner, Prince Philip scowled gloomily.

Princess Margaret and Antony Armstrong-Jones moved into Kensington Palace in July. Their sumptuously furnished rooms, filled with priceless antiques, were a marvel of the decorator's art. Armstrong-Jones himself supervised the painting, and laid out a lavish display of flowers from Constance Spry to greet his wife when he carried her over the threshold. He had fixed the exact time of meeting her at the door, since both had pressing and unavoidable engagements that day. However, Margaret, not always ideally punctual by nature, arrived too early. Armstrong-Jones had not yet given her the key. Therefore, the Princess was compelled to ring the bell.

She asked if her husband had arrived. The staff informed her he also had come early and, not finding her there, had become most annoyed and driven back to Clarence House. Margaret told her butler, Thomas Cronin, to telephone Armstrong-Jones and tell him that the Princess had arrived, but would not enter the house until he had carried her over the threshold. He raced back and performed his husbandly duty.

Although the apartments were spacious by most people's standards, Margaret and her husband felt extremely cramped, due to the amount of furniture that crammed the rooms, the dozens of family photographs, and the necessity to house a full office staff. The couple talked of being the occupants of "a doll's house." So numerous were the wedding gifts, they had to be piled in the hallway, obstructing passage, and a great many had to be stored.

Noise was another problem. The pampered Princess complained to friends that she could hear the heavy steps of the servants in the rooms above her. There were further problems. Thomas Cronin, an imposing, portly figure in his impeccable suitings, had, like most British butlers, a very special role in the Royal Household. He was accustomed to engaging or firing staff, issuing instructions to the housekeeper, and maintaining specific disciplines within the home. Even when working for John Hay Whitney, U.S. Ambassador to the Court of St. James's, he had been allowed his peculiar privileges. However, Armstrong-Jones felt it necessary to assert himself in his own home. He overrode Cronin (the latter alleged), and made his life difficult. The two clashed violently when he called Armstrong-Jones "Mr. Jones," and was instructed by Princess Margaret to address him in the future as "sir." Cronin told Associated Press:

I was not allowed to employ my staff. I didn't pay them their wages, and many other matters were not left in my hands as they should have been. When I worked for Mr. Whitney, I had charge of thirty-seven employees, and that's the right way to run a household.

To my mind there is only one person to whom a new employee should be responsible—the butler. Otherwise there must be an unfortunate division of authority. The master of the house must recognize this.

Cronin was anxious to point out that Princess Margaret (who, of course, was totally experienced in the specific prerogatives of a royal butler) had never interfered with him or tried to usurp his duties, but he reported that she, also, clashed with the servants.

Cronin grumbled about a number of things. He could not get used to Armstrong-Jones invading the kitchen and the servants' quarters. He hated the fact that Armstrong-Jones went around in an unbuttoned leather jacket and jeans; that he approved his being paid seven pounds a week (about twenty-one dollars), and it was only with difficulties that he was raised to twelve pounds.

Cronin also complained (incorrectly) that he was not allowed to enter the drawing room without knocking first. He said that in his thirty years in service, he had never been issued such an instruction; he was told that only bedroom doors should be knocked on. Surprisingly, at least according to Cronin, Armstrong-Jones yielded in the matter and Cronin was permitted to enter the drawing room whenever he chose. One amusing event occurred during his residence. The Queen came on a brief visit. As she chatted with Princess Margaret, a storm broke outside the Palace. The time came for her to leave. Antony Armstrong-Jones grabbed an umbrella from the stand and opened it to shelter her as she walked to the royal car. It was so motheaten with age that it was about as protective as a sieve. Cronin wrote in a reminiscence, "It acted merely as a water distributor all over Her Majesty." "Really, Cronin, I must have that umbrella recovered," Princess Margaret said. The last straw came when Princess Margaret and Armstrong-Jones kept singing day and night, greatly distracting the oversensitive butler, grumbled loudly about the cost of the wine he had been sent to acquire, and complained bitterly when he refused to buy shelves for the wine cellar. Cronin packed up his things and left.

Armstrong-Jones was back in the news for acts of defiance, including turning up at the Royal Highland Games at Braemar in Scotland wearing trousers instead of a kilt. Following the euphoria of marriage to the woman he loved, and the happy and spectacular honeymoon, Armstrong-Jones suffered from having to escort Princess Margaret at every occasion, without being able to pursue his career as a leading photographer. He could not help but be fretful in private. He was held back from making independent public appearances or engagements. He wondered what kind of job he could get, and faced criticism that was not only vicious but totally unfounded, that he would soon obtain major photographic assignments through his wife's influence. He had, of course, already been able to obtain access to anyone he wanted because of his reputation. The Queen tried to mollify his restlessness. On one occasion, he spilled a drink on his trousers. Embarrassed, flustered, he went to see one of the Queen's maids in her room. She told him to take his trousers off and she would clean the stain. As he stood there in shirt and undershorts, the door flew open and the Queen stood in the doorway.

She looked him up and down, as the horrified, blushing Armstrong-Jones stood there undressed. "What happened?" the Queen asked. He told her, and she burst out laughing and disappeared.

The Princess and her husband were at Balmoral for the summer holidays. Again, Armstrong-Jones felt awkward, wondering what he would be doing for a living. There was much discussion of a peerage. But neither Margaret nor Armstrong-Jones was anxious for this to happen. It would have looked too much like buying the privilege through marriage.

Back in London, Princess Margaret liked to be up very late at night, partying, entertaining her old beaux and other guests until 4 A.M., with loud rock music played on the phonograph. Armstrong-Jones liked to retire by midnight, and, always concentrating on his health, would tire easily. This led to drastic arguments. The couple had to undertake official engagements, though not nearly as many as Prince Philip. The endless shaking of hands, smiling into boring officials' faces, and making meaningless remarks in praise of everything grated on Armstrong-Jones's intelligent, sensitive, and enlightened mind. He had perhaps rashly, but certainly decently, agreed to pay for certain minor expenses out of his royalties from photographs done before the wedding, and this proved to be a drain on his pocket. Royal funds were used to run the household.

In October, England came to the edge of finding itself without a monarch or a consort: the royal couple was in Germany following a visit to Denmark when two West German fighter planes, straying off course, flew within less than two thousand feet of the royal aircraft. Although the British and West German governments issued a joint statement that the Queen was not in danger, very few believed it.

It was a year crowded with events. On October 1, Nigeria, with its 34 million people, achieved independence. Soon, Sierra Leone would join the Commonwealth—a further indication of Great Britain's achievement in turning over the former Empire to its peoples without undue distress or bloodshed.

Conscription ended in November 1960; it had lasted without a break from 1939. This decision of the Prime Minister and War Ministry was reached because it was understood that the emphasis in the future would be upon missiles and nuclear submarines. Although Blue Streak, which was to have been the nation's major ballistic instrument, was no longer to be manufactured. October saw the launching of the first British nuclear underwater craft. The dominance of America in the national defense system remained a bone of contention. America had supplied four Thor missile squadrons; Polaris missiles were aboard U.S. submarines moored in Holy Loch on the River Clyde in Scotland.

Major strides were made in the opening up of religious boundaries. In late November, the Archbishop of Canterbury visited Turkey, obtaining many valuable connections with Islam, and then, after meetings with Jewish leaders in the Holy Land, broke all tradition by following the Queen Mother and Princess Margaret's earlier visit in a historic meeting with the Pope at the Vatican. No British church leader had met with the Supreme Pontiff since the Reformation. These powerfully forged links between different faiths can be seen as a desire to weld not only the military and material, but the spiritual forces of the West against the Soviet Union. With the increase in the

Cold War, following the period of moderate thaw, Khrushchev saw these moves for what they were, while himself sustaining a pretense that the U.S.S.R. was the sole supporter of peace in the new decade, and that American capitalism and imperialism were the only serious blocks to satisfactory resolutions of international conflicts.

The year had brought the death of Prince Philip's brother-in-law, Prince Gottfried von Hohenlohe-Langenburg, whose role in the German Army in World War II continued to be overlooked by supporters of the British royal family. He had been head of the house of Hohenlohe since 1953, when his father had died.

The royals spent Christmas at Sandringham, Antony Armstrong-Jones not too comfortably in their midst. He had been more fretful than ever, consoled only by the fact that his *avant garde* design of the new aviary at the London Zoo in Regent's Park had been accepted. The peculiarity of his position can be illustrated by the fact that he had decided to fly with Princess Margaret to Birr Castle in Ireland for the New Year's holiday on economy-class tickets, but, to his embarrassment, the airline instead converted the first-class section into the couple's private living room. He was appalled to find that the entire rest of the plane had been booked by members of the press. The result was an unpleasant journey, a struggle against a tide of question-firing reporters and brutal cameramen.

The Queen was busy throughout the Christmas season preparing for a tour of India, Pakistan, Nepal, and Iran. As she and Prince Philip arrived in New Delhi on January 23, it was announced that they would be guests of the Maharajah of Jaipur at his hunting lodge. Immediately, animal lovers began to protest loudly.

It turned out that the famous wild-game hunter Col. Keshari Singh had done his utmost to arrange for the royal couple to attend the shooting of a number of tigers. On the first day of their arrival, the royal couple were involved in a hunt, but despite the efforts of some two hundred Indian beaters, only one tiger was seen, and it rapidly got away. Prince Philip was disappointed.

He had better luck the next day. The royal couple, after shooting numerous partridges and grouse, were delighted to hear that the beaters had seen two tigers prowling the edge of the jungle. The Duke immediately raced up the steps of a tall

wooden tower arranged to assist him in the shoot. The Queen
watched from some thirty feet away. She also was in a wooden
tower.

As the royal party watched, a male and a female beast
appeared in a large clearing. Rear Admiral Bonham-Carter,
royal treasurer, felled the tigress. The Duke then leveled the
male tiger with a direct shot into the center of the forehead.

Immediately, wildlife conservationists were again heard
from, but not in sufficient volume, or with sufficient publicity,
to make themselves felt. For days, Aamritlal Gindal, the young
leader of the anti-violence Ahimsak party, had been fasting,
threatening not to cease the fast for a week because of his
disgust at the royal action. He was as good as his word, but few
people seemed to care. In the London *Times,* D. E. Adams, a
reader in Reading, wrote:

> Is it not a matter for concern to humane people that
> members of the royal family should find pleasure in the
> destruction of wildlife?
>
> Deer-stalking, hunting, and shooting in Britain and now, in
> a country where great poverty exists, no expense is spared to
> make tigers an easy target for royal guns. We read that calves
> are sacrificed to provide live bait. How long will it be before
> man makes the tiger another extinct species?

Prince Philip would, in due course, be president of the World
Wildlife Fund.

The Queen and her husband, scarcely ruffled by such
protests, continued to Agra, where, perhaps because of the tiger
incident, or perhaps because of local ill feeling for the former
rule of the Raj, the few people watching them were either
coolly unenthusiastic or overtly displeased. It was one of the
most unfriendly welcomes the royal couple had ever received.
The Queen, with her customary shrewdness, added some words
in Hindustani to the speech she delivered when received by the
mayor of Delhi before a crowd of something approaching half
a million people. But although the crowd responded with
laughter and applause to the Queen's command of language,
the overall mood was restless and sullen. Several people sent
protests about the tiger shoot to the Queen, but there is no
evidence there was any response. The biggest problem was the

sheer mass of photographers and press the couple had to
endure.

The royal couple arrived, as guests of the Maharaja of
Mewar, at Udaipur, a magnificent setting of islands in an
exquisite lake. The Duke killed a crocodile from the Maharaja's
launch. The couple drove under clumsy arches fashioned
of the skins of tigers and leopards, vegetables, and even a
canopy of strung-together bicycles. They were received at the
Palace in a magnificence of jewelry and gilded robes. They
picnicked at the delectable Water Palace of Jag Nivas, a marble
floating dream over the water. They were loaded with gifts.
That same day, the animal welfare organizations of the state of
Victoria in Australia sent a joint telegram expressing their
concern over the matter of the tigers.

Several people were arrested for threatening to intercept the
royal progress, which continued on schedule. A Nepal rhinoceros
shoot put a further dent in the royal reputation among
animal lovers. The couple proceeded to a visit to Italy to
cement the Archbishop of Canterbury's revolutionary relationship
with the Pope.

The Queen and Prince Philip flew in to a base near Cagliari
on April 30. Always hating to fly, the Queen, despite her
courageous smile, looked visibly shaken as the aircraft landed
amid turbulence in thirty-knot winds, thunder, and lightning; as
she stepped down the gangway, she was greeted by so severe
a gust that she was almost drenched, her umbrella barely
surviving. Very pale, she forced herself to go through the
inspection of an Italian Air Force Honor Guard. The Queen
Mother, who had arrived almost simultaneously from an Italian
tour of her own, had to push her way through the storm to have
a brief meeting with her daughter and son-in-law.

The royal yacht *Britannia* sailed toward Sardinia on April
30, her cable twisting and fouling a propeller, her decks lashed
by rain. Fortunately, the Queen was a much better sailor now
than she had been; there were no reports that she was seasick.
In Rome, the Queen visited the British Minister for the Holy
See, Sir Peter Scarlett. In the late morning, the Queen, in a
full-length black lace dress and black lace veil, wearing the
Order of the Garter, the Duke in the uniform of Admiral of the
Fleet, proceeded through the crowded streets to the Vatican,
where an immense number of Roman Catholics from every part
of the Commonwealth joined the Italians in receiving her. The

royal audience with the Supreme Pontiff was warm; the couple joined him in the Throne Room without any attendants for just under half an hour. Afterward, the Pope gave an official speech of welcome before assembled clerks and laity, delighting the Queen when he said that the innumerable Roman Catholic subjects of the Commonwealth shared with their Protestant brothers absolute loyalty to the British crown. The gifts exchanged were, in view of the extraordinary wealth of the two great figures of Commonwealth and Church, impressively parsimonious. The Pope gave the Queen twenty rather ordinary coins discovered in an old, recently excavated catacomb, and the Queen handed over an African mahogany walking stick. Unhappily, in view of her present position as the target of the conservationists, the handle was made from the horn of a rare rhinoceros.

That afternoon, the Queen and her husband were treated to a somewhat tactless display of the original love letters of Henry VIII to Anne Boleyn, and some equally ill-advised presentations of documents in which the much-married Tudor monarch gave sycophantic and meaningless dedications of manuscripts to the Pope—a product of his marriage of convenience to Catherine of Aragon. What the couple made of these uniquely inappropriate documents can only be conjectured. It was the first visit of the British monarch to a Pontiff since King George V's ill-advised visit during the Mussolini regime.

It is also odd that the couple toured those very places in Venice in which Prince Philip, as a young and somewhat untrammeled Don Juan, cut a swathe through various members of the female international set in 1938.

The trip, of course, involved leaving their children, including Prince Andrew, who was not yet one year old, and it even precluded their attending his first birthday. Once again, royalty put the priorities of official visits before their concern for themselves or their family. When they returned to London, the Queen and Prince Philip were apprised that Princess Margaret would now be officially announcing her expectation of her first child that fall.

Shortly before the royal tour, Armstrong-Jones had taken up his position on the Board of the Council of Industrial Design in London. At last, Armstrong-Jones felt he could make something out of his life. He would work without compensation; he would also have substantial duties on the Council of the Royal

Academy of Dramatic Art. He had not achieved overwhelming popularity, perhaps because he had an intellectual air along with his looks and charm. He was suffering from much the same blight that had affected Prince Philip's career. Those who were not gifted with particularly ingratiating manners in public were seldom favored by either populace or press.

That summer, the Queen was happy to welcome President John F. Kennedy, who had entered office in January. Following a triumphant visit to Paris, Kennedy had had a disastrous meeting with Khrushchev in Vienna, and arrived in London on June 4, in agony from his old spinal problems caused by injuries in World War II. He seemed almost naively appalled by Khrushchev's tough attitude, which undoubtedly stemmed from the U-2 incident as well as internal pressures in Moscow. In the wake of his visit, the Queen was advised by Macmillan that there was a threat of possible world war. In addition to meeting with the Queen, Macmillan continued to supplement his personal observations with valuable letters. He was seized by pessimism: that this was not without foundation could be seen when the Communist government of East Germany hastily erected the notorious Berlin Wall. Thousands of refugees fled into West Germany. In October, there was an unprecedented confrontation of U.S. and Russian tanks at the Wall. From the Bay of Pigs incident that spring to the end of the year, the international situation could not have been much more grave. In her public appearances, the Queen looked more sobered by events than she had ever been before. She cannot have been pleased by the fact that South Africa became a notoriously racist republic, failing to join the Commonwealth on May 31.

With the birth of Princess Margaret's baby imminent, the Queen and Macmillan felt very strongly that Antony Armstrong-Jones should, despite his continuing objections, be raised to the peerage, if only to secure titles for the children. He yielded shortly after the summer holidays; it was decided he would be known as the Earl of Snowdon, also Viscount Linley of Nymans. Princess Margaret, supported strongly by the Prime Minister, was the weighing factor in her husband's acceptance of the Earldom. Not only would she be more comfortable with the name Countess of Snowdon, but also her children would be appropriately titled; if she had a son, he would be Viscount Linley.

The choice of Snowdon was a deliberate reference to Armstrong-Jones's Welsh connections and origins. Linley was the family name of Armstrong-Jones's mother, while Nymans was his mother's house at Staplefield, Sussex. Margaret would use the title Her Royal Highness, the Princess Margaret, Countess of Snowdon.

By late summer, the Princess had virtually suspended all of her official engagements. As so often before in royal history, the anticipated birth was darkened by a death; the Queen Mother's brother, Sir David Bowes-Lyon, passed away in mid-September. Simultaneously, the Queen was extremely busy preparing for the much-delayed trip to the troubled country of Ghana. Scene of much anti-British feeling, that nation was considered to be dangerous and threatening to royalty, a double reason for the Queen to want to go there, with her abiding concern with suppressing untoward elements in the expanding Commonwealth.

It was decided, because of the cramped quarters at Kensington Palace, and Princess Margaret's continuing fretfulness and dissatisfaction with that residence, that her child should be born at Clarence House. The impending and actual birth excited remarkably little public enthusiasm. Even when the bulletins began to be posted at Clarence House shortly before midday on November 3, 1961, very few were gathered outside in the icy, clinging, damp cold. The birth was without complications or problems, the child born at 10:45 A.M. It was a boy. Both parents were overjoyed. They had wanted a son. He would be named David Albert Charles, after the Duke of Windsor (despite his disgraceful political history), Albert (after King George VI), and Charles (after David's famous cousin). He, weighing six pounds, four ounces, would be fifth in line for the throne.

The Queen ordained that the parents should move to the apartment known as 1A Clockcourt at Kensington Palace, a more capacious residence, with twenty-one rooms and large staff quarters, which had originally been designed for King William of Orange by Sir Christopher Wren. Part of it had been occupied by the Duchess of Kent, who had run short of money following her husband's death in the air crash in 1942. It had been empty for many years. The exquisitely hand-carved fittings and handsome, well-proportioned living and dining room were attractive to the royal couple; but the condition of the property was appalling. Gas lamps were still fixed into the walls; there were mildewed, ancient portraits, bricked-up windows, and floors that had totally decayed and were unsafe to walk on. The government had to lay out the equivalent of about $238,000 to remodel everything. Yet again, there was protest in Parliament; undisturbed by the criticisms, Lord Snowdon supervised the redecoration, throwing himself heart and soul into the task of remodeling, at last finding an outlet for his fierce and driving energy. In his shirtsleeves, covered in paint and dust, surrounded by workmen's ladders, he, with the Queen's keen support, did a fine job of turning gloomy, rotting chambers into bright, vivid, exciting rooms.

Meanwhile, in November, the Queen and Prince Philip arrived in Ghana. In one of her rare quoted statements, the monarch said that she wanted to appear there before Khrushchév, who might try to upstage her. Also, and more seriously, she and Macmillan felt that if she failed to go it would indicate that she was opposed to Ghana being part of the Commonwealth. "That would be a very grave step," Macmillan wrote to her.

It was a bold decision. President Kwame Nkrumah was a belligerent individual who had apparently fallen under the influence of Khrushchev and had been vigorously objecting to both British military figures and Conservative British politicians who were in there as representatives of the British Government. There was a feeling that Nkrumah might be assassinated, and, shortly before the Queen's arrival, the military police arrested fifty dissidents; there were bomb explosions in Accra. The Queen and Prince Philip can actually be said to have taken a very grave risk in going there; surely no greater proof is needed of the fact that the Commonwealth remained the Queen's greatest concern, and she was prepared to put her life on the line in order to sustain it.

On the early morning of November 9, thousands of Ghanans crammed the roads outside the city as they walked or struggled in trucks and cheap automobiles toward the airport to greet the Queen. When she and her husband landed that night, the crowd screamed ecstatically, and a sea of umbrellas, multicolored and in many cases clumsily patched, rippled in torchlight as she appeared on the gangway. Chieftains in dazzling colors of orange, red, yellow, and green, with gold crowns and bracelets, jumped up and down in welcome in the darkness caused by a sudden electrical failure. A powerful roll of drums burst out like thunder from the surrounding fields. The Queen was almost swamped as hundreds burst the police cordon and swept down on her, barely checked by another line of officials. The next days were ablaze with ceremonies.

The Queen, with immense cleverness, actually risked widespread criticism by dancing with Nkrumah at a ball, while Prince Philip danced with Nkrumah's wife. The achievement of this skillfully engineered visit was that Ghana remained firmly within the Commonwealth, keeping at arm's distance from Moscow, which might easily have absorbed it. Although Macmillan bragged in a telephone call to President Kennedy, saying, "I have risked my Queen; you must risk your money!" the truth is that Elizabeth was far more than a royal piece in a Prime Ministerial chess game played against the Soviet leader. True, Macmillan had advised her to undertake the visit; true, he had opposed most radically those in government who had feared the consequences of it. But, in the last analysis, the Queen's decision to accept Nkrumah's invitation was hers and hers alone. Only a fool would have doubted her symbolic, as well as her personal, importance in African politics.

The Queen's Ghanan adventure shone like a good deed in a naughty world; but it could not alone stem the tide of serious and violent upheavals throughout the African continent. The "winds of change" of which Macmillan had spoken in a famous speech had turned decidedly bleak.

On the domestic scene, following her return and the customary Christmas at Sandringham, the Queen and her husband were forced to decline an invitation to the wedding of his cousin Princess Sophie of Greece. However, the Queen saw a good deal of Philip's mother when she was in London; and, despite Princess Alice's deafness, still managed to keep up a friendly relationship with her.

At the beginning of February 1962, Prince Charles was seized with stomach pains in the dormitory at Cheam. Dr. Basil Philips, of the Cheam medical staff, immediately called in the Queen's special pediatrician, Sir Wilfred Sheldon, who confirmed a case of appendicitis. The Queen was advised; the Prince was rushed to the Children's Hospital in London, where there was an operation. With normal royal rigor, Prince Philip did not return from a trip to Latin America to be by his son's side, receiving bulletins by telegram or telephone every day, daringly piloting his own plane over the Andes, visiting Bolivia, Chile, Uruguay, Brazil, and Argentina before leaving to join his beloved family in Germany. Prince Charles robustly recovered, showing, at age thirteen, evidence that he had inherited his mother's sturdy constitution. By March 1, he was skating on the ice at Richmond Park, then flew to join his father on the German visit. Unfortunately, the Queen approved the trip, including a stay with Aunt Sophie, Princess of Hanover. Charles hobnobbed with his cousins, including Karl Adolf, named for Hitler. He joined his father, on a visit to his aunt Theodora, Margravine of Baden.

Prince Philip's reputation among reporters did not improve, partly because of murmurings about the German visit and his association with former servants of the Third Reich (which, however, conveniently did not appear in the press), as rumors still continued of his involvement in questionable parties at the Monday Club, involving women of low repute. It was stated that he was friendly with a certain Dr. Stephen Ward, but it was not until a year later that that name would be internationally notorious.

The Earl of Snowdon agreed to become special adviser to the color supplement of the London *Sunday Times*. The appointment was confirmed in January 1962, and was approved by the Queen. He would retain as assistant and secretary Dorothy Everard, who had been with him for many years. His private suite of offices in the basement of Kensington Palace included a studio and a darkroom, as well as printing facilities. He was a much happier man now, far more his own master, and busily contributing very valuable, handsomely achieved photographs which greatly enhanced the newspaper. On March 1, 1962, he took his seat in the House of Lords, and proved to be a vigorous member of the National Union of Journalists, despite its strong opposition to his joining. His list of public engagements notably increased that spring.

He faced a major problem when he escorted his wife to State luncheons presided over by the Queen. He invariably timed his photographic appointments around these occasions. However, the Queen often enjoyed herself so much that she would linger on quite excessively over the time allowed, talking away cheerfully to everyone, and he found himself unable, because of the rule that no one could leave the Queen's presence before she herself departed, to break away. He couldn't even get to a telephone to make a phone call; when she at last left, he had to make frantic efforts to rearrange his afternoons.

Protocol at Kensington Palace was very strict. On one occasion, when she was very busy, Dorothy Everard contacted the resident chef, asking him to serve her a light snack for lunch, as she could not leave the office. For six weeks, he sent up a maid with a tray, the dishes laid out with exquisitely prepared tidbits. Delighted, Miss Everard sent a personal thank-you note to the chef. Princess Margaret reprimanded her for breaking protocol in this manner. She was informed that she was required to ask a housekeeper to relay the message to the chef.

The question arose of where Prince Charles should be educated upon leaving Cheam that summer. At the age of thirteen, he was ready for public school. The ideal choice would have been Eton, which was very close to Windsor Castle, and which the Queen is believed to have favored. He had, in fact, had his name put down at birth for that most distinguished of English schools. However, by the summer of 1962 the Queen had changed her mind. She knew that every time he went from the Castle to Eton, he would be besieged by reporters and photographers every inch of the way. Prince Charles was interested in going to Charterhouse, to join some close friends from Cheam. However, Prince Philip was determined Charles would go to Gordonstoun. It had not improved since Prince Philip's days there: a boot camp for the rich and privileged, still run on autocratic Germanic lines, rather like a Hitler Youth training camp, with a grim emphasis on Strength through Joy.

Although Hahn was no longer headmaster, his humpbacked presence was strongly felt in the school. He had been astonishingly busy from the period before World War II, badgering the Foreign Office to appease Germany by appealing to the more moderate political elements there, playing a role behind the scenes in the plot against Hitler's life, turning up after the war to visit the French zone of Germany to investigate conditions at Salem, taking stock of the future of former Nazi schools in West Germany, and assisting in the taking over of Salem by Prince Philip's brother-in-law, the Prince of Baden,

as the Prince's father had done. There was controversy as to
whether Gordonstoun had been used as a locale for German
agents in World War II, and whether Hahn himself had assisted
the Germans, even to the extent that he had been accused of
being a spy. All of this nonsense added considerable notoriety
to Gordonstoun, and made it the center of gossip and a hive of
busy discussion among its own students.

One advantage of Gordonstoun, apart from its comparative
remoteness from public and press, was that it could be reached,
very comfortably, in a short drive from Balmoral. Prince Philip
took his son on a tour of the school before he actually moved
him in; Charles shuddered at the sight of its concentration-
camp-like, gloomy atmosphere. The Queen can only have
suffered inwardly over his dread of it. Prince Philip, with his
sturdy Christian muscularity, his exhausting emphasis on
fitness, vigor, and toughness, saw the school as a way of
making his son into a man.

The headmaster was Robert Chew. He had been promoted
recently from housemaster. He was there to greet Prince Philip
and his son when they drove off the highway through trees to
the grand old mansion that formed the center of the school.
Philip had lunch with Chew, then drove away. He flew his own
plane off a nearby airstrip, buzzing Windmill Lodge, where
Prince Charles was now resident, with a loud roar of the
propeller and a ceremonial dipping of the wings. This did
nothing to raise Prince Charles's spirits. He hated Windmill
Lodge, an ugly wood and stone building with a roof lined with
asbestos. The dormitory had no carpets, no paint, no shades on
the light bulbs, and crude, spring, double bunk beds, one above
the other. There were twenty in Prince Charles's dorm.

The pupils were wakened at 6:45 A.M. with a yell, and then
sent out for a 150- to 200-yard run, followed by a hot and then
a cold shower. Prince Charles joined the other boys in relays as
waiters in the dining room; he helped to clean and dust and he
weeded the garden. The future King of England was relegated
to emptying out the trash cans.

English, Latin, French, history, and geography were interrupted by running, jumping, discus, javelin throwing, and
assault courses. Apart from the normal athletics, cricket in
summer and rugby football in winter, as well as tennis and
hockey, there was weekly training in seamanship, scouting,
putting fires out, saving lives in an icy Scottish sea, and sailing

through rough waves as volunteer Coast Guard watchers. Cold showers took place repeatedly.

The boys were in bed by 9:15 P.M., and lights were firmly snapped out at 9:30. At one stage, there was a ghastly trip by canoe along a windswept, grim shore. Prince Charles almost fell to the ground with exhaustion at the end of the journey. He hated every minute of the experience. It was repellent, harrowing, and soul-destroying. Yet he was sufficiently royal not to attempt to run away or even to complain bitterly to his parents. Even the Queen could not have intervened if she had felt he was being ill-treated. It had been agreed from the outset that Prince Philip would be in sole charge of their son's education.

Michael Varney, a Norfolk police constable, and member of the Royal Protection Group of the Metropolitan Police, soon after was appointed to Gordonstoun as Charles's personal bodyguard. He was housed disagreeably in a converted kennel. Despite his own rigorous training, he was appalled by the sight of Prince Charles running stripped to the waist in savagely cold winds and plunging into icy showers. He noted in his memoirs: "[Such activities] smacked of the philosophy that cold showers and a couple of turns around the playing field would help keep growing boys' minds off sex. As if anything could!"

18

***

PRINCE CHARLES, PRINCESS ANNE, and Prince Andrew were in bouncing high spirits at Christmas. The Queen, in her sixth month of pregnancy, looked healthy and relaxed in spite of everything; and Prince Philip was as hearty and vigorous as ever. The feasting at Sandringham, the walks on chilly mornings, the presents heaped around the giant Christmas tree in the ballroom, all had the same glow of good cheer that had not varied in years. The Queen Mother was in especially good form as she approached her sixty-fifth year.

Nineteen sixty-four began quietly, with no royal news more momentous than Prince Charles doing the fashionable Twist, made popular by Chubby Checker, at the Christmas residence. Back at Gordonstoun, he played the trumpet in the orchestra. The death of King Paul of Greece at the beginning of March was distressing to some. The birth of the Queen's fourth child, on March 10, was, despite her age of thirty-seven, without any unusual problems. Once more, it was a boy; he was named Edward Antony (for Armstrong-Jones) Richard (for Prince Richard, younger son of the Duke of Gloucester, Louis (for Mountbatten). It was very exciting for Charles, Anne, and Andrew to see their brother for the first time. So strict were the rules at Gordonstoun, that Prince Charles was not released to visit his mother at Buckingham Palace until the school holiday on March 14.

In the wake of the new Prince's birth, the Queen was ordered to have an almost complete rest; she was somewhat tired and weak, and her doctors told her to suspend all official engagements for the immediate future. She stayed at Buckingham Palace, with weekends at Windsor Castle. Prince Philip flew to Athens to the funeral of King Paul, conducted with great ceremony and no doubt provoking in him many disturbing memories.

Early in March, Sir Roger Hollis and the Attorney General, Sir John Hobson (who had played so crucial a role in putting together Profumo's lying statement to the House of Commons just over a year before), acted on the damaging information that made it impossible to avoid closing in on the Surveyor of the Queen's Pictures, Sir Anthony Blunt, who was also a Russian spy. They decided that instead of arresting him and putting him on trial for treason, they would offer him immunity, thus ensuring that the government would not again be embarrassed. The condition would be that Blunt "confessed."

Hollis and Sir Charles Cunningham of the Home Office summoned Sir Michael Adeane to a meeting; Adeane asked, "What should the Queen do?" Hollis replied, "The Queen should do nothing." Hollis added, "If he is dismissed from the Palace it might alert other Soviet agents." Adeane so advised the Queen, and on April 23, the Attorney General, quite without authorization from the Prime Minister, offered Blunt immunity and received his "confession," which was largely useless. Later, he was to admit that he had spied for the KGB and named two accomplices.

It was customary procedure to confront a suspected agent; Blunt, a weak man, would probably have admitted everything. Why then was it necessary to conceal him through granting him immunity? Because he had several royal flushes up his sleeve.

It will be remembered that, in 1945, he had served the royal family by going to the Schloss Krönberg in Germany and retrieving the incriminating letters from Ribbentrop and Hitler to the Duke of Windsor, and Windsor's replies. As the MI5 officer in charge of intercepting neutral couriers and opening and examining all correspondences in the diplomatic bags, he must have learned during World War II that members of the British and Greek royal families (including the Duchess of Kent, the Mountbattens, and King George of Greece) were in breach of the Trading with the Enemy Act by corresponding with their relatives, enemy nationals, through Crown Princess Louise, later Queen of Sweden, via the Swedish diplomatic bags, and that one of these relatives was the wife, and later the widow, of Prince Christopher of Hesse, Goering's secret service chief and high-ranking SS official for Himmler. Sir Michael Adeane specifically asked MI5 not to bring this subject up with Blunt. References to this highly sensitive correspondence to Germany may be found not only in the Mountbatten Archives at the University of Southampton, England, but in Stella King's *Princess Marina, Her Life and Times:*

> [The Duchess's] only communication with her family [in Germany] was by letters sent through Queen Louise of Sweden . . . her sister Elizabeth was married to a German (Count Toerring) and therefore could be considered an enemy . . . he was an officer in the German army.

In E. H. Cookridge's *From Battenberg to Mountbatten,* it is stated:

> [Prince Philip's] three sisters [were] in Germany. Philip had only infrequent news from them, sent through neutral Sweden, where his aunt Louise Mountbatten was the wife of the Crown Prince.

Had Blunt been exposed to the public it would have been revealed that the security at MI5 was so lax he had been able to advise his Russian contacts on British codes; Britain had kept those secret codes from Russia, thereby risking the lives of large numbers of Russian troops. His fellow officials at MI5 had not acted on his statements—made at the end of World War II—that he had given the Russians the names of all of them. Above all, a trial would reveal the secret plans being made by Britain and America through neutral countries to turn the war against Russia by making negotiated peace with Germany. And it might reveal, even more embarrassingly, that Blunt had greatly helped Britain by exposing such German spies as JOSEFINE through examining the diplomatic bags.

Blunt is also likely to have been in possession of information regarding the activities of the Queen's friend R. A. Butler in negotiating for peace with Hitler via Sweden after war broke out. Butler's first wife was Sydney Courtauld, daughter of Samuel, the head of the giant corporation that had founded the Courtauld Institute. Samuel Courtauld was known to have connections to I. G. Farben, and was believed to have provided backing for the fascist Sir Oswald Mosley; such a background was not appealing, and it was unfortunate that Butler was close to the Queen; his second wife was Mollie, the widow of another Courtauld. As we shall see from statements made by Senator Thomas J. McIntyre of New Hampshire and Congressman Silvio O. Conte in 1971, the Queen and her family held a major shareholding in Courtaulds, a fact not supposed to be made public.

In an interview on BBC radio on November 18, 1979, George Young, deputy head of MI6, the Secret Intelligence Service, was asked if Home knew about Blunt. His reply was:

There's a curious convention in Whitehall, you can inform a prime minister without telling him. This may have happened or it may be that Sir Alec was rather dim, I cannot remember.

How could a Prime Minister let such a piece of information—that the Surveyor of the Queen's Pictures was a Russian secret agent—go "in one ear" (to use Young's expression) and out the other? And how could the Queen be advised of the matter and then be forced out of her constitutional role so that she could not advise and warn Home at meetings but must pretend she knew nothing?

Asked whether he had informed Harold Wilson, when Wilson became Prime Minister in 1964, Young replied:

I would be rather hesitant to have informed Harold Wilson. The higher reaches of the Civil Service undoubtedly make most of the decisions for ministers. They put them in front of them and say, Ministers, do you agree? The ethos of the higher reaches of the Civil Service is not one of stirring up hornets' nests, particularly if some of your best friends are hornets, but in my experience of dealing with Ministers—and I've met a fair amount off and on over the past few years—they don't hear what you say . . .

In a Parliamentary debate on the matter many years later, on November 21, 1979, when Blunt was at last after years of concealment exposed, Mrs. Thatcher said:

It was for the Home Secretary to decide whether the Prime Minister should be informed. There is no record on this point. Neither Lord Brooke nor Lord Home can recall discussing this matter.

In other words, like Powell, she did not say that Home knew; only that (improbably) Home did not recall discussing the matter as Young said. Asked directly whether he did know, Lord Home replied to Charles Higham from the House of Lords on February 24, 1990, that he was "away on holiday" when Blunt's treachery was exposed. According to Home, the Home Secretary, Henry Brooke, dealt with the matter appropriately, and Home got to know about it when he came home in the evening.

That might settle the matter, but for certain residual questions. Why did Lord Home not remember being told in 1979, but remember in 1990? And if he did remember at that earlier date, why did the normally careful Mrs. Thatcher not say that he had remembered? Apparently everyone in power knew; and they cast a ring of steel around Blunt. It seemed only appropriate that Mrs. Thatcher should be approached directly to ask her why Lord Home had not recollected the matter in 1979 but did in 1990. Mrs. Thatcher responded through her Principal Private Secretary, Andrew Turnbull, on March 23, 1990, the letter sent to Charles Higham via the British Embassy in Washington, D.C. Mr. Turnbull, writing for Mrs. Thatcher, said that Higham may have misunderstood Lord Home's letter. Mr. Turnbull continued, stating that Lord Home had been contacted and had confirmed that he did not know of Blunt's treason at the time he was Prime Minister, and first learned of it at the time of Mrs. Thatcher's statement to Parliament in November 1979. The cause of the misunderstanding, Mrs. Thatcher alleged, might have been that Lord Brooke (he had now been elevated to the peerage) wrote to Lord Home in November 1979 to explain the background.

In strict fairness to all parties, their positions are presented here as clearly as possible. The reader may draw his own conclusions.

The truth was not kept from Prime Ministers Edward Heath and James Callaghan, as they stated on November 21.

For the next fifteen years, the monarch, whose hatred of communism matched her dislike of Nazism, would have to hold continuing meetings with a confessed Soviet spy. She would have to discuss exhibitions at the Queen's Gallery, Blunt's continuing cataloging of the immense royal collection of paintings and furniture, and what works of art should be obtained to augment the collection. Sir Roger Hollis had made the Queen an accessory. The Queen Mother and Prince Philip were apparently not to be advised, which placed the Queen in an even more delicate position since she would have to act toward those nearest and dearest to her as though she knew nothing.

The excuse for Blunt's not being asked to leave the Palace—that this action would alert other Soviet agents in London and cause them to leave the country—does not hold water: the only important person who was under suspicion at the time was Sir Roger Hollis.

In April 1963, the week of Blunt's confession, Prince Charles began several days of basic Naval training at the Naval College at Portsmouth, where his father had been a pupil. Prince Philip was delighted with his progress; although Prince Charles was, and would be later, somewhat of a disappointment to Philip because of his shyness, sensitivity, and artistic nature, Philip was delighted to note that, after his early bouts of seasickness, Prince Charles was proving to be a good sailor. And Princess Anne was a tornado of energy at Benenden.

Prince Edward was baptized two days after Princess Margaret's child Lady Sarah Armstrong-Jones was born on May 1. There was much discussion of the Queen going to French Canada in the fall. It was widely believed that, at a time of violent secessionism in the French Canadian communities, she might be in danger. She was even warned that if she went to Montreal or Quebec she might be assassinated. She clearly felt that, as on her visit to Ghana, she could cement rifts in the Commonwealth. Other threats accompanied the announcement that she was seriously considering a visit to West Germany, for which Prince Philip had been pressing for years; left-wing and Jewish groups might object to the thought of her meeting with Prince Philip's sisters and their families, although in fact, as we know, those individuals had been received by the royal family, both privately and at official occasions such as weddings and funerals, for years. There were those who felt that the Queen should not be going to Canada just before the crucial election period. Needless to say, she was not prepared to alter any of her plans, regardless of what anybody said.

In late July, Prince Charles fell ill. The weakness in the Windsors, bronchial trouble, flared up, and what appeared to be a simple cold turned into influenza and then into pneumonia.

The trouble began following a fishing expedition in which Charles, standing in the icy water of the River Esk, had insisted on continuing until the small hours of the morning in order to bring back a catch.

His bodyguard, Michael Varney, called the Queen's doctor, Sir George Middleton, who, Varney says, failed to turn up and take care of the matter, even though his home was a mere nine miles away. Varney recalled in his memoirs telephoning Chief Superintendent Albert Perkins, to whom he was directly responsible, at Buckingham Palace. Perkins was out. The young bodyguard insisted on talking to the Queen. She took the call, and Varney told her her son was seriously ill. Apparently, she couldn't get through to Middleton until late morning; the physician at last arrived at Gordonstoun, but instead of diagnosing pneumonia said that a second opinion would be required. Varney suggested a hospital, but Middleton did not respond. Finally, Middleton called in Dr. David Short of Aberdeen Royal Infirmary and, at this surprisingly late moment, Charles was taken by ambulance to the Watson-Frazer Nursing Home at Aberdeen. The Queen, greatly concerned, arrived at the hospital with flowers; soon afterward, the Prince was transferred to Windsor Castle to recover. The whole experience drew attention to the fact that the Prince lacked his father's extremely robust constitution, emphasizing a certain delicacy not only in his nature but in his health.

In August, Princess Margaret was with her husband in Sardinia for a vacation, on board the lavish yacht *Amaloun* as guests of the Aga Khan. The vessel struck a rock near the island of Mortario, forcing the Princess and Snowdon to jump overboard in life preservers, making their way ashore by dinghy. That same week, two chauffeurs quit Balmoral, during the Queen's summer holiday, announcing that they were dissatisfied with the "medieval hours and conditions." They complained that their duties were not confined to driving cars, but to picking up groceries, running errands for Prince Charles, and performing menial tasks; they claimed they were treated like "second-class peasants." They were paid the equivalent of only thirty dollars a week. They had the distinction of being of the handful of disgruntled royal servants who did not publish their reminiscences in a popular newspaper.

There was much industrial unrest. The Mods and Rockers, long-haired, garishly dressed and hysterically violent, ram-

paged through the seaside towns of Margate, Brighton, and
Bournemouth, sacking houses, smashing shop windows, and
fighting with the police. One hundred and twenty-nine thousand mail deliverers and sorters went on strike, effectively
closing down the postal service for three days. Another
problem emerged to concern the Queen: excluded from the
Commonwealth conference in the first two weeks of July, at
Marlborough House in London, Southern Rhodesia's newly
appointed and high-powered rebel Prime Minister, Ian D.
Smith, of whom much more would shortly be heard, insisted
upon full independence from the Commonwealth. Jomo Kenyatta, Prime Minister of Kenya, and seven other African
Commonwealth Premiers, assailed Smith, opposing the idea of
independence for what was predominantly a white government.
Kenyatta insisted on a constitutional conference to be held in
Salisbury, in which there would be a charter set up calling for
majority rule government in a country of 3.9 million Africans
and 221,000 whites.

On July 15, Douglas-Home stated, after consulting with the
Queen on the matter, that Britain agreed with these demands.
But Smith refused to comply, and decided to announce a
unilateral declaration of independence based on white suprem-
acy. This was unthinkable, and the Queen joined with her
Prime Minister in fighting such a policy. One of the great
achievements of her reign was that, despite many criticisms
and many problems in independent government, one African
nation after another had been handed over to black rule while
remaining happily within the Commonwealth. Both the Queen
and Douglas-Home placed this transference of power at the top
of the agenda. The affair was particularly vexing since, earlier
that year, Zanzibar had been granted recognition following a
rebellion, and had merged with Tanganyika to become the
Republic of Tanganyika and Zanzibar or Tanzania. Nyasaland
had become Malawi on July 6, and a follow-up visit there by
Prince Philip was highly strategic. Plans were already afoot for
Northern Rhodesia to become Zambia in October.

On September 18, in Athens, Prince Philip was present at the
nuptials of King Constantine and Princess Anne-Marie of
Denmark. Later that month, strict security precautions were
undertaken in advance of the royal tour of Canada, where there
were problems with militant separatists.

The arrival in Quebec was painful. Instead of flags and

flowers and bleachers filled with excited people, there were barriers with police signs on them and squads of officials wandering around checking on everyone. For the second time in her life, the Queen experienced hoots and boos of anger. She had trained herself to show no response. As she arrived at the Legislative Building, separatists yelled at her, screaming in French, "Québec for the *Québécois!*" The Royal Canadian Mounted Police rounded up the demonstrators with nightsticks and bundled several extremists into cars.

The Queen and Prince Philip returned the day before the British elections. Labor won. Sir Alec Douglas-Home fought vigorously, but Harold Wilson carried the day.

When Wilson arrived at the Palace for the "kissing-of-hands" ceremony, he was accompanied by his wife, the glum and unaccommodating Mary Wilson, his father, and his two sons. Her Majesty would, of course, not receive the Wilson family, who were appropriately placed in an equerry's room while the new Prime Minister saw the Queen alone. When he made a mistake in referring to a particular constituency, she briskly corrected him. She wasn't over Macmillan yet.

Wilson's new Cabinet, few of whom had been accustomed to high office, found it difficult to adjust to the rituals of royalty. Richard Crossman, arguably the most intellectually gifted of Wilson's Cabinet Ministers, recalled in his memoirs the ceremony of becoming a Privy Counsellor. "I don't suppose anything more dull, pretentious, or plain silly has ever been invented." He added:

> There we were, sixteen grown men, for over an hour we were taught how to stand up, how to kneel on one knee on a cushion, how to raise the right hand with the Bible in it, how to advance three paces towards the Queen, how to take the hand and kiss it, how to move back ten paces without falling over the stools—which had been carefully arranged so that you *did* fall over them.

The rehearsal took place one morning from eleven-ten to twelve-fifteen, whereupon the counsellors drove to the Palace and went through the ritual all over again in a drawing room. All present were miserably uncomfortable, including the Queen. But at the end, with everyone flustered, the Queen said, with an enchanting laugh, "You all moved backward very nicely!'' Everyone relaxed; they were immediately fond of her.

The monarch would not only have to get used to Mrs. Wilson, but also to the real power behind the Prime Minister, the remarkable secretary Marcia Williams. Good-natured and generous, toothily charming, she was ready to deal with everyone and everything in the best of spirits.

The new Prime Minister, in the Alice-in-Wonderland world of British politics, was genial Carpenter to Macmillan's busy Walrus; in the same context, Sir Alec Douglas-Home was a grinning Cheshire Cat. Within days of assuming office, Wilson began to look tired. His round shoulders were more marked, his sharp blue eyes looked strained. This vigorous moralistic critic of government was finding out what government entailed; though he looked tougher than Macmillan, he wasn't. His habit of constantly smoking pipes in public (and Churchillian cigars in private), and his restriction of all exercise to solo golf on the drawing room floor, scarcely helped. He was faced with many enemies, not only Douglas-Home but such entrenched Tories as Lord Cromer, the stubborn and imperious governor of the Bank of England, who made him realize that he would have to toe the line to the conservative old guard in clubland and the City's financial circles, or be in grave difficulties.

The vast debts with which the Maudling chancellorship had saddled him, the threat of Ian Smith in Rhodesia to go independent, and the difficulty at first of relating to the Queen at the Tuesday meetings, were added to by his wife's constant complaints that she had to move into 10 Downing Street. She must have been among the few women in England who would not welcome being installed in the most famous private home in the nation. In desperation, to escape his wife's temper (she could not get over having to store the furniture from her own house), the Prime Minister's Tuesday evenings with the Queen were sometimes extended to an unprecedented two hours or more, and she seemed to warm to his bluff Yorkshire temperament as time went on. When Wilson returned, barely in time for dinner at seven-thirty, Mrs. Wilson would snap, ''I suppose you've been with your girlfriend again!''

The new government faced a terrifying run on sterling, the money reserves of about $3 billion disappearing at the rate of $50 million a day, recalling the financial nightmare that had followed Britain's defeat at Suez. The unhappy Wilson was compelled to go to the hated Lord Cromer so that the Bank of

England could whip up thousands of millions, much of it coming from the American Federal Reserve Bank and the International Monetary Fund. The Queen was disturbed to find that her country was now hundreds of millions in debt and the stock market was on the verge of collapse. At last, the crisis eased; but Cromer's measures constituted no more than thumbs in the cracks in a dam; England itself was being hocked to America.

Almost from the beginning, Wilson emerged as a more conservative Prime Minister than Macmillan; the Labor party ironically was further to the right of center than all except the extremist front benches behind Lord Home. President Johnson treated Wilson with little respect, rebuking him like a disobedient lackey for not supporting the Vietnam War.[1] And he had to pursue the Conservative policy of building more Polaris submarines in Scotland, with America still holding the trigger. His policy on Rhodesia would, of course, remain that of Macmillan. The difference between the Labor and Tory government was that, whereas Macmillan's and Home's were largely run by the public school/university Mafia with a heavy lacing of Etonians—traditionally paternalistic, mutually protective, and casually interrelated—the Labor government was, ironically, a true oligarchy, with the power pyramid narrower at the top, and the Prime Minister a tougher if benign dictator. Labor had become a form of Toryism; genuine Whigs were rare. Behind Wilson's violent attacks on Douglas-Home in the Commons that autumn and winter lay a true-blue respect for tradition and a deep-seated "conservative" mistrust in the fast-on-their-feet manipulators of the national economy in the City.

The Queen was exceedingly busy in November, preparing an important exhibition, with Sir Anthony Blunt, at the Queen's Gallery, and checking the text of a subsequent picture book. She had finally yielded to pressure from West Germany (and, surely, Prince Philip, who dreamed of a united Germany) to visit that country and her husband's controversial sisters. In view of the increasing importance of West Germany in terms of its confrontational position against the Soviet bloc, the symbolic importance of the trip apparently outweighed in the

1. At one stage, Johnson slammed down the hot-line telephone in annoyance at Wilson's stance.

Queen's mind the thought that she would be received by the widows of important SS and military officials in Hitler's government.

By the end of the year, the troublesome Ian Smith was at the top of the Queen's and Prime Minister's agenda. Rugged and rangy, of old farming stock, the inflexible, hard-bitten (if soft-spoken) Smith had to consider his own electorate, composed not only of rugged farming stock, as many of the public believed, but of post-war British immigrants from the public school class, who had gone to Rhodesia to escape British austerity and get rich quick with unlimited black servants in a California climate where a colonial atmosphere prevailed. The society of Salisbury, Rhodesia's capital, was predominantly smart and raffish, mercenary, and upwardly mobile. Smith was riding on the independence ticket; his role as lean, hard Rhodesian rebel appealed to his expatriate supporters and their children. Smith was furious that when he dismissed Major General John Anderson, Chief of Staff of military forces, 10 Downing Street was displeased; he was annoyed that Wilson should treat his country as a colony; he disliked being told that he should extend voting rights to the millions of blacks who formed the majority, and who would surely pitch him and his government out of office.

There could be no doubt that Rhodesia was a thorn in the Queen's heart: she had worked so hard to maintain black-run nations in the Commonwealth, had so tirelessly advised her Prime Ministers that incorporation of black rule was the only peaceable alternative to the loss of Empire—she, who was so utterly her father's daughter. And she dreaded the thought that Rhodesia might become another South Africa, whose menacing government ruled to the very southern border of Smith's aggressive tobacco province.

The Queen was not without domestic problems as well. A search had been going on since mid-September for a missing exercise book in which Prince Charles had written essays on the uses of power and other subjects indicative of his adolescent liberalism. The book had been stolen from his locker. Late in October, the police, who had proved so useful to the monarch in retrieving the damaging photographs from Odham's Press and in closing the inconvenient Museum Street Galleries exhibition of Stephen Ward's royal portraits, now proved invaluable again. Acting under royal instruction through the Home Secretary, they found that two Gordonstoun boys were responsible, one of whom had sold the book to the Mercury Press in Lancashire. Arriving at the offices with the appropriate warrant, they seized the book. Terence Smith, owner of Mercury, was made of sterner stuff than the directors of Odham's. He sued the police for wrongful seizure. Not surprisingly, the case failed in the Queen's courts.

Smith had the last laugh. The enterprising publisher had sold the exercise book to a formidable array of publications including *Life* magazine, *Paris-Match*, and the German photo-magazine *Der Stern. Der Stern* scooped the others, bringing out lengthy excerpts on November 17. The overall headline was, absurdly, "The Confessions of Prince Charles." The essays looked forward to Prince Charles's later position in life; they were drawn in part from a book by the historian William Lecky. The Prince called for the government to grant freedom to the press (an idea scarcely appealing to his father) so that politicians' improprieties would be exposed; he wrote how important it was to judge Parliamentary candidates not on the lines of reform they chose to peddle, but on their actual merits. *Der Stern* accompanied the excerpts with the unwarranted statement that the Prince had sold the material because he wasn't getting enough pocket money. *Time* magazine repeated the canard, whereupon the Queen issued a furious denial. The freedom of the press that Prince Charles so rashly called for resulted in stories that, in a time of financial desperation in England, he was cavorting around Windsor Castle in a Beatle wig and had demanded a very expensive guitar and electric organ as his Christmas gifts.

At the same time, the Queen was involved in a prolonged fight with the British Press Council, through Commander Colville, signing the first royal complaint ever lodged with that body. She was exasperated by photographs that had appeared in the *Sunday Express* and *The People*, showing her water-skiing with her sister on the lake at Sunninghill Park, near Ascot. Commander Colville appeared before the council to state that photographers had been seen shooting the Queen changing her clothes in a hut; the council upheld the complaint.

The Christmas festivities that year were held not at Sandringham, but at Windsor.[2]

Princess Margaret and Lord Snowdon were in Dublin early in January when an Irish Republican Army bomb exploded, shaking the house and resulting in a search for several men. Another bomb blew up a transformer, plunging the house into darkness. Yet another was thrown at a police car. The culprits were not caught. A futile conflict between Indonesia and Malaysia taxed the government that week.

Sir Winston Churchill, aged ninety, died at the end of January. He had already, with his customary theatrical skill, arranged his own memorial service at St. Paul's Cathedral; the Queen selected Saturday, January 30, for the occasion. She had decided long since that she would attend the service, the first British monarch ever to appear at a memorial for a commoner. She broke precedent by visiting Westminster Hall when the body lay in state; she turned up with Princess Margaret and other royal family members, the long line of people temporarily held back, staring in disbelief, as she made her way into the hall in deep mourning. She stood silently before the coffin of the great man who had guided her with such devotion and affection from her earliest girlhood. There was no mistaking the dark grief in her face. She had instructed that the floor be lined in felt, thus muffling the footsteps of the 132,000 people who streamed silently past the catafalque.

An icy gale and rain lashed London at the solemn State memorial the following day. The Queen again broke precedent by arriving ahead of the coffin and before the official mourners—not last, as was customary at royal funerals. She and Prince Philip were followed by the twelve pallbearers, who included a bent and withered Earl Attlee, and a shaky, pale, and shockingly aged former Sir Anthony Eden, the Earl of Avon. To the muffled thunder of drums outside, the coffin was laid

2. It was not so cheerful at 10 Downing Street. Lady Home had not advised Mrs. Wilson that the cost of Christmas cards and stamps came out of the central office government purse, or that she could be helped with the mailings. As a result, with important political business pressing, Marcia Williams and the entire staff had to sit on the floor amid vast piles of envelopes, stamping them at Wilson's own expense, then stagger out with bags to mail them. Mrs. Wilson was, quite visibly, Not Amused.

upon Christopher Wren's memorial inscription; heralds made a blaze of color against the dark columns, and, with a Churchillian flourish, the "Battle Hymn of the Republic" was played in honor of his American mother, and a trumpeter dramatically played the "Last Post" in a medieval tunic from the Whispering Gallery, followed by the "Reveille," sounded by a royal hussar's trumpeter against the tall west window. As the coffin was carried down the Thames to its final resting place in the humble village churchyard of Bladon, near Blenheim Palace, ancestral home of the Marlboroughs, the workmen on the great river lowered their cranes in silent homage. It was the last great imperial ceremony of death in England.

Ian Smith was invited to the funeral, and even he, belligerent though he was, could not refuse to come. However, at the elaborate reception at Buckingham Palace, attended by many heads of state and royal persons, the Queen, who never missed anything, observed that one face was absent from the sea of distinguished countenances. She asked Harold Wilson, "Where is Ian Smith?"

Wilson replied, "I don't know." She sent him to the telephone. He located Smith at the restaurant of the Park Lane Hotel. Smith claimed he had not received the invitation. According to Wilson, it was in his pocket. He was forced to make an awkward apology to the monarch when he finally arrived at the Palace. The Queen was unimpressed. Smith denies the story.

That same evening, the Queen's uncle, the Duke of Gloucester, together with the Duchess, drove home to Barnwell Manor, in Northamptonshire, in their gray Rolls-Royce. The Duke had been suffering for some time from dizzy spells and periods of incoherence, indicative of a severe illness. But he was of stubborn character, and, for no particular reason, decided to drive, putting the chauffeur in the back seat alongside the Duchess. While he was speeding through country lanes, he crashed the car; it fell upside down into a field. Although he was not severely injured, only bruised, the Duchess suffered from several fractures and her face was badly gashed. She had to have fifty-seven stitches; she was furious with the Duke; the Queen called anxiously to Bedford Hospital, but fortunately the Duchess was not in any danger.

In February, the Queen made a quick trip to Ethiopia, where Prince Philip misbehaved badly. He ran into a highly placed

Canadian diplomat in the capital of Addis Ababa, and, referring indirectly to Canadian economic interests in the region, taste-lessly observed, ''Oh, you're one of the neocolonialists!'' Shown through the important Ethnic Museum in the same city, he said to its locally respected curator, ''If you gave a seven-year-old a brush and paints, he'll produce something like these paintings.'' He was observed to ignore the Queen, walk ahead of her, fail to open a car door for her when no official was available to do so, and speak sharply to her on several occasions.

While Prince Philip went on to an exhausting tour of the Orient and Australia, the Queen returned to distressing news of the illness of her uncle David, Duke of Windsor. He was in a private room at the London clinic. An awkward situation emerged, handled by her with great dignity. The Duchess of Windsor was at the London Clinic daily with her husband. For the Queen pointedly to ignore her, or not permit her presence in the room during the royal visits, would undoubtedly attract unfortunate comment, since the public had a short memory and few remembered in detail the Duchess's role of Nazi collabo-ration in World War II. A royal snub would have made the Duchess a martyr. Therefore, the Queen sensibly organized it so that she would confer briefly with the controversial Duch-ess, even at the risk of the press announcing (as in fact it did) a reconciliation.

At one visit, the Duke fragilely and pathetically asked the Queen if his wife could be granted the privilege of a royal memorial service and could be buried next to him. The monarch promised to give the matter her consideration. This certainly was a quandary for her. It cannot have pleased her, or especially her mother, that this wretched woman should be given so great an honor. However, she could scarcely resist the Duke's miserable pleas, or (again) risk public criticism, since undoubtedly the Duchess would make headlines out of any refusal. The Queen granted permission.

A grievous blow struck the royal family late in March, when the Princess Royal, only daughter of King George V and Queen Mary, and the Queen's beloved aunt, died of a heart attack while walking through the gardens of her estate, Harewood House, near Leeds in Yorkshire. The hard-pressed monarch was faced with another severe problem of protocol. Although she had avoided comment by speaking with the Duchess of Windsor at the hospital, she could scarcely face the thought of being seated near her in the Royal Gallery in Westminster Abbey for the memorial service. She disrupted precedent in reaching her solution. She arranged for the funeral to be held on the same day as the memorial service. This would mean that she, her husband, and her aunt's bereaved family would go to Leeds, some considerable distance from London, while the Windsors would go to Westminster Abbey. The public did not get onto this plan, and the press chose to overlook it. Since even the peripatetic Duke and Duchess of Windsor could not be in more than one place at a time, the problem was solved.

It was not the only bereavement in March. Earlier that month, Lord Louis Mountbatten's sister and Prince Philip's aunt, Queen Louise of Sweden, had passed away in Stockholm, the funeral attended, alone of the royal circle, by the Princess Royal. Louise had grown increasingly eccentric with time, displaying temper fits and traveling around London with a piece of paper in her handbag which said, in case she should suffer from illness or accident and not be recognized, "I am the Queen of Sweden." No obituary writer recalled her ambiguous role vis-à-vis Hitler or knew of her misbehavior at the funeral of the dowager Marchioness of Milford Haven, when she vandalized the Marchioness's papers and ripped dedications from her books, presumably in an effort to conceal awkward political liaisons which her mother had established during the war.

That week, the Queen, according to protocol, had to receive at the Palace the new Ambassador for the Federal Republic of West Germany, Herr Blankenhorn. Questions were asked in the House of Commons concerning what MP Tom Driberg (later disclosed to be a Soviet agent) described as Blankenhorn's "former support of Hitler and the ideology and policies of the Nazi Party." Foreign Secretary Michael Stewart denied that the Ambassador was in any way questionable. However, Renée Short, MP, whose reputation was impeccable, was to bring the subject up again on May 3. She asked Stewart:

Is my honorable friend aware that [Blankenhorn] joined the Nazi Party in 1938 when he was employed at the German Embassy in Washington [where] he could have sought asylum if he had been opposed to the Nazi ideology? Is he also aware that this man was sufficiently highly placed to be sent to inspect the Warsaw Ghetto in 1941? And that after then [sic] he continued to serve Hitler in Switzerland in the German Embassy there, where he could have sought political asylum . . .

Mrs. Short had not even finished the sentence when the Speaker made her stop; George Thomson, MP, responded to her, remarking that later in the war Blankenhorn was associated with an anti-Hitler group.

The royal family was far more than marginally involved in international geopolitics. Hence, when Prince Philip left for Como, Italy, on April 2, he attended, one assumes with the Queen's approval, a meeting of the mysterious and powerful Bilderberg group, a precursor of the extraordinary Trilateral Commission. According to authorities on the Bilderbergers, he would attend future meetings, and was supportive of their purposes. This was unheard of for a British royal person.

The founder of the Bilderbergers (they held their first meetings at Oosterbeck, Holland, in 1954) and a committed member of the board of the commission was Prince Bernhard of the Netherlands, who was German: the Prince of Lippe Biesterfeld. He had been a close friend of Prince Philip and allegedly shared the use of an apartment with him in Paris. In the mid-1930s, he had joined I. G. Farben, the German chemicals trust which backed Hitler and later ran the Buna rubber factories of Auschwitz. He was a key figure in NW7, the Intelligence branch of Farben, under Franz Fahle, Lockheed's West German agent after World War II.

The Bilderbergers and the Trilateral Commission, of which they were progenitors, formed a secret financial world government. They were devoted to the unification of all conflicting empires in a generalized financial community. It was reported in the book *Trilateralism* by Holly Sklar:

Top executives from the world's leading multinational corporations meet with national political figures at Bilderberg meetings to consider jointly the immediate and long-term problems facing the West. Bilderberg itself is not an executive agency. However, when Bilderberg participants reach a form of consensus about what is to be done, they have at their disposal powerful transnational and national instruments for bringing about what it is they want to come to pass.

Among those attending the meeting at the Villa d'Este Hotel, in Lake Como, favorite haunt of the Duke and Duchess of Windsor and of many such internationalists, were Lord Mountbatten, who accompanied Prince Philip on the trip, Denis Healey, Minister of Defense in the Wilson government, Prince Bernhard, and his daughter Princess Beatrix, George Ball, American Under Secretary of State, Signor Brosio, Secretary General of NATO, Robert Marjolin, vice president of the Executive Commission of the EEC, and Signor Carli, governor of the Bank of Italy.

A theme of the meeting, as of most Bilderberger meetings, was unification of Europe and the operations of NATO. E. H. van der Breugel, president of KLM Dutch Airlines, was treasurer. He was later head of the International Institute of Strategic Studies in London, founded by Denis Healey in 1958. Lord Home, in due course, would be chairman. Joseph E. Johnson of the Council of Foreign Relations was U.S. Secretary of the Bilderbergers; Arthur Dean, of the law firm of Sullivan and Cromwell, who had helped negotiate the end of the Korean War and was alleged to have CIA connections, was co-chairman; the members were only those who could further the aim of the Bilderbergers "through their special knowledge or experience, their personal contacts and their influence in national and international circles."

The power of the Bilderbergers was astonishing: President Kennedy had filled the State Department with them: Dean Rusk as Secretary of State, George W. Ball, his Under Secretary, McGeorge Bundy, Walter Rostow, George McGhee, Arthur Dean—all were Bilderbergers; years later, President Carter would fill his administration with others: Vance, Mondale, Brzezinski, Blumenthal. The previous year, 1964, three British Prime Ministers attended.

In the wake of her forgiveness of the Windsors, and of her reception at the Palace of a diplomatic representative who had allegedly been a Nazi, the Queen was increasingly being placed in a most invidious position. She was, of course, not remotely supportive of anything approaching National Socialism, indeed the mere thought is absurd. However, in the interest of securing a *cordon sanitaire* in Western Europe against the Soviets, she, the Queen on the chess board, was rapidly coming to resemble a mere pawn. Wilson's policy, and that of his Foreign Secretary, was unequivocally for the future reunion of East and West Germany; the speeches that were drafted for the Queen in conference with Michael Stewart and with Sir Michael Adeane, and which she would deliver on public occasions during her forthcoming German tour, pressed for that reunification. And it is known that Prince Philip, and not merely because of his familial ties, was personally anxious to bring about this melding of conflicting and divided states.

The question is, how could such a reunification be achieved? A limited war was obviously not in the cards in view of the nuclear deterrent. There was no record of any plan to bring about a *coup d'état* in East Germany. Reunification was a pipe dream, a vision intended to inspire hope in the repressed victims of communism, twenty-five years before freedom.

The Queen may have been sympathetic to the idea of a restoration of the German royal family, a restoration which would, of course, enormously benefit her husband's relatives.[3]

At the beginning of May, elaborate preparations were made throughout Germany for the royal visit. Munich was *en fête* with an Italian week, another reminder of past fascist connections. A sixteen-foot-high reproduction of Michelangelo's *David* set before the Cenotaph had to be removed before the Queen arrived because of the exposed genitals. Attempts to save the day by daubing the offending member with red paint proved to be futile. One girl's remark as the statue was removed was widely quoted: "If that's David, I'd certainly like to see Goliath!"

Desperate efforts were made to avoid any Nazi overtones. The Haus der Kunst, Hitler's art gallery, still containing at this late date his personal selection of paintings, was omitted from the royal itinerary. So was the Bavarian State Museum, containing three thousand paintings seized by Goering. Crowds were ordered by public proclamation not to issue cries of *"Sieg Heil!"* Instead, they must call the Queen's name. There was a heavy emphasis on royal ties; the Queen had over four hundred German relatives, of whom she could only meet a handful.

3. According to the Grand Duke Otto von Hapsburg, Winston Churchill often spoke of placing the Queen's cousin, Ernst August of Hanover (or Lord Louis Mountbatten), on the throne of a post-war united Germany.

The Queen, looking tense and grim, evidently in a state of stress over the whole matter, her husband grinning cheerfully, flew through a storm to Bonn, on May 15, where the crowds were impressively quiet and subdued. At a banquet that night at Brühl Castle, where her great-great grandmother Queen Victoria had once stayed, she addressed President Heinrich Lübke and six hundred guests in words of enthusiasm, words undermined by a curious flatness and detachment in her delivery. Members of the Hohenzollern, Hanover, and Glucksburg families were present in their finery, hanging onto her every word as she spoke, almost unconstitutionally, of uniting Europe "on as broad a base as possible." She went on to state, unhesitatingly, her "wholehearted support of your natural wish for peaceful reunification." World War II was, of course, far too inconvenient a subject for her to touch upon: the ghosts of 6 million Jews were just over the Queen's shoulder. She continued the tour, managing not to wince as the Army and Air Force bands blared out *"Deutschland Uber Alles."* During the prolonged journey, she visited Hanover, where there were many of her husband's family.

There were fireworks; there was a triumphal journey up the Rhine past castles and gardens of rich flowers and vineyards; there was dinner at Schloss Wolfsgarten, near Darmstadt, scene of so much of Prince Philip's childhood, where the royal couple were the guests of the British-born Margaret Geddes, daughter of Sir Auckland Geddes, and her husband Prince Ludwig of Hesse and by Rhine, the former chargé d'affaires for Joachim von Ribbentrop, Hitler's Ambassador to London in the 1930s.

Munich was a blaze of flags and bunting as the Queen emerged on the balcony of the State Chancellery; she was given a letter from the pro-Nazi Richard Strauss on the subject of his opera *Der Rosenkavalier*. That evening, the opera itself was performed in full.

She left with the Prince for Salem that same night. The royal couple spent the weekend there, on the glowing shores of Lake Constance, housed in a suite in the former Cistercian monastery where Prince Philip had been schooled. They were met at the station by the Margrave Max of Baden, son of Prince Philip's sister Theodora; Max had succeeded his recently deceased father Gottfried as head of the noble house. They made the journey to Salem romantically in a large black hunting coach drawn by two magnificent chestnut stallions, their arrival accompanied by a twenty-one-gun salute and three brass bands blaring out traditional martial themes.

That evening, the Margrave and his mother presided over a dinner party at the Castle, at which Prince Philip's eldest sister, Princess Margarita von Hohenlohe-Langenburg, and his youngest sister, Sophie, Princess Georg Wilhelm of Hanover, were prominent among the guests. The stay continued until Monday, when the Queen proceeded to Marbach, and then to meet the Kaiser's daughter, the pro-Nazi Princess Viktoria Luise, at Herrenhausen; the old lady had made a lengthy journey at the Queen's personal invitation. The meeting was very exciting for her, and she wrote of it glowingly in her memoirs. Prince Philip had last seen her at the marriage of King Constantine of Greece.

The British press dealt with the tour discreetly; this was, after all, a time of Cold War, and it was scarcely desirable to bring up the subject of Nazism or of dinner parties with the widows or wives of former members of Hitler's SS and armed services. It was left to the socialist *New Statesman* to level anything approaching a degree of criticism. The *Sunday Times* of London described the visit as "a sign that this country has at last realigned its views about the Germans and accepts them genuinely as allies and human beings." Unhappily though, due to some editorial mishap, the same newspaper featured soon after in its color supplement a rediscovered blacklist issued by the Nazis during World War II, singling out those individuals who would be disposed of immediately when Hitler took up the occupancy of Buckingham Palace. The aforementioned Herr Blankenhorn informed the newspaper's editor-in-chief that he was most displeased and Mercedes canceled an advertisement.

Back in London, after a choppy voyage on the royal yacht *Britannia* from Hamburg, the Queen and Prince Philip were given a tumultuous welcome. Germany basked in self-congratulations, and the Queen's statement that an unfortunate history that had begun fifty years before (i.e., in 1915, an odd choice of date) had come to an end, was quoted everywhere in a glow of self-approval; Foreign Secretary Michael Stewart's accompaniment of the Queen everywhere was considered a major feather in his cap.

In June, the Queen honored the Beatles with an MBE. The ceremony was, as usual, at Buckingham Palace. The Beatles were dismayed to find, instead of being presented with the insignia, they had to pick them up from a table where they were displayed. They grumbled about this, and also the fact that their manager, the celebrated Brian Epstein, was not so honored. A few years later, they would, notoriously, return their MBEs to the Queen.

Not long after the royal couple arrived home, Prince Philip made a disastrous mistake. Although he was not constitutionally bound to silence on political issues, he was supposed not to express his opinion upon them. Restless and bored at the restrictions of his role in life, he tended to express himself too freely in private, but seldom allowed his statements to reach a wider audience. In mid-July, he addressed three hundred students at the University at Edinburgh on the subject of Commonwealth relations. Reading from a prepared speech, mostly his own work, he stated that he would not be commenting upon Rhodesia, where, following Ian Smith's triumphal election that spring, the situation was more volatile than ever, and Smith's threats to leave the Commonwealth more drastic than hitherto. Instead of holding to the text of his address, the Prince suddenly thrust it aside, to the students' evident delight, and began vigorously breaking protocol. He said:

> I recognize the impressions of many Africans about Rhodesia. But I think that it is better to spin out the solution of these difficulties with patience, and with a bit of luck get a better result rather than risk a bloodbath by forcing a pace.

The statement caused a furor. A Labor member of Parliament, Hugh Jenkins, tabled a motion in the House of Commons charging that "it is a condition of Constitutional monarchy that royalty should not give public expression to contentious political opinions." Lord Brockway, Chairman of the Movement for Colonial Freedom, said, "The Duke has unhappily given encouragement to Mr. Smith, whose whole strategy is to seek delay." External Affairs Minister of Kenya, Joseph Murumbi, snapped, "It is hard to imagine how the Duke of Edinburgh, who has never been exposed to the hard realities of Toryism, can speak authoritatively on Rhodesia." Cecil King, chairman of I.P.C., owner of the *Daily Mirror*, in a letter to Harold Wilson dated July 13, 1965, and referring to the onslaught of the press, explained:

Our attack on Prince Philip was not really caused by his pretty innocuous remarks about Rhodesia. But a few days earlier he had been the guest at lunch of Denis Hamilton (of the *Sunday Times*) at which various newspapermen were present . . . At this lunch Prince Philip's main theme . . . was the urgent importance of the reunification of Germany. Hugh Cudlipp [of the *Mirror*] thought that we cannot have Prince Philip saying in public anything like what he had said in private at this lunch. Hence the decision to seize on his remarks about Rhodesia as an opportunity to fire a shot across his bows. We are informed from the Palace that the point has been taken.

King knew, as any shrewd Fleet Street newspaper figure would know, that whatever the press had done to whitewash the royal visit, in the interests of the West, the public as a whole in England was unhappy with the mere idea of a united Germany; the Queen had managed to escape calumny because it was known she was a mouthpiece of government. But if it were to be discovered that Prince Philip actually held such views on his own, and that by some unthinkable extension the Queen might share those views, the consequences could have been dire. Hence, the need of Cecil King and his colleagues to protect Prince Philip by means of an indirect warning.

That same month, the Queen, no doubt somewhat put about by her husband's loquacity, had a lesser but still pressing problem to deal with: Prince Charles's O-levels, the exams necessary to admit him to higher education (which, it would soon emerge, would include six months at the Australian equivalent of a boot camp). At a State banquet for the President of Chile, Barbara Castle, distinguished member of the Privy Council and Cabinet as Minister of Overseas Development, was talking to the Queen. A footman appeared in the middle of the conversation and whispered to the Queen, who laughed that "poor Charles" needed reassurance before he took the exams, got up, and left. When she returned, having more or less soothed the nervous Prince, she said to Mrs. Castle, "Aren't these exams awful?" Then she turned to Princess Margaret and added, "You and I would never have got into university, would we?"

Charles managed to scrape through, but failed in two subjects, one of which was mathematics, the bane of his existence.

On July 22, the Queen was advised that Sir Alec Douglas-

Home had resigned as leader of the Opposition and of the Conservative party. Soon, he would be replaced by Edward Heath. He had been under an almost continuous barrage of criticism and had been subjected to many cruel squibs by cartoonists. He simply lacked that harsh necessity of political leadership required in the new world of the media: a strong and warm television personality (his Cheshire-cat smile simply didn't do the trick) and his apparent air of dry detachment combined with an equally apparent inability to match Harold Wilson in Commons debates produced an unsatisfactory result. A decent, thoughtful, and very proper Scottish gentleman, he was out of place in contemporary politics.

Sir Robert Menzies, former Prime Minister of Australia, came to Balmoral in August to discuss details of Prince Charles's transfer to Timbertop, the rugged up-country branch of Geelong Church of England Grammar School in Melbourne. The Prince would be exchanged for a Geelong boy, who would spend an equivalent six months at Gordonstoun. Prince Charles was not at all happy about this decision, on which he had not been consulted. But his father was adamant that he must go ahead. Although physically fit, and a decent weight for his height, Prince Charles still had a soft, boyish look at sixteen. Even the grueling training at Gordonstoun had failed to turn him into a rugged, powerful youth. His lamentable performance at several sports had made him the despair of his father. Prince Philip was determined on a sink-or-swim effort to bring about a transformation in his eldest boy that might force him to measure up to Philip's harsh standards. Timbertop was known as the ultimate and most harrowing of training schools; the Australians were notably lacking in delicacy when it came to dealing with the British, especially British royals. He was scheduled to go to Australia at the beginning of 1966.

The Queen was pleased with the progress of Princess Anne, who, as horse-mad as herself, a veritable hippophile, continued to do splendidly at Benenden. She was fifteen now, as spirited, vigorous, and impertinent as ever. She was pushing her way up to be captain of her house and housemother, both of which positions she would assume a year later. Prince Andrew was starting to emerge with a personality of his own. He was much closer to Anne than Charles. Not a beautiful child, he was aggressive, strong, and opinionated, taking after his father. He had enormous energy, running everybody in the family off their feet. The Queen Mother especially adored him. Prince Edward was a bouncing delight, adored by everyone.

October brought the Rhodesia crisis to a peak. On the eighth, negotiations toward an avoidance of a unilateral declaration of independence broke down in London. Ian Smith flew back to Salisbury, dismissing Prime Minister Wilson's warning that, were he to proceed, Rhodesia would be regarded as a rebel state, and there was more than a hint of charges of treason in the air. Two weeks later, Wilson was in Rhodesia, trying to avert the tragic consequences of what was generally known as UDI. Smith charged that Britain was imposing unfair conditions on a royal commission set up to resolve the issue; he had just declared a state of emergency. On November 11— ironically, Armistice Day—Smith finally and boldly declared Rhodesia's independence.

Wilson, joined by the government and unquestionably with the support of the Queen, let it be announced that Smith had committed an act of treason. The question arose whether force should be used; whether Britain should send in the Royal Air Force with paratroopers, in an attempt to crush the rebellious government. However, this was not by any means an easy prospect, and, despite fierce demands both from the right wing and the left, Wilson hung back. He, of course, had not forgotten Suez; in the admittedly unlikely event that Rhodesia should defeat the landing force on the ground, Britain's humiliation would be absolute. Furthermore, this was not an attack upon an Arab country, where deaths, no matter how numerous, could scarcely cause mourning in the cities, towns, and villages of England. Many Rhodesian residents had close relatives in Britain, and killing Rhodesians would be painfully offensive to a large proportion of the electorate.

There was fear also that, encouraged by the attack, the radical elements in the Rhodesian black population would be unleashed in the bloodbath to which Prince Philip had so rashly referred.

Wilson's dilemma was agonizing. His visits to the Queen went beyond the usual Tuesday evenings, and at least one of these took place at Buckingham Palace very late at night. There can be little doubt that she also was under great stress in the matter. Privy Council meetings were highly charged. The fact that there was no means of enforcing law and order was frustrating. The discussions in Cabinet rambled on and on,

Wilson still seeking negotiation, Barbara Castle and other powerful members of the Cabinet demanding severe action. Sanctions seemed to be the only form of punishment readily available.

Rhodesia depended to a great extent on its exports, notably of tobacco, and while an oil embargo was exercised, tobacco was stopped from coming into England. All of these efforts were halfhearted and generally useless, since, in fact, Ian Smith turned to South Africa for his oil supplies, cementing an alliance with an aggressive racist republic whose policies were in direct opposition to Britain's. By late November, just three weeks after the unilateral Declaration of Independence, talk of military intervention began to recur in Whitehall. But again, Wilson stood firm against any such suggestion.

Meanwhile, in Rhodesia itself, Smith was more popular than ever among his devoted white following. Even in the face of devastating criticism not only from the Commonwealth but from other nations as well, he rejoiced, knowing that he was supported not only by his personal popularity among the rank and file property owners, but also by the fear, endemic and perpetual from border to border on his landlocked nation, of what would become of those selfsame people if the blacks should take over.

Princess Margaret and Lord Snowdon took off to the United States on an expensive and controversial tour that fall. Princess Margaret's friend Sharman Douglas had been in the forefront of those Americans who had wanted the Princess to visit their country. The trip, which took in both coasts, was a marvel of extravagance: an Andover of the Queen's Flight was used for eight trips, only three of which were part of the official itinerary. The Andover, with a seven-man crew, had to be flown to different locations, including California, to supplement the Snowdons' trip in a Lockheed Jet Star which President Johnson had supplied. In addition, BOAC supplied a Super-VC-10; the royal party was ten strong and included a fashionable Mayfair hairdresser, René Moulard. There were also, the vigilant *New Statesman* recorded, "two menservants, two maids, a detective, a secretary, a lady-in-waiting, Princess's Principal Private Secretary, and the Deputy Captain of the Queen's Flight." A brief stopover at the Arizona Inn in Phoenix cost £3,000, or at least three to four times that much in contemporary money. The BOAC fare alone involved commandeering the entire plane and came to £11,000; the royal wardrobe cost £4,000.

Had Princess Margaret arrived in less than the grand style, Americans would have not appreciated it. The only valid criticism seemed to be that the tour was not undertaken as a result of an invitation by President Johnson, but instead was engineered by the Princess herself, who excused the costs of the trip on a necessity to attend the English-speaking Union and to incorporate the Society of London Fashion Designers' shows in San Francisco and Los Angeles. The rest of the trip looked rather like self-indulgence.

If that were the case (and the jury is still out on the matter), then that self-indulgence cost Princess Margaret dearly. After only three days in New York City, she became exhausted, canceled the meeting with architect Philip Johnson, and was driven to John Hay Whitney's estate at Manhasset, where she rested, canceling several engagements in Connecticut. In Los Angeles, there was an unseemly struggle among those who wished to be presented to her; at a party at the Bistro, she danced with Fred Astaire, Gene Kelly, and, most notably, her old friend Danny Kaye, while Lord Snowdon partnered Shirley MacLaine. The anti-royalist Marlon Brando characteristically backed out of the party at the last minute.

When the Princess and her husband returned to London in the third week of November, rude questions were asked about the trip in the House of Commons.

On December 20, Prince Charles won a silver medal, appropriately the Duke of Edinburgh's Award, following a severe test of endurance in athletics, first aid, mountain training, and pottery making at Gordonstoun. Two days later, the Queen and Prince Philip entertained a distinguished group to dinner at Buckingham Palace to discuss Charles's academic future.

Harold Wilson, the Archbishop of Canterbury, the Dean of Windsor, the principal of Gloucester University, and, last but by no means least, Lord Mountbatten entered into a brisk discussion. Harold Wilson thought it might be a good idea for the boy to go to a so-called "redbrick" university. Provincial education establishments that were allegedly of more democratic character than Oxford or Cambridge contained a large proportion of grammar-school products. Mountbatten said, succinctly, "Trinity, Dartmouth and the Royal Navy." He was,

of course, referring to Trinity College, Cambridge, where King
George VI and King Edward VII had been students and the
controversial R. A. Butler was now in charge; an overlooked
detail was that Anthony Blunt had agreed to become a fellow
at Trinity the following year.

Prince Philip was keen on Trinity, and so was the Queen.
Robin Woods, Dean of Windsor, went to Cambridge to test the
water; he returned, recommending strongly that Trinity should
be the choice. Butler recommended that Prince Charles should
not, in common with his grandfather, live away from the
college, but in fact should have rooms in it like any other
undergraduate. Prince Philip agreed; he continued to want his
son to have the most normal upbringing possible for a young
man. Luckily, the Prince was able to satisfy the requirements
for admission by scraping in on two A-levels.

Prince Charles flew to visit the Prince of Lichtenstein and his
family. There, he was reunited with his cousins, the children of
Prince Philip's sisters, who skied with him. They included
Prince Welf and Prince Georg Paul, who were, respectively,
eighteen and sixteen. Apparently unaware that their late father
had been involved in the bombing of London, Prince Charles
was very close to the two boys. Dermot Morrah, authorized
biographer of Prince Charles, wrote in his *To Be a King:*

> From a personal point of view it is fortunate that the old
> princely families have been largely excluded from the polit-
> ical life of the new Germany since the downfall of the
> Hohenzollern Empire in 1918.

Morrah added:

> The Prince of Wales [became] extremely fond of all three of
> his aunts. He finds them all completely different; although
> they share one characteristic, a mischievous sense of humor.
> There is always great excitement at Balmoral when any of
> them are coming to stay, and no less when there is a chance
> to go to stay with them. The cousins, too, fourteen of them,
> are exceedingly popular. Every one of them the Prince of
> Wales finds marvelous and funny . . .

19
***

IN JANUARY 1966, THE Queen and Prince Philip were pleased to see Charles fly off to Timbertop; a few days later, the couple left for a Caribbean tour. British Guiana, which had been a trouble spot for some time, was almost omitted from the schedule when the Opposition party announced a boycott. There were threats in Trinidad and Jamaica; the latter island, where the Rastafari group was creating problems, was left off the itinerary.

Prince Philip couldn't resist a quip during a visit to a hospital at Roseau, Dominica, when the matron said to him, "We have trouble with mosquitoes." Prince Philip replied, "You may have mosquitoes, but we have the press!" Immediately, the London newspapers flew into an uproar and demanded an apology which, very surprisingly, was actually made. But the Prince was soon in trouble again when he undertook a solo tour of the United States. He was extremely testy, bored, and irritable, and was annoyed with himself for having agreed to undertake the trip, which was to raise funds for charities run by Variety Clubs International. Reporters following him around needled him to the point that he frequently lost his temper. While he was in Miami, the Hotel Fontainebleu was picketed by angry Cubans who were yelling about British indifference and colonialism. The Prince was asked, "Do you approve of Britain trading with North Vietnam in the midst of the Vietnam War?" He snapped, "If I did give an opinion it wouldn't make the slightest bit of difference one way or the other." When a five-year-old child, Sharon Smith, was introduced to him, the child said she had never met a prince before. Philip made a rude gesture at the photographers, and said, irritably, "Never mind! These camera bugs have never met a prince before either!''

In Houston, he came perilously close to attacking the press corps with his bare fists. Asked about the Beatles, he said sourly, ''I'd rather people go around making noise, even idiots' noise, rather than [sic] fighting.'' This didn't go down with admirers of the Beatles, or with the American establishment, which was still committed to the Vietnam War. He seemed to be almost deliberately setting out to displease everyone. When a radio reporter pushed a microphone into his face, he pushed it aside, saying, ''Stuff it up your you-know-what!'' When Harry Gould, paper box tycoon, said, ''Your Highness, my house is at least as nice as yours,'' Prince Philip replied, ''Am I to consider that a secondhand invitation?'' Gould angrily shouted at him, ''Who writes your material?'' Mrs. Gould screamed, ''You mustn't talk like that to His Majesty [sic]!''

That same month, by happy coincidence, the Queen Mother was in Australia at the same time as Prince Charles. She met Charles in Canberra, the nation's capital, and they had talked several times on the telephone. Democratic and liberal in character, he enjoyed the fact that he was called ''mate,'' by average Australians, that there was no fuss and bother, snobbery, or sycophancy in their attitude toward him. The clean air and water, the immense blue skies with their dramatic cloud formations, the haunting, olive-green bush, the scent of eucalyptus trees, and the unrivaled taste of a heavily barbecued T-bone steak won him completely. Far from the claustrophobic castles and somber palaces of England, far from the depressing austerity of Gordonstoun, Timbertop was situated strikingly in the foothills of the Great Dividing Range, surrounded by immense gum-tree forests. Self-reliance was even more the order of the day than at Gordonstoun. There was a blessed lack of cold, snobbish, authoritarian teachers; the boys (Charles was accompanied by his handsome equerry Squadron Leader David Checketts) clubbed in together to repair broken pipes, cut and stack timber for fires, and repair cars, trucks, and equipment.

It was, of course, not a comfortable experience. Prince Charles later told a BBC interviewer, Jack De Manio, in March 1969:

The first [cross-country expeditions] I had when I got there were absolutely horrifying. It was 90 degrees in the shade and flies everywhere, and you sort of ran around amongst the kangaroos and things. Dust and everything . . .

But he added:

[The Australians] were very, very good and marvelous people. Very genuine. Said exactly what they thought . . . I walked into the unit one evening and I had an umbrella with me—it had been raining quite heavily, and they all looked rather quizzically at the strange English thing and, as I walked out, having turned the lights out, there were marvelous shouts of "Oh, Pommy bastard."

Calling the heir to the throne of England a "Pommy bastard" was the ultimate compliment. The term "Pommy" came from remarks made about the early settlers from England, who had apples in their cheeks; the French word for apple was, of course, *pomme*.

Charles also enjoyed a visit to New Guinea, where he was received at a native feast by the local chief and his followers dressed in feathers and beating drums and, quite suddenly, singing "God Save the Queen." Prince Charles said:

It was the most moving, touching thing I have ever experienced . . . to see these native people, miles from Britain, singing the national anthem. And the tears practically rolled down my cheeks.

He shared his mother's deep love of the Commonwealth, of the way in which the most far-ranging peoples were united, without being victims of Empire, in devotion toward his mother. Undoubtedly, the experience strengthened him in the thought that one day, probably when he was already in middle age, he would become King.

Prime Minister Wilson decided on an election in March. Labor polled 47.9 percent of the votes, returning with a majority of 97 in the House of Commons, the Conservative vote having fallen by 550,000. The Queen announced, in her gracious speech, that plans were now far advanced to nationalize most of the steel industry, set up a land commission to collect a levy on development values and the sale of land, and establish a prices and incomes policy.

The Queen was forty years of age. She had reigned for fourteen years. She was as beautiful as ever, her figure untouched by time or weight. Precisely how she achieved this marvelous result nobody could understand. Perhaps she simply willed herself to be the way she was.

In May, Princess Margaret and Lord Snowdon ran into more controversy. Arriving forty minutes late for a crowded showing of the British movie *Modesty Blaise* at the Palais des Festivales, they stood to receive the expected burst of applause, only to find themselves booed and hissed by the obstreperous audience. They shrugged it off: the behavior was typical of the international riffraff that jammed the city at festival time. The Queen is said to have found the occasion equally amusing; and she is sure to have been entertained by the fact that, in an introduction to *Debrett's Peerage, Baronetage, Knightage and Companionage,* the editor, P. Montague-Smith, revealed that not only was she descended from William the Conqueror, but from his defeated enemy King Harold. Montague-Smith also determined the Queen was descended from Lady Godiva, famous for her nude horse ride, which brought some ribald comments from comedians in view of the Queen's support of horse racing, and her ardent love of riding.

The Queen was less amused when she and Philip started a tour of western England farming districts, and a Vietnam War protester sat down in the road in front of her car and had to be dragged out of the way by police; and she did not appear to be delighted when a number of letters appeared in the press claiming that her private train left a trail of lobster and shrimp shells crawling with flies, beer cans, wine bottles, toilet paper, lettuce, eggshells, and newspapers all over the western countryside. Asked to comment, a Palace spokesman said, "Take it up with British Railways!"

The relationship of the Snowdons ran into trouble: while Snowdon was absent in India on a photographic expedition, the Princess was the object of constant gossip in society. She was supposed to be romantically involved with a wine merchant, the good-looking Anthony Barton, who was godfather to her daughter Sarah; he was a married man, which increased the intensity of the adverse comment. Snowdon and the Princess were seen arguing over where they should live in the country;

after all these years of marriage, they still had no private residence outside of London. He wanted to live in a house that had belonged to Oliver Messel, in Sussex; she favored a large home in Sunninghill Park. He won, but she hated the place; she found it too small and too modest for her tastes. The quarrels were violent and lethal, and the Queen and the Queen Mother must have found them distressing. There was more adverse comment when she abruptly canceled a lunch in her honor and left with Snowdon for another vacation with the Aga Khan. When she returned, she was seen frequently at parties with a new beau, Sir Alec Douglas-Home's neurotic, manic-depressive son, Robin.

The Queen made a two-day visit to Northern Ireland at the beginning of July, quite ignoring threats of violence against her. The route was very heavily guarded; it was a tense and uncomfortable visit. There was a radical demonstration, connected more to the Vietnam issue than to IRA objections to the stay. There was an unpleasant episode when Rex McCandless, who had designed a rather shaky helicopter, crashed his aircraft right in front of the royal couple. And a youth, age seventeen, flung a concrete block in an attempt to injure the Queen as she drove through the streets; a chambermaid tossed a bottle, hitting a car window.

Looking somewhat disgruntled after this experience, Prince Philip was not pleased when, on his return to London, he was informed that the Institute of Physics and the Physical Society, which had invited him to be an honorary member because of his continuing interest in science, now refused him permission to join, by a vote of 850–250 against.

Prince Philip was again embattled. He had flown to Buenos Aires for a semi-official visit; the country was in an uproar over an incident in which twenty nationalists had hijacked an Argentine airliner and had arrived in the Falkland Islands to claim them from Britain. Armed with rifles, they had made an audacious landing on a rain-swept racecourse near the governor's residence. Royal Marines surrounded the plane, finally arresting the hijackers.

Prince Philip heard pistol shots as he dressed for dinner on his first night in Rosario, the second-largest city in the nation. A gang of students burst into the British Consulate carrying guns, wrecked the offices, tore and burned important documents, and raised the Argentinean flag on the roof. Death threats rained down on the residence where Prince Philip was staying, and hundreds of leaflets were flung at him as he went out by car. Prince Philip told reporters, ''This is like a television installment thriller.'' No one was allowed to shake his hand at a British Chamber of Commerce dinner in case someone should attempt something against him. Actually, he went unharmed, the worse injury he suffered being a heavy fall from his horse at a celebrity polo match, and some stress in his hands (he would later be afflicted by painful arthritis) when, to boos and screams, he laid a foundation stone for a new British Embassy, certainly not the best of timing in the circumstances. It would be sixteen years before a more serious incident led to war between Britain and Argentina.

The bumpy year for the royal family continued in the late fall and early winter as the Queen Mother became ill. She was suffering from what may have been cancer of the bowel, and at the least, from a severe benign tumor which called for a radical colostomy. The Queen visited her repeatedly in the hospital, where she rallied with her customary bravery, good humor, and considerable strength. Prince Charles was also able to visit her; on his eighteenth birthday in November, he had displaced his father as possible regent should his mother become incapacitated; he had been made for the first time Counsellor of State, the first of six members of the family who would act for the Queen should she be abroad; his income was doubled to the equivalent of $84,000.

At the beginning of December, an attempt was made to resolve the chronic problem with Rhodesia; with the Queen's evident approval, Harold Wilson flew to a high-level meeting with Ian Smith aboard the HMS *Tiger* off Gibraltar. The encounter took place in severe weather conditions; the meeting was scarcely less turbulent. With various members of the party, including Wilson, intermittently seasick, and only the strapping Ian Smith, to the annoyance of the Londoners, proving healthy and vigorous, the discussions ended in a stalemate. Smith seemed to be agreeing to concessions, but in the end did not. Wilson was compelled to return to England empty-handed, which did not help his already strained popularity. In January, he drastically reshuffled his Cabinet, but it didn't seem to help.

Both the Queen and Princess Margaret were ill at the beginning of the new year, from internal problems; the Queen in particular suffered severely from gastroenteritis.

Princess Margaret was rumored to have taken an overdose of sleeping tablets in an attempt to commit suicide; she had been having major problems with Snowdon, and there were reports of violent arguments at Kensington Palace. She was restless and unhappy in her marriage, perhaps in part because she simply didn't have the deep cultural knowledge and intellectual range of her husband, who became increasingly distressed by her antic, superficial, and somewhat giddy way of life. She suffered badly from the near-loss of one of her favorite dogs, which fell under a train.

Prince Philip had his own distractions that winter: his mother was still living in Athens, where the political situation was rapidly deteriorating and was potentially extremely dangerous. There were violent meetings of left-wing members of the Greek Youth Movement at which King Constantine and his mother, Queen Friederike, were strongly insulted. A court-martial ended after ten weeks of hearings; twenty-eight military officers had been tried for treason over a bomb plot against former Prime Minister Papandreou, then was reopened as new witnesses turned up. Fifteen officers were sentenced to between two and eighteen years; others were acquitted; but the nation was in an uproar over the matter, and the Premier, Paraskevopoulos, was forced to resign in March. In the midst of this critical situation, Prince Philip visited his mother in February, hoping to persuade her to return to England to live. She was offered a permanent place at Buckingham Palace or any other royal residence should she wish to take sanctuary.

On March 8, there was a curious little incident at the Victoria and Albert Museum in London. The fail-safe alarm system was triggered off accidentally when the Queen and Princess Margaret (Prince Philip was in Australia), the Soviet Ambassador, senior Russian diplomatists, and others were visiting an exhibition of joint Great Britain-Russian exhibits. They were trapped in the building and couldn't get out. The Queen and the other members of the party remained calm until they were released.

Meantime, the royal family was troubled with a serious matter. The Earl of Harewood, well-known patron of music, and son of Queen Elizabeth's aunt, the late Princess Royal, was sued for divorce for adultery. Even though Harewood was first cousin of the Queen, this was not a drastically serious matter. In view of the fact that Harewood was not in direct line to the throne, there could clearly be special arrangements if the Queen was willing to make them. And this despite the continuing existence of the Royal Marriage Act, which had destroyed Princess Margaret's chance for happiness.

The problem was that Lady Harewood charged that the Earl, and his alleged mistress, the Australian musician Patricia Tuckwell, had an illegitimate son, who was now two and a half years old. This presented the Queen with a very uncomfortable situation, and brought untold amounts of adverse publicity, fiercely stimulated by the popular press. Much sympathy was drawn to Lady Harewood, herself a former musician; she was the former Marion Stein, daughter of a distinguished Jewish music publisher and a woman of great elegance and distinction. The Queen promised to give her decision as soon as possible on whether the divorce would be granted.

Following a meeting of the Privy Council, the Queen consented to Lord Harewood marrying Patricia Tuckwell. However, the couple could not be married in the British Isles, and had to be wed in the United States. The wedding took place at a mansion in New Canaan, Connecticut, on July 31.

Prince Charles himself was showing musical ability: he played the cello in a Gordonstoun school concert in Edinburgh in late February, and later appeared in Gilbert and Sullivan's comic opera *The Pirates of Penzance.* He emulated his father in falling off a horse at polo at the end of April; chose his courses at Trinity College in May, and was informed he would be named Prince of Wales in 1969. He would be Counsellor of State during the Queen's visit to Canada later in the year.

Early in May, the Queen was compelled to invite the Duke and Duchess of Windsor to an occasion at which a plaque would be unveiled in memory of the late Queen Mary; the Windsors accepted. The ceremony, held on June 7, was the first public recognition of the Windsors by the Palace to date; the plaque was installed on a wall of Marlborough House, Queen Mary's former residence; it is to be noted, though, that the further step was not taken: the Windsors were not invited to attend the Derby with the Queen that afternoon, and instead they went to Kensington Palace to join Princes Marina, Duchess of Kent.

Outside the confines of the royal family, the world was no less troubled than before. Britain's efforts to enter the European Economic Community were still being thwarted. Charles de Gaulle was still a stubborn obstacle. Israel crushed Egypt,

Syria, and Jordan in the Six-Day War; British Foreign Secretary George Brown, with the approval of Prime Minister and Queen, failed to bring England in. Aden became independent following widespread revolutionary activity; there was civil war in Nigeria; the economy, despite clearing of heavy debts to the American Federal Reserve Bank, was still an ailing invalid. It was so drab and depressing a year that even the Queen's launching of the celebrated ship *Queen Elizabeth 2* became almost excessively reported as a good and glorious event.

Meanwhile, in Greece, the militant colonels formed a fascistic junta to cancel popular elections, suppress free thought, imprison radicals, and essentially turn the nation into a gross equivalent of its 1936 situation, in which a similar military government had been set up. There were protests in London and New York, and other world capitals, as purges began, removing people disloyal to the regime or to national ideals. The movie star Melina Mercouri was charged with treason. A control board formed during the Nazi occupation was restored. There were boycotts of Greek theater, and other arts throughout the world. Princess Alice was in constant danger in Athens, as the rebels threatened the safety of any member or associate of the royal family.

On October 8, 1967, with Princess Anne doing extremely well in her last year at Benenden, and he himself emerging a highly successful Guardian, or head boy, of his house at Gordonstoun, Prince Charles was driven to Trinity College, Cambridge, by Squadron Leader David Checketts. He was, by his own wish, housed in unexceptional quarters, not much more elaborate than might be found in a middle-class London flat. Whereas all other freshmen had to share a bathroom, he had his own, which only one other student used.

Over a thousand were waiting for him, cheering ecstatically, including a large number of mini-skirted girls screaming loudly; it took the efforts of a number of college porters to push the gates shut to prevent the screaming females flowing in. It was a proud day for the Queen and Prince Philip. But problems lay ahead: there was much criticism of his just getting in on two A-levels; his choice of subjects, archaeology and anthropology, seemed marginal; it was wondered whether he would be able to obtain a deep learning of British history or of international politics. Oddly, though, nobody seemed to raise the issue of the situation in which his master would be R. A. Butler, whose political background of appeasement to Germany before and even during World War II was scarcely desirable. Also, the intermittent presence of Sir Anthony Blunt as fellow soon afterward might have given pause had anyone known about him.

Michael Varney, Charles's bodyguard, recalled in his book that he was faced with the peculiar problem that the university was in the heart of the town, and that, since the Prince would be riding a bicycle, or walking, he could always be vulnerable to assault or kidnap. Moreover, whereas before Prince Charles had lived in a totally male environment at Gordonstoun and Timbertop, he would now undoubtedly be dating girls, many of whom could be predatory and drawing him into a dangerous situation; if one of these girls were to become pregnant, she might have a chance to be the future Queen of England. Prince Charles could scarcely be expected to live a celibate existence, no matter how devoted he might be to the throne.

At the end of the year, the military junta in Greece discovered an attempted counter-*coup d'état* by King Constantine, and summarily drove him, his wife, his mother Queen Friederike, and Prince Philip's mother Princess Alice, into exile. In a repetition of the event of 1922, they were assisted by the Pope, and took sanctuary in Rome, whence Princess Alice, at the Queen and Prince Philip's urgent invitation, proceeded to London. She was housed at Buckingham Palace, in almost complete secrecy, perhaps because of fears of a repetition of earlier political incidents in London; in her gray nun's habit, for she was still Mother Alice Elizabeth of the Sisterhood of Martha and Mary, she drifted about the Palace corridors like a ghost, a spectral figure addressed by everyone in sign language or deafening shouts, smoking, coughing, speaking in her odd, nervous voice, almost never seen, even at a window, by the most urgent royal watchers. It is hard to believe that she was not a thorough nuisance, irritating everyone, but some hardworking publicist, or possibly the Press Secretary, issued the statement that she was proving to be an "admirable adviser to the Queen."

The new year of 1968 began in a swirl of controversy. Enoch Powell fervently attacked the overwhelming wave of black immigration into England, seeking a clampdown on Asians arriving from Kenya. He was supported by Duncan Sandys in compelling Wilson's government to bring in emergency legislation to curb the flow. There was great fear of severe racial disharmony and explosions, in a nation which was yet again suffering from economic and industrial blight. The response was that thousands of Kenyan immigrants rushed the airports, seeking to obtain entry before the bill was passed. The country was torn apart on the issue, charges of racism fiercely leveled against Powell, Sandys, and even the embattled Harold Wilson; demonstrators appeared at Buckingham Palace and at 10 Downing Street, demanding that Wilson bring about the bar on "Negroes and coloreds." The bill was passed in the Commons 372–62, with 180 MPs abstaining, and hard-liners like Maudling and Michael Foot, on opposite sides of the House, demurring strongly.

In March, George Brown furiously resigned as Foreign Secretary because Wilson had decided to close the London gold market. Brown raged that Wilson was at least partly responsible for the cynicism in England, and that he would bring about an urgent campaign to restore confidence in the government. He stayed on as Labor party deputy leader. That same month, the government was defeated in four by-elections, and Heath vigorously called for Wilson to resign and his government to admit that it was finished. Wilson reshuffled the Cabinet, making controversial appointments.

All of this upheaval stemmed from the disastrous devaluation of the pound. On March 19, Chancellor of the Exchequer Roy Jenkins produced the most harrowing peacetime budget to date. Taxes were increased by £775 million with surtax on investments, corporation tax, purchase tax, selective employment tax, and wine and liquor taxes. Tobacco, gasoline, and gambling were extremely heavily taxed. The country's mood was utterly depressed, recalling the worst days of the Attlee administration. People felt defeated, hopeless, painfully aware that Canada and Australia, to mention only two Commonwealth countries, were enormously more prosperous and were enjoying comparatively trouble-free existence. The executive class was devastated by the budget. There were murmurings of revolution, of mutiny in the forces, of a violent overthrow of the government itself.

Cecil King, megalomaniac chairman of the International Publishing Corporation, became the self-appointed spokesman of a wide area of the tax-crippled establishment. With reckless folly, he began indulging in the pipe dream of a full-scale military *coup d'état* similar to that in Greece. The almost unwritten Constitution of England indicated that only the Queen herself could dismiss the government or allow the creation of a temporary military or police state. Certainly, the Queen was "in charge" of the Army when untoward exhibitions of paintings or the seizure of essays by royal Princes needed to be appropriately dealt with.

How King, who was scarcely popular at the Palace, could possibly have hoped to inspire anyone at the highest level to bring about such a coup remains inexplicable. Except that he seemed to have lost all sense of proportion and of reasonably achievable probabilities. Cecil King selected Lord Mountbatten as the instrument of his absurdist plan. He also sought the support of Hugh Cudlipp, co-publisher with him of the magazine *Encounter,* which was believed to have CIA connections, and joint managing director (later chairman) of *Daily Mirror* newspapers. King urged Cudlipp to arrange a meeting with Mountbatten, and this was fixed at Mountbatten's country estate at Broadlands. Mountbatten agreed with his visitors that the nation was in an appalling state. His own tax bills can only have provoked such an opinion, though his political leanings were known to be toward the left. King earnestly proposed that the Queen should seek Wilson's resignation and that there should be drastic changes in the economic structure of the country. Lord Mountbatten could scarcely agree with such revolutionary statements. However, he very much wanted the deep cynicism and gloom in England to be relieved.

Another meeting was arranged between Mountbatten, King, and a reluctant Cudlipp at Mountbatten's house on May 8. King, on this occasion, added another to the party: Sir Solly Zuckerman, distinguished Chief Scientific Adviser to the government. Zuckerman arrived late. King delivered a prolonged diatribe, dragging out a whole succession of hobby horses. He promised a major national crisis, in which Wilson's government would collapse, people would be shot in the city streets, and anarchy would break loose. He felt that Mountbatten should head up the military takeover, restoring confidence in the people.

Zuckerman arrived in the midst of this ill-advised peroration. Mountbatten, instead of denouncing King on the spot on behalf of the Queen (as he should have done), displayed the same shilly-shallying he had shown at Suez. He asked Zuckerman what he thought. Zuckerman denounced the entire scheme as "rank treachery." He called King's mention of machine guns on the streets "appalling." He was, after all, a servant to the government, and dismissed the whole idea out of hand. Mountbatten agreed. Mountbatten's Head of Naval Retinue, William Evans, wrote in his memoirs:

> Lord Louis came dashing out to the bedroom where I was working and said: "This man is insane—he wants *me* to organize a coup, throw out the government and worse, put armed troops on the street . . . Me? Overthrow the crown? *Me?* Give me about two or three minutes and then come in and get rid of him."

Zuckerman had already walked out. Disgusted, Cudlipp followed. Evans said, "I regret to say, Your Lordship, you are required at the Ministry of Defense." It was the customary line, prearranged at all times, used to get rid of unwelcome guests.

One who took the plot seriously, perhaps too seriously, was Marcia Williams, Harold Wilson's secretary, who apparently spoke to the press at a later stage, talking of Mountbatten as "a prime mover in the plan." She added:

> Mountbatten had a map on the wall of his office showing how it could be done. Harold and I used to stand in the State Room at Number Ten and work up where they would put the guns. We reckoned then they would site them in the Horse Guards.

She made the statement many years later. It is hard to believe that her memory was not at fault, assuming she was accurately quoted.

The only result of this nonsense was that King had to resign as chairman of IPC, and his career did not recover. What the episode does illustrate is that a number of rational individuals, above all Lord Mountbatten, were in a state of unique disaffection, deeply unhappy with Wilson and appalled by the state of the nation. So desperate was the campaign against Wilson that an old canard was revived, that he was a Soviet agent. The hysteria that seemed perpetually to underlie the well-groomed, smooth, and impeccably polished surface of the English ruling class, had seldom threatened to burst forth with such frenzy. Wilson's plight can only have attracted the Queen's sympathy; and her feelings for England must have made 1968 one of her very worst years.

Civil war in Nigeria that summer of 1968 was another of her burdens. And her health was known to be less than perfect: she had a recurrence of sinus trouble and internal problems. Also, there were threats against Prince Charles, who was to become Prince of Wales the following year. Welsh nationalists stated that he might be injured or blown up at the ceremony. In mid-June, he was invested as a Knight of the Order of the Garter, facing a new barrage of threats; when he arrived at the Welsh Office in Cardiff, to be indoctrinated in Welsh affairs, he was rudely heckled by a hostile crowd, and notes arrived again threatening his life should he be invested. Apparently he was impressed by criticism that he was not studying modern and constitutional history, and decided to take up a course in those subjects instead of archaeology and anthropology.

Princess Anne was finishing up successfully at Benenden. She had passed her first driving test in mid-April. Though not beautiful, she was attractive, forceful, and sharp-witted; although she still irritated many people, and bored more, particularly with her constant interest in horses, the majority were intrigued, even captivated by her. They liked her spirit and her energy. She remained closer to her father, as did Prince Andrew, while Prince Edward took after his eldest brother.

The Queen was as fiercely protective of her family's privacy as before. She was furious when the *Daily Express* gave over almost half of its front page to a picture, originally published in *Paris-Match,* of herself holding Prince Edward in her arms in bed shortly after his birth four years earlier. The newspaper categorically refused to drop the photograph.

In the fall, Prince Philip was in Mexico. Prince Philip also made a visit to Acapulco. He renewed an earlier and most affectionate relationship with the Anglo-Indian motion picture star Merle Oberon. Miss Oberon, a great friend of the Duchess of Kent and Lord Mountbatten, had visited the royal couple in London preceding her marriage in July 1957, to the multimillionaire Italian-Mexican Bruno Pagliai. The Pagliais had adopted two children. Her friends agree that Miss Oberon was in love with Prince Philip. He even stayed at her Acapulco house when her husband was in Mexico City; it was an exquisite home, designed by her in the Persian mode, and the Prince was captivated with it. He arrived at the airport; Miss Oberon greeted him in her limousine. The British Ambassador to Mexico advised her that the Prince would be taking a limousine to her house. She was furious and told him, "Prince Philip will ride in *my* car!" The Ambassador replied, "Mrs. Pagliai, that is emphatically not the correct protocol where royalty is concerned." Merle snapped back, "Then I suggest you go and look for a place for Prince Philip to stay, because it will *not* be at my house!" The Ambassador shuddered and backed down. Miss Oberon walked up to the plane, curtsied, twirled her parasol, and greeted the Prince.

He enjoyed his stay. Pictures of the Queen and his family were placed by his bed. He telephoned the Queen just before her departure from Heathrow. According to a very close friend of Miss Oberon:

> I do not know whether Merle had an affair with Prince Philip. But she certainly liked to give the impression that they were lovers. She was very romantic, and may have invented it, but many of us felt that it had happened.

Whatever the truth, they certainly had a very close relationship. Prince Philip was, at forty-seven, still very handsome, and Merle Oberon was at the height of her beauty. If indeed a liaison developed—Prince Philip did return on other occasions (on one of them sailing into Acapulco Bay aboard the royal yacht *Britannia* and firing a romantic salute below Miss Oberon's windows)—it can only have been an extremely dangerous situation for both. If the gossips on both sides of the Atlantic were to be believed, Prince Philip's other affairs with women were brief, insignificant, and could never be publicly known. But even in her declining, almost vanished career, Miss Oberon remained a name to conjure with, and not only that, she had a jealous and possessive husband, quite devoid of Prince Philip's looks, possessed of an Italian's pride and hatred of being cuckolded.

Prince Philip left after a very short stay, for Brazil, to join his wife on an official State visit. He proved to be as bouncingly tactless as ever. Introduced to the admiral of the Brazilian fleet, he asked him if he had won his gun battles on a lake. The admiral replied to the effect that it was obvious Prince Philip had had to win his in the royal bedroom. Always a good sport, despite his testy character, the Prince was compelled to laugh.

For the first time in her life, the Queen was visibly exasperated during the tour; Brazilian inefficiency infuriated her, and when plans were changed for a reception, she outright berated the Embassy staff; during that same reception, the lights failed, and there was a deafening silence. Suddenly, the Queen's high, sharp voice was heard uttering the words, "Where's Cawston?" Almost nobody knew what she was talking about. "Cawston, Cawston?" the Brazilian guests repeated in the darkness. She was referring to Richard Cawston, director of a film, *Royal Family,* in which she had appeared.

In Chile, the crowds were cheerful and enthusiastic; the Queen looked notably glum in all except the official photographs. She showed one of her rare displays of open concern when, during a procession through the streets in a nineteenth-century French coach, an enormous dog leaped through the Army guard line and furiously bit one of the horses drawing the vehicle along. The horse reared, and the coach lurched violently; a policeman kicked the intruding animal and it fled, yelping loudly.

A week after their return to London, no doubt much to the royals' annoyance, the British Press Council rejected the Palace's complaints against the *Daily Express* for publishing pictures of the Queen in bed with her youngest son. But the Queen was visibly amused when, at a party at the Palace in honor of members of Britain's Olympic team, twenty-eight-year-old champion runner Jim Adler sat down firmly on the throne and picked at a chicken leg with his teeth. Such events provided a welcome light relief; trouble was still threatened from Wales, and in fact, in her gracious speech in Parliament at the end of October, the Queen felt constrained to reassert the ancient ties that bound Wales, Scotland, and Northern Ireland to the throne. She was clearly nervous about what might happen when her son became Prince of Wales the following summer. And right up to the end of the year, the country's mood remained restive, the continuing reshuffles of the Labor government indicative that much was still unwell in the body politic.

20

***

PRINCE CHARLES'S FORTHCOMING INVESTITURE as Prince of Wales continued to attract the serious criticism of Welsh nationalists. The Prince issued a statement, saying that he did not blame the Welsh for demonstrating against him, but hoped that things might improve after he had been in Wales for eight weeks, in preparation for the occasion. Privately, he was annoyed at the interruption to his studies at Cambridge, which might seriously handicap him in pursuit of a degree; already very much a modern man, he anxiously desired to be considered seriously, but at the same time knew that tradition would bind him into the investiture, and there was no escaping it. And it is reasonable to deduce that a part of him quickend to the idea of so ceremonial a presentation to his mother's people.

Meanwhile, the Queen, concerned for national unity in the face of increasing separatism in Scotland as well as in Wales, became the first reigning monarch since the crowns of Scotland and England were joined in 1603 to open the Session of the Church of Scotland General Assembly. Dissentients were few, and there were no scenes of violence. The Queen had recently returned from Austria, where she had made history by being the first reigning British monarch to go to that country officially in sixty-six years.

Prince Philip continued to sustain his image of a jocular, opinionated humorist; at the annual dinner of the Royal College of Science Union in London, he said, "I am delighted to find the Union so broad-minded and tolerant, especially considering how many of the officers are from Wales." He added, *inter alia:* "I am one of those stupid bums that never went to a university—and a fat lot of harm it did me." Shortly afterward,

343

he addressed the students of Edinburgh University; repeatedly hissed and booed, he was heckled by one youth who was annoyed that all the questions had been vetted in advance and insisted upon an "open discussion." At last, the Prince lost control and shouted at him, quite unroyally, "Shut up and grow up!" The incident caused much criticism. So did one in which Prince Charles visited a Welsh mining village and spoke to two poverty-stricken children. His lack of a grasp on reality was shown when he asked a woman accompanying them, "Are you their nanny?" There was further hostility toward the royal family when word leaked out that the Queen intended to intervene in the continuing struggle over the issue of Rhodesian independence. Ian Smith expressed disbelief and dismay at the suggestion; he was referring to the possibility that she might issue a broadcast appeal for loyalty following Smith's announcement that he would introduce apartheid in his troubled nation. She was directly attacked by Lance Smith, Minister of Internal Affairs in Salisbury, with the words:

> She is a figurehead and mouthpiece of whatever government is in power. Our people cannot look to the Great White Queen for protection. We should declare ourselves a republic.

Lance Smith accused the Queen of playing a part in "the handing over of Kenya to the criminals of the Mau Mau." He made an indirect reference to the surrender of Zanzibar to Communist influences.

At last, on July 1, Prince Charles underwent the ceremony of investiture at Caernarvon Castle. Right up to the last minute, there were explosions and gunshots, threatening and disturbing to the royal family. No less than nine separate explosions were traced to activist sources. On the morning of the investiture, two men were killed in an attack on a government office, and a post office building in Cardiff was shattered by a time bomb.

Even on the royal train itself, a bomb was located, and the royal family had to be stopped at the town of Crewe while it was dismantled. It was found to be harmless, but the episode scarcely was encouraging. As they arrived, there was word that a large party tent, constructed for a post-investiture event, was burned to the ground. The city was jammed with thousands of people for the royal arrival. The progress began at a local factory; as the fleet of cars proceeded to the Castle, a railway siding blew up and a young man smashed an egg on the hood of the royal Rolls-Royce. The crowd screamed, "Lynch him!" and "Traitor!" as he was hurried off by police.

Lord Snowdon, shrewdly chosen for the task of organizing the great occasion, had, in concert with the Duke of Norfolk, Earl Marshal, skillfully staged the pageantry, recalling the glamour and excitement of the present Duke of Windsor's investiture by Winston Churchill in 1911. The gloom and drizzle of the morning were relieved by a blaze of multicolored banners streaming down the ancient Castle walls with motifs of bears, lions, wolves, ravens, and even severed heads, the heraldic emblems of generations of nobility.

Prince Charles arrived first, still looking touchingly boyish with his soft, pink, seemingly beardless cheeks, slight figure, and carefully plastered-down hair. He had even now not acquired the size and ruggedness he would have as a fully grown man. He walked gingerly, nervously, his deportment becomingly modest; he was accompanied by two baronets carrying banners, and was escorted by the burnished glitter of the Household Cavalry. He looked up, shyly startled and pleased by the trumpet fanfare delivered by heralds from the Eagle Tower. A twenty-one-gun salute greeted the Queen and Prince Philip. As the Queen's carriage jolted to a halt outside the Castle gate, an equerry delivered a time-honored request for the custodian to open the entrance.

As the Queen walked in, impeccably dignified, looking astonishingly young and trim, Lord Snowdon handed her the six and one-half pound official key, which she received, and handed back. She and her husband stepped up to the thrones, which had a primitive look, rather like (as the London *Times* observed) Stonehenge. They were sheltered from the increasing drizzle by a canopy; the vast crowd of dignitaries was not as fortunate, and no one, apparently, had the temerity to open an umbrella. The Queen Mother, Princess Anne, and Princess Margaret made their own ascent as the Queen instructed Garter King of Arms to fetch her son, who walked solemnly inward to the low platform, accompanied by notables who carried sword, coronet, golden rod, and ring.

The Prince, now flushing visibly, in his purple velvet and ermine, three times made a bow to those around him, and then knelt before his mother, who, with great poise, invested him as the Letters Patent were read aloud. As she placed the golden coronet with its fringing of ermine upon his head, he fixed it in position, afraid it might fall off. He declared to her his devotion as "your liege man of life and limb and earthly worship," and they exchanged kisses. Prince Charles read the Response to the Address of the University College of Wales president in Welsh, which brought a strong ripple of approval from the crowd. The drizzle turned to rain as the religious service proceeded.

As he left for what would be four days of official appearances, the Prince apparently forgot to wave to the people, and his mother tenderly raised his right hand in reminder. Planes flew past, dipping their wings, the blare of trumpets acting in counterpoint to the loud scream of the engines. The procession was gone.

Despite more bomb scares and threats, the Prince continued on his progress aboard the *Britannia.* Numerous pretty girls were in the royal party, causing some unnecessary comments in the press. The Queen caught cold as a result of the chilly conditions at Caernarvon and had to cancel a dinner party in honor of Tricia, daughter of President Nixon, scheduled for the following night. She was busy after that preparing for a cruise of the Norwegian fjords; she worked hard on a microdot message which was taken to the moon by U.S. astronauts in mid-July.

The Norwegian cruise aboard the *Britannia* and, later, the Norwegian royal yacht *Norge,* proved a welcome break in a strenuous and threatening year. King Olav was loved by the whole royal family, to which he was related. When the Queen returned to London, she had a long rest from official engagements, suggesting that her health was still in question. In October, Prince Philip was once again in the news, talking in Vienna of the necessity for unification; he was said to be still connected to the Bilderbergers. And at the same time, there were the murmurings, which would soon swell to a loud clamor, of the improprieties of Prince Bernhard vis-à-vis Lockheed, with which he had become deeply involved; Prince Philip, who now played a dominant role in the World Wildlife Fund headed by Bernhard, would soon be in danger of being charged with a most undesirable partnership, and there was much talk of his sharing the use of an apartment in Paris with the husband of the Netherlands Queen.

On his birthday on November 14, Prince Charles made a decent gesture, whether it was prompted by his mother or not—a gesture which undoubtedly helped to make him among the most beloved of the royal family. In view of the state of the British finances, he agreed to give back to the Treasury 50 percent of his $72,000 allowance from the Duchy of Cornwall. The remaining $456,000 of Duchy income would be paid to the Queen as part of the $1,140,000 accorded to her by the Civil List since 1952. It was a time of much discussion of the royal family's financial problems. Prince Philip said on an American television show that he and the Queen might have to leave Buckingham Palace, that considerable corners had to be cut, and that a yacht had had to be sold; he might also have to give up polo. (Actually, he had already been advised by his doctors not to continue with the sport in view of severe arthritis in his left hand.) He even, perhaps in jest, mentioned in the interview that the Queen might have to abdicate. Buckingham Palace on the Queen's instruction said that no such question had in fact arisen. The government was aggravated by Prince Philip's TV appearance, even the most ardent royalists objecting to his discussion of private matters and absurd pleading of poverty when his wife was the richest woman in the world.

He at least succeeded in his purpose to this extent: Harold Wilson agreed to set up a committee which would study the question of royal moneys (Wilson rejected the suggestion that there should be an immediate increase, and he pointed out that there were great surpluses for at least another year, and that the Queen would scarcely be left in poverty). A few days after the Parliamentary debate, Prince Philip ostentatiously booked a $5.40 room at the second-best hotel in Stranraer, Scotland; the Queen must have been embarrassed to receive a large number of donations from her people, ranging from a few pence to £1 per person.

She seemed to have been disaffected by all of this unwarranted public discussion, to the point that she made the unprecedented announcement she was canceling her annual Christmas broadcast to the nation and would instead make a statement that would be relayed through the press. Despite numerous protests, she categorically would not be shaken.

On December 5, Princess Alice of Greece, Mother Alice Elizabeth, died at Buckingham Palace at the age of eighty-four, only a few weeks after her daughter, Prince Philip's sister Theodora, Margravine of Baden. Following the funeral at St. George's Chapel, Windsor, she was held in a receiving vault in

London for eighteen years until at last, in 1988, she was interred alongside her mother's sister, the Grand Duchess Elizabeth, founder of the Sisterhood of Martha and Mary, in the church near the Mount of Olives in Jerusalem.

The ironies and contrasts of character in Prince Philip remained numerous. Although he was head of the World Wildlife Fund, he was still subjected to constant attacks from the League Against Cruel Sports; it was charged that, during shooting parties at Balmoral, not only the old, lame, and sick stags and deer were culled by shots to the head, the creatures driven out by the beaters. Also, it was alleged that the Duke was selling pheasant at two pounds a brace from the royal shops, and later it would be stated that he, finding a glut in the market, ordered the pheasants raised for shooting burned or placed in burial mounds. Michael Varney stated in his book of memoirs in 1989 that he actually saw the Prince furiously screaming at a lame pheasant, and when it failed to fly, he brutally mowed it down at point-blank range.

The League Against Cruel Sports again objected vigorously to Prince Philip pushing his children into fox hunts, having them blooded with the fox's brush when the creatures were killed, and in general subjecting the foxes to misery. There were even suggestions that eagles and other predators of pheasants were being killed when they were endangered species. There were frequent claims at the league's meetings that Prince Philip had actually killed the rarest of white rhinoceroses on a hunt in Africa. Grouse, also, were being massacred, and by no means always for food.

At the same time, critics of the Prince noted that in 1970, at the headquarters of the World Wildlife Fund in Morges, Switzerland, he became a founder member of the mysterious 1,001 Club, co-founded by Prince Bernhard, Peter Scott, a close friend of Prince Philip's noted for his bird conservation, and Anton Rupert, head of Rothman's tobacco in South Africa. This club, composed of some of the thousand richest people in the world, for a $10,000 membership fee, included on its board the criminal Robert Vesco, who fled to Guatemala when the U.S. Securities and Exchange Commission threatened to prosecute him on the grounds of defrauding thousands of stockholders. Among those who belonged to the club were members of the Astor, Rockefeller, and Rothschild families. Two of the companies with whom Prince Bernhard was entangled were represented in 1,001 Club: Courtlandt Gross, head of Lockheed, and Thomas Jones, president of Northrop. Another member was Fred Meuser, sales agent for Lockheed; Michael Parker, Prince Philip's former equerry, was not mentioned in the list of members but was still hard at work at Lockheed. The alleged purpose of the 1,001 Club was to assist in the preservation of endangered species. Stephen Aris and Paul Eddy, of the London *Sunday Times*, effectively explored the history of the company. Though they did not emphasize it, they succeeded in establishing a most inconvenient connection between Prince Philip and Prince Bernhard and the two companies, which were to be the subject of calumny in the late 1970s.

The 1,001 Club was linked directly to the Bilderbergers through interlocking memberships and, in due course, would also be connected to the 1972 Trilateral Commission, which, three years later, would include on its board such figures associated with the Queen's royal enterprises as the Earl of Cromer, sometime governor of the Bank of England and adviser to Baring Brothers; Ronald Grierson, director of General Electric, London, in which the Queen remained deeply involved to the tune of about £1 million, and which would later be a chief backer of Margaret Thatcher; Sir Arthur Knight, chairman of Courtaulds; and Sir Mark Turner, later board member and chairman of Rio Tinto-Zinc.

On February 11, 1970, Prince Charles ceremonially took his seat in the House of Lords before a crowd of over one thousand peers. Squadron Leader Checketts walked before him, carrying the royal coronet; Charles was accompanied by the Duke of Beaufort and the Duke of Kent, his first cousin, and was followed by a long procession of noblemen in ermine, scarlet, and gold; the Prince handed the Lord Chancellor, Lord Gardiner, the document known as the Writ of Summons, enabling any peer to be permitted to take his place in the House. The Prince promised his allegiance to his mother, her heirs, and all successors.

In February, Prince Philip was back in Mexico, visiting with Merle Oberon, swimming with her, adoring her. He played polo, despite warnings from his physicians, at a high and risky altitude in Mexico City. Prince Philip was not well: he collapsed during a match on March 1, and had to be given oxygen. But he recovered quickly, and the royal couple embarked on an Australian tour. In March, they were in New Zealand. A heavy storm besieged them, as the *Britannia* sailed into Cook Strait, between the North and South islands of New Zealand. Vast waves swept across the decks, hurling three sailors overboard. One man was never seen again. Prince Philip took the bridge with the commander, Rear Admiral Patrick Morgan, during the terrible crossing, and helped supervise a dramatic rescue of two men struggling in the water; a helicopter sent down a rope and they pulled themselves up hand over hand. The Queen was too sick and distressed by the conditions to leave her cabin.

There were more bomb threats, but these proved to be meaningless. The visit to the Antipodes brought about for the first time a certain degree of skepticism and even criticism; there was much publicity when a Sydney schoolgirl declined to use the term "I serve my Queen" in a classroom ritual. There was talk of Republicanism. A Gallup poll revealed that "God Save the Queen" was no longer acceptable as the national anthem; 51 percent voted against it.

During the royal tour, word reached the Queen and Prince Philip that the Marquess of Milford Haven, Philip's controversial first cousin David, had died of a heart attack at Liverpool Street railway station in London. His behavior had been embarrassing from the days in which he was best man at the royal wedding. His appearance at questionable parties, his involvement with Prince Philip in the Thursday and Monday Clubs, his connections to Stephen Ward, and his unfortunate marriage to an American woman, who had obtained a Mexican divorce from him in 1954, had scarcely endeared him to supporters of propriety in the royal circles. His heroism in World War II aboard Naval destroyers had largely been eclipsed by his subsequent misbehavior.

The royal couple were back in England on May 4. The following month, with the surplus in balance of payments vanished and a £31 million deficit declared, the election resulted in a victory for the Conservatives, who obtained a majority of thirty-one. The new Prime Minister was Edward Heath, who appointed Iain Macleod Chancellor of the Exchequer, Reginald Maudling Home Secretary, and Sir Alec Douglas-Home Foreign Secretary. Douglas-Home made himself almost immediately unpopular once again by announcing that he would be prepared to discuss selling arms to the republic of South Africa, a statement which resulted in his widespread excoriation.

In July, the royal couple, with Prince Charles and Princess Anne, embarked on an adventurous tour to the Northwest Territories of Canada and the Artic Circle; the royal children left their parents and continued on their own to Washington, D.C., as guests of President Nixon's daughters and David Eisenhower. They were visiting in an unofficial capacity, and the emphasis during their trip was on the image of youth they presented, contradictory to public feeling that Britain was an old and broken country deserving only of condescension and pity. In the circumstances, it was vitally important that the image of enlightenment and youthfulness be sustained, and at a lavish dinner dance at the White House, 564 under-thirty members of society were present. It was an exciting visit, marred by Princess Anne's gaucherie. She had the nerve to criticize the bald eagle as the American symbol, addressing a rather startled Speaker of the House with her untoward remark. Prince Charles seemed, at worst, cheerfully inept: looking at a large painting depicting a battle in the Revolutionary War, he asked Gerald R. Ford, minority leader, "Is that General Cornwallis?" Ford, embarrassed, was forced to reply that it was not; he tactfully improved the situation by saying, "Cornwallis was sick that day." Prince Charles replied, "Now I know why we lost the battle." Unfortunately, when he entered the living room of Mount Vernon, he made the mistake of asking, "Is this Republican taste?" Some people forced a smile. Given two volumes of Senate Rules, he said, "Oh, I see. Three easy lessons."

The Prince and Princess returned home to a hail of criticism of their ineptitude. The *New York Times* reported that Princess Anne didn't live up to Americans' impression of how a Princess should act. This episode made her very unpopular in the United States.

Three days after their return, there was an incident in the House of Commons when a demonstrator flung gas bombs. Several members were reduced to crawling on the floor, seeking first aid. The incident was apparently caused by an Irish activist, using gas that had been widely employed in battles in Belfast.

On July 30, Prince Philip was guiding Prince Charles in a flying lesson in a Royal Air Force Bassett airplane in Sussex when a small private plane headed straight for it. A collision was narrowly avoided; it was Prince Charles's second brush with death that year; he had been in a Royal Air Force helicopter in June when it almost crashed into an Army plane. A spokesman for the Ministry of Defense at the time was compelled to criticize Charles with the words, "His [aircraft] did not take any avoiding action," a roundabout way of saying that he had failed to respond properly in the emergency, and that, had the pilot of the other plane not banked away, he would have been killed. On July 31, Lord Snowdon narrowly escaped death as he and an unnamed blond woman crashed into a fire engine just outside London. The police did nothing about this.

In August 1970, Prince Philip again secretly attended a meeting of the mysterious Bilderberg group, of which he was now a registered permanent member. The Bilderberg meeting dealt with the general unification of Western Europe and in particular Germany. The meeting was held at The Hague—on Prince Bernhard's home territory. Among those present were the banker Herman J. Abs, now of the Deutsche Bank; Dean Acheson of Cobington and Burling, of Washington, D.C., who had played a crucial role in the attempted suppression after World War II of the German Foreign Office Documents implicating the Windsors in collaboration with the enemy government; Giovanni Agnelli; Ludwig Erhard; and the Portuguese banker Manuel Ricardo Espirito Santo Silva, whose family had major Windsor connections going back to World War II.

That year Prince Philip and Prince Bernhard were seen on visits not always reported by the press, quite frequently in Mexico City, where they were entertained lavishly at the Jockey Club and the British Club. They mingled with many internationalist figures, some of whom had played both ends against the middle during the war, and whose raffish cosmopolitanism recalled the figures in the popular film *Casablanca*.

In October, the royal couple were back in the news: the Queen broke all precedent by joining President and Mrs. Nixon for lunch at Prime Minister Heath's country house at Chequers, the first time a sovereign had ever entered the historic home for such an occasion. In October, Prince Philip was in Rome when a BBC correspondent asked him the color of the bears he saw in a zoo that morning. He replied, typically, "Only such a mammoth organization as the BBC could think of asking such a bloody silly question!'' In those days, words of that sort were never heard from royalty, and there was the usual minor furor over the Prince's unbridled tongue.

There was much discussion of the increasingly severe problems in Princess Margaret's marriage. Almost nothing of this conflict appeared in print. One unpublicized episode occurred at a party given by the wealthy Marquess and Marchioness of Dufferin and Ava, celebrated scions of the Guinness family. No sooner did the Snowdons arrive at the Dufferin and Ava house in the early hours of the morning than they started to quarrel in front of the guests. They spent most of the occasion glaring at each other, moving from room to room looking increasingly tense and angry.

A few days later, the Snowdons arrived at an art gallery opening. According to the owner, Snowdon stood gazing admiringly at a painting of a naked man. He said to his wife, ''I think we should buy it. What do you think?'' She replied, ''Isn't it a bit much?'' He shouted at her, ''A bit much indeed! What do you know about art anyway?''

Another argument took place at a ballet at Covent Garden. Somebody asked the Princess her opinion of the performance; she praised everything except the sets and costumes, which she said she disliked. Lord Snowdon snapped, ''Nonsense! The sets and costumes were good. Everything else was terrible.'' Princess Margaret stared angrily at him.

During a country visit to the home of a well-known nobleman, their host assembled a number of wealthy and attractive socialites. The drawing room was turned into a ballroom. About midnight, the host was talking to Snowdon; suddenly the latter announced that he wanted to discuss an important matter in the library. The two men began to leave the drawing room when the Princess furiously insisted that Snowdon should dance with her. ''Go away, you bore me!'' he said in front of everyone, and continued into the library.

There was much talk in London that the Snowdons invited themselves to parties; but this was probably apocryphal. Another subject of gossip was the Queen's very close friendship, wrongly believed to be more than that, with Patrick, seventh Baron Plunket, who was Deputy Master of her Household. Wealthy, educated at Eton and Cambridge, wounded in World War II, Lord Plunket had been equerry to King George VI, and had obtained his present appointment in 1954. He had a particular talent for royal occasions, described by the historian Kenneth Rose in *Kings, Queens and Courtiers:*

> There would be vast pyramids of white flowers: delphiniums and eremurus and peonies; or a whole syringa tree in bloom, rising from a great malachite pot. And along the tables would be arranged treasure troves of silver, unused since the reign of George IV. Sometimes he would create a palace, sometimes a country house; never an hotel.

He had much to do with the Queen's Gallery, in which he worked in harness with Sir Anthony Blunt. He was slender, handsome, with thinning dark hair and an aristocratic profile. The Queen was deeply fond of him and perhaps in love with him. Even if her royal duty had not been utterly binding, she could have never entered into an emotional relationship with him because he was homosexual.

For years, she followed a strict and quite unreported ritual. On Monday evenings when she was in London, she would often go with him, driving her simple Rover automobile, a scarf over her head, quite unrecognized, to movie performances, usually at the Odeon Cinema in the Kings Road, Chelsea. Even when the theater cashiers seemed to recognize her, they cast the thought from their minds, deciding she was a look-alike. After the film, the Queen and Plunket would go across the road to the popular Raffles Club, which was set up rather like a library, with books and wood paneling. They would find tables at the back of the dining room, shrouded in almost complete darkness, and again, perhaps because of the sheer improbability involved, no waiter would recognize her. These nocturnal escapades were unique in her life, and probably among her most enjoyable experiences.

She gradually got used to her new Prime Minister. Edward Heath was very different from the bluff, tough, warmly cordial Harold Wilson, with his unstuffy, down-to-earth Yorkshire humor. A scholarship boy who had had a considerable success at Oxford, becoming Union president, Heath distinguished himself by opposing appeasement before World War II. He was also very much against Franco during the Spanish Civil War. Thus, his political background was impeccably decent; yet he was not a warm or accommodating man, and to many he appeared cold and haughty, lacking in the common touch.

Unmarried, a confirmed bachelor, he was never known to have had an affair with a woman. His chief passions seemed to be music and yachting, and he was at his happiest when he was pounding away with more energy than brilliance at a church organ or a grand piano or enthusiastically conducting amateur choirs.

Heath has confirmed in a letter that the Queen Mother formed a friendship with him because of their mutual love of music. Standing in shorts, a somewhat unathletic figure, upon the deck of his boat, he would often be carefully framed for publicity reasons with an eligible, bikini-clad blonde. He was a close friend of President Nixon. He was also for sales of armaments to South Africa. He was very much for joining the European Economic Community. It is doubtful whether the Queen warmed to him strongly. In early 1971, despite the fact that he had so easily won the election, he rapidly became a victim of the extraordinarily mercurial mood of the British electorate; in May, the Labor party would win a landslide victory in local elections, gaining 2,000 seats, while the conservatives lost 1,800. To a logical, cool, and dedicated Conservative, this fickleness of the public was a grating irritation.

In April 1971, the Queen celebrated her forty-fifth birthday. Her character had undergone major changes in the previous few years. It had broadened from that of a shy and nervous young monarch; now she was a worldly-wise mother of the great Commonwealth. She had attained a formidable and matchless knowledge of government and of all constitutional affairs. As head of the House of Windsor, she was sharply aware that she was solely responsible for this enormous family and was required to deal with and find solutions for all of its countless troubles, anxieties, and setbacks. Immensely rich, with vast properties abroad, she had, through the international firm of Courtaulds, whose institute, art gallery, and museum Sir Anthony Blunt continued to run, obtained, according to statements in the *Congressional Record*, in 1968 one of the world's largest cotton plantations in Scott, Mississippi, a community situated on the banks of the Mississippi River, right on the border of Arkansas. It was known as the Delta and Pine Land Company, or "The Queen's Farm." It consisted of thirty-eight thousand acres of rich soil and a factory as well as a mill; it was worth about $44.5 million at the time and employed hundreds of black laborers. It had originally been established in the last century, merging in 1919 with the company known as the Fine Spinners and Doublers of Manchester, England. From 1968, it had been subsidized by the U.S. Department of Agriculture, drawing from a substantial fund, to the tune of $1.5 million. This was quite inappropriate for a property owned by the British royal family.

First to draw attention to the anomaly was Senator Thomas McIntyre of New Hampshire, who mentioned it in session on April 16, 1970, while introducing a bill relating to limitations on farm payments. Stating that the government was improperly using funds to featherbed rich property owners, he said that a new bill would save 200 million dollars' worth of taxpayers' money. He added: "In 1969, seven farm companies received in excess of $1 million each in farm payments, 14 received between a half a million and a million, and 54 between a quarter and a half a million dollars. We paid the Queen of England $120,000 for not planting cotton on the farmland she owns in Mississippi." In other words, he charged, the Queen, via Courtaulds, was being underwritten so that the land could be left fallow in the normal cycle of crops. "Payments continue to go to many unusual farm factories, including heavy payments to a farm in which the Queen of England and her family are major investors."

It is worth nothing that, in 1968, when Courtaulds bought the property, the Queen's friend, Lord Butler, was a director of Courtaulds. Congressman Silvio O. Conte of Massachusetts asserts that at the time the Queen secretly owned a major shareholding in Courtaulds; it was headed by Lord Kearton, who, starting as an atomic energy expert, stopped ICI from taking the company over in 1962, and expanded hugely thenceforth, with interests in every country in the world, even Ian Smith's Rhodesia and the hated South Africa; it was an empire of fibers, synthetics, cotton, wool, and paint; many directors were prominent in Special Operations in World War II.

Exactly how the Queen was able to obtain American properties through her major interest in Courtaulds, which also had immense holdings in South Africa, that rebel against the Commonwealth, is unclear. The Crown Lands remained "Crown" property, despite many published statements to the contrary, only the interest being surrendered *after maintenance* in return for the Civil List. The Queen Mother was said to own a building on Broadway in New York City, in which Jack Dempsey, the famous boxer, had a restaurant and bar; he often bragged to people that she was his landlady; also holdings on Eighth and Ninth avenues and the West Forties from Forty-first to Forty-eighth Streets. The firms of Baring Brothers and Rowe and Pitman handled the royal investments, which included heavyweight holdings in such firms as Rio Tinto-Zinc and General Electric. Her bankers remained Coutts.

There is no doubt that she kept a firm eye on every penny she invested and, in particular, not only her strings of racehorses, but also Ascot itself, which she owned outright. She was extremely shrewd, and also knew how to take the best advice. Her jewelry, according to the jewel historian Leslie Field, amounted to more than 250,000 separate items. There was, of course, no way of calculating the value of the incredible collection of paintings which the inescapable Sir Anthony Blunt, still head of the Courtauld Institute, was busy cataloging on her behalf.

The Queen had grown calmer and more measured with the passing of time, and had developed a very keen sense of humor which brought much joy and laughter to her family and limited inner circle of friends. She was at her funniest when imitating people she had met in her line of duty, including Lord Mayors, officials, and heads of companies. She was impatient with the giddy foolishness of the typical society debutante, and for years had stopped official presentations at court. However, there was no escaping the hordes of pretty but uninformed young women who poured into her gardens each year in the summer or danced with the young bucks at various elaborate balls.

The garden parties were crowded with as many as four thousand people at a time, and civil servants and lesser dignitaries who would not have dreamed of shaking hands with the Queen were catered to inconspicuously at these events.

The Queen enjoyed shopping expeditions to Harrods and Fortnum & Mason each year about two and a half weeks before Christmas; accompanied by a small entourage, she walked from department to department selecting gifts. Sometimes, she would sit in a department manager's office while individual items were brought to her for closer inspection. She was particularly fond of the Book Department, where she would buy Bibles or atlases for her two younger children, cousins, nephews, and nieces. In later years, Harrods brought its goods to her.

Her clothing was often unfairly criticized. She dressed practically, smartly, but never ostentatiously, still avoiding the vulgar glitter that might have made her more admired by the fashion magazines. Only her pillbox or cabbage-like hats, which were devised to show off her face, might be justly criticized, although sometimes Norman Hartnell and his associate Ian Thomas would err in making her look a little too formal and severe. All her clothes had to be tailor-made. She preferred to wear clothes which were of no particular time or period, so that she could continue to wear them for three or four years. She preferred colors that would make her stand out in a crowd, seldom black or navy blue. Norman Hartnell would go to Buckingham Palace with suitcases full of manufacturers' samples of cloth, so that the Queen could choose something she liked. Her designers would then work on the actual clothes, and have further conferences with her until the actual fittings. During those fittings, she would always talk to the staff in the most casual and informal way, never forgetting their names, and asking them about their children, husbands or wives, never failing to be concerned if someone was ill. She had a particular dressing room she used for these sessions. She did not welcome being interrupted, even by close family members. She would chat with them, but she was visibly impatient because she was so completely dedicated to perfection and to doing one thing at a time.

She was an English size twelve, with an exquisite back and perfectly trim waist. Year after year, her flawless complexion never faded. She would never dress or undress in front of Hartnell or Thomas; they would wait until they were informed by a lady-in-waiting that she was ready. Only the fitters were in the room. She was amazingly correct, and sweetly exacting; she knew precisely what the dressmaking team was doing, when it picked up a shoulder or tweaked a skirt or a sleeve. She knew every bit as much as the team working on her, and sometimes her eye was even sharper than theirs. Once a dress was finished, she would walk up and down in it, watching the fall of the clothes and the fit in mirrors, going back again and again to make everything perfect. She was especially thorough over dresses to be worn on State occasions.

Bobo MacDonald, still with the Queen after forty-five years, was almost always present, hovering, offering help. Tiny, tidy, very neat and meticulous, she never let a detail slip past her. The packing of the clothes for a tour was a staggering achievement, in which Hartnell's help, and above all that of Bobo MacDonald, was essential. Into the scores of suitcases, amounting to as much as six tons for an extended tour, hats, gloves, frocks, shoes, gloves, and stockings by the dozen had to be laid out, with tissue paper in layers, the whole operation exhausting for the tiny Scotswoman and the fashion house team. Only in one respect were the Hartnell group treated with less than an absolute sense of their importance. They always entered the dressing room through the back door.

Since the Queen did not touch her own investments to run her palaces and staffs (with over four hundred housed in Buckingham Palace alone), she was by now seriously feeling the pinch of which Prince Philip had loudly complained the previous year. The money she was receiving from the Civil List was not enough to maintain her residences, and in June, at about the time of her official birthday celebrations, there was much discussion of her request for an increase. She wanted to have her annual allowance doubled from the equivalent of $12 million to $24 million. Parliament agreed to consider the request, which yet again brought savage criticism from, among others, Richard Crossman, editor of the *New Statesman*. John Colville, former Secretary to Winston Churchill and to the Queen when she was Princess Elizabeth, was now a director of Coutts (the royal) bank; he attacked Crossman, making the outrageous statement, "If the Queen's got more than £2 million of her own, I'll eat my hat." Somebody should have made him eat it in a public place.

The Queen was as close as ever to her mother and sister, and would often drive herself unrecognized in her Rover across a short cut through Hyde Park to Kensington Palace for afternoon visits with Princess Margaret. The sisters would sit in the garden listening to a transistor radio playing their favorite programs, a seemingly interminable BBC series, "The Archers," and taking tea. Years later, Princess Margaret would actually appear in the show as an actress.

Friends were limited. But the Queen certainly was very fond of Lord and Lady Rupert Nevill, Mr. and Mrs. John Wills, and Marmaduke and Lady Susan Hussey, as she and Prince Philip would attend informal dinner parties at their homes. She also would go with her husband to Broadlands, to visit Lord Mountbatten, with whom Prince Charles, totally unpublicized, would live for long periods during his college vacation.

The Queen would telephone her mother whenever she left Buckingham Palace in the Rover to drive to Clarence House. In an unfailing ritual, the Queen Mother would, upon receiving the call, walk into the garden and climb onto an orange box placed by the wall overlooking the Mall so she could wave to her daughter. The Queen always looked back, barely able to see the small hand as it extended over the wall.

Almost incredibly, the Queen still did not understand the love of the people that swelled in their hearts, and she was extremely conservative and cautious in not taking for granted the greetings she received wherever she went. She was conscious that she was the monarch first, and a person second, and she knew only too well that she could only expect cupboard love and applause from overawed people. She was trying now to encourage her family to start what were known as "walkabouts" in which they could meet and shake hands with the people. She had begun these in 1970, and, more than anything, the walkabouts endeared her to the people. Even the increasing signs of terrorism had not yet suppressed the custom, which would sadly have vanished by 1990. The Queen was careful never to appear as an upper-class woman, encouraging a vision of being middle class. She remained middle-of-the-road in politics and life. She still did not carry money, a passport, or a driver's license, and when she speeded, which was not too frequently, the police had to turn the other way.

The Queen never lost sight of her prerogatives. We have already learned how she received Lord Home as Prime Minister when her Principal Private Secretary had not properly canvassed the Conservatives. In 1967, Harold Wilson, backing Barbara Castle as Secretary of State for employment when she wanted to obtain reforms in trade unions, and finding much criticism, had sought to dissolve Parliament, even though that might lead to a general election unfavorable to his party. The Queen, through her Secretary, made it known to Wilson that he did not have the constitutional right to presume that she would consent to a dissolution. Such an intervention would have been considered extraordinary had the public heard about it. She always had the right, and retains it to this day, to decline a dissolution if she so pleases. And, in a very few years' time, she also had the capacity to dismiss an Australian Prime Minister, and did so in short order.

The Queen Mother remained as hard-working, lovable but strong-tempered, and powerful as ever. Not intellectual, she was cheerful, very Scots, healthy, robust, and outgoing, and no one but a fool would have the temerity to irritate her or cross her. Clarence House was run gently and firmly with a rod of iron. She loved to fish and go picnicking, she shared her daughter's passion for racehorses, and she had a delightfully unpretentious attitude to her status. Kenneth Rose tells the story that when she was at Kempton Park Racetrack, somebody put on a television set and she could hear a football crowd singing "God Save the Queen." "Oh, do turn it off!" she said. "It's so embarrassing unless one is there—like hearing the Lord's Prayer when playing canasta." Members of the Clarence House staff were often traditionally gay. On one occasion, two members of the staff were quarreling. One called the other "You stupid old queen!" The Queen Mother walked in. She said, "There's only one Queen here, and she's hungry. I want some supper!"

Prince Philip was as impatient, easily bored, frustrated, and drastically impetuous as ever. He has emerged so far as a somewhat boorish figure, constantly committing social and political gaucheries. Yet there was more to him than that: as Kenneth Rose has pointed out, he mastered "an impressive range of subjects: education, health, science, conservation, industrial relations, sport. He [knew] whose brains [were] worth picking and how to distill those loans into well-shaped and fluently delivered speeches." Rose points out that Prince Philip designed a charming new fountain for the Windsor Castle gardens and had a flair for landscape painting; he was quite able to exchange detailed comments with clerics of the Church of England on the subject of Christian doctrine. Along with his brusque character, he was not unthoughtful; but the sense of harshness in his private and public demeanor is impossible to overcome. And he remained very strict with his children.

In addition to the friendship with Prince Bernhard, Prince Philip was drawn by the presence at Lockheed of his oldest and one of his closest friends, his former equerry, Michael Parker, who had entertained Prince Bernhard when he piloted a

Lockheed Jet Star into London on May 11, 1962. Prince Philip was godfather to Parker's daughter Julie, who married Timothy Buxton, son of Aubrey Buxton, another close friend of Prince Philip's who had founded the World Wildlife Fund. On October 6, 1961, Parker testified in a court case in London in which Marcel Mann, an expatriate Rumanian businessman, sued Royal Dutch Shell Petroleum, charging breach of contract; under oath, Parker stated that he had gone with Mann to Cuba in 1959, at the beginning of Castro's regime, to persuade Fidel Castro not to nationalize Shell; Mann claimed the boycott was lifted. Michael Parker was constantly in the press, in stories that carried a heavy suggestion of very high-level contacts; *Private Eye*, on October 1, 1970, asked why there were no press pictures of Michael Heseltine, controversial former Secretary of State for Air, with Parker, "Lockheed spokesman."

Prince Charles continued to do well at Cambridge; Princess Anne was noisily out and about; Prince Andrew was flourishing (and improving in looks) rapidly at his preparatory school Heatherdown at Ascot; Prince Edward would soon be at school in London, at Gibb's. All four young family members enjoyed extraordinary good health, and despite the apparent fling with Merle Oberon and the occasional visits to young women, Prince Philip firmly retained the family solidarity.

In th midst of the controversy over the royal moneys, the matter of the Delta and Pine Land Company had cropped up at a major congressional debate in Washington on May 26, 1970.

The result of the debate, at which Congressman Silvio O. Conte made the statement, "We hear occasional reports of the rising cost of upkeep for Buckingham Palace, but I think the American taxpayer would have grave misgivings about this form of foreign aid," was that farming subsidies were cut from $55,000 to $20,000 per farm. Conte's mention of the Queen brought about the defeat of many supporters of the government to retain the higher subsidies. Later, the Senate restored the subsidies by rejecting the decision of the House; threatened in 1978 with a bill which would expose all foreign ownerships in America, Courtaulds, presumably with royal authorization, sold the property for $44.5 million to a New York corporation named Southwide, which, in turn, sold all except the cottonseed business to the British company of Prudential Insurance, in which there were said to be royal interests. Thus, the money flowed by a different route back into Britain.

The Queen's advisers obtained safety from disclosure by entering her investments under the unusual name of Houblon Nominees, transferring them to the umbrella group known as the Bank of England Nominees, which also protected foreign heads of state and royal family members from the provisions of the Companies Act. Mrs. Doreen Archer Houblon, granddaughter of the sixth Earl of Carrick, had strong racing and personal connections to the royal family and had received the MVO from the Queen in 1954 and then the CVO in 1969, both awards indicative of significant services to the crown. She was a leading authority on sidesaddle horsemanship, and her classic book *Side Saddle* was a favorite of the Queen's as a teenager. For eighteen years she prepared the Queen's horse for her birthday parades; she was a friend of the Queen, a judge of major equestrian events in which Princess Anne had taken part, and her pioneering of organic farming would have been of great interest to Prince Charles. She died childless in 1977.

Houblon, whose royal assets were changed over to the Bank of England Nominees, was, it is curious to relate, itself a part of the Bank of England (a Houblon had been involved in the bank's founding). The investments were merely shifted from one element in the Bank of England to another, revealing that in fact, before the Companies Act, the Queen was already protected by that nationalized British institution. The reason for the change is somewhat obscure, although possibly it may have been intended to indicate that Houblon was a separate investment group. The directors of Houblon were all directors of the Bank of England, including John Stanton Fleming, Richard E. Williams, George Malcolm Gill, and the Duke of Somerset. Houblon Nominees was originally founded on February 9, 1965.

The Bank of England Nominees were headed by J. W. McMahon, a director of the Royal Opera Trust, of which Prince Charles is today the chairman. Strand Nominees handled investments for the royal children. With other members of the royal family, it had, not insignificantly, as a director, the Honorable Michael Albemarle Bowes-Lyon; the connection to the Queen Mother scarcely needs stressing. Strand Nominees was, in effect, part of the royal bank of Coutts, whose address, at 440 The Strand, it shared.

Throughout 1971, Princess Anne increasingly took part in

equestrianism; she took the lead at the Badminton horse trials; she had a spectacular twenty-first birthday party aboard the royal yacht *Britannia,* with over one hundred guests and a dance band, and appeared effectively in a thirty-minute color documentary for the Save the Children Fund, of which she was president. In August, she fell suddenly ill; seized with intense pain, she was admitted to the King Edward VII Hospital. What was described as an ovarian cyst was removed. She fought back in order to enter the European riding championships. Riding her horse Doublet (incredibly in view of her recently weakened condition), she became European champion after Doublet successfully cleared twelve successive fences. The Queen was ecstatic, throwing all royal reserve to the winds, as she gave her the prize. She was voted Sports Personality of the Year, and was granted the national press Sportswoman of the Year title, as well as the Sports Writers Award.

Prince Charles made a major mark that year, beginning his training as a jet pilot and parachutist; he joined the Ten Ton Club, restricted to men who had flown at supersonic speeds or those over one thousand miles an hour. He attracted enormous public excitement when he successfully parachuted twelve hundred feet over the English Channel, and splashed down without injury. He had volunteered for the jump, although some effort was made to dissuade him because of his position as heir to the throne. The Queen backed him nervously, but with total commitment; she had to give permission herself. After his career at Cambridge (he obtained a B.A.), he followed his father in entering Dartmouth Naval College for six weeks of training in September. His parents gloried in his improvement.

In November, the Queen contracted chicken pox for the first time, having missed it, perhaps because of her extraordinary isolated existence, as a child. Recovering, she was pleased to learn that the House of Commons committee had recommended the 106 percent pay raise she had sought. Labor critics who had protested were overruled; picketers gathered outside the Commons with placards, shouting about the appalling conditions of so many people, and the unhappiness and unrest in the labor unions. Just before Christmas, the House ruled that the committee's recommendations had been accepted.

Meantime, at the end of October, the Commons approved, over the objections of the still-influential Enoch Powell, British membership in the European Economic Community. This was a stunning victory for Prime Minister Heath, the one unequivocal triumph of his administration. Wilson attacked the Prime Minister in a prolonged six-day debate, threatening outright that if he were returned to power his government would insist on a renegotiation of terms. Laborite turned against Laborite, charging betrayal of the cause by supporting the government; in particular Deputy Leader Roy Jenkins was singled out with cries of "Traitor!" as he stood and left the chamber. Difficult and complicated legislation lay ahead in order to allow Britain to conform with the EEC. The Queen appears to have taken a neutral position in the matter, her chief concern being that the special relationship with the Commonwealth would not suffer from Britain's membership. But the controversy over EEC raged on into the new year.

At that time, Lord Louis Mountbatten involved himself in a complex personal intrigue to ensure that his name would not be confined to the present restrictions in its use in the royal descent, but would instead be used by all of the children of the Queen. Retired now, still frustratedly seeking influence and power, he was a man obsessed. So extreme was his obsession that he actually committed an act which was, to put it mildly, questionable. *The Genealogist's Magazine* was considered to be of major importance, and its editor, mindful of the extended public interest in the royal titles and lineage, had written to Mountbatten, asking him if he would be interested in contributing a piece on the occasion of the forthcoming silver wedding anniversary of the Queen and Prince Philip. Afraid of showing his hand, Mountbatten declined the invitation, but was not unaware of the advantages of such a piece appearing under a respectable name, if it could be circulated to all family members and would push his own cause.

He had a discussion with Mrs. Mollie Travis, archivist of his large collection of papers at his estate, Broadlands. Mrs. Travis's daughter, the genealogist Clare Forbes Turner, was selected by Mrs. Travis to write the piece; Lord Mountbatten and Mrs. Travis agreed that the article should be published under Mrs. Forbes Turner's name, and that all correspondence with the editor should emanate not from Broadlands, but from Mrs. Forbes Turner's home in the north of England.

Mountbatten put together the piece, which had a number of errors in it, including the statement that Prince Philip relinquished his Greek royal inheritance upon becoming a British

subject in World War II. In fact, the Greek law of the time did
not admit of such an action, and the truth was that Philip
remained an heir to the Greek throne, a detail the Machiavellian King George II had overlooked. Lord Mountbatten pointed
out in the article that, by virtue of the Queen marrying a
Mountbatten, her direct descendants were Mountbattens.

Between the authorship of the piece and its publication,
much would go on. Mountbatten was extremely nervous over
his deception, chopping and changing elements in the article;
for instance, he would urge Mollie Travis to have Clare Forbes
Turner state that the information about Prince Philip giving up
his claim to the throne was based only on hearsay and not
written evidence. There was a change of editor at the journal in
the midst of the flurry of notes.

The new editor, Patrick Montague-Smith, insisted on certain
corrections being made. He pointed out that Prince Philip was
still heir to the Greek (and also the Danish) thrones. He might
have rejected the appropriate titles, but this still did not prevent
him from being "in remainder" to the thrones. After all, there
were many in line for the British throne who were not
themselves British. He also pointed out that it was royal custom
for a female in line to take a father's name rather than a
husband's. Suggestions made in the piece that there were
precedents based upon Prime Ministerial advice should be
categorically removed. Any suggestion that Queen Elizabeth II
continue to retain the Mountbatten surname for more than two
months after her accession should be eliminated. There were
other changes, all referring directly to Mountbatten's quite
improper effort to shoehorn the changes without satisfactory
precedents.

Throughout this correspondence, Mrs. Travis showed considerable nervousness, quite understandable in the circumstances. In one of her letters to Clare, she wrote, there was little
chance that she would be traced as being her daughter, and
went on to say that if there should be some leak, Clare was to
assert that she had done some research for her mother.
Somewhat in desperation, the correspondents kept bringing up
the name of the constitutional legal expert Edward F. Iwi,
presumably on the theory that if all else failed he could be cited
in support of what can only appear the most undesirable
argument.

The end result of all this intrigue, which dragged on up to

and beyond the article's publication in time for the silver wedding anniversary, was that Princess Anne would eventually enter the name Mountbatten-Windsor on her marriage certificate. At least, the Machiavellian Mountbatten achieved that end; apparently, his careful circulation of the piece to Prince Charles, Princess Anne, and all the other royal children, as well as to the Queen and Prince Philip, served its dubious purpose. However, all subsequent marriage and birth certificates were correctly presented with the name of Windsor alone. How Mountbatten got away with the deception is something of a mystery, but it might be noted that Mountbatten's authorized biographer, Philip Ziegler, with delicacy, omitted any mention of the correspondence, which no doubt, given his usual diligence, he found snugly, if unwisely, housed at the Broadlands archives.

The Queen was very much worn down that winter of 1971 by the illness of her beloved friend Lord Plunket. He would soon be in the merciless grip of cancer. The strain on her was terrible, and in mid-January, she was ill. She was determined to go ahead with an extensive tour of Southeast Asia.

The tour lasted forty-seven grueling days. Princess Anne was also on the journey. The heat in Thailand was considerable, and there was an unpleasant moment when King Phumiphol's royal automobile broke down in Bangkok, and the royal party had to wait, quite uncomfortably, and dressed ceremonially for the evening, in the street, while another car was found. There is no record of a precedent for such an incident, and there was widespread criticism both in Thailand and abroad. It was a marvelous trip.

The Queen and Princess Anne returned to London in late March, Prince Philip proceeding to Africa to visit a wild game preserve. Back in London, the Queen had unsettling news: she learned that her uncle David, the Duke of Windsor, was gravely ill. He had not fully recovered from a hernia operation, and was suffering from advanced cancer. Fortuitously, the Queen had already planned a State visit to France; she was able to attend his sickbed in Paris. She was grieved when he passed away late in May, and, with consideration, arranged for the Duchess of Windsor to be brought to Buckingham Palace, where she was housed in the State Suite. The Duchess would also, of course, be attending the funeral. The Queen's birthday parade on June 3 was not canceled; the Queen combined the

ceremony with a tribute to the deceased Duke. Prince Charles
was especially saddened by the death.

The summer passed without major incident. There were
widespread demands that government members should be
forced to reveal their business interests, and there were many
indications that the government would be undergoing a cleanup
operation. At the same time, MI5 was starting a smear
campaign, apparently instigated by certain Soviet agents. Once
more, as during the Profumo affair, with its absurd security
issues played up out of all proportion, these MI5 agents, never
discovered, or, if discovered, never named, were busy spread-
ing rumors of moral and political turpitude concerning not only
Prime Minister Heath, whose private life was exposed to much
scurrilous gossip, but also Harold Wilson. The matter did not
surface until as late as 1990, when Colin Wallace, former press
officer, revealed that he had been in charge of an MI5-
sponsored disinformation campaign. At the time, and lamentably, no serious effort appears to have been made by the Prime
Minister to explore the sources of this lying and vicious war
against the establishment. Indeed, as late as 1989, Mrs.
Thatcher made a firm stand against disclosure, or, to give the
most charitable interpretation, she was not informed until an
embarrassingly late moment in Parliamentary debates.

Apparently, the royal family was able to remain above this
tidal wave of lies, unless the numerous rumors about Prince
Charles's personal affairs could be considered to emanate from
such a questionable source. The worst that could be leveled
against Princess Anne was that she was an extremely bad
driver. She tended to drive recklessly, somewhat headily
overexcited by her possession of a new Scimitar sports car. The
police were forced to charge her twice with exceeding the
speed limit, and there was talk of having her license suspended;
seemingly, royal influence overcame this.

In August, there was a family tragedy when the young and
charming, much beloved Prince William of Gloucester, son of
the ailing Duke, and first cousin of the Queen, was killed in an
air race. In October, the Queen had a disturbing visit to Stirling
University, Scotland. She was received by a crowd of angry
students, yelling "Out with the monarchy!" and breaking
through the police lines. She acted with superb control and
decorum. When one youth shouted "Cunt!" at her, she calmly
asked him to step aside as she wished to have a few words with

him. The crowd fell utterly silent. In full hearing of everyone, she asked him what his complaint was, and he was shamed into an embarrassed apology. With great expertise and control, and much to the dismay of her equerries and personal bodyguards, she stopped to talk to various students, again requesting them to specify their grievances. Lieutenant General Lang put his arm around her, a most unusual action, as they told her they had no personal animosity against her, but were furious that so much money had been spent on her visit when welfare on their behalf was meager and grants and financial supports of all kinds were almost nonexistent. So absolute was her victory over the protesters and anarchistic screamers that no less than 930 young people signed a document apologizing profusely for what they had put her through.

Two days later, the Queen, with Prince Philip and Princess Anne, flew to Yugoslavia to a magnificent reception from President Tito. It was her first visit to a Communist country. The royals made a 780-mile tour of the scenically beautiful country, planted a peace tree in Friendship Park near the River Danube, walked through the ancient walled streets of Dubrovnik, toured the precipitous roads above it, and had a glorious day in Zagreb; they enjoyed their trip enormously.

Back in London, the royal couple's twenty-fifth silver wedding anniversary celebrations were held. The Queen had decided to use the occasion to mingle with her people as she had never done before. While she spent a weekend with her husband at Luton Hoo, the Bedfordshire home of their dear friends Sir Harold and Lady Zia Wernher, grouse shooting and walking through the woods, foreign royals were present in the capital, headed by King Constantine and Queen Anne-Marie of Greece, Crown Prince Carl Gustav of Sweden, and Prince Harald and Princess Sonja of Norway. The royal family gathered for a group portrait, taken at Windsor Castle, with everyone smiling radiantly, except for a sullen Lord Snowdon. The Queen Mother, just behind the Queen to her right, had a particularly triumphant look, and the Queen, smiling broadly, looked incredibly youthful, her younger children appearing remarkably robust and healthy.

The silver wedding service was held at Westminister Abbey, and was deliberately unostentatious. The procession by coach through the streets, greeted by the joyful population, was not marked by unusually elaborate ceremoniousness. It was followed by the Queen's and Prince Philip's daring and unprecedented walk among the crowds, beautifully judged to match the increasing, democratization of the 1970s. The Queen delighted the world when, responding with humor and charm to the many parodists who seized upon her much-quoted words "My husband and I," she made a direct reference to this in a clever and touching speech at the Guildhall luncheon.

She also said, "When the bishop was asked what he thought about sin, he replied with simple conviction that he was against it. If I am asked today what I think about family life after twenty-five years of marriage, I can answer with equal simplicity and conviction. I am for it." The laughter and applause were deafening.

The stiffness so often found in her addresses, the occasional hint of shrillness and sharpness which sprang from her painful shyness in front of live audiences, had been replaced by a slightly tremulous, but far more human, warmth. It was as though the glass screen that separated her from the rest of humanity was showing a crack or two. It is almost certain that she had never been as popular as she was at the Christmas season of 1972. Through all Britain's years of economic suffering, through all the broken promises of government and the bitternesses of labor, she alone seemed a consistent and marvelous, unchangeable being. No matter how gauche or grotesque her husband's behavior, she, certainly, always gave her best.

21

***

BRITAIN CELEBRATED NEW YEAR'S Day, 1973, by joining the European Economic Community, and the Prime Minister rashly forecast a better future. Labor boycotted the British delegation to the European Parliament; at the end of the month, the Vietnam War, in which Britain had firmly and honorably refused to take part, ended with a cease-fire. It was a happy beginning to what was in many ways a very unpleasant year.

The Queen was once again forced to watch the continuing tragedy of her nation, in which many of the labor rank and file remained unhappy, shattered by inflation, barely able to survive, lacking in morale, and depressed by the mediocrity and lack of inspiration and leadership in middle and top management. Edward Heath failed to produce even the modest degree of leadership provided by Wilson; he was far from being comparable to Macmillan in Macmillan's early and less tired days. To convert the latter's most famous statement, the British had never had it so bad. The country was old, sick, and broke. The public was weary of struggling with the government's numerous shortcomings. In February, the National Gas Workers struck and six hundred industrial plants were compelled to close. The first civil servant strike in history took place later that month. The budget was hopelessly uninspiring, and few believed that inflation would be checked. It was hard to believe any promises in that year of sadness.

Princess Anne was enjoying a romance with Captain Mark Phillips, a handsome, dashing, well-built young Army officer, for whom she overthrew a number of suitors, including at least one with whom she was in love—Brian Alexander, son of the military hero Earl Alexander of World War II fame. Phillips had much in common with her. In their first meeting at the

Mexico Olympic Games in 1968, she had found herself irresistibly drawn to this sporty country gentleman, who shared her passion for horses and was himself an expert equestrian. His admiration for her, his psychological support of her, continually appealed; he was present whenever possible during her racing events, and provided a shoulder to lean on when she was harried by police for her inept performances at the wheel. Finally, Phillips plucked up enough courage to approach Prince Philip to ask for Princess Anne's hand in marriage. He was petrified, rigid, during the meeting, but, as it turned out, Prince Philip was quite aware of the inevitability of the wedding, and, without hesitation, gave his consent. The Palace announced the engagement on May 29; the couple would be married in November.

Princess Anne was determined that in marrying a commoner no special privileges should be accorded to her husband or children as they had been to Lord Snowdon. Very much a lover of the common people, and deeply middle class in her nature and behavior, Princess Anne made it clear to her parents that Phillips should not be elevated to the peerage and her children would not receive royal titles. Her urge was to live the life of a country gentlewoman, running a farm, raising horses and chickens, surveying her properties, living unpretentiously. The Queen supported her in this desire. The worst criticism of the couple was that they went fox-hunting together, at the same time that Prince Philip was head of the British branch of the World Wildlife Fund. Many of the public were touched by Phillips's devotion, as he flew home weekend after weekend from his military post in Germany to see the woman he loved. In the midst of so many unpleasant scandals, the public longed for a fairy-tale romance, for something clean and beautiful in an increasingly ugly world.

In April, Prince Charles was progressing well in the Royal Navy. He had spent some months as acting sublieutenant aboard the HMS *Norfolk,* a destroyer equipped with nuclear missiles. He had taken part in NATO exercises in the Mediterranean, greatly annoying the Spanish Government when he came ashore at Gibraltar; this was felt to provide a direct act of hostility against Spain, which was continually nibbling at the British occupancy of the city. At the end of April, his wage was increased to the equivalent of $6,625 a year. Characteristically, he gave it all to charity. He was transferred to HMS *Minerva,* a well-equipped frigate, aboard which he traveled to the West Indies. He also visited Portsmouth, New Hampshire, Naval Shipyard to join the populace in celebrating the town's three hundred and fiftieth anniversary.

In August, Prince Philip made a disastrous appearance before the students of the University of Edinburgh. Talking about the political scene of the moment, he brought a gasp, hisses, and boos when he unwisely said, "Nationalism and socialism produced Nazis and fascists." This came ill from a man whose favorite sister had been married to a high-ranking Nazi and whose favorite cousin Friederike, Queen of Greece, had been a member of Hitler Youth, quite apart from his misquotation of Dr. Johnson's "Patriotism is the last refuge of a scoundrel," as "Nationalism is the scoundrel's last resort." It was also a deliberate kick in the teeth for Scottish independence, and it followed untimely on a visit to fascist Portugal.

The Prince, somewhat ironically, made a royal visit to the Soviet Union. This was at the invitation of Premier Kosygin who, on April 18, had received the British Trade Minister, thus preventing an eighteen-month return of the Cold War and a freezing of commercial dealings. Yet again, a royal personage was playing a role in cementing foreign policy both actually and symbolically. Prince Philip added his own incomparable dramatic touch by flying his own plane to Moscow. This was most carefully framed not as a private visit, but simply as a gesture of friendship which would confirm Prime Minister Heath's expressions of goodwill—expressions, it should be added, which were far more intense than those proffered by the allegedly left-wing Harold Wilson.

Warmly received at the Kremlin, Philip spoke of what he hoped to see as improved British-Soviet relations, and gave more than a hint that the Queen would follow him. This was indeed an extraordinary statement, in view of the fact that the Russian Communists had murdered the Queen's great-uncle, Czar Nicholas of Russia, and also her husband's aunts, Czarina Alix and Grand Duchess Elizabeth. Prince Philip would not have been himself if there had not been an "incident" during his stay: he was being driven in a horse-drawn carriage through the streets when he suddenly took it into his head to seize the reins. The driver stubbornly refused him permission, and not without a degree of wisdom, since the Prince was a notoriously wild driver and would soon upset a similar conveyance in

England. There was a loud quarrel which did little to enhance Russian-British relations.

He flew to Kiev, where Princess Anne was already present in training for the trials of the International Equestrian Federation events.

Shortly afterward, the Queen and her husband visited Australia. Word came there of the death of King Gustav Adolf of Sweden, and the Queen ordered certain reluctant members of her family to wear mourning. In November, the Queen opened the new session of Parliament; opinion polls showed that the British were more dissatisfied than ever with both Conservatives and Laborites, and perhaps would like to see a coalition government for the first time since World War II. The atmosphere of disillusionment and discontent was sharp. In view of the general disenchantment, the marriage of Princess Anne to Captain Phillips could only seem a shining sop to the public, a temporary chance to escape into fantasy. Even the simple matter of the now very handsome young Prince Andrew being admitted to the dreaded Gordonstoun in September had been given an exceptional amount of weight by the popular press to relieve the overall gloom.

At Princess Anne's request, the wedding would be less lavish than previous royal nuptials. Besides England being in grave economic difficulties, Princess Anne ranked low in the lists of royal favorites, and her behavior at Kiev, when she shouted at reporters after falling off a horse, "Sorry to disappoint you, but I'm not seriously hurt!" had not endeared her to anyone. Quite a few were unkindly amused when, shortly after the Russian visit, her father compared her to a horse herself. Only Princess Margaret was less liked.

Nevertheless, large crowds did turn out for the big occasion. The Queen's Household Cavalry once again rode out, the splendid horse-drawn carriages rolled up to Westminster Abbey. At the ceremony, Princess Anne's train was carried by Prince Edward and Lady Sarah Armstrong-Jones, both nine years old. Characteristically, the Princess had declined to have the dress made by Norman Hartnell, and instead had bought it at an ordinary fashion house. Her only concession to grand tradition was to have a myrtle sprig in her bouquet that was a descendant of Queen Victoria's own bouquet myrtle, and a fragment of white heather tucked in among the white roses, the traditional Scottish good-luck symbol.

In the brilliant sunshine, the radiant Princess and her husband stepped out on the Palace balcony and laughed at a banner that read, "It's never too late to say neigh!" The couple were driven through the streets and then left for their honeymoon at the house of Princess Alexandra of Kent and the Hon. Angus Ogilvy; they took off for Barbados for a honeymoon voyage aboard the *Britannia* which included Central America and the Galápagos Islands.

The Queen and her people were soon forced back into reality with power shortages, a fall on the London Stock Exchange, and a three-day week for employees of commerce and industry; electricity users would only be allowed 65 percent of normal consumption. Just before a gloomy Christmas, countless homes were lit by candles. It was like the deadliest days of the Second World War. Yet, all through December, there was much discussion of the Queen wanting even more money to sustain her incomparable lifestyle.

At the outset of 1974, as the economic crisis dragged on, the Queen and her husband went to New Zealand to attend the Commonwealth Games. Shortly before they left, there was talk of Heath calling for a dissolution of Parliament. Anthony Wedgwood Benn, Minister of Power, recorded in his diary a curious conversation at a lunch in honor of Harold Wilson at the Iranian Embassy in which the question of dissolution came up. Benn spoke to Sir Martin Charteris, the monarch's Principal Private Secretary, who confirmed that the Queen still had the absolute right of authorizing to dissolve. Benn suggested that she might call in the Speaker, while preserving that right. Charteris, in a unique example of a Principal Private Secretary revealing something personal about his royal mistress, said, "We must preserve her right, because I think there has to be some risk attached in order to provide excitement for the monarchy. And of course, in the end, the Queen's judgment will have to be tested by the events." Benn took this to mean that if the Queen refused a dissolution and Heath was defeated, the Palace would be embarrassed.

Harold Wilson had announced "a great new social contract" with the unions in a preelection speech, which he reworked repeatedly, if somewhat unconvincingly in view of his known dislike of being blackmailed by the work force. Polling day brought a strong turnout with the country, as expected, divided almost equally. The depressing thought on most middle-class minds was that whichever party gained power would have to meet the demands of the labor unions or put up with a total collapse of the economy.

As the result came in, it appeared there was a deadlock. Wilson held a very tiny majority, but it was by no means certain that he could govern on the strength of the results. Definitively, Heath stripped of his majority, informed the monarch that he would not resign his post; she accepted his decision, not calling for his resignation as she might well have done. Heath broke precedent by saying that he would attempt to govern with the support of the minority parties, a statement that instantly aroused criticism, and not only in Labor. Wilson charged that the Conservatives lacked the authority to lead the country, while many Conservatives argued that the people had not declared for a Labor government.

A new count showed Labor with 301 seats, Conservatives with 296, Liberals with 14; the extraordinary crisis dragged on and on, with no real winner. Heath was expected to remain in office until the new Parliament convened on March 12; if his program were to be defeated, the Queen would then ask Wilson to form a new government.

In the midst of this, the Queen was compelled, yet again in her life, to continue her commitments to the Commonwealth. It must have been agonizing for her that she had to leave England without a definite Prime Minister, and clearly, she might have to return very suddenly and under strenuous conditions, should the situation call for it. Finally, Wilson managed to squeeze in on his dangerously narrow majority and a general, if shaky, vote of confidence; his would be the first Cabinet in forty-five years to lack majority in the House of Commons, and he would clearly have to call a new election within eighteen months. The Queen, without Philip, flew to London. Only minutes after Heath met her and tendered his resignation, Wilson strode into her rooms and "kissed hands."

The Queen flew back at once to rejoin Prince Philip at Bali, Indonesia, an improbably remote location, given the circumstances. On the way there, she was very nearly killed. Her VC-10 British Airways jet wandered into a restricted flight over Germany used for NATO Air Force maneuvers and was mistaken for a target dummy. Only at the last minute did the attacking planes turn away before firing.

Shortly after 7 P.M. on March 20, while the Queen was in Djakarta, Indonesia, Princess Margaret was in the West Indies, and Prince Charles was in Los Angeles, Princess Anne and Mark Phillips were headed up the Mall on their way to Buckingham Palace, when a man named Ian Ball, driving a white Ford Escort, suddenly cut in front of them as they headed toward the gates. The royal chauffeur slammed his foot on the brake. James Beaton, the Princess's bodyguard, jumped out; at the same moment Ball pushed a revolver into the chauffeur's face and told him to switch off the ignition. Then he aimed the gun at the Princess and said, "Come with me, I only want you for two days."

Beaton confronted Ball, who shot him twice; one bullet penetrated a lung. When Beaton tried to fire back, his revolver jammed. The chauffeur tried to seize Ball's gun. Ball fired at him, directly into his chest. Rowena Brassey, lady-in-waiting, got out, so that Princess Anne, who was seated next to her, could run, but Ball reached in, grabbed the Princess, and ordered her out. He warned Beaton that unless the bodyguard dropped the gun, he would kill the Princess.

Ball began dragging the Princess out; Phillips pulled her back, talking incessantly to Ball. "Where do you want to take me?" the Princess asked, coldly furious. Phillips managed to close the door, whereupon Ball said he would kill him if he didn't open it again.

Beaton tried to block the shot that was about to come, and his hand was blasted open. Ball shot him in the stomach. A policeman appeared and Ball shot him also. Journalist Brian McConnell heard the commotion, stopped his taxi, and confronted Ball, who fired into his chest; businessman Ronald Russell struck Ball across the head as Ball still struggled with Phillips to pull open the door. But Ball managed to wrench it open and again began pulling the Princess. "Why don't you go away?" the cool Princess snapped. "What good is this going to do?"

As others, from Cabinet ministers to Scottish students, had been silenced by the Queen, so Ball was stilled by the majestic detachment of his intended victim. The Princess and her husband climbed out the other side; Ronald Russell struck Ball to the ground. Ball fled; the Princess yelled to the arriving police, "Get him!" He was seized by an officer. She was angrier than she had ever been in her life; not frightened—she was her mother's daughter—just infuriated.

Ball was caught. A ransom note calling for £2 million (or $4.8 million) was found in his possession, addressed to the Queen. He had drugs, two sets of revolvers, handcuffs, and leg shackles. He pleaded guilty; a schizophrenic, he would be sent to a mental institution; the Queen would award James Beaton with the George Cross and others involved received other rewards for their heroism. None had died as a result of their injuries.

Maintaining her composure, Princess Anne immediately went to Clarence House to reassure her grandmother that all was well and she was unharmed; she telephoned her mother, who was still in Djakarta, on her way to visit a temple. The Queen listened to the extraordinary story with detached concern and announced unhesitatingly that she would proceed with her schedule and would not be returning to England. Prince Charles was in Hollywood at the time, on leave from his vessel to make a tour of MCA Universal Studios. He had been on the set of the television series "Kojak," starring Telly Savalas, and was now completing a conversation with Barbra Streisand on the set of *Funny Lady*. When he was brought the news, he acted with great control, and, like the Queen, was instantly placed under maximum security guard. It was feared that the kidnapping attempt might be the work of an international gang which would strike at the other members of the family. Police officials rushed him off to his ship immediately.

Rather embarrassingly, Princess Margaret was living under the same roof in the Caribbean island of Mustique with a new friend, Roderic Llewellyn, son of a landowner, Sir Harry Llewellyn, who had distinguished himself in equestrian events at the 1952 Olympic Games. The Princess and Llewellyn were enjoying a three-week vacation at her house. She was put under tight control by military and civil officials; word leaked out of the ménage, and, inevitably, the press created the illusion that she was involved in a passionate relationship. Actually, although she was in love with Llewellyn, her royal caution and religious principles kept her from consummating the relationship, which was to remain platonic.

Of the whole royal family, only the Queen Mother was present to ease Princess Anne's understandably jangled nerves.

The Princess and her husband closed themselves off at their home in Sandhurst, near London.

Prince Charles appeared on the floor of the House of Lords to give his maiden speech in mid-June, the first by any member of the royal family in almost a century. A few weeks later, Marcia Williams, now Lady Falkender of West Haddon, took her seat in the Lords.

At almost exactly the same time as Prince Charles's address, the Duke of Gloucester, who had never recovered from his severe car crash several years before, and had become increasingly senile and comatose, finally died of complications from Parkinson's disease. Days later, the most ferocious street battle in years erupted in London as left-wing demonstrators clashed with the National Front, a somewhat fascist organization; when police tried to break them up, thirty-nine officers and patrolmen were badly injured. The issue was the same so bitterly fought by such figures as Enoch Powell; Wilson had agreed that black immigrants, wetbacks from the Commonwealth who had been smuggled into the British Isles, should be given a total amnesty. There was also a revolution in the Church: for four hundred and fifty years, bishops had been chosen by the Prime Minister, and the King or Queen had approved the appointment. Now, the Church voted to separate the ecclesiastical and secular, and to ensure that a bishop would be subject only to a religious consensus.

Prince Andrew was settling in well at Gordonstoun. His headmaster was the genial John Kempe. Kempe ran the school with much less severe a hand than his predecessors, Kurt Hahn or Robert Chew. Prince Andrew was, of course, treated like other boys, sharing a dormitory and showers and taking the usual two-hundred-yard morning run. His private detective was always present, but as unobtrusively as possible. During Prince Andrew's stay, Gordonstoun would become coeducational. This made a big difference, relaxing the grim, spartan, somewhat homoerotic atmosphere that had existed under Hahn. The Queen and Prince Philip made private visits to the school, which, by arrangement, were seldom mentioned in the press. They attended plays and chapel services, strolling about so informally that on more than one occasion a parent was startled by bumping into the monarch, who, impeccably good-

mannered, usually apologized herself. The Queen made Kempe
understand that her son, who would soon be followed by Prince
Edward, was not to be given any special privileges. They were
called Andrew and Edward by the boys, Prince Andrew and
Prince Edward by the staff. They never took advantage of their
royal position. Prince Andrew was a great enthusiast, an
athletic and healthy extrovert who enjoyed the outdoors even
more than Prince Charles.

One of the difficulties for Prince Andrew was finding
sufficient time, with so many distractions and private and
public occasions, to keep up his studies and vacation
periods. Prince Charles did his best to help him over this
problem; he himself enjoyed descending on the school by
helicopter.

Kempe enjoyed the custom of having Prince Andrew to tea;
this continued during his first term. He was given the duty of
taking care of guests to the school, and, finally, was appointed
Captain of Guests, sensitively and expertly taking care of their
needs. On one occasion, he was in charge of his own mother as
she toured Cumming House, of which he was a resident. It was
decided he would go to Canada for further schooling, because
his mother wanted him to have a keen grasp of Commonwealth
experience and teaching.

As expected, the general election took place on October 10.
The public expressed only apathy, gloom, and boredom. The
malaise was absolute; no government could alleviate it. There
had been a great to-do when the Conservative party's election
manifesto was leaked to three newspapers, apparently after it
was stolen from the printer's. As it turned out, it seemed not far
removed from the Labor manifesto, which called for national
unity, conciliation with the trade unions, and determination to
deal with inflation. In the wake of the announcement, Wilson
kept up his own proposals, and made sure that his press
conferences were as lively, boisterous, and colorful as old-
fashioned music hall performances, while Edward Heath conducted his own with cold solemnity, rather like gatherings of
high-ranking clerics. When the Queen dissolved Parliament on
September 20, it had been the shortest sitting in a hundred
years.

There was no way to make it a cheerful election. Wilson won
again, and thus became the first Prime Minister since Glad-
stone to triumph in four elections. But his was, again, a very

narrow victory; he only had a three-seat majority. Seven percent fewer voters had appeared at the polls. Could Wilson rescue the country from its appalling crisis?

Mary Wilson made a characteristic announcement in the wake of her husband's new victory; she stated that she hated 10 Downing Street as much as ever. She had refused to move into it after his triumph in February, and she certainly would not move into it now. The statement scarcely added to her popularity.

The Queen once again enjoyed her lingering late afternoons with Wilson, apparently still finding him more appealing than Heath.

Meantime, Prince Charles had remained aboard *Jupiter,* mostly in charge of Fleet Air Arm FAA. Back in England, at Davenport, he continued his work, and then went to Yeovil to obtain his helicopter license. The grueling forty-five-day course involved risky landings in aircraft that were already deliberately set on fire; he proceeded to Lympstone for a full-scale boot-camp training as a commando. He hugely enjoyed the whole experience, and, physically, he was at last changing rapidly, becoming now a broad-shouldered, powerful-chested, strapping young man with no hint of the soft, pampered, overgrown schoolboy he had been at his inauguration as Prince of Wales. On December 12, he obtained his helicopter pilot's license. He was known as a Red Dragon. The Queen had to accept the constant danger he risked. Prince Philip was extremely proud of him, though still irritated by his continuing sensitivity, sense of delicacy, and sweetness. He could never be tough enough for his father.

During this period, strange rumors began to circulate about Lord Mountbatten. In the wake of his peculiar exercise in the matter of the family surname, he had become radically eccentric. He had made bizarre expeditions to the Duchess of Windsor's house in Paris, apparently authorizing the burglary of her safe, and making off with all manner of documents, letters, and diaries, which he had quite improperly transferred (according to the Duchess's lawyer, Maître Suzanne Blum) to the Round Tower of Windsor Castle. A long-term member of his personal staff began telling people that his master was indulging in sadomasochistic activities, reminiscent of the dubious stories to be found in the pages of the pornographic volumes owned by the Milford Havens for two generations. He was said to have been seen furiously riding his horses in black leather, accompanied by similarly garbed women of the nobility, driving spurs into the horses' flanks until they bled, and whipping himself into an orgasmic frenzy as he did so. He would apparently subject his female partners to picturesque punishments, all of which the staff member diligently recorded. As if all this activity was not enough for an elderly gentleman of great distinction and uneven health, he was supposed to be indulging in affairs with handsome young men who sought advancement in the armed services. A certain amusement could be gleaned from these stories, true or false: they conjured up an image of amazing septuagenarian energy, at once dubious and enviable; what the Queen, and in particular Prince Philip, made of these antics cannot, of course, be determined. One only hopes that Prince Charles, whose visits to Broadlands were more and more frequent, was not exposed to them.

In February 1975, the extremely left-wing publication *Morning Star* published charges that the Queen's vast private share-holdings were being hidden deliberately by the Bank of England, Edward Heath, and the Palace. The paper referred to a letter dated December 5, 1973, from Robert Armstrong, Heath's Principal Private Secretary, to Robert Hird, of the Department of Trade and Industry. The letter contained a statement that Heath attached great importance to protecting the Queen's share-holdings from public disclosure. She would not be required to make public those holdings, as would other figures of industry, as a result of the Companies Bill, which was passed that December. In Subsection 8 of the bill, it was stated that the Secretary of State, after consultation with the governor of the Bank of England, could preclude selected individuals from the requirement to go public. The newspaper asked, what were the Queen's share-holdings, in which companies did she have a share, and would she be protected indefinitely?

At the *Morning Star*'s forty-fifth birthday rally at London's Festival Hall, the newspaper's editor, Tony Chater, spoke again, and loudly, of the cover-up. Harold Wilson became the butt of the charges. The audience cheered as Chater demanded Wilson not improve the Queen's finances any further. Labor members of Parliament on February 24 supported the newspaper in its position. Wilson had been forced to admit the authenticity of the cover-up letters. Wilson condemned the leak. At this stage, Margaret Thatcher, who had replaced Heath as leader of the Conservatives, the first woman in history to lead any political party in England, expressed her concern that the documents should have fallen into unauthorized hands.

An energetic debate continued on a proposed £420,000 pay raise for the monarch. James Wellbeloved, Labor MP for Erith and Crayford, called for the increase to be annulled; he added that the British people were being asked to tighten their belts while this extravagance was going on. Although the ghost of Marie Antoinette hovered over the Commons, most agreed with Paul Dean, Conservative MP for Somerset North, who said:

> The Queen brightens our lives on great ceremonial occasions. She also delighted people with her walkabouts, and she entertained at Buckingham Palace round about 30,000 each year. She is an asset beyond price.

The result of the debate was a vote for the increase.

The Queen returned to England, after a visit to Mexico, with a severe chill brought on by the strain of the long flight, with a change from hot weather to cold. She and Prince Philip made a State visit to Hong Kong and Japan in May. Few felt offended by her being received by the Emperor, despite the great loss of life of British troops to the Japanese during World War II. The visit was a great success, and included a tea ceremony, a visit to the Imperial Palace of Kyoto, and the planting of a memorial oak sapling. Upon her return she installed Prince Charles as Great Master of the Order of the Bath. There was sad news; Lord Plunket died, followed by Sir Richard Colville, the Queen's trusted Press Secretary from 1952 until 1968. The Queen was deeply grieved. She provided a memorial site to honor the memory of Lord Plunket in one of his favorite spots, the beautiful Valley Gardens in Windsor Great Park. Plunket's friends provided a small temple, fashioned of wood, that was built in the gardens with a view of Virginia Water. It was a serene and lovely monument to a man she deeply responded to emotionally.

The Queen was doing very well financially. Not only had she managed to bring off the *coup* (aided by the loud complaints of her husband) of doubling her already substantial Civil List income, but her immense personal fortune was amplified by a most shrewd investment that was now paying off substantially. For some years, she had been an important shareholder in General Electric and in the colossal international corporation known as Rio Tinto-Zinc, or RTZ. Her long-term Principal Private Secretary, Sir Martin Charteris, who, in 1978, would be created Lord Charteris of Amisfield, would soon be on the Board of Directors of RTZ. The sheer range and size of RTZ was (as it remains) astounding. It had vast holdings in Canada and Australia. Lead, zinc, copper, iron ore, bauxite, aluminum, coal and coke, tin, salt, stainless steel, magnetite, borax, sulfuric acid, glass, wood, and all manner of minerals were grist to the massive mill, operated from luxurious offices at 6 St. James's Square, London. RTZ was never free of controversy during the 1970s. In the spring of 1974, there was a conflict in Newfoundland, when the government threatened to take over all shares of the RTZ subsidiary Brinco, which controlled much of the electricity in the province, if RTZ did not agree to sell its 40.2 percent interest to the government. It offered $7.07 a share for Rio Tinto's 11.3 million shares; the offer was made to American, Canadian, and British shareholders, including the Queen. Brinco declared it would accept the offer but would make a counterproposal. Premier Frank Moores of Newfoundland announced that he would proceed with the takeover, supplying a total of $180 million from the Bank of Nova Scotia.

The discovery of oil in the North Sea had proved to be a potential boost to the British economy. Norway and Holland rapidly benefited from discoveries in their own waters. Rio Tinto-Zinc was in right at the beginning, as one might expect. The Queen undoubtedly approved the heavy investment, which would enrich her in the immediate future. Conjointly with Texaco, RTZ was the spearhead, that June of 1975, as it shipped from the Argyll Field, as it was known, to the refineries of British Petroleum, in which the Queen was also believed to have interests. Also that month, Prime Minister Wilson proved helpful to the Queen and RTZ's cause by advising his new Secretary of State for Energy, Anthony Wedgwood Benn, to put every ounce of effort behind bringing up as much oil as possible. Benn, who was known to be sympathetic to the Labor work force, determinedly set about meeting with as many oil-rig workers as possible to appease conflicts that occurred among them and members of the competitive teams.

Meanwhile, Harold Lever, Chancellor of the Duchy of Lancaster, and thus directly concerned with the vast land holdings of the Queen, although in many ways his appointment was a sinecure, and the Paymaster General Edmund Dell, were in charge of government negotiations with RTZ, Texaco, British Petroleum, and the other companies involved. Wedgwood Benn himself, in a ceremony on June 18, turned the valve which caused the first North Sea oil to flow from tanker to refinery. He was turning the tap on for not only the national, but specifically the Queen's, benefit.

At the end of July, Lord Kearton resigned as chairman of Courtaulds, which, it will be recalled, according to Senator McIntyre and Congressman Conte, was effectively running a Mississippi plantation for the Queen, and was named head of the British National Oil Corporation, through which the government itself would obtain a 51 percent interest in the oil fields. By September, 32,500 barrels were being supplied from Transworld 58 every day; RTZ shared two thirds of the profits with Associated Newspapers and Kleinwort Benson, the remaining third taken by Hamilton Brothers Oil, which discovered and ran the Argyll Field.

Nor was the Queen's benefit by any means restricted to this staggering upsurge of petroleum through the ocean wave. It was discovered in 1976, during the course of the U.S. Senate Foreign Relations Committee hearing under Joint Chairmen U.S. Attorney General Edward H. Levi and Senator Frank Church, that an international cartel, of which RTZ was a major partner, had been formed in 1971 to fix the world's uranium prices. A federal grand jury, seeking to determine whether there had been a violation of U.S. anti-trust laws, obtained minutes of a meeting in Johannesburg, South Africa, in 1974, of Rio Tinto-Zinc executives with Australian, Canadian, French, and South African delegates to discuss a corner in the substance. A letter was subpoenaed from Louis C. Mezel of Rio Tinto to Harold F. Melouney of Mary Kathleen Uranium of Australia discussing this exclusive consortium designed to control the commodity's prices. Further documents emerged from an Australian mining company's files, published in the French newspaper *Le Monde.* The Queen was doing as well out of uranium as she was out of oil.

In view of all this, one could scarcely be amazed by a statement made to Geoffrey Smith of *Forbes,* for its issue of October 16, 1978. Alluding discreetly, Smith wrote, to the widely held belief that the Queen was a major RTZ shareholder with the Bank of England, Sir Mark Turner, the then chairman, said astonishingly, in the course of an interview, "You're running into problems of what the government is going to say [about the Queen's involvement]. [RTZ] is one of the great assets of the country."

As a footnote to this whole matter, the Queen had a special interest, above and beyond her political concerns, that the still extant Rhodesian problem might finally be solved. Ian Smith was talking of expropriating the Rhodesian holdings of RTZ (since the unilateral Declaration of Independence in 1965, they had remained in a holding company, out of touch with London); absolute nationalization might follow. There was also talk of Southwest Africa and Papua/New Guinea expropriating RTZ. But in the end the Queen's personal commonwealth of investments stayed intact, and the various threats against RTZ came to nothing.

In addition to her investments in Rio Tinto-Zinc, the Queen held over $2 million in General Electric shares. This put her into a peculiar relationship with Mrs. Thatcher, since General Electric was the largest financial supporter of the Conservative party in 1980, and hence, of course, of Mrs. Thatcher's electoral campaigns. In his book *Thatcher and Friends: The Anatomy of the Tory Party,* John Ross stated:

> At the time of her election, Thatcher . . . had no more openly proclaimed admirer in industry than the head of General Electric, Lord Weinstock.

Except for a brief period during the 1981 recession, when General Electric was forced to withdraw from support, Weinstock remained unrelentingly the main backer of the Tories. Anthony Sampson wrote of the company in which the Queen had so substantial an investment:

> Weinstock's preoccupation with profits soon made him a bogeyman as he closed down whole plants and eliminated

tens of thousands of jobs, so that by 1980 labor . . . demanded [General Electric's] nationalization.

By contrast, the threat to expose Prince Philip's secret connections through the 1,001 Club with Prince Bernhard of the Netherlands was never far away. By the setting up of the special Houblon and Bank of England Nominees trust group, which was precluded from disclosure, the Queen's continuing involvement in Rio Tinto was obscured; Prince Philip's personal if innocent links to the troubled Netherlands Prince Consort could not be quite hidden, and yet the British press remained extremely subdued in the matter.

There was much interparty strife in Labor that September. Chancellor of the Exchequer Denis Healey, that key figure of the Bilderberg group, left the Labor party's ruling council. There was a controversy that fall over the publication of the Richard Crossman diaries, with their unflattering accounts of Privy Council meetings with the Queen. Harold Wilson backed the Attorney General, Sam Silkin, in an effort to stop publication of this, one of the most important records of an era, and it is likely that the Queen approved Wilson's move. The publishers were threatened with injunctions, but finally publication went ahead, so ordered by the High Court. The government did not appeal the decision.

Princess Anne remained obsessed, like her mother, with horses. In June, she became the first member of a British royal family ever to appear in an American equestrian event: Ledyard Farm Horse Trials at Wenham, Massachusetts. Just before her and her husband's departure, there was a ghastly moment: on May 30, during the Silverstone Race Circuit in London, with the Princess watching from the stands, Captain Phillips crashed his car while rounding a bend; she, for once, lost composure and cried out in distress, but he was unhurt.

The couple made a dashing impression at Wenham and at Hamilton, Massachusetts; Phillips, to his wife's ecstatic delight, won the opening-day dressage prize at the Myopia Hunt Club; the Princess sportingly shrugged as she came in thirteenth; later, the roles were reversed when she came in tenth and his horse, much to his fury, failed three times to make it over a fence. (In October, in England, there was an odd aftermath: as Captain Phillips and she rode against each other in a cross-country event, they collided head-on, and were bruised. She fell off her horse.)

Prince Charles was busy, too. Among other appearances, he was in India with Lord Mountbatten, to attend the coronation of King Birendra of Nepal, an occasion reminiscent of the great age of the Maharajahs; he lunched with Prime Minister Indira Gandhi and paid homage at Mahatma Gandhi's tomb.

In Parliament there was a powerful attempt to appease Scottish and Welsh nationalists with talk of home rule, and the Queen spoke of the matter in her gracious speech in November. In a white paper that month, the government, undoubtedly with the Queen's support, decided that, while Scotland and Wales would obtain far more autonomy than hitherto, they would still be part of the United Kingdom. Many in both countries objected that the North Sea oil fields would be strictly under London, not joint Welsh, Scottish, and British, control.

The Queen was feeling unusually strong that month. She extended her privileges by declining to consult with either the Prime Minister or Cabinet when she exercised her royal privilege in sending Prince Philip to Madrid to attend the accession ceremony of Don Juan Carlos of Spain, whose wife was her relative by marriage.

She even expressed her opinion in public. When she received hundreds of letters protesting against a film that would show Jesus Christ having sexual intercourse, she issued a statement: "I find the proposal as obnoxious as most of my subjects do."

The Queen was compelled late in 1975 to contribute the equivalent of $300,000, followed by $240,000 in 1976, from her own pocket to supplement the Civil List. Harold Wilson described it as "a generous gesture." Her money would be used to cover allowances for the Dukes of Kent and Gloucester, Princess Alexandra of Kent, and the venerable Princess Alice of Athlone, granddaughter of Queen Victoria, who was over ninety years old. Thus, they became direct dependents of the monarch, a unique happenstance in British history. At another discussion in Parliament, several members took up the question of the succession to the throne, claiming that there was discrimination against women, and that in fact Princess Anne should not be behind her younger brothers Andrew and

Edward, but as the second-born should take the appropriate position in line of succession. Nothing came of this; the laws remained the same.

Prince Charles was nearing the end of his Naval service; in February 1976, he became commander of HMS *Bronington,* a tiny, 360-ton mine hunter with only three other officers and thirty-three ratings aboard. This uncomfortable tub, which wallowed alarmingly in heavy swells, and offered a cramped and unaccommodating galley, traveled mostly through the North Sea, very close to RTZ's oil fields, sweeping mines. The Queen Mother also had her maritime moments, dropping her handbag in the sea when she climbed aboard a barge, or making a trip to Holland, to see (rather boldly, in view of the scandals surrounding the Netherlands Government) Queen Juliana and Prince Bernhard. Prince Andrew, long since recovered from such uncomfortable moments at Gordonstoun as a nasty dormitory rag in which he was severely struck on the head by three other boys, continued to do extremely well, joined now by his younger brother Edward. Kurt Hahn finally died in 1974, to the end a mystery, exiled overseas, his precise role in secret peace negotiations in World War II never fully known.

The pincers of the Prince Bernhard affair began to close in. On February 6, during an investigation by a Senate subcommittee in Washington, A. C. Kotchian, president of Lockheed Aircraft Corporation, revealed that $1.1 million was paid to "a member of the Netherlands royal family," in his role as Inspector General of the Dutch Army, Navy, and Air Force, in order to secure contracts for the Starfighter jets. Later, the *New York Times* obtained confirmation that the official was Prince Bernhard. A massive controversy blew up. In order to bring Prince Bernhard to trial, his wife, the Queen, would have to sign documents, and it was, of course, unlikely that she would do so. The Dutch Cabinet called for an "independent investigation." The Prince stated he had never received or accepted money. He was linked to secret deals with Northrop, also for military aircraft. And, of course, he still remained head of the World Wildlife Fund with Prince Philip, his partner in the 1,001 Club and his associate in the Bilderbergers, as British leader. Yet no hint of scandal touched Philip in the matter; there was no evidence that he had been involved in any inappropriate deals in England.

Prince Bernhard laughed off all the criticism, but, not insignificantly, he canceled a proposed journey to Hot Springs, Virginia, in April, when he was to have been president of the latest Bilderberg conference. Prince Philip was also not present. Eventually, Prince Bernhard would be compelled to resign from Bilderberg, to be replaced by Lord Home as chairman.

While the Netherlands affair bubbled on, there was much else to preoccupy followers of economic and political history in the making. Returning from India to London, former Prime Minister Harold Macmillan assumed the mantle of prophecy and announced that Margaret Thatcher would soon be Prime Minister. Wilson's short-lived Labor government crashed in March, defeated in the Commons because it had planned to slice public service costs. Mrs. Thatcher had issued the demand that either Wilson resign or obtain a vote of confidence. In a second vote the following day, Wilson's move was passed. Mrs. Thatcher was temporarily thwarted. But, stricken with serious illness that was not made public, the Prime Minister resigned anyway, advising the Queen that he had no alternative, and revealing that, for two years, he had set this as his moment to step down. Of his successors, the most likely to be chosen seemed to be Foreign Secretary James Callaghan, Bilderberger/Chancellor of the Exchequer Denis Healey, and Home Secretary Roy Jenkins. The left wing of the party favored Anthony Wedgwood Benn. In the wake of the resignation, stock prices fell drastically. Everyone was stunned, shocked, staggered—even Wilson's worst enemies.

That the Queen held Wilson in higher regard than any other of her Prime Ministers since Churchill was conclusively proven by the fact that she, for the first time since Churchill retired twenty-one years earlier, actually went with her husband to 10 Downing Street for dinner.

An odd little scene took place after the meal. Everyone went upstairs from the table; other people arrived. Harold Wilson had asked Lady Falkender to introduce the guests to the Queen, but she became involved in talking to Prince Philip and forgot. Lady Wilson also seemed to be engaged. As a result, Wilson, most embarrassed, had to go from person to person saying, "Do you want to meet the Queen?" When they (naturally) replied that they did, he had, most laboriously, to introduce them one by one.

Yet again in the Queen's reign, a ballot was taken for Wilson's successor. The voting narrowed down to Callaghan and Michael Foot, Secretary of Employment. Callaghan won. The ailing Wilson presented his resignation to the Queen.

Callaghan was a man of great ability, polished, probably the best-dressed British Prime Minister since Lord Avon, Anthony Eden; he was seen as a unifier and moderator of dissident elements in his party, not radically upsetting to anyone, earning respect at party conferences.

In a not unfamiliar political pattern, no sooner had Callaghan assumed high office, his plump, jovial face and his wife's broadly grinning suburban visage appearing on television and in newspapers all over the world, than the Conservatives suddenly gained in the by-elections. Typically, Mrs. Thatcher demanded that Callaghan, who had barely been in office for a month, should call a general election. She was setting the pattern of her career as a ruthless politician, impatient for power and unable to wait for her adversaries to lie down so that she might walk, in her sturdy high heels, all over them.

In late August, the Lockheed/Bernhard matter came dangerously close to the government, if not the throne. Ernest Hauser, former sales executive for Lockheed, stated that "an unnamed British Cabinet Minister" had been in receipt of no less than $1 million to ensure that the company's airplanes should be made available in Great Britain. Hauser stated that fifty Tristar Airbuses were optioned by Air Holdings, Ltd., which controlled British United Airways, now subsumed into British Caledonian. The money was allegedly delivered to the Minister in cash in four suitcases, each carried by Lockheed officials. Nothing came of this. Who was responsible for burying the matter was never revealed.

Princess Anne was making news in the equestrian field that year; so complete was her obsession by now that she would spend an entire dinner party talking to a horse breeder on one side while ignoring a guest with different interests on the other. One night, she had behaved so rudely that when she asked the neglected guest for some sugar for her coffee, he held his hand open, with two lumps in the palm.

She had a worse mishap: at the Portman Horse Show Trial in April she was thrown and cracked a vertebra in her spine, and was hospitalized. But she was discharged quickly; nothing would hold her; she would compete or die. Distressed because two friends' favorite horses had died during racing events, she failed at a cross-country race in May, but pulled herself together, buoyed by news that the Queen had bought for the equivalent of $1.3 million the magnificent estate Gatcombe Park, in Gloucestershire, for her and her husband; the seller was the ever-useful Lord Butler. She again fell at a race in July, and did not do well at the Montreal Olympics where her mother watched as she came in twenty-fourth.

Mrs. Thatcher was still furiously reshuffling her shadow Cabinet, pressing Callaghan to the edge over controversial legislation on the nationalizing of ship-building and aircraft.

Meantime, the Queen had made a six-day summer visit to the United States, her first in nineteen years, for the bicentennial, during which she met Muhammad Ali and her own and her son's admired television star, Telly Savalas, at a reception and banquet given by President Gerald Ford at the White House; then she flew to Montreal to open the Games.

Prince Charles, Prince Edward, and Prince Andrew were also there; only the Queen Mother of the immediate family remained in London. A few days later, Prince Charles, still serving on his minesweeper, accepted the position of chancellor of the University of Wales.

The Lockheed scandal would not die down. On August 30, the Dutch Parliament voted (and quite disgracefully) against a left-wing motion for the Prince to be prosecuted. They announced that "Constitutional considerations" justified their approach to the matter. And this despite the fact that the Commission of Inquiry had a letter Prince Bernhard had sent to one of the heads of Lockheed, asking for between $4 million and $6 million, but agreeing to $1 million in return for a sale of thirteen Orion airplanes. Two members of the government were revealed as being involved in the sales promotions of Orion. It was also revealed that Bernhard had asked West German Chancellor Helmut Schmidt, who had been Defense Minister, to buy Northrop airplanes. It will be recalled that the heads of Lockheed and Northrop were co-members with Bernhard and Prince Philip in the 1,001 Club. There were even suggestions that funds raised by the World Wildlife Committees were making their way into Prince Bernhard's pocket, but these charges did not stand up. However, the grave issue could not entirely be suppressed, and Prince Bernhard resigned as international president of the organization. Soon, the Netherlands Government would place a huge order with Lockheed.

That year was a tragic one for Princess Margaret and Lord Snowdon. It was now quite clear that they would be unable to salvage their marriage. The Princess was continuing to spend much time with Roddy Llewellyn, and Snowdon with Lucy Lindsay Hogg, former wife of the stage and film director Michael Lindsay Hogg, son of the Irish-American actress Geraldine Fitzgerald. Princess Margaret had never been able to marry her royal status to her longed-for association with ordinary people, and it was her strict adherence to royal behavior, never ceasing to make her husband aware of the difference in their station, that helped to break the marriage. Lord Snowdon had most ably and expertly combined his new position in the royal family with his career as a great photographer, able to deal with people at all levels, as totally at ease with the Queen as he was with tradesmen or workers.

Paradoxically, it was he who was the better mannered of the two; Princess Margaret had been brought up spoiled; yet at the same time she was always aware of her subsidiary status, and therefore overcompensated with violent displays of ''royal'' arrogance, unlike her composed and secure elder sister. It was the impetuous Princess who ruled her staff fiercely, not Lord Snowdon, whom people like fired ex-butlers and footmen from Thomas Cronin on tended to excoriate in their published memoirs. A decision that her children would not be given ''royal'' titles was typical, and was a way of putting down the very husband she had chosen to share her life with. He was always painfully aware that he did not have the rights of landlord a normal male would enjoy, but, instead, was a tenant in a Royal Household, and a nonpaying one at that. He was thus his wife's vassal, and his masculinity kicked at that; furthermore, much as he adored the Queen Mother, and was genuinely fond of the Queen, he still had no rapport with Prince Philip, who, on at least one memorable occasion, had told him to ''stick to your bloody camera in your shooting!'' when he proved to be (and God be praised) a clumsy hand at deerstalking.

The Snowdons did not want a divorce; not really. A divorce meant an admission of defeat and a horrendous appeal to the

Queen the Princess loved more than any other human being to get over the still punitive terms of the dreaded Royal Marriage Act. But they had grown inexorably apart. It was impossible to sustain a marriage in which the husband was constantly traveling about at the very top of his profession, from country to country, eclipsing such previous notables as Karsh of Ottawa as probably the most penetrating and audacious camera portraitist of a generation.

The Princess greatly resented her husband's absences, not so much the career. But the career caused the absences, and was finally resented itself.

She had increasingly found, in her boring and sadly meaningless career, less and less time to devote to the requirements of a royal person, and her visits to the Commonwealth were undistinguished and quite infrequent. A trip to Australia at the time was perfunctory and marred by local displays which indicated that she was not entirely popular. Mustique in the Caribbean remained her place of escape, her own personal island, the land for her house given to her long ago for her wedding by Colin Tennant. Her favorite pastime was sitting or lying in the sun, dreaming away the long days with her swimsuited set of friends, who grew browner and browner and less and less brilliant with each passing, self-indulgent hour. She would sip pink gins, smoke through her familiar holder, solve the London *Times* crossword puzzle flown in daily, and play cards, until the velvet nights closed in and the long dinners went on and on, playing havoc with her once-perfect figure.

Roddy Llewellyn and she still did not enjoy a physical relationship, and she remained, despite all of her hedonism, a constant attendant at the local church and a giver of tithes.

To Lord Snowdon, the life on Mustique was totally unappealing; he hated the heat and humidity, the emptiness and pointlessness. It was stated in Christopher Warwick's authorized biography that, exasperated by a picture of Margaret lounging with Llewellyn in Mustique, Snowdon moved out of Kensington Palace bag and baggage. Shortly before, in a violent quarrel with the Princess, he had shattered the mirrors in her bedroom.

While Snowdon retreated to his cottage near Uckfield in Sussex (he soon afterward bought a house in Kensington), the miserable separation went on. Princess Margaret made State visits to Morocco and Tunisia, meaningless locations that were painfully indicative of her marginal status. Still, no divorce was announced. It would be delayed until after the royal jubilee celebrations the following summer.

22

***

THE SILVER JUBILEE, COMMEMORATING the twenty-fifth year of the Queen's reign, was not to display the overwhelming opulence of her wedding or Coronation. This she decreed from the outset. In view of the country's still lamentable condition, both economically and politically, this was probably a wise decision. Throughout the last three months of 1976, an extensive itinerary was planned for her, so that she could tour more of England at one time than she had ever done before. But borough councils were instructed not to provide lavish decorations and motifs of the national flag; a vigorous scrubbing of sooty, grimy buildings would be enough. Thousands of homes would be repainted, and those selected for her private visits, mostly to the poor and underprivileged, would be spruced up at the councils' expense.

In December 1976, Prince Charles finally left the Navy. The Queen, Prince Philip, and other family members came aboard his minesweeper, cramming tightly into the mess room. Hugely popular with the officers and crew, Prince Charles announced in a farewell speech that he would give everyone on board a specially struck medal. A crew member was sent to his cabin saying they would rather have an autographed picture; later, he supplied them with both.

In farewell, the men sent him sliding down the gangplank on a toilet seat with a roll around his neck. He shouted with laughter; he was always happiest skylarking around as one of the boys. The royals laughed uproariously.

Immediately after the 1976 Christmas holidays, Prince Andrew flew to Canada, where he was happily enrolled at school, Lakefield College, Lakefield, Ontario. Within a few days of his arrival he had enlisted in the ice hockey team and the skiing team, and, during May, he took part in a school play. He shared his elder brother's, mother's, and aunt's skill as an actor. Strikingly handsome, lean, and fit, he made a strong impression, especially on the local girls. He would return to Gordonstoun later. Meanwhile, as if to indicate her intention to be less formal in keeping with the attitudes of the newest generation, the Queen was seen entering a movie theater in Leicester Square, London. She was noticed driving to visit with her old friends Lord and Lady Porchester and Lord and Lady Rupert Nevill at their country homes. The death of Lord Avon in January seemed to leave her unmoved. In May, she would be present at the opening of Sandringham to the public for the first time, thus breaking all tradition in an effort to raise money to pay for expensive repairs.

As the first of several jubilee-year tours, the Queen and Prince Philip left for Australia at the end of the winter. They returned to England to authorize the public announcement of Princess Anne's pregnancy. The Princess herself had also been threatened loudly: on a trip to Belfast in the third week of March, there was a severe threat from IRA terrorists. This also came to nothing.

In May, Rio Tinto-Zinc was in considerable difficulties. Against the triumph of RTZ's pioneer oil shipments from the troublesome North Sea, international legal actions were beginning to cast a shadow over the Queen's celebratory anniversary. Power companies had brought charges against Westinghouse Electric Corporation in the United States, claiming that Westinghouse had failed to meet uranium supplies according to contract. Westinghouse, on its part, alleged that RTZ and other corporations had formed a uranium cartel that was forcing up world prices to the detriment of Westinghouse, preventing the company from meeting its contracts. The matter was before the Court of Appeal in London. Certain of RTZ's directors, gravely concerned about having to appear before the courts, had appealed strongly against giving depositions; they also were fighting yielding up documentary evidence. In an extraordinary move, they went to the American Embassy in Grosvenor Square to plead the Fifth Amendment. Promised immunity from prosecution if they were to testify, they still felt the Fifth Amendment was necessary to protect the confidentiality of their arrangements with several European governments.

This was certainly a rare, if not unknown, use by British

businessmen of a right due to the American citizen; in England, the Civil Evidence Act of 1968 provided a similar protection.

Were they to have testified, there is no doubt that the RTZ accounts, including details of shareholders, would have had to have been made public in America, though perhaps protected in Britain by the Companies Act. Therefore, the Queen might not have escaped exposure in the U.S.A., and, while the directors undoubtedly had in mind not only their own protection but that of their particular arrangements with foreign governments, they had the Queen to consider as well when they lodged the appeal before the court under Lord Denning.

Denning refused the appeal. In a long speech, he gave a history of the uranium cartel, citing Australian documents and naming Australia itself, Canada, South Africa, France, and England as members of the secret consortium. Denning went beyond the U.S. charges by saying that Common Market law under Article 85 of the EEC Treaty was designed to prohibit cartels and would be free under a general commission to impose fines on government members of the EEC who intentionally or negligently broke the rules.

While a further court hearing at the American Embassy was being scheduled, the Queen, by a peculiar irony, began to get ready for the ceremony of the Silver Jubilee. On June 6, dressed with deliberate casualness in a scarf, green topcoat, and sensible shoes, she climbed up Snow Hill, near Windsor Castle, and lit a thirty-foot-high bonfire with a flaring torch. She was surrounded by thousands of children, also carrying torches, as the rain-dampened timber crackled and flickered into flame. A fireworks display filled the sky; the Household Cavalry Band gave a vivid performance of the Queen's favorite march, Elgar's "Pomp and Circumstance." As at the time of her birth, and on other royal occasions, fires, from Scotland to the Scilly Isles, illuminated the nation. Again, for a short moment, the country's troubles were dissolved in an orgy of excitement.

Despite a drizzle, London was alive with excitement, even delirium, the following day. Over a million people, perhaps exceeding the number which had attended the Coronation, crammed the Mall and flowed over into Trafalgar Square. It was like the old times as, for the first time since the glorious days of 1953, the gilded State coach carried the Queen and Prince Philip from the Palace gates, lumbering behind the traditional eight Windsor gray horses, grooms in scarlet and gold uniforms walking beside. The Queen, serious at first, now smiled and waved to her people. Prince Philip was dressed as Admiral of the Fleet. Prince Charles followed, on the back of a powerful black stallion, dressed resplendently in his scarlet uniform and black bearskin hat, in his role as recently appointed Colonel-in-Chief of the Welsh Guards. The Queen Mother, Princess Margaret, and the Princes Andrew and Edward followed in the two-mile journey to St. Paul's; at the Queen's special request, the cavalrymen of the Royal Canadian Mounted Police were delegated to accompany her.

In 1953, the State coach had only to make the journey to Westminster Abbey, but in this case it had to go up Ludgate Hill, a modest rise that nevertheless called for (on the Queen's advice) sand to be laid down on the street in case the horses should slip.

The royal coach stopped at Temple Bar, at the edge of the City of London; Sir Robin Gillett, Lord Mayor, gave the Queen her namesake monarch's original sword, and Elizabeth handed it back to him with ceremony. As the procession arrived at the cathedral, there was a temporary hitch: Prince Charles found himself unable to dismount. The Queen grinned affectionately, and the people clapped delightedly as he was brought down. "At least I didn't fall off it," the laughing Prince said later.

The service lasted fifty minutes. The royal party was greeted with an eight-trumpet fanfare, and, before an assemblage of over 2,700 people, the Queen and Prince Philip sat in rich red and gold armchairs. The Most Reverend Donald Coggan, Archbishop of Canterbury, spoke of the Queen's devotion to duty, her "service untiringly done." Following the Archbishop's pronunciation of the blessing, the ancient dome of the great building resounded to the strains of "God Save the Queen," and the trumpets blended with the organ in a magnificent burst of music. For almost the first time in her life, the Queen had to fight back tears before her people. She had lived through so much; she had suffered and rejoiced with her troubled populace; far more remained to be done.

The Queen began the "walkabout" to which she had most looked forward. The love of her people for the first time in her life now completely overwhelmed her. As Lord Mountbatten said later,[1] she was so modest, that, incredible though it might seem, she had no idea the people were so fond of her. They touched her clothes; in her pink hat and coat, she provided a flash of color among the many drably dressed citizens, strolling all the way to the Guildhall. She talked to many, including a bearded student, a nun, and elderly women, especially singling out blacks for her attention. At luncheon at the Guildhall, she made jokes, in her most relaxed and charming speech to date, about "my husband and I," and the use of the royal plural; she referred wryly to former jubilees as occasions for "rest, mercy and pardon." There would be nothing restful about this particular year. She said, "This is not exactly a period of rest for us." Everyone laughed. She laughed with them. She had never looked happier, nor had Prince Philip.

On the journey back to Buckingham Palace, she and Prince Philip went in a horse-drawn 1902 landau, surrounded by the thousands waving their Union Jacks. That week saw the Queen's celebratory voyage on the River Thames, in a river pageant accompanied by ships' sirens and whistles and cries from the shore; over the houses of Parliament, in the icy summer rain, fireworks blazed and fountained. Among the vast number of craft that saluted the Queen were boats used to take British soldiers away from Dunkirk in the memorable evacuation of 1940. Everyone who could master a vessel was out there in the water. Kites flew above; guns rang out; there was a chorus, from ships' horns, of "Cock-a-Doodle-Doo."

The blazing beacons, the jubilant crowd, the flashing rockets in the sky, the faces flushed with pleasure at the sight of her, now totally engulfed the monarch. According to Lord Mountbatten, she was determined to increase her schedule for the next several months, planning more and more provincial visits, no matter how great the risk to her health and strength. If she could have, he felt, she would have seen every single one of her people.

In the wake of the jubilee celebration, Rio Tinto-Zinc was in further trouble. The executive directors tried to have the hearing at the U.S. Embassy held *in camera,* but Judge Robert Merhigh said that there was no reason why the matter should be held in secret. Sir Mark Turner, RTZ chairman, flatly refused

1. In an interview with Roy Moseley.

to release a transcript. He continued to deny liability in the Westinghouse case. The board was granted the Fifth Amendment.

On June 16, in further hearings under the U.S. House Interstate and Foreign Commerce Subcommittee on Oversight and Investigations, Jerry McAfee, chairman of Gulf Oil Corporation, admitted that the cartel in which RTZ was his partner had in fact increased the world price of uranium. At the same time, the Tennessee Valley Authority was suing RTZ and its partners for tens of millions of dollars over the same matter. A total figure of $6 billion could be awarded should RTZ and the others be found guilty. Further hearings took place at the U.S. Embassy. There was much discussion of what was to become popularly known in high-level industrial circles as The Club. This was the consortium concerned; The Club correctly summarized its chummy character.

In Washington, D.C., on June 16, documents were released from Gulf Oil which helped to cement the case against RTZ and one of its subsidiaries, Rio Algom. Documents were produced by Friends of the Earth, an Australian environmental agency, which protested the severe danger to the atmosphere coming from leaks, actual or potential, in nuclear reactors. RTZ's Rio Algom was charged with being in contempt of court for failing to produce appropriate documents. The documents were produced.

In July, the U.S. Attorney General overruled the Fifth Amendment and demanded the RTZ directors testify under immunity in London.

Even when, in an attempt at obtaining crucial information, the U.S. Government granted immunity from prosecution to RTZ's executives should they give evidence, they did not proceed with the arrangement, and instead made the extraordinary move of appealing directly via the Attorney General (on behalf of the government) to the House of Lords to overrule the U.S. courts in the matter.

During this darkly threatening series of legalistic goings-on, the Queen was in Belfast for a perilous thirty-eight hours, threatened every moment with death. An IRA spokesman announced that a bomb had been placed at the new University of Ulster in Coleraine, and that it was ''not a hoax.'' In fact, no bombs were there. The Queen traveled by royal yacht *Britannia* and by helicopter (she hated this latter form of travel more than any other); on advice, she was not conveyed by road, as she could easily be shot. Exhausted, according to Lord Mountbatten, by these eight months of endless journeying, the Queen, with Prince Philip, went to rest at Balmoral. Hours after they left, the threatened bomb went off at the University of Ulster.

But the Queen had much good news that year. Her filly Dumfernline spectacularly triumphed in both the coveted Oaks and St. Leger races. Rio Tinto-Zinc, with Texaco, Associated Newspapers, and Kleinwort Benson, was still doing well in the North Sea oil field. Their jointly owned Transworld 58 was ahead in pumping in the region. The Argyll Field was doing splendidly, producing thirty-two thousand barrels a day. Aside from minor accidents like cables snarled and cranes breaking, everything continued to go well, though other oil companies were pouring in.

In October the Queen traveled to Canada for six days; on November 15, 1977, the Queen's first grandchild was born: Master Peter Phillips. He was the first direct descendant of Queen Victoria who was not accorded a title. Mark Phillips was present at the birth, according to modern custom; it was admirably supervised by the Queen's own gynecologist, George Pinker, at St. Mary's Hospital, Paddington. The Queen arrived in the evening, her eyes bright with excitement, smiling happily, waving to the hundreds who crowded outside the hospital. The Duke of Edinburgh was in Germany, Prince Charles in Yorkshire, Prince Andrew at Gordonstoun with his brother Prince Edward. According to tradition, a forty-one-gun salute was fired from the Tower of London, but a second salute proved impossible because the Royal Horse Artillery had to be available in case of a fire; the London firemen had gone on strike.

At the same time, Lord Dilhorne, whose role in the Macmillan ballot of 1963 will be recalled, Lord Wilberforce, Lord Diplock, Lord Frazer of Tullybelton, and Lord Keith of Kinkel reached their decision in the matter of the appeal by the RTZ executives against appearing before an American court. The appellate law lords ruled that RTZ would not have to give evidence; they described the U.S. court's demand for it as ''an unacceptable invasion of British sovereignty''; there the matter seemed to lie. But, useful though it was to the Queen and the other shareholders, the law lords' decision came too late to prevent crucial RTZ correspondence from being published in the U.S. House Committee hearings volumes. They may be examined in the document rooms of most well-stocked American libraries today. The financial cliffhanger over, her interest still carefully hidden, the Queen could relax at the end of the jubilee year at Christmas at Windsor.

For the first time in decades, the United Kingdom boomed in 1978. The Queen's investment in North Sea oil paid off for herself; RTZ's and its associates' involvement paid off for the kingdom. Industrial output rose almost 6 percent during the next twelve months. Spending power increased. Earnings rose tremendously and taxes were reduced. Under the moderate James Callaghan, and his most able Chancellor of the Exchequer, there was a strong sense of promise and renewal in the air.

Princess Margaret came under cruel fire from left-wing elements in April for spending public money—it was her own—on a Caribbean vacation with Roddy Llewellyn; Bishop Graham Leonard of Truro, chairman of the Church of England's Board for Social Responsibility, attacked this trip, describing it as "very foolish." He suggested unfairly that the Princess should leave public life for good. The Bishop of Southwark rushed to Margaret's defense, while Peregrine Worsthorne of the *Sunday Telegraph* talked of her "sad lack of private decorum in her choice of companion" and said that her life was "far from edifying." American readers, learning of these matters from such diligent correspondents as R. W. Apple of the *New York Times,* wrote in letters to its press, stating that the Princess had every right to live her own life if she wanted to. She was dubbed a parasite, an embarrassment, and a number of other things. She was not in the best of health, and seemed fretful and isolated, her existence pointless.

Some much needed light relief was supplied in May, when the Queen, at the Royal Windsor Horse Show, acted with impressive bravery. A spirited team of horses, drawing one of her party's coaches, managed to snap the leads and overturn the vehicle. They began to gallop, pulling the coach with them. To the astonishment of the crowd, and a chorus of cries of terror, the Queen walked right in front of the horses, and yelled at them to stop. She seized the reins, coming narrowly close to being trampled; Prince Philip dashed to her side, and the horses were reigned in.

That same week, Princess Margaret was severely ill with hepatitis and gastroenteritis, and had to cancel all her engagements. From her sickbed, she was compelled to announce her divorce. Labor party members called for a salary cut once the divorce had taken place. It was an unhappy time for her; it cannot have been pleasant that Snowdon, for whom she still cared, was in love with another woman (she was certainly not in love with Roddy Llewellyn) and planned to marry her, and for the two children, David and Sarah, it must have been a torment. More than ever, people felt that, as more than one headline put it, the Princess was "the unlucky sister of the Queen."

But she was fortunate in one respect: the normally creaky wheels of bureaucracy were efficiently oiled to allow the divorce to go through smoothly on May 24. She was not present in court, but instead was represented by Matthew Farrer, her attorney. On July 11, she was informed of the decree absolute.

The Queen appears to have been happy that her sister was free. She now had to deal with the question of the marriage of Prince Michael of Kent and the Roman Catholic Baronness Marie-Christine von Reibnitz, who had been granted a dissolution of a previous marriage. The Pope refused to allow this second matrimonial alliance to take place in the Catholic Church; permission had to be obtained from the Queen, who granted it. This aroused much controversy. It was discovered later that Marie-Christine's father had served in Hitler's armed services.

The Queen and Prince Philip traveled to Berlin for a special birthday parade in late May. The Queen again moved to the edge of privilege by telling a large crowd, "We in Britain will defend your freedom." This seemed a curiously belligerent anti-Russian statement to come from a royal person. They returned to her London celebrations. Princess Anne was back in the news, jeered by members of anti-animal-cruelty organizations, who were attacking her for continuing to support fox-hunting. She was believed wrongly to be the model for a nude statue done by the royal sculptor David Wynne.

The Queen and her husband undertook yet another trip to Canada, with their younger sons; Prince Philip and Prince Edward toured a potash mine, of which 60 percent was in the process of being sold by Rio Tinto-Zinc to the Potash Corporation of Saskatchewan. RTZ would retain a percentage.

Prince Andrew was busy all year long at a course in parachuting at Brize Norton in England. He had received his first parachute wings, the day after the Queen's birthday, on April 22. He passed his medical exam for the Royal Navy at the end of the year. Unlike his elder brother and father, he had decided to make the Navy his full career.

There was an unpleasant incident in November when Princess Anne, as President of the Save the Children Fund, went to Oslo to raise money. Walking into a local hospital, with TV cameras following her, she noticed a bedridden little boy, who stretched out his arms to her. Even though the world would see her behavior, she coldly ignored him. *Verdens Gang,* the Oslo newspaper, reported numerous angry telephone calls from viewers of the program, which, fortunately for the British royal family, was not shown in England. (In August, in Canada, the Queen had had to reprimand Prince Andrew for staring too overtly at a beautiful harpist named Gianetta Baril during a banquet in Edmonton, Alberta.) Compared to the subdued and considerate Prince Charles and the reserved and sensitive Prince Edward, the other royal children were beginning to emerge as brazen as their Aunt Margaret.

In February, the Queen and Prince Philip embarked on a three-week tour of the Arab kingdoms; it had been planned originally under James Callaghan, but had been postponed when the Shah of Iran's regime was in grave difficulties and there was fear that Her Majesty might be in some degree of danger. Following the revolution in Iran in 1978, it was felt that it would be diplomatically advisable for the Queen to, in the words of a Foreign Office official talking to R. W. Apple of the *New York Times,* ''settle the nerves of the Arab rulers, who have been badly disturbed by the earthquake just across the gulf.''

The royal couple flew to Kuwait with Foreign Secretary David Owen on February 12, proceeding along the gulf aboard the royal yacht *Britannia.* Norman Hartnell and Ian Thomas followed strict Arabian custom by designing dresses for the Queen and her ladies-in-waiting which would not reveal arms or legs, and the hats were draped with silk scarves that would do service as veils. It was understood that Prince Philip would, as usual, have to walk three paces behind the Queen, even though Arab rules dictated that a female always followed a male.

There was another reason for the visit. Through her interests in minerals, oil, and textiles, and through the nation's extensive investments and exports of over $4 billion in 1978, she had already obtained a spiderweb of connections, sustaining them despite her own strong support of the Jews and of Israel. Old enmities and tensions forgotten, the Queen received a most enthusiastic welcome as she proceeded from Kuwait to Saudi Arabia, whose King Khalid amnestied twenty-six British prisoners in celebration. As she proceeded through the Emirates, she was showered with extraordinary gifts, the tributes of oil and feudal power: a sapphire-and-diamond necklace, including some four hundred separate gems; a tray mounted by camels of rich gold standing in the shade of palm trees, also fashioned of gold; another golden palm, each date represented by priceless pearls; and a magnificent sailing-ship brooch, ablaze with rubies and diamonds.

She received pearls, incense burners encrusted with jewels, a falcon-shaped gold jug, cups also of gold. She was like a potentate in the Middle Ages, a Sultana to whom nation after nation gave their obeisance. In response, she provided somewhat parsimonious gifts, including silver trays with the *Britannia* embossed upon them, and her autographed photograph in silver frames. Nobody seemed to be offended.

The Queen was banqueted with spiced lamb, under tent-like draperies of blue silk; she was walked through gardens ablaze with marigolds and jasmine, and shown a painting of herself as an Arab with dark skin and pursed lips. She attended a race conducted in sand dunes, saw women spinning in wild dances, and received a British family group which had galloped toward her across the desert for the moment of their lifetimes. Everywhere, there was the perfume of rich flowers, guards in turbans and sabers, and clothes of gold and emerald. The Sheik tried to draw the reluctant monarch onto a flat stretch of sand to join him in a frenzied dance; he was severely shocked when she would not respond.

Prince Philip was as testy as ever. In a place called Firq, the Queen unwisely embarked on a walkabout in which she almost got swallowed up in an enormous crowd. Maddened by the situation, unable to find his wife, the Prince yelled at a police car, ordering it to "shut that fucking siren off." He was flustered; the Queen hugely enjoyed the whole experience, as covered in dust as she had been in Kenya on the unforgettable trip just before her father died.

The royal yacht *Britannia* sailed home stuffed with treasures; England had been suffering from an atrociously severe winter and a gasoline delivery drivers' strike that stranded motorists and almost wrecked industry. It was followed by strikes by train drivers, the British Leyland Car Factory, and other radical disputes. Worse still, hospitals went on one-day stoppages, and trash collectors left the cities' street strewn with windblown rubbish. The public was furious at the apparent callousness toward, and abandonment of, the impoverished and the ill. Prime Minister Callaghan was in appalling trouble, with Scots and Welsh in revolt. It was obvious that he would have to ask the Queen to dissolve Parliament; essentially still a caretaker, besieged relentlessly by Margaret Thatcher, he was compelled to yield absolutely when a motion of no confidence was carried in Parliament, if only by a single vote. An election was announced for May 3.

It was Mrs. Thatcher's hour, and she seized it. Unlike the Queen, she was bored by the Commonwealth, irritated by Britain's membership in the European Economic Community, and determined that Britain would emerge as a special, individual major power, unique unto itself and, in essence, serving under her benign dictatorship. Her election promises were bold and sweeping; most members of the British upper and middle classes were thoroughly disgusted with the unions, and foresaw that she would tolerate no further nonsense from the work force. She called for radical change in every sense. She would put the power back in the hands of the ruling class and not allow common workers to hold the government to ransom. Though cool and composed, she knew exactly what she was talking about. The middle class was tired, not to say exhausted, and desperate for a change. It was as though people wanted another Queen in England, and for many men who had been to preparatory and public schools, and they were numbered in the millions, Mrs. Thatcher was a kind of glorified school matron, peremptory, dominating, attractively severe, doling out punishments and privileges with imperious detachment. And her physical beauty, even in middle age, her smart clothes and composed deportment, made her deeply intriguing. It seemed incredible that a country run by men who had been raised in a strictly male public school society would ever tolerate being ruled by a woman. But she was more than a woman: she was a self-created institution, sturdily built from the ground up.

Her relationship with the Queen, or rather, the Queen's with Mrs. Thatcher, could be summarized by an anecdote told by Kenneth Rose:

> It is said that Mrs. Thatcher felt embarrassed at a public ceremony because her [dress] closely resembled that of the Queen. Afterward, Downing Street discreetly asked the Palace whether there was any way in which the Prime Minister could know of the Queen's choice on such occasions. The reply was both reassuring and dismissive: "Do not worry. The Queen does not notice what other people are wearing."

Several members of the royal family were on the move. Prince Charles, after taking instruction from James Callaghan in the last days before Mrs. Thatcher's triumph, and actually attending a Cabinet meeting, set out soon afterward on a fact-finding tour, as Colonel-in-Chief of the Gordon Highlanders. Princess Margaret again fled to Mustique. She was adrift, devoid of any official engagements until she made a tour of the United States later in the year. Prince Andrew was accepted as a trainee helicopter pilot in the Navy; Princess Anne was as busy as ever with horses. On June 8, the Queen received the saddening news that Sir Norman Hartnell had died of a heart attack. This was a great blow to her.

In July, the Queen set out with Prince Philip and Prince Andrew to Zambia, Africa, where she would attend the Commonwealth Conference. She was most annoyed when Mrs. Thatcher tried to dissuade her from the trip; she was not going to be put off. Zambia was a trouble spot at the time; there was potential danger of assassination; but such threats had never deflected the Queen, who was adamant she would go ahead. She was entirely confident that there would be no problem.

Neighboring Rhodesia/Zimbabwe, torn by violent conflict, its government under Ian Smith still illegal and treasonable, was the main topic in the capital city of Lusaka on August 1. It was a rare opportunity for the Queen to exert her personal influence and power, and she seized it with both hands. She went to the edge of her constitutional rights to talk to the various Prime Ministers, to appease contradictory feelings, and suggest means of settling the perilous issue. She was utterly determined that, *pace* Mrs. Thatcher, who had no strong commitments to Commonwealth policy, Zimbabwe would be a strong member of her community of nations and that the government would have to yield at last to black rule.

In discussions outside the conference (which she, of course, could not attend), especially with Kenneth D. Kaunda, she secured what she sought; she laid the groundwork, with matchless tact and expertise, for the Lancaster House conference in London at which the future of Zimbabwe was settled firmly according to her wishes. In her own way, she was as much of a leader as her Prime Minister; and, that year and later, she would also, in very carefully worded statements, make clear that, despite her sympathy for Scottish and Welsh nationalists, she was crowned Queen of the United Kingdom, and that the kingdom would remain united, as long as she lived. Anyone who doubted that she was Queen in more than name should have been silent in those hours.

But another specter sill hung over the Queen: the Irish Republican Army was as aggressive as ever. After years of threatening, the IRA at last decided to select a victim within the British royal family. They chose Lord Mountbatten. The reason probably had more to do with geography and accessibility than with any sense that he was an ideal target politically. On August 27, with several members of his family, his daughter and son-in-law, Lord and Lady Brabourne, Lord Brabourne's mother, and the twin Brabourne boys, he set out in his fishing boat, *Shadow V,* at Mullaghmore, Ireland. The vessel took off cleanly, Mountbatten, as impatient as ever, vigorously forcing the *Shadow V*'s hard-pressed outboard motor. Everyone was busy laying the lobster pots. Suddenly, a violent explosion blasted everyone aboard into the sea and shattered the small craft into a thousand pieces. Lord Mountbatten died instantly. The bomb had been placed under the planks between his feet. Fourteen-year-old Nicholas, his grandson, died at once. So did a boat boy, Paul Maxwell. The dowager Lady Brabourne was severely injured and would die after a few hours. Timothy, Nicholas's twin brother, was injured; the Brabournes were torn apart by pieces of metal and fragments of the deck planks, their legs smashed violently.

The Queen and Prince Philip were deeply distressed when they heard the news. But, aware of the requirements of their public personae, they resolutely decided to show no grief in public. Prince Charles was unable to endure the news. He was in Iceland at the time. He broke into helpless tears; he flew back by the Queen's Flight to London to be with his parents; Prince Philip was adamant that Charles must suppress his natural distress in a manner befitting a future king. But nothing and no one could console him. He loved his great-uncle more dearly than he loved himself.

Princess Anne and the younger boys were more stoical; they had not been as intimately close to Lord Louis as Charles.

While the desperately injured Mountbatten kindred struggled to recover in Sligo Hospital, Ireland, the dead bodies were flown to Dublin, where they were accorded a military ceremony. With customary foresight, Mountbatten had laid out every detail of his funeral. It was to take place in Westminster Abbey.

Like Churchill, the grandiose near-monarch, in his own mind at least, had planned a procession and service that would rival the Duke of Wellington's.[2] Both were opulent, magnificent, and expensive. Even the weather obliged him: as the funerary cortege left St. James's Palace for the journey to the Abbey, down the Mall and Whitehall, the sun blazed in a dazzling blue sky. The coffin was draped with the Union Jack, and was surmounted by the ceremonial hat Mountbatten had worn as Admiral of the Fleet, his gold stick, and the City of London's sword of honor. To the loud tolling of bells, past a congregation that included eighteen members of European royal houses and all surviving former British Prime Ministers in the company of Mrs. Thatcher, the draped box containing the dead man's shattered remains was placed upon a catafalque. A Marine band provided a military fanfare; Prince Charles tenderly read Psalm 107 from the Holy Bible, speaking of "they that go down to the sea in ships," and, again according to Mountbatten's written instructions, the choir ravishingly sang that notable hymn for all men who sail upon the ocean waves, "Eternal Father, Strong to Save." And now the coffin was taken on the final stage of its journey to Romsey. Lord Mountbatten lay in the south transept of Romsey Abbey, so placed that he would forever face the ocean he loved.

2. He excluded a Japanese representative from the event.

At the memorial service at St. Paul's a few weeks later, Prince Charles was devastated, tears rolling down his cheeks during his address from the pulpit, as, ashen gray, furious at his son's lack of composure, Prince Philip glared directly at the altar. Charles dried his tears and finished the address.

With miraculous bravery, Lord and Lady Brabourne, now Countess Mountbatten of Burma, handicapped, wheelchaired, actually received the mourners outside St. Paul's, a sight few who saw it would ever forget.

Prince Charles leaned heavily on his mother, and even more upon the Queen Mother, in those terrible weeks. He was sustained by a profound religious belief, a conviction of life in the hereafter.

Princess Margaret also found religious consolation, but her anger was very intense. Shortly before leaving for her American tour in October, she made some unflattering remarks; and then, in Chicago, entertained by the prominent hostess Mrs. Abra Anderson, she allegedly said to Chicago mayor Jane Byrne, "The Irish are pigs." The remark earned her headlines; Jane Byrne was Irish-American. The Princess insisted she was only talking about the IRA, but she was made to learn, and not for the first or last time, that royal persons were not supposed to express their opinions on anything.

The turmoil in Britain in the wake of Mrs. Thatcher's appointment as Prime Minister was very severe. In November, thousands marched through London's streets screaming abuse at the national leader and denouncing severe cuts in government spending.

On September 13, Prince Andrew, to his parents' delight, was enrolled at Dartmouth, and in October and November was in full training in the wake of his father and elder brother, destined to be posted for Naval flying training the following year.

In November 1979, Ted Leadbitter, MP, asked Mrs. Thatcher in the House of Commons whether she would make a statement on the recent evidence, obtained by the author Andrew Boyle, concerning the "actions of an individual, whose name has been supplied to her, in relation to the security of the United Kingdom." In response, the Prime Minister named Sir Anthony Blunt. She gave a summary of his career as a secret agent, already supplied in these pages, adding that his role in the Royal Household "carried with it no access to classified information and no risk to security, and the security authorities thought it desirable not to put at risk his cooperation in their continuing investigations.'' This was a somewhat different version of the much-quoted official view, which was that Blunt was being protected so that other Soviet agents in MI5 would not be alerted and compelled to leave the country. It is interesting, not least because by this stage certain individuals who might have been considered questionable were dead.

It says much for the character of the British establishment that, despite his subsequent disgrace, prolonged public confession, stripping of his knighthood by the Queen, and banishment into the outer darkness, Blunt remained on the board of the Royal Academy, and his fellow directors categorically refused to consider asking for his resignation until he at last had the decency to offer it. When he died, some years later, the Courtauld Institute, at which he remained as a learned professor, saw fit to mourn his passing in printed words of praise passed out to supporters and members of the public. He never revealed, given the reasonable assumption that he knew it, the royal family's substantial investment in Courtaulds itself.

By year's end, Britain was in the grip of a profound recession; it was destined to be the worst since the Depression of the 1930s.

In February, a magazine poll found that most people in England felt the Queen should herself abdicate by 1990;[3] some chose the year 1986, when she would be sixty. There was a general feeling that Prince Charles should be given his chance to be King. There were popular speculations about whom Prince Charles would eventually marry. There was talk of his interest in an attractive Princess Marie-Astrid of Luxembourg, and in several other young women, including Lady Jane Wellesley, daughter of the Duke of Wellington, but these were all make-believe; the truth was that Prince Charles was in love with none of them, and was playing a cautious game, knowing that there could be no official separation or divorce as long as he lived; that whichever woman he committed to, he would be committing to for life. He was acutely aware of the

3. Queen Juliana of the Netherlands abdicated on April 30, her seventy-first birthday.

importance of the role of the Prince of Wales and did not wish to bring disgrace to the title and position as others before him had done. He was now over thirty, and his father was getting increasingly restive about his apparent continuing celibacy and apparent inability to find an appropriate bride. The Queen may have been somewhat concerned herself; and certainly the constant garish publicity about this or that girlfriend was exceedingly annoying to her. Everyone was fascinated when at long last Prince Charles began to show a serious interest in one very attractive young woman.

Lady Diana Spencer lived, as a child, next door to Sandringham, and she and her family certainly knew the royals; although it was frequently denied, it has been said that she in fact played with Andrew and Edward when she was a little girl. She was said to have an innocent romantic interest in Andrew, who was close to her own age.

Born on July 1, 1961, she was one of three daughters (she also had a younger brother) born to the eighth Earl of Spencer, who was, at the time of her birth, Lord Edward John Althorp; he had been in attendance with Peter Townsend as a royal equerry at the Coronation. Her parents broke up when she was a young girl, and her mother Frances married a businessman and settled in Scotland. Diana suffered considerably from the divorce; her father married the divorced Countess of Dartmouth, daughter of the celebrated romantic novelist Barbara Cartland.

Diana was not in any way outstanding as a young girl; she was not very popular at her schools, where she was considered, to quote one fellow pupil at West Heath, to be "rather large and extremely bossy." She grew up quite tall for a girl, rather like Alice in Wonderland after drinking the contents of the bottle; she was plumpish then, with a long, craning neck, and walked as though to compensate for her height, with her head down, her neck stretched out, and her shoulders pushed forward. Though domineering by nature, she adored children, and this deep love endeared her to those who might have been most critical of her. She worked in London as a teacher. Her father bought her a three-bedroom flat in Earl's Court, which she shared with two female boarders. All the shopkeepers in the neighborhood liked her very well, and not only because she was constantly in and out, buying something or other.

She met Prince Charles several times, turning up in a party

of young people as the guest of Lady Sarah Armstrong-Jones on board the royal yacht *Britannia* at Cowes in August 1980. Very pretty now, she captivated everyone with her easy, effortless charm. The following month, she was a guest at Balmoral during the royal vacation period. Everyone began whispering that she would make an ideal match for the Prince.

In October, she stayed with the Queen Mother at Birkhall, accompanied by her grandmother, Lady Fermoy, the Queen Mother's lady-in-waiting. It is pleasant to record that neither at Balmoral nor Birkhall would she join in the deerstalking— then.[4] Inevitably, Charles and Diana were attracted to each other. The two most serious contenders for his hand, the Princess of Luxembourg and Lady Jane Wellesley, were firmly ruled out, the first because she was a Roman Catholic, and the second because she was working in television. Diana Spencer was from an impeccably Protestant background, and her royal origins almost rivaled those of the royal family itself. Furthermore, she was understood to be a virgin. The one handicap to a relationship, that her parents had been divorced, was overcome by the Queen Mother, who in particular liked Diana.

It cannot be said that, romantic myths notwithstanding, the couple fell violently in love. In fact, their growing friendship had to be conducted with the utmost discretion, and there could be no question of a physical relationship before marriage. It is virtually certain that Prince Charles was as lacking in sexual experience with women as she was with men, and that all his "affairs" with women were sheer invention. There was certainly no strong emotion on either side. Diana had concerns about whether she could face a life for which she was little prepared, that would give her no freedom and would expose her to the constant attentions of press and public. She was somewhat shy, and of a nervous, high-strung temperament, and the thought of her privacy being permanently invaded did not appeal to her. Prince Charles also had much to give up: he enjoyed the company of women; he liked the variety of a blameless romantic career surrounded by female beauty. Yet the time had come, and he knew it. The royal ranks began to close in on the couple; they began to see each other regularly.

The generation gap showed. Charles was years older, and his

4. A later effort at killing a deer ended in a horrifying disaster.

character was fully formed as a civilized, cultured, deeply serious lover of opera and classical theater. As patron of the Royal Opera, he was noted for his keen support, and he was a most critical opponent of the ugliness of contemporary British architecture, the overdevelopment of the British countryside by unscrupulous builders. Diana was not interested in many things beyond discos and rock bands; she was particularly fond of Phil Collins (her favorite), Elton John, and Eric Clapton, who years later would receive a miniature gold guitar from Charles and herself. She enjoyed swimming, tennis, but was not (a problem in her relationship with the Queen and Princess Anne) deeply interested in horses.

From the beginning of their relationship, Charles and Diana were under siege by reporters and photographers. Yet Diana refused to begin dressing in a manner that might become a Princess; she was certainly no Princess Grace, a close friend of the royal family who is said to have encouraged the romance. She liked to wear sweaters, open-necked blouses, and long, sweeping skirts, slightly Bohemian and not at all fashionable. She was annoyed at being invaded by reporters at the Young England Kindergarten, where she worked. She hated the endlessly flashing cameras that made her life unpleasant. Michael Shea, the Queen's Press Secretary, kept denying anything was going on between the pair; there was talk that they had spent a night together on the royal train in Wiltshire. "I wish the bloody press would leave Diana alone," Prince Charles is said to have told his valet, Stephen Barry. It was a vain hope in the circumstances.

By fall of 1980, the Queen was being eclipsed by her own son and by a previously unknown young girl; the engagement would soon be announced. Her visit to the Pope on October 17 created little attention, and her three-day trip to Tunisia was easily outdistanced by stories of Diana's movements. Only the announcement that Princess Anne was expecting a second child in May created a comparable flurry. There were rumors that Anne was having an extramarital affair with a policeman, but even this was eclipsed by the royal romance.

In mid-December, Buckingham Palace issued an official protest, joined by Diana's mother, accusing several newspapers of printing lies and hounding the unhappy young woman, making her life impossible. Few editors responded to such an unrealistic grumble.

Mrs. Thatcher's policies of building a capital-owning economy with incentives to business and a tough attitude to the work force was creating a new breed of upwardly mobile, smart, raffish, and ambitious young businessmen, ruthlessly on the make in imitation of New York models, indifferent to problems of the working class. In the face of severe urban decay and unemployment (the highest since 1937), the Thatcherites were everywhere, smartly suited, brisk, pushy, and extravagant. The Prime Minister's tax incentives would bring back many exiles from the Bahamas and other tax-free zones, and even from Australia, to which many had fled in the long austerity years, to a Britain where at least the ambitious and forceful now stood a chance. And they did not have to be of necessity highly born. In a sense, Diana Spencer, though not of their number, because she was born to privilege, became a symbolic representation of what a dominating and upthrusting woman might achieve. She became an idol of what would later be known as yuppies, far more than Princess Anne, whose haughty royal behavior (which would soon improve) distanced her from the majority.

Lady Diana was exceedingly uneasy, all too aware of the overwhelming future. Her nervousness and insecurity even seemed to affect the monarch, who was severely rattled by the press pursuing her at Sandringham at the outset of 1981. The Queen was at a pheasant shoot when a crowd of reporters and photographers followed her through the woods, finally confronting her with the question of whether Diana was accompanying Charles as a member of the royal party. Scarfed, overcoated, in Wellington boots, her face twisting in displeasure, the Queen stood four square before her pursuers and shouted at them, "I wish you would go away!" Only a few did.

Once more, despite a lifetime of being exposed to constant attention, the Queen could not deal with the brutalities of life in the media-ridden late twentieth century. Prince Philip's language on this occasion need scarcely be evoked. It was decided to move Diana into Buckingham Palace, where she would be fully protected and would be instructed in how to deal with what would face her for years to come. The engagement was announced on February 14, Valentine's Day.

After two days at Clarence House with the Queen Mother, from whom she had learned many secrets of composure, posture, and correct deportment, she went to live at Buckingham Palace and underwent months of the most meticulous grooming and prepa-

ration. Whereas the Queen had been trained from birth on how to
be a royal person, and even Princess Margaret and Prince Philip
were not without their basic preparation, Diana had to cram what
would have been nineteen years of hard work into no more than
five months.

Obviously, the Queen could not spare an enormous amount
of time to educate the nervous girl in protocol. Oliver Everett,
a great expert in the field, had been at the Embassy in Spain,
dealing with the difficult King Juan Carlos, who had already
announced that he would not attend the wedding if the royal
couple kept their promise and made Gibraltar the first stop of
the *Britannia*'s honeymoon voyage. Everett instructed Diana
on all of the difficult procedures of receptions, garden parties,
and banquets. She must learn to make conversation with
representatives of the Commonwealth in foreign countries, and
would have to obtain at least a superficial knowledge of each
foreign Prime Minister or royal family member, their families,
and the political situations in their countries.

Diana would have to know to whom she would give honor
and to whom she would be necessarily cool. She would learn
proper carriage, using her height instead of overcompensating
for it. She must never show grief in public, she must always
remain composed in the face of danger, even if there were an
attempted assassination. She must avoid discussion of controversial matters, and she must remember that her opinion on
most issues would have to be tempered by deep consideration.

She set herself to obtain the best possible grooming, settling
upon young designers and hairdressers, rather than on the
veterans who took care of the Queen. Much to their disappointment, she sidestepped Norman Hartnell's right-hand man and
successor Ian Thomas, and Hardy Amies, and, instead, turned
to twenty-eight-year-old David Emanuel, and his twenty-
seven-year-old wife Elizabeth, whose audacious, striking styles
were the talk of London; they were among the most popular of
designers for the very youthful and the very rich. Their clothes
were known as sexy, voluptuous, and evocative of the seventeenth century. As hairdresser, Diana chose Kevin Shanley,
who was also extremely young, at twenty-five. He further
enhanced her already celebrated layered cut, exquisitely suited
to her face, with its strong features; she was busy dieting,
shedding a few pounds, and the stress and tension and
sleeplessness of those many weeks of waiting for the big

occasion of her life made her thinner still; by late spring, she was so emaciated she was verging on anorexia.

It was decided that the wedding would take place at St. Paul's Cathedral on July 29. The announcement was made at the beginning of March. The hard-pressed Michael Shea announced three days later that Diana would be known as Her Royal Highness, the Princess of Wales; fortunately, he corrected his earlier and most ridiculous statement that she would be called Princess Charles. The couple made their first official public appearance on March 9 at the Goldsmiths' Hall in London. Three days later, Mrs. Thatcher announced that the wedding day would be a public holiday. The overexuberant Prince was fortunate that he proceeded to the wedding without serious injury. Right after Mrs. Thatcher's announcement, in a steeplechase race at Sandown Park, in full view of his future wife, he fell off his horse twice.

At the same time, the Queen received the bad news from her investment counsellors. After a prolonged struggle with Westinghouse and the Tennessee Valley Authority, in which the company continued to deny culpability in the matter of uranium price fixing, Rio Tinto-Zinc gave in and settled with the suing corporations out of court; the agreements were signed in London; RTZ was liable, along with the other companies defending, for a staggering $100 million in the TVA case and $29 million in the Westinghouse case. In addition, a 1974 contract between Rio Algom and TVA for 17 million pounds of uranium was nullified.

The curious, ancient custom of the Queen giving official permission for her son's marriage took place at the end of March; Diana had been wearing her magnificent engagement ring for several weeks. It was unfortunate for her that the usual demands upon royalty compelled Prince Charles to go to New Zealand, Australia, Venezuela, and the United States immediately after that. She missed him, but her closeness to the Queen and the Queen Mother, who continued to work on her during every spare minute, kept her preoccupied.

In May, there were disturbing noises from the IRA. There was an explosion at the British Petroleum Oil Terminal of Sullom Voe, Scotland, during the Queen's visit there. She did not suffer harm, but the pointedness of the gesture couldn't be missed: RTZ was still deeply involved with British Petroleum in the North Sea. Just before that episode, a letter bomb in a parcel addressed to Prince Charles, whose absence abroad had apparently not been noted by the Irish terrorists, was defused at the last minute.

At the end of May, Prince Charles, his fiancée, and the Queen finally concluded the selection of 2,500 guests. The Queen took the lion's share of the invitations, granting Prince Charles 300 and Diana only 100. Richly gold-embossed, they were sent out by the Lord Chamberlain. This saved the royal family some money. Just six days later, at the beginning of June, Ronald Zen, an American citizen, was arrested for announcing that he would kill the couple on their wedding day. On June 4, the first official photograph appeared in the papers of the Queen, Queen Mother, Prince Charles, Princess Margaret, and Diana in a family group. A stamp was issued, showing the engaged couple: in view of his royal position, the Prince was made to appear taller than his future bride, though there was not an inch between them.

On June 13, the Queen rode sidesaddle on a favorite horse, Burmese, as she left the gates of Buckingham Palace, with a full Guard's escort, for the Horse Guards Parade, where the customary large crowd was gathered for the Trooping of the Color. Prince Andrew and Lady Diana had preceded the Queen in an open carriage, and Prince Philip and Prince Charles were riding just behind the monarch. Something made the Queen glance up. Suddenly, she saw a young man, just ten feet from her, gripping a large 9-mm pistol firmly in both hands, ready to shoot. He was in the crowd, pushed up against the wooden barrier. Before she could do anything, the man fired directly at her. Her horse reared. Someone screamed, "Kill him!" Six shots rang out, emptying the chamber. The Queen looked startled, but had long since learned not to look terrified. People began screaming, and, more startled by the yells than by the shots, her mount actually stumbled, and only with great difficulty was she able to rein it in. Police seized the seventeen-year-old man, and the Queen, with a nod, made it clear that the procession would continue as before. She went through the Trooping the Color looking serious, pale, and subdued, but showing no indication that she was very badly shaken.

The assailant was identified as Marcus Simon Sergeant, and the bullets were shown to be blanks. He had no connection with the Irish Republican Army. He had been in the Air Training Corps and was a member of the Anti-Royalist Movement. There was nothing in his previous history to suggest so violent an expression of his disapproval of royalty. He was taken in charge.

On June 26, a nineteen-year-old woman flung a package into the Queen's car when she was driving to the Portland Naval Base. It was discovered that the package only contained an appeal for support for anti-leukemia funds. Another, less serious threat came from Mrs. Ronald Reagan, who announced that she would neither curtsy nor bow to the Queen when she came to London. She was criticized, but curtsying was not required of wives of heads of state. She was seen to resemble Barbra Streisand, who had shattered all protocol by speaking to the Queen before she was spoken to during a royal premiere, and had asked the monarch why there should be the custom of wearing gloves in the royal presence, a custom to which she, as a Hollywood royal, severely objected. (Martha Mitchell, controversial wife of former U.S. Attorney General John Mitchell, had also, with customary vulgarity, declined to curtsy to the Queen.)

While Diana continued to undergo her training for the wedding, she influenced Prince Charles in many ways. She forced him to abandon the ghastly custom of shooting deer; when she had made an effort at this, she had made a horrible botch of it, and the poor creature had to be shot twice. She also forbade him to steeplechase. She was supportive of him—the Queen and Prince Philip were not—when he took up holistic medicine, almost complete vegetarianism, and organic farming at his estates, including his country home of Highgrove. The couple went fishing together, flew in and out of Highgrove by helicopter, and had some understandable disagreements over the somewhat shabby decor of the estate.

As the great day grew closer, Diana, for all her careful preparation, grew increasingly uneasy. She was tense when Mrs. Thatcher and other political leaders arrived at Buckingham Palace to offer their formal congratulations; she attended a traditional Buckingham Palace garden party, smiling often, but also frowning when the cameras were not turning. She was distracted by her father's condition: he had recovered from a severe stroke that had almost killed him, and she was worried that it might be difficult for him to conduct her up the aisle.

In those last weeks, Diana was constantly shopping, attending fittings of her wedding dress, which was magnificently designed, with a billowing, cloud-like veil as voluminous as a parachute, always using her own or her family's money. She spent as much time as possible driving to Highgrove in her Mini Metro, working desperately hard on repainting and decorating with the aid of a friend, the well-known interior designer Dudley Poplak. She chose subtle, delicate colors, achieving impressive results. But the work took its toll, and she was often, even at her age, exhausted.

The wedding gifts poured in in late June and right up until late July. They included a superb bracelet, watch, necklace, and earrings designed by Cartier on behalf of King Khalid of Saudi Arabia. A snowstorm of diamonds, a green blaze of emeralds, a red river of rubies descended upon the fortunate young woman. While she sifted through these treasures, Prince Charles consulted closely with William Mathias, professor of music at the University College of North Wales, on the anthem that would be played as the couple entered the nave. The Prince also selected the entire musical program, which was to end with the magnificent "I Vow to Thee, My Country." Its words exactly expressed his profound patriotism. Kiri Te Kanawa, internationally famous Maori star, was selected to perform at the service. Meanwhile, a 168-pound wedding cake was devised, about four and a half feet in height; there would be 49 pounds of icing and 50 pounds of marzipan, providing a total of about four hundred thousand calories.

It was decided that Queen Elizabeth's glass coach would be used for her future daughter-in-law, despite the potential danger. The most intense police guard ever to accompany a royal wedding or other ceremonial occasion would be used. The Queen boldly announced she would ride in an open carriage.

By July, the sheer weight of the preparation at last snapped Diana's stretched-out nerves. Attending a polo match, which always made her uneasy because of the punishing stress it imposed upon Prince Charles, she was suddenly mobbed by the press and cameramen and, throwing up her arms, cried out and burst into helpless tears. No doubt this display appalled the Queen, but she was lovingly sympathetic and did everything she could to console her. Diana also showed great distress when she attended the wedding rehearsals, and was most annoyed when she was not allowed to go to Hyde Park to see the magnificent display of fireworks, perhaps the most splendid ever seen in England. She had to watch as best she could from a window of Clarence House.

The display of pyrotechnics was overwhelming; a virtually exact copy of the 1749 show of rockets that celebrated the termination of the War of the Austrian Succession. The Guards and Household Cavalry bands joined in a superb rendition of Handel's *Music for the Royal Fireworks.*

Prince Charles lit the first of a hundred and one bonfires that would blaze across the nation; cannons roared and scores of thousands crammed the parks as the whole sky exploded in rivers and fountains of fire. It was another occasion when, in the face of rioting and class hatred and murmurs of civil war, the English could enjoy being English, and the royals shone brightly in a ghastly world.

The royal banquets and receptions were finally over; the great day of July 29, 1981, dawned. The Queen was up early, but Diana rose ahead of her, at 6:30 A.M. The Queen did not vary her usual sparse breakfast; Diana ate an enormous amount, lashings of eggs and bacon and toast and jam, and at the end of it felt so full that she was somewhat more composed. Her hairdresser Kevin Shanley arrived, and after he had gone over her hair, she put on a superb tiara that had come down in the Spencer family for generations. The expert Barbara Daly did her makeup; it took about forty-five minutes. Prince Charles called her at Clarence House as soon as she was done. She had had at least ten fittings for her wedding dress. It was of ivory silk taffeta, augmented with antique lace once worn by Queen Mary. The twenty-five-foot train, which she had walked with repeatedly, was longer even than the Queen's and Princess Margaret's. Just as Norman Hartnell had sewn a four-leaf clover into the Queen's gown, so Diana's thoughtful mother personally sewed in a gold and diamond horseshoe. The overall effect was dazzling, voluminous, floating, cloud-like. It matched in perfection even Princess Margaret's wedding dress. It may be seen today on exhibition at Kensington Palace.

The bouquet appropriately contained Mountbatten roses, lilies of the valley, orchids, gardenias, and the same myrtle from which Princess Anne had drawn.

At exactly ten twenty-two, the carriages rolled out of the Palace on the way to St. Paul's. For the first time in history, certain footmen accompanying the monarch were armed police. Casting off months of stress and tension and worry, Diana at last seemed cheerful and composed as, accompanied by her father, she walked into the gold coach. She did not seem at all startled by the incredible number of people who cheered her as she emerged. The procession went down the Mall and the strand, via Fleet Street, to Ludgate Hill and the cathedral. To keep her spirits up, Diana, according to the author Ralph G. Martin, sang the words of an ice cream commercial jingle during the ride.

The television cameras bristled as the royal party arrived; millions all over the world would witness the glorious occasion. Everywhere there were banners and flowers and bells and trumpets, and the fairy-tale glass coach glittered as Cinderella made her way up the steps, her veil billowing behind her in a light breeze. The Queen looked extremely serious, almost grim in her aquamarine clothes; Prince Philip was alternately grinning and severe. Whether the royal mood was affected by fears of possible IRA action or some last-minute misgivings was unclear at first; but that in the Queen's case it was due chiefly to nerves and a dislike of the cameras was shown when somebody accidentally dislodged a lampshade and she burst into spontaneous laughter.

The ceremony lasted seventy minutes. Its most pleasant feature was the tenderness shown by bride and groom for each other in the way in which Prince Charles gripped his wife's hand strongly and reassuringly. He looked handsome, confident, and relaxed in his Naval uniform. Even the Archbishop of Canterbury couldn't resist saying that the wedding was "the stuff of which fairy tales are made." He was stifling his own annoyance that the wedding had not taken place in Westminster Abbey.

As the vows were taken, Diana again looked uneasy and tense. Prince Charles fluffed a line, saying, "All thy goods with thee I share," instead of "All my worldly goods with thee I share"; Diana got his names mixed up, calling him "Philip Charles Arthur George." Several people smiled at this display of human frailty in the face of so great an occasion. Now, Prince Charles put the ring on his wife's finger; it came from the same nugget as the rings of all other members of the royal family. After the wedding, the Princess of Wales curtsied gracefully to the Queen, whose tension dissolved in a glowing smile.

IRA or no IRA, the Prince and Princess rode back to the

Palace in an open landau. They appeared repeatedly on Buckingham Palace's balcony, and when the thousands screamed, "Kiss her!" and the Prince kissed his wife on her hand, they demanded that he kiss her on the lips. Prince Charles glanced at the Queen, who indicated that it was all right. Then, for the first time in history, the royal couple actually kissed each other on the lips in front of the public. The screams went up to the sky.

At the wedding breakfast, 118 family members devoured mountains of chicken and strawberries and swallowed oceans of champagne. The Princess personally inscribed the "Just Married" sign on the royal car in her favorite lipstick. As the country celebrated, and the royal family held another festive event at Claridge's, the honeymoon couple appropriately traveled, like Prince Charles's parents, to Mountbatten's estate of Broadlands for the night. It was a decision of which the late intriguer would heartily have approved.

That night, the Queen's cousin Lady Elizabeth Shakeley, sister of the Earl of Lichfield, presided over a large party in the ballroom of Claridge's. Most of the guests were foreign royalty; the Queen of the Netherlands was absent and so was the Queen Mother, who was too tired to attend. The Queen and Prince Philip were happy, laughing, joking, affectionate toward each other, and as excited as though it were their own wedding. Princess Margaret acted like the drag hero of *Charley's Aunt;* Nancy Reagan was the great success of the evening. She succeeded in charming the Queen; it was the basis for a warm friendship in the years to come. The men were given cardboard hats with "Charles and Diana" printed on them.

As the royal party left, Prince Philip stuck his hat inside his tuxedo to look pregnant; the Queen jokingly pulled it away as Lady Elizabeth Shakeley curtsied low, kissed the Queen and Prince Philip on both cheeks, and ushered them into the car.

The young couple flew to Gibraltar after two days. Riotously welcomed, they joined the newly refitted *Britannia* for the long Mediterranean voyage, the Princess converting the Queen's bedroom into a dressing room. They spent most of the voyage sunbathing; Diana, much the better swimmer, spent hours bobbing about in the waves. The voyage took in the coast of North Africa, where *Britannia* would put in for hours at a time so the royals could enjoy picnic barbecues. At night, they watched video tapes of the wedding ceremony and burst into

laughter every time Diana was seen scrambling Prince Charles's
name. The sounds of Elton John, the Beach Boys, and Supertramp
floated above the vessel, alternating with Prince Charles's pref-
erences, classical concerts, Barbra Streisand, and Donna Summer.
The entire crew was captivated with the Princess's easy charm
and constant consideration of their needs. They often acted like
happy children, pouring cold water over each other or attacking
each other with ice cubes. At Port Said, President Anwar el-Sadat
and his wife Jihan came aboard for dinner, but otherwise the
couple avoided all entertainment. They especially enjoyed the
Greek islands, riding donkeys up the volcanic hills of Santorini,
barbecuing at Cape Grabuza, Crete, and relishing Rhodes. It was
a glorious trip, in which the royal couple and the entire crew were
like a joyous family, totally informal and eating their way through
large quantities of ice cream. On the final night of the voyage, the
sailors and royal staff put on a marvelous concert, in which one
man, in drag as the Princess, cavorted with royal valet Stephen
Barry in a number entitled "We Are Loafing." Everyone was
tipsy, and next morning, happily hung-over as the royal couple
disembarked at Hurgharda, Egypt.

23

***

THAT WINTER, AN ODD incident, reported in the *New York Times,* involved the Queen. She had been to visit Princess Anne at Gatcombe Park, and was being driven by her chauffeur, with an auxiliary driver, two detectives, a lady-in-waiting, and an equerry, on a journey that took her through Chipping Sodbury. She had stubbornly set out, despite several warnings, in the teeth of a fierce blizzard. Much to her annoyance, nature proved impervious to her royal position and the car became totally snowbound, unable to move.

The Queen was forced to do the unthinkable and take refuge in the only hotel within a convenient distance, the sixteenth-century Cross Hands, a fairly modest hostelry; the owner, Roberto Cadei, and his wife had decided to watch a replay on television of the royal wedding when suddenly a small group of figures appeared at his front door seeking refuge. According to the *Times,* a man asked to speak to Cadei and uttered the astonishing words, "Her Majesty the Queen is here. Can you accommodate her?" Cadei felt faint for a moment, then wondered if it was a practical joke. He was astonished when, completely covered in snowflakes, Her Majesty emerged through the gloom. The question was, how could she be smuggled upstairs to his one unoccupied room without every-one in the hotel mobbing her? The servants' entrance, marked by stone steps, was completely covered in snow. Cadei worked desperately hard to clear it with a spade; meantime, the royal party shivered behind the hotel, hoping nobody would notice them.

The Queen made her way up the steps, and found herself in an extremely modest, old-fashioned room, Number 15, with matching rosebud-covered wallpaper and bedspreads on the twins. She was pleased to observe there was an automatic coffee maker and a TV set. There was no telephone in the room. The embarrassed Mrs. Cadei bustled about in jeans and a T-shirt, making the greatly amused Queen an afternoon cup of tea. At last the snow stopped falling and the party continued on its way. It is doubtful if the Queen had had as much fun in years.

By contrast, she was tense and irritable when she summoned the newspaper editors in December and asked them to cease and desist from harassing Princess Diana, who was almost hysterical with distress. They were understandably compelled not to comply with her wishes.

Nineteen eighty-two would be known as the year of the Falklands War; that extraordinary conflict, raging eight thousand miles from England in the icy South Atlantic, would galvanize the nation as no other recent event had done. It gave a much-needed boost to Mrs. Thatcher's election chances in the immediate future, brought about a wave of patriotism that temporarily subdued the militant elements in the work force, and provoked much grief among the enlightened over the severe loss of young men's lives.

The Falkland Islands, scarcely changed in hundreds of years, are a bleak, sparsely populated group of windswept rocky outcrops, the total area approximately the same as Northern Ireland. Slightly under two thousand farmers of mostly Scottish and Welsh origin struggled with adverse weather conditions and a reluctant soil to eke out a living while, on bitter, stormy nights, the governor and his immediate entourage sat down in black-tie to gourmet food and the best of wines imported from London or Buenos Aires. For as long as anyone could remember, the ownership of this godforsaken spot was a matter of severe controversy; the British had proved remarkably cavalier toward the Falklanders, not allowing them full rights as British citizens unless a grandparent were born in England. The islanders depended utterly upon Argentina for their sustenance. In December 1980, Margaret Thatcher, apparently irritable over the constant arguments as to whether the United Kingdom or the Argentinean government should be in charge, had unsuccessfully put forward a lease-back arrangement which would grant Argentina sovereignty providing the British would be allowed to continue to administer the region.

The Falklanders felt little attachment to England, and in fact, lacked in any strong sense of nationality; loners by nature, they simply wanted to be allowed to live their harsh, disconnected existence in peace. Certainly, they did not enjoy being perpetually at the storm center of two militant nations.

At the end of March 1982, Argentinean civilians, armed with a contract, landed on South Georgia Island; they were commissioned to dismantle an abandoned whaling station. They had applied for permission to do so sometime earlier, but had not so far had a favorable response and had decided to act anyway. The President of Argentina, Leopoldo Galtieri, a Mussolini-style fascist running a grossly suppressive militaristic regime through a powerful junta, needed a fillip to his administration; he decided to invade the Falklands. President Juan Perón before him had tried to buy the islands from the Attlee government without success; Galtieri was bent on stronger measures. Unhappily, despite the existence of satellite technology, and presumably some MI6 agents in Argentina, British Intelligence failed lamentably to inform Mrs. Thatcher and the Ministry of Defense of the approaching danger. Argentinean fleet maneuvers should at the very least have indicated the problem, and provoked the Prime Minister and the Admiralty into sending out certain vessels in a defensive strategy. Mrs. Thatcher might have laid the groundwork for an appropriate approach to the United Nations Security Council in the event of a serious crisis. She must have been aware of the strategic position of the Falklands vis-à-vis Cape Horn and the Strait of Magellan, its direct entrée to the Antarctic, and its potential as a minerals center, quite apart from her imperial concerns and probable sympathy for quiet, peace-loving farming folk huddled on cold nights by their peat fires. But there is every reason to believe she was taken completely by surprise when, on April 2, thousands of Argentinean troops overcame a small group of eighty-four British Marines and on the third took over Falkland, South Sandwich, and South Georgia. The Marines struggled bravely, amid flying mortar and shattered buildings, and most of the inhabitants of the capital, Port Stanley, fled to the remotest farms. Within three hours, the Argentinean flag was being raised.

Mrs. Thatcher immediately consulted the Queen; diplomatic relations were broken with Argentina, and, at a moment's notice, an existing aircraft carrier task force off the British coast was assembled for action. The Prime Minister summoned an emergency Cabinet meeting and conferred with President Reagan, who had tried until the last minute to avoid the invasion. The United States had colossal investments in Argentina, and would suffer economically if President Galtieri should renounce his nation's enormous debts. The United Nations Security Council urged an immediate end to hostilities, insisted that Galtieri withdraw, and called for diplomatic negotiation toward a solution. Mrs. Thatcher had no patience for that. She immediately sent the task force to the South Atlantic, froze all Argentinean assets in Britain, and imposed severe economic sanctions. Diplomats were expelled from both countries as Rex Hunt, the Falklands governor, turned up with his family and eighty Marines who had been evacuated, somewhat mysteriously, in Montevideo, Uruguay. He was replaced by the Argentinean governor, General Mario Benjamin Menéndez.

Lord Carrington resigned as Foreign Secretary; he was appalled by what he called the "humiliating affront" of the seizure. The aircraft carriers would take two weeks to reach the South Atlantic. Meanwhile, the Organization of American States, at a meeting in Washington, D.C., criticized Britain's claim of sovereignty and stated that the consensus in Latin America was that Britain no longer had a real claim to the islands. President Reagan instructed Secretary of State Alexander M. Haig to do everything possible to settle the matter; meantime, the EEC proved slow and reluctant with sanctions, limiting them to specific periods and not extending them indefinitely. Mrs. Thatcher made clear that any Argentinean ship that came within two hundred miles of the islands after the morning of April 12 would be instantly sunk. Neither at this stage nor later was war actually declared.

Alexander Haig was in London, urgently trying to reach a settlement; at the same time, Argentina shipped as many as ten thousand troops to await the British Navy's arrival. Haig continued to Buenos Aires, but could achieve little. Argentinean troops trudged the six miles of road on Falkland, inspected the farms for hidden soldiers, exchanged Spanish with the inhabitants, most of whom spoke it fluently, and watched while the sheep were rounded up in the icy, damp, vulture-haunted hills.

By April 12, Britain had imposed a full blockade, waiting to see if any warship dared enter the two-hundred-mile limit. Within three days, eight thousand new troops were airlifted from Argentina and were encamped on the island group. They worked round the clock extending the Port Stanley Airport runway so that their fighter bombers could land comfortably. On April 14, two Argentinean Coast Guard patrol boats raced through the blockade, but were not sunk. By now, British national enthusiasm was running high, many people irritated by what they took to be the lack of commitment of President Reagan and Secretary Haig, and in particular expressing annoyance at Jeane J. Kirkpatrick, U.S. Ambassador to the United Nations, who they felt was overly concerned about Pan-American diplomacy and was notably lax in dealing with the crisis.

Haig's talks with Argentinean leaders limped on through mid-April. Saying the "time is running out," he left for Washington after a prolonged struggle to resolve the matter; the same day, twenty thousand Spaniards marched through the streets of Madrid, many of them crying out for Gibraltar to be surrendered to the Spanish King.

Days went by with nothing significant taking place. The Queen remained constantly anxious, watching every telecast, listening to the radio; and she also had a concern that was deeply personal. Prince Andrew was a sublieutenant, flying helicopters from the pitching decks of the 19,500-ton aircraft carrier *Invincible*. Even given her extraordinary stoicism and strength, it must have been agonizingly painful for the Queen, who had never forgotten the horrors of World War II, or her father's reminiscences of World War I, to think that her beloved son would be risking his life. But she also must have taken great pride in the potentiality: the tradition of Naval heroism exemplified by her father, who had so gallantly fought against personal frailty to serve at sea, was undoubtedly an inspiration to her in that difficult hour. It is certain that Prince Philip was excited by the prospect of seeing his son's manhood tested in mortal conflict.

The tedious days went on in the grim and uninviting war zone. Argentina's entire fleet, with the exception of a small handful of vessels, patrolled eight hundred miles north of the Falklands. On April 24, Argentine officials announced that two British warships had violated the Argentinean defense zone by sailing within fifty miles of South Georgia Island. As the Haig talks dragged on, the Argentineans more stubborn than ever, Mrs. Thatcher could no longer tolerate the delay, and ordered British troops to land and recapture South Georgia. After a two-hour battle, the Argentinean invaders admitted defeat, and an Argentinean submarine limped off, badly damaged. The Argentineans suspended peace talks. The Prime Minister, again in consultation with the Queen, announced that there would be further military action unless certain requirements were met at the diplomatic level.

At the end of April, the Organization of American States passed a resolution 17–0 calling for a truce and withdrawal of all British and Argentinean forces, the entire matter to be placed under the United Nations Security Council. The United Nations' powerlessness in the matter was still appalling; Mrs. Thatcher was obdurate.

As the cruelest month drew toward its end, Prince Andrew took part in anti-submarine exercises, flew his Sea King helicopter, practiced depth charges, and disrupted or decoyed enemy communications.

At the beginning of May, Mrs. Thatcher issued an order for which she would be castigated in years to come. The Argentinean cruiser *General Belgrano,* outside the two-hundred-mile blockade zone, was sailing northwest of the islands back to port in Argentina when it was torpedoed by a British submarine and sank with the loss of hundreds of lives, many of the crew teenage recruits with almost no experience of seamanship. Blasted to death or flung overboard and burned in oil or drowned in the freezing sea, the crew was decimated; Rodolfo Baltierrez, Argentinean Secretary of Information, condemned the attack, which horrified many in the House of Commons and provoked an immediate investigation, conducted by a Scottish member of Parliament, Tam Dalyell, into the tragedy. This seemingly unprovoked and quite improper action was followed by a British helicopter sinking an Argentinean patrol vessel on May 3. President Reagan expressed deep regret over the *Belgrano* incident, a statement which must have greatly provoked his belligerent friend Mrs. Thatcher.

That same week, Prince Andrew was flying helicopter patrols from the *Invincible;* but he was not involved in the attacks on Argentinean shipping, which could have risked his life. The Queen managed to keep in touch with him aboard the *Invincible* by satellite radio telephone, shouting loudly through the deafening static and offering her heartfelt encouragement and good wishes.

In reprisal against the *Belgrano* destruction, an Argentinean jet fighter disabled the British destroyer *Sheffield,* which was abandoned with at least thirty lives lost. By May 6, all negotiations between the United States and the Argentinean Government had disintegrated; two British Sea Harrier jets were lost, the crew swept away in the fierce Atlantic currents. Local government elections in England showed passionate support for Mrs. Thatcher; the public was incensed, angry, and fiercely patriotic. References to "our boys" recalled the mood of World War II, and Labor politicians who evoked the dreaded name of Suez in criticizing the Prime Minister got short shift from many of the electorate.

Libya poured armaments into Argentina; Israel announced that it would continue shipping previously contracted arms. This caused much annoyance in Whitehall. Freelance arms suppliers in the United States had a field day, breaking through the embargoes imposed by the EEC and the United States. Many would later be punished for this.

By May 10, British warships and helicopters were involved in a full-scale attack upon the main island; they shot down an Argentinean helicopter, and captured an Argentinean boat. The air over Port Stanley was torn apart by explosions; the bombardment was relentlessly consistent. An Argentinean ship, identified as an oil tanker, was sunk between the east and west islands; on May 12, the *QE2,* largest oceangoing liner in the world, set out, crammed to the gunwales with three thousand troops and a squadron of journalists. On the day of sailing, two Argentinean A-4 Skyhawk planes were blasted out of the sky when they attempted an attack on the British fleet at Falkland.

The United States position in the matter remained difficult. Reagan and Haig were still determined to maintain their political, financial, and strongly anti-Communist commitment to the nations south of Panama. At the same time, they wanted to maintain a special relationship with Great Britain, giving as much support as they dared without risking being drawn into the war or infuriating the other Latin American countries. Pope John Paul II held a mass for peace, and there were prayers throughout Europe for a solution short of further bloodshed. By May 21, the British troops had established a beachhead, despite damage to five vessels and the loss of a Sea Harrier jet. The landing at Port San Carlos resulted in severe casualties on both sides. It was a constant struggle to maintain any kind of foothold in the rugged, damp terrain. As the war dragged on, the British public was joined in the grave concern not only for many loved ones but also for Prince Andrew, who was still not in any actual danger, despite an Argentinean Air Force attack on all the British ships. None of these were sunk, and seven Argentinean war planes were shot down. So far, British losses amounted to one hundred, with twenty-five wounded; several hundred Argentineans were dead.

On May 28, it was announced that the British paratroopers and Marines, at least three thousand strong, were sweeping in from the San Carlos Bay beachhead in a full-scale attack. The same day, Queen Elizabeth, addressing a meeting in the north of England, said she was praying for victory and for the safety of the task force and of her son.

The British recaptured Douglas and Teal Inlet, hundreds of prisoners were taken, and twelve British lives were lost. The Queen had a terrible moment when, on the last day of the month, Argentina reported that it had hit and crippled the *Invincible,* using French Exocet missiles, but this turned out to be a false alarm; actually, one of Prince Andrew's worst experiences was seeing a vessel attacked by Exocets from his helicopter.

Mrs. Thatcher ordered a full assault on Port Stanley at the beginning of June. She found President Reagan firmly behind her; she was exasperated by word that Israel, Libya, Brazil, Peru, and Venezuela were still honoring previous arms contracts; it made her very unhappy that French missiles were in use by the enemy. When Argentinean planes damaged the British frigate *Plymouth* and two amphibious vessels, as well as a frigate, she was angrier than ever. By June 12, a bitter struggle was going on over Port Stanley, with outstanding displays of bravery on both sides. The Argentineans were ferocious in their attacks; the light cruiser *Glamorgan* was shattered by gunfire, with the loss of nine sailors; ambulance planes flew out every day with injured British troops; but at last by mid-June the struggle was over. The Argentineans gave up, over thirteen thousand surrendering in one night. It was Mrs. Thatcher's great triumph; although General Galtieri threatened that there would be more conflict if Britain restored colonial rule, no one believed him. Next year, he would be court-

martialed for the unforgivable offense of losing. The chief
problem facing the British forces was to deal with fifteen
thousand prisoners of war who were desperately ill from
starvation, dysentery, and scurvy.

The Prime Minister's victory was not unmixed. Tam Dalyell,
MP, headed a number of militant left-wingers in the Labor
party in seeking to expose the improper sinking of the
Belgrano; Mrs. Thatcher's critics felt that the war was unnecessary, that she was simply using it as a political stunt, ensuring
her future when the country was in upheaval, cynically
exploiting long-buried British patriotism for her own purposes.
For the masses of people, it was glorious to be English at that
hour. The tumultuous welcome for the returning troops, to be
followed shortly by the birth of Princess Diana's first child—an
almost theatrically perfect example of timing—made millions
swell with pride, quite overlooking the terrible deaths of so
many youths in burning seas.

Even the timing of the birth was perfect according to the
calendar: it took place on the first day of summer, June 21. The
Princess was admitted to St. Mary's Hospital, Paddington, with
labor pains at 5 A.M.; a simple room had been reserved for her
in the Lindo Wing; the Queen's favorite gynecologist, George
Pinker, was again in charge.

The birth took place at 9:03 that night. The child was a boy:
he weighed seven pounds, one and a half ounces. The crowd
outside the hospital received the news with great enthusiasm.
Prince Charles called his mother at the Palace, and one of his
staff advised Prince Philip at St. John's College, Cambridge.

A forty-one-gun salute rang out across London, and bells
resounded all through the noon hour the following day. The
heir to the throne was named William Arthur Philip Louis. His
godparents were ex-King Constantine of Greece; Princess
Alexandra of Kent; Lord Romsey; Prince Charles's friend and
mentor, the author Sir Laurens van der Post; the Duchess of
Westminster; and the Queen's lady-in-waiting, Lady Susan
Hussey.

The advent of the Queen's new grandchild bound the family
together very strongly. The Queen seemed to be in exceptional
spirits. She was overjoyed to pick up the healthily bawling
baby. He was to be known as Prince William of Wales.

Arrangements had been made to house the future King and
Queen in accommodations equal to their station. Kensington

Palace, already a rabbit warren of royals, would have to be sufficient on the Queen's orders. Since 1975, an army of architects, staffs, carpenters, and painters had been at work combining Apartments 8 and 9, derelict for many years, into a resplendent dwelling; at a cost to the taxpayers of almost £1 million. Princess Diana was constantly present, calling for a bewildering number of changes; informed that the apartments would contain offices, she objected loudly and insisted that "the shop" be at Buckingham Palace; she didn't want her home to be a workplace.

Dudley Poplak, that hard-working South African, was in charge of the decorations, incorporating some of the wedding gifts of furniture to try to save money; but any hope of economy was dashed when Princess Diana added a bathroom here, enlarged a room there—Poplak told the author Andrew Morton that working with this demanding young lady was "two years before the mast."

On the morning of July 9, just eighteen days after Prince William's birth, with preparations advanced for the christening, the Queen was sleeping peacefully (and alone) in her bedroom at Buckingham Palace. She would be awakened according to strict tradition at exactly 7:30 A.M. Her maid would come in with tea and biscuits and draw the curtains, and her bath would be run and tested with a thermometer.

A sound disturbed her; quite suddenly she found herself awake. A thin young man in his early thirties was standing near the window—he had drawn the curtains—looking directly at her as she lay against the pillows. Controlled and calm though she had been trained to be, she cannot have failed to feel a sense of terror, since it was well known that she was considered the most important of all targets by the Irish Republican Army. The young man began talking to her, saying, at first, "I am not here to harm you." Repeatedly, he said, in a tense, disturbed voice, "I love you, I love you, I love you." One of his thumbs was dripping blood on the carpet. In his other hand, he held a piece of a broken cut-glass ashtray. Disheveled and poorly dressed, he was visibly a vagrant. She pressed an alarm button. Nothing happened. All the time keeping the intruder engaged in conversation, answering questions as best she could in the circumstances about Prince Charles, Princess Diana, and the rest of the family, she picked up the bedside telephone, an extremely courageous thing to do in the circumstances, and asked the switchboard operator to contact security. This was at seven-eighteen. Nothing happened; she called again at seven twenty-four. Still, there was no response.

Glancing at her watch, the Queen counted every minute until the instant when her ever-reliable maid would actually enter. There seemed no way of reaching her otherwise. Prince Philip was, according to one report, present and fast asleep in his own room, which was divided from the Queen's by a sitting room; but, according to a confidential Palace source, he was spending the night at his club.

At last, after much awkward and desultory conversation, as the intruder sat on the bed, blood flowing onto the sheet until it soaked through, the maid came in with the breakfast tray. She almost dropped it, saying, "Oh, bloody 'ell, Ma'am!" The Queen's glance stilled the maid's panic; the Queen got out of bed, put on a dressing gown, and suggested to the intruder that he might like to have a cigarette. He said that he would, and she told him that the cigarettes were in the pantry. She and the maid guided him into it. The footman, who had been walking the Queen's corgis, mercifully appeared and kept the trespasser from breaking out.

Only now did a policeman turn up. The furious Queen made clear her annoyance with the lack of security protecting her. Several heads would fall.

As the story began to emerge in the Scotland Yard investigation, it became more and more incredible. The intruder's name was Michael Fagan. An unemployed vagrant obsessed with the Queen, he had expressed his love for her on several occasions to his greatly irritated wife. He had appeared in court on June 26 on charges that he had stuck a screwdriver in the neck of his fifteen-year-old stepson. After cutting his wrist with a broken bottle during the hearing, he had been committed to the psychiatric wing of Brixton Prison and had been released on bail. On June 7, he managed to break into Buckingham Palace and steal a bottle of white wine from the top of a filing cabinet in one of the Prince Charles's rooms.

At 6:35 A.M. on July 9, the police saw this mumbling and visibly crazed person climbing over the Palace railings on the south side of the building. The officer reported the sighting to a colleague in the Palace control room, but the man did nothing. Fagan made his way through a half-open window into the Stamp Room, housing the royal family's priceless collection. As he opened the door, an alarm was set off, but the police who heard it took no notice. He climbed a drainpipe over a large stone portico surmounting the Ambassador's Entrance. He found himself on a flat roof; taking off his socks and sandals, he managed to get through a second-floor window. Now he was standing in the office of Vice Admiral Sir Peter Ashmore, Master of the Household. There was no one to intercept him; even though a maid saw him walking down the corridor, with bare feet and messy hair, talking to himself, she failed to raise an alarm. He strode along the Picture Gallery, following the pictures one by one until he reached the North Wing. He pushed open a door, apparently at random (though this seems highly improbable), found a small sitting room with a large glass ashtray on a table, and broke it. Holding a sliver of glass, pricking a thumb, he walked into the Queen's bedroom.

The whole story has the sinister charm of a fairy tale. How could Fagan, given his mental condition and lack of knowledge of the Palace's architecture, have achieved what he did without inside help? Is it possible that a policeman he met in a pub actually tipped him off to the location of the Queen's bedroom? Whatever the truth, the laxity of the police staff was demonstrably shocking. Fagan later said that he had undertaken the trespass simply to show the Queen's lack of safety; this may have been patently absurd, but he certainly did achieve his purpose.

One police officer after another was dismissed or sent to outside duties by the angry Queen.

Just eleven days after this extraordinary incident, an IRA group of terrorists planted bombs. In Hyde Park, soldiers in the Queen's Household Cavalry were killed when a car exploded as they rode to the Changing of the Guard. In Regent's Park, a bomb exploded under the bandstand as the royal Greenjackets played. Six musicians were blown to pieces and several of the audience were injured.

This horrifying act of murder can only have enhanced the acute distress of the monarch, who was depressed and annoyed now in the wake of the joy she had experienced in her grandson's birth. She was also embarrassed by increasingly lurid press stories of Prince Andrew's alleged affair with an inconsequential Hollywood girl, Koo Stark.

Fagan was not charged with trespass; it took a jury barely

twenty minutes to acquit him on the charge of stealing the wine bottle, and after a period in a psychiatric ward he obtained a job singing in a punk rock band, introducing mention of his intrusion into the Palace into the songs. Palace security was tripled as a result. The Queen was angry for weeks afterward. So, undoubtedly, was Prince Philip, whose name, significantly or not, was excluded from every account of what followed the morning's events.

The Home Secretary, William Whitelaw, faced a storm of abuse from members of Parliament. Harassed, exhausted, he never recovered completely from the calumny; security was his ultimate responsibility.

In late July, the Queen was so worn out that she canceled a visit to Goodwood Races, and the extraction of a wisdom tooth did not help her condition. But she managed to attend a memorial service for the dead servicemen of the Falklands at St. Paul's Cathedral.

The troops' return from the Falkland Islands aboard the *Invincible* in late September was moving and spectacular. Grandparents, parents, wives, brothers, sisters, and sweethearts crowded onto the dock at Portsmouth, waving flags, wild with excitement. They strained against the long rope barrier, cheering, singing, and calling the names of their loved ones. Suddenly, and without warning, the Queen and Prince Philip arrived, with a minimal escort, and were greeted with rapturous cries of welcome. There was an overwhelming sense of patriotism in the crowd, and love of the royal couple who had shared their agony and the horrifying news of sinkings and mass deaths.

The royal couple went up the gangway; there, they greeted their handsome son with pride. Now, for the onlookers, every member of the officer corps and crew emerged on the decks, leaning over the guns, clinging to the rigging, straining, bending over the rails as they waved, shouted, and sang out to each family in turn as these were identified on the wharf.

Prince Andrew brought a burst of applause and cheering as he raced, looking extremely fit in his uniform, down the gangway. He leaned against the rope, reaching out to the people. They asked him about individual boys and he pointed the young men out from a sea of faces on the decks. He shook hands and talked with hundreds gathered there.

The Queen and Prince Philip stepped onto the dock and

began walking rather haltingly behind Prince Andrew, slightly to his left and very close to the hull of the ship. So intense was the cry of love that came from the crowd that the royal couple completely abandoned protocol and simply moved toward the crowd without ceremony, sharing their happiness. It was better than any victory parade; nothing else was needed.

The Queen began preparing for a tour of the Caribbean, Mexico, and, for the first time, the West Coast of America. She was looking forward to the trip; Prince Philip had been in San Francisco and Los Angeles on Naval duty during World War II, and she had heard much of the region from other family members. She was eager to visit with President and Mrs. Reagan, both of whom she was fond of now.

Stories of differences between Princess Anne and Mark Phillips filled the press that fall and into the winter. Phillips was absent from many of the Princess's official engagements. He had not been present at the Buckingham Palace garden party in July or with the family at Balmoral for the summer holidays. Stories of her alleged relationship with police Sergeant Peter Cross could not be suppressed. Every day, the Queen had to pick up newspapers with garish headlines bringing serious charges against not only her personal security force but also her family.

Princess Diana sacked two members of her husband's staff and reorganized much of the help at Kensington Palace. A staggering list of engagements was arranged for her; she bore up well, looking more glamorous every day. It was decided that Prince Charles and she would undertake an Australian tour at the same time the Queen and Prince Philip were in Mexico and California. The Princess broke royal tradition by insisting on taking Prince William with her; this was a far cry from the days when the Queen Mother as Duchess of York had had to say good-bye to her own eldest child when she left for an Antipodean excursion, and from the countless times when the Queen and her husband had left their own offspring for trips abroad. Diana was very much in tune with modern custom, which called for babies to enter deeply into their parents' experiences.

The Queen and Prince Philip sailed aboard the *Britannia,* on February 13, for Jamaica via the Cayman Islands through the Panama Canal to Acapulco, where they were received by

President de la Madrid at an official dinner. They continued to Puerto Vallarta and La Paz in Baja, California. Santa Barbara Harbor had been dredged for the Queen and Philip's arrival from Mexico. But by an unfortunate quirk of nature, the royal couple, instead of being greeted by the expected golden sunshine, were lashed with winds and rain as they stepped off the royal yacht at San Diego amid a flag-flying flotilla of the U.S. Pacific Fleet and hundreds of yachts, launches, and small fishing boats. Accompanied by an entourage of forty, they had a pleasant day in an old Navy bus slicing through flood water, visiting the aircraft carrier *USS Ranger* at North Island Naval Air Station, where they inspected 2,800 crew and met 900 visitors and 1,000 civilian guests; they were entertained to lunch by Admiral Sylvester R. Foley, Commander-in-Chief of the Pacific Fleet. Only the mayor touching the Queen was provoking to her.

Prince Philip made a separate trip to the San Diego Zoo to see a rare Arabian oryx. The couple squeezed in a tour of the Old Globe Theater, a replica of Shakespeare's sixteenth-century theater in London, and walked through the Scripps Institute of Oceanography.

There was no hotel ballroom sufficiently large to accommodate the enormous press of guests as well as the royal party in Los Angeles. Since the Queen had expressed a desire to see a movie set, the movie industry reception took place on the soundstage of 20th Century-Fox, where the television series "M*A*S*H" was being shot. Among those present were Bette Davis, Frank Sinatra (supposedly upset because he had not been invited to an exclusive luncheon aboard the *Britannia*), Fred Astaire, Gene Kelly, Lucille Ball, Loretta Young, and Julie Andrews. Armand Hammer, a great friend of Prince Charles, and Henry Kissinger were there. Due to a ghastly error, only British stars were presented to the Queen; Bette Davis and the other Americans were shocked and angered.

A performance was put on. Perry Como sang and George Burns told jokes. The Queen looked glum throughout, barely managing a smile; she was not fond of this type of entertainment, and even when Frank Sinatra delivered several numbers with great skill, she merely stared at him. The royal party left at exactly eleven through a hideous decor which included plastic trees covered in colored bulbs, a statue of a plump, unclad Bacchus, god of wine, on AstroTurf, and paper lanterns flanking a period fountain for *Hello, Dolly* discovered in the prop room.

The grisly event was followed by a new ordeal as the royals made their way to the Reagan ranch near Solvang, the imitation Danish model town. In rain and wind, the road to the ranch house was almost impassable and dangerous, filled with huge potholes and threatening all but the most sturdy jeep or powerful official automobile. The Secret Service told the Queen she shouldn't risk the journey. But she was determined to go ahead, and regarded the whole experience as a most enjoyable adventure. Normally furious (as she had been particularly during the Brazilian tour of some years earlier) at mishaps or changes, the Queen seemed to welcome everything going wrong. Clad in a mackintosh and Wellington boots, she and Prince Philip made the harrowing journey by four-wheeler up Refugio Road, where floods had washed away parts of the hillside. A presidential Mexican meal of tacos, enchiladas, guacamole, and refried beans awaited them.

The couple were delighted to be with their great and good friends, the Reagans. However, they were disappointed that weather conditions precluded them from sailing to San Francisco. They flew there by *Air Force 2;* hasty arrangements had been made for their accommodations. The Reagans placed them in the Presidential Suite of the Westin St. Francis Hotel on Union Square.

At a reception at City Hall given by Mayor Dianne Feinstein, Mary Martin was about to sing when an Irish activist, Seamus Gibney, jumped up and screamed at the Queen, ''Stop the torture!'' Prince Philip led a rhythmical clapping that drowned out Gibney's cries as he was led out. There was a presidential banquet at the De Young Museum in Golden Gate Park, the Queen resplendent in a pearl-and-diamond tiara. Harpsichordist Tamara Loring played Bach and Rameau, while two quartets, one woodwind and one strings, also supplied a musical accompaniment as seven thousand Irish-Americans demonstrated outside. The unusual decision was made to entertain the royals at Trader Vic's restaurant.

The royal couple enjoyed the Hawaiian food, but security called for them to be hustled in and out through the kitchen door. Next day, there was a visit to Sacramento; it was boycotted by Assemblyman Tom Hayden, husband of Jane Fonda, who was protesting against the British activities in

Northern Ireland. At last the weather had cleared, and on the night of March 3, the Queen and Prince Philip were able to give a banquet for President and Mrs. Reagan aboard the *Britannia* in celebration of their thirty-first wedding anniversary.

A fireworks display rounded off a most enjoyable evening. But the rain came down again, and as the royal couple left for Yosemite National Park it was described in the press as "a soggy farewell." Tragically, as the couple passed through Coulterville, a sheriff's patrol car filled with police crashed into a Secret Service automobile and three agents were killed. The royal party headed north for Seattle.

A curious incident occurred as the royal couple were leaving Seattle Harbor. They were waving on the deck for the official photographs when one of the cameramen's equipment failed. Sportingly, the Queen resumed her laugh and her wave for the shot. The rain teemed fiercely down. The light was so bad it rendered the photograph difficult, and the cameraman once again begged for another shot. Prince Philip lost his temper and walked into his cabin, leaving the Queen behind. She glared. Instantly, Michael Shea, Press Secretary, did the unthinkable and took the Prince's place, waving with the Queen. Prince Philip was annoyed, and it is doubtful if the Queen was amused.

The royal visit to California was an unqualified success. The Queen's wit and presence of mind were felt constantly, and she dealt readily with the weather problem more than once by referring to it as a British import. She also, discreetly but firmly, talked of the Falklands War, stating that the principle of self-determination had been satisfied, and she thanked the American government for its support. She, of course, was choosing to overlook the ambiguous attitude of the President and Alexander Haig, who had struggled so long to protect substantial American investments in Argentina and had infuriated many in England by not supplying an outright military backup in the conflict. As always, she was a supreme diplomat, knowing exactly how to cement national bonds and not cause reanalysis of attitudes and events of the past.

In her absence, Prince Charles and Princess Diana's tour of Australia had been no less triumphant, a dazzle of brilliant receptions, enthusiastic trips through beautiful and varied regions, and wild enthusiasm from all except stern-hearted republicans. Mrs. Thatcher, with great shrewdness, had turned up in the

Falklands in January. Now she embarked upon plans for an electoral campaign, which she kept announcing or threatening would take place shortly, thus keeping everyone on tenterhooks. When the royal couple returned to London, she had firmly decided to go to the country. Despite the fact that her administration had been in many ways a disaster, with appalling unemployment figures, serious unrest at every level of working-class society, and conflicts in her own ranks, she banked on her own powerful personality and capacity as a leader to swing the public. She did not have much to oppose her. Michael Foot, the Labor leader, was not a particularly inspiring figure. The advent of the young and hard-working Neil Kinnock did not provide a serious threat. Moreover, the socialist ideals of Labor had long since been swallowed up in what was in effect a pale imitation of Conservatism.

The Prime Minister campaigned vigorously for reelection; her opponents made the serious mistake of castigating her over the Falklands War; although they made some useful points about waste and loss of life, they made the fatal error of flying in the face of a mass emotional reaction to what was felt to be British heroism and a revival of the spirit of World War II. They overdid the criticisms and infuriated the families of those who had served. By contrast, Mrs. Thatcher managed once more to achieve a messianic prophetic force of utterance, as she sought to awaken the lethargic and disappointed with promises to give England a vigorous and exciting future. Like so many Prime Ministers before her, she succeeded in giving the impression that whatever disasters had befallen England during her regime were due to the errors made by previous administrations. There was something in the British character that could not resist iron strength, and the sheer boldness (some might call it effrontery) of her approach carried the day. People were entertained by her audacious attack on Francis Pym, Foreign Secretary, for saying on television, "It is undesirable for our government to have too large a majority." Such folly earned its own reward. The public got the impression that ineptitude, featherbedding, and mollycoddling would be things of the past; that she would sack and sack again if anyone in her Cabinet should cross her.

Her victory was overwhelming. She was the first Prime Minister in over eighty years to win so huge a margin that she was virtually guaranteed her entire five-year second term; what was more, the 140-seat Conservative majority was the most crushing since 1922.

There was a burden that fall: the United States Marines invaded Grenada to overthrow the left-wing government that had been thrown up to displace the British; the Foreign Secretary, Sir Geoffrey Howe, was caught off guard, having made the unwise pronouncement the day before that there would be no intervention by Mr. Reagan. Three hours later, he was proven to be deficient in the art of prophecy, and Mrs. Thatcher got on the hot-line to President Reagan to no avail. After the Marines had landed, she neglected to attend a House of Commons debate on the subject; how she managed to dodge the issue, given her stance of absolute control of everything, remains mysterious; but evidently, in view of her special relationship with the American President, there was very little she could do. She made some token noises, but this gross breach of normal conditions, and this disrespect for the United Nations Security Council and Commonwealth hegemony, should normally have provoked her to drastic lengths. The Queen cannot have been pleased at the failure of Britain either to oppose the invasion and call on the United Nations Security Force or to insist that the United States troops leave and the British supplant them. In any event, Grenada was certainly not a subject that could have appealed strongly, for some time to come, to Buckingham Palace.

There were consolations at home in the thriving young Prince William; and the fact that Prince Charles, with great effectiveness, was taking up much of the burden of local appearances from his parents. He grew every day more confident, solid, and dependable; he began to look as though one day he would make a very good King.

Shortly after the Christmas holidays, the Queen was delighted to learn that Diana was pregnant again. She rejoiced in appointing Prince Andrew her personal *aide de camp*. She was happy with Prince Edward's glowing record as a schoolteacher at Wanganui, New Zealand; this two-year appointment there echoed Prince Charles's tuition at Timbertop, symbolizing once more the Queen's determination to have her children fully conversant with the far-flung regions of the Commonwealth. Meanwhile, Princess Anne, very much estranged from Mark Phillips, was constantly on the move for the Save the Children Fund, dividing her time almost equally between visits to areas such as Morocco and Gambia to observe the fund in action, and attending horse racing events, with a special emphasis on riding for the disabled.

There were indications of serious attempts at *détente* with the Soviet Union, and in July Sir Geoffrey Howe, Foreign Secretary, was in Moscow for meetings with Soviet leaders. The euphoria following the Falklands victory and the 1983 election was dissolved in increases in bank and mortgage rates, the miserable state of the stock market, the weakness of the pound, coal mine and dock strikes, and conflicts with the government of Nigeria. Prices began to explode, contradicting Mrs. Thatcher's claims that she had quelled inflation. She was back at the wrong end of the news when, in August, Clive Ponting, Assistant Secretary of the British Ministry of Defense, insisted that the Prime Minister had no right to authorize the firing of the torpedoes that destroyed hundreds of innocent lives.

On September 15, Princess Diana gave birth to a healthy second baby boy, Prince Henry. The couple seemed much closer now than ever before, and even their taste in music coincided in some areas: they both had a passion for Neil Diamond. Princess Anne made a great success plowing through rain-swept conditions on a visit to the United States, which included a visit to Roanoke Island, scene of the first British colony.

If little was good about the body politic, the Queen had seldom been happier with her family situation than she was that year. Prince Edward was installed at Cambridge; the Queen accepted an invitation to visit China; she opened a bridge, attended military ceremonies, visited a nursing home; she had not been as active in two years.

The question came up of whether she and Prince Philip, who had been busy as chancellor of Edinburgh University, riding in carriage-driving competitions, not always without mishap, as usual causing provocation by calling for the abolishing of income tax, should go to Canada for an official visit. The new leader of the Canadian Liberal party might call a general election, in which case the tour would certainly have to be postponed. But at the last minute it was decided to go ahead. The couple were in towns that stretched along the St. Lawrence Seaway, and in Toronto for a resplendent military pageant (she was said to have been furious when the Minister of Transport touched her elbow), faced a barrage of criticism over her clothes, and, after the Duke moved on to Egypt, where he visited the tombs of the Pharaohs, she continued to the best part of the trip.

This was a visit she had been looking forward to for years. It was her first journey as a private citizen of the British Commonwealth to the United States. Aboard a DC-10 RAF jet, accompanied by her Principal Private Secretary, Sir Philip Moore, and her lady-in-waiting, Lady Angela Oswald, she flew in to Lexington, Kentucky, on October 7. There, she would be able to see her beloved mare, Highclere, victor of the race at Chantilly years before, which was being used for breeding foals. The Queen had boarded brood mares at the rate of one a year in Lexington for twenty years. She was dreaming that one of the foals might grow up to fulfill her one great dream: winning the Derby.

She also wanted to view stallions that would be suitable for importing to England in order to sire possible future winners. Lord Porchester, her robust and controversial racing manager, a close friend, had already arrived in Lexington to preselect appropriate horses for viewing; her stud manager, Michael Oswald, husband of Lady Angela, would also be available to assist her.

As she stepped out of her VC-10 at Bluegrass Airport, the weather was appropriately "British": cool, gray, drizzling, and cloudy. The mayor, "Scotty" Baesler, stepped forward to greet her. Looking up at the sky, she said, with a smile, "I imagine you need rain." "Thank you for bringing it, Your Majesty," he replied.

She was greeted also by her subdued host, the wealthy Texan, Standard Oil of New Jersey heir, William S. Farish (whose grandfather's unfortunate role in assisting the German Government before and during World War II was presumably not known to the Queen) and his wife. It was understood that the press would, according to custom, not be permitted to ask questions of Her Majesty, even on this uniquely informal occasion. She waved to the six hundred people, most of them in Hawaiian shirts and jeans, straining against the chain-link fence as, with her small entourage, very simply dressed, she walked, glowing with good cheer, to the first of a nine-car procession, a black Cadillac limousine. She talked animatedly with the Farishes as the automobile swept her through the

pleasant, pale gray, rolling countryside with its rich soil to the
magnificent Farish farm, Lane's End, Versailles, Woodford
County.

She had seldom seemed more content or at home than she
was in the sprawling ranch house, with its unpretentious
all-American decor, chatting informally with her host and
hostess and the tiny handful of privileged friends who were
admitted at night; she played Scrabble with enthusiasm; she
even fixed her own hair. The next few days, she was extremely
busy, viewing twenty-four prime stallions at six farms, including the world-famous Secretariat, who was now at stud. She
was especially fascinated by a computerized blood stock
service installed at Corporate Center, and watched with intense
interest as, on the screen, she was shown how stallions' blood
lines were analyzed and reanalyzed along with those of choice
mares to ensure a perfect mating and a solid chance for foals
that would prove to be major winners. She was only too well
aware from her own infinite experience of the staggering costs
of such matings: somewhere in the region of half a million
dollars for each given situation; as in England, a prime horse
could be worth as much as $50 million, and often was divided
between more than one owner.

With a pack of German shepherd dogs sniffing every inch of
the way ahead of her for possible hidden bombs, the Queen
continued on her semi-private excursion through stable after
stable, as Porchester, beaming and cheery-faced, drew her
attention to the particular points of each recommended stallion.
The high spot of the trip was the celebrated Queen Elizabeth II
Challenge Cup Stakes horse race at Keeneland, arguably the
most beautiful track in America. She was entertained to lunch
in the racecourse dining room, chatting away joyfully with the
other owners. The odds were on Sintra, owned by the Hancock
family of Claiborne Farm, one of her favorite spots of the trip.
Wives had been spending hours in beauty parlors preparing
for her arrival, and she herself had never been as totally at
ease, even with the reporters who at last were allowed to come
close to take pictures. She took her favorite gin and tonic
before luncheon, and ate the well-prepared meal with considerable zest. Only twice did she show a royal touch: when a
steward began to pour her water, she produced her own bottle
of Malvern water, and when another steward tried to remove

her red wine, she put her hand over it. "I haven't finished yet," she said, with unmistakable firmness.

The race was exciting, held as it was under perfect blue skies with just a few flecks of cloud, the hundreds gathered to watch pleasantly adrift on champagne, everyone cheering lustily and Sintra bouncing cheerfully through under her expert jockey Keith Allen. The three-year-old roan was visibly hard-pressed, but brought rapturous excitement and very few torn-up tickets as she finally romped home at the end of the one-and-one-sixteenth-mile race. The Queen is said to have bet on Sintra herself; she turned to Seth Hancock, its ecstatic owner, and he could barely resist the impulse to hug her.

The Queen had one of the best times of her life to date, and instantly marked down plans for two future visits. It was good to be away from all the troubles of home. But her joy was only temporary; toward the end of her stay, she received appalling news. She was informed that, during a Conservative party conference at Brighton, an IRA bomb shattered several rooms of the Grand Hotel, injuring at least twenty people in the process. Mrs. John Wakeham, wife of the Chief Whip, was killed, and Norman Tebbit, Secretary of the Department of Trade and Industry, was severely wounded, a particular blow because he was felt to be Mrs. Thatcher's possible successor should she ever need to be replaced. His wife was paralyzed. Although the Queen was devastated by the news and angry with the Irish terrorists, who were preparing an autumn offensive, she announced immediately through Michael Shea that she would not consider changing any of her plans, and continued to receive selected local citizens brought to her by the Farishes.

A lavish party at Lane's End Farm marked her departure for the next important stage of her visit, which was to Wyoming, where she would be the guest of Senator Malcolm Wallop, grandson of the Earl of Portsmouth, who owned a magnificent ranch at Big Horn. Wallop's sister was Lady Porchester.

The Queen had always had rushed visits to United States; they were far less comfortable than her Commonwealth trips. But now, as she relaxed in the warmth and hospitality of her hosts, she felt an overwhelming love for America, and enjoyed, as never before (so she conveyed to her friends), the sheer size, openness, and freshness of the nation. Just as in California, every burst of rain and gust of wind seemed to amuse and delight her, so now did she revel in the abrupt changes of weather, and the clean, bright air of the Northwest. Again, she would long to return.

Prince Andrew had not behaved as well on his American visit earlier that year. In California to promote British products, he had sprayed paint on the press in an action which, though claimed to be accidental, only too clearly reflected his father's temperament and attitude to reporters, and resulted in claims for damages. He was in the news to an extent, which must have embarrassed his mother: he audaciously turned up at the home of his girlfriend Katie Rabett, in a sober, middle-class house in London, for his twenty-fourth birthday, at which Miss Rabett's parents entertained him. This was unheard of; after midnight, reporters noted he kissed Miss Rabett good night on the doorstep. When pictures appeared in the press of the young model nude, her father, responding to her statement that she had not done anything of the sort, announced, "If she has not told me the truth, I shall smack her bottom." Such vulgarisms could not have gone down well at Buckingham Palace. Prince Andrew was also seen rather too often with Noelle Williams, daughter of the singer Andy Williams and the controversial Claudine Longet, during the trip to Los Angeles. He appeared at School Dinners, a London club in which the members were punished by waitresses with a cane if they were seen to have misbehaved. Three waitresses held him down over some ridiculous infringement, and thrashed him with what was popularly known in England as "six of the best." In the circumstances, it was probably just as well that the Queen had her furlough in Kentucky and Wyoming.

In 1985, Prince Charles was tirelessly involved in a crushing round of activities. He led an appeal to raise £6.5 million to save the spire of Salisbury Cathedral, he called for landowners to preserve old buildings, he urged farming estates to improve the labor situation by creating extra jobs, he joined with medical students in discussions of holistic and homeopathic medicine, he led a blood donation drive, sang with the Bach Choir, worked hard on Sunday service appeals for repairs to Hereford Cathedral, gave money for the restoration of bells at a church near his house in Gloucestershire, and granted interviews confirming that his marriage was good and sound. An Australian tour with Princess Diana was marred only by a Philippian moment when he could not resist soaking reporters

in water from a large ornamental fountain, and by a demonstration of IRA supporters in Melbourne.

He had established a love affair with Italy; his "walkabout"
in Milan with the Princess enchanted the local populace; he
enthusiastically inspected the great art treasures of Florence,
the Princess dutifully following along; and he had a happy
meeting with the Pope, though he was annoyed that there had
been some suggestion that he should not attend mass and have
breakfast with him, supposedly emanating from the Church of
Scotland, which denied the charge. It was thought that the
Queen had intervened in the matter.

Prince Charles made a much stronger impression in Italy
than Princess Diana. Although she was felt to be simple,
charming, and clever, and had certainly memorized information on the places and people they would encounter, it was he
who had a true and deep feeling for Italian culture. During the
tour, he made many friends and set a course for the future of
what would undoubtedly be a lifelong love affair with the
Italian nation. In the course of the trip, while in Florence, the
couple stayed at the Villa la Pietra, home of the legendary
author and aesthete Sir Harold Acton. Prince Charles, always
eager to learn from the elderly and the learned, proved to be a
disciple of Acton's; from him, he obtained a fuller grasp of
Italian painting and sculpture. Prince Charles and Princess
Diana also visited the home of the Frescobaldis, a very
distinguished Italian family. There, they formed a particular
rapport with the Marchesa Bona Frescobaldi (an attractive and
ambitious socialite whose success fueled envious and vicious
gossip in Italian aristocratic circles) and her beautiful daughter,
Fiammetta, a gifted, cultured, intelligent, and profoundly
reserved young woman. In the years to come, there would be
much speculation concerning an affair between Prince Charles
and either the mother or daughter; these were totally invented,
and, unfortunately, not sufficiently discouraged by Bona Frescobaldi. When Prince Charles returned in later years, the gossip
intensified because he was not accompanied by Princess Diana.
The reason had entirely to do with Princess Diana's minimal
interest in local culture and history, and nothing to do with
either an emotional separation or Prince Charles's infatuation
with the brilliant Italian woman.

In fact, the matter of touring separately, which gave rise to
similar tittle-tattle, was a royal custom, time-honored as well as

convenient. It had been understood for years that, if they chose, the Queen and Prince Philip would travel separately or begin a tour together and then divide their itineraries. Not only did the sheer pressure of invitations call for this, but also it was a given in circles from the aristocracy upward that couples would live their own lives, follow their own pursuits, and simply form an alliance for the sake of the dynasty and for the image of propriety which the public required of them.

Princess Margaret was ill in January. She was suffering from chest pains, and had to be admitted to the hospital to have part of her lung removed; a lifelong smoker, albeit with a holder, she must have feared cancer, but the tissue was (officially) said to be afflicted only with a benign growth.

Prince Edward appeared in an obscure, much-criticized amateur production of *The Taming of the Shrew* in Scotland as Biondello, a buffoon, at one stage clowning as another actor struck him with a stick. He was showing keen interest in getting into work in the theater.

Of all the family, arguably the busiest was Princess Diana, whose schedule in 1985 was nothing short of staggering. This mother of two was perpetually on the move, punishingly busy in every direction, matching even Prince Philip at his most involved. She visited youth associations, a foundation for the study of infant deaths, a gala jazz concert, a charities trust pop concert, premieres of the films *Amadeus* and *A Passage to India;* she opened a dance studio, acted as Colonel-in-Chief of the Royal Hampshire Regiment, attended services for Dr. Barnado's Volunteer Year, appeared in a TV program on drug abuse, walked through hospital wards visiting the survivors of the Manchester air crash, and undertook at least fifty more engagements. Merely to list them is exhausting; to have experienced them must have been crushing. But she insisted on accepting virtually every invitation sent to her. She weathered the usual amount of criticism: for firing gays from the Palace, for dismissing Edward Adeane, who had been Prince Charles's friend and private secretary since 1979, for allegedly being tough with her staff at Kensington Palace, and for getting rid of, among others, the secretary Oliver Everett, the bodyguards David Robinson and John Brownridge, the butler Alan Fisher, the cook Roseanna Lloyd, and a nanny. In many cases, these individuals had chosen to resign for various reasons. For instance, Fisher was incensed at the way Diana was changing names and places just before dinner parties, but Princess Diana was charged with eliminating them all.

At times, she was sharply reminded of protocol. When she accepted a $13,000 ring by the French jeweler Louis Gerard, the Palace informed her that she should not have done so, and the ring had to be returned.

In October 1985, Prince William was admitted to Mrs. Mynors' Nursery School. He would be taught according to the time-honored methods of Maria Montessori, who had pioneered open instruction of children and the encouragement of their personal interests against grimly prescribed studies.

By now, Princess Diana and Princess Anne had become close friends; Diana was also very fond of Carolyn Herbert, Lord Porchester's daughter, and Lady Penelope Romsey, granddaughter-in-law of Lord Mountbatten, who frequently entertained Charles and Diana at Broadlands. Princess Margaret and Antony Armstrong-Jones's son Viscount Linley was making his name as a furniture maker, as democratically spirited and lacking in royal affectation as his father.

In November, aggravated by constant criticism and what they felt to be false stories in the press, the Prince and Princess gave their first interview on television in four years. Sir Alastair Burnet's questions were prepared well in advance, and Sir Richard Attenborough (whose film *Gandhi* was much admired) prepared the Princess for the experience. The program was appealing, charming, very successful, and the public relations device paid off. The Princess blushed occasionally, denied she was domineering, but admitted she was a perfectionist. Prince Charles denied he had ever toyed with a Ouija Board or had tried to get in touch with his dead uncle Lord Mountbatten. Diana said she was not anorexic but kept thin through exercise. She did not deny she slept with a Walkman on her head. The couple admitted that Princess Diana frequently criticized her husband's shoes. Prince Charles said he was close to being a vegetarian; when he said that the couple occasionally fought, Diana denied it.

It was all harmless pablum for the masses, seemingly revealing, but in fact charmingly closing a door on reality. This was just as well, in view of a further succession of unhappy events under the Thatcher regime: in September, a woman named Cherry Groce was accidentally killed by police as they searched her house in Brixton, and there was yet another

outbreak of violence in that neighborhood. There were riots at
Broadwater Farm Estate in Tottenham, North London, and a
policeman was slain by a knife-wielding mob. There were
threats of gas and bullets being used as Mrs. Thatcher stated
that the police should have a blank check to suppress any
further upheavals. And in December, there was the beginning
of a huge scandal when the Westland Helicopter Company
turned down a European takeover bid.

In October, the Queen was in the Caribbean, somehow
enduring a roasted rodent served up to her at dinner in Belize,
Honduras; she rather boldly went to Grenada, after visiting her
sister's favorite spot of Mustique. At a speech in Grenada, she
congratulated the local populace for getting through the recent
ordeal of invasion and for committing itself to the future of
democracy, an interesting way of setting the seal on a brief but
irritating crisis.

The Queen Mother was in the news that year: a guardsman
was put in prison for breaking into Clarence House and causing
a fire, and one of her chauffeurs was tried and acquitted for
being in possession of a dangerous weapon. Her health
remained extraordinary in her mid-eighties. Prince Philip made
headlines; he flew into a temper in Melbourne and almost
walked out of a press conference when he disliked some
questions. But he was little heard from otherwise. He had
begun to take a back seat in family affairs, and appeared to be,
at least temporarily, semi-retired.

24
***

NINETEEN EIGHTY-SIX BEGAN ON an ominous note. The much embattled and somewhat obscure British helicopter company named Westland had run into severe difficulties, and the question came up of how it might be bailed out. The British Secretary of State for Defense, Michael Heseltine, had obtained from a consortium of European airplane companies an offer that he considered appropriate for the purchase of Westland; Mrs. Thatcher was accused of misleading the House of Commons in the matter, as a violent conflict arose between Heseltine and Westland's directors, who backed an alternate purchase by Sikorsky, a U.S. corporation. A leaked letter involving the insolvent company brought about a furor; Heseltine resigned, and Mrs. Thatcher was roughly in the position of a person lined up against a wall, waiting for the action of a firing squad.

However, with her customary ability to survive almost every kind of charge against her administration (an ability she shared with her friend President Ronald Reagan) she emerged only slightly scathed by the issue. Like her or hate her, there was in fact nobody to take her place.

The Queen's preoccupations in the first weeks of 1986 were dominated by the matter of Prince Andrew's rapidly developed love affair, the most serious emotional commitment of his life. The procession of inconsequential, not to say common, young women with whom he had been linked had undoubtedly aggravated her, and she was as anxious to get him settled down as she had been in the case of her oldest son.

The monarchical attitude to marriage was similar to that which was applied to stud farming. But it was not always possible to find an appropriate aristocrat with whom the Queen could mate her offspring. She found herself settling for Sarah Ferguson, daughter of Major Ronald Ferguson, the Prince of Wales's polo manager, and Susan Barrantes, who had divorced her husband and married the celebrated Argentinean polo player Hector Barrantes. Once again, the monarch was forced to stretch her standards to include a child of divorce.

However, in certain respects Sarah Ferguson was considered a suitable match. She had the romantic background of being a descendant of King Charles II and one of his mistresses. She had a decided advantage in the Queen's eyes: a horsewoman, she had appropriately met Prince Andrew for the first time on intimate terms at Ascot. Breezy, outgoing, dominating, and strident, Fergie, as she became known, was redheaded and freckle-faced; she was certainly not a beauty. However, there was something about her pushy, forceful character that appealed at the same time as it provoked; she was greatly supported by Princess Diana, who had in mind not only obtaining a valuable ally, but also an ideal wife for the errant brother-in-law.

Her background did not have the virginal appeal of Diana's. She had lived with two men several years older than herself; she was thought of as something of a playgirl. All this might have been shocking to the Queen, but somehow Miss Ferguson overcame any natural objections and, with extraordinary single-mindedness, set out toward her target. Certainly, she would not be in the least afraid of the media, as Princess Diana still was to a degree, and the royal family did need at least one member who could absorb the constant attention of the popular newspapers. When she went riding with the Queen, Fergie was home free.

As the Queen celebrated her sixtieth birthday, few, including the Queen, could have imagined the brilliant celebrations that had been organized. Thousands of children came running down the Mall in the middle of the afternoon; the Queen waved cheerfully from the balcony of the Palace, accompanied only by Prince Andrew and Sarah Ferguson. Each child was wearing one daffodil that seemed to complement the Queen's yellow suit perfectly. The pure spectacle of the occasion was happy and dramatic, and as children at the front clung to the railings of the Palace, the Queen instructed that all gates should be opened. The children poured into the courtyard and when TV cameras tried to find the Queen on the balcony, she had gone to the courtyard of the Palace to be surrounded by the children who loved her and who represented all her loyal and devoted subjects in England and throughout the Commonwealth. She walked on a carpet of daffodils. For evening celebration, Princess Margaret had collaborated with the Royal Opera House, Covent Garden, to produce the most impressive program of opera and ballet in even that opera house's great history. The program began, instead of ended, with the national anthem (which was not played again at the end of the performance), and the Queen and the privileged audience were given programs only at the end of an evening of brilliant song and dance. All the royal family were assembled in the circle, as Prince Philip escorted the Queen to her central seat. At the end of the evening, which Jessye Norman brought to a tumultuous and triumphant finish, the cast and audience rose to salute the Queen, who did not disguise the happy tears in her eyes. Never before had the monarch been so showered with love.

And now she was forced to confront another problem: Mrs. Thatcher had strongly supported President Reagan's bombing of Libya, and London was torn apart by explosions that were apparently acts of revenge. The British Airways building was ripped apart by bombs, and nearby stores were also shattered, with glass strewn all over the street. In the midst of these expressions of violence, the Duchess of Windsor, whose life had been itself stormy and catastrophic, died, and the Queen kept her promise that she would be buried next to the Duke at the cemetery at Frogmore. The funeral service was attended by the royal family, although, either by accident or design, the Duchess's name was omitted from the service. It cannot have appealed to the Queen or the Queen Mother that they would have to solemnize in this manner and commemorate in a spectacle a nefarious career devoted to the downfall of England during World War II; the Duchess had consistently schemed to have her husband return to the British throne and replace King George VI. But to have failed to make this an appropriate funerary occasion would have been to render the Duchess a martyr in the eyes of the public.

Soon afterward, Michael Bloch, with the authorization of Maître Suzanne Blum, the Duchess's lawyer, would publish much of the Duchess's personal correspondence with the Duke, all of it of a highly embarrassing character, and containing more than enough evidence of the couple's fretful and contentious attitude to the British royals. A deafening silence was heard from the Palace when the letters appeared.

Prince Edward gained an honors degree in history at Cambridge; it was not a First, but at least was respectable evidence of his devotion to his studies. He planned a career in the theater. In May, the Queen was back in Lexington, again visiting her mares and making a very rare appearance in a church outside the royal domain; she was actually seen putting American money in the collection box, certainly a precedent. Once more, she was delighted with her hosts, Mr. and Mrs. Farish. She discovered that Highclere had now been bred successfully to the stallion Nureyev. This was a great pleasure to her.

That summer was filled with the exhaustive preparations for Prince Andrew's royal wedding, and, at the same time, with an increasing and inflammatory controversy concerning the matter of sanctions to be applied against South Africa. As always in the Queen's life, political tension contrasted with personal rejoicing; not only did she have to fill the role of considerate and thoughtful mother, brooding over the complex arrangements for a Westminster Abbey marriage, but she also had (mindful of her constitutional limitations) to face up to the formidable Mrs. Thatcher, who differed radically from her in the matter of sanctions.

The Queen, it is safe to say, was adamantly set upon punishing South Africa through restricting the supplies of goods, and may even have thought of encouraging British companies to boycott that nation, whose withdrawal from the Commonwealth had been a perennial thorn in her side.

Despite the curious fact that certain companies in which she invested had substantial interests in that region, she was radically opposed to President P. W. Botha, with his vicious policy of apartheid, suppression of free thought, and imprisonment of critics of his government. She would no more tolerate his racism than she would tolerate it in one of her own Prime Ministers.

On the other hand, Mrs. Thatcher, not unsupported by respectable opinion, felt strongly that sanctions would lead to only mass unemployment of blacks, while at the same time the immensely rich dynasties that ruled the southern nation would scarcely be hurt. Even in the matter of imports, it was doubtful that British sanctions would be radically destructive except to the well-being of the people themselves.

The Queen, with her mystical sense of unification of black and white nations, her One-World vision, could not accept such an argument, which was also maintained by President Reagan, who, as during the Falklands crisis and war, bore in mind American investments and the U.S. debt situation.

In the third week of May, the squatter camp named Cross-roads erupted in so severe a succession of fights that thirty thousand people were driven homeless into the night, and thirty people lay dead on the ground. Like Alexander Haig before him, George Shultz, U.S. Secretary of State, sought a peaceful ending to the rioting and murders, but again supported his President in opposing sanctions and pulling out investments.

By mid-June, with plans for the royal wedding far advanced, South Africa was in a state of civil war. There was talk of the Commonwealth being rent apart as several member nations spoke of sanctions and others, of whom Britain was by far the most prominent, opposed. The shrewd and practical pointed out that Britain had $9.1 billion invested in Botha's republic, or over 40 percent of all foreign investments there, a consideration that cannot have failed to weigh with the Prime Minister in this extreme hour. Botha pushed through grim security measures allowing the police a totally free hand. Curfews were announced in many districts; the slightest sign of unrest was brutally stamped out. Early in July, Mrs. Thatcher made her position clear: she announced that it would be immoral and repugnant to cause unemployment among Africans by imposing sanctions. There is no doubt the Queen remained drastically opposed to her.

The state of national emergency in the republic continued throughout July. Deeply troubled, the Queen, as strong as ever, conducted her Tuesday meetings with her Prime Minister in a manner which is reputed to have been entirely composed, calm, and not unfriendly. However, the Sunday *Times* of London reported, on July 20, 1986, that the Queen was determined to use her influence to prevent a breakup of the Commonwealth. She was concerned by the fact that India, Bangladesh, and several other countries boycotted the Commonwealth Games in protest against Britain's adamant stand. The influential newspaper tended to support Mrs. Thatcher, quoting with approval a statement by Zulu leader Chief Buthelezi that sanctions would only result in scorched earth policies. The newspaper may not have taken full account of the peculiar role of tribal chiefs, not dissimilar to that taken in Rhodesia, as occupying a middle ground between white and black interests.

It was claimed in a statement to the newspaper, the source a secret (it was rumored to be either Prince Philip or Prince Charles), that the Queen would work hard on the situation and hoped that she might be of assistance as she had been during the Lusaka Commonwealth Prime Ministers' conference of 1979. Apparently, the Queen was annoyed by the leak and furiously called for it to be denied, but the Palace had great difficulty in obtaining anything even approaching a retraction. By July 20, sixteen countries in all had boycotted the Games, including Zambia, Zimbabwe, Swaziland, Jamaica, and Trinidad. Still Mrs. Thatcher would not be shaken.

And it was in the midst of this situation that at last Prince Andrew married the ineffable Sarah Ferguson. Every effort had been made to have the occasion informal, although, much to the annoyance of millions of British workers, the Queen had elected not to declare July 23, the wedding day, a national holiday. Miss Ferguson went out of her way to behave in as unroyal a manner as possible: at the rehearsal, she did the unthinkable and threw off her shoes because they pinched, and, discussing the musical program, she sat down at the Westminster Abbey organ and pounded out a melody for the astonished Archbishop of Canterbury.

A television film was made before the wedding, in the course of which the Prince and Miss Ferguson were seen hitting each other, the prince sending his fiancée flying into an undignified descent from a wall into the soft earth of a flower bed. The wedding day was bright and sunny, the crowds predictably large, Miss Ferguson in a voluminous gown lacking in the exquisite elegance of those worn by her royal predecessors, Prince Andrew in Naval uniform. Just hours before, the Queen, with great generosity, bestowed upon her son her father's title of Duke of York. Despite all her problems with Mrs. Thatcher, the Queen seemed exceptionally happy both before and during the ceremony, and younger than she had looked in two years. The four pages dressed in Naval blues were a nice touch.

Prince William, eldest son of Prince Charles and Princess Diana, stole the show with an astonishing display of childish

bad manners, chewing the string of his hat or winding it three
times around his nose; *Time* magazine reported:

> Undaunted by baleful stares from his mother and grand-
> mother, [the Prince] pulled out his miniature ceremonial
> dagger and began poking holes in the dress of Diana's niece,
> Laura Fellowes, age six. When his victim wagged a finger of
> rebuke, the second in line for the British throne trumped her
> with a silent but definitive Bronx cheer.

Somehow, this display of impudence fitted the marriage of a
royal bride who only a week beforehand had accompanied
Princess Diana to Annabel's in London disguised in a police
uniform.

As the family left the Abbey, Prince William suddenly
darted forward out of the correct order; the Queen, who had
seldom been seen behaving with equal informality except at the
races, ran forward with surprisingly brisk athleticism to retrieve her grandson. The royal combination of a laugh and a
grimace was very characteristic of her.

The royal couple left for a holiday in the most obscure place
they could think of, the Azores, but they were not to be left
alone there. Fortunately, neither of them shared the same horror
of the press as the Queen and Princess Diana, and they made
the best of the situation. They were, above all, good sports,
healthy, extroverted, bouncingly unneurotic, and, though Sarah
Ferguson often grated, the public fell in love with her more
than ever now that they were married.

The Commonwealth Prime Ministers' Conference in London
in August deeply absorbed the Queen's attention. Australia, the
Bahamas, Canada, India, Zambia, and Zimbabwe adopted a
resolution calling for eleven severely punitive measures against
South Africa. Mrs. Thatcher stubbornly agreed to only two
provisions, but there was little she could do to stem the tide of fury
in Europe, where EEC sanctions would inevitably be applied. At
least, the result of the meeting was that the Commonwealth was
not actually rifted apart; sanctions were applied, though not
perhaps to the overwhelming extent the Queen had wished, and
there the matter rested for the time being, with the South African
people as jeopardized and miserable as ever.

In September, Prince Edward began training as a Royal
Marine, taking part in a dramatic struggle against drug runners

in Belize, Honduras, as well as undertaking further adventures in Latin America. Though humorously dubbed Mr. Puniverse by his fellows, he was in fact a vigorous and committed soldier, physically strong and capable of dealing with many adverse conditions. But he quickly saw there could be no future in the job, and, unlike Prince Andrew, who was fated to a life in the Navy, he dreamed of London's Shaftesbury Avenue and the West End theater.

In October, the Queen and Prince Philip were in China, where they were rushed through a very heavy schedule; Prince Philip was again at his worst while addressing Scottish students, who always seemed to bring out the provocative in him. Echoing his misbehavior on more than one occasion at the University of Edinburgh, he told a student in a group in the city of Xian, that Beijing was "ghastly," and that if he was to stay in China too long, the boy would return to Scotland with "slitty eyes." This breach of etiquette and abandonment of common politeness justly earned him international vilification. No doubt the pressure of the trip, the constant trudging through museums and palaces, few of which would interest him, and, perhaps, the monolithic character of the Communist state provoked him to the misguided outburst. Yet again, he seemed superfluous in the scheme of things, a mere adjunct, frustrated and weighed down by the knowledge that, as a man, he would be perpetually thwarted.

Another controversial member of the family was in trouble following the royal couple's return in England. Princess Michael of Kent did not get on with the Queen, who said repeatedly that the Princess was "too grand for the likes of us." There was a revelation that her father had been in the SS. So harsh were her statements about other members of the family that Prince Philip dubbed her "Motor Mouth." She groused incessantly about the fact that she was not included in the Civil List and had to make money by writing books, and, following her endless grousing some years earlier over the remodeling of Kensington Palace to accommodate Prince Charles and Princess Diana, she fussed and fretted over noise from their home, which adjoined hers.

On a television program, she committed the ultimate sin in the Queen's eyes by saying that the corgis ought to be shot. She was charged with plagiarism when the London *Observer* matched passages in her book *Crowned in a Far Country* with those in two other works; when she cried during an interview in mentioning her father, the Queen was furious.

By the time Princess Michael attended the royal Christmas gathering at Windsor Castle, the Queen appeared to have had enough of her. She dared to offend the monarch by refusing to attend the traditional dinner and sulking in a tower room. The Queen dictated a memorandum to her secretary which read, "It is understood that in the future you will join the rest of the family for dinner." The Princess, according to some reports, left at once for London; according to others, she obeyed. Andrew Morton, royal historian, states that for some time afterward the Queen addressed all her requirements to the Princess in writing, spoke only minimally to her in person, and absolutely never addressed her by telephone.

Prince Edward elected to leave the Marines early in the year. The Duke of Norfolk and Andrew Morton confirm that the Prince was deeply admired from the House of Lords down for having stood up to Prince Philip, who certainly opposed the decision. Edward had almost completed training, and his decision was acceptable to the Queen. He was still determined to enter the theater. He would later join Andrew Lloyd Webber's Really Useful Theater Company as a production assistant. Sweet-natured, warm, and kind, immensely attractive and hard-working, he would captivate everyone with whom he worked.

In June, Mrs. Thatcher was reelected, confirming her as the longest-lasting Prime Minister of the century.

In 1987 most of the royal activity was undertaken by the Prince and Princess of Wales. They toured tirelessly, the Prince again taking the leading role in restoring cathedrals and churches, supporting AIDS research and hospital wards, visiting a leech farm and uncomfortably treading on one which had got free, traveling through the Kalahari Desert with Laurens van der Post. And above all embarking on what would probably be a lifelong campaign against the depressed standards of British architecture. Constitutionally able to speak his mind, unlike his mother, he followed his uncle David and his father in loudly expressing his opinions whenever he could. He likened one new microchip factory to a Victorian prison, he attacked a development plan for impersonal office structures which would flank the scene of his marriage—his beloved St. Paul's Cathedral; he seared developers with his tongue, strafing those architects of the fifties who had changed the subdued, gray, Georgian or Victorian look of London as "worse than the Luftwaffe." His war was not one-sided; it would be hard to remember any royal figure who had attracted so extreme a barrage of public criticism as he; the fact that the criticism emerged from the front ranks of the architectural community did not lessen its effectiveness and, embattled, he repeatedly struck back. Nor were his visits abroad without controversy. Despite the fact that King Juan Carlos of Spain had boycotted their wedding, Charles and Princess Diana stayed in Madrid as guests of the royal couple, breaking protocol by arriving late for the State banquet when Prince Charles could not tear himself away from the paintings in the celebrated art gallery of the Prado.

In Germany in November, the Prince provoked some comment by openly discussing his family's local connections, and by actually confirming Mrs. Thatcher's defense policies as he addressed the cadets of the German Army.

There was one uncomfortable matter which excited some minor interest that year: Katherine Bowes-Lyon, first cousin to the Queen, was discovered to be in a mental hospital where she had remained hidden since 1941. Her sister Nerissa had died there in 1986. But the story, and all the suggestions of familial neglect, amounted to nothing; the unhappy Miss Bowes-Lyon had been given the best of care. More serious was the matter of an intruder at Sandringham who had managed to get within five feet of the Queen; from an upstairs window she had seen him rushing across the lawn; with great dispatch, she made her way downstairs and locked the door as a policeman tackled him and threw him to the ground. This was yet another case of the very poor state of royal security being exposed.

In the late 1980s, the Queen's business was conducted as ceremoniously, and at as vast a cost, as ever. She continued to employ over 420 staff; those at Buckingham Palace alone were numbered in scores, still run by the Master of the Household, the Palace Steward, the Housekeeper; armies of cleaners and polishers, electricians and plumbers were constantly on call. The private post office still handled thousands of letters a day; the Queen was still not required to pay for stamps. Organizing State banquets continued to have a Victorian solemnity and complexity: well over 100 liveried servants were called on to attend to the guests at the great horseshoe-shaped central banqueting table in the Palace ballroom; Peter Russell, former royal butler, had recorded that a system of traffic lights, amber for staff to prepare to serve, green for the actual serving and clearing, was introduced. A total of 76 were required to take care of the evening, all in full livery.

Christmas had scarcely varied in thirty years; the luncheon was usually of lobster; dinner the traditional turkey and Christmas pudding, and the staff, Russell reported, was never made to feel less than festive—except when served the traditional sugared almonds on cardboard plates, while the royal family ate them from priceless silver dishes. December 26 was occupied with a pheasant shoot; there was invariably a film screening in the evening, all of this at Windsor Castle before the usual trip to Sandringham. Because of security, the Queen no longer shopped at Harrods, but instead the store was brought to her; gifts were set out on long tables, from which she could select. Travel still involved vast retinues, private trains, processions of trucks, flocks of movable human beings.

The 1980s were not easy for the Queen. As she retreated more and more from public life, only breaking her comparative degree of seclusion to go abroad—she went to Australia for the bicentennial celebrations—she suffered from more than her share of personal stress. She saw the Secretary of the Cabinet reduced to powder by the brilliant Australian lawyer Malcolm Turnbull when the publication of *Spycatcher,* former British secret agent Peter Wright's exposé of the flaws in security in Great Britain, was prevented from taking place in London and Wright became the subject of a court action.

In March 1988, Prince Charles had a narrow escape from death at Klosters, Switzerland, when a sudden avalanche killed a favored friend and equerry and injured a young woman in the royal party; and Princess Anne's troubled marriage to Captain Mark Phillips ended painfully, with much unwelcome gossip about her supposed relationship with her former bodyguard, Peter Cross. Princess Anne, it was claimed, had received a number of love letters from another man indicating an adulterous affair; yet, in fact, those letters were written by a close friend seeking advice on his emotional and psychological difficulties.

The Queen also had to contend with the matter of Marina Ogilvy, daughter of Princess Alexandra of Kent, who admitted that she was pregnant out of wedlock and pleaded unsuccessfully at first to the monarch for consideration. There was not an hour when the Queen was not acutely aware that, protected though she was, she could not escape from the increasingly squalid gossip that was commonplace in the last two decades of the century.

Mrs. Thatcher's increasing belligerence and determined attempts to reduce aid to the aged and infirm also cannot have pleased (though her restoration of hereditary peerages did). Nor can the anger and ridicule that continued to greet Prince Charles as he nostalgically sought a return to a more noble and beautiful England.

It is not surprising that, at a Commonwealth conference in Malaysia in 1989, the Queen drew a parallel between the troubled family of the nations of which she was titular head, and her own disturbed clan, when she said, "Like all the best families, we have our share of eccentricities, of impetuous and wayward youngsters, and of family disagreements."

And so, battered by a storm of adverse comment, the Queen had to cling to excellences within her own clan: above all, the full emergence of Prince Charles, whose persuasive book and television documentary *A Vision of Britain* was the summation of his thoughts on architecture. This work can only have pleased her, given the much changed townscape visible from the windows of the British royal residences: the featureless and charmless skyscrapers that had mushroomed all over London, the monotony and drabness to which the town of Windsor had been reduced. The number of royal residences in royal Gloucestershire spoke for itself: it was necessary to travel that far from London to find unspoiled countryside and an atmosphere not too appallingly changed from pre-World War II days.

The Queen can only have smiled upon Prince Charles's increasing passion for Italy, and his extraordinary and profound knowledge of that country's history and architecture. It was typical of him that, when he visited the medieval town of Monte San Marino, he singled out a church in order to see a triptych by Crivelli, by no means a fashionable artist today. Like Prince Philip and Winston Churchill, he became an acceptable amateur painter, exhibiting his watercolors of Italian landscapes in that country. Inspired by meetings with the legendary author Iris Origo, at her magical home near Siena, and armed with the authoritative advice of the American art critic Milton Gendel, he still more extensively developed his knowledge of a culture he found desirable, far removed from the modern Dark Age in which fate had placed him for all of his young life. He supported his mother's desire for ecumenicism, a blending of religions in a unified world.

EPILOGUE
* * *

THERE HAS BEEN MUCH discussion, from the outset, about the marriage of Charles and Diana. In 1992, many royal-watchers assumed that Diana cooperated with the journalist Andrew Morton on a book about her marriage. Unwisely, and with offense to the Royal Family, she allowed her late father, her brother, Charles, the ninth Earl of Spencer, her best friend and roommate, Caroline Bartholomew, and her close male companion, James Gilbey, among others, to discuss her intimate life with Morton.

On royal tours, the family always looks at the gathered reporters in order to locate a familiar and friendly face. For Diana, Morton was always the most favored and most adoring fan. Without the knowledge of any member of the Royal Family, in what may have been a historically unique breach of royal protocol and accepted rules of behavior, many believe that Diana defiantly gave Morton access to privileged information concerning her husband and his parents. This was, in effect, stabbing them in the back. No royal person in England's history had committed so gross a breach of conduct. For her to have done so may have been calculated to bring down the throne. It was inspired by her hatred of her husband and her loathing of the anachronistic and hidebound dynasty in which she had, with such reckless ambition, landed herself.

Not only did she open the floodgates to Morton, she allegedly told him and her own family that she was sick and tired of her fake romantic marriage and of the phony manner in which the Queen ran her offspring—that is to say, without any degree of understanding or sympathy, and according to outworn Victorian principles.

The book provides a harrowing portrait that insured the

469

author a bestseller. In it, Morton writes that Diana had attempted suicide on six separate occasions. In fact, the account of these efforts reads, to say the least, questionably. She is supposed to have flung herself down a staircase at Sandringham without causing a miscarriage of her expected elder son; actually, there are contrasting reports, probably more reliable, that say that she slipped down just a few steps and fell at the feet of the Queen Mother, who was understandably shaken but calmly called for a doctor. No damage had been done; had she fallen in the manner she described, she would almost certainly have lost the baby.

Even more dubious is the account of trying to kill herself with the edge of a lemon slicer, which, in fact, has no edge. She is supposed to have cut herself with a penknife, an action from which generations of schoolchildren have recovered. Most extreme of all, she is said to have flung herself against a glass cabinet in the apparent hope that she would be cut to pieces, whereas, in fact, the wooden partitioning of the cabinet would have protected her from harm. These childish demonstrations, if true, suggest nothing more than the tantrums of a foolish young woman trying to attract sympathy from an understandably bored husband. Displays of this sort would surely justify Prince Charles's much emphasized annoyance with, and withdrawal from, his wife.

As for her alleged bulimia, and severe depression following Prince William's birth, these are common symptoms in young mothers and in fashionable young women concerned over their post-natal figures. The medication taken in such circumstances, whether for weight loss or for emotional disturbance, or, for that matter, weight gain, can easily upset the endocrine balance of the subject and create emotional disturbances. In order to provoke and upset her husband and his family, Princess Diana may have allowed Morton to make it seem that such upsets of the nervous system were unique, strange, and provoked by royal cruelty.

The actual causes of the unhappy marriage and its gradual and finally its virtual complete breakdown are as follows: Originally, her older sister, Lady Sarah Spencer, had dreamed of marrying Charles. But she had realized, on careful reflection, that the union with him would stifle her as a human being and limit her personal happiness. As she got to know Charles, she realized his intrinsic coldness, his inability to love deeply and fully, and his severity, inherited from his parents. She came to understand that his intellectual interests would conflict with her more relaxed and casual way of living.

After the birth of Prince Harry, Charles's attitude toward Diana changed drastically. He found he could no longer accept the charade of his marriage. He knew now that he was married, not to the fairytale princess of public fantasy, but to a hysterical, bad-tempered and conceited shrew. Diana's self-obsessive egotism was abhorrent to him; she kept a set of scrapbooks of everything she had done and endlessly leafed through them. He hated this; he found it unroyal and ridiculous.

The traditional, intimate Sunday dinner parties given by the couple continued for a time for appearance's sake, but Diana would even scribble on the invitation notes in her own hand remarks such as, "Don't dress, it's only the usual macaroni and cheese!" This was a direct, and rude, reference to her husband's plain British taste in food. Finally, the Prince apparently could no longer endure living under the same roof as his wife. It came as a great shock, not only to her, but to the Queen and Prince Philip, when Charles announced that he would run his office from their country residence, Highgrove, and not from either Buckingham Palace or Kensington Palace. Thus, he could stay at the house all week long and avoid her, since she would be in London. For the children's sake, he would have her stay over the weekends.

The Prince of Wales began the separation long before the public found out. Diana was shocked by his decision to spend five days out of seven apart from her. She became ill from the stress. Finally, she confronted the Prince by asking him whether he loved her. He replied with a categorical, "No." She still had not understood, after numerous explanations, that royal marriages are, and always have been, designed for the dynasty and not for romantic fulfillment, that royal princesses are not supposed to become emotional, and, most of all, she hadn't grasped that she hadn't been able to change the Prince's nature to conform with her unroyal own. Ignoring the rules, she felt scorned. She grew to hate—deeply, fiercely—both her husband and her parents-in-law. Revenge was at the top of her agenda. With surprising brilliance, she worked out a scheme of causing them great distress. First, she made sure that she was the most popular and glittering member of the royals, and the most publicly accepted in centuries. Then, she turned to her family in order to destroy Charles, the Queen, and Prince Philip via Andrew Morton.

The unhappy matter of the younger royals has filled the columns and astonished the public. Princess Anne's disastrous marriage to Captain Mark Phillips ended in the midst of the Charles-Diana fracas. They lost any physical attraction for each other after 15 years of marriage and lived in separate quarters at their Gloucestershire estate, Gatcombe Park. Once again, much to the Queen's chagrin, they had ignored the rules of royalty—remain together for appearance's sake after romance has burned out. One would believe that Princess Anne's effrontery in ending a marriage that was no longer convenient must have caused the Queen considerable anguish. Anne had broken the rules as much as Princess Diana, and with even less of an excuse since she was her mother's daughter.

The Queen, with surprising compliance, quite against her rulebook practices, accepted her daughter's lover, Commander Timothy Laurence of the Royal Navy. In order to overcome the restrictions of the Royal Marriage Act, they were to be married, at the time of writing in Scotland, outside British church jurisdiction, in the autumn of 1992. The divorce from Phillips became final during the Diana crisis.

At the same time, the Queen had yet another major burden to bear. Her second daughter-in-law, the dreaded Fergie, decided, again in breach of royal rules, simply, and impetuously, to shed her husband, the Duke of York, after the birth of their second daughter, Princess Eugenie. The Queen reacted in a calm manner. With quiet persuasiveness, she brought the couple together again. As of July 1992, it was uncertain whether this reunion would work. Once again, Fergie ignored, as flagrantly as Diana and Princess Anne, every tenet of royal behavior laid down for centuries. The reason for her desire for divorce was a sense of isolation from a husband who spent most of the year away from her on naval duties, and, like Charles, had the peculiar coldness of Windsor husbands. Unlike Charles, he did publicly declare his continuing love for his wife. The duchess's alleged involvement with several men was offensively over-emphasized, and, disgracefully, she did nothing to suppress the rumors, and behaved with an absence of taste surpassing Diana's or another royal person's since King George IV.

As for Prince Edward, his unmarried state has given rise to uncomfortable rumors. Will he, at 33, be forced into a marriage as Charles was? And would it not be a reasonable guess that he would refuse so artificial an arrangement? It is unfortunate that, in view of his interest in the public arts, his resignation from Sir Andrew Lloyd Webber's Really Useful Company has not been followed by a suitable appointment on the board of, for example, the Royal National Theater where his presence would be valuable and influential. He remains the most natural, unaffected, charming and popular of the Queen's children, and, it must be added, apart from Charles, the only one to keep his dignity and protect his privacy.

Princess Margaret's life today is humdrum, unexciting, and far removed from the glamour of the past. To this day, she is still mourning over her sister's decision that prevented her from marrying Peter Townsend. She has declared that her children, Viscount Linley and Lady Sarah Armstrong-Jones (he makes furniture, both he and Lady Sarah are still unmarried), are not royals, which is as absurd as Princess Anne disestablishing her own offspring. Such statements scarcely improve the solidity of the dynasty.

What is the future for British royalty? With the advent of the European Economic Community, will the Queen, who recently celebrated 40 years on the throne, no longer have a *raison d'être*? Already, the Republicans are being heard loudly calling for a dissolution of the whole structure of the family. This is no more than hot air. The British people, if asked by referendum whether they would wish to see the monarchy abolished, would undoubtedly give a resounding, "No." The latest flurries, scandal-mongering and circulation-building stunts have increased the average Englishman's sympathy and support for the Queen. And, of course, for the Prince of Wales, who has fortunately chosen to remain silent during his wife's tasteless behavior.

One more thing is certain. Charles and Diana's first born will one day be king. Whatever Diana may have done in a futile effort to shake the throne, she has provided its future occupant. It is an irony she must live with for the rest of her days.

ACKNOWLEDGMENTS

***

Four Prime Ministers responded to letters promptly and invaluably. Their names are included among the following, who were especially helpful: Rupert Allason, MP (Nigel West), Nicholas Armstrong, Richard Babcock, Dr. Beatrice Berle, Gary Brown, Lord Callaghan of Cardiff, Lord Carrington, Ned Comstock, Dora Contreras, Tamar Cooper, John Costello, Jenny Davis, Lord Denning of Whitchurch, Richard Dreyfus, Richard Goetz, Professor John-Peter Grill, Roger Hall, Gabriel Hardmann, the Rt. Hon. Edward Heath, MP, Lord Home of the Hirsel, Gina Johnson, Christopher Kloes, Johnny Lail of Glendale, Estelle Laurence, John Leach, Edward H. Levi, Phyllis Milberger, Peter Moore, Kathy Nicastro, Chapman Pincher, the Rt. Hon. Enoch Powell, Stephen Rattey, Daniel Re'em, Dan Rightmyer, Kenneth Rose, Harold Schwab, George Selden, Peter Seyderhelm, Lord Shackleton, Bernard Sharpe, Victoria Shellin, the Hon. Ian Smith, Paul Stewart, Robert Stewart, John Taylor, the Rt. Hon. Margaret Thatcher, MP, Gerald Turbow, Andrew Turnbull, Robert Uher, George Ungar, Joseph and Dee Wambaugh, the Hon. Gough Whitlam, Lord Wilson of Rievaulx, the staffs of USC Doheny Library, the Library of Congress, the National Archives, UCLA Research Library, the New York Public Library, the Public Record Office in London, the memorial libraries of President Roosevelt, Eisenhower, Kennedy, Johnson, Nixon, Ford, and Reagan.

Note: It should be noted that numerous individuals who do not wish to be named contributed a substantial portion of the previously unknown material in this book. Because of the peculiar rules applying to individuals who are close to the Palace, they may not be quoted directly, and the authors have respected their requirement of anonymity. A special debt is due to Professor Stanford Shaw of UCLA and General Necip Torumtay for obtaining the unique documents on Prince Andrew, Prince Philip's father, which have been declassified for the authors for the first time. Also, from the above list, the authors would like to give a special acknowledgment to Paul Stewart, who admirably handled the difficult and exhausting task of obtaining very large numbers of documents, previously unexamined by historians, from the Public Record Office, Kew, London.

SELECTIVE
BIBLIOGRAPHY
* * *

ADAMS, MICHAEL, *Suez and After: Year of Crisis*. Boston: Beacon Press, 1958.

AIRLIE, MABELL, Countess of. *Thatched with Gold*. London: Hutchinson, n.d.

ALEXANDRA, QUEEN OF YUGOSLAVIA. *Prince Philip: A Family Portrait*. New York: Bobbs-Merrill, 1959.

ALLEN, GARY. *None Dare Call It Conspiracy*. Rossmore, Calif.: Concord Press, c. 1971.

ANDREW, PRINCE OF GREECE. *Towards Disaster*. London: John Murray, 1930.

ARNOLD, BRUCE. *Margaret Thatcher: A Study in Power*. London: Hamish Hamilton, 1984.

ASQUITH, LADY CYNTHIA. *The Duchess of York*. London: Hutchinson, 1927.
———. *The Family Life of Queen Elizabeth*. London: Hutchinson, 1927.
———. *The King's Daughters*. London: Hutchinson, 1938.
———. *The Married Life of the Duke of York*. London: Hutchinson, 1937.
———. *The Queen*. London: Hutchinson, 1937.

BARRY, STEPHEN. *Royal Service*. New York: Macmillan, 1983.

BEATON, CECIL. *Self Portrait with Friends*. New York: Times Books, 1979.

BEAUFRE, ANDRE. *The Suez Expedition: 1956*. New York: Praeger, 1969.

BENN, TONY. *Against the Tide: Diaries 1973–1976*. London: Hutchinson, 1989.

BERKSON, SIMON. *Their Majesties*. New York: Stat Poll, 1938.

BERTIN, CELIA. *Marie Bonaparte, A Life*. New Haven, Conn.: Yale University Press, 1987.

BERTON, PIERRE. *The Royal Family*. New York: Knopf, 1955.

BOOTHROYD, BASIL. *Prince Philip: An Informal Biography*. New York: McCall Books, 1971.

BOULTON, DAVID. *The Lockheed Papers*. London: Cape, 1978.

BROAD, LEWIS. *Queens, Crowns and Coronations*. London: Hutchinson, 1952.

BROUGH, JAMES. *Margaret: The Tragic Princess*. New York: Putnam, 1978.

CALVOCORESSI, PETER. *Suez: Seven Years After*. New York: Pantheon Books, 1967.

CATHCART, HELEN. *Princess Margaret*. London: W. H. Allen, 1974.

CHANNON, SIR HENRY. *Chips: The Diaries of Sir Henry Channon*. London: Weidenfeld and Nicolson, 1967.

CHURCHILL, RANDOLPH S. *The Fight for the Tory Leadership*. London: Heinemann, 1964.

COLVILLE, JOHN. *Footprints in Time*. London: Collins, 1976.

COOKRIDGE, E. H. *From Battenberg to Mountbatten*. London: Arthur Barker, 1966.

CORBITT, FREDERICK. *My Twenty Years in Buckingham Palace*. New York: D. McKay, 1956.

CORDET, HELENE. *Born Bewildered*. London: Peter Davies, 1961.

COSGRAVE, PATRICK. *The Lives of Enoch Powell*. London: The Bodley Head, 1989.

COSTELLO, JOHN. *Mask of Treachery*. New York: Morrow, 1969.

CRAWFORD, MARION. *The Little Princesses*. New York: Harcourt Brace Jovanovich, 1950.

DEAN, JOHN. *Prince Philip, Duke of Edinburgh, A Portrait by His Valet*. London: Robert Hale, n.d.

DEMPSTER, NIGEL. *Princess Margaret: A Life Unfulfilled*. Toronto: Totem Books, 1983.

DENNIS, GEOFFREY. *Coronation Commentary*. New York: Dodd Mead, 1937.

DONALDSON, FRANCES. *Edward VIII*. New York: Ballantine Books, 1970.

DROVER, G.M.F. *Neil Kinnock, the Path to Leadership*. London: Weidenfeld and Nicolson, 1984.

EGYPT, MINISTRY OF FOREIGN AFFAIRS. *White Paper on the Nationalization of the Suez Canal Maritime Company*. Cairo: Government Press, 1956.

EILERS, MARLENE E. *Queen Victoria's Descendants*. Baltimore: Genealogical Publishing Company, 1987.

EVANS, WILLIAM. *My Mountbatten Years*. London: Headline, 1989.

FARNIE, D. A. *East and West of Suez*. Oxford: Clarendon Press, 1969.

FIELD, LESLIE. *The Queen's Jewels*. New York and London: Weidenfeld and Nicolson, 1987.

FITZGERALD, PERCY. *The Great Canal at Suez*. New York: AMS Press, 1978.

FLICKE, WILHELM F. *War Secrets in the Ether*. 2 vols. Laguna Hills, Calif.: Aegean Park Press, 1977.

Fodor's Royalty Watching. New York and London: Fodor's Travel Publications, 1987.

FOOTE, GEOFFREY. *A Chronology of Post-War British Politics*. London: Croom Helm, 1988.

FREEDMAN, LAWRENCE. *Britain at the Falklands War*. Oxford: Basil Blackwell, 1988.

FRERE, JAMES A. *The British Monarchy at Home*. London: Anthony Gibbs and Phillips, n.d.

GIBBS, SIR PHILIP. *The Book of the King's Jubilee: The Life and Times of the King and Queen and Their People.* London: Hutchinson, 1935.

GILBERT, MARTIN. *Churchill.* Garden City, N.Y.: Doubleday, 1980–89.

GOLDSMITH, BARBARA. *Little Gloria . . . Happy at Last.* New York: Knopf, 1980.

GORE, JOHN. *King George V: A Personal Memoir.* New York: Scribner, 1941.

GRAVES, CHARLES. *Champagne and Chandeliers: The Story of the Café de Paris.* London: Odhams, 1958.

HALL, UNITY. *Philip: The Man Behind the Monarchy.* London: Michael O'Mara Books, 1987.

HAMILTON, ALAN. *Royal Watching.* London: Mitchell Beazley, 1985.

HARRIS, KENNETH. *Thatcher.* Boston: Little Brown, 1988.

HARTNELL, NORMAN. *Silver and Gold.* New York: Pitman, 1956.

HAXEY, SIMON. *Tory M.P.* London: Victor Gollancz, 1939.

HEIKAL, MOHAMMED. *The Cairo Documents.* Garden City, N.Y.: Doubleday, 1973.

HORNE, ALISTAIR. *Macmillan.* London: Macmillan, 1989.

HOUBLON, LADY ALICE. *The Houblon Family, Its Story and Times.* London: Constable, 1907.

HOUBLON, DOREEN ARCHER. *Side-saddle.* London: Country Life, 1938.

HOUGH, RICHARD. *Mountbatten.* New York: Random House, 1981.

———. *Margaret, the Tragic Princess.* New York: Putnam, n.d.

INSIGHT TEAM, London *Sunday Times. War in the Falklands.* New York: Harper and Row, 1982.

JAMES, PAUL. *Anne: The Working Princess.* London: Pan Books, 1988.

——— AND PETER, RUSSELL. *At Home with the Royal Family.* New York: Harper and Row, 1986.

JAMES, ROBERT RHODES. *Anthony Eden.* New York: McGraw-Hill, 1986.

JOHNSON, PAUL. *A History of the English People.* New York: Harper and Row, 1972.

———. *Modern Times.* New York: Harper and Row, 1983.

JUDD, DENIS. *Prince Philip Duke of Edinburgh.* New York: Atheneum, 1980.

KAY, ERNEST. *Pragmatic Premier: An Intimate Portrait of Harold Wilson.* London: Frewin, 1967.

KERR, SIR JOHN. *Matters for Judgment.* Australia: Macmillan, 1988.

KHRUSHCHEV, NIKITA. *Khrushchev Remembers.* Boston: Little, Brown, 1970.

KIDD, CHARLES, AND SMITH, MONTAGUE. *Royal Children.* New York: Morrow, 1982.

KILLEARN, LORD. *The Killearn Diaries.* London: Sidgwick and Jackson, 1972.

KING, STELLA. *Princes Marina, Her Life and Times.* London: Castle, 1969.

LACEY, ROBERT. *Majesty.* New York: Harcourt Brace Jovanovich, 1977.

LAIRD, DOROTHY. *How the Queen Reigns.* Cleveland: World Publishing Company, 1959.

LEIGH, DAVID. *The Wilson Plot*. London: Heinemann, 1988.

LLOYD, SELWYN. *Suez 1956*. London: Cape, 1978.

LONGFORD, ELIZABETH. *The Queen*. New York: Knopf, 1983.

MACMILLAN, HAROLD. *At the End of the Day*. New York: Harper and Row, 1973.

———. *Blast of War*. New York: Harper and Row, 1968.

———. *Pointing the Way*. New York: Harper and Row, 1972.

———. *Riding the Storm*. New York: Harper and Row, 1971.

———. *Tides of Fortune*. New York: Harper and Row, 1969.

———. *War Diaries: Politics and War in the Mediterranean 1943–1945*. New York: St. Martin's Press, 1984.

———. *Winds of Change*. New York: Harper and Row, 1966.

MACVEIGH, A. *An Ambassador Reports: Greece, 1933–1947*. Princeton, N.J.: Princeton University Press, 1980.

MARTIN, RALPH G. *Charles and Diana*. New York: Putnam, 1985.

MAX OF BADEN, PRINCE. *Memoirs*. New York: Scribner, 1928.

MAYOR, ALLAN J. *Madam Prime Minister: Margaret Thatcher and Her Rise to Power*. New York: Newsweek Books, 1979.

MENKES, SUZY. *The Royal Jewels*. London: Grafton Books, 1985.

MILLAR, OLIVER. *The Queen's Pictures*. New York: Macmillan, 1977.

MILLER, HARRY T. *Undoubted Queen*. London: Hutchinson, 1958.

MORRAH, DERMOT. *To Be a King*. London: Arrow Books, 1969.

MORROW, ANN. *The Queen*. New York: Morrow, 1983.

MORTIMER, PENELOPE. *Queen Elizabeth, a Portrait of the Queen Mother*. New York: St. Martin's Press, 1986.

MORTON, ANDREW. *Inside Kensington Palace*. London: Michael O'Mara Books, 1987.

———. *Theirs Is the Kingdom: The Wealth of the Windsors*. London: Michael O'Mara Books, 1989.

NERF, DONALD. *Warriors at Suez*. New York: Linden Press/Simon & Schuster, 1981.

NICKOLLS, L. *The Queen's Majesty: A Diary of the Royal Year*. London: MacDonald, 1957.

NICOLSON, HAROLD. *King George V: His Life and Reign*. Garden City, N.Y.: Doubleday, 1953.

NUTTING, ANTHONY. *Nasser*. New York: Dutton, 1972.

———. *No End of a Lesson: The Story of Suez*. New York: Potter, 1967.

PACKARD, JERROLD W. *The Queen and Her Court*. New York: Scribner, 1981.

Papers Relating to the Foreign Relations of the U.S. Government. Washington, D.C.: U.S. Government Printing Office, 1938.

PINCHER, CHAPMAN. *Too Secret, Too Long*. New York: St. Martin's Press, 1984.

POPE-HENNESSEY, JAMES. *Queen Mary 1867–1953*. New York: Knopf, 1960.

QUIGLEY, CARROLL. *Tragedy and Hope*. New York: Macmillan, 1966.

Records of the Department of State Relating to Internal Affairs of Greece. Washington, D.C.: National Archives, 1963.

RITTER, GERHARD. *The Sword and the Scepter.* Miami: University of Miami Press, 1969.

ROBERTSON, TERRENCE. *Crisis: The Inside Story of the Suez Conspiracy.* London: Hutchinson, 1964.

ROHRS, HERMAN. *Kurt Hahn.* London: Routledge and Kegan Paul, 1970.

ROSE, KENNETH. *King George V.* New York: Knopf, 1984.

―――. *Kings, Queens and Courtiers.* London: Weidenfeld and Nicolson, 1985.

ROSS, JOHN. *Thatcher and Friends: The Anatomy of the Tory Party.* London: Pluto Press, 1983.

ROTH, ANDREW. *Enoch Powell: A Biography.*

SAKOL, JEANNE, AND LATHAM, CAROLINE. *Royals.* London: W. H. Allen, 1987.

SAMPSON, ANTHONY. *The Arms Bazaar: From Lebanon to Lockheed.* New York: Viking, 1977.

―――. *The Changing Anatomy of Britain.* London: Coronet Books, 1982.

SCHEIDEMANN, PHILLIP. *The Making of the New Germany.* New York: D. Appleton, 1929.

SCHÖLL, HEINZ. *Bilderberg and Trilaterale.* Köln: VZD, 1972.

SEVERAL HANDS. *The Story of the Princess Elizabeth.* London: Rembrandt, 1934.

SHEW, BETTY. *The Royal Wedding.* London: MacDonald, 1947.

SHUCKBURGH, EVELYN. *Descent to Suez, Foreign Office Diaries, 1951–1956.* New York: Norton, 1986.

SKLAR, HOLLY. *Trilateralism.* Boston: South End Press, 1980.

Suez in the Middle East: Documents, November 5–December 6, 1956. London: Soviet News, 1956.

SUMMERS, ANTHONY, AND DORRIL, STEPHEN. *Honeytrap: The Secret Worlds of Stephen Ward.* London: Weidenfeld and Nicolson, 1987.

THOMAS, HUGH. *The Suez Affair.* Harmondsworth: Penguin Books, 1970.

TISDALL, E. E. *Royal Destiny: The Royal Hellenic Cousins.* London and New York: S. Paul, 1955.

TOWNSEND, PETER. *Time and Chance.* (Published in Great Britain.)

UNITED STATES. Congress. House. Committee on Interstate and Foreign Commerce. Subcommittee on Oversight and Investigations. International uranium supply and demand: hearing before the Subcommittee on Oversight and Investigations of the Committee on Interstate and Foreign Commerce, House of Representatives, Ninety-fourth Congress, second session, on allegations that uranium prices and markets have been influenced by a foreign producer's cartel and other factors . . . November 4, 1976. Washington, D.C.: U.S. Government Printing Office, 1977.

VARIOUS. *Royal Homes (Illustrated).* London: Odhams, n.d.

VARNEY, MICHAEL (WITH MAX PHILLIPS). *Bodyguard to Charles.* London: Hale, 1989.

VIKTORIA LUISE, H.M. *The Kaiser's Daughter.* New York: Prentice-Hall, 1965.

WALES, PRINCE OF. *A Vision of Britain.* New York: Doubleday, 1989.

WARWICK, CHRISTOPHER. *George and Marina, the Duke and Duchess of Kent.* London: Weidenfeld and Nicolson, 1988.

————. *Princess Margaret.* London: Weidenfeld and Nicolson, n.d.

WHEELER-BENNETT, SIR JOHN. *King George VI.* New York: St. Martin's Press, 1958.

WHITE, RALPHE M., AND FISHER, GRAHAM. *The Royal Family: A Portrait.* New York: David McKay, 1969.

WILLIAMS, MARCIA. *Inside Number Ten.* New York: Howard McCann and Geoghegan, 1972.

WILSON, EDGAR. *The Myth of the British Monarchy.* London: Journeyman Republic, 1989.

WOODHOUSE, C. M. *The Story of Modern Greece.* London: Faber and Faber, 1968.

XYDIS, STEPHEN G. *Greece and the Great Powers.* Thessaloniki, Greece: Institute for Balkan Studies, 1967.

ZIEGLER, PHILIP. *Mountbatten.* London: Collins, 1985.

NOTES ON
SOURCES
***

INTRODUCTION

Three filing cabinets of some thousands of Xeroxed reports, articles, and documents have been assembled in order to provide the tapestry of this chronicle. The method has not been to rely on single sources; hence, a listing of the basis of each piece of information would be impossibly lengthy. The London *Times* and *New York Times*, the latter seldom used by British historians, are the backbone of the work; but over three hundred books amounting to millions of words have been drawn from, and the Public Record Office has yielded much that has been invaluable; so has the National Archive in Washington. Hansard, the official record of the Parliamentary debates, has been read for a sixty-four-year period. What follows is meant only as an indication, a guidepost, to further exploration by scholars; it is also intended as a *vade mecum* for the general reader, to glance at if he is concerned about the authenticity of a fact.

CHAPTER ONE

Sir John Wheeler-Bennett's authorized biography of King George VI is still the best available on the subject. We are without a satisfactory biography of the Queen Mother, so that the particulars of her life have been drawn largely from Wheeler-Bennett and from Kenneth Rose's *Kings, Queens and Courtiers*, the best general work available on the royal family.

For the debates on the royal income in the House of Commons, Hansard, the convenient general title for the Parliamentary debates from the beginning to the present day, supplies the record. A very large portion of this book has been drawn from Hansard. The *New York Times* also, in several issues preceding the wedding, gave exhaustive details of the wedding cakes and gifts, these articles not drawn from by previous historians. The rehearsal for the wedding was described in the *New York Times* and London *Times*. Leslie Field's *The Queen's Jewels* is indispensable on the wedding gifts. The pre-wedding party comes from the *New York Times* and the London *Times;* the wedding itself was best described in both newspapers. Public Record Office files have been consulted. The story about the Duchess's unpunctuality has been common coin in court circles. The African tour was best covered by the London *Times* on various days that year. The *New York Times* covered the royal moves from house to house.

CHAPTER TWO

Descriptions of the birth of Princess Elizabeth are to be found in Ann Morrow's *The Queen* and in the *New York Times* and London *Times;* other British newspapers have been consulted, as well as the *Illustrated London News* for that week. An identical survey was made of the press for the consequences of the birth. See also, in particular, the *New York Times.* The *New York Times* was much the most vivid on the christening ceremony. The descriptions of Buckingham Palace at the time have been drawn from John Gore's *King George V* and from confidential sources. John Gore was indispensable on mealtime rituals. The threat of kidnapping comes from the *New York Times;* so does the ritual at Glamis Castle. Gore was excellent on the King's routines. Also, the Christmas ceremonies. The royal tour of Australia was covered expertly by Wheeler-Bennett, the London *Times*, the *New York Times*, the *Illustrated London News*, the *Sydney Morning Herald,* and newspapers in Auckland and Wellington, New Zealand. The debate is in Hansard. Princess Elizabeth's first birthday and all subsequent childhood birthdays were vividly described in the *New York Times.* The necklace story was in the *New York Times.* The return to London was best described in the *New York Times.* An anonymous book entitled *The Story of the Princess Elizabeth,* which apparently emanated unofficially from Buckingham Palace, has proved an irreplaceable source on details of 145 Piccadilly and all particulars of Elizabeth as a small child. The author(s) evidently had access to records no one else has been admitted to. The painting story did not appear in England and was published in the *New York Times.* Kenneth Rose in *Kings, Queens and Courtiers* and his *King George V* provided the dog and pram stories. Rose is the best source on the King's illness. The royal chandeliers anecdote comes from *The Story of the Princess Elizabeth.*

CHAPTER THREE

Again, Kenneth Rose is best on the King's condition. The *New York Times* is splendid on birthday gifts. *The Story of the Princess Elizabeth* dealt with the portrait sittings. Penelope Mortimer and the London *Times* are best on the Italian visit. The Princess's birthday is described in the *New York Times* and *The Story of the Princess Elizabeth;* see also Kenneth Rose. The *New York Times Magazine* contained the article on the Princesses by Virginia Pope; for the details of the birth of Princess Margaret, see Christopher Warwick's authorized biography, but more details are in the *New York Times* for July and August; the *Illustrated London News* and *The Sphere* were consulted. For the christening, see the

New York Times, London *Times,* Brough, and other London newspapers. The *New York Times* was best on the killer fog.

Wheeler-Bennett provided the description of Royal Lodge. *The Story of the Princess Elizabeth* supplied the early reading and doll-throwing stories, supplemented by the *New York Times.*

CHAPTER FOUR

Marion Crawford's *The Little Princesses* remains a good general source on the children's upbringing. She supplied the horse-driving story. Details of *Y Bwthyn Bach* are to be found in the *New York Times,* and not in as much detail elsewhere. For more particulars of the royal upbringing, see the London *Times,* Elizabeth Longford's *The Queen,* Ann Morrow, and *The Little Princesses.* Some of this material has been drawn from confidential sources. The Christmas Day broadcast was best evoked in the *New York Times.* See Marion Crawford and *The Story of the Princess Elizabeth* for childhood reading habits. Also Lady Longford's *The Queen* (entitled *Elizabeth R* in England). On the 1934 royal speech, again see the *New York Times* for December 26. The diary of Henry Channon supplies the lunch party story. Christopher Warwick, the London *Times,* and the *New York Times* have been drawn from for the royal curriculum, supplemented by Crawford. See *Sunday Express* for the security problems; the wedding of the Duke and Duchess of Kent is to be found described in the *New York Times,* London *Times, Illustrated London News,* and Warwick's *George and Marina.* Once again, the *New York Times* is much the best source. The same is true of the description of the Silver Jubilee (*New York Times,* May 7, 1935).

CHAPTER FIVE

Kenneth Rose and Wheeler-Bennett are best on the King's illness. For the funeral, see the London *Times* and *New York Times.* For details of the new King, Edward VIII, see Lady Longford's life of him. Wheeler-Bennett is best on the King's vocal training. See the London *Times* for royal movements. The *New York Times* may be consulted on the abdication crisis.

The *New York Times* and London *Times* dealt with the beginning of the new reign in more detail than any biography. Crawford provided the collapsing chair story and the descriptions of a cheerless Buckingham Palace. Princess Margaret's own story was told on the BBC in her only broadcast interview so far. Many details in this chapter, including Princess Elizabeth's response to the new reign, are from confidential sources as well as Crawford. The royal income comes from the *Statesman's Year Book.* The big party at the Palace is in the *New York Times,* and again the account of the Coronation is best described in that newspaper. Leslie Field is the source on the royal jewels. The Countess of Oxford and Asquith's description comes from a book of memoirs. The *New York Times* was virtually alone in describing Princess Margaret's misbehavior at Westminster Abbey. Kenneth Rose is the best source on the mishaps of the Coronation, his published information supplemented in a personal interview.

CHAPTER SIX

For the party following the Coronation, see the *New York Times*. For the Queen's influence on her husband, see Pierre Berton's excellent *The Royal Family*, a much neglected source. See the London *Times* for Chamberlain's policies. Also, other political details of that year. Princess Margaret recalled her love of "King Cotton" in her BBC interview. For the Spithead review see the *New York Times*. The story of the children watching the newsreel is from a confidential source. For royal engagements in 1938 see the London *Times* and the Court Circular. The Paris tour was in the London *Times* and *New York Times*, the *Illustrated London News*, *The Sphere*, and *Figaro* and other French newspapers. The Suffolk tour was in the *New York Times*. Princess Margaret's birthday was in the *New York Times;* the London *Times* for October 3 covered the King's speech. See the *New York Times*, the London *Times*, and other newspapers for the events of 1939. The silk stocking story was from the *New York Times*. Again, confidential sources have enriched this information; the royal calendar is drawn from the Court Circular. The American tour was covered by all newspapers, seven of which have been searched for the description. The mishap at Hyde Park comes from Eleanor Roosevelt's diaries housed at that address in the Roosevelt Memorial Archive. See the London *Times* and *New York Times* for the return to London. The Foreign Office document signed R. W. Mountbeck is in the Public Record Office, Kew, London.

CHAPTER SEVEN

The *Literary Digest* yields additional information. Summarizing Prince Philip's family life and ancestry involved reading some thirty-seven books, scores of newspaper articles, and the enormous files on the Greek royal family contained at the Public Record Office and no longer restricted by the Official Secrets Act. E. H. Cookridge's *From Battenberg to Mountbatten* has proved to be a backbone. A set of documents is available in the Charles Higham Collection at Occidental College, Eagle Rock, California. The *New York Times* and London *Times* covered the day-to-day events. The unique information on Prince Andrew's abandonment of his duties, unavailable to researchers until the present, with the opening of the Turkish archives for the first time, was obtained with the assistance of the authority Professor Stanford Shaw at UCLA and of General Necip Torumtay, Commanding General of the Turkish forces, whose staff spent seventeen weeks delving through seized Greek archives in order to obtain this crucial information. The description of the trial has been obtained from Greek newspapers and the *New York Times* as well as Foreign Office documents including reports in the French language and Jefferson Caffery's telegraphed reports obtained from the State Department archives in Washington, D.C. Particulars of the transportation arrangements of the Greek royal family, train ticket prices, telegrams, diplomatic wires, and interoffice memoranda of the Foreign Office are indexed and filed at the Public Record Office at Kew, London. See the *New York Times* for Prince Andrew's visit to the United States. Details of King George II of Greece have been obtained from confidential sources and from *Current Biography*. For the particulars of the Milford Haven ménage, the reader is referred to Barbara Goldsmith's *Little Gloria . . . Happy at Last*. Prince Andrew's letters are to be found in the Public Record Office at Kew, London. For details of Kurt Hahn, see Philipp Scheidemann's *The Making of the New Germany*. T. C. Worsley's *Flanneled Fool* is to be read with caution and has not been included in the bibliography. Details of Hahn have been filled out in a lengthy interview with a confidential source. For the Hohenlohe-Langenburg affair, see Goldsmith. Particulars of Prince Christopher of Hesse are in Wilhelm F. Flicke's seldom-read *War Secrets in the Ether* (two volumes). Flicke had access to secret German files that appear not to have been examined by other historians. The *New York Times* is the best source on the plane crash that killed Prince Philip's sister.

CHAPTER EIGHT

The early relationship of Elizabeth and Philip has been drawn from confidential sources, as well as from the Public Record Office, Kew, London, and Mountbatten archives files that have been neglected by historians. Foreign Office documents, though much weeded, can still be examined for the correspondence through Stockholm. For the general background, see Martin Gilbert's life of Winston Churchill, drawn from letters, diaries, and other intimate records. The *New York Times* gave the East Midlands tour story. Also the bomb explosion. The "Children's Hour" broadcast is in the BBC archives in London. The *New York Times* is best on Christmas 1940. See the Channon diaries for the meeting with Prince Philip in Athens. Logs of Philip's vessels have been obtained by Paul Stewart from Admiralty archives in London. They may be consulted in the Charles Higham collection at Occidental College. For details on the situation in Greece at the time, see the Public Record Office files, Kew, London. Also *Time* magazine and the Mountbatten archives, which include letters from Prince Philip to his uncle Lord Mountbatten. For particulars of R. A. Butler's wartime dealings with Germany, see John Costello's *Ten Days that Saved the West* (New York: Morrow, 1991), and documents at the National Archives in Washington. Eleanor Roosevelt's diaries describe her visit to London. See the *New York Times* for the Thanksgiving party at Buckingham Palace.

See the London *Times* and the Court Circular for *Sleeping Beauty;* see the London *Times* and the *New York Times* for the Greville will; associated information is from confidential sources, also the King's factory work, and Lord Woolton. For the Sea Ranger story, see the *New York Times*. See the London *Times* for details of the cathedral service. See the *New York Times* for play visit; the Foreign Office document of February 15, 1943, is in the

Foreign Office files at the Public Record Office, Kew, London. The debate on the Regency Bill is in Hansard. See Mountbatten to the dowager Marchioness of Milford Haven, Mountbatten archives, October 24, 1943, for the letter about Princess Sophie. Hansard covered the King's gracious speech; see the *New York Times* and London *Times Aladdin.* For the King George II appeals to the King re Philip, see Cookridge *From Battenberg to Mountbatten* and the Mountbatten archives, also the King's letter to Queen Mary of March 17, 1944. Much of the subsequent material on Princess Elizabeth is from confidential sources. The Channon diaries describe the meeting at Coppins; see Cookridge for the discussion of the marriage idea. The meeting in Cairo is fully detailed in the Mountbatten archives; for some reason, Philip Ziegler, authorized biographer of Mountbatten, omitted any mention of the meeting in his book.

CHAPTER NINE

Harold Macmillan's diaries of World War II provide the information on his meetings with the Greek royals in Athens. The February 9, 1945, note is at the Mountbatten archives. For a list of Princess Elizabeth's engagements in 1945, see the London *Times* and Court Circular. Frederick Corbitt's memoirs are indispensable on this period. The *New York Times* in November and December 1945 is best on Princess Elizabeth's Army training. The description of VE Day is drawn from the *New York Times,* London *Times,* and all other New York and London newspapers, as well as radio broadcasts. Both Princess Margaret in her BBC interview and the present Queen have discussed their experiences. The second victory celebrations have been drawn from the same sources as the first. See Hansard for October 17, 1945, for the discussion of Philip's nationality. The *New York Times* article "Marriage à la Mode" appeared on September 17, 1945. The Blunt mission to Germany is described by John Costello in *Mask of Treachery;* first to break the story were Philip Knightly and the Insight team of the London *Sunday Times.* For details of Prince Philip in London, see Helene Cordet's *Born Bewildered,* and Queen Alexandra of Yugoslavia's biography of Philip. The King's letter to his brother from January 21, 1946, is quoted in Wheeler-Bennett. Again, see *Statesman's Yearbook* for the royal income. The Victory Parade was reported in the *New York Times* and the London *Times,* etc. Alexandra of Yugoslavia was again the main source on Philip in England. Ralphe M. White expertly described Balmoral visit. John Dean, Philip's valet, was indispensable on further details of Philip's life. The royal film performance description is from a confidential eyewitness. The royal variety performance is from a former manager of the London Palladium.

CHAPTER TEN

For the royal tour of South Africa, all British and American newspapers have been consulted, as well as a selection of South African newspapers, these too numerous to list. In view of the lack of a full description in any book, a complex jigsaw puzzle of information had to be assembled. Norman Hartnell described his search for the wedding dress design in his memoir *Silver and Gold;* the *New York Times* described the Princess's meeting with her future mother-in-law. The *New York Times* was again indispensable in dealing with the wedding cake. The material on the preparation for the wedding has been drawn in part from confidential sources. Leslie Field is the source on the jewel gifts. Sir John Colville's memoirs and *Time* magazine are main sources on the party at the Palace; again, sources on preparations for the royal wedding are too numerous to list; Colville again was the source of the necklace story. Kenneth Rose supplied the tiara anecdote. For the order of the wedding, see particulars at the Public Record Office, Kew, London, supported by all newspapers.

CHAPTER ELEVEN

John Dean and Charles Smith are the sources on the honeymoon; both are excellent on the early days of the marriage. See the *New York Times* and London *Times* and the *Illustrated London News* for the royal tour, and see E. E. Tisdall's *Royal Destiny* for details of Philip's mother's convent. The particulars of Michael Parker are in the detailed files compiled by the English author Stephen Dorril and supplied to Charles Higham. Details of Princess Margaret are from confidential sources. The romance with Danny Kaye is from confidential sources. John Dean supplements the major newspapers on details of Prince Charles's birth. See the *New York Times* for the playhouse article. The same for the christening. The Café de Paris evening is described in *Champagne and Chandeliers* by Charles Graves. He noted the presence of Profumo. For the redecoration of Clarence House see all major newspapers. Major Alfred Briffa, OBE, of the Knights of Malta, was the source on the royal stay in Malta.

The movements here of Philip are in the ships' logs obtained by Paul Stewart in London; details of Prince Charles's life were published in the *New York Times;* again for the King's illness see the *New York Times* and London *Times;* also Wheeler-Bennett and Kenneth Rose; the Canadian tour is in all newspapers and Public Record Office files, Kew, London; John Dean is the source on the practical jokes; the American tour is best covered in the *Washington Post;* the *New York Times* described the departure.

CHAPTER TWELVE

See Wheeler-Bennett and John Dean, all newspapers (including Kenyan) for the African tour; the King's death was in all newspapers; the *East African Standard* is the best source on the story of the Queen being informed; see also books by Morrow and Longford on the Queen; the events in London are in the *New York Times* and London *Times;* protocol described here is from a confidential source; the *New York Times* described the drive to Sandringham; the funeral is in the *New York Times,* London *Times,* and the *Illustrated London News;* again, protocol is from private sources; Pierre Berton's book on the royals is invaluable here; Peter

Russell's books supply the bulk of the material on the order of the Palace staff; for the Queen Mary and Mountbatten conflict see books by Richard Hough and by Philip Ziegler, also a biography of Queen Mary by James Pope-Hennessey; the behavior of Prince Philip at the Palace is described by John Dean and Peter Russell; see articles by William Ellis, the warden of Windsor Castle, for the story about the building's problems (*Sunday Pictorial,* January 11, 1959); see the *New York Times* for the Queen's daily rituals; Hartnell's *Silver and Gold* is good on the preparations for the Coronation; Christopher Warwick's book on Princess Margaret is indispensable on this period; for the fullest account of the Royal Marriage Act, Hansard debates of the period are to be consulted; Kenneth Rose has supplied material on the issues involved.

CHAPTER THIRTEEN

Much the best source on the Coronation, accounts of which are greatly at variance, is the very large file at the Public Record Office, Kew, London, of Coronation Council meetings, of which minutes were kept; the charts of the placements in the cathedral of the attendants to the Queen; the film *The Queen Is Crowned;* the *New York Times,* London *Times* and all newspapers; Charles Higham's interviews with Kenneth Rose, who supplied witty anecdotes; Cecil Beaton described the scene after the ceremony in his memoirs.

CHAPTER FOURTEEN

The *New York Journal-American, The People, The Sunday Pictorial,* London *Times,* and *New York Times* are prime sources on the Townsend affair, supported further by the books on Princess Margaret by Christopher Warwick and Richard Hough and most usefully Peter Townsend's still irreplaceable *Time and Chance.* Particulars of the Queen's racehorses are in the *New York Times;* for details of the Thursday and Monday clubs see *Honeytrap* by Anthony Summers and Stephen Dorril; the Regency Bill debate is in Hansard; details of Charles's childhood are best given in Dermot Morrah's *To Be a King;* the Australasian tour was covered in the *Fiji Times* (courtesy Len Usher); also the New Zealand and Australian journals, especially the *Melbourne Age;* the story of the episode in Malta comes from Major Alfred Briffa; more details of races (Aureole) from the *New York Times; The Frog* was largely ignored; for the Canadian tour see the *Toronto Star;* again, for details of Charles see Morrah; again, see chiefly *Time and Chance* for Princess Margaret; the Crichel Downs affair was in the London *Times* and Dorset papers; Philip's Newspaper Press Fund address was reported in the *New York Times.*

CHAPTER FIFTEEN

The account of the Suez crisis has been drawn from over one hundred sources, of which the most reliable will be found in the bibliography; Hansard was a rich source; also the reminiscences of several participants, including Anthony Nutting, Lord Avon, Lord Stockton (formerly Sir Harold Macmillan), R. A. Butler, Lord Hailsham, etc., histories in French and English of the Suez Canal Company; declassified Cabinet meetings records; and Egyptian sources. The great book on the crises remains to be written.

CHAPTER SIXTEEN

For the Queen's situation at the time, see the *New York Times* and London *Times;* the polo match stories are from confidential sources; see Summers and Dorril for the Thursday Club; general news of the period is gleaned from a large number of newspapers; Prince Philip's Indian tour is from the *New York Times* and the *Times of India;* the details of the progressive affair of Princess Margaret and Armstrong-Jones are from confidential sources and from a series of articles by David-John Payne, not published in England, that appeared in *France-Dimanche,* November–December 1960; see the *New York Times* and London *Times* for the Canadian tour; for the private screenings and cross-dressing stories see Payne; for Macmillan's Prime Ministerial career see Alistair Horne's authorized biography; also Macmillan's memoirs; see Public Record Office, Kew, London, for details of the succession; see Hartnell and *Time and Chance* and the *New York Times* for preparations for the marriage; the wedding was best described in the *New York Times,* London *Times, Time,* and *Newsweek.*

CHAPTER SEVENTEEN

The Gary Powers incident was widely reported at the time; for the summit meeting see Macmillan's and Khrushchev's memoirs; the royal tour of the Caribbean is in the *New York Times* and other American papers; for the Thomas Cronin matters see Associated Press, date given; the marriage of Armstrong-Jones and Margaret is drawn from confidential sources as well as Warwich, Hough, and Dempster; the Indian tour is in the *New York Times;* also the London *Times;* also the Italian tour; for the royal birth see the *New York Times* and London *Times;* the Ghanian tour is dealt with in the *New York Times* and London *Times;* Prince Charles's illness is best described in Morrah; again, confidential sources are used in the Snowdon marriage; the Hahn material and all Gordonstoun details are from confidential sources.

CHAPTER EIGHTEEN

See the *New York Times* and London *Times* for the royal birth; again see Costello, and also Chapman Pincher's *Too Secret, Too Long* for the Blunt affair; the King and Cookridge sources are given on the correspondence via Sweden; Prince Charles's illness is in Morrah; the Rhodesian crisis was internationally reported; details of Wilson are from confidential sources and from Marcia Williams's *Inside Number Ten;* the theft story is in Morrah; the death of Churchill is drawn from the *New York Times* and

London *Times;* the Ethiopian tour is in contemporary issues of *Der Stern;* see Hansard for the Blankenhorn matter; the Bilderberg meeting was (amazingly) mentioned in the London *Times* for April 2, 1945; see also Holly Sklar: *Trilateralism;* also see Heinz Schöll, *Bilderberg und Trilaterale.* The *New York Times* covered the royal tour of Germany and the dinner at Salem; also see Princess Viktoria Luise's *The Kaiser's Daughter,* a much-neglected text; see Cecil King's diaries for the episode with Prince Philip at the luncheon; the meeting on Prince Charles's future is best described in Morrah; so is the trip to Lichtenstein.

CHAPTER NINETEEN

Morrah is best on Prince Charles at Timbertop; Nigel Dempster deals with Princess Margaret's extramarital interests; Prince Philip's visit to Rio is in the *New York Times;* the Queen Mother's illness is in the *New York Times* and London *Times;* the *Tiger* meeting is vividly described in Marcia Williams's *Inside Number Ten;* the *New York Times* covered the Greek crisis; the Victoria and Albert Museum incident was in the London *Times;* the Harewood divorce was reported in all newspapers; Prince Charles and music is in Morrah and also in Holden; the plaque incident is in *The Duchess of Windsor* by Higham; Michael Varney best described Charles at Cambridge; the race problems are dealt with best by Andrew Roth in *Enoch Powell;* the episode involving Cecil King and the planned revolution is sensibly dealt with by Ziegler in *Mountbatten* and in an article by Cudlipp in *Encounter;* see also the William Evans memoir of his years with Mountbatten; for Princess Anne's development, see Paul James's biography; the Oberon-Prince Philip friendship is confirmed by confidential sources and by Luis Estevez, fashion designer and friend of Miss Oberon; the Brazilian tour is in the *New York Times.*

CHAPTER TWENTY

Prince Philip's speech at the Science Union is in the *New York Times;* the Mountbatten intrigue over the royal titles is recorded in numerous letters and other documents at the Broadlands Archives, University of Southampton, England; the illness of Plunket is recorded in Kenneth Rose's *Kings, Queens, and Courtiers;* the investiture of Prince Charles as Prince of Wales is best described in the London *Times* and seen in various documentary film materials; it was seen on television; the *New York Times* covered the royal family's alleged financial difficulties; the Mexican and Australian tours were in the *New York Times* and the London *Times;* the Canadian and American tours are in the *New York Times* and the *Washington Post;* also *Newsweek* and *Time;* the arguments between Princess Margaret and Armstrong-Jones were recorded in an anonymous article in the *Ladies' Home Journal* for August 1970, written by a peer whose name was not disclosed but who was privy to the events described; the friendship with Plunket is from confidential sources; the Courtaulds matter is to be found in the *Congressional Record* on the dates supplied in the text; the Queen's days are again drawn from confidential sources; so are details of her clothing fittings and her investments; the arguments over her income are recorded in Hansard; the "Archers" story is from confidential sources; so is the story of the Queen Mother's waving; the stories of the Queen Mother that follow are from Kenneth Rose; details of Michael Parker are from the personal files of Stephen Dorril; again see the *Congressional Record* for arguments over the Queen's farm (and note the absolute silence of the Houses of Commons and Lords on the delicate matter); the Malaysian tour is in the *New York Times* and the London *Times;* the dirty tricks smear campaign is in Stephen Dorril's files; it was a main issue in the British press in 1990; the driving episodes were recorded in the *New York Times,* underplayed in England; the student confrontation is from confidential sources and the *New York Times;* the Yugoslavian tour is from the *New York Times;* also the silver wedding anniversary, well described by R. W. Apple.

CHAPTER TWENTY-ONE

The fox-hunt matter and royal tours are in the *New York Times* and the London *Times;* the speech in Edinburgh was in the *New Statesman* anti-jubilee issue, July 7, 1977; the *New York Times* covered the royal visit to Russia; the *New York Times* (Apple), *Newsweek,* and *Time* covered Princess Anne's wedding; see Tony Benn's memoirs for the story of the royal privilege; the *New York Times* covered the New Zealand tour; the near mishap in Germany also; the story of the Ball attempt on Princess Anne was in all newspapers; details of Prince Andrew at school are from confidential sources; the Mountbatten misbehavior is recorded in an as yet unpublished memoir by a member of his personal staff and from confidential sources; see cited issues of the *Morning Star* for arguments over the Queen's income; also Hansard for the debate; details of the dedications to Lord Plunket are in Rose's *Kings, Queens, and Courtiers;* the RTZ matters are contained in British Law Reports 1978 AC; also the Hearing before the Subcommittee on Oversight and Investigations Serial 94–150, November 4, 1976, Washington, D.C.; for the 1,001 Club see articles in the London *Sunday Times;* the Lockheed affair is fully reported in the *New York Times, Washington Journal,* and in Boulton's *The Lockheed Papers.* The dinner party scene at Number 10 is from a confidential source; the Callaghan period is covered simply in the London *Times,* the *Sunday Times,* and British newspapers as a whole; much of the Armstrong-Jones/Princess Margaret relationship here is from a confidential source.

CHAPTER TWENTY-TWO

The farewell of the crew to Prince Charles is from a confidential source; also the Queen's movements at the time; the RTZ matter was again reported in detail in the *Sunday Times,* U.S. House Committee reports, and in the aforementioned Law Reports; the Silver Jubilee was effectively reported by the *New York Times,* London *Times, Newsweek, Time,* etc.

Observations on the Queen that year are drawn from confidential sources and from an interview with Earl Mountbatten of Burma by Roy Moseley; details of Princess Margaret at the time are from the *New York Times* and the London *Times* as is the episode of the Queen and the horses; the *New York Times* reported Princess Anne's visit to the Oslo hospital; the Middle Eastern tour is in the *New York Times* and London *Times;* also in Lady Longford's biography; see the *New York Times* and London *Times* for royal tours; the death of Mountbatten is best described in the *New York Times* and London *Times* (not, oddly enough, in detail in Ziegler's authorized work); the funeral and memorial service are described by confidential eyewitnesses, the *New York Times* and London *Times;* Princess Margaret in Chicago is in the *Chicago Tribune;* on Prince Charles's early romantic life see Morrah and Holden; on Diana, also; the newspapers uniformly followed every detail of the couple's romance, condensed in Ralph G. Martin's dual biography; the Queen's clash with the press is in the *New York Times* and *Newsweek;* the settlement of the RTZ case is reported in the *New York Times;* also in *The Wall Street Journal;* the attempt on the Queen's life was reported in all journals; also the inner city riots and the royal wedding; the party at Claridge's is from a confidential source; also the honeymoon voyage, but Ralph G. Martin got the details right.

CHAPTER TWENTY-THREE

The incident at Chipping Sodbury was in the *New York Times;* the Falklands War was best described in the *New York Times*, also in the *Sunday Times* Insight team book on the conflict; however, a complete account of the war with all its political and economic ramifications explored needs to be written; the *New Statesman* and Hansard debates need to be read for the whole period; the story of the intruder into the Queen's bedroom was in all newspapers; see the *New York Times* and London *Times* for the IRA attacks; the American tour was covered by the *Los Angeles Times, New York Times,* and London *Times;* the tour of Australia by Prince Charles and Princess Diana was best described in the *Sydney Morning Herald* and *Melbourne Age;* see the *New York Times;* again, the tours are described in the *New York Times* and London *Times;* the Lexington visit was in all local papers in that area; but it is greatly supplemented by a confidential source; the London *Times* detailed the Brighton explosion; Prince Andrew's goings-on were the joy of the transatlantic tabloids for months; Prince Charles's Italian visits are admirably supplied by Donatella Ortona Ferrario; Princess Diana's behavior at the time was recorded widely; the TV interview of the Prince and Princess has been examined.

CHAPTER TWENTY-FOUR

On the Westland affair, see Hansard; on Sarah Ferguson see all newspapers; the sixtieth birthday ceremony is drawn from eyewitnesses; the clash between the Queen and Mrs. Thatcher over sanctions was fully reported by the *Sunday Times;* see *Time* and *Newsweek* for the best reports on the royal wedding; for the goings-on of Princess Michael of Kent see Andrew Morton's *Inside Kensington Palace;* the matter of the Bowes-Lyons is in all newspapers; again, Donatella Ortona Ferrario is the best source on Prince Charles in Italy; the anecdote about Mrs. Thatcher listening to the Queen is from a confidential source.

INDEX
* * *